31.95

KIA
SEPHIA, SPECTRA & S
1994-10 REPAIR MANUAL

CHILTON'S

Covers all U.S. and Canadian models of
Kia Sephia (1994 through 2001),
Spectra (2000 through 2009)
& Sportage (2005 through 2010)

by Joe L Hamilton

CHILTON *Automotive Books*
PUBLISHED BY **HAYNES NORTH AMERICA, Inc.**

Haynes ®

APAA
AUTOMOTIVE
PARTS &
ACCESSORIES
ASSOCIATION MEMBER

Manufactured in USA
©2011 Haynes North America, Inc.
ISBN-13: 978-1-56392-960-1
ISBN-10: 1-56392-960-0
Library of Congress Control Number 2011942854

Haynes Publishing Group
Sparkford Nr Ycovil
Somerset BA22 7JJ England

Haynes North America, Inc
861 Lawrence Drive
Newbury Park
California 91320 USA

ABCDE
FGHIJ
KLM

4R5-2

Contents

INTRODUCTORY PAGES

About this manual – 0-5
Introduction – 0-5
Vehicle identification numbers – 0-6
Buying parts – 0-8
Maintenance techniques, tools and
    working facilities   0-9
Jacking and towing – 0-17

Booster battery (jump) starting – 0-18
Automotive chemicals and lubricants – 0-19
Conversion factors – 0-20
Fraction/decimal/millimeter
    equivalents – 0-21
Safety first! – 0-22
Troubleshooting – 0-23

1 TUNE-UP AND ROUTINE MAINTENANCE – 1-1

2 FOUR-CYLINDER ENGINES – 2A-1
V6 ENGINE – 2B-1
GENERAL ENGINE OVERHAUL PROCEDURES – 2C-1

3 COOLING, HEATING AND AIR CONDITIONING SYSTEMS – 3-1

4 FUEL AND EXHAUST SYSTEMS – 4-1

5 ENGINE ELECTRICAL SYSTEMS – 5-1

6 EMISSIONS AND ENGINE CONTROL SYSTEMS – 6-1

MANUAL TRANSAXLE – 7A-1
AUTOMATIC TRANSAXLE – 7B-1

7

CLUTCH AND DRIVELINE – 8-1

8

BRAKES – 9-1

9

SUSPENSION AND STEERING SYSTEMS – 10-1

10

BODY – 11-1

11

CHASSIS ELECTRICAL SYSTEM – 12-1
WIRING DIAGRAMS – 12-23

12

GLOSSARY – GL-1

GLOSSARY

MASTER INDEX – IND-1

MASTER INDEX

Mechanic and photographer with a 1999 Kia Sephia

ACKNOWLEDGEMENTS

Technical writers who contributed to this project include Robert Maddox, John Wegmann and Mike Stubblefield. We are grateful to Solution Builders (Sephia/Spectra) and Vally Forge Technical Information Services (Sportage) for the origination of wiring diagrams.

About this manual

ITS PURPOSE

The purpose of this manual is to help you get the best value from your vehicle. It can do so in several ways. It can help you decide what work must be done, even if you choose to have it done by a dealer service department or a repair shop; it provides information and procedures for routine maintenance and servicing; and it offers diagnostic and repair procedures to follow when trouble occurs.

We hope you use the manual to tackle the work yourself. For many simpler jobs, doing it yourself may be quicker than arranging an appointment to get the vehicle into a shop and making the trips to leave it and pick it up. More importantly, a lot of money can be saved by avoiding the expense the shop must pass on to you to cover its labor and overhead costs. An added benefit is the sense of satisfaction and accomplishment that you feel after doing the job yourself.

USING THE MANUAL

The manual is divided into Chapters. Each Chapter is divided into numbered Sections. Each Section consists of consecutively numbered paragraphs.

At the beginning of each numbered Section you will be referred to any illustrations which apply to the procedures in that Section. The reference numbers used in illustration captions pinpoint the pertinent Section and the Step within that Section. That is, illustration 3.2 means the illustration refers to Section 3 and Step (or paragraph) 2 within that Section.

Procedures, once described in the text, are not normally repeated. When it's necessary to refer to another Chapter, the reference will be given as Chapter and Section number. Cross references given without use of the word "Chapter" apply to Sections and/or paragraphs in the same Chapter. For example, "see Section 8" means in the same Chapter.

References to the left or right side of the vehicle assume you are sitting in the driver's seat, facing forward.

Even though we have prepared this manual with extreme care, neither the publisher nor the author can accept responsibility for any errors in, or omissions from, the information given.

➡ **NOTE**

A *Note* provides information necessary to properly complete a procedure or information which will make the procedure easier to understand.

❋❋ **CAUTION**

A *Caution* provides a special procedure or special steps which must be taken while completing the procedure where the Caution is found. Not heeding a Caution can result in damage to the assembly being worked on.

❋❋ **WARNING**

A *Warning* provides a special procedure or special steps which must be taken while completing the procedure where the Warning is found. Not heeding a Warning can result in personal injury.

Introduction

These models are available in four-door sedan, hatchback and SUV body styles.

The transversely mounted inline four-cylinder and V6 engines used in these models are equipped with electronic fuel injection.

The engine drives the front wheels through either a five-speed manual or a four-speed automatic transaxle via independent driveaxles. On 4WD Sportage models, the rear wheels are also propelled, via a transfer case, driveshaft, rear differential and independent driveaxles.

Independent suspension, featuring coil spring/shock absorber units, is used on all four wheels. The power-assisted rack-and-pinion steering unit is mounted behind the engine.

The brakes are disc at the front and either disc or drum at the rear, with power assist standard. Some models are equipped with an Anti-lock Braking System (ABS).

Vehicle identification numbers

Modifications are a continuing and unpublicized process in vehicle manufacturing. Since spare parts manuals and lists are compiled on a numerical basis, the individual vehicle numbers are essential to correctly identify the component required.

VEHICLE IDENTIFICATION NUMBER (VIN)

This very important number is stamped on the firewall in the engine compartment and on a plate attached to the dashboard inside the windshield on the driver's side of the vehicle. The VIN also appears on the Vehicle Safety Certification label and the Vehicle Certificate of Title and Registration. It contains information such as where and when the vehicle was manufactured, the model year and the body style (see illustrations).

VIN year and engine codes

Two particularly important pieces of information located in the VIN are the model year and engine codes. Counting from the left, the engine code is the eighth digit and the model year code is the 10th digit.

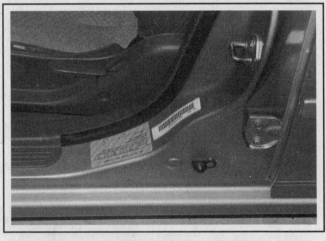

The Vehicle Safety Certification label is affixed to the bottom of the driver's door pillar

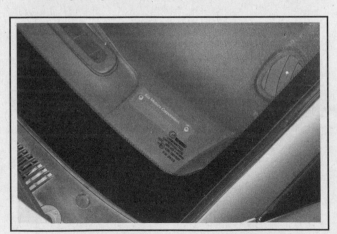

The Vehicle Identification Number (VIN) is stamped into a metal plate fastened to the dashboard on the driver's side - it is visible through the windshield

The engine code number is located near the exhaust manifold

Engine codes - Sephia/Spectra

1 (1994 and 1995)
1.6L Single Overhead Camshaft (SOHC)
3, 4 (1995 through 1997)
1.6L Double Overhead Camshaft (DOHC)
5 (1995 through 1997)
1.8L Double Overhead Camshaft (DOHC)
1 (1998 through 2004)
1.8L Double Overhead Camshaft (DOHC)
1 (2004 and later)
2.0L Double Overhead Camshaft (DOHC)
2 (2004 and later)
2.0L Double Overhead Camshaft (DOHC) SULEV

Engine codes - Sportage

2 (Federal models)
2.0L Double Overhead Camshaft (DOHC)
4 (Four-cylinder California models)
2.0L Double Overhead Camshaft (DOHC) four-cylinder
3 (2005 and later)
2.7L Double Overhead Camshaft (DOHC) V6

Model year codes

R	1994
S	1995
T	1996
V	1997
W	1998
X	1999
Y	2000
1	2001
2	2002
3	2003
4	2004
5	2005
6	2006
7	2007
8	2008
9	2009
A	2010

Buying parts

Replacement parts are available from many sources, which generally fall into one of two categories - authorized dealer parts departments and independent retail auto parts stores. Our advice concerning these parts is as follows:

Retail auto parts stores: Good auto parts stores will stock frequently needed components which wear out relatively fast, such as clutch components, exhaust systems, brake parts, tune-up parts, etc. These stores often supply new or reconditioned parts on an exchange basis, which can save a considerable amount of money. Discount auto parts stores are often very good places to buy materials and parts needed for general vehicle maintenance such as oil, grease, filters, spark plugs, belts, touch-up paint, bulbs, etc. They also usually sell

tools and general accessories, have convenient hours, charge lower prices and can often be found not far from home.

Authorized dealer parts department: This is the best source for parts which are unique to the vehicle and not generally available elsewhere (such as major engine parts, transmission parts, trim pieces, etc.).

Warranty information: If the vehicle is still covered under warranty, be sure that any replacement parts purchased - regardless of the source - do not invalidate the warranty!

To be sure of obtaining the correct parts, have engine and chassis numbers available and, if possible, take the old parts along for positive identification.

MAINTENANCE TECHNIQUES

There are a number of techniques involved in maintenance and repair that will be referred to throughout this manual. Application of these techniques will enable the home mechanic to be more efficient, better organized and capable of performing the various tasks properly, which will ensure that the repair job is thorough and complete.

Fasteners

Fasteners are nuts, bolts, studs and screws used to hold two or more parts together. There are a few things to keep in mind when working with fasteners. Almost all of them use a locking device of some type, either a lockwasher, locknut, locking tab or thread adhesive. All threaded fasteners should be clean and straight, with undamaged threads and undamaged corners on the hex head where the wrench fits. Develop the habit of replacing all damaged nuts and bolts with new ones. Special locknuts with nylon or fiber inserts can only be used once. If they are removed, they lose their locking ability and must be replaced with new ones.

Rusted nuts and bolts should be treated with a penetrating fluid to ease removal and prevent breakage. Some mechanics use turpentine in a spout-type oil can, which works quite well. After applying the rust penetrant, let it work for a few minutes before trying to loosen the nut or bolt. Badly rusted fasteners may have to be chiseled or sawed off or removed with a special nut breaker, available at tool stores.

If a bolt or stud breaks off in an assembly, it can be drilled and removed with a special tool commonly available for this purpose. Most automotive machine shops can perform this task, as well as other repair procedures, such as the repair of threaded holes that have been stripped out.

Flat washers and lockwashers, when removed from an assembly, should always be replaced exactly as removed. Replace any damaged washers with new ones. Never use a lockwasher on any soft metal surface (such as aluminum), thin sheet metal or plastic.

Fastener sizes

For a number of reasons, automobile manufacturers are making wider and wider use of metric fasteners. Therefore, it is important to be able to tell the difference between standard (sometimes called U.S. or SAE) and metric hardware, since they cannot be interchanged.

All bolts, whether standard or metric, are sized according to diameter, thread pitch and length. For example, a standard 1/2 - 13 x 1 bolt is 1/2 inch in diameter, has 13 threads per inch and is 1 inch long. An M12 - 1.75 x 25 metric bolt is 12 mm in diameter, has a thread pitch of 1.75 mm (the distance between threads) and is 25 mm long. The two bolts are nearly identical, and easily confused, but they are not interchangeable.

In addition to the differences in diameter, thread pitch and length, metric and standard bolts can also be distinguished by examining the bolt heads. To begin with, the distance across the flats on a standard bolt head is measured in inches, while the same dimension on a metric bolt is sized in millimeters (the same is true for nuts). As a result, a standard wrench should not be used on a metric bolt and a metric wrench should not be used on a standard bolt. Also, most standard bolts have slashes

radiating out from the center of the head to denote the grade or strength of the bolt, which is an indication of the amount of torque that can be applied to it. The greater the number of slashes, the greater the strength of the bolt. Grades 0 through 5 are commonly used on automobiles. Metric bolts have a property class (grade) number, rather than a slash, molded into their heads to indicate bolt strength. In this case, the higher the number, the stronger the bolt. Property class numbers 8.8, 9.8 and 10.9 are commonly used on automobiles.

Strength markings can also be used to distinguish standard hex nuts from metric hex nuts. Many standard nuts have dots stamped into one side, while metric nuts are marked with a number. The greater the number of dots, or the higher the number, the greater the strength of the nut.

Metric studs are also marked on their ends according to property class (grade). Larger studs are numbered (the same as metric bolts), while smaller studs carry a geometric code to denote grade.

It should be noted that many fasteners, especially Grades 0 through 2, have no distinguishing marks on them. When such is the case, the only way to determine whether it is standard or metric is to measure the thread pitch or compare it to a known fastener of the same size.

Standard fasteners are often referred to as SAE, as opposed to metric. However, it should be noted that SAE technically refers to a non-metric fine thread fastener only. Coarse thread non-metric fasteners are referred to as USS sizes.

Since fasteners of the same size (both standard and metric) may have different strength ratings, be sure to reinstall any bolts, studs or nuts removed from your vehicle in their original locations. Also, when replacing a fastener with a new one, make sure that the new one has a strength rating equal to or greater than the original.

Tightening sequences and procedures

Most threaded fasteners should be tightened to a specific torque value (torque is the twisting force applied to a threaded component such as a nut or bolt). Overtightening the fastener can weaken it and cause it to break, while undertightening can cause it to eventually come loose. Bolts, screws and studs, depending on the material they are made of and their thread diameters, have specific torque values, many of which are noted in the Specifications at the end of each Chapter. Be sure to follow the torque recommendations closely. For fasteners not assigned a specific torque, a general torque value chart is presented here as a guide. These torque values are for dry (unlubricated) fasteners threaded into steel or cast iron (not aluminum). As was previously mentioned, the size and grade of a fastener determine the amount of torque that can safely be applied to it. The figures listed here are approximate for Grade 2 and Grade 3 fasteners. Higher grades can tolerate higher torque values.

Fasteners laid out in a pattern, such as cylinder head bolts, oil pan bolts, differential cover bolts, etc., must be loosened or tightened in sequence to avoid warping the component. This sequence will normally be shown in the appropriate Chapter. If a specific pattern is not given, the following procedures can be used to prevent warping.

Initially, the bolts or nuts should be assembled finger-tight only. Next, they should be tightened one full turn each, in a criss-cross or diagonal pattern. After each one has been tightened one full turn, return to the first one and tighten them all one-half turn, following the same

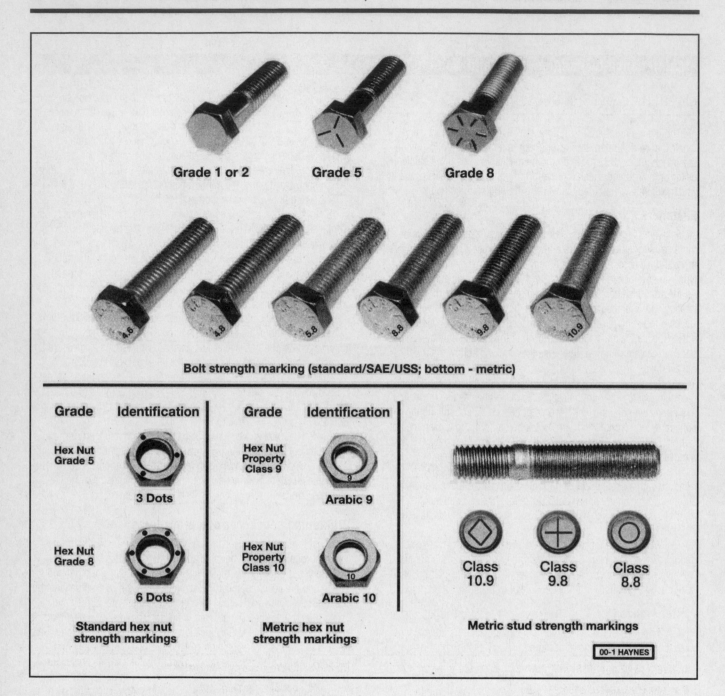

Grade 1 or 2   Grade 5   Grade 8

Bolt strength marking (standard/SAE/USS; bottom - metric)

Grade	Identification	Grade	Identification
Hex Nut Grade 5	3 Dots	Hex Nut Property Class 9	Arabic 9
Hex Nut Grade 8	6 Dots	Hex Nut Property Class 10	Arabic 10

Standard hex nut strength markings

Metric hex nut strength markings

Class 10.9   Class 9.8   Class 8.8

Metric stud strength markings

00-1 HAYNES

pattern. Finally, tighten each of them one-quarter turn at a time until each fastener has been tightened to the proper torque. To loosen and remove the fasteners, the procedure would be reversed.

Component disassembly

Component disassembly should be done with care and purpose to help ensure that the parts go back together properly. Always keep track of the sequence in which parts are removed. Make note of special characteristics or marks on parts that can be installed more than one way, such as a grooved thrust washer on a shaft. It is a good idea to lay the disassembled parts out on a clean surface in the order that they were removed. It may also be helpful to make sketches or take instant photos of components before removal.

When removing fasteners from a component, keep track of their locations. Sometimes threading a bolt back in a part, or putting the washers and nut back on a stud, can prevent mix-ups later. If nuts and bolts cannot be returned to their original locations, they should be kept in a compartmented box or a series of small boxes. A cupcake or muffin tin is ideal for this purpose, since each cavity can hold the bolts and nuts from a particular area (i.e. oil pan bolts, valve cover bolts, engine

Metric thread sizes

	Ft-lbs	Nm
M-6	6 to 9	9 to 12
M-8	14 to 21	19 to 28
M-10	28 to 40	38 to 54
M-12	50 to 71	68 to 96
M-14	80 to 140	109 to 154

Pipe thread sizes

1/8	5 to 8	7 to 10
1/4	12 to 18	17 to 24
3/8	22 to 33	30 to 44
1/2	25 to 35	34 to 47

U.S. thread sizes

1/4 - 20	6 to 9	9 to 12
5/16 - 18	12 to 18	17 to 24
5/16 - 24	14 to 20	19 to 27
3/8 - 16	22 to 32	30 to 43
3/8 - 24	27 to 38	37 to 51
7/16 - 14	40 to 55	55 to 74
7/16 - 20	40 to 60	55 to 81
1/2 - 13	55 to 80	75 to 108

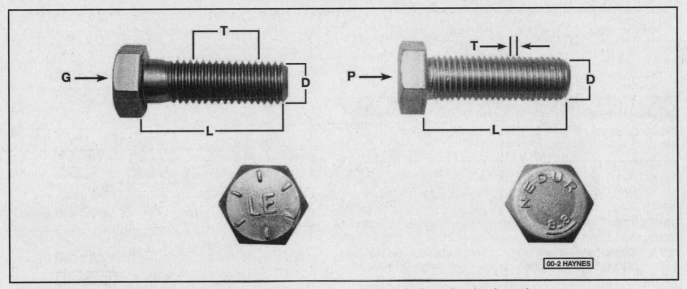

00-2 HAYNES

Standard (SAE and USS) bolt dimensions/grade marks

G   Grade marks (bolt strength)
L   Length (in inches)
T   Thread pitch (number of threads per inch)
D   Nominal diameter (in inches)

Metric bolt dimensions/grade marks

P   Property class (bolt strength)
L   Length (in millimeters)
T   Thread pitch (distance between threads in millimeters)
D   Diameter

mount bolts, etc.). A pan of this type is especially helpful when working on assemblies with very small parts, such as the carburetor, alternator, valve train or interior dash and trim pieces. The cavities can be marked with paint or tape to identify the contents.

Whenever wiring looms, harnesses or connectors are separated, it is a good idea to identify the two halves with numbered pieces of masking tape so they can be easily reconnected.

Gasket sealing surfaces

Throughout any vehicle, gaskets are used to seal the mating surfaces between two parts and keep lubricants, fluids, vacuum or pressure contained in an assembly.

Many times these gaskets are coated with a liquid or paste-type gasket sealing compound before assembly. Age, heat and pressure can sometimes cause the two parts to stick together so tightly that they are very difficult to separate. Often, the assembly can be loosened by striking it with a soft-face hammer near the mating surfaces. A regular hammer can be used if a block of wood is placed between the hammer and the part. Do not hammer on cast parts or parts that could be easily damaged. With any particularly stubborn part, always recheck to make sure that every fastener has been removed.

Avoid using a screwdriver or bar to pry apart an assembly, as they

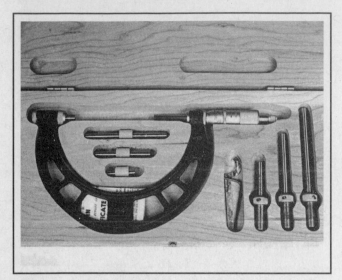

Micrometer set

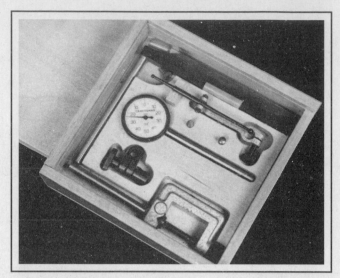

Dial indicator set

can easily mar the gasket sealing surfaces of the parts, which must remain smooth. If prying is absolutely necessary, use an old broom handle, but keep in mind that extra clean up will be necessary if the wood splinters.

After the parts are separated, the old gasket must be carefully scraped off and the gasket surfaces cleaned. Stubborn gasket material can be soaked with rust penetrant or treated with a special chemical to soften it so it can be easily scraped off.

⁂ CAUTION:

Never use gasket removal solutions or caustic chemicals on plastic or other composite components.

A scraper can be fashioned from a piece of copper tubing by flattening and sharpening one end. Copper is recommended because it is usually softer than the surfaces to be scraped, which reduces the chance of gouging the part. Some gaskets can be removed with a wire brush, but regardless of the method used, the mating surfaces must be left clean and smooth. If for some reason the gasket surface is gouged, then a gasket sealer thick enough to fill scratches will have to be used during reassembly of the components. For most applications, a non-drying (or semi-drying) gasket sealer should be used.

Hose removal tips

⁂ WARNING:

If the vehicle is equipped with air conditioning, do not disconnect any of the A/C hoses without first having the system depressurized by a dealer service department or a service station.

Hose removal precautions closely parallel gasket removal precautions. Avoid scratching or gouging the surface that the hose mates against or the connection may leak. This is especially true for radiator hoses. Because of various chemical reactions, the rubber in hoses can bond itself to the metal spigot that the hose fits over. To remove a hose, first loosen the hose clamps that secure it to the spigot. Then, with slip-joint pliers, grab the hose at the clamp and rotate it around the spigot. Work it back and forth until it is completely free, then pull it off. Silicone or other lubricants will ease removal if they can be applied

between the hose and the outside of the spigot. Apply the same lubricant to the inside of the hose and the outside of the spigot to simplify installation.

As a last resort (and if the hose is to be replaced with a new one anyway), the rubber can be slit with a knife and the hose peeled from the spigot. If this must be done, be careful that the metal connection is not damaged.

If a hose clamp is broken or damaged, do not reuse it. Wire-type clamps usually weaken with age, so it is a good idea to replace them with screw-type clamps whenever a hose is removed.

TOOLS

A selection of good tools is a basic requirement for anyone who plans to maintain and repair his or her own vehicle. For the owner who has few tools, the initial investment might seem high, but when compared to the spiraling costs of professional auto maintenance and repair, it is a wise one.

To help the owner decide which tools are needed to perform the tasks detailed in this manual, the following tool lists are offered: *Maintenance and minor repair, Repair/overhaul and Special.*

The newcomer to practical mechanics should start off with the *maintenance and minor repair* tool kit, which is adequate for the simpler jobs performed on a vehicle. Then, as confidence and experience grow, the owner can tackle more difficult tasks, buying additional tools as they are needed. Eventually the basic kit will be expanded into the *repair and overhaul* tool set. Over a period of time, the experienced do-it-yourselfer will assemble a tool set complete enough for most repair and overhaul procedures and will add tools from the special category when it is felt that the expense is justified by the frequency of use.

Maintenance and minor repair tool kit

The tools in this list should be considered the minimum required for performance of routine maintenance, servicing and minor repair work. We recommend the purchase of combination wrenches (box-end and open-end combined in one wrench). While more expensive than open end wrenches, they offer the advantages of both types of wrench.

Combination wrench set (1/4-inch to 1 inch or 6 mm to 19 mm)
Adjustable wrench, 8 inch
Spark plug wrench with rubber insert

Spark plug gap adjusting tool
Feeler gauge set
Brake bleeder wrench
Standard screwdriver (5/16-inch x 6 inch)
Phillips screwdriver (No. 2 x 6 inch)
Combination pliers - 6 inch
Hacksaw and assortment of blades
Tire pressure gauge
Grease gun

Oil can
Fine emery cloth
Wire brush
Battery post and cable cleaning tool
Oil filter wrench
Funnel (medium size)
Safety goggles
Jackstands (2)
Drain pan

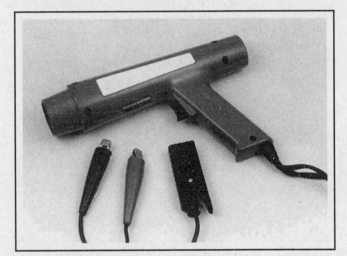

Dial caliper

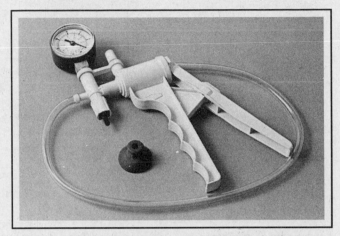

Hand-operated vacuum pump

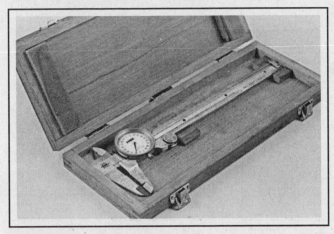

Timing light

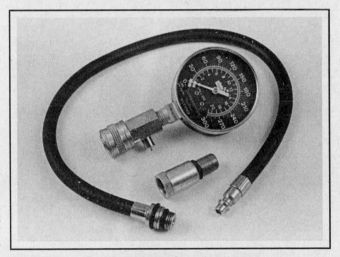

Compression gauge with spark plug hole adapter

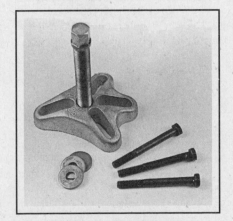

Damper/steering wheel puller

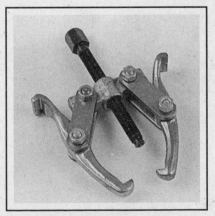

General purpose puller

Hydraulic lifter removal tool

➡ Note: If basic tune-ups are going to be part of routine maintenance, it will be necessary to purchase a good quality stroboscopic timing light and combination tachometer/dwell meter. Although they are included in the list of special tools, it is mentioned here because they are absolutely necessary for tuning most vehicles properly.

Repair and overhaul tool set

These tools are essential for anyone who plans to perform major repairs and are in addition to those in the maintenance and minor repair tool kit. Included is a comprehensive set of sockets which, though expensive, are invaluable because of their versatility, especially when various extensions and drives are available. We recommend the 1/2-inch drive over the 3/8-inch drive. Although the larger drive is bulky and more expensive, it has the capacity of accepting a very wide range of large sockets. Ideally, however, the mechanic should have a 3/8-inch drive set and a 1/2-inch drive set.

Valve spring compressor

Valve spring compressor

Ridge reamer

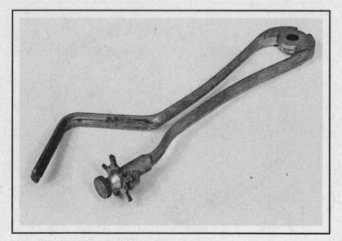

Piston ring groove cleaning tool

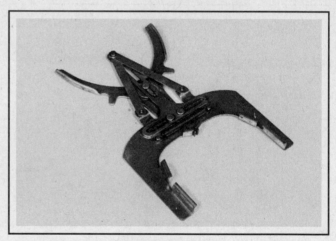

Ring removal/installation tool

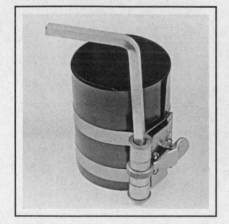

Ring compressor

Cylinder hone

Brake hold-down spring tool

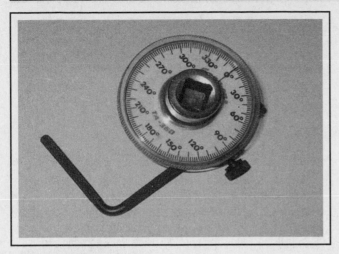

Torque angle gauge

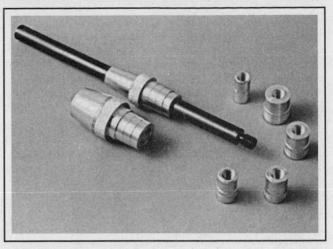

Clutch plate alignment tool

Socket set(s)
Reversible ratchet
Extension - 10 inch
Universal joint
Torque wrench (same size drive as sockets)
Ball peen hammer - 8 ounce
Soft-face hammer (plastic/rubber)
Standard screwdriver (1/4-inch x 6 inch)
Standard screwdriver (stubby - 5/16-inch)
Phillips screwdriver (No. 3 x 8 inch)
Phillips screwdriver (stubby - No. 2)
Pliers - vise grip
Pliers - lineman's
Pliers - needle nose
Pliers - snap-ring (internal and external)
Cold chisel - 1/2-inch
Scribe
Scraper (made from flattened copper tubing)
Centerpunch
Pin punches (1/16, 1/8, 3/16-inch)
Steel rule/straightedge - 12 inch
Allen wrench set (1/8 to 3/8-inch or 4 mm to 10 mm)
A selection of files
Wire brush (large)
Jackstands (second set)
Jack (scissor or hydraulic type)

➡Note: Another tool which is often useful is an electric drill with a chuck capacity of 3/8-inch and a set of good quality drill bits.

Special tools

The tools in this list include those which are not used regularly, are expensive to buy, or which need to be used in accordance with their manufacturer's instructions. Unless these tools will be used frequently, it is not very economical to purchase many of them. A consideration would be to split the cost and use between yourself and a friend or friends. In addition, most of these tools can be obtained from a tool rental shop on a temporary basis.

This list primarily contains only those tools and instruments widely available to the public, and not those special tools produced by the vehicle manufacturer for distribution to dealer service departments. Occasionally, references to the manufacturer's special tools are included in the text of this manual. Generally, an alternative method of doing the job without the special tool is offered. However, sometimes there is no alternative to their use. Where this is the case, and the tool cannot be purchased or borrowed, the work should be turned over to the dealer service department or an automotive repair shop.

Valve spring compressor
Piston ring groove cleaning tool
Piston ring compressor
Piston ring installation tool
Cylinder compression gauge
Cylinder ridge reamer
Cylinder surfacing hone
Cylinder bore gauge
Micrometers and/or dial calipers
Hydraulic lifter removal tool
Balljoint separator
Universal-type puller
Impact screwdriver
Dial indicator set
Stroboscopic timing light (inductive pick-up)
Hand operated vacuum/pressure pump
Tachometer/dwell meter
Universal electrical multimeter
Cable hoist
Brake spring removal and installation tools
Floor jack

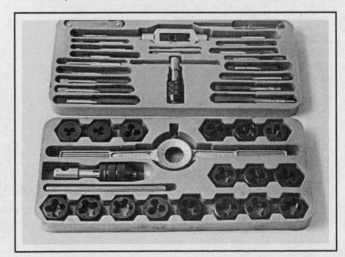

Tap and die set

Buying tools

For the do-it-yourselfer who is just starting to get involved in vehicle maintenance and repair, there are a number of options available when purchasing tools. If maintenance and minor repair is the extent of the work to be done, the purchase of individual tools is satisfactory. If, on the other hand, extensive work is planned, it would be a good idea to purchase a modest tool set from one of the large retail chain stores. A set can usually be bought at a substantial savings over the individual tool prices, and they often come with a tool box. As additional tools are needed, add-on sets, individual tools and a larger tool box can be purchased to expand the tool selection. Building a tool set gradually allows the cost of the tools to be spread over a longer period of time and gives the mechanic the freedom to choose only those tools that will actually be used.

Tool stores will often be the only source of some of the special tools that are needed, but regardless of where tools are bought, try to avoid cheap ones, especially when buying screwdrivers and sockets, because they won't last very long. The expense involved in replacing cheap tools will eventually be greater than the initial cost of quality tools.

Care and maintenance of tools

Good tools are expensive, so it makes sense to treat them with respect. Keep them clean and in usable condition and store them properly when not in use. Always wipe off any dirt, grease or metal chips before putting them away. Never leave tools lying around in the work area. Upon completion of a job, always check closely under the hood for tools that may have been left there so they won't get lost during a test drive.

Some tools, such as screwdrivers, pliers, wrenches and sockets, can be hung on a panel mounted on the garage or workshop wall, while others should be kept in a tool box or tray. Measuring instruments, gauges, meters, etc. must be carefully stored where they cannot be damaged by weather or impact from other tools.

When tools are used with care and stored properly, they will last a very long time. Even with the best of care, though, tools will wear out if used frequently. When a tool is damaged or worn out, replace it. Subsequent jobs will be safer and more enjoyable if you do.

HOW TO REPAIR DAMAGED THREADS

Sometimes, the internal threads of a nut or bolt hole can become stripped, usually from overtightening. Stripping threads is an all-too-common occurrence, especially when working with aluminum parts, because aluminum is so soft that it easily strips out.

Usually, external or internal threads are only partially stripped. After they've been cleaned up with a tap or die, they'll still work. Sometimes, however, threads are badly damaged. When this happens, you've got three choices:

1) *Drill and tap the hole to the next suitable oversize and install a larger diameter bolt, screw or stud.*

2) *Drill and tap the hole to accept a threaded plug, then drill and tap the plug to the original screw size. You can also buy a plug already threaded to the original size. Then you simply drill a hole to the specified size, then run the threaded plug into the hole with a bolt and jam nut. Once the plug is fully seated, remove the jam nut and bolt.*

3) *The third method uses a patented thread repair kit like Heli-Coil or Slimsert. These easy-to-use kits are designed to repair damaged threads in straight-through holes and blind holes. Both are available as kits which can handle a variety of sizes and thread patterns. Drill the hole, then tap it with the special included tap. Install the Heli-Coil and the hole is back to its original diameter and thread pitch.*

Regardless of which method you use, be sure to proceed calmly and carefully. A little impatience or carelessness during one of these relatively simple procedures can ruin your whole day's work and cost you a bundle if you wreck an expensive part.

WORKING FACILITIES

Not to be overlooked when discussing tools is the workshop. If anything more than routine maintenance is to be carried out, some sort of suitable work area is essential.

It is understood, and appreciated, that many home mechanics do not have a good workshop or garage available, and end up removing an engine or doing major repairs outside. It is recommended, however, that the overhaul or repair be completed under the cover of a roof.

A clean, flat workbench or table of comfortable working height is an absolute necessity. The workbench should be equipped with a vise that has a jaw opening of at least four inches.

As mentioned previously, some clean, dry storage space is also required for tools, as well as the lubricants, fluids, cleaning solvents, etc. which soon become necessary.

Sometimes waste oil and fluids, drained from the engine or cooling system during normal maintenance or repairs, present a disposal problem. To avoid pouring them on the ground or into a sewage system, pour the used fluids into large containers, seal them with caps and take them to an authorized disposal site or recycling center. Plastic jugs, such as old antifreeze containers, are ideal for this purpose.

Always keep a supply of old newspapers and clean rags available. Old towels are excellent for mopping up spills. Many mechanics use rolls of paper towels for most work because they are readily available and disposable. To help keep the area under the vehicle clean, a large cardboard box can be cut open and flattened to protect the garage or shop floor.

Whenever working over a painted surface, such as when leaning over a fender to service something under the hood, always cover it with an old blanket or bedspread to protect the finish. Vinyl covered pads, made especially for this purpose, are available at auto parts stores.

Jacking and towing

JACKING

WARNING:

The jack supplied with the vehicle should only be used for changing a tire or placing jackstands under the frame. Never work under the vehicle or start the engine while this jack is being used as the only means of support.

The vehicle should be on level ground. Place the shift lever in Park, if you have an automatic, or Reverse if you have a manual transaxle. Block the wheel diagonally opposite the wheel being changed. Set the parking brake.

Remove the spare tire and jack from stowage. Remove the wheel cover and trim ring (if so equipped) with the tapered end of the lug nut wrench by inserting and twisting the handle and then prying against the back of the wheel cover.

CAUTION:

On some models the wheel cover can't be removed by prying; the wheel nuts must be removed first. Loosen, but do not remove, the lug nuts (one-half turn is sufficient).

Place the scissors-type jack under the side of the vehicle and adjust the jack height until the slot in the jack head engages with the rocker panel flange, between the two raised areas, nearest the wheel to be changed. There is a front and rear jacking point on each side of the vehicle (see illustration).

Turn the jack handle clockwise until the tire clears the ground. Remove the lug nuts and pull the wheel off. Replace it with the spare.

Install the lug nuts with the beveled edges facing in. Tighten them snugly. Don't attempt to tighten them completely until the vehicle is lowered or it could slip off the jack. Turn the jack handle counterclockwise to lower the vehicle. Remove the jack and tighten the lug nuts in a criss-cross pattern.

The jacking points are located near the front and rear wheel on each side of the vehicle

Install the cover (and trim ring, if used) and be sure it's snapped into place all the way around.

Stow the tire, jack and wrench. Unblock the wheels.

TOWING

Sephia/Spectra/2WD Sportage

As a general rule, the vehicle should be towed with the front (drive) wheels off the ground (the best method is to have the vehicle placed on a flat-bed tow truck). If they can't be raised, place them on a dolly. The ignition key must be in the OFF position, since the steering lock mechanism isn't strong enough to hold the front wheels straight while towing.

Vehicles equipped with an automatic transaxle can be towed from the front with all four wheels on the ground, provided that speeds don't exceed 35 mph and the distance is not over 50 miles. Before towing, check the transmission fluid level (see Chapter 1). If the level is below the HOT line on the dipstick, add fluid or use a towing dolly. Additionally, perform the following steps:

    a) *Release the parking brake*
    b) *Start the engine*
    c) *Move the transaxle gear selector into D, then to Neutral*
    d) *Turn off the engine*
    e) *Place the ignition key in the OFF (not the LOCK position)*

CAUTION:

Never tow a vehicle with an automatic transaxle from the rear with the front wheels on the ground.

When towing a vehicle equipped with a manual transaxle with all four wheels on the ground, be sure to place the shift lever in neutral and release the parking brake.

4WD Sportage

4WD Sportage models must be towed with all four wheels off the ground. A flat-bed car carrier is the preferred method, but a wheel-lift type tow truck will work, as long as the rear wheels are placed on a dolly.

2WD Sportage models can be towed with the rear wheels on the ground and the front wheels off the ground.

CAUTION:

Never tow the vehicle backwards, with the rear wheels raised and the front wheels on the ground.

All models

Never have the vehicle towed by a tow truck with a sling-type lift. Equipment specifically designed for towing should be used. It should be attached to the main structural members of the vehicle, not the bumpers or brackets.

Safety is a major consideration when towing and all applicable state and local laws must be obeyed. A safety chain system must be used at all times. Remember that power steering and power brakes will not work with the engine off.

Booster battery (jump) starting

Observe these precautions when using a booster battery to start a vehicle:

a)   *Before connecting the booster battery, make sure the ignition switch is in the Off position.*

b)   *Turn off the lights, heater and other electrical loads.*

c)   *Your eyes should be shielded. Safety goggles are a good idea.*

d)   *Make sure the booster battery is the same voltage as the dead one in the vehicle.*

e)   *The two vehicles MUST NOT TOUCH each other!*

f)   *Make sure the transaxle is in Neutral (manual) or Park (automatic).*

g)   *If the booster battery is not a maintenance-free type, remove the vent caps and lay a cloth over the vent holes.*

Connect the red jumper cable to the positive (+) terminals of each battery (see illustration).

Connect one end of the black jumper cable to the negative (-) terminal of the booster battery. The other end of this cable should be connected to a good ground on the vehicle to be started, such as a bolt or bracket on the body.

Start the engine using the booster battery, then, with the engine running at idle speed, disconnect the jumper cables in the reverse order of connection.

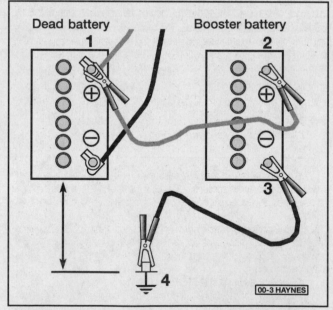

Make the booster battery cable connections in the numerical order shown (note that the negative cable of the booster battery is NOT attached to the negative terminal of the dead battery)

Automotive chemicals and lubricants

A number of automotive chemicals and lubricants are available for use during vehicle maintenance and repair. They include a wide variety of products ranging from cleaning solvents and degreasers to lubricants and protective sprays for rubber, plastic and vinyl.

CLEANERS

Carburetor cleaner and choke cleaner is a strong solvent for gum, varnish and carbon. Most carburetor cleaners leave a dry-type lubricant film which will not harden or gum up. Because of this film it is not recommended for use on electrical components.

Brake system cleaner is used to remove brake dust, grease and brake fluid from the brake system, where clean surfaces are absolutely necessary. It leaves no residue and often eliminates brake squeal caused by contaminants.

Electrical cleaner removes oxidation, corrosion and carbon deposits from electrical contacts, restoring full current flow. It can also be used to clean spark plugs, carburetor jets, voltage regulators and other parts where an oil-free surface is desired.

Demoisturants remove water and moisture from electrical components such as alternators, voltage regulators, electrical connectors and fuse blocks. They are non-conductive and non-corrosive.

Degreasers are heavy-duty solvents used to remove grease from the outside of the engine and from chassis components. They can be sprayed or brushed on and, depending on the type, are rinsed off either with water or solvent.

LUBRICANTS

Motor oil is the lubricant formulated for use in engines. It normally contains a wide variety of additives to prevent corrosion and reduce foaming and wear. Motor oil comes in various weights (viscosity ratings) from 0 to 50. The recommended weight of the oil depends on the season, temperature and the demands on the engine. Light oil is used in cold climates and under light load conditions. Heavy oil is used in hot climates and where high loads are encountered. Multi-viscosity oils are designed to have characteristics of both light and heavy oils and are available in a number of weights from 0W-20 to 20W-50.

Gear oil is designed to be used in differentials, manual transmissions and other areas where high-temperature lubrication is required.

Chassis and wheel bearing grease is a heavy grease used where increased loads and friction are encountered, such as for wheel bearings, ball-joints, tie-rod ends and universal joints.

High-temperature wheel bearing grease is designed to withstand the extreme temperatures encountered by wheel bearings in disc brake equipped vehicles. It usually contains molybdenum disulfide (moly), which is a dry-type lubricant.

White grease is a heavy grease for metal-to-metal applications where water is a problem. White grease stays soft under both low and high temperatures (usually from -100 to +190-degrees F), and will not wash off or dilute in the presence of water.

Assembly lube is a special extreme pressure lubricant, usually containing moly, used to lubricate high-load parts (such as main and rod bearings and cam lobes) for initial start-up of a new engine. The assembly lube lubricates the parts without being squeezed out or washed away until the engine oiling system begins to function.

Silicone lubricants are used to protect rubber, plastic, vinyl and nylon parts.

Graphite lubricants are used where oils cannot be used due to contamination problems, such as in locks. The dry graphite will lubricate metal parts while remaining uncontaminated by dirt, water, oil or acids. It is electrically conductive and will not foul electrical contacts in locks such as the ignition switch.

Moly penetrants loosen and lubricate frozen, rusted and corroded fasteners and prevent future rusting or freezing.

Heat-sink grease is a special electrically non-conductive grease that is used for mounting electronic ignition modules where it is essential that heat is transferred away from the module.

SEALANTS

RTV sealant is one of the most widely used gasket compounds. Made from silicone, RTV is air curing, it seals, bonds, waterproofs, fills surface irregularities, remains flexible, doesn't shrink, is relatively easy to remove, and is used as a supplementary sealer with almost all low and medium temperature gaskets.

Anaerobic sealant is much like RTV in that it can be used either to seal gaskets or to form gaskets by itself. It remains flexible, is solvent resistant and fills surface imperfections. The difference between an anaerobic sealant and an RTV-type sealant is in the curing. RTV cures when exposed to air, while an anaerobic sealant cures only in the absence of air. This means that an anaerobic sealant cures only after the assembly of parts, sealing them together.

Thread and pipe sealant is used for sealing hydraulic and pneumatic fittings and vacuum lines. It is usually made from a Teflon compound, and comes in a spray, a paint-on liquid and as a wrap-around tape.

CHEMICALS

Anti-seize compound prevents seizing, galling, cold welding, rust and corrosion in fasteners. High-temperature anti-seize, usually made with copper and graphite lubricants, is used for exhaust system and exhaust manifold bolts.

Anaerobic locking compounds are used to keep fasteners from vibrating or working loose and cure only after installation, in the absence of air. Medium strength locking compound is used for small nuts, bolts and screws that may be removed later. High-strength locking compound is for large nuts, bolts and studs which aren't removed on a regular basis.

Oil additives range from viscosity index improvers to chemical treatments that claim to reduce internal engine friction. It should be noted that most oil manufacturers caution against using additives with their oils.

Gas additives perform several functions, depending on their chemical makeup. They usually contain solvents that help dissolve gum and varnish that build up on carburetor, fuel injection and intake parts. They also serve to break down carbon deposits that form on the inside surfaces of the combustion chambers. Some additives contain upper cylinder lubricants for valves and piston rings, and others contain chemicals to remove condensation from the gas tank.

MISCELLANEOUS

Brake fluid is specially formulated hydraulic fluid that can withstand the heat and pressure encountered in brake systems. Care must be taken so this fluid does not come in contact with painted surfaces or plastics. An opened container should always be resealed to prevent contamination by water or dirt.

Weatherstrip adhesive is used to bond weatherstripping around doors, windows and trunk lids. It is sometimes used to attach trim pieces.

Undercoating is a petroleum-based, tar-like substance that is designed to protect metal surfaces on the underside of the vehicle from corrosion. It also acts as a sound-deadening agent by insulating the bottom of the vehicle.

Waxes and polishes are used to help protect painted and plated surfaces from the weather. Different types of paint may require the use of different types of wax and polish. Some polishes utilize a chemical or abrasive cleaner to help remove the top layer of oxidized (dull) paint on older vehicles. In recent years many non-wax polishes that contain a wide variety of chemicals such as polymers and silicones have been introduced. These non-wax polishes are usually easier to apply and last longer than conventional waxes and polishes.

CONVERSION FACTORS

LENGTH (distance)

Inches (in)	X	25.4	= Millimeters (mm)	X 0.0394	= Inches (in)
Feet (ft)	X	0.305	= Meters (m)	X 3.281	= Feet (ft)
Miles	X	1.609	= Kilometers (km)	X 0.621	= Miles

VOLUME (capacity)

Cubic inches (cu in; in³)	X	16.387	= Cubic centimeters (cc; cm³)	X 0.061	= Cubic inches (cu in; in³)
Imperial pints (Imp pt)	X	0.568	= Liters (l)	X 1.76	= Imperial pints (Imp pt)
Imperial quarts (Imp qt)	X	1.137	= Liters (l)	X 0.88	= Imperial quarts (Imp qt)
Imperial quarts (Imp qt)	X	1.201	= US quarts (US qt)	X 0.833	= Imperial quarts (Imp qt)
US quarts (US qt)	X	0.946	= Liters (l)	X 1.057	= US quarts (US qt)
Imperial gallons (Imp gal)	X	4.546	= Liters (l)	X 0.22	= Imperial gallons (Imp gal)
Imperial gallons (Imp gal)	X	1.201	= US gallons (US gal)	X 0.833	= Imperial gallons (Imp gal)
US gallons (US gal)	X	3.785	= Liters (l)	X 0.264	= US gallons (US gal)

MASS (weight)

Ounces (oz)	X	28.35	= Grams (g)	X 0.035	= Ounces (oz)
Pounds (lb)	X	0.454	= Kilograms (kg)	X 2.205	= Pounds (lb)

FORCE

Ounces-force (ozf; oz)	X	0.278	= Newtons (N)	X 3.6	= Ounces-force (ozf; oz)
Pounds-force (lbf; lb)	X	4.448	= Newtons (N)	X 0.225	= Pounds-force (lbf; lb)
Newtons (N)	X	0.1	= Kilograms-force (kgf; kg)	X 9.81	= Newtons (N)

PRESSURE

Pounds-force per square inch (psi; lbf/in²; lb/in²)	X	0.070	= Kilograms-force per square centimeter (kgf/cm²; kg/cm²)	X 14.223	= Pounds-force per square inch (psi; lbf/in²; lb/in²)
Pounds-force per square inch (psi; lbf/in²; lb/in²)	X	0.068	= Atmospheres (atm)	X 14.696	= Pounds-force per square inch (psi; lbf/in²; lb/in²)
Pounds-force per square inch (psi; lbf/in²; lb/in²)	X	0.069	= Bars	X 14.5	= Pounds-force per square inch (psi; lbf/in²; lb/in²)
Pounds-force per square inch (psi; lbf/in²; lb/in²)	X	6.895	= Kilopascals (kPa)	X 0.145	= Pounds-force per square inch (psi; lbf/in²; lb/in²)
Kilopascals (kPa)	X	0.01	= Kilograms-force per square centimeter (kgf/cm²; kg/cm²)	X 98.1	= Kilopascals (kPa)

TORQUE (moment of force)

Pounds-force inches (lbf in; lb in)	X	1.152	= Kilograms-force centimeter (kgf cm; kg cm)	X 0.868	= Pounds-force inches (lbf in; lb in)
Pounds-force inches (lbf in; lb in)	X	0.113	= Newton meters (Nm)	X 8.85	= Pounds-force inches (lbf in; lb in)
Pounds-force inches (lbf in; lb in)	X	0.083	= Pounds-force feet (lbf ft; lb ft)	X 12	= Pounds-force inches (lbf in; lb in)
Pounds-force feet (lbf ft; lb ft)	X	0.138	= Kilograms-force meters (kgf m; kg m)	X 7.233	= Pounds-force feet (lbf ft; lb ft)
Pounds-force feet (lbf ft; lb ft)	X	1.356	= Newton meters (Nm)	X 0.738	= Pounds-force feet (lbf ft; lb ft)
Newton meters (Nm)	X	0.102	= Kilograms-force meters (kgf m; kg m)	X 9.804	= Newton meters (Nm)

VACUUM

Inches mercury (in. Hg)	X	3.377	= Kilopascals (kPa)	X 0.2961	= Inches mercury
Inches mercury (in. Hg)	X	25.4	= Millimeters mercury (mm Hg)	X 0.0394	= Inches mercury

POWER

Horsepower (hp)	X	745.7	= Watts (W)	X 0.0013	= Horsepower (hp)

VELOCITY (speed)

Miles per hour (miles/hr; mph)	X	1.609	= Kilometers per hour (km/hr; kph)	X 0.621	= Miles per hour (miles/hr; mph)

FUEL CONSUMPTION *

Miles per gallon, Imperial (mpg)	X	0.354	= Kilometers per liter (km/l)	X 2.825	= Miles per gallon, Imperial (mpg)
Miles per gallon, US (mpg)	X	0.425	= Kilometers per liter (km/l)	X 2.352	= Miles per gallon, US (mpg)

TEMPERATURE

Degrees Fahrenheit = (°C x 1.8) + 32   Degrees Celsius (Degrees Centigrade; °C) = (°F - 32) x 0.56

*It is common practice to convert from miles per gallon (mpg) to liters/100 kilometers (l/100km), where mpg (Imperial) x l/100 km = 282 and mpg (US) x l/100 km = 235

FRACTION/DECIMAL/MILLIMETER EQUIVALENTS

DECIMALS TO MILLIMETERS

Decimal	mm	Decimal	mm
0.001	0.0254	0.500	12.7000
0.002	0.0508	0.510	12.9540
0.003	0.0762	0.520	13.2080
0.004	0.1016	0.530	13.4620
0.005	0.1270	0.540	13.7160
0.006	0.1524	0.550	13.9700
0.007	0.1778	0.560	14.2240
0.008	0.2032	0.570	14.4780
0.009	0.2286	0.580	14.7320
		0.590	14.9860
0.010	0.2540		
0.020	0.5080		
0.030	0.7620		
0.040	1.0160	0.600	15.2400
0.050	1.2700	0.610	15.4940
0.060	1.5240	0.620	15.7480
0.070	1.7780	0.630	16.0020
0.080	2.0320	0.640	16.2560
0.090	2.2860	0.650	16.5100
		0.660	16.7640
0.100	2.5400	0.670	17.0180
0.110	2.7940	0.680	17.2720
0.120	3.0480	0.690	17.5260
0.130	3.3020		
0.140	3.5560		
0.150	3.8100	0.700	17.7800
0.160	4.0640	0.710	18.0340
0.170	4.3180	0.720	18.2880
0.180	4.5720	0.730	18.5420
0.190	4.8260	0.740	18.7960
0.200	5.0800	0.750	19.0500
0.210	5.3340	0.760	19.3040
0.220	5.5880	0.770	19.5580
0.230	5.8420	0.780	19.8120
0.240	6.0960	0.790	20.0660
0.250	6.3500		
0.260	6.6040		
0.270	6.8580	0.800	20.3200
0.280	7.1120	0.810	20.5740
0.290	7.3660	0.820	21.8280
		0.830	21.0820
0.300	7.6200	0.840	21.3360
0.310	7.8740	0.850	21.5900
0.320	8.1280	0.860	21.8440
0.330	8.3820	0.870	22.0980
0.340	8.6360	0.880	22.3520
0.350	8.8900	0.890	22.6060
0.360	9.1440		
0.370	9.3980		
0.380	9.6520		
0.390	9.9060	0.900	22.8600
0.400	10.1600	0.910	23.1140
0.410	10.4140	0.920	23.3680
0.420	10.6680	0.930	23.6220
0.430	10.9220	0.940	23.8760
0.440	11.1760	0.950	24.1300
0.450	11.4300	0.960	24.3840
0.460	11.6840	0.970	24.6380
0.470	11.9380	0.980	24.8920
0.480	12.1920	0.990	25.1460
0.490	12.4460	1.000	25.4000

FRACTIONS TO DECIMALS TO MILLIMETERS

Fraction	Decimal	mm	Fraction	Decimal	mm
1/64	0.0156	0.3969	33/64	0.5156	13.0969
1/32	0.0312	0.7938	17/32	0.5312	13.4938
3/64	0.0469	1.1906	35/64	0.5469	13.8906
1/16	0.0625	1.5875	9/16	0.5625	14.2875
5/64	0.0781	1.9844	37/64	0.5781	14.6844
3/32	0.0938	2.3812	19/32	0.5938	15.0812
7/64	0.1094	2.7781	39/64	0.6094	15.4781
1/8	0.1250	3.1750	5/8	0.6250	15.8750
9/64	0.1406	3.5719	41/64	0.6406	16.2719
5/32	0.1562	3.9688	21/32	0.6562	16.6688
11/64	0.1719	4.3656	43/64	0.6719	17.0656
3/16	0.1875	4.7625	11/16	0.6875	17.4625
13/64	0.2031	5.1594	45/64	0.7031	17.8594
7/32	0.2188	5.5562	23/32	0.7188	18.2562
15/64	0.2344	5.9531	47/64	0.7344	18.6531
1/4	0.2500	6.3500	3/4	0.7500	19.0500
17/64	0.2656	6.7469	49/64	0.7656	19.4469
9/32	0.2812	7.1438	25/32	0.7812	19.8438
19/64	0.2969	7.5406	51/64	0.7969	20.2406
5/16	0.3125	7.9375	13/16	0.8125	20.6375
21/64	0.3281	8.3344	53/64	0.8281	21.0344
11/32	0.3438	8.7312	27/32	0.8438	21.4312
23/64	0.3594	9.1281	55/64	0.8594	21.8281
3/8	0.3750	9.5250	7/8	0.8750	22.2250
25/64	0.3906	9.9219	57/64	0.8906	22.6219
13/32	0.4062	10.3188	29/32	0.9062	23.0188
27/64	0.4219	10.7156	59/64	0.9219	23.4156
7/16	0.4375	11.1125	15/16	0.9375	23.8125
29/64	0.4531	11.5094	61/64	0.9531	24.2094
15/32	0.4688	11.9062	31/32	0.9688	24.6062
31/64	0.4844	12.3031	63/64	0.9844	25.0031
1/2	0.5000	12.7000	1	1.0000	25.4000

Regardless of how enthusiastic you may be about getting on with the job at hand, take the time to ensure that your safety is not jeopardized. A moment's lack of attention can result in an accident, as can failure to observe certain simple safety precautions. The possibility of an accident will always exist, and the following points should not be considered a comprehensive list of all dangers. Rather, they are intended to make you aware of the risks and to encourage a safety conscious approach to all work you carry out on your vehicle.

ESSENTIAL DOS AND DON'TS

DON'T rely on a jack when working under the vehicle. Always use approved jackstands to support the weight of the vehicle and place them under the recommended lift or support points.

DON'T attempt to loosen extremely tight fasteners (i.e. wheel lug nuts) while the vehicle is on a jack - it may fall.

DON'T start the engine without first making sure that the transmission is in Neutral (or Park where applicable) and the parking brake is set.

DON'T remove the radiator cap from a hot cooling system - let it cool or cover it with a cloth and release the pressure gradually.

DON'T attempt to drain the engine oil until you are sure it has cooled to the point that it will not burn you.

DON'T touch any part of the engine or exhaust system until it has cooled sufficiently to avoid burns.

DON'T siphon toxic liquids such as gasoline, antifreeze and brake fluid by mouth, or allow them to remain on your skin.

DON'T inhale brake lining dust - it is potentially hazardous (see Asbestos below).

DON'T allow spilled oil or grease to remain on the floor - wipe it up before someone slips on it.

DON'T use loose fitting wrenches or other tools which may slip and cause injury.

DON'T push on wrenches when loosening or tightening nuts or bolts. Always try to pull the wrench toward you. If the situation calls for pushing the wrench away, push with an open hand to avoid scraped knuckles if the wrench should slip.

DON'T attempt to lift a heavy component alone - get someone to help you.

DON'T rush or take unsafe shortcuts to finish a job.

DON'T allow children or animals in or around the vehicle while you are working on it.

DO wear eye protection when using power tools such as a drill, sander, bench grinder, etc. and when working under a vehicle.

DO keep loose clothing and long hair well out of the way of moving parts.

DO make sure that any hoist used has a safe working load rating adequate for the job.

DO get someone to check on you periodically when working alone on a vehicle.

DO carry out work in a logical sequence and make sure that everything is correctly assembled and tightened.

DO keep chemicals and fluids tightly capped and out of the reach of children and pets.

DO remember that your vehicle's safety affects that of yourself and others. If in doubt on any point, get professional advice.

STEERING, SUSPENSION AND BRAKES

These systems are essential to driving safety, so make sure you have a qualified shop or individual check your work. Also, compressed suspension springs can cause injury if released suddenly - be sure to use a spring compressor.

AIRBAGS

Airbags are explosive devices that can CAUSE injury if they deploy while you're working on the vehicle. Follow the manufacturer's instructions to disable the airbag whenever you're working in the vicinity of airbag components.

ASBESTOS

Certain friction, insulating, sealing, and other products - such as brake linings, brake bands, clutch linings, torque converters, gaskets, etc. - may contain asbestos or other hazardous friction material. Extreme care must be taken to avoid inhalation of dust from such products, since it is hazardous to health. If in doubt, assume that they do contain asbestos.

FIRE

Remember at all times that gasoline is highly flammable. Never smoke or have any kind of open flame around when working on a vehicle. But the risk does not end there. A spark caused by an electrical short circuit, by two metal surfaces contacting each other, or even by static electricity built up in your body under certain conditions, can ignite gasoline vapors, which in a confined space are highly explosive. Do not, under any circumstances, use gasoline for cleaning parts. Use an approved safety solvent.

Always disconnect the battery ground (-) cable at the battery before working on any part of the fuel system or electrical system. Never risk spilling fuel on a hot engine or exhaust component. It is strongly recommended that a fire extinguisher suitable for use on fuel and electrical fires be kept handy in the garage or workshop at all times. Never try to extinguish a fuel or electrical fire with water.

FUMES

Certain fumes are highly toxic and can quickly cause unconsciousness and even death if inhaled to any extent. Gasoline vapor falls into this category, as do the vapors from some cleaning solvents. Any draining or pouring of such volatile fluids should be done in a well ventilated area.

When using cleaning fluids and solvents, read the instructions on the container carefully. Never use materials from unmarked containers.

Never run the engine in an enclosed space, such as a garage. Exhaust fumes contain carbon monoxide, which is extremely poisonous. If you need to run the engine, always do so in the open air, or at least have the rear of the vehicle outside the work area.

THE BATTERY

Never create a spark or allow a bare light bulb near a battery. They normally give off a certain amount of hydrogen gas, which is highly explosive.

Always disconnect the battery ground (-) cable at the battery before working on the fuel or electrical systems.

If possible, loosen the filler caps or cover when charging the battery from an external source (this does not apply to sealed or maintenance-free batteries). Do not charge at an excessive rate or the battery may burst.

Take care when adding water to a non maintenance-free battery and when carrying a battery. The electrolyte, even when diluted, is very corrosive and should not be allowed to contact clothing or skin.

Always wear eye protection when cleaning the battery to prevent the caustic deposits from entering your eyes.

HOUSEHOLD CURRENT

When using an electric power tool, inspection light, etc., which operates on household current, always make sure that the tool is correctly connected to its plug and that, where necessary, it is properly grounded. Do not use such items in damp conditions and, again, do not create a spark or apply excessive heat in the vicinity of fuel or fuel vapor.

SECONDARY IGNITION SYSTEM VOLTAGE

A severe electric shock can result from touching certain parts of the ignition system (such as the spark plug wires) when the engine is running or being cranked, particularly if components are damp or the insulation is defective. In the case of an electronic ignition system, the secondary system voltage is much higher and could prove fatal.

HYDROFLUORIC ACID

This extremely corrosive acid is formed when certain types of synthetic rubber, found in some O-rings, oil seals, fuel hoses, etc. are exposed to temperatures above 750-degrees F (400-degrees C). The rubber changes into a charred or sticky substance containing the acid. *Once formed, the acid remains dangerous for years. If it gets onto the skin, it may be necessary to amputate the limb concerned.*

When dealing with a vehicle which has suffered a fire, or with components salvaged from such a vehicle, wear protective gloves and discard them after use.

Troubleshooting

CONTENTS

Section Symptom

Engine

1 Engine will not rotate when attempting to start
2 Engine rotates but will not start
3 Engine hard to start when cold
4 Engine hard to start when hot
5 Starter motor noisy or excessively rough in engagement
6 Engine starts but stops immediately
7 Oil puddle under engine
8 Engine lopes while idling or idles erratically
9 Engine misses at idle speed
10 Engine misses throughout driving speed range
11 Engine stumbles on acceleration
12 Engine surges while holding accelerator steady
13 Engine stalls
14 Engine lacks power
15 Engine backfires
16 Pinging or knocking engine sounds during acceleration or uphill
17 Engine runs with oil pressure light on
18 Engine diesels (continues to run) after switching off

Engine electrical systems

19 Battery will not hold a charge
20 Alternator light fails to go out
21 Alternator light fails to come on when key is turned on

Fuel system

22 Excessive fuel consumption
23 Fuel leakage and/or fuel odor

Cooling system

24 Overheating
25 Overcooling
26 External coolant leakage
27 Internal coolant leakage
28 Coolant loss
29 Poor coolant circulation

Clutch

30 Pedal travels to floor - no pressure or very little resistance
31 Fluid in area of master cylinder dust cover and on pedal
32 Fluid on release cylinder
33 Pedal feels spongy when depressed
34 Unable to select gears
35 Clutch slips (engine speed increases with no increase in vehicle speed
36 Grabbing (chattering) as clutch is engaged
37 Transaxle rattling (clicking)
38 Noise in clutch area
39 Clutch pedal stays on floor
40 High pedal effort

Section Symptom

Manual transaxle

41 Knocking noise at low speeds
42 Noise most pronounced when turning
43 Clunk on acceleration or deceleration
44 Clicking noise in turns
45 Vibration
46 Noisy in neutral with engine running
47 Noisy in one particular gear
48 Noisy in all gears
49 Slips out of gear
50 Leaks lubricant
51 Locked in gear

Automatic transaxle

52 Fluid leakage
53 Transaxle fluid brown or has burned smell
54 General shift mechanism problems
55 Transaxle slips, shifts roughly, is noisy or has no drive in forward or reverse gears

Driveaxles

56 Clicking noise in turns
57 Shudder or vibration during acceleration
58 Vibration at highway speeds

Brakes

59 Vehicle pulls to one side during braking
60 Noise (high-pitched squeal when the brakes are applied)
61 Brake roughness or chatter (pedal pulsates)
62 Excessive pedal effort required to stop vehicle
63 Excessive brake pedal travel
64 Dragging brakes
65 Grabbing or uneven braking action
66 Brake pedal feels spongy when depressed
67 Brake pedal travels to the floor with little resistance
68 Parking brake does not hold

Suspension and steering systems

69 Vehicle pulls to one side
70 Abnormal or excessive tire wear
71 Wheel makes a thumping noise
72 Shimmy, shake or vibration
73 Hard steering
74 Poor returnability of steering to center
75 Abnormal noise at the front end
76 Wander or poor steering stability
77 Erratic steering when braking
78 Excessive pitching and/or rolling around corners or during braking
79 Suspension bottoms
80 Cupped tires
81 Excessive tire wear on outside edge
82 Excessive tire wear on inside edge
83 Tire tread worn in one place
84 Excessive play or looseness in steering system
85 Rattling or clicking noise in rack and pinion

This section provides an easy reference guide to the more common problems which may occur during the operation of your vehicle. These problems and their possible causes are grouped under headings denoting various components or systems, such as Engine, Cooling system, etc. They also refer you to the chapter and/or section which deals with the problem.

Remember that successful troubleshooting is not a mysterious black art practiced only by professional mechanics. It is simply the result of the right knowledge combined with an intelligent, systematic approach to the problem. Always work by a process of elimination, starting with the simplest solution and working through to the most complex - and never overlook the obvious. Anyone can run the gas tank dry or leave the lights on overnight, so don't assume that you are exempt from such oversights.

Finally, always establish a clear idea of why a problem has occurred and take steps to ensure that it doesn't happen again. If the electrical system fails because of a poor connection, check the other connections in the system to make sure that they don't fail as well. If a particular fuse continues to blow, find out why - don't just replace one fuse after another. Remember, failure of a small component can often be indicative of potential failure or incorrect functioning of a more important component or system.

ENGINE

1   Engine will not rotate when attempting to start

1   Battery terminal connections loose or corroded (Chapter 1).
2   Battery discharged or faulty (Chapters 1 and 5).
3   Automatic transaxle not completely engaged in Park (Chapter 7) or clutch pedal not completely depressed (Chapter 6).
4   Broken, loose or disconnected wiring in the starting circuit (Chapters 5 and 12).
5   Starter motor pinion jammed in flywheel ring gear (Chapter 5).
6   Starter solenoid faulty (Chapter 5).
7   Starter motor faulty (Chapter 5).
8   Ignition switch faulty (Chapter 12).
9   Starter pinion or flywheel teeth worn or broken (Chapter 5).

2   Engine rotates but will not start

1   Fuel tank empty.
2   Battery discharged (engine rotates slowly) (Chapter 5).
3   Battery terminal connections loose or corroded (Chapter 1).
4   Leaking fuel injector(s), faulty fuel pump, pressure regulator, etc. (Chapter 4).
5   Broken or stripped timing belt (Chapter 2A) or broken timing chain (Chapter 2B).
6   Ignition components damp or damaged (Chapter 5).
7   Worn, faulty or incorrectly gapped spark plugs (Chapter 1).
8   Broken, loose or disconnected wiring in the starting circuit (Chapter 5).
9   Broken, loose or disconnected wires at the ignition coil or faulty coil (Chapter 5).
10   Defective crankshaft or camshaft sensor (Chapter 6).

3   Engine hard to start when cold

1   Battery discharged or low (Chapter 1).
2   Malfunctioning fuel system (Chapter 4).
3   Faulty coolant temperature sensor or intake air temperature sensor (Chapter 6).
4   Faulty ignition system (Chapter 5).

4   Engine hard to start when hot

1   Air filter clogged (Chapter 1).
2   Fuel not reaching the fuel injection system (Chapter 4).

3   Corroded battery connections, especially ground (Chapter 1).
4   Faulty coolant temperature sensor or intake air temperature sensor (Chapter 6).

5   Starter motor noisy or excessively rough in engagement

1   Pinion or flywheel gear teeth worn or broken (Chapter 5).
2   Starter motor mounting bolts loose or missing (Chapter 5).

6   Engine starts but stops immediately

1   Loose or faulty electrical connections at ignition coil or alternator (Chapter 5).
2   Insufficient fuel reaching the fuel injector(s) (Chapters 1 and 4).
3   Vacuum leak at the gasket between the intake manifold/plenum and throttle body (Chapter 4).

7   Oil puddle under engine

1   Oil pan gasket and/or oil pan drain bolt washer leaking (Chapter 2).
2   Oil pressure sending unit leaking (Chapter 2).
3   Valve cover leaking (Chapter 2).
4   Engine oil seals leaking (Chapter 2).
5   Oil pump housing leaking (Chapter 2).

8   Engine lopes while idling or idles erratically

1   Vacuum leakage (Chapters 2 and 4).
2   Leaking EGR valve (Chapter 6).
3   Air filter clogged (Chapter 1).
4   Malfunction in the fuel injection or engine control system (Chapters 4 and 6).
5   Leaking head gasket (Chapter 2).
6   Timing belt or chain and/or sprockets worn (Chapter 2).
7   Camshaft lobes worn (Chapter 2).

9   Engine misses at idle speed

1   Spark plugs worn or not gapped properly (Chapter 1).
2   Faulty spark plug wires (Chapter 1).
3   Vacuum leaks (Chapter 1).
4   Incorrect ignition timing (Chapter 1).
5   Uneven or low compression (Chapter 2).
6   Problem with the fuel injection system (Chapter 4).

10 Engine misses throughout driving speed range

1   Fuel filter clogged and/or impurities in the fuel system (Chapters 1 and 4).
2   Low fuel pressure (Chapter 4).
3   Faulty or incorrectly gapped spark plugs (Chapter 1).
4   Leaking spark plug wires (Chapters 1 or 5).
5   Faulty emission system components (Chapter 6).
6   Low or uneven cylinder compression pressures (Chapter 2).
7   Weak or faulty ignition system (Chapter 5).
8   Vacuum leak in fuel injection system, intake manifold, air control valve or vacuum hoses (Chapters 4 and 6).

11 Engine stumbles on acceleration

1   Spark plugs fouled (Chapter 1).
2   Problem with fuel injection or engine control system (Chapters 4 and 6).
3   Fuel filter clogged (Chapters 1 and 4).
4   Intake manifold air leak (Chapters 2 and 4).
5   Problem with the emissions control system (Chapter 6).

12 Engine surges while holding accelerator steady

1   Intake air leak (Chapter 4).
2   Fuel pump or fuel pressure regulator faulty (Chapter 4).
3   Problem with the fuel injection system (Chapter 4).
4   Problem with the emissions control system (Chapter 6).

13 Engine stalls

1   Idle speed incorrect (Chapter 1).
2   Fuel filter clogged and/or water and impurities in the fuel system (Chapters 1 and 4).
3   Distributor components damp or damaged (Chapter 5).
4   Faulty emissions system components (Chapter 6).
5   Faulty or incorrectly gapped spark plugs (Chapter 1).
6   Faulty spark plug wires (Chapter 1).
7   Vacuum leak in the fuel injection system, intake manifold or vacuum hoses (Chapters 2 and 4).

14 Engine lacks power

1   Obstructed exhaust system (Chapter 4).
2   Defective spark plug wires or faulty coil (Chapters 1 and 5).
3   Faulty or incorrectly gapped spark plugs (Chapter 1).
4   Problem with the fuel injection system (Chapter 4).
5   Plugged air filter (Chapter 1).
6   Brakes binding (Chapter 9).
7   Automatic transaxle fluid level incorrect (Chapter 1).
8   Clutch slipping (Chapter 8).
9   Fuel filter clogged and/or impurities in the fuel system (Chapters 1 and 4).
10 Emission control system not functioning properly (Chapter 6).
11 Low or uneven cylinder compression pressures (Chapter 2).

15 Engine backfires

1   Emission control system not functioning properly (Chapter 6).
2   Problem with the fuel injection system (Chapter 4).
3   Vacuum leak at fuel injector(s), intake manifold, air control valve or vacuum hoses (Chapters 2 and 4).
4   Valve clearances incorrectly set and/or valves sticking (Chapter 2).

16 Pinging or knocking engine sounds during acceleration or uphill

1   Incorrect grade of fuel.
2   Fuel injection system faulty (Chapter 4).
3   Improper or damaged spark plugs or wires (Chapter 1).
4   Knock sensor defective (Chapter 6).
5   EGR valve not functioning (Chapter 6).
6   Vacuum leak (Chapters 2 and 4).

17 Engine runs with oil pressure light on

1   Low oil level (Chapter 1).
2   Idle rpm below specification (Chapter 1).
3   Short in wiring circuit (Chapter 12).
4   Faulty oil pressure sender (Chapter 2).
5   Worn engine bearings and/or oil pump (Chapter 2).

18 Engine diesels (continues to run) after switching off

1   Idle speed too high (Chapter 1).
2   Excessive engine operating temperature (Chapter 3).

ENGINE ELECTRICAL SYSTEMS

19 Battery will not hold a charge

1   Alternator drivebelt defective or not adjusted properly (Chapter 1).
2   Battery electrolyte level low (Chapter 1).
3   Battery terminals loose or corroded (Chapter 1).
4   Alternator not charging properly (Chapter 5).
5   Loose, broken or faulty wiring in the charging circuit (Chapter 5).
6   Short in vehicle wiring (Chapter 12).
7   Internally defective battery (Chapters 1 and 5).

20 Alternator light fails to go out

1   Faulty alternator or charging circuit (Chapter 5).
2   Alternator drivebelt defective or out of adjustment (Chapter 1).
3   Alternator voltage regulator inoperative (Chapter 5).

21 Alternator light fails to come on when key is turned on

1   Warning light bulb defective (Chapter 12).
2   Fault in the printed circuit, dash wiring or bulb holder (Chapter 12).

FUEL SYSTEM

22 Excessive fuel consumption

1 Dirty or clogged air filter element (Chapter 1).
2 Emissions system not functioning properly (Chapter 6).
3 Fuel injection system not functioning properly (Chapter 4).
4 Low tire pressure or incorrect tire size (Chapter 1).

23 Fuel leakage and/or fuel odor

1 Leaking fuel feed or return line (Chapters 1 and 4).
2 Tank overfilled.
3 Evaporative canister filter clogged (Chapters 1 and 6).
4 Problem with the fuel injection system (Chapter 4).

COOLING SYSTEM

24 Overheating

1 Insufficient coolant in system (Chapter 1).
2 Water pump drivebelt defective or out of adjustment (Chapter 1).
3 Radiator core blocked or grille restricted (Chapter 3).
4 Thermostat faulty (Chapter 3).
5 Electric coolant fan inoperative or blades broken (Chapter 3).
6 Radiator cap not maintaining proper pressure (Chapter 3).

25 Overcooling

1 Faulty thermostat (Chapter 3).
2 Inaccurate temperature gauge sending unit (Chapter 3).

26 External coolant leakage

1 Deteriorated/damaged hoses; loose clamps (Chapters 1 and 3).
2 Water pump defective (Chapter 3).
3 Leakage from radiator core or coolant reservoir (Chapter 3).
4 Engine drain or water jacket core plugs leaking (Chapter 2).

27 Internal coolant leakage

1 Leaking cylinder head gasket (Chapter 2).
2 Cracked cylinder bore or cylinder head (Chapter 2).

28 Coolant loss

1 Too much coolant in reservoir (Chapter 1).
2 Coolant boiling away because of overheating (Chapter 3).
3 Internal or external leakage (Chapter 3).
4 Faulty radiator cap (Chapter 3).

29 Poor coolant circulation

1 Inoperative water pump (Chapter 3).
2 Restriction in cooling system (Chapters 1 and 3).
3 Water pump drivebelt defective/out of adjustment (Chapter 1).
4 Thermostat sticking (Chapter 3).

CLUTCH

30 Pedal travels to floor - no pressure or very little resistance

1 Master or release cylinder faulty (Chapter 8).
2 Hose/pipe burst or leaking (Chapter 8).
3 Connections leaking (Chapter 8).
4 No fluid in reservoir (Chapter 8).
5 If fluid level in reservoir rises as pedal is depressed, master cylinder center valve seal is faulty (Chapter 8).
6 If there is fluid on dust seal at master cylinder, piston primary seal is leaking (Chapter 8).
7 Broken release bearing or fork (Chapter 8).
8 Faulty pressure plate diaphragm spring (Chapter 8).

31 Fluid in area of master cylinder dust cover and on pedal

Rear seal failure in master cylinder (Chapter 8).

32 Fluid on release cylinder

Release cylinder plunger seal faulty (Chapter 8).

33 Pedal feels spongy when depressed

Air in system (Chapter 8).

34 Unable to select gears

1 Faulty transaxle (Chapter 7).
2 Faulty clutch disc or pressure plate (Chapter 8).
3 Faulty release lever or release bearing (Chapter 8).
4 Faulty shift lever assembly or control cables (Chapter 8).

35 Clutch slips (engine speed increases with no increase in vehicle speed)

1 Clutch plate worn (Chapter 8).
2 Clutch plate is oil soaked by leaking rear main seal (Chapters 2 and 8).
3 Clutch plate not seated (Chapter 8).
4 Warped pressure plate or flywheel (Chapter 8).
5 Weak pressure plate diaphragm spring (Chapter 8).
6 Clutch plate overheated. Allow to cool.

36 Grabbing (chattering) as clutch is engaged

1 Oil on clutch plate lining, burned or glazed facings (Chapter 8).
2 Worn or loose engine or transaxle mounts (Chapter 2).
3 Worn splines on clutch plate hub (Chapter 8).
4 Warped pressure plate or flywheel (Chapter 8).
5 Burned or smeared resin on flywheel or pressure plate (Chapter 8).

37 Transaxle rattling (clicking)

1 Release lever loose (Chapter 8).
2 Clutch plate damper spring failure (Chapter 8).

38   Noise in clutch area

1   Fork shaft improperly installed (Chapter 8).
2   Faulty bearing (Chapter 8).

39   Clutch pedal stays on floor

1   Clutch master cylinder piston binding in bore (Chapter 8).
2   Broken release bearing or fork (Chapter 8).

40   High pedal effort

1   Piston binding in bore (Chapter 8).
2   Pressure plate faulty (Chapter 8).
3   Incorrect size master or release cylinder (Chapter 8).

MANUAL TRANSAXLE

41   Knocking noise at low speeds

1   Worn driveaxle constant velocity (CV) joints (Chapter 8).
2   Worn side gear shaft counterbore in differential case (Chapter 7A).*

42   Noise most pronounced when turning

Differential gear noise (Chapter 7A).*

43   Clunk on acceleration or deceleration

1   Loose engine or transaxle mounts (Chapter 2).
2   Worn differential pinion shaft in case.*
3   Worn side gear shaft counterbore in differential case (Chapter 7A).*
4   Worn or damaged driveaxle inboard CV joints (Chapter 8).

44   Clicking noise in turns

Worn or damaged outboard CV joint (Chapter 8).

45   Vibration

1   Rough wheel bearing (Chapter 10).
2   Damaged driveaxle (Chapter 8).
3   Out-of-round tires (Chapter 1).
4   Tire out of balance (Chapters 1 and 10).
5   Worn CV joint (Chapter 8).

46   Noisy in neutral with engine running

1   Damaged input gear bearing (Chapter 7A).*
2   Damaged clutch release bearing (Chapter 8).

47   Noisy in one particular gear

1   Damaged or worn constant mesh gears (Chapter 7A).*
2   Damaged or worn synchronizers (Chapter 7A).*

3   Bent reverse fork (Chapter 7A).*
4   Damaged fourth speed gear or output gear (Chapter 7A).*
5   Worn or damaged reverse idler gear or idler bushing (Chapter 7A).*

48   Noisy in all gears

1   Insufficient lubricant (Chapter 7A).
2   Damaged or worn bearings (Chapter 7A).*
3   Worn or damaged input gear shaft and/or output gear shaft (Chapter 7A).*

49   Slips out of gear

1   Worn or improperly adjusted linkage (Chapter 7A).
2   Shift linkage does not work freely, binds (Chapter 7A).
3   Input gear bearing retainer broken or loose (Chapter 7A).*
4   Worn shift fork (Chapter 7A).*

50   Leaks lubricant

1   Side gear shaft seals worn (Chapter 7).
2   Excessive amount of lubricant in transaxle (Chapters 1 and 7A).
3   Loose or broken input gear shaft bearing retainer (Chapter 7A).*
4   Input gear bearing retainer O-ring and/or lip seal damaged (Chapter 7A).*

51   Locked in gear

Lock pin or interlock pin missing (Chapter 7A).*
Although the corrective action necessary to remedy the symptoms described is beyond the scope of this manual, the above information should be helpful in isolating the cause of the condition so that the owner can communicate clearly with a professional mechanic.

AUTOMATIC TRANSAXLE

➡**Note: Due to the complexity of the automatic transaxle, it is difficult for the home mechanic to properly diagnose and service this component. For problems other than the following, the vehicle should be taken to a dealer or transmission shop.**

52   Fluid leakage

1   Automatic transaxle fluid is a deep red color. Fluid leaks should not be confused with engine oil, which can easily be blown onto the transaxle by air flow.
2   To pinpoint a leak, first remove all built-up dirt and grime from the transaxle housing with degreasing agents and/or steam cleaning. Then drive the vehicle at low speeds so air flow will not blow the leak far from its source. Raise the vehicle and determine where the leak is coming from. Common areas of leakage are:
   a) *Dipstick tube (Chapters 1 and 7)*
   b) *Transaxle oil lines (Chapter 7*
   c) *Speed sensor (Chapter 6*
   d) *Driveaxle oil seals (Chapter 7).*

53 Transaxle fluid brown or has a burned smell

Transaxle fluid overheated (Chapter 1).

54 General shift mechanism problems

1   Chapter 7, Part B, deals with checking and adjusting the shift linkage on automatic transaxles. Common problems which may be attributed to poorly adjusted linkage are:

　　a) Engine starting in gears other than Park or Neutral.
　　b) Indicator on shifter pointing to a gear other than the one actually being used.
　　c) Vehicle moves when in Park.

2   Refer to Chapter 7B for the shift linkage adjustment procedure.

55 Transaxle slips, shifts roughly, is noisy or has no drive in forward or reverse gears

There are many probable causes for the above problems, but the home mechanic should be concerned with only one possibility - fluid level. Before taking the vehicle to a repair shop, check the level and condition of the fluid as described in Chapter 1. Correct the fluid level as necessary or change the fluid and filter if needed. If the problem persists, have a professional diagnose the cause.

DRIVEAXLES

56 Clicking noise in turns

Worn or damaged outboard CV joint (Chapter 8).

57 Shudder or vibration during acceleration

1   Excessive toe-in (Chapter 10).
2   Worn or damaged inboard or outboard CV joints (Chapter 8).
3   Sticking inboard CV joint assembly (Chapter 8).

58 Vibration at highway speeds

1   Out-of-balance front wheels and/or tires (Chapters 1 and 10).
2   Out-of-round front tires (Chapters 1 and 10).
3   Worn CV joint(s) (Chapter 8).

BRAKES

➡Note: Before assuming that a brake problem exists, make sure that:

　　a) The tires are in good condition and properly inflated (Chapter 1).
　　b) The front end alignment is correct.
　　c) The vehicle is not loaded with weight in an unequal manner.

59 Vehicle pulls to one side during braking

1   Incorrect tire pressures (Chapter 1).
2   Front end out of alignment (have the front end aligned).
3   Front, or rear, tire sizes not matched to one another.
4   Restricted brake lines or hoses (Chapter 9).
5   Malfunctioning drum brake or caliper assembly (Chapter 9).
6   Loose suspension parts (Chapter 10).
7   Excessive wear of brake shoe or pad material or disc/drum on one side (Chapter 9).
8   Contamination (grease or brake fluid) of brake shoe or pad material or disc/drum on one side (Chapter 9).

60 Noise (high-pitched squeal when the brakes are applied)

Front brake pads worn out. Replace pads with new ones immediately (Chapter 9).

61 Brake roughness or chatter (pedal pulsates)

1   Excessive lateral runout (Chapter 9).
2   Uneven pad wear (Chapter 9).
3   Defective disc (Chapter 9).

62 Excessive brake pedal effort required to stop vehicle

1   Malfunctioning power brake booster (Chapter 9).
2   Partial system failure (Chapter 9).
3   Excessively worn pads or shoes (Chapter 9).
4   Piston in caliper or wheel cylinder stuck or sluggish (Chapter 9).
5   Brake pads or shoes contaminated with oil or grease (Chapter 9).
6   Brake disc grooved and/or glazed (Chapter 9).
7   New pads or shoes installed and not yet seated. It will take a while for the new material to seat against the disc or drum.

63 Excessive brake pedal travel

1   Partial brake system failure (Chapter 9).
2   Insufficient fluid in master cylinder (Chapters 1 and 9).
3   Air trapped in system (Chapter 9).

64 Dragging brakes

1   Incorrect adjustment of brake light switch (Chapter 9).
2   Master cylinder pistons not returning correctly (Chapter 9).
3   Restricted brakes lines or hoses (Chapter 9).
4   Incorrect parking brake adjustment (Chapter 9).

65 Grabbing or uneven braking action

1   Binding brake pedal mechanism (Chapter 9).
2   Contaminated brake linings (Chapter 9).

66 Brake pedal feels spongy when depressed

1   Air in hydraulic lines (Chapter 9).
2   Master cylinder mounting bolts loose (Chapter 9).
3   Master cylinder defective (Chapter 9).

67   Brake pedal travels to the floor with little resistance

1   Little or no fluid in the master cylinder reservoir caused by leaking caliper or wheel cylinder piston(s) (Chapter 9).
2   Loose, damaged or disconnected brake lines (Chapter 9).

68   Parking brake does not hold

Parking brake linkage improperly adjusted (Chapter 9).

SUSPENSION AND STEERING SYSTEMS

➡**Note: Before attempting to diagnose the suspension and steering systems, perform the following preliminary checks:**

a) Tires for wrong pressure and uneven wear.
b) Steering universal joints from the column to the rack and pinion for loose connectors or wear.
c) Front and rear suspension and the rack and pinion assembly for loose or damaged parts.
d) Out-of-round or out-of-balance tires, bent rims and loose and/or rough wheel bearings.

69   Vehicle pulls to one side

1   Mismatched or uneven tires (Chapter 10).
2   Broken or sagging springs (Chapter 10).
3   Wheel alignment incorrect. Have the wheels professionally aligned.
4   Front brake dragging (Chapter 9).

70   Abnormal or excessive tire wear

1   Wheel alignment out-of-specification. Have the wheels aligned.
2   Sagging or broken springs (Chapter 10).
3   Tire out-of-balance (Chapter 10).
4   Worn strut damper (Chapter 10).
5   Overloaded vehicle.
6   Tires not rotated regularly.

71   Wheel makes a thumping noise

1   Blister or bump on tire (Chapter 10).
2   Improper strut damper action (Chapter 10).

72   Shimmy, shake or vibration

1   Tire or wheel out-of-balance or out-of-round (Chapter 10).
2   Worn wheel bearings (Chapter 10).
3   Worn tie-rod ends (Chapter 10).
4   Worn balljoints (Chapters 1 and 10).
5   Excessive wheel runout (Chapter 10).
6   Blister or bump on tire (Chapter 10).

73   Hard steering

1   Lack of lubrication at balljoints and/or tie-rod ends (Chapter 10).
2   Wheel alignment out-of-specifications. Have the wheels professionally aligned.

3   Low tire pressure(s) (Chapter 1).
4   Worn steering gear (Chapter 10).

74   Poor returnability of steering to center

1   Lack of lubrication at balljoints and tie-rod ends (Chapter 10).
2   Binding in balljoints (Chapter 10).
3   Binding in steering column (Chapter 10).
4   Lack of lubricant in steering gear assembly (Chapter 10).
5   Wheel alignment out-of-specifications. Have the wheels professionally aligned.

75   Abnormal noise at the front end

1   Lack of lubrication at balljoints and tie-rod ends (Chapters 1 and 10).
2   Damaged strut mounting (Chapter 10).
3   Worn control arm bushings or tie-rod ends (Chapter 10).
4   Loose stabilizer bar (Chapter 10).
5   Loose wheel nuts (Chapter 1).
6   Loose suspension bolts (Chapter 10).

76   Wander or poor steering stability

1   Mismatched or uneven tires (Chapter 10).
2   Lack of lubrication at balljoints and tie-rod ends (Chapters 1 and 10).
3   Worn strut assemblies (Chapter 10).
4   Loose stabilizer bar (Chapter 10).
5   Broken or sagging springs (Chapter 10).
6   Wheels out of alignment. Have the wheels professionally aligned.

77   Erratic steering when braking

1   Wheel bearings worn (Chapter 10).
2   Broken or sagging springs (Chapter 10).
3   Leaking wheel cylinder or caliper (Chapter 10).
4   Warped rotors or drums (Chapter 10).

78   Excessive pitching and/or rolling around corners or during braking

1   Loose stabilizer bar (Chapter 10).
2   Worn strut dampers or mountings (Chapter 10).
3   Broken or sagging springs (Chapter 10).
4   Overloaded vehicle.

79   Suspension bottoms

1   Overloaded vehicle.
2   Sagging springs (Chapter 10).

80   Cupped tires

1   Front wheel or rear wheel alignment out-of-specifications. Have the wheels professionally aligned.
2   Worn strut dampers or shock absorbers (Chapter 10).
3   Wheel bearings worn (Chapter 10).
4   Excessive tire or wheel runout (Chapter 10).
5   Worn balljoints (Chapter 10).

81   Excessive tire wear on outside edge

1   Inflation pressures incorrect (Chapter 1).
2   Excessive speed in turns.
3   Wheel alignment incorrect (excessive toe-in). Have professionally aligned.
4   Suspension arm bent or twisted (Chapter 10).

82   Excessive tire wear on inside edge

1   Inflation pressures incorrect (Chapter 1).
2   Wheel alignment incorrect (toe-out). Have professionally aligned.
3   Loose or damaged steering components (Chapter 10).

83   Tire tread worn in one place

1   Tires out-of-balance.
2   Damaged or buckled wheel. Inspect and replace if necessary.
3   Defective tire (Chapter 1).

84   Excessive play or looseness in steering system

1   Wheel bearing(s) worn (Chapter 10).
2   Tie-rod end loose (Chapter 10).
3   Steering gear loose (Chapter 10).
4   Worn or loose steering intermediate shaft U-joint (Chapter 10).

85   Rattling or clicking noise in steering gear

1   Steering gear loose (Chapter 10).
2   Steering gear defective.

Section

1   Maintenance schedule
2   Introduction
3   Tune-up general information
4   Fluid level checks
5   Tire and tire pressure checks
6   Engine oil and oil filter change
7   Windshield wiper blade inspection and replacement
8   Battery check, maintenance and charging
9   Cooling system check
10 Tire rotation
11 Seat belt check
12 Brake system check
13 Steering, suspension and driveaxle boot check
14 Underhood hose check and replacement
15 Fuel and exhaust system checks
16 Cabin air filter replacement
17 Air filter replacement
18 Drivebelt check, adjustment and replacement
19 Brake fluid change
20 Cooling system servicing (draining, flushing and refilling)
21 Timing belt check
22 Positive Crankcase Ventilation (PCV) valve - check and replacement
23 Spark plug check and replacement
24 Spark plug wire, distributor cap and rotor - check and replacement
25 Idle speed check and adjustment
26 Automatic transaxle fluid change
27 Manual transaxle lubricant change
28 Transfer case lubricant change (4WD models)
29 Differential lubricant change (4WD models)
30 Fuel filter replacement

Reference to other Chapters

CHECK ENGINE light on - See Chapter 6

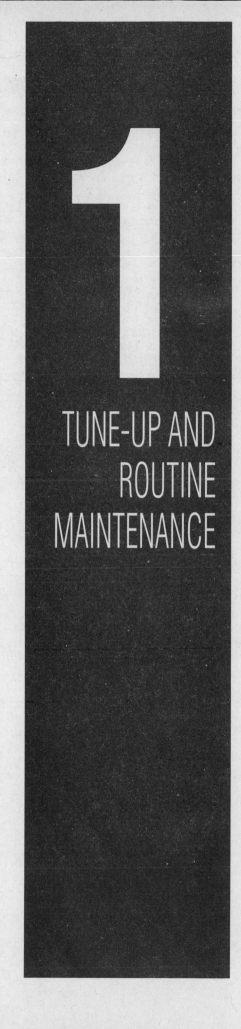

1

TUNE-UP AND ROUTINE MAINTENANCE

1 · Maintenance schedule

The maintenance intervals in this manual are provided with the assumption that you, not the dealer, will be doing the work. These are the minimum maintenance intervals recommended by the factory for vehicles that are driven daily. If you wish to keep your vehicle in peak condition at all times, you may wish to perform some of these procedures even more often. Because frequent maintenance enhances the efficiency, performance and resale value of your car, we encourage you to do so. If you drive in dusty areas, tow a trailer, idle or drive at low speeds for extended periods or drive for short distances (less than four miles) in below freezing temperatures, shorter intervals are also recommended.

When your vehicle is new, it should be serviced by a factory authorized dealer service department to protect the factory warranty. In many cases, the initial maintenance check is done at no cost to the owner.

EVERY 250 MILES (400 KM) OR WEEKLY, WHICHEVER COMES FIRST

Check the engine oil level (see Section 4)
Check the engine coolant level (see Section 4)
Check the brake/clutch fluid level (see Section 4)
Check the power steering fluid level (see Section 4)
Check the windshield washer fluid level (see Section 4)
Check the automatic transaxle fluid level (see Section 4)
Check the tires and tire pressures (see Section 5)
Check the operation of all lights
Check the horn operation

EVERY 3000 MILES (4800 KM) OR 3 MONTHS, WHICHEVER COMES FIRST

All items listed above, plus:
Change the engine oil and filter (see Section 6)

EVERY 7500 MILES (12,000 KM) OR 6 MONTHS, WHICHEVER COMES FIRST

All items listed above, plus:
Inspect (and replace, if necessary) the windshield wiper blades (see Section 7)
Check and service the battery (see Section 8)
Check the cooling system (see Section 9)
Rotate the tires (see Section 10)
Check the seatbelts (see Section 11)
Inspect the brake system (see Section 12)
Inspect (and replace, if necessary) the air filter element (see Section 17)

EVERY 15,000 MILES (24,000 KM) OR 12 MONTHS, WHICHEVER COMES FIRST

All items listed above, plus:
Check the manual transaxle lubricant level (see Section 4)

Check the transfer case lubricant level (4WD models) (see Section 4)
Check the rear differential lubricant level (4WD models) (see Section 4)
Check the suspension, steering components and driveaxle boots (see Section 13)*
Inspect underhood hoses (see Section 14)
Check the fuel system hoses and connections for leaks and damage (see Section 15)
Check the exhaust pipes and hangers (see Section 15)

EVERY 30,000 MILES (48,000 KM) OR 24 MONTHS, WHICHEVER COMES FIRST

All items listed above, plus:
Replace the cabin air filter (see Section 16)
Replace the air filter element (see Section 17)*
Check (and replace/adjust, if necessary) the drivebelts (see Section 18)
Change the brake fluid (see Section 19)
Service the cooling system (drain, flush and refill) (see Section 20)
Inspect (and replace, if necessary) the timing belt (see Section 21)
Check (and replace, if necessary) the PCV valve (see Section 22)
Replace the spark plugs (see Section 23)
Inspect and replace, if necessary, the spark plug wires, distributor cap and rotor (see Section 24)
Check and adjust, if necessary, the idle speed (see Section 25)

EVERY 60,000 MILES (96,000 KM) OR 36 MONTHS, WHICHEVER COMES FIRST

All items listed above, plus:
Change the automatic transaxle fluid (see Section 26)**
Change the manual transaxle lubricant (see Section 27)
Change the transfer case lubricant (4WD models) (see Section 28)
Change the rear differential lubricant (4WD models) (see Section 29)
Replace the fuel filter (see Section 30)
This item is affected by "severe" operating conditions as described below. If your vehicle is operated under "severe" conditions, perform all maintenance indicated with an asterisk (*) at 3000 mile/3 month intervals (unless otherwise specified in the schedule). Severe conditions are indicated if you mainly operate your vehicle under one or more of the following conditions:
Operating in dusty areas
Towing a trailer
Idling for extended periods and/or low speed operation
Operating in extended temperatures below freezing and when most trips are less than five miles
**If operated under one or more of the following conditions, change the or automatic transaxle fluid lubricant every 30,000 miles:*
In heavy city traffic where the outside temperature regularly reaches 90-degrees F (32-degrees C) or higher
In hilly or mountainous terrain
Frequent towing of a trailer

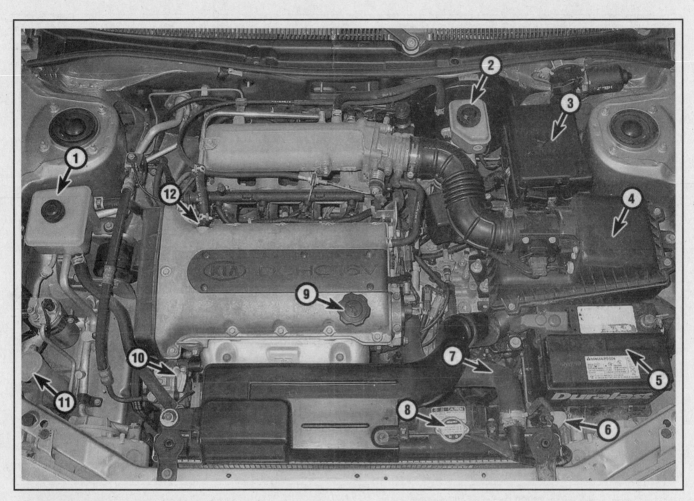

Engine compartment layout (1999 model shown)

1 Power steering fluid reservoir
2 Brake master cylinder reservoir
3 Underhood fuse/relay block
4 Air filter housing
5 Battery

6 Coolant reservoir (location
   varies by year - see Section 4)
7 Upper radiator hose
8 Radiator cap
9 Engine oil filler cap

10 Engine oil dipstick
11 Windshield washer fluid reservoir
12 Positive Crankcase Ventilation
    (PCV) valve

Engine compartment layout (2009 Sportage V6 model shown)

1	Power steering fluid reservoir	5	Battery	9	Engine oil filler cap
2	Brake master cylinder reservoir	6	Coolant reservoir	10	Engine oil dipstick
3	Underhood fuse/relay block	7	Upper radiator hose	11	Windshield washer fluid reservoir
4	Air filter housing	8	Radiator cap	12	Positive Crankcase Ventilation (PCV) valve

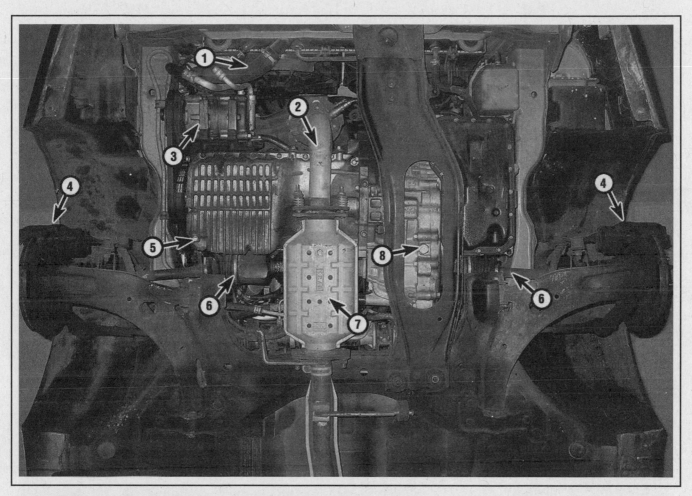

Typical engine compartment underside components (Sephia and Spectra models)

1	Lower radiator hose	4	Front disc brake caliper	7	Catalytic converter
2	Exhaust pipe	5	Engine oil drain plug	8	Automatic transaxle drain plug
3	Air conditioning compressor	6	Driveaxle		

Typical engine compartment underside components (2009 Sportage V6 4WD model shown, other Sportage models similar)

1	Engine oil drain plug	6	Exhaust pipe	10	Outer CV joint
2	Engine oil filter	7	Downstream catalytic converter	11	Front disc brake caliper
3	Transfer case drain plug (4WD models)	8	Inner CV joint	12	Transfer case (4WD models)
4	Transfer case fill plug (4WD models)	9	Driveaxle	13	Driveshaft (4WD models)
5	Automatic transaxle drain plug				

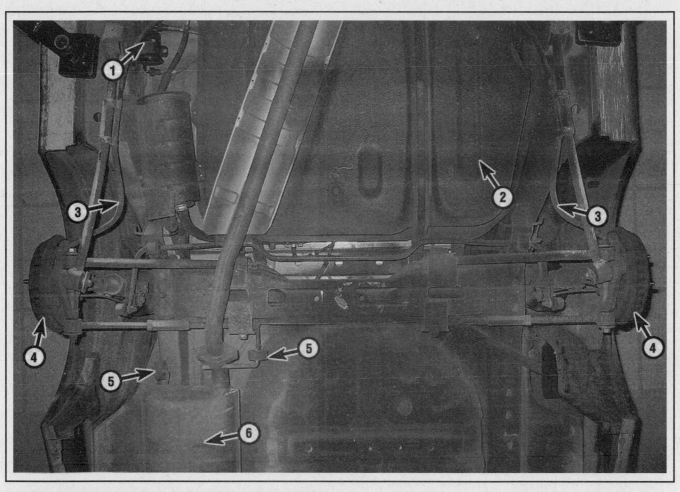

Typical rear underside components (Sephia and Spectra models)

1	Fuel filter	3	Parking brake cable	5	Exhaust system hanger
2	Fuel tank	4	Drum brake assembly	6	Muffler

Typical rear underside components (2009 Sportage 4WD model shown, other Sportage models similar)

1	Fuel tank	4	Muffler	7	Outer CV joint boot (4WD models)
2	Parking brake cable	5	Rear driveaxle (4WD models)	8	Rear differential drain plug
3	Exhaust system hanger	6	Inner CV joint boot (4WD models)		(4WD models)

2   Introduction

This Chapter is designed to help the home mechanic maintain the Sephia, Spectra and Sportage with the goals of maximum performance, economy, safety and reliability in mind.

Included is a master maintenance schedule, followed by procedures dealing specifically with each item on the schedule. Visual checks, adjustments, component replacement and other helpful items are included. Refer to the accompanying illustrations of the engine compartment and the underside of the vehicle for the locations of various components.

Servicing your vehicle in accordance with the mileage/time maintenance schedule and the step-by-step procedures will result in a planned maintenance program that should produce a long and reliable service life. Keep in mind that it's a comprehensive plan, so maintaining some items but not others at the specified intervals will not produce the same results.

As you service your vehicle, you will discover that many of the procedures can - and should - be grouped together because of the nature of the particular procedure you're performing or because of the close proximity of two otherwise unrelated components to one another.

For example, if the vehicle is raised for chassis lubrication, you should inspect the exhaust, suspension, steering and fuel systems while you're under the vehicle. When you're rotating the tires, it makes good sense to check the brakes since the wheels are already removed. Finally, let's suppose you have to borrow or rent a torque wrench. Even if you only need it to tighten the spark plugs, you might as well check the torque of as many critical fasteners as time allows.

The first step in this maintenance program is to prepare yourself before the actual work begins. Read through all the procedures you're planning to do, then gather up all the parts and tools needed. If it looks like you might run into problems during a particular job, seek advice from a mechanic or an experienced do-it-yourselfer.

OWNER'S MANUAL AND VECI LABEL INFORMATION

Your vehicle owner's manual was written for your year and model and contains very specific information on component locations, specifications, fuse ratings, part numbers, etc. The Owner's Manual is an important resource for the do-it-yourselfer to have; if one was not supplied with your vehicle, it can generally be ordered from a dealer parts department.

Among other important information, the Vehicle Emissions Control Information (VECI) label contains specifications and procedures for applicable tune-up adjustments and, in some instances, spark plugs. The information on this label is the exact maintenance data recommended by the manufacturer. This data often varies by intended operating altitude, local emissions regulations, month of manufacture, etc.

This Chapter contains procedural details, safety information and more ambitious maintenance intervals than you might find in manufacturer's literature. However, you may also find procedures or specifications in your Owner's Manual or VECI label that differ with what's printed here. In these cases, the Owner's Manual or VECI label can be considered correct, since it is specific to your particular vehicle.

3   Tune-up general information

The term tune-up is used in this manual to represent a combination of individual operations rather than one specific procedure.

If, from the time the vehicle is new, the routine maintenance schedule is followed closely and frequent checks are made of fluid levels and high wear items, as suggested throughout this manual, the engine will be kept in relatively good running condition and the need for additional work will be minimized.

More likely than not, however, there will be times when the engine is running poorly due to lack of regular maintenance. This is even more likely if a used vehicle, which has not received regular and frequent maintenance checks, is purchased. In such cases, an engine tune-up will be needed outside of the regular routine maintenance intervals.

The first step in any tune-up or diagnostic procedure to help correct a poor running engine is a cylinder compression check. A compression check (see Chapter 2C) will help determine the condition of internal engine components and should be used as a guide for tune-up and repair procedures. If, for instance, a compression check indicates serious internal engine wear, a conventional tune-up will not improve the performance of the engine and would be a waste of time and money. Because of its importance, the compression check should be done by someone with the right equipment and the knowledge to use it properly.

The following procedures are those most often needed to bring a generally poor running engine back into a proper state of tune.

MINOR TUNE-UP

Check all engine-related fluids (Section 4)
Clean, inspect and test the battery (Section 8)
Check the cooling system (Section 9)
Check all underhood hoses (Section 14)

MAJOR TUNE-UP

All items listed under Minor tune-up, plus . . .
Replace the air filter (Section 17)
Check the drivebelts (Section 18)
Replace the PCV valve (Section 22)
Replace the spark plugs (Section 23)
Check the charging system (Chapter 5)

4   Fluid level checks (every 250 miles [400km] or weekly)

1   Fluids are an essential part of the lubrication, cooling, brake and windshield washer systems. Because the fluids gradually become depleted and/or contaminated during normal operation of the vehicle, they must be periodically replenished. See *Recommended lubricants and fluids* in this Chapter's Specifications before adding fluid to any of the following components.

➡**Note: The vehicle must be on level ground when fluid levels are checked.**

ENGINE OIL

▸ **Refer to illustrations 4.2a, 4.2b and 4.4**

2   The oil level is checked with a dipstick, which is attached to the engine block (see illustrations). The dipstick extends through a metal tube down into the oil pan.

3   The oil level should be checked before the vehicle has been driven, or about 5 minutes after the engine has been shut off. If the oil is checked immediately after driving the vehicle, some of the oil will remain in the upper part of the engine, resulting in an inaccurate reading on the dipstick.

4   Pull the dipstick out of the tube and wipe all the oil from the end with a clean rag or paper towel. Insert the clean dipstick all the way back into the tube and pull it out again. Note the oil at the end of the dipstick. At its highest point, the level should be between the FULL and LOW marks on the dipstick (see illustration).

5   It takes one quart of oil to raise the level from the LOW mark to the FULL mark on the dipstick. Do not allow the level to drop below the LOW mark or oil starvation may cause engine damage. Conversely, overfilling the engine (adding oil above the FULL mark) may cause oil fouled spark plugs, oil leaks or oil seal failures. Maintaining the oil level above the FULL mark can cause excessive oil consumption.

6   To add oil, remove the filler cap from the valve cover. After adding oil, wait a few minutes to allow the level to stabilize, then pull out the dipstick and check the level again. Add more oil if required. Install the filler cap and tighten it by hand only.

7   Checking the oil level is an important preventive maintenance step. A consistently low oil level indicates oil leakage through damaged seals, defective gaskets or past worn rings or valve guides. If the oil looks milky in color or has water droplets in it, the cylinder head gasket(s) may be blown or the head(s) or block may be cracked. The engine should be checked immediately. The condition of the oil should also be checked. Whenever you check the oil level, slide your thumb and index finger up the dipstick before wiping off the oil. If you see small dirt or metal particles clinging to the dipstick, the oil should be changed (see Section 6).

ENGINE COOLANT

▸ **Refer to illustrations 4.10a and 4.10b**

✲✲ WARNING:

Do not allow antifreeze to come in contact with your skin or painted surfaces of the vehicle. Flush contaminated areas immediately with plenty of water. Don't store new coolant or leave old coolant lying around where it's accessible to children or pets - they're attracted by its sweet smell. Ingestion of even a small amount of coolant can be fatal! Wipe up garage floor and drip pan spills immediately. Keep antifreeze containers covered and repair cooling system leaks as soon as they're noticed.

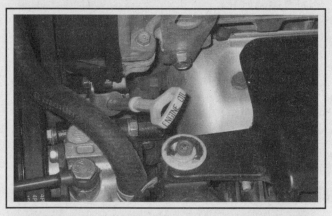

4.2a The oil dipstick is located at the right front corner of the engine (four-cylinder)

4.2b Locations of the engine oil dipstick (A) and automatic transaxle fluid dipstick (B) - Sportage V6 model

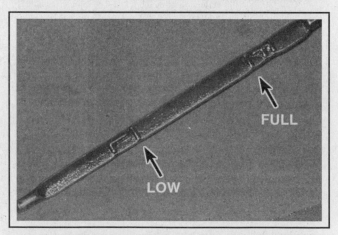

4.4 The oil level should be between the two marks on the dipstick - if it's below the LOW mark, add enough oil to bring it up to or near the FULL mark

8   All vehicles covered by this manual are equipped with a coolant recovery system. A coolant reservoir is attached to the right side of the engine compartment on 1994, 1995 and 2003 and later models, or on the left side on 1996 through 2002 models, and is connected by a hose to the radiator filler neck. As the engine warms up, the system pressure increases causing some coolant to escape through a valve in the radiator cap and travel through the hose and into the coolant reservoir. As the engine cools, the coolant in the reservoir is automatically drawn back into the cooling system via the vacuum created by the contracting coolant. This recovery type system maintains the maximum amount of coolant available at all times.

✖✖ WARNING:

Never remove the radiator cap to add coolant while the engine is warm! If the cap feels even slightly warm, wrap a towel or rag around the cap and open it very slowly.

9   With the engine cold, remove the radiator cap. The coolant level should be up to the cap seat inside the filler neck. If it is low, add a mixture of high-quality antifreeze/coolant and water in the ratio specified on the antifreeze container or in this Chapter's Specification Section to bring it up to the correct level.

10   The coolant level in the reservoir should be checked while the engine is at normal operating temperature. Simply note the fluid level on the side of the reservoir (1994, 1995 and 2003 and later models) or on the dipstick (1996 through 2002 models) - it should be at or close to the FULL HOT or MAX mark when the engine is at normal operating temperature (see illustrations).

11   If only a small amount of coolant is required to bring the system up to the proper level, ordinary tap water may be used. However, to maintain the proper antifreeze/water mixture in the system, a blend of high-quality antifreeze/coolant and water in the ratio specified on the antifreeze container or in this Chapter's Specification Section should be added.

12   As the coolant level is checked, note the condition of the coolant as well. It should be relatively clean and the color of new antifreeze. If it's brown or rust colored, the system should be drained, flushed and re-filled (see Section 20).

13   If the coolant level drops consistently, there is a leak in the system. Check the radiator, hoses, filler cap, drain plugs and water pump (see Section 9). If no leaks are noted, have the radiator cap and coolant system pressure tested by your dealer service department or other qualified service station.

BRAKE AND CLUTCH FLUID

▶ **Refer to illustration 4.16**

14   The brake master cylinder is mounted on the front of the power booster unit in the engine compartment. The hydraulic clutch master cylinder used on manual transaxle vehicles is located next to the brake master cylinder.

15   On early models, the clutch fluid reservoir is located on the clutch master cylinder. On later models the brake master cylinder and the clutch master cylinder share a common reservoir. To check the fluid level of either system, simply look at the MAX and MIN marks on the reservoir.

16   The fluid level should be maintained at the upper (FULL or MAX) mark on the reservoir (see illustration).

17   If additional fluid is necessary to bring the level up, use a rag to clean all dirt off the top of the reservoir to prevent contamination of the system. Also, make sure all painted surfaces around the reservoir are covered, since brake fluid will ruin paint. Carefully pour new, clean brake fluid obtained from a sealed container into the reservoir. Be sure the specified fluid is used; mixing different types of brake fluid can cause damage to the system. See *Recommended lubricants and fluids* in this Chapter's Specifications or your owner's manual.

18   While the reservoir cap is removed, inspect the master cylinder reservoir for contamination. If deposits, dirt particles or water droplets are present, the system should be drained and refilled.

19   After filling the reservoir to the proper level, make sure the lid is properly seated to prevent fluid leakage.

20   The fluid in the brake master cylinder will drop slightly as the brake pads at each wheel wear down during normal operation. If the master cylinder requires repeated replenishing to keep it at the proper level, this is an indication of leakage in the brake or clutch system, which should be corrected immediately. If the brake system shows an indication of leakage check all brake lines and connections, along with the calipers, wheel cylinders and booster (see Section 12 for more

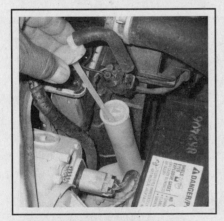

4.10a Maintain the coolant level near the upper FULL mark on the reservoir dipstick (1996 through 2002 models)

4.10b On 1994 and 1995, and 2003 and later models, maintain the coolant level between the LOW and FULL marks (2009 Sportage model shown)

4.16 The brake fluid should be kept between the MIN and MAX marks on the reservoir

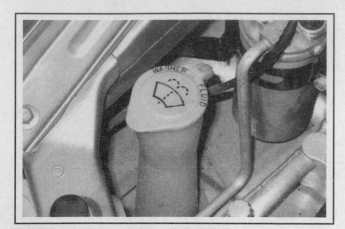

4.22 Flip up the cap to add washer fluid

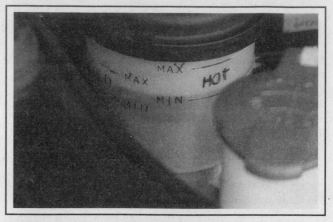

4.26 At normal operating temperature, the power steering fluid level should be between the FULL and LOW (or MIN and MAX) marks

information). If the hydraulic clutch system shows an indication of leakage check all clutch lines and connections, along with the clutch release cylinder (see Chapter 8 for more information).

21 If you discover that the reservoir is empty or nearly empty, the system should be thoroughly inspected, refilled and then bled (see Chapter 8 for clutch system bleeding and Chapter 9 for brake system bleeding).

WINDSHIELD WASHER FLUID

▶ **Refer to illustration 4.22**

· 22 Fluid for the windshield washer system is stored in a plastic reservoir located at the right front of the engine compartment (see illustration).

23 In milder climates, plain water can be used in the reservoir, but it should be kept no more than 2/3 full to allow for expansion if the water freezes. In colder climates, use windshield washer system antifreeze, available at any auto parts store, to lower the freezing point of the fluid. Mix the antifreeze with water in accordance with the manufacturer's directions on the container.

✳✳ CAUTION:

Do not use cooling system antifreeze - it will damage the vehicle's paint.

POWER STEERING FLUID

▶ **Refer to illustration 4.26**

24 Check the power steering fluid level periodically to avoid steering system problems, such as damage to the pump.

✳✳ CAUTION:

DO NOT hold the steering wheel against either stop (extreme left or right turn) for more than five seconds. If you do, the power steering pump could be damaged.

25 The power steering reservoir, located at the right side of the

engine compartment. The power steering fluid level can be checked with the engine either hot or cold.

26 On later models the power steering fluid reservoir is translucent and the level can be checked without removing the cap (see illustration). On these models it's a simple matter to make sure the fluid level is within the proper range.

27 On earlier models the fluid level is checked with a dipstick. With the engine off, use a rag to clean the reservoir cap and the area around the cap. This will help prevent foreign material from falling into the reservoir when the cap is removed.

28 Turn and pull out the reservoir cap, which has a dipstick attached to it. Wipe the fluid at the bottom of the dipstick with a clean rag. Reinstall the cap to get a fluid level reading. Remove the cap again and note the fluid level. It should be at the appropriate mark on the dipstick in relation to the engine temperature; near the MIN mark if the fluid is cold, and near the MAX mark if the fluid is hot.

29 If additional fluid is required, pour the specified type fluid (see *Recommended lubricants and fluids* in this Chapter's Specifications or your owner's manual directly into the reservoir using a funnel to prevent spills.

30 If the reservoir requires frequent topping up, all power steering hoses, hose connections, the power steering pump and the steering gear should be carefully examined for leaks.

AUTOMATIC TRANSAXLE FLUID

▶ **Refer to illustrations 4.34a and 4.34b**

31 The level of the automatic transaxle fluid should be carefully maintained. Low fluid level can lead to slipping or loss of drive, while overfilling can cause foaming, loss of fluid and transaxle damage.

32 The transaxle fluid level should only be checked when the transaxle is hot (at its normal operating temperature). If the vehicle has just been driven over 10 miles (15 miles in a frigid climate), and the fluid temperature is 160 to 175-degrees F, the transaxle is hot.

✳✳ CAUTION:

If the vehicle has just been driven for a long time at high speed or in city traffic in hot weather, or if it has been pulling a trailer, an accurate fluid level reading cannot be obtained. Allow the fluid to cool down for about 30 minutes.

4.34a The automatic transaxle dipstick is located on the left side of the engine compartment

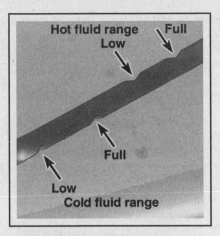

4.34b Check the fluid with the transaxle at normal operating temperature - the level should be kept in the HOT range

4.45 The lubricant level should be between the indicated marks on the side of the drive gear assembly

33 If the vehicle has not just been driven, park the vehicle on level ground, set the parking brake and start the engine. While the engine is idling, depress the brake pedal and move the selector lever through all the gear ranges, beginning and ending in Park.

34 With the engine still idling, remove the dipstick from its tube (see illustration). Check the level of the fluid on the dipstick (see illustration) and note its condition.

35 Wipe the fluid from the dipstick with a clean rag and reinsert it back into the filler tube until the cap seats.

36 Pull the dipstick out again and note the fluid level. The fluid level should be in the operating temperature range (the cross-hatched area). If the level is at the low side of either range, add the specified automatic transaxle fluid through the dipstick tube with a funnel.

37 Add just enough of the recommended fluid to fill the transaxle to the proper level. It takes about one pint to raise the level from the low mark to the high mark when the fluid is hot, so add the fluid a little at a time and keep checking the level until it is correct.

38 The condition of the fluid should also be checked along with the level. If the fluid at the end of the dipstick is black or a dark reddish brown color, or if it emits a burned smell, the fluid should be changed (see Section 27). If you are in doubt about the condition of the fluid, purchase some new fluid and compare the two for color and smell.

MANUAL TRANSAXLE LUBRICANT

➡**Note: It isn't necessary to check this lubricant weekly; every 15,000 miles (24,000 km) or 12 months will be adequate.**

39 The manual transaxle does not have a dipstick.

1997 and earlier models

◗ **Refer to illustration 4.45**

40 On 1997 and earlier models, the oil level is checked by removing the speedometer cable and driven gear from the transaxle in the engine compartment. The speedometer cable and driven gear are located at the left rear of the engine compartment on the top of the transaxle.

41 Park the vehicle on level ground and set the parking brake firmly. Turn the engine off.

42 Disconnect the speedometer cable by turning the knurled nut securing it to the driven gear assembly.

43 Remove the fastener securing the driven gear assembly to the transaxle and slowly pull the driven gear assembly from the transaxle.

44 Wipe the driven gear clean and reinsert the assembly in the transaxle.

45 Pull it out again. The oil level should be between L (Low) and F (Full) (see illustration).

46 If the oil level is low, add oil through the speedometer gear hole until it is at the proper level.

❋❋ **WARNING:**

Do not overfill.

47 Inspect the O-ring seal on the driven gear. Replace it if it appears damaged, flattened or age hardened. Re-install the driven gear in the transaxle and tighten the retaining bolt securely. Then re-install the speedometer cable. Drive the vehicle a short distance, then check for leaks.

1998 and later models

48 Raise the vehicle and support it securely on jackstands. On the transaxle housing, remove the fluid fill plug. If the lubricant level is correct, it should be up to the lower edge of the hole.

49 If the transaxle needs more lubricant (if the level is not up to the hole), use a syringe or a gear oil pump to add more. Stop filling the transaxle when the lubricant begins to run out the hole.

50 Install the plug and tighten it securely. Drive the vehicle a short distance, then check for leaks.

TRANSFER CASE LUBRICANT (4WD MODELS)

◗ **Refer to illustration 4.52**

➡**Note: It isn't necessary to check this lubricant weekly; every 15,000 miles (24,000 km) or 12 months will be adequate.**

51 Raise the vehicle and support it securely on jackstands.

52 Unscrew the check/fill plug from the transfer case (see illustration).

53 Use your little finger to reach inside the housing to feel the lubricant level. The level should be at or near the bottom of the plug hole. If it isn't, add the recommended lubricant through the plug hole with a syringe or squeeze bottle.

54 Install the plug and tighten it to the torque listed in this Chapter's Specifications. Check for leaks after the first few miles of driving.

DIFFERENTIAL LUBRICANT (4WD MODELS)

♦ **Refer to illustration 4.56**

➡**Note: It isn't necessary to check this lubricant weekly; every 15,000 miles (24,000 km) or 12 months will be adequate.**

55 Raise the rear of the vehicle and support it securely on jackstands.

56 Unscrew the check/fill plug from the rear differential (see illustration).

57 Use your little finger to reach inside the housing to feel the lubricant level. The level should be at or near the bottom of the plug hole. If it isn't, add the recommended lubricant through the plug hole with a syringe or squeeze bottle.

58 Install the plug and tighten it to the torque listed in this Chapter's Specifications. Check for leaks after the first few miles of driving.

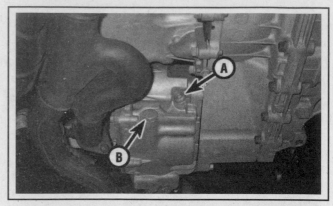

4.52 Transfer case check/fill plug (A) and drain plug (B) (4WD models)

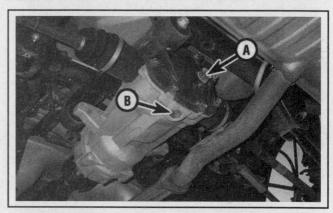

4.56 Rear differential check/fill plug (A) and drain plug (B) (4WD models)

5 Tire and tire pressure checks (every 250 miles [400 km] or weekly)

♦ **Refer to illustrations 5.2, 5.3, 5.4a, 5.4b and 5.8**

1 Periodic inspection of the tires may spare you from the inconvenience of being stranded with a flat tire. It can also provide you with vital information regarding possible problems in the steering and suspension systems before major damage occurs.

2 Normal tread wear can be monitored with a simple, inexpensive device known as a tread depth indicator (see illustration). When the tread depth reaches the specified minimum, replace the tire(s).

3 Note any abnormal tread wear (see illustration). Tread pattern irregularities such as cupping, flat spots and more wear on one side than the other are indications of front end alignment and/or balance problems. If any of these conditions are noted, take the vehicle to a tire shop or service station to correct the problem.

4 Look closely for cuts, punctures and embedded nails or tacks. Sometimes a tire will hold its air pressure for a short time or leak down very slowly even after a nail has embedded itself into the tread. If a slow leak persists, check the valve core to make sure it is tight (see illustration). Examine the tread for an object that may have embedded itself into the tire or for a "plug" that may have begun to leak (radial tire

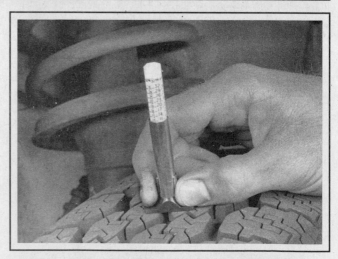

5.2 A tire tread depth indicator should be used to monitor tire wear - they are available at auto parts stores and service stations and cost very little

5.3 This chart will help you determine the condition of your tires, the probable cause(s) of abnormal wear and the corrective action necessary

UNDERINFLATION

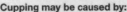
CUPPING

OVERINFLATION

Cupping may be caused by:
- Underinflation and/or mechanical irregularities such as out-of-balance condition of wheel and/or tire, and bent or damaged wheel.
- Loose or worn steering tie-rod or steering idler arm.
- Loose, damaged or worn front suspension parts.

INCORRECT TOE-IN OR EXTREME CAMBER

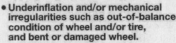
FEATHERING DUE TO MISALIGNMENT

5.4a If a tire loses air on a steady basis, check the valve core first to make sure it's snug (special inexpensive wrenches are commonly available at auto parts stores)

5.4b If the valve core is tight, raise the corner of the vehicle with the low tire and spray a soapy water solution onto the tread as the tire is turned slowly - slow leaks will cause small bubbles to appear

5.8 To extend the life of your tires, check the air pressure at least once a week with an accurate gauge (don't forget the spare!)

punctures are repaired with a plug that is installed in a puncture). If a puncture is suspected, it can be easily verified by spraying a solution of soapy water onto the puncture area (see illustration). The soapy solution will bubble if there is a leak. Unless the puncture is inordinately large, a tire shop or gas station can usually repair the punctured tire.

5   Carefully inspect the inner side of each tire for evidence of brake fluid leakage. If you see any, inspect the brakes immediately.

6   Correct tire air pressure adds miles to the lifespan of the tires, improves mileage and enhances overall ride quality. Tire pressure cannot be accurately estimated by looking at a tire, particularly if it is a radial. A tire pressure gauge is therefore essential. Keep an accurate gauge in the glovebox. The pressure gauges fitted to the nozzles of air hoses at gas stations are often inaccurate.

7   Always check tire pressure when the tires are cold. "Cold," in this case, means the vehicle has not been driven over a mile in the three hours preceding a tire pressure check. A pressure rise of four to eight pounds is not uncommon once the tires are warm.

8   Unscrew the valve cap protruding from the wheel or hubcap and push the gauge firmly onto the valve (see illustration). Note the reading on the gauge and compare this figure to the recommended tire pressure shown on the tire placard on the left door jamb. Be sure to reinstall the valve cap to keep dirt and moisture out of the valve stem mechanism. Check all four tires and, if necessary, add enough air to bring them up to the recommended pressure levels.

9   Don't forget to keep the spare tire inflated to the specified pressure (consult your owner's manual). Note that the air pressure specified for the compact spare is significantly higher than the pressure of the regular tires.

6 Engine oil and oil filter change (every 3000 miles [4800 km] or 3 months)

▶ Refer to illustrations 6.2, 6.3, 6.7, 6.12 and 6.14

➡ Note: While the vehicle is raised, be sure to check the manual transaxle fluid level (if equipped).

1 Frequent oil changes are the best preventive maintenance the home mechanic can give the engine, because aging oil becomes diluted and contaminated, which leads to premature engine wear.

2 Make sure you have all the necessary tools before you begin this procedure (see illustration). You should also have plenty of rags or newspapers handy for mopping up any spills.

3 Raise the front of the vehicle and place it securely on jackstands. Remove the engine under cover (see illustration), if equipped.

4 If this is your first oil change, get under the vehicle and familiarize yourself with the locations of the oil drain plug and the oil filter. The engine and exhaust components will be warm during the actual work, so try to anticipate any potential problems before the engine and accessories are hot.

5 Park the vehicle on a level spot. Start the engine and allow it to reach its normal operating temperature. Warm oil and sludge will flow out more easily. Turn off the engine when it's warmed up. Remove the filler cap from the valve cover.

6 Raise the vehicle and support it securely on jackstands.

✳✳ WARNING:

Never get beneath the vehicle when it is supported only by a jack. The jack provided with your vehicle is designed solely for raising the vehicle to remove and replace the wheels. Always use jackstands to support the vehicle when it becomes necessary to place your body underneath the vehicle.

7 Being careful not to touch the hot exhaust components, place the drain pan under the drain plug in the bottom of the pan and remove the plug (see illustration). You may want to wear gloves while unscrewing the plug the final few turns if the engine is hot.

8 Allow the old oil to drain into the pan. It may be necessary to

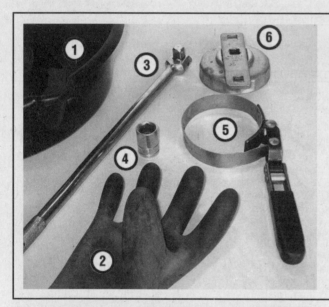

6.2 These tools are required when changing the engine oil and filter

1 **Drain pan** - It should be fairly shallow in depth, but wide in order to prevent spills
2 **Rubber gloves** - When removing the drain plug and filter, it is inevitable that you will get oil on your hands (the gloves will prevent burns)
3 **Breaker bar** - Sometimes the oil drain plug is pretty tight and a long breaker bar is needed to loosen it
4 **Socket** - To be used with the breaker bar or a ratchet (must be the correct size to fit the drain plug)
5 **Filter wrench** - This is a metal band-type wrench, which requires clearance around the filter to be effective
6 **Filter wrench** - This type fits on the bottom of the filter and can be turned with a ratchet or breaker bar (different size wrenches are available for different types of filters)

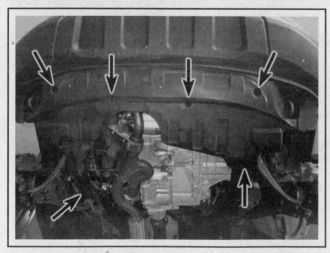

6.3 Engine under-cover fasteners (Sportage model shown)

6.7 Use a proper size box-end wrench or socket to remove the oil drain plug and avoid rounding it off

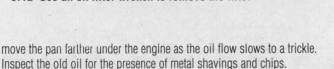

6.12 Use an oil filter wrench to remove the filter

6.14 Lubricate the oil filter gasket with clean engine oil before installing the filter on the engine

move the pan farther under the engine as the oil flow slows to a trickle. Inspect the old oil for the presence of metal shavings and chips.

9   After all the oil has drained, wipe off the drain plug with a clean rag. Even minute metal particles clinging to the plug would immediately contaminate the new oil.

10 Clean the area around the drain plug opening, reinstall the plug and tighten it to the torque listed in this Chapter's Specifications.

11 Move the drain pan into position under the oil filter.

12 Loosen the oil filter (see illustration) by turning it counterclockwise with an oil filter wrench. Once the filter is loose, use your hands to unscrew it from the block. Keep the open end pointing up to prevent the oil inside the filter from spilling out.

☀☀ WARNING:

The exhaust system may still be hot, so be careful.

13 With a clean rag, wipe off the mounting surface on the block. If a residue of old oil is allowed to remain, it will smoke when the block is heated up. Also make sure that none of the old gasket remains stuck to the mounting surface. It can be removed with a scraper if necessary.

14 Compare the old filter with the new one to make sure they are the same type. Smear some clean engine oil on the rubber gasket of the new filter (see illustration).

15 Attach the new filter to the engine, following the tightening directions printed on the filter canister or packing box. Most filter manufac-

turers recommend against using a filter wrench due to the possibility of overtightening and damaging the seal.

16 Remove all tools, rags, etc. from under the vehicle, being careful not to spill the oil in the drain pan, then lower the vehicle.

17 Add new oil to the engine through the oil filler cap in the valve cover. Use a funnel, if necessary, to prevent oil from spilling onto the top of the engine. Pour three quarts of fresh oil into the engine. Wait a few minutes to allow the oil to drain into the pan, then check the level on the oil dipstick (see Section 4). If the oil level is at or near the FULL mark on the dipstick, install the filler cap hand tight, start the engine and allow the new oil to circulate.

18 Allow the engine to run for about a minute. While the engine is running, look under the vehicle and check for leaks at the oil pan drain plug and around the oil filter. If either is leaking, stop the engine and tighten the plug or filter.

19 Wait a few minutes to allow the oil to trickle down into the pan, then recheck the level on the dipstick and, if necessary, add enough oil to bring the level to the FULL mark on the dipstick.

20 During the first few trips after an oil change, make it a point to check frequently for leaks and proper oil level.

21 The old oil drained from the engine cannot be reused in its present state and should be disposed of. Check with your local auto parts store, disposal facility or environmental agency to see if they will accept the oil for recycling. After the oil has cooled it can be drained into a container (capped plastic jugs, topped bottles, milk cartons, etc.) for transport to one of these disposal sites. Don't dispose of the oil by pouring it on the ground or down a drain!

7 Windshield wiper blade inspection and replacement (every 7500 miles [12,000 km] or 6 months)

♦ **Refer to illustrations 7.5a and 7.5b**

1   The windshield wiper and blade assembly should be inspected periodically for damage, loose components and cracked or worn blade elements.

2   Road film can build up on the wiper blades and affect their effi-

ciency, so they should be washed regularly with a mild detergent solution.

3   The action of the wiping mechanism can loosen bolts, nuts and fasteners, so they should be checked and tightened, as necessary, at the same time the wiper blades are checked.

4   If the wiper blade elements are cracked, worn or warped, or no longer clean adequately, they should be replaced with new ones.

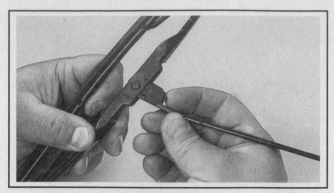

7.5a Depress the release lever . . .

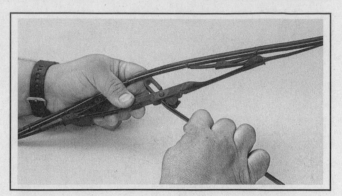

7.5b . . . and slide the wiper element down out of the hook in the end of the arm

5   Lift the arm assembly away from the glass for clearance, press on the release lever, then slide the wiper blade assembly out of the hook at the end of the arm (see illustrations).

6   Attach the new wiper to the arm. Connection can be confirmed by an audible click.

8   Battery check, maintenance and charging (every 7500 miles [12,000 km] or 6 months)

▶ Refer to illustrations 8.1, 8.6a, 8.6b, 8.7a and 8.7b

✳✳ WARNING:

Certain precautions must be followed when checking and servicing the battery. Hydrogen gas, which is highly flammable, is always present in the battery cells, so keep lighted tobacco and all other open flames and sparks away from the battery. The electrolyte inside the battery is actually diluted sulfuric acid, which will cause injury if splashed on your skin or in your eyes. It will also ruin clothes and painted surfaces. When removing the battery cables, always detach the negative cable first and hook it up last!

1   A routine preventive maintenance program for the battery in your vehicle is the only way to ensure quick and reliable starts. But before performing any battery maintenance, make sure that you have the proper equipment necessary to work safely around the battery (see illustration).

2   There are also several precautions that should be taken whenever battery maintenance is performed. Before servicing the battery, always turn the engine and all accessories off and disconnect the cable from the negative terminal of the battery (see Chapter 5, Section 1).

3   The battery produces hydrogen gas, which is both flammable and explosive. Never create a spark, smoke or light a match around the battery. Always charge the battery in a ventilated area.

4   Electrolyte contains poisonous and corrosive sulfuric acid. Do not allow it to get in your eyes, on your skin on your clothes. Never ingest it. Wear protective safety glasses when working near the battery. Keep children away from the battery.

5   Note the external condition of the battery. If the positive terminal and cable clamp on your vehicle's battery is equipped with a rubber protector, make sure that it's not torn or damaged. It should completely cover the terminal. Look for any corroded or loose connections, cracks in the case or cover or loose hold-down clamps. Also check the entire length of each cable for cracks and frayed conductors.

6   If corrosion, which looks like white, fluffy deposits (see illustration) is evident, particularly around the terminals, the battery should

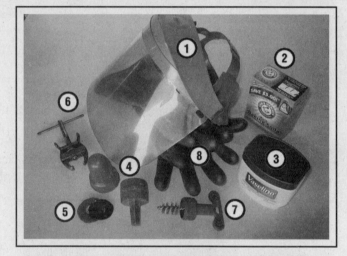

8.1 Tools and materials required for battery maintenance

1   *Face shield/safety goggles - When removing corrosion with a brush, the acidic particles can easily fly up into your eyes*

2   *Baking soda - A solution of baking soda and water can be used to neutralize corrosion*

3   *Petroleum jelly - A layer of this on the battery posts will help prevent corrosion*

4   *Battery post/cable cleaner - This wire brush cleaning tool will remove all traces of corrosion from the battery posts and cable clamps*

5   *Treated felt washers - Placing one of these on each post, directly under the cable clamps, will help prevent corrosion*

6   *Puller - Sometimes the cable clamps are very difficult to pull off the posts, even after the nut/bolt has been completely loosened. This tool pulls the clamp straight up and off the post without damage*

7   *Battery post/cable cleaner - Here is another cleaning tool which is a slightly different version of number 4 above, but it does the same thing*

8   *Rubber gloves - Another safety item to consider when servicing the battery; remember that's acid inside the battery*

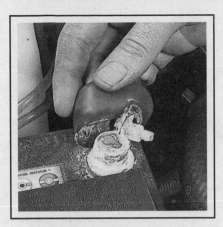

8.6a Battery terminal corrosion usually appears as light, fluffy powder

8.6b Removing a cable from the battery post with a wrench - sometimes a pair of special battery pliers are required for this procedure if corrosion has caused deterioration of the nut hex (always remove the ground (-) cable first and hook it up last!)

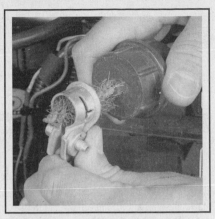

8.7a When cleaning the cable clamps, all corrosion must be removed (the inside of the clamp is tapered to match the taper on the post, so don't remove too much material)

8.7b Regardless of the type of tool used to clean the battery posts, a clean, shiny surface should be the result

be removed for cleaning. Loosen the cable clamp bolts with a wrench, being careful to remove the ground cable first, and slide them off the terminals (see illustration). Then disconnect the hold-down clamp bolt and nut, remove the clamp and lift the battery from the engine compartment.

7   Clean the cable clamps thoroughly with a battery brush or a terminal cleaner and a solution of warm water and baking soda (see illustration). Wash the terminals and the top of the battery case with the same solution but make sure that the solution doesn't get into the battery. When cleaning the cables, terminals and battery top, wear safety goggles and rubber gloves to prevent any solution from coming in contact with your eyes or hands. Wear old clothes too - even diluted, sulfuric acid splashed onto clothes will burn holes in them. If the terminals have been extensively corroded, clean them up with a terminal cleaner (see illustration). Thoroughly wash all cleaned areas with plain water.

8   Make sure that the battery tray is in good condition and the hold-down clamp fasteners are tight. If the battery is removed from the tray, make sure no parts remain in the bottom of the tray when the battery is reinstalled. When reinstalling the hold-down clamp bolts, do not overtighten them.

9   Information on removing and installing the battery can be found in Chapter 5. If you disconnected the cable(s) from the negative and/or positive battery terminals, see Chapter 5, Section 1. Information on jump starting can be found at the front of this manual.

10   Corrosion on the hold-down components, battery case and surrounding areas can be removed with a solution of water and baking soda. Thoroughly rinse all cleaned areas with plain water.

11   Any metal parts of the vehicle damaged by corrosion should be covered with a zinc-based primer, then painted.

CHARGING

✳✳ WARNING:

When batteries are being charged, hydrogen gas, which is very explosive and flammable, is produced. Do not smoke or allow open flames near a charging or a recently charged battery. Wear eye protection when near the battery during charging. Also, make sure the charger is unplugged before connecting or disconnecting the battery from the charger.

12   Slow-rate charging is the best way to restore a battery that's discharged to the point where it will not start the engine. It's also a good way to maintain the battery charge in a vehicle that's only driven a few miles between starts. Maintaining the battery charge is particularly important in the winter when the battery must work harder to start the engine and electrical accessories that drain the battery are in greater use.

13   It's best to use a one or two-amp battery charger (sometimes called a "trickle" charger). They are the safest and put the least strain on the battery. They are also the least expensive. For a faster charge,

you can use a higher amperage charger, but don't use one rated more than 1/10th the amp/hour rating of the battery. Rapid boost charges that claim to restore the power of the battery in one to two hours are hardest on the battery and can damage batteries not in good condition. This type of charging should only be used in emergency situations.

14 The average time necessary to charge a battery should be listed in the instructions that come with the charger. As a general rule, a trickle charger will charge a battery in 12 to 16 hours.

9 Cooling system check (every 7500 miles [12,000 km] or 6 months)

◆ **Refer to illustration 9.4**

1 Many major engine failures can be attributed to a faulty cooling system. The cooling system also cools the transaxle fluid and thus plays an important role in prolonging transaxle life.

2 The cooling system should be checked with the engine cold. Do this before the vehicle is driven for the day or after the engine has been shut off for at least three hours.

3 Remove the radiator cap by turning it to the left until it reaches a stop. If you hear a hissing sound (indicating there is still pressure in the system), wait until it stops. Now press down on the cap with the palm of your hand and continue turning to the left until the cap can be removed. Thoroughly clean the cap, inside and out, with clean water. Also clean the filler neck on the radiator. All traces of corrosion should be removed. The coolant inside the radiator should be relatively transparent. If it's rust colored, the system should be drained and refilled (see Section 20). If the coolant level isn't up to the top, add additional antifreeze/coolant mixture (see Section 4).

4 Carefully check the large upper and lower radiator hoses along with the smaller diameter heater hoses which run from the engine to the firewall. Inspect each hose along its entire length, replacing any hose which is cracked, swollen or shows signs of deterioration. Cracks may become more apparent if the hose is squeezed (see illustration). Regardless of condition, it's a good idea to replace hoses with new ones every two years.

5 Make sure that all hose connections are tight. A leak in the cooling system will usually show up as white or rust colored deposits on the areas adjoining the leak. If wire-type clamps are used at the ends of the hoses, it may be a good idea to replace them with more secure screw-type clamps.

6 Use compressed air or a soft brush to remove bugs, leaves, etc. from the front of the radiator or air conditioning condenser. Be careful not to damage the delicate cooling fins or cut yourself on them.

7 Every other inspection, or at the first indication of cooling system problems, have the cap and system pressure tested. If you don't have a pressure tester, most gas stations and repair shops will do this for a minimal charge.

Check for a chafed area that could fail prematurely.

Overtightening the clamp on a hardened hose will damage the hose and cause a leak.

Check each hose for swelling and oil-soaked ends. Cracks and breaks can be located by squeezing the hose

Check for a soft area indicating the hose has deteriorated inside.

9.4 Hoses, like drivebelts, have a habit of failing at the worst possible time - to prevent the inconvenience of a blown radiator or heater hose, inspect them carefully as shown here

10 Tire rotation (every 7500 miles [12,000 km] or 6 months)

◆ **Refer to illustrations 10.2a and 10.2b**

1 The tires should be rotated at the specified intervals and whenever uneven wear is noticed. Since the vehicle will be raised and the tires removed anyway, check the brakes (see Section 12) at this time.

2 Radial tires must be rotated in a specific pattern (see illustration). Most models are equipped with non-directional tires, but some models may have directional tires, which have a different rotation pattern (see illustration). When rotating tires, examine the sidewalls. Directional tires have arrows on the sidewall that indicate the direction they must turn. The left and right side tires must not be rotated to the other side.

3 Refer to the information in *Jacking and towing* at the front of this manual for the proper procedures to follow when raising the vehicle and changing a tire. If the brakes are to be checked, do not apply the parking brake as stated. Make sure the tires are blocked to prevent the vehicle from rolling.

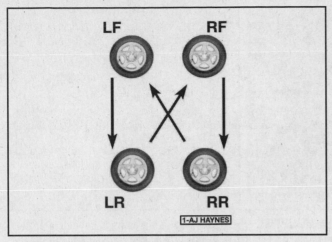

10.2a The recommended rotation pattern for non-directional radial tires

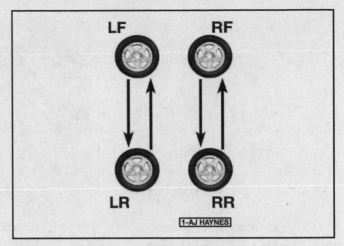

10.2b The recommended rotation pattern for directional radial tires

4   Preferably, the entire vehicle should be raised at the same time. This can be done on a hoist or by jacking up each corner and then lowering the vehicle onto jackstands placed under the frame rails. Always use four jackstands and make sure the vehicle is firmly supported.

5   After rotation, check and adjust the tire pressures as necessary

and be sure to check the lug nut tightness. Ideally, lug nuts should be tightened to the torque listed in this Chapter's Specifications with a torque wrench, and rechecked after 25 miles of driving.

6   For further information on the wheels and tires, refer to Chapter 10.

11 Seat belt check (every 7500 miles [12,000 km] or 6 months)

1   Check seat belts, buckles, latch plates and guide loops for obvious damage and signs of wear.

2   See if the seat belt reminder light comes on when the key is turned to the Run or Start position. A chime should also sound. On passive restraint systems, the shoulder belt should move into position in the A-pillar.

3   The seat belts are designed to lock up during a sudden stop or impact, yet allow free movement during normal driving. Make sure the retractors return the belt against your chest while driving and rewind the belt fully when the buckle is unlatched.

4   If any of the above checks reveal problems with the seat belt system, replace parts as necessary.

12 Brake system check (every 7500 miles [12,000 km] or 6 months)

✳✳ WARNING:

The dust created by the brake system is harmful to your health. Never blow it out with compressed air and don't inhale any of it. An approved filtering mask should be worn when working on the brakes. Do not, under any circumstances, use petroleum-based solvents to clean brake parts. Use brake system cleaner only!

➡Note: For detailed photographs of the brake system, refer to Chapter 9.

1   In addition to the specified intervals, the brakes should be inspected every time the wheels are removed or whenever a defect is suspected.

2   Any of the following symptoms could indicate a potential brake system defect: The vehicle pulls to one side when the brake pedal is depressed; the brakes make squealing or dragging noises when applied; brake pedal travel is excessive; the pedal pulsates; or brake fluid leaks, usually onto the inside of the tire or wheel.

DISC BRAKES

▶ **Refer to illustrations 12.6a and 12.6b**

3   Disc brakes can be visually checked without removing any parts except the wheels. Remove the hub caps (if applicable) and loosen the wheel lug nuts a quarter turn each.

4   Raise the vehicle and place it securely on jackstands.

✳✳ WARNING:

Never work under a vehicle that is supported only by a jack!

5   Remove the wheels. Now visible is the disc brake caliper which contains the pads. There is an outer brake pad and an inner pad. Both must be checked for wear.

12.6a With the wheel off, measure the thickness of the inner pad lining material through the inspection hole

12.6b Measure the thickness of the outer brake pad from the metal backing

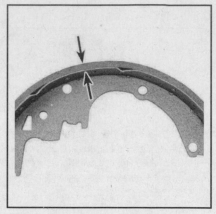

12.14 If the lining is bonded to the brake shoe, measure the lining thickness from the outer surface to the metal shoe; if the lining is riveted to the shoe, measure from the lining outer surface to the rivet head

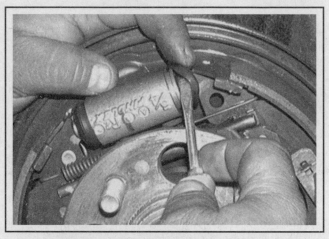

12.16 Carefully peel back the wheel cylinder boot and check for leaking fluid, indicating that the cylinder must be replaced

6   Measure the thickness of the outer pad at each end of the caliper and the inner pad through the inspection hole in the caliper body (see illustrations). Compare the measurement with the limit given in this Chapter's Specifications; if any brake pad thickness is less than specified, then all brake pads must be replaced (see Chapter 9).

7   If you're in doubt as to the exact pad thickness or quality, remove them for measurement and further inspection (see Chapter 9).

8   Check the disc for score marks, wear and burned spots. If any of these conditions exist, the disc should be removed for servicing or replacement (see Chapter 9).

9   Before installing the wheels, check all the brake lines and hoses for damage, wear, deformation, cracks, corrosion, leakage, bends and twists, particularly in the vicinity of the rubber hoses and calipers.

10   Install the wheels, lower the vehicle and tighten the wheel lug nuts to the torque given in this Chapter's Specifications.

DRUM BRAKES

♦ **Refer to illustrations 12.14 and 12.16**

11 On models with rear drum brakes, make sure the parking brake is

off then tap on the outside of the drum with a rubber mallet to loosen it.

12 Remove the brake drums. If the drum still won't come off, refer to Chapter 9.

13 With the drums removed, carefully clean the brake assembly with brake system cleaner.

❊❊ WARNING:

Don't blow the dust out with compressed air and don't inhale any of it (it is harmful to your health).

14 Note the thickness of the lining material on both front and rear brake shoes (see illustration). Compare the measurement with the limit given in this Chapter's Specifications; if any lining thickness is less than specified, then all of the brake shoes must be replaced (see Chapter 9). The shoes should also be replaced if they're cracked, glazed (shiny areas), or covered with brake fluid.

15 Make sure all the brake assembly springs are connected and in good condition.

16 Check the brake components for signs of fluid leakage. With your finger or a small screwdriver, carefully pry back the rubber cups on the wheel cylinder located at the top of the brake shoes (see illustration). Any leakage here is an indication that the wheel cylinders should be replaced immediately (see Chapter 9). Also, check all hoses and connections for signs of leakage.

17 Wipe the inside of the drum with a clean rag and denatured alcohol or brake cleaner. Again, be careful not to breathe the dangerous brake dust.

18 Check the inside of the drum for cracks, score marks, deep scratches and "hard spots" which will appear as small discolored areas. If imperfections cannot be removed with fine emery cloth, the drum must be taken to an automotive machine shop for resurfacing.

19 Repeat the procedure for the remaining wheel. If the inspection reveals that all parts are in good condition, reinstall the brake drums, install the wheels and lower the vehicle to the ground.

BRAKE BOOSTER CHECK

20 Sit in the driver's seat and perform the following sequence of tests.

21 With the brake fully depressed, start the engine - the pedal should move down a little when the engine starts.

22 With the engine running, depress the brake pedal several times - the travel distance should not change.

23 Depress the brake, stop the engine and hold the pedal in for about 30 seconds - the pedal should neither sink nor rise.

24 Restart the engine, run it for about a minute and turn it off. Then firmly depress the brake several times - the pedal travel should decrease with each application.

25 If your brakes do not operate as described, the brake booster has failed. Refer to Chapter 9 for the replacement procedure.

PARKING BRAKE

26 Slowly pull up on the parking brake and count the number of clicks you hear until the handle is up as far as it will go. The adjustment is correct if you hear the specified number of clicks (see this Chapter's Specifications). If you hear more or fewer clicks, it's time to adjust the parking brake (see Chapter 9).

27 An alternative method of checking the parking brake is to park the vehicle on a steep hill with the parking brake set and the transaxle in Neutral. If the parking brake cannot prevent the vehicle from rolling, it is in need of adjustment (see Chapter 9).

---

13 Steering, suspension and driveaxle boot check (every 15,000 miles [24,000 km] or 12 months)

➡**Note: For detailed illustrations of the steering and suspension components, refer to Chapter 10.**

WITH THE WHEELS ON THE GROUND

1 With the vehicle stopped and the front wheels pointed straight ahead, rock the steering wheel gently back and forth. If freeplay is excessive, a front wheel bearing, steering shaft universal joint or lower arm balljoint is worn or the steering gear is out of adjustment or broken. Refer to Chapter 10 for the appropriate repair procedure.

2 Other symptoms, such as excessive vehicle body movement over rough roads, swaying (leaning) around corners and binding as the steering wheel is turned, may indicate faulty steering and/or suspension components.

3 Check the shock absorbers by pushing down and releasing the vehicle several times at each corner. If the vehicle does not come back to a level position within one or two bounces, the shocks/struts are worn and must be replaced. When bouncing the vehicle up and down, listen for squeaks and noises from the suspension components.

4 Check the struts and shock absorbers for evidence of fluid leakage. A light film of fluid is no cause for concern. Make sure that any fluid noted is from the shocks and not from some other source. If leakage is noted, replace the shocks as a set.

5 Check the shocks to be sure they are securely mounted and undamaged. Check the upper mounts for damage and wear. If damage or wear is noted, replace the shocks as a set (front and rear).

6 If the shocks must be replaced, refer to Chapter 10 for the procedure.

UNDER THE VEHICLE

▶ **Refer to illustrations 13.9, 13.10 and 13.11**

7 Raise the vehicle and support it securely on jackstands. See *Jack-*

ing and towing at the front of this book for the proper jacking points.

8 Check the tires for irregular wear patterns and proper inflation. See Section 5 in this Chapter for information regarding tire wear and Chapter 10 for information on hub bearing replacement.

9 Inspect the universal joint between the steering shaft and the steering gear housing. Check the steering gear housing for lubricant leakage. Make sure that the dust seals and boots are not damaged (see illustration) and that the boot clamps are not loose. Check the steering linkage for looseness or damage. Check the tie-rod ends for excessive play. Look for loose bolts, broken or disconnected parts and deteriorated rubber bushings on all suspension and steering components. While an assistant turns the steering wheel from side to side, check the steering components for free movement, chafing and binding. If the steering components do not seem to be reacting with the movement of the steering wheel, try to determine where the slack is located.

10 Check the balljoints for wear by trying to move each control arm up and down with a pry bar (see illustration) to ensure that its balljoint has no play. If any balljoint does have play, replace it. See Chapter 10

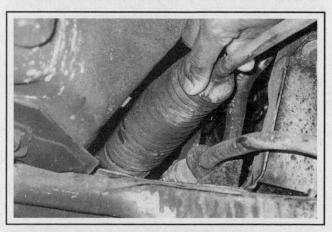

13.9 Check the steering gear boots for damage

13.10 To check the balljoint for wear, try to pry the control arm up and down to make sure there is no play in the balljoint (if there is, replace it)

13.11 Check the balljoint boot for damage

13.14 Flex the driveaxle boots by hand to check for cracks and/or leaking grease

for the balljoint replacement procedure.

11 Inspect the balljoint boots for damage and leaking grease (see illustration). Replace the balljoints with new ones if they are damaged (see Chapter 10).

12 At the rear of the vehicle, inspect the suspension arm bushings for deterioration. Additional information on suspension components can be found in Chapter 10.

DRIVEAXLE BOOT CHECK

▶ **Refer to illustration 13.14**

➡**Note: For detailed illustrations of the driveaxles, refer to Chapter 8.**

13 The driveaxle boots are very important because they prevent dirt, water and foreign material from entering and damaging the constant velocity (CV) joints. Because it constantly pivots back and forth following the steering action of the front hub, the outer CV boot wears out sooner and should be inspected regularly.

14 Inspect the boots for tears and cracks as well as loose clamps (see illustration). Don't forget to inspect the inner and outer boots of the rear driveaxles on 4WD Sportage models. If there is any evidence of cracks or leaking lubricant, they must be replaced as described in Chapter 8.

14 Underhood hose check and replacement (every 15,000 miles [24,000 km] or 12 months)

❊❊ WARNING:

Replacement of air conditioning hoses must be left to a dealer service department or air conditioning shop that has the equipment to depressurize the system safely. Never remove air conditioning components or hoses until the system has been depressurized.

GENERAL

1 High temperatures under the hood can cause deterioration of the rubber and plastic hoses used for engine, accessory and emission systems operation. Periodic inspection should be made for cracks, loose clamps, material hardening and leaks.

2 Information specific to the cooling system hoses can be found in Section 9.

3 Most (but not all) hoses are secured to the fittings with clamps. Where clamps are used, check to be sure they haven't lost their tension, allowing the hose to leak. If clamps aren't used, make sure the hose has not expanded and/or hardened where it slips over the fitting, allowing it to leak.

PCV SYSTEM HOSE

4 To reduce hydrocarbon emissions, crankcase blow-by gas is vented through the PCV valve in the valve cover to the intake manifold via a rubber hose. The blow-by gases mix with incoming air in the intake manifold before being burned in the combustion chambers.

5 Check the PCV hose for cracks, leaks and other damage. Disconnect it from the valve cover and the intake manifold and check the inside for obstructions. If it's clogged, clean it out with solvent. See Chapter 6 for more information on the PCV system.

VACUUM HOSES

6 It's quite common for vacuum hoses, especially those in the emissions system, to be color coded or identified by colored stripes molded into them. Various systems require hoses with different wall thickness, collapse resistance and temperature resistance. When replacing hoses, be sure the new ones are made of the same material.

7 Often the only effective way to check a hose is to remove it completely from the vehicle. If more than one hose is removed, be sure to label the hoses and fittings to ensure correct installation.

8　When checking vacuum hoses, be sure to include any plastic T-fittings in the check. Inspect the fittings for cracks and the hose where it fits over each fitting for distortion, which could cause leakage.

9　A small piece of vacuum hose (1/4-inch inside diameter) can be used as a stethoscope to detect vacuum leaks. Hold one end of the hose to your ear and probe around vacuum hoses and fittings, listening for the "hissing" sound characteristic of a vacuum leak.

✳✳ WARNING:

When probing with the vacuum hose stethoscope, be careful not to come into contact with moving engine components such as drivebelts, the cooling fan, etc.

FUEL HOSE

✳✳ WARNING:

Gasoline is flammable, so take extra precautions when you work on any part of the fuel system. Don't smoke or allow open flames or bare light bulbs near the work area, and don't work in a garage where a gas-type appliance (such as a water heater or clothes dryer) is present. Since fuel is carcinogenic, wear fuel-resistant gloves when there's a possibility of being exposed to fuel, and, if you spill any fuel on your skin, rinse it off immediately with soap and water. Mop up any spills immediately and do not store fuel-soaked rags where they could ignite. The fuel system is under constant pressure, so, if any fuel lines are to be disconnected, the fuel pressure in the system must be relieved first (see Chapter 4 for more information). When you perform any kind of work on the fuel system, wear safety glasses and have a Class B type fire extinguisher on hand.

10　The fuel lines are usually under pressure, so if any fuel lines are to be disconnected be prepared to catch spilled fuel.

✳✳ WARNING:

Your vehicle is equipped with fuel injection and you must relieve the fuel system pressure before servicing the fuel lines. Refer to Chapter 4 for the fuel system pressure relief procedure.

11　Check all flexible fuel lines for deterioration and chafing. Check especially for cracks in areas where the hose bends and just before fittings, such as where a hose attaches to the fuel pump, fuel filter and fuel injection unit.

12　When replacing a hose, use only hose that is specifically designed for your fuel injection system.

13　Spring-type clamps are sometimes used on fuel return or vapor lines. These clamps often lose their tension over a period of time, and can be "sprung" during removal. Replace all spring-type clamps with screw clamps whenever a hose is replaced. Some fuel lines use spring-lock type couplings, which require a special tool to disconnect. See Chapter 4 for more information on this type of coupling.

METAL LINES

14　Sections of metal line are often used for fuel line between the fuel pump and the fuel injection unit. Check carefully to make sure the line isn't bent, crimped or cracked.

15　If a section of metal fuel line must be replaced, use seamless steel tubing only, since copper and aluminum tubing do not have the strength necessary to withstand vibration caused by the engine.

16　Check the metal brake lines where they enter the master cylinder and brake proportioning unit (if used) for cracks in the lines and loose fittings. Any sign of brake fluid leakage calls for an immediate thorough inspection of the brake system.

15　Fuel and exhaust system checks (every 15,000 miles [24,000 km] or 12 months)

FUEL SYSTEM CHECK

✳✳ WARNING:

Gasoline is flammable, so take extra precautions when you work on any part of the fuel system. Don't smoke or allow open flames or bare light bulbs near the work area, and don't work in a garage where a gas-type appliance (such as a water heater or clothes dryer) is present. Since fuel is carcinogenic, wear fuel-resistant gloves when there's a possibility of being exposed to fuel, and, if you spill any fuel on your skin, rinse it off immediately with soap and water. Mop up any spills immediately and do not store fuel-soaked rags where they could ignite. When you perform any kind of work on the fuel system, wear safety glasses and have a Class B type fire extinguisher on hand. The fuel system is under constant pressure, so, before any lines are disconnected, the fuel system pressure must be relieved (see Chapter 4).

1　If you smell gasoline while driving or after the vehicle has been sitting in the sun, inspect the fuel system immediately.

2　Remove the fuel filler cap and inspect if for damage and corrosion. The gasket should have an unbroken sealing imprint. If the gasket

is damaged or corroded, install a new cap.

3　Inspect the fuel feed line for cracks. Make sure that the connections between the fuel lines and the fuel injection system are secure and dry.

✳✳ WARNING:

Your vehicle is fuel injected, so you must relieve the fuel system pressure before servicing fuel system components. The fuel system pressure relief procedure is outlined in Chapter 4.

4　Since some components of the fuel system - the fuel tank and the fuel lines, for example - are underneath the vehicle, they can be inspected more easily with the vehicle raised on a hoist. If that's not possible, raise the vehicle and support it on jackstands.

5　With the vehicle raised and safely supported, inspect the gas tank and filler neck for punctures, cracks and other damage. The connection between the filler neck and the tank is particularly critical. Sometimes a rubber filler neck will leak because of loose clamps or deteriorated rubber. Inspect all fuel tank mounting brackets and straps to be sure that the tank is securely attached to the vehicle.

Do not, under any circumstances, try to repair a fuel tank (except rubber components); the fuel tanks in these vehicles are made of plastic and must be replaced if damaged.

6   Carefully check all hoses and lines leading away from the fuel tank. Check for loose connections, deteriorated hoses, crimped lines and other damage. Repair or replace damaged sections as necessary (see Chapter 4).

EXHAUST SYSTEM CHECK

▸ **Refer to illustration 15.8**

7   With the engine cold (at least three hours after the vehicle has been driven), check the complete exhaust system from the engine to the end of the tailpipe. Ideally, the inspection should be done with the vehicle on a hoist to permit unrestricted access. If a hoist isn't available, raise the vehicle and support it securely on jackstands.

8   Check the exhaust pipes and connections for evidence of leaks, severe corrosion and damage. Make sure that all brackets and hangers are in good condition and tight (see illustration).

9   At the same time, inspect the underside of the body for holes, corrosion, open seams, etc. which may allow exhaust gases to enter the passenger compartment. Seal all body openings with silicone or body putty.

15.8 Be sure to check each exhaust system rubber hanger for damage

10 Rattles and other noises can often be traced to the exhaust system, especially the mounts and hangers. Try to move the pipes, muffler and catalytic converter. If the components can come in contact with the body or suspension parts, secure the exhaust system with new mounts.

11 Check the running condition of the engine by inspecting inside the end of the tailpipe. The exhaust deposits here are an indication of engine state-of-tune. If the pipe is black and sooty or coated with white deposits, the engine may need a tune-up, including a thorough fuel system inspection and adjustment.

16 Cabin air filter replacement (every 30,000 miles [48,000 km] or 24 months)

➡**Note: 2008 and 2009 Spectra and all Sportage models are equipped with a cabin air filter located behind the glovebox.**

1   Open the glovebox door. Pull the elastic cord, rotate the assembly until it lines up with the notch in the glovebox and push it through the opening. Lower the glovebox door.

2   Remove the stoppers from each side and swing the glovebox door completely down.

3   Remove the cabin air filter cover by releasing the tabs.

4   Slide the cabin air filter from the HVAC housing.

5   Installation is the reverse of removal.

17 Air filter replacement (every 30,000 miles [48,000 km] or 24 months)

▸ **Refer to illustrations 17.1a, 17.1b and 17.1c**

1   The air filter is located inside a housing inside of the engine compartment. To remove the air filter, loosen the clamp securing the inlet tube to the air filter cover, remove the screws or clips securing the two halves of the air filter housing together, then remove the cover halves and remove the air filter element (see illustrations).

2   Inspect the outer surface of the filter element. If it is dirty, replace it. If it is only moderately dusty, it can be reused by blowing it clean from the back to the front surface with compressed air. Because it is a pleated paper type filter, it cannot be washed or oiled. If it cannot be cleaned satisfactorily with compressed air, discard and replace it. While the cover is off, be careful not to drop anything down into the housing.

Never drive the vehicle with the air cleaner removed. Excessive engine wear could result and backfiring could even cause a fire under the hood.

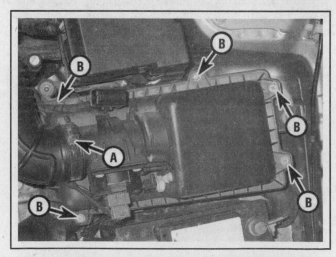

17.1a Loosen the intake hose clamp (A), then remove the fasteners securing the air filter housing cover (B) . . .

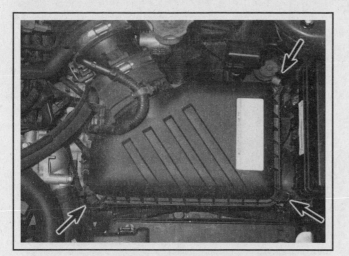

17.1b . . . or, if the filter housing cover is secured by clips instead of screws, release the clips . . .

17.1c . . . then pull the cover out of the way and lift out the filter element

3 Wipe out the inside of the air cleaner housing.

4 Place the new filter into the air cleaner housing, making sure it

seats properly.

5 Installation of the housing is the reverse of removal.

18 Drivebelt check, adjustment and replacement (every 30,000 miles [48,000 km] or 24 months)

FOUR-CYLINDER MODELS

✳✳ WARNING:

The electric cooling fan(s) on these models can activate at any time the ignition switch is in the ON position. Make sure the ignition is OFF when working in the vicinity of the fan(s).

1 The drivebelts are located at the front of the engine and play an important role in the operation of the vehicle and its components. Due to their function and material makeup, the belts are prone to failure after a period of time and should be inspected and adjusted periodically to prevent major damage.

2 The drive belts drive the alternator, power steering pump and air conditioning compressor (if equipped), as well as the water pump. The engine has two belts: one for the water pump and alternator, and one for the air conditioning compressor and power steering pump.

Check

▶ Refer to illustrations 18.3 and 18.4

3 With the engine off, open the hood and use your fingers (and a flashlight, if necessary), to move along the belt checking for cracks and separation of the belt plies. Also check for fraying and glazing, which gives the belt a shiny appearance. Also check the ribs on the underside of the belt. They should all be the same depth, with none of the surface uneven (see illustration).

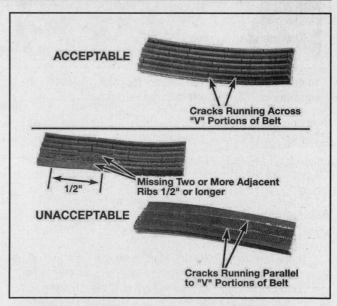

18.3 Here are some of the more common problems associated with drivebelts (check the belts very carefully to prevent an untimely breakdown)

4 The tension of each belt is checked by pushing on it at a distance halfway between the pulleys. Apply about 20 pounds of force with your thumb and see how much the belt moves down (deflects). Measure the

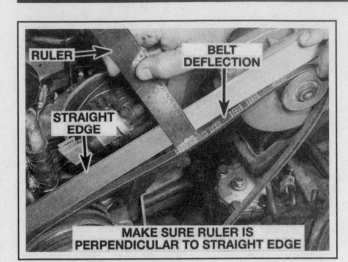

18.4 Measure drivebelt deflection with a straightedge and ruler - make sure the ruler is perpendicular to the straight edge (typical)

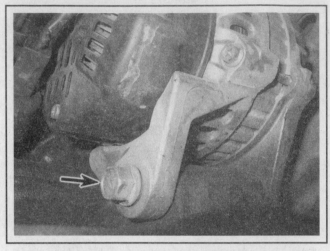

18.6a To adjust the alternator/water pump belt, loosen the pivot bolt or nut . . .

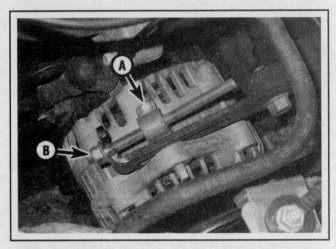

18.6b . . . then loosen the adjuster lock bolt (A) and turn the adjusting bolt (B) to adjust the drivebelt tension

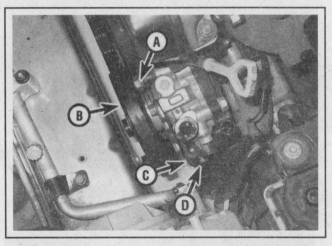

18.6c To adjust the power steering pump/air conditioning compressor belt, loosen the pivot bolt (A), the bracket nut (B) and lock nut (C), then turn the adjusting bolt (D) (bracket nut and lock nut not visible)

deflection with a ruler (see illustration). The belt should deflect about 1/4-inch if the distance between pulleys is between 7 and 11 inches and around 1/2-inch if the distance is between 12 and 16 inches.

Adjustment

♦ Refer to illustrations 18.6a, 18.6b and 18.6c

5   Depending on the belt being adjusted, you may have to raise the vehicle and support it securely on jackstands.

6   Drivebelt tension adjustment is made by moving the component position with an adjuster after loosening the pivot bolt (see illustrations). Loosen the adjuster lock bolt or nut and turn the adjuster bolt as necessary to move the component away from the engine (to tighten the belt) or toward the engine (to loosen the belt) to achieve the correct drivebelt tension. Tighten the pivot bolt/nut and lock bolt securely.

Replacement

7   To replace a drivebelt, follow the procedures for drivebelt adjustment, except loosen the adjustment enough to allow you to slip the

drivebelt off the pulleys to remove it. Because drivebelts tend to wear out equally, it's a good idea to replace all belts at the same time. As they are removed, identify each belt as to its appropriate drive function (PS-A/C or ALT-WP) so the replacement belts can be installed in their proper positions.

8   Take the old drivebelts with you when you go to the auto parts store in order to make a direct comparison for length, width and design.

9   Install the new drivebelts. Make sure they are routed correctly and properly centered in each pulley.

10   Adjust the drivebelts as described earlier in this Section. After the drivebelts have been in service for approximately fifteen minutes, check the drivebelt tension again and adjust if necessary, as new drivebelts tend to stretch after initial installation.

V6 (SPORTAGE) MODELS

11   The V6 engine on these models uses a single drivebelt. Belt tension is maintained by an automatic spring-loaded adjuster.

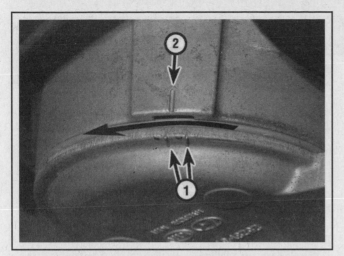

18.13 Automatic tensioner details (Sportage V6 models):

1 *The area between these two marks indicates the acceptable range of drivebelt stretch*
2 *When the area indicated by the two marks moves past this stationary mark, replace the drivebelt*

18.18 Drivebelt tensioner mounting bolt (V6 Sportage models)

Check

▶ **Refer to illustration 18.13**

12 Inspect the condition of the drivebelt the same way that you would check a conventional drivebelt (see Step 3).

13 As the belt stretches over time, the tensioner pulley arm moves in a counterclockwise direction. The acceptable range of drivebelt stretch is indicated by the area between two marks on the tensioner pulley arm (see illustration). When the acceptable tension range moves beyond the stationary mark on top of the tensioner, the drivebelt is worn out.

Replacement

Drivebelt

14 Before removing the old drivebelt, note how it is routed. To help you remember the belt routing, make a sketch.

15 Insert a ratchet or breaker bar into the square-drive hole at the end of the tensioner arm, rotate the tensioner pulley arm clockwise and pull the belt off the power steering pump pulley, then release the tensioner pulley arm and remove the belt from the other pulleys.

16 Installation is the reverse of removal. Route the new belt onto all the pulleys, rotate the tensioner pulley arm clockwise, place the belt over the tensioner pulley, then release the pulley arm.

Tensioner

▶ **Refer to illustration 18.18**

17 Remove the drivebelt (see Steps 14 and 15).

18 Remove the tensioner mounting bolt (see illustration) and remove the tensioner.

19 Installation is the reverse of removal.

19 Brake fluid change (every 30,000 miles [48,000 km] or 24 months)

※※ **WARNING:**

Brake fluid can harm your eyes and damage painted surfaces, so use extreme caution when handling or pouring it. Do not use brake fluid that has been standing open or is more than one year old. Brake fluid absorbs moisture from the air. Excess moisture can cause a dangerous loss of braking effectiveness.

1 At the specified intervals, the brake fluid should be drained and replaced. Since the brake fluid may drip or splash when pouring it, place plenty of rags around the master cylinder to protect any surrounding painted surfaces.

2 Before beginning work, purchase the specified brake fluid (see *Recommended lubricants and fluids* in this Chapter's Specifications).

3 Remove the cap from the master cylinder reservoir.

4 Using a hand suction pump or similar device, withdraw the fluid from the master cylinder reservoir.

5 Add new fluid to the master cylinder until it rises to the base of the filler neck.

6 Bleed the brake system as described in Chapter 9 at all four brakes until new and uncontaminated fluid is expelled from the bleeder screw. Be sure to maintain the fluid level in the master cylinder as you perform the bleeding process. If you allow the master cylinder to run dry, air will enter the system.

7 Refill the master cylinder with fluid and check the operation of the brakes. The pedal should feel solid when depressed, with no sponginess.

※※ **WARNING:**

Do not operate the vehicle if you are in doubt about the effectiveness of the brake system.

20 Cooling system servicing (draining, flushing and refilling) (every 30,000 miles [48,000 km] or 24 months)

※※ WARNING:

Do not allow antifreeze to come in contact with your skin or painted surfaces of the vehicle. Rinse off spills immediately with plenty of water. Antifreeze is highly toxic if ingested. Never leave antifreeze lying around in an open container or in puddles on the floor; children and pets are attracted by its sweet smell and may drink it. Check with local authorities about disposing of used antifreeze. Many communities have collection centers which will see that antifreeze is disposed of safely. Never dump used antifreeze on the ground or pour it into drains.

1   Periodically, the cooling system should be drained, flushed and refilled to replenish the antifreeze mixture and prevent formation of rust and corrosion, which can impair the performance of the cooling system and cause engine damage. When the cooling system is serviced, all hoses and the radiator cap should be checked and replaced if necessary.

DRAINING

▶ Refer to illustrations 20.3 and 20.4

2   Apply the parking brake and block the wheels.

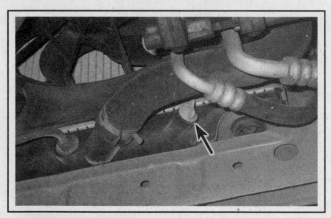

20.3 The drain fitting is located at the lower corner of the radiator

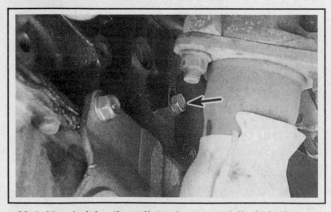

20.4 After draining the radiator, be sure to fully drain the cooling system by removing the block drain plug located on the side of the engine block

※※ WARNING:

If the vehicle has just been driven, wait several hours to allow the engine to cool down before beginning this procedure.

Turn the heater control to maximum heat.

3   Move a large container under the radiator drain to catch the coolant. The radiator drain plug is located on the right side lower corner of the radiator (see illustration). Unscrew the drain plug until coolant starts flowing from the drain hole (a pair of pliers may be required to turn it).

4   Remove the radiator cap and allow the radiator to drain, then, move the container under the engine, loosen the engine block drain plug (if equipped) and allow the coolant in the block to drain (see illustration).

5   While the coolant is draining, check the condition of the radiator hoses, heater hoses and clamps (refer to Section 9 if necessary).

6   Replace any damaged clamps or hoses. Close the drain plugs.

FLUSHING

▶ Refer to illustration 20.9

7   Once the system is completely drained, remove the thermostat from the engine (see Chapter 3), then reinstall the thermostat housing without the thermostat. This will allow the system to be thoroughly flushed.

8   Turn the heating system controls to Hot, so that the heater core will be flushed at the same time as the rest of the cooling system.

9   Disconnect the upper radiator hose from the radiator, then place a garden hose in the upper radiator inlet and flush the system until the water runs clear at the upper radiator hose (see illustration).

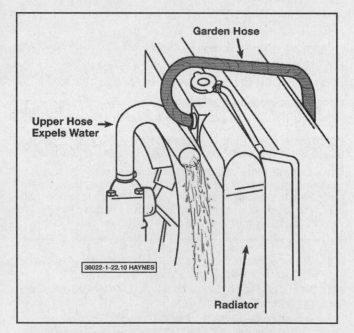

20.9 After removing the thermostat, disconnect the upper radiator hose from the radiator and flush the radiator and engine block with a garden hose

10 In severe cases of contamination or clogging of the radiator, remove the radiator (see Chapter 3) and have a radiator repair facility clean and repair it if necessary.

11 Many deposits can be removed by the chemical action of a cleaner available at auto parts stores. Follow the procedure outlined in the manufacturer's instructions.

➡**Note: When the coolant is regularly drained and the system refilled with the correct antifreeze/water mixture, there should be no need to use chemical cleaners or descalers.**

12 Remove the overflow hose from the coolant recovery reservoir. Drain the reservoir and flush it with clean water, then reconnect the hose.

REFILLING

13 Reconnect the upper radiator hose and reinstall the thermostat.

14 Fill the cooling system with the proper type and mixture of anti-freeze (see this Chapter's Specifications), up to the base of the radiator cap filler neck. Loosely install the radiator cap.

15 Start the engine and run it at approximately 1500 rpm until the radiator fan comes on two times. Feel the upper radiator hose - it should be warm, indicating the thermostat has opened.

16 Turn off the engine and let it cool down. Slowly remove the radiator cap and check the coolant level, adding as necessary.

❊❊ WARNING:

If you hear a hissing sound as you unscrew the cap, STOP. Let the engine cool down longer.

Fill the coolant reservoir up to the MIN mark, if necessary.

17 Start the engine, allow it to reach normal operating temperature once again and check for leaks.

21 Timing belt check (every 30,000 miles [48,000 km] or 24 months)

1   Remove the timing belt upper cover, then check the tension of the timing belt. If you're working on a four-cylinder engine, see Chapter 2A, Section 7, Step 43 (SOHC engine) or Step 52 (DOHC engines). If you're working on a V6 engine, refer to Chapter 2B, Section 7

2   If the belt deflection is not correct, adjust the belt tension as described in Chapter 2A, Section 7.

22 Positive Crankcase Ventilation (PCV) valve check and replacement (every 30,000 miles [48,000 km] or 24 months)

▶ **Refer to illustration 22.2**

1   The PCV valve is usually located in the valve cover.

2   With the engine idling at normal operating temperature, pull the valve (with hose attached) from the valve cover (see illustration).

3   Place your thumb over the valve opening. If there's no vacuum, check for a plugged hose, manifold port, or the valve itself. Replace any plugged or deteriorated hoses.

4   Turn off the engine and shake the PCV valve, listening for a rattle. If the valve doesn't rattle, replace it with a new one.

5   To replace the valve, pull it from the end of the hose, noting its installed position.

6   When purchasing a replacement PCV valve, make sure it's for your particular vehicle and engine size. Compare the old valve with the new one to make sure they're the same.

7   Push the valve into the end of the hose until it's seated.

8   Inspect all rubber hoses and grommets for damage and hardening. Replace them, if necessary.

9   Press the PCV valve and hose securely into position.

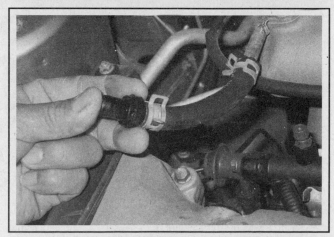

22.2 The PCV valve is located in the valve cover - with the engine running, put your finger over the end of the PCV valve; you should feel vacuum

23 Spark plug check and replacement (every 30,000 miles [48,000 km] or 24 months)

▶ **Refer to illustrations 23.2, 23.5a, 23.5b, 23.8, 23.10, 23.12a and 23.12b**

1   The spark plugs are located in the center of the cylinder head.

2   In most cases the tools necessary for spark plug replacement include a spark plug socket which fits onto a ratchet (this special socket is padded inside to protect the porcelain insulators on the new plugs and hold them in place), various extensions and a feeler gauge to check and adjust the spark plug gap (see illustration). Since these engines are equipped with an aluminum cylinder head, a torque wrench should be

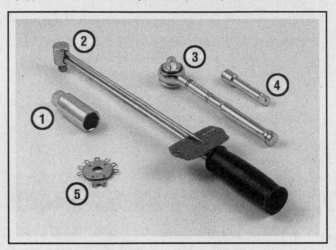

23.2   Tools required for changing spark plugs

1   Spark plug socket - This will have special padding inside to protect the spark plug's porcelain insulator
2   Torque wrench - Although not mandatory, using this tool is the best way to ensure the plugs are tightened properly
3   Ratchet - Standard hand tool to fit the spark plug socket
4   Extension - Depending on model and accessories, you may need special extensions and universal joints to reach one or more of the plugs
5   Spark plug gap gauge - This gauge for checking the gap comes in a variety of styles. Make sure the gap for your engine is included

used when tightening the spark plugs.

3   The best approach when replacing the spark plugs is to purchase the new spark plugs beforehand, adjust them to the proper gap and then replace each plug one at a time. When buying the new spark plugs, be sure to obtain the correct plug for your specific engine. This information can be found in this Chapter's Specifications or in your owner's manual.

4   Allow the engine to cool completely before attempting to remove any of the plugs. During this cooling off time, each of the new spark plugs can be inspected for defects and the gaps can be checked.

5   The gap is checked by inserting the proper thickness gauge between the electrodes at the tip of the plug (see illustrations). The gap between the electrodes should be as listed in this Chapter's Specifications or in your owner's manual. Also, at this time check for cracks in the spark plug body (if any are found, the plug must not be used).

6   Cover the fender to prevent damage to the paint. Fender covers are available from auto parts stores but an old blanket will work just fine.

7   Remove the screws and detach the spark plug cover from the valve cover.

8   On 1997 and earlier models, work on one spark plug at a time to prevent the possibility of mixing up the spark plug wires. Remove the wire and boot from one spark plug. Grasp the boot, not the cable, give it a half twist and pull straight up. On 1998 and later models, remove the coil mounting bolts and remove the coil/plug wire assembly (see Chapter 5).

9   If compressed air is available, use it to blow any dirt or foreign material away from the spark plug area. The idea here is to eliminate the possibility of material falling into the cylinder through the spark plug hole as the spark plug is removed.

✳✳ WARNING:

Wear eye protection!

10   Place the spark plug socket over the plug and remove it from the engine by turning it in a counterclockwise direction (see illustration).

11   Compare the spark plug with the chart on the inside back cover of

23.5a   Using a wire-type gauge to check the spark plug gap - if the wire doesn't slide between the electrodes with a slight drag, adjustment is required

23.5b   To change the gap, bend the side electrode only, and be very careful not to crack or chip the porcelain insulator surrounding the center electrode

23.10   Use a socket with a long extension to unscrew the spark plugs

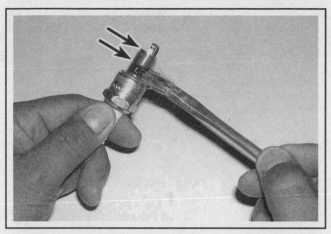

23.12a Apply a thin film of anti-seize compound to the spark plug threads, being careful not to get any near the electrodes (in the area indicated by the arrows)

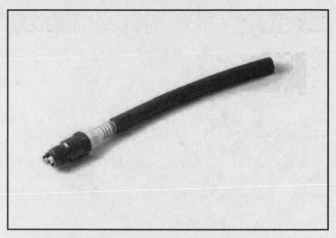

23.12b A length of rubber hose will save time and prevent damaged threads when installing the spark plugs

this manual to get an indication of the overall running condition of the engine.

12 Apply a small amount of anti-seize compound to the spark plug threads (see illustration). Install one of the new plugs into the hole until you can no longer turn it with your fingers, then tighten it with a torque wrench (if available) or the ratchet. It is a good idea to slip a short length of rubber hose over the end of the plug to use as a tool to thread

it into place (see illustration). The hose will grip the plug well enough to turn it, but will start to slip if the plug begins to cross-thread in the hole - this will prevent damaged threads and the accompanying repair costs.

13 Attach the coil/plug wire to the new spark plug using a twisting motion until it is firmly seated on the end of the spark plug.

14 Repeat the procedure for the remaining spark plugs.

24 Spark plug wire, distributor cap and rotor check and replacement (every 30,000 miles [48,000 km] or 24 months)

➡Note: On 1998 and later models, there is no conventional distributor. The spark plugs are fired by two coil-packs that mount directly over the plugs on the valve cover. Each coil-pack serves two cylinders, with one cylinder using a plug wire from the coil to the plug and the other cylinder having a direct boot from the bottom of the coil-pack to the plug.

1 The spark plug wires should be checked whenever new spark plugs are installed.

2 Begin this procedure by making a visual check of the spark plug wires while the engine is running. In a darkened garage (make sure there is ventilation) start the engine and observe each plug wire. Be careful not to come into contact with any moving engine parts. If there is a break in the wire, you will see arcing or a small spark at the damaged area. If arcing is noticed, make a note to obtain new wires, then allow the engine to cool and check the distributor cap and rotor.

3 The spark plug wires should be inspected one at a time to prevent mixing up the order, which is essential for proper engine operation. Each original plug wire should be numbered to help identify its location. If the number is illegible, a piece of tape can be marked with the correct number and wrapped around the plug wire.

4 Disconnect the plug wire from the spark plug. A removal tool can be used for this purpose or you can grasp the rubber boot, twist the boot half a turn and pull the boot free. Do not pull on the wire itself.

5 Check inside the boot for corrosion, which will look like a white crusty powder.

6 Check the resistance of the spark plug wires. If the indicated resistance is more than the maximum value listed in this Chapter's Specifications, replace the wires.

7 Push the wire and boot back onto the end of the spark plug. It should fit tightly onto the end of the plug. If it doesn't, remove the wire and use pliers to carefully crimp the metal connector inside the wire boot until the fit is snug.

8 Using a clean rag, wipe the entire length of the wire to remove built-up dirt and grease. Once the wire is clean, check for burns, cracks and other damage. Do not bend the wire sharply, because the conductor might break.

9 Disconnect the wire from the distributor cap or from the ignition coil. Again, pull only on the boot. Check for corrosion and a tight fit. Replace the wire in the distributor cap.

10 Inspect the remaining spark plug wires, making sure that each one is securely fastened at the distributor and spark plug when the check is complete.

11 If new spark plug wires are required, purchase a set for your specific engine model. Pre-cut wire sets with the boots already installed are available. Remove and replace the wires one at a time to avoid mix-ups in the firing order.

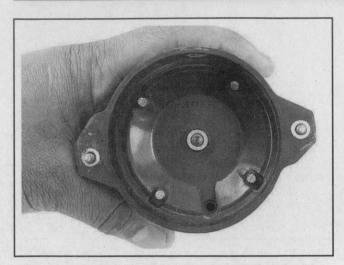

24.12 Inspect the distributor cap for carbon tracks, charred or eroded terminals and other damage (if in doubt about its condition, install a new one)

24.13 Check the rotor for damage, wear and corrosion (if in doubt about its condition, buy a new one)

MODELS EQUIPPED WITH A DISTRIBUTOR

▶ **Refer to illustrations 24.12 and 24.13**

12 Detach the distributor cap by removing the two retaining screws. Look inside it for cracks, carbon tracks and worn, burned or loose contacts (see illustration).

13 Pull the rotor off the distributor shaft and examine it for cracks and carbon tracks (see illustration). Replace the cap and rotor if any damage or defects are noted.

14 When installing a new cap, remove the wires from the old cap one at a time and attach them to the new cap in the exact same location - do not simultaneously remove all the wires from the old cap or firing order mix-ups may occur.

---

25 Idle speed check and adjustment (every 30,000 miles [48,000 km] or 24 months)

▶ **Refer to illustrations 25.4 and 25.5**

➡ **Note: The idle adjustment procedure applies to 1994 through 1997 models. You can check the idle speed on 1998 and later models but you can't adjust it.**

1 Engine idle speed is the speed at which the engine operates when no accelerator pedal pressure is applied, as when stopped at a traffic light. The speed is critical to the performance of the engine itself, as well as many subsystems. Before checking or adjusting the idle speed make sure the CHECK ENGINE light in not on, the air cleaner and spark plugs are in good condition, the PCV system is operating properly and the ignition timing is correct.

2 Set the parking brake firmly and block the wheels to prevent the vehicle from rolling. Place the transaxle in Neutral (manual transaxle) or Park (automatic transaxle).

3 Connect a hand-held tachometer in accordance with the tool manufacturer's instructions.

4 Locate the Data Link Connector (DLC) on the firewall. Open the DLC's protective lid and install a jumper wire between the ENGINE TEST and GROUND terminals (see illustration).

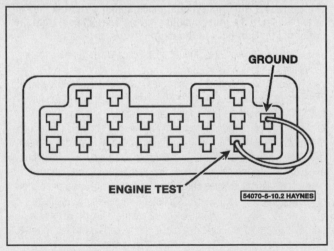

25.4 Install a jumper wire between the ENGINE TEST and GROUND terminals

5   Start the engine and allow the idle to stabilize for one minute. Note the idle speed on the tachometer and compare it to that listed on the VECI label or in this Chapter's Specifications.

 a) *If the idle speed listed on the VECI label is different than that listed in this Chapter's Specifications, use the specification shown on the VECI label.*

 b) *On 1994 through 1997 models, if the idle speed is too low or too high, remove the cap and turn the idle adjust screw to obtain the specified idle speed (see illustration). Make changes slowly in 1/4-turn increments only.*

 c) *On 1998 and later models, if the idle speed is too low or too high, there could be a problem with the IAC system (see Chapter 6) or the intake manifold may have a leak (see Chapter 2A).*

25.5 To obtain the specified idle speed, turn the idle adjust screw slowly in 1/4-turn increments

26 Automatic transaxle fluid change (every 60,000 miles [96,000 km] or 36 months)

⯈ **Refer to illustration 26.6**

1   The automatic transaxle fluid should be changed at the recommended intervals.

2   Before beginning work, purchase the specified transaxle fluid (see *Recommended lubricants and fluids* in this Chapter's Specifications).

3   Other tools necessary for this job include jackstands to support the vehicle in a raised position, wrenches, drain pan capable of holding at least four quarts, newspapers and clean rags.

4   The fluid should be drained immediately after the vehicle has been driven. Hot fluid is more effective than cold fluid at removing built up sediment.

❄❄ WARNING:

Fluid temperature can exceed 350-degrees F in a hot transaxle. Wear protective gloves.

5   After the vehicle has been driven to warm up the fluid, raise the front of the vehicle and support it securely on jackstands.

❄❄ WARNING:

Never work under a vehicle that is supported only by a jack!

6   Place the drain pan under the transaxle drain plug and remove the drain plug (see illustration). Be sure the drain pan is in position, as fluid will come out with some force. Once the fluid is drained, reinstall the drain plug securely. Measure the amount of fluid drained and write down this figure for reference when refilling.

7   Lower the vehicle.

8   With the engine off, add new fluid to the transaxle through the dipstick tube (see *Recommended lubricants and fluids* for the recommended fluid type). Begin the refill procedure by initially adding 1/3 of the amount drained. Then, with the engine running, add 1/2-pint at a time (cycling the shifter through each gear position between additions) until the level is correct on the dipstick.

9   If desired, repeat Steps 5 through 8 once to flush any contaminated fluid from the torque converter.

10   The old oil drained from the transaxle cannot be reused in its present state and should be disposed of. Check with your local auto parts store, disposal facility or environmental agency to see if they will accept the oil for recycling. After the oil has cooled it can be drained into a container (capped plastic jugs, topped bottles, milk cartons, etc.) for transport to one of these disposal sites. Don't dispose of the oil by pouring it on the ground or down a drain!

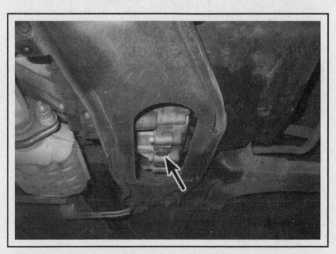

26.6 Location of the automatic transaxle fluid drain plug

27 Manual transaxle lubricant change (every 60,000 miles [96,000 km] or 36 months)

1   Raise the vehicle and support it securely on jackstands in a level position.

✳✳ WARNING:

Never work under a vehicle that is supported only by a jack!

2   Remove the fill plug (1998 and later models), followed by the drain plug. Drain the fluid into a suitable container capable of holding at least four quarts.

3   After the fluid has completely drained, install the drain plug and tighten it to the torque given in this Chapter's Specifications.

4   Fill the transaxle with the recommended lubricant (see *Recommended lubricants and fluids* in this Chapter's Specifications). On 1997 and earlier models, add new oil to the transaxle through the speedometer driven gear case hole. Use a funnel to prevent spills. It is best to add a little oil at a time, continually checking the level (see illustration 4.45). Inspect the O-ring seal on the driven gear. Replace it if it appears damaged, flattened or age hardened. Re-install the driven gear in the transaxle and tighten the retaining bolt securely. Then re-install the speedometer cable.

5   On 1998 and later models, use a syringe or a gear oil pump to add lubricant through the fill plug. Stop filling the transaxle when the lubricant begins to run out the hole. Install the plug and tighten it securely.

6   The old oil drained from the transaxle cannot be reused in its present state and should be disposed of. Check with your local auto parts store, disposal facility or environmental agency to see if they will accept the oil for recycling. After the oil has cooled it can be drained into a container (capped plastic jugs, topped bottles, milk cartons, etc.) for transport to one of these disposal sites. Don't dispose of the oil by pouring it on the ground or down a drain!

28 Transfer case (Sportage 4WD models) - lubricant change (every 60,000 miles [96,000 km] or 36 months)

1   Drive the vehicle for at least 15 minutes to warm the lubricant in the case.

2   Raise the vehicle and support it securely on jackstands.

3   Remove the check/fill plug, then the drain plug and allow the old lubricant to drain completely (see illustration 4.52).

4   After the lubricant has drained completely, reinstall the plug and tighten it securely.

5   Fill the case with the specified lubricant until it is level with the lower edge of the filler hole.

6   Install the check/fill plug and tighten it securely.

7   Drive the vehicle for a short distance, then check the drain and fill plugs for leakage.

29 Rear differential (Sportage 4WD models) - lubricant change (every 60,000 miles [96,000 km] or 36 months)

1   Drive the vehicle for at least 15 minutes to warm the lubricant in the differential.

2   Raise the vehicle and support it securely on jackstands.

3   Remove the check/fill plug, then the drain plug and allow the old lubricant to drain completely (see illustration 4.56).

4   After the lubricant has drained completely, reinstall the plug and tighten it securely.

5   Fill the differential with the specified lubricant until it is level with the lower edge of the filler hole.

6   Install the check/fill plug and tighten it securely.

7   Drive the vehicle for a short distance, then check the drain and fill plugs for leakage.

30 Fuel filter replacement (every 60,000 miles [96,000 km] or 45 months)

▶ Refer to illustration 30.4

✳✳ WARNING:

Gasoline is extremely flammable, so take extra precautions when you work on any part of the fuel system. Don't smoke or allow open flames or bare light bulbs near the work area, and don't work in a garage where a gas-type appliance (such as a water heater or clothes dryer) is present. Since fuel is carcinogenic, wear latex gloves when there's a possibility of being exposed to fuel, and, if you spill any fuel on your skin, rinse it off immediately with soap and water. Mop up any spills immediately and do not store fuel-soaked rags where they could ignite. When you perform any kind of work on the fuel system, wear safety glasses and have a Class B type fire extinguisher on hand.

➡Note: 2.0L models and all Sportage models have a returnless fuel system. This system uses a fuel filter that is an integral component of the fuel pump, which is mounted in the fuel tank and is not normally serviced. Refer to Chapter 4 for information about servicing the fuel pump and fuel tank.

1   The fuel filter is mounted under the vehicle on the right side, near the gas tank.

2   Relieve the fuel system pressure (see Chapter 4), then disconnect the cable from the negative terminal of the battery (see Chapter 5, Section 1).

3   Raise the vehicle and support it securely on jackstands. Inspect the fittings at both ends of the filter to see if they're clean. If more than a light coating of dust is present, clean the fittings before proceeding.

4   Disconnect the fuel lines at the fuel filter (see illustration). Detach the lines, one at a time; be prepared for fuel spillage.

5   After the lines are detached, check the fittings for damage and

30.4 To disconnect the quick-connect fittings from the fuel filter, depress the two release buttons on the sides of the fitting (this disengages the locking mechanism inside the fitting from the raised ridge on the pipe)

distortion. If they were damaged in any way during removal, new ones must be used when the lines are reattached to the new filter. Also inspect the condition of the O-ring inside the fitting. If it's cracked, torn or otherwise deteriorated, replace it.

6   Remove the fuel filter from the mounting clamp, while noting the direction the fuel filter is installed.

7   Install the new filter in the same direction. Carefully push each hose onto the filter until it's seated against the collar on the fitting. Pull on the hoses to make sure the fittings have completely engaged with the pipes - if they come off, the hoses could back off the filter and a fire could result!

8   Start the engine and check for fuel leaks.

Specifications

Recommended lubricants and fluids

➡️**Note: The fluids and lubricants listed here are those recommended by the manufacturer at the time this manual was written. Vehicle manufacturers occasionally upgrade their fluid and lubricant specifications, so check with your local auto parts store for the most current recommendations.**

Engine oil	
Type	API "Certified for gasoline engines"
Viscosity	See accompanying chart
Automatic transaxle fluid	
1995 and earlier models	DEXRON® IIE or equivalent
1996 through 2000 models	DEXRON® III or equivalent
2001 and later models	SK ATF SP-III or Diamond ATF SP-III
Manual transaxle lubricant	
All except Sportage	API GL-4 or GL-5, SAE 75W-90 gear oil
Sportage	API GL-4, SAE 75W-85
Transfer case lubricant (4WD models)	GL-5, SAE 80W-90

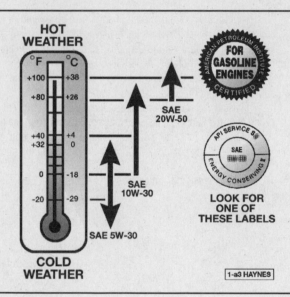

ENGINE OIL VISCOSITY CHART

For best fuel economy and cold starting, select the lowest SAE grade for the expected temperature range

Rear differential lubricant (4WD models)	GL-5 hypoid gear oil, SAE 80W-90
Brake fluid type	DOT 3 or DOT 4 brake fluid
Clutch fluid type	DOT 3 brake fluid
Power steering system fluid	
2001 and earlier models	DEXRON® IIE or equivalent
2002 and later models	PSF-III or equivalent
Fuel type	Unleaded gasoline, 87 octane or higher
Engine coolant	50/50 mixture of ethylene-glycol based antifreeze/coolant and distilled water

Capacities*

Engine oil (including oil filter)

1.6L SOHC and DOHC	3.4 quarts (3.2 liters)
1.8L DOHC	4.0 quarts (3.8 liters)
2.0L DOHC	
All except Sportage	4.3 quarts (4.1 liters)
Sportage	4.2 quarts (4.0 liters)
2.7L V6	4.8 quarts (4.5 liters)

Automatic transaxle fluid (drain and refill)**

1995 and earlier models	6.7 quarts (6.3 liters)
1996 and later models (except 2.0L DOHC)	5.7 quarts (5.4 liters)
2.0L DOHC	
2004 and 2005	8.2 quarts (7.8 liters)
2006 and later	
All except Sportage	6.5 quarts (6.2 liters)
Sportage	8.2 quarts (7.8 liters)
2.7L V6	8.2 quarts (7.8 liters)

Manual transaxle lubricant (drain and refill)

All except 2.0L DOHC and Sportage	2.8 quarts (2.7 liters)
2.0L DOHC (except Sportage)	2.30 quarts (2.15 liters)
Sportage	
2.0L DOHC	2.22 quarts (2.10 liters)
2.7L V6	2.30 quarts (2.15 liters)

Transfer case fluid (Sportage 4WD)	0.85 quart (0.80 liter)
Rear differential fluid (Sportage 4WD)	0.85 quart (0.80 liter)

Cooling system

All except 2.0L DOHC and Sportage	
Automatic transaxle models	6.3 quarts (6.0 liters)
Manual transaxle models	
1995 and earlier	5.3 quarts (5.0 liters)
1996 and later	6.3 quarts (6.0 liters)
2.0L DOHC (except Sportage)	
2004 through 2007 models	8.6 quarts (8.14 liters)
2008 and later models	7.0 quarts (6.5 liters)
Sportage	
Four-cylinder engine	6.3 quarts (6.0 liters)
V6 engine	7.4 quarts (7.0 liters)

* All capacities approximate. Add as necessary to bring to appropriate level.

** If you want to flush the converter during a fluid change, purchase twice the amount of fluid listed here.

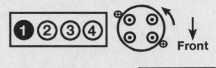

Cylinder numbering and distributor rotation - four-cylinder engines (1998 and later models do not have a distributor)

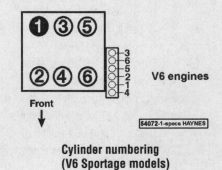

Cylinder numbering (V6 Sportage models)

Ignition system

Spark plug type and gap (all except Sportage)

Type

1997 and earlier models	NGK BKR5E-11
1998 through 2004 models (except 2.0L DOHC)	NGK BKR6E
2.0L DOHC	
NGK platinum-coated	PFR5N-11
NGK iridium-coated (2004 through 2006)	IFR5G-11
NGK iridium-coated (2007 and later)	IZFR5L-11
Champion platinum-coated	RC10PYPB4

Gap

1997 and earlier models	0.039 to 0.043 inch (1.0 to 1.1 mm)
1998 through 2004 models (except 2.0L DOHC)	0.028 to 0.032 inch (0.7 to 0.8 mm)
2.0L DOHC	0.039 to 0.043 inch (1.0 to 1.1 mm)

Spark plug type and gap (Sportage)

Type

2.0L DOHC	
Champion	RC10PYB4
NGK	PFR5N-11
2.7L V6	
NGK	IFR5G-11
Gap (both engines, all plugs)	0.039 to 0.043 inch (1.0 to 1.1 mm)
Spark plug wire resistance	Less than 25,000 ohms

Engine firing order

Four-cylinder engines	1-3-4-2
V6 engine	1-2-3-4-5-6

Engine idle speed (in Park or Neutral)

1997 and earlier models	
1.6L DOHC engine w/manual transaxle	700+/-50 rpm
All other models	750+/-50 rpm
1998 and later models	Not applicable (electronically controlled)

Cooling system

Accessory drivebelt deflection

All except 2.0L DOHC and Sportage	
New belt	0.31 to 0.35-inch (8 to 9 mm)
Used belt	0.35 to 0.39-inch (9 to 10 mm)
2.0L DOHC (except Sportage)	
New belt	0.16 to 0.20 inch (4 to 5 mm)
Used belt	0.20 to 0.24 inch (5 to 6 mm)
Sportage	
2.0L DOHC	
New	0.16 to 0.20 inch (4.0 to 5.0 mm)
Used	0.20 to 0.23 inch (5.0 to 6.0 mm)
2.7L V6	Automatically tensioned

Brakes

Disc brake pad minimum thickness
      All models through 2004 (except 2.0L DOHC)   1/16 inch (1.6 mm), front and rear
      2.0L DOHC and 2.7L V6   5/64 inch (2.0 mm), front and rear
Drum brake shoe minimum lining thickness
      All models through 2004 (except 2.0L DOHC)   5/64 inch (2.0 mm)
      2.0L DOHC   3/64 inch (1.0 mm)
Parking brake adjustment
      1997 and earlier models   6 to 8 clicks
      1998 through 2004 models (except 2.0L DOHC)   5 to 7 clicks
      2.0L DOHC
            Models with rear disc brakes
                  All except Sportage   8 to 9 clicks
                  Sportage   7 to 8 clicks
            Models with rear drum brakes   8 clicks

Torque specifications	Ft-lbs	Nm
Engine oil drain plug		
1994 through 2004 (except 2.0L DOHC)	22 to 30	29 to 41
2.0L DOHC and 2.7L V6	30 to 33	39 to 44
Automatic transaxle drain plug		
1994 through 2004 (except 2.0L DOHC)	29 to 40	39 to 54
2.0L DOHC		
2004 and 2005	20 to 24	29 to 34
2006 and later (except Sportage)	25 to 32	35 to 45
Sportage (all)	29 to 36	40 to 50
Manual transaxle drain and filler plugs		
1994 through 2004 (except 2.0L DOHC)	29 to 43	40 to 58
2.0L DOHC (except Sportage)	22 to 45	30 to 35
Sportage (2.0L DOHC and 2.7L V6)		
Drain plug	22 to 25	30 to 35
Filler plug	25 to 33	35 to 45
Transfer case (4WD models)		
Drain plug	29 to 43	39 to 59
Filler plug	29 to 43	39 to 59
Rear differential (4WD models)		
Differential cover bolts	29 to 36	40 to 50
Filler plug	29 to 40	40 to 55
Spark plugs		
1997 and earlier models	11 to 17	15 to 23
1998 through 2004 (except 2.0L DOHC)	18 to 22	25 to 30
2.0L DOHC (except Sportage)	See owner's manual	
Sportage	15 to 21	20 to 30
Wheel lug nuts		
1995 and earlier models	65 to 87	88 to 118
1996 and later models (except Sportage)	76	103
Sportage (all models, 2WD and 4WD)	66 to 81	90 to 110

Notes

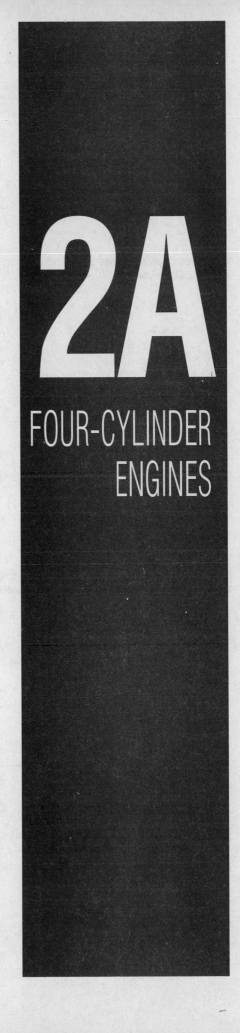

2A
FOUR-CYLINDER ENGINES

Section

1   General information
2   Repair operations possible with the engine in the vehicle
3   Top Dead Center (TDC) for number one piston - locating
4   Valve cover - removal and installation
5   Intake manifold - removal and installation
6   Exhaust manifold - removal and installation
7   Timing belt and sprockets - removal, inspection and installation
8   Camshaft oil seal(s) - replacement
9   Crankshaft pulley and front oil seal - removal and installation
10   Camshaft(s), lifters and rocker arms - removal, inspection, installation and adjustment
11   Cylinder head - removal and installation
12   Oil pan - removal and installation
13   Oil pump - removal, inspection and installation
14   Flywheel/driveplate - removal and installation
15   Rear main oil seal - replacement
16   Engine mounts - check and replacement

Reference to other Chapters

CHECK ENGINE light on - See Chapter 6
Cylinder compression check - See Chapter 2C
Drivebelt - check, adjustment and replacement - See Chapter 1
Engine - removal and installation - See Chapter 2C
Engine oil and filter change - See Chapter 1
Engine overhaul - general information - See Chapter 2C
Spark plug replacement - See Chapter 1
Water pump - removal and installation - See Chapter 3

1 General information

This Part of Chapter 2 is devoted to in-vehicle repair procedures for all four-cylinder engines. All information concerning engine removal, Installation and overhaul can be found in Part C of this Chapter.

The following repair procedures are based on the assumption that the engine is installed in the vehicle. If the engine has been removed from the vehicle and mounted on a stand, many of the Steps outlined in this Part of Chapter 2 will not apply.

The Specifications included in this Part of Chapter 2 apply only to the procedures contained in this Part.

2 Repair operations possible with the engine in the vehicle

Many major repair operations can be accomplished without removing the engine from the vehicle.

Clean the engine compartment and the exterior of the engine with some type of degreaser before any work is done. It will make the job easier and help keep dirt out of the internal areas of the engine.

Depending on the components involved, it may be helpful to remove the hood to improve access to the engine as repairs are performed (refer to Chapter 11 if necessary). Cover the fenders to prevent damage to the paint. Special pads are available, but a substitute such as a thick bedspread or blanket will also work.

If vacuum, exhaust, oil or coolant leaks develop, indicating a need for gasket or seal replacement, the repairs can generally be made with the engine in the vehicle. The intake and exhaust manifold gaskets, oil pan gasket, crankshaft oil seals and cylinder head gasket are all accessible with the engine in place.

Exterior engine components, such as the intake and exhaust manifolds, the oil pan, the oil pump, the water pump, the starter motor, the alternator, the distributor and the fuel system components can be removed for repair with the engine in place.

Since the cylinder head can be removed without pulling the engine, camshaft and valve component servicing can also be accomplished with the engine in the vehicle. Replacement of the timing belt and sprockets is also possible with the engine in the vehicle.

In extreme cases caused by a lack of necessary equipment, repair or replacement of piston rings, pistons, connecting rods and rod bearings is possible with the engine in the vehicle. However, this practice is not recommended because of the cleaning and preparation work that must be done to the components involved.

3 Top Dead Center (TDC) for number one piston - locating

1 Top Dead Center (TDC) is the highest point in the cylinder that each piston reaches traveling up-and-down as the crankshaft turns. Each piston reaches TDC on the compression stroke and again on the exhaust stroke, but TDC generally refers to piston position on the compression stroke.

2 Positioning the piston(s) at TDC is an essential part of many procedures such as camshaft and timing belt/sprocket removal and distributor removal, on models so equipped.

1994 THROUGH 1997 MODELS

▶ **Refer to illustration 3.8**

➡**Note: The following procedure is based on the assumption that the distributor is correctly installed. If you are trying to locate TDC to install the distributor correctly, piston position must be determined by feeling for compression at the number one spark plug hole, then aligning the ignition timing marks as described in Step 8.**

3 Before beginning this procedure, be sure to place the transmission in Neutral and apply the parking brake or block the rear wheels. Also, disable the ignition system by detaching the primary (low voltage) wires from the coil (see Chapter 5). Remove the spark plugs (see Chapter 1). If, in the next Step you will be rotating the engine using the starter motor, disable the fuel system by removing the rear seat cushion and unplugging the fuel pump electrical connector (see Chapter 4, Section 2).

4 In order to bring any piston to TDC, the crankshaft must be turned using one of the methods outlined below. When looking at the front of the engine, normal crankshaft rotation is clockwise.

   a) *The preferred method is to turn the crankshaft with a socket and ratchet attached to the bolt threaded into the front of the crankshaft.*

   b) *A remote starter switch, which may save some time, can also be used. Follow the instructions included with the switch. Once the piston is close to TDC, use a socket and ratchet as described in the previous paragraph.*

   c) *If an assistant is available to turn the ignition switch to the Start position in short bursts, you can get the piston close to TDC without a remote starter switch. Make sure your assistant is out of the vehicle, away from the ignition switch, then use a socket and ratchet as described in Paragraph a) to complete the procedure.*

5 Note the position of the terminal for the number one spark plug wire on the distributor cap. If the terminal is not marked, follow the plug wire from the number one cylinder spark plug to the cap.

6 Use a felt-tip pen or chalk to make a mark on the distributor body and the cap - directly at the terminal.

7 Detach the cap from the distributor and set it aside (see Chapter 1 if necessary).

3.8 To bring the number one piston to TDC, align the timing notch on the edge of the crankshaft pulley with the T mark (1.6L SOHC engine shown)

3.15 To bring the number one piston to TDC, align the timing notches on the edge of the crankshaft pulley with the T mark and the 10-degree BTDC mark (1.8L DOHC T8 engine shown, 2.0L DOHC engine similar)

8   Turn the crankshaft (see Step 3) until the notch in the crankshaft sprocket is aligned with the T on the timing plate (located at the front of the engine) (see illustration).

9   Look at the distributor rotor - it should be pointing directly at the mark you made on the distributor body.

10 If the rotor is 180-degrees off, the number one piston is at TDC on the exhaust stroke. To get the piston to TDC on the compression stroke, turn the crankshaft one complete turn (360-degrees) clockwise. The rotor should now be pointing at the mark on the distributor.

11 When the rotor is pointing at the number one spark plug wire terminal in the distributor cap and the ignition timing marks are aligned, the number one piston is at TDC on the compression stroke.

➡ **Note: If it is impossible to align the ignition timing marks when the rotor is pointing at the mark on the distributor body, the timing belt may have jumped the teeth on the sprockets or may have been installed incorrectly.**

12 After the number one piston has been positioned at TDC on the compression stroke, TDC for any of the remaining pistons can be located by turning the crankshaft 180-degrees at a time and following the firing order.

1998 AND LATER MODELS

▶ **Refer to illustration 3.15**

13 Remove the ignition coils and spark plug wires (see Chapter 5).

14 Remove the spark plugs and install a compression gauge in the number one cylinder. Turn the crankshaft clockwise with a socket and breaker bar attached to the large bolt threaded into the front of the crankshaft.

15 When the piston approaches TDC, compression will be noted on the compression gauge. Continue turning the crankshaft until the notch in the crankshaft pulley is aligned with the TDC mark on the front cover (see illustration). At this point, number one cylinder is at TDC on the compression stroke.

16 After the number one piston has been positioned at TDC on the compression stroke, TDC for any of the remaining pistons can be located by turning the crankshaft 180-degrees at a time and following the firing order.

4   Valve cover - removal and installation

REMOVAL

1   Disconnect the cable from the negative battery terminal (see Chapter 5, Section 1).

2   Remove the engine cover, if equipped. Detach the PCV (Positive Crankcase Ventilation) valve and breather hoses from the valve cover (see Chapter 6).

SOHC models

▶ **Refer to illustrations 4.4 and 4.5**

3   Disconnect the spark plug wires from the clips.

4   Remove the two upper bolts from the timing belt cover (see illustration). Loosen, but do not remove the lower timing belt cover bolts.

4.4 Remove the timing belt cover bolts (1.6L SOHC engine shown)

4.5 Remove the valve cover bolts (1.6L SOHC engine shown)

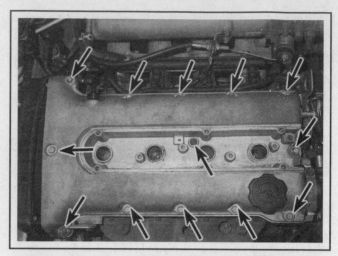

4.12a Location of the valve cover bolts (1.8L DOHC T8 engines)

4.12b Location of the valve cover bolts (2.0L DOHC engine)

4.15 Install the valve cover gasket into the groove around the perimeter of the valve cover and, on DOHC models, around the spark plug openings

5   Remove the valve cover bolts (see illustration).

6   Lift the valve cover from the cylinder head. If it sticks, knock it loose with a rubber mallet or a hammer and a block of wood. Don't pry between the sealing surfaces.

7   Check the valve cover gasket for damage and to ensure that it has not hardened and is still flexible; it can be reused if it's in good shape.

DOHC models

♦ **Refer to illustrations 4.12a and 4.12b**

8   Label the spark plug wires, then remove them from the spark plugs (see Chapter 1).

9   On 1995 through 1997 models, remove the distributor (see Chapter 5).

10   On 1998 through 2004 models (except 2.0L DOHC models), remove the ignition coil-packs from the top of the valve cover (see Chapter 5).

11   Remove the bolts attaching the upper timing belt cover, then remove the cover (see Section 7).

12   Remove the bolts holding the valve cover in place (see illustrations), disconnect any tubing or other connected components and move them out of the way, and remove the valve cover.

13   If the cover sticks, knock it loose with a rubber mallet or a hammer and a block of wood. Do not pry between the sealing surfaces.

14   Check the valve cover gasket for damage and to ensure that it has not hardened and is still flexible; it can be reused if it's in good shape.

INSTALLATION

♦ **Refer to illustration 4.15**

15   Clean the groove in the valve cover and the mating surface of the cylinder head. Press the gasket into the groove (see illustration).

16   On DOHC models, apply a light coating of silicone sealant to the areas directly adjacent to the camshaft caps at the sprocket end, and to the exhaust camshaft cap at the left end of the cylinder head.

17   Position the valve cover in place and insert the bolts by hand, starting the threads several turns before using a wrench.

18   Tighten the valve cover bolts in several steps to the torque listed in this Chapter's Specifications.

19   Installation of the remaining parts is the reverse of removal.

20   Run the engine and check for oil leaks.

5   Intake manifold - removal and installation

✳✳ WARNING 1:

Gasoline is extremely flammable, so take extra precautions when you work on any part of the fuel system. Don't smoke or allow open flames or bare light bulbs near the work area, and don't work in a garage where a gas-type appliance (such as a water heater or clothes dryer) is present. If you spill any fuel on your skin, rinse it off immediately with soap and water. When you perform any kind of work on the fuel system, wear safety glasses and have a Class B type fire extinguisher on hand.

✳✳ WARNING 2:

Wait until the engine is completely cool before beginning this procedure.

REMOVAL

◆ Refer to illustrations 5.5, 5.6, 5.10, 5.11a and 5.11b

1   Relieve the fuel system pressure (see Chapter 4).
2   Disconnect the cable from the negative battery terminal (see Chapter 5, Section 1).

3   Remove the engine cover, if equipped. Remove the air intake duct and the upper half of the air filter housing (see Chapter 4).
4   Disconnect the accelerator cable, cruise control cable and the throttle cable, as equipped, from the throttle body, then unbolt the cable bracket from the intake plenum (upper intake manifold) (see Chapter 4).
5   Clamp off the coolant hoses leading to the throttle body (see illustration), then loosen the clamps and disconnect the hoses from the throttle body.
6   Label and detach all wire harnesses, control cables and hoses (see illustration) connected to the intake manifold.
7   On 1.6L SOHC models, remove the alternator (see Chapter 5) and the alternator bracket.
8   Remove the fuel rail and injectors (see Chapter 4).
9   Raise the vehicle and support it securely on jackstands.
10   Remove the engine splash shields (see Section 7). Working under the intake manifold, remove the intake manifold support bracket, as applicable (see illustration). While you're underneath the vehicle, remove the row of bolts/nuts securing the bottom of the intake manifold to the cylinder head.
11   Remove the intake manifold upper mounting bolts/nuts (see illustrations), then remove the intake manifold.

➡Note: On models equipped with a two-piece manifold, separate the upper intake manifold from the lower intake manifold with the assembly on the bench.

5.5 Coolant hoses and power brake booster hose (2.0L DOHC engine)

5.6 PCV hose connection (2.0L DOHC engine)

5.10 Location of the intake manifold support bracket bolts on a 1.8L DOHC T8 engine (typical)

5.11a Location of the intake manifold upper mounting bolts and nuts on a 1.8L DOHC T8 engine (lower bolts not visible in this photo)

5.11b Location of upper and lower intake manifold mounting nuts (2.0L DOHC engine)

INSTALLATION

12 Carefully use a gasket scraper to remove all traces of old gasket material and any sealant from the manifold and cylinder head, then clean the mating surfaces with gasket cleaner or solvent - be careful to not gouge the gasket surfaces when cleaning. If the gasket was leaking, have the manifold checked for warpage at an automotive machine shop and resurfaced if necessary.

13 Install a new gasket, then position the manifold on the head and install the nuts/bolts.

14 Tighten the nuts/bolts in three or four equal steps to the torque listed in this Chapter's Specifications. Work from the center out towards the ends, while alternating upper to lower bolts/nuts to avoid warping the manifold.

15 Reinstall the remaining parts in the reverse order of removal.

16 Check the coolant level, adding as necessary to bring it to the appropriate level.

17 Before starting the engine, check the throttle linkage for smooth operation.

18 Run the engine and check for coolant and vacuum leaks.

19 Road test the vehicle and check for proper operation of all accessories, including the cruise control system (if equipped).

6 Exhaust manifold - removal and installation

❖❖ WARNING:

The engine must be completely cool before beginning this procedure.

REMOVAL

♦ Refer to illustrations 6.3, 6.6, 6.7a and 6.7b

1 Disconnect the cable from the negative battery terminal (see Chapter 5, Section 1).

2 Unplug the oxygen sensor electrical connector from the exhaust manifold. If you are installing a new manifold, remove the sensor (see Chapter 6).

3 Remove the heat shield bolts and remove the heat shield from the manifold (see illustration).

4 Apply penetrating oil to the exhaust manifold mounting bolts/nuts and to the exhaust pipe nuts.

5 Raise the vehicle and support it securely on jackstands. Remove the engine splash shields (see Section 7).

6 Disconnect the exhaust pipe from the exhaust manifold (see illustration). Lower the vehicle.

7 Remove the manifold nuts and detach the manifold from the cylinder head (see illustrations).

➡Note: If any nuts are difficult to remove, reapply penetrating oil to the bolts/nuts and let them soak for at least 15 minutes. If any bolts or studs break during removal, you may be able to use locking pliers after the manifold is removed to unscrew the broken bolt/stud. If unable to remove the broken bolt/stud, see your automotive parts store for stud removal tools. Replace any damaged parts with factory parts, or parts specifically designed for exhaust system application.

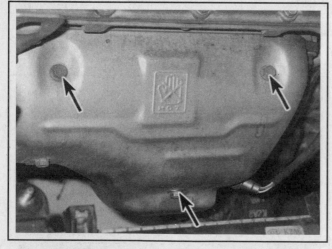

6.3 Remove the exhaust manifold heat shield bolts (typical)

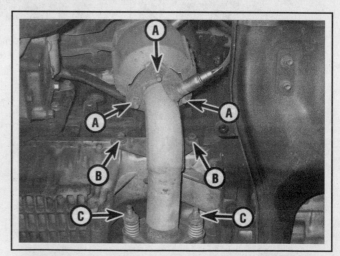

6.6 Remove the exhaust pipe flange nuts (A), the exhaust pipe bracket bolts (B) and the catalytic converter flange nuts (C), then separate the exhaust pipe from the exhaust manifold and the catalytic converter (1.8L DOHC T8 engine shown)

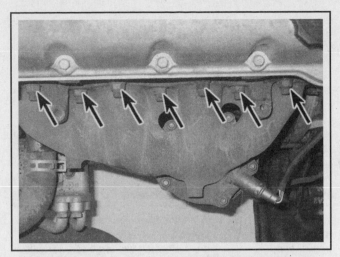

6.7a Location of the exhaust manifold mounting nuts on a 1.8L DOHC T8 engine

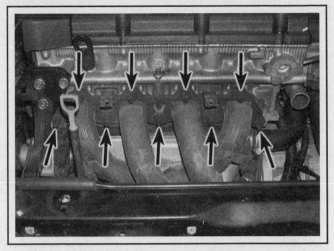

6.7b Location of the exhaust manifold mounting nuts (2.0L DOHC engine)

INSTALLATION

8   Use a scraper to remove all traces of old gasket material and carbon deposits from the manifold and cylinder head mating surfaces. If the gasket was leaking, have the manifold checked for warpage at an automotive machine shop and resurfaced if necessary.

✳✳ CAUTION:

When scraping, be very careful not to gouge or scratch the delicate aluminum cylinder head.

9   Position a new exhaust manifold gasket over the studs on the cylinder head.
10 Install the manifold and thread the nuts into place.
11 Working from the center out, tighten the nuts to the torque listed in this Chapter's Specifications in several equal steps.
12 Reinstall the remaining parts in the reverse order of removal. If reinstalling the oxygen sensor, use a special anti-seize thread lubricant available at your automotive parts store.
13 Run the engine and check for exhaust leaks.

7   Timing belt and sprockets - removal and installation

ALL EXCEPT 2.0L DOHC ENGINE

Removal

▸ **Refer to illustrations 7.3a and 7.3b**

✳✳ CAUTION:

The timing system is complex. Severe engine damage will occur if you make any mistakes. Do not attempt this procedure unless you are highly experienced with this type of repair. If you are at all unsure of your abilities, consult an expert. Double-check all your work and be sure everything is correct before you attempt to start the engine.

1   Disconnect the cable from the negative battery terminal (see Chapter 5, Section 1).
2   Block the rear wheels and set the parking brake. Loosen the right front wheel lug nuts, raise the front of the vehicle and support it securely on jackstands, then remove the wheel.
3   Remove the engine splash shields (see illustrations).

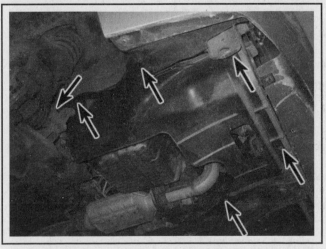

7.3a Location of the right side engine splash shield retaining pins on a late model

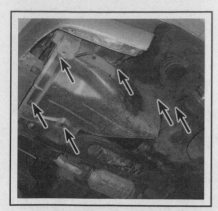

7.3b Location of the left side engine splash shield retaining pins on a late model

7.8 Remove the center bolt from the crankshaft pulley boss using a large socket and ratchet or breaker bar

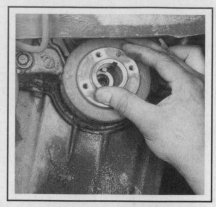

7.9 Slide the pulley boss from the crankshaft - if necessary, carefully pry it off using two large screwdrivers or small prybars

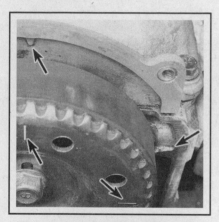

7.11a Camshaft sprocket alignment marks (1.6L SOHC engines) - when the proper mark is aligned with the pointer on the valve cover, the other mark will be in the 3 o'clock position, in alignment with the pointer on the cylinder block

7.11b Crankshaft sprocket alignment marks (1.6L SOHC engines)

7.14 To release the tension on the timing belt, loosen the timing belt tensioner pulley bolt, rotate the pulley away from the belt and retighten the bolt

4   Remove the drivebelts (see Chapter 1).

5   Remove the spark plugs from all cylinders (see Chapter 1).

6   Remove the water pump pulley bolts and remove the water pump pulley (see Chapter 3).

SOHC models

▶ Refer to illustrations 7.8, 7.9, 7.11a, 7.11b and 7.14

7   Unscrew the four crankshaft pulley bolts and remove the crankshaft pulley.

8   Remove the bolt from the crankshaft pulley boss (see illustration).

➡ **Note: To prevent the crankshaft from turning, remove the flywheel/driveplate access cover and carefully wedge a screwdriver between the ring gear teeth and the engine block.**

9   Remove the crankshaft pulley boss (see illustration). If necessary, carefully pry it off using two large screwdrivers or small prybars.

10 Remove the timing belt upper and lower covers.

11 Confirm that the crankshaft and camshaft sprocket timing marks are properly aligned with their corresponding marks (see illustrations). If they aren't, temporarily reinstall the crankshaft pulley boss bolt, rotate the engine to align the crankshaft and camshaft sprocket marks. The crankshaft sprocket Woodruff key should be facing upwards.

12 Remove the crankshaft bolt if it was reinstalled in the previous Step.

13 If reusing the timing belt, paint match marks on the sprockets and belt and an arrow indicating direction of travel on the belt.

14 Loosen the timing belt tensioner (see illustration), move it away from the belt and temporarily tighten the tensioner with the spring fully extended. Remove the timing belt.

15 If it is necessary to remove the camshaft sprocket to replace the seal, remove the valve cover (see Section 4) and unscrew the camshaft sprocket bolt while preventing the camshaft from turning by placing a wrench on the hexagonal portion cast into the camshaft. Carefully pry off the sprocket with two prybars.

DOHC models

▶ Refer to illustrations 7.17, 7.19a, 7.19b, 7.20a, 7.20b, 7.20c, 7.22 and 7.24

16 Remove the engine oil dipstick.

17 Remove the four crankshaft pulley bolts and remove the pulley (see illustration).

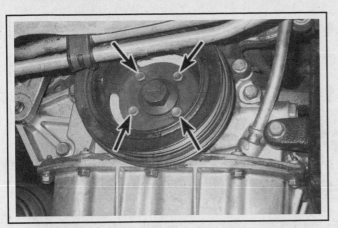

7.17 Remove the four crankshaft pulley bolts

7.19a Locations of the timing belt cover bolts accessible from above (1.8L DOHC T8 engine)

7.19b Locations of the timing belt cover bolts accessible from below (1.8L DOHC T8 engine)

7.20a Crankshaft sprocket alignment marks - 1.8L DOHC T8 engine

7.20b Camshaft sprocket alignment marks - 1.8L DOHC T8 engine (the tool shown here prevents the camshafts from turning after the belt has been removed)

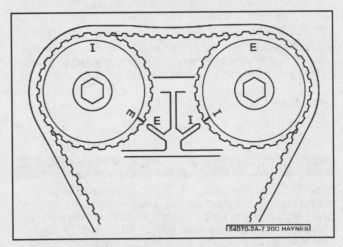

7.20c Camshaft sprocket alignment marks - 1.6L B6 and 1.8L BP DOHC engines

18 Support the engine from below with a jack or from above with an engine support fixture and remove the right (passenger's side) engine mount (see Section 16).

19 Remove the timing belt covers (see illustrations).

20 Confirm that the crankshaft and camshaft sprocket timing marks are properly aligned with their corresponding marks (see illustrations). If they aren't, rotate the engine to align the crankshaft and camshaft sprocket marks.

21 If reusing the timing belt, paint match marks on the pulley and belt and an arrow indicating direction of travel on the belt.

7.22 To release the tension on the timing belt, loosen the timing belt tensioner pulley bolt, rotate the pulley away from the belt using a ratchet and hex drive socket and retighten the bolt - 1.8L DOHC T8 engine shown

7.24 To remove the camshaft sprocket, hold the camshaft with a wrench on the hex while unscrewing the sprocket bolt

7.26 The tensioner and idler pulleys are each retained by a single bolt

22 Loosen the timing belt tensioner (see illustration). Push the tensioner pulley away from the belt and temporarily tighten the bolt in this position.

➡ **Note: These models are equipped with different tensioners: 1995 through 1997 models are equipped with separate tensioner and spring components, while 1998 and later models are equipped with a tensioner assembly with an internally mounted spring.**

23 Remove the timing belt.

24 If it is necessary to remove the camshaft sprocket(s) to replace the seal(s), remove the valve cover (see Section 4) and unscrew the camshaft sprocket bolt(s) while preventing the camshaft from turning by placing a wrench on the hexagonal portion cast into the camshaft (see illustration). Carefully pry off the sprocket with two prybars.

25 If it is necessary to remove the crankshaft sprocket, remove the crankshaft sprocket center bolt and carefully pry it off with two prybars.

➡ **Note: To prevent the crankshaft from turning, remove the flywheel/driveplate access cover and wedge a screwdriver between the ring gear teeth and the engine block.**

Inspection

♦ **Refer to illustration 7.26**

✳ CAUTION:

Do not bend, twist or turn the timing belt inside out. Do not allow it to come in contact with oil, coolant or fuel. Do not use timing belt tension to keep the camshaft or crankshaft from turning when installing the sprocket bolt(s). Do not turn the crankshaft or camshaft more than a few degrees (necessary for tooth alignment) while the timing belt is removed.

26 Remove the tensioner and idler pulleys (see illustration) and check the bearings for smooth operation and excessive play. Inspect the tensioner spring for damage.

27 If the timing belt was broken during engine operation, the belt may have been fouled by debris or may have been damaged by a defective component in the area of the timing belt; check for belt material in the teeth of the sprockets. Any defective parts or debris in the sprockets

must be cleaned out of all the sprockets before installing the new belt or the belt will not mesh properly when installed. Also check for oil residue - if the area is oily, replace the camshaft seals and crankshaft front oil seal (see Sections 8 and 9).

28 If the belt teeth are cracked or pulled off, the distributor, water pump, oil pump or camshaft(s) may have seized.

29 If there is noticeable wear or cracks in the belt, check to see if there are nicks or burrs on the sprockets.

30 If there is wear or damage on only one side of the belt, check the belt guide and the alignment of all sprockets.

31 Replace the timing belt with a new one if obvious wear or damage is noted or if it is the least bit questionable. Correct any problems which contributed to belt failure prior to belt installation.

➡ **Note: We recommend replacing the belt whenever it is removed, since belt failure can lead to expensive engine damage.**

Installation

✳ CAUTION:

Before starting the engine, carefully rotate the crankshaft by hand through at least two full revolutions (use a socket and breaker bar on the crankshaft pulley center bolt). If you feel any resistance, STOP! There is something wrong - most likely, valves are contacting the pistons. You must find the problem before proceeding. Check your work and see if any updated repair information is available.

32 Remove all dirt and oil from the timing belt area at the front of the engine.

33 If they were removed, install the idler pulleys and tensioner, tightening the bolts to the torque listed in this Chapter's Specifications.

➡ **Note: On 1998 and later models, it will be necessary to install a new tensioner spring to the tensioner before reassembly.**

34 If they were removed, install the sprock-et(s) to the camshaft(s) and crankshaft. When installing the crankshaft sprocket, make sure the sprocket Woodruff key is installed with the tapered side toward the oil pump body. Tighten the sprocket bolt(s) to the torque listed in this Chapter's Specifications while preventing the camshaft(s) or crankshaft from turning by using one of the methods described during removal.

35 Recheck the camshaft sprocket and crankshaft sprocket timing marks to be sure they are properly aligned (see illustrations 7.11a, 7.11b, 7.20a, 7.20b and 7.20c).

36 Slip the timing belt over the crankshaft sprocket, the idler pulley, the exhaust camshaft, the intake camshaft and tensioner on DOHC engines (or simply over the camshaft on SOHC engines), in that order, and make sure there is no slack on the side opposite the tensioner pulley. If the original belt is being reinstalled, align the marks made during removal with the marks on the sprockets, and be sure to install the timing belt so that it will rotate in the same direction as removed (the direction of rotation was marked during removal).

SOHC models

37 Install the crankshaft pulley boss and crankshaft sprocket bolt.

38 Rotate the crankshaft two turns clockwise and align the crankshaft sprocket timing marks.

❈❈ CAUTION:

If you feel resistance while rotating the engine by hand, do not continue. The valves may be contacting the pistons due to incorrect valve timing. Recheck the camshaft and crankshaft sprockets to be sure they are correctly aligned with their marks.

39 Verify the camshaft sprocket marks are properly aligned (see illustration 7.11a).

40 Loosen the tensioner (idler) pulley bolt to apply tension to the timing belt.

➥Note: The tensioner pulley spring applies the proper tension to the belt.

41 Tighten the tensioner pulley bolt to the torque listed in this Chapter's Specifications.

42 Again, rotate the crankshaft two turns clockwise, align the crankshaft sprocket timing marks and verify the camshaft sprocket marks are aligned with the marks on the cylinder head.

43 Check the timing belt tension by applying moderate force by hand (about 20 pounds of force) midway between the crankshaft sprocket and camshaft sprocket (not the tensioner pulley side) and measure the belt deflection. Deflection should be as listed in this Chapter's Specifications.

44 If belt deflection is not correct, loosen the tensioner pulley bolt, set the tensioner pulley with the spring fully extended and temporarily tighten the tensioner pulley bolt. Repeat Steps 38 through 43. If the proper tension is still not obtained, replace the tensioner spring with a new spring and reset belt tension as described above.

45 Tighten the crankshaft sprocket bolt to the torque listed in this Chapter's Specifications.

46 Reinstall the remaining parts in the reverse order of removal. Run the engine and check for proper operation.

❈❈ CAUTION:

DO NOT start the engine until you are absolutely certain that the timing belt is installed correctly. Serious and costly engine damage could occur if the belt is improperly installed.

DOHC models

▶ Refer to illustration 7.52

47 Install the timing belt guide, if equipped, and crankshaft sprocket bolt.

48 Loosen the tensioner pulley bolt. Allow the tensioner spring to apply tension to the timing belt.

49 Tighten the tensioner pulley bolt to the torque listed in this Chapter's Specifications.

50 Verify that the crankshaft sprocket timing mark and the camshaft sprocket timing marks are correctly aligned (see illustrations 7.20a, 7.20b and 7.20c). If the timing marks do not align, remove the timing belt and repeat the installation procedure.

51 Rotate the crankshaft two complete revolutions clockwise and recheck the timing marks. If the timing marks do not align, remove the timing belt and repeat the installation procedure.

❈❈ CAUTION:

If you feel resistance while rotating the engine by hand, do not continue. The valves may be contacting the pistons due to incorrect valve timing. Recheck the camshaft and crankshaft sprockets to be sure they are correctly aligned with their marks.

52 Check the timing belt tension by applying moderate force by hand (about 20 pounds force) midway between the camshaft sprockets. The belt deflection should be as listed in this Chapter's Specifications.

➥Note: On 1995 through 1997 models, rotate the crankshaft 1-5/6 turns clockwise before checking the belt deflection (see illustration).

53 If belt deflection is not correct, repeat the installation procedure. If the proper tension is still not obtained, replace the tensioner spring with a new one and reset belt tension as described above.

54 Tighten the crankshaft sprocket bolt to the torque listed in this Chapter's Specifications.

55 Reinstall the remaining parts in the reverse order of removal. Run the engine and check for proper operation.

❈❈ CAUTION:

DO NOT start the engine until you are absolutely certain that the timing belt is installed correctly. Serious and costly engine damage could occur if the belt is improperly installed.

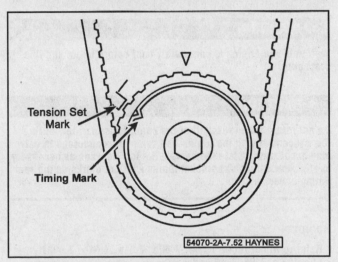

7.52 On 1.6L DOHC B6 and 1.8L DOHC BP engines, rotate the crankshaft clockwise 1-5/6 turns and align the crankshaft sprocket timing mark with the Tension Set Mark. Then check the belt tension between the camshaft sprockets

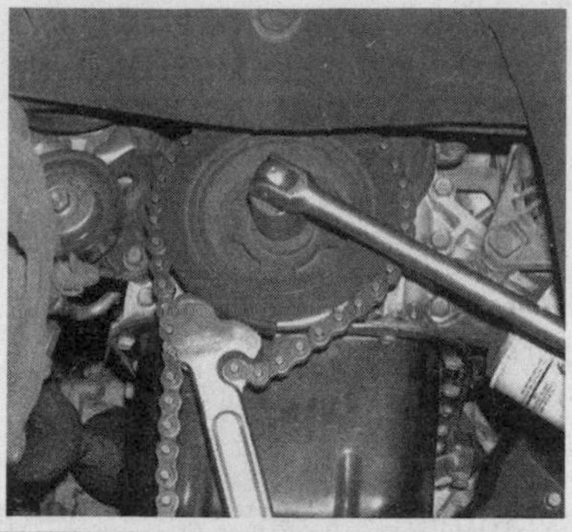

7.60a Using a chain wrench or a strap wrench to hold the crankshaft pulley, loosen the crank pulley bolt, then remove the pulley bolt and the crank pulley

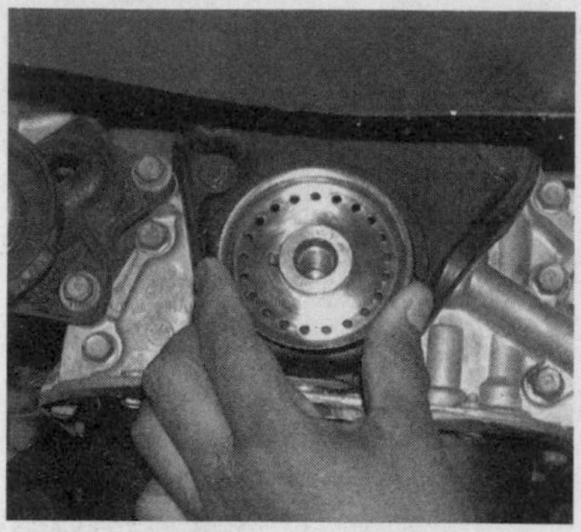

7.60b After removing the crankshaft pulley, remove the timing belt retainer/guide flange

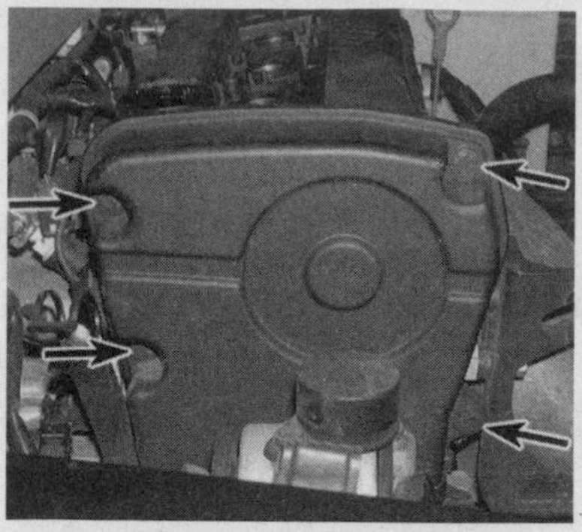

7.61a Upper timing belt cover fasteners (2.0L DOHC)

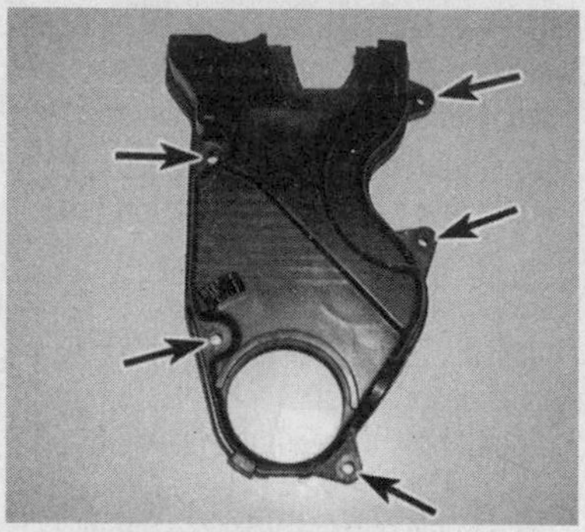

7.61b Lower timing belt fastener locations, cover removed for clarity (2.0L DOHC)

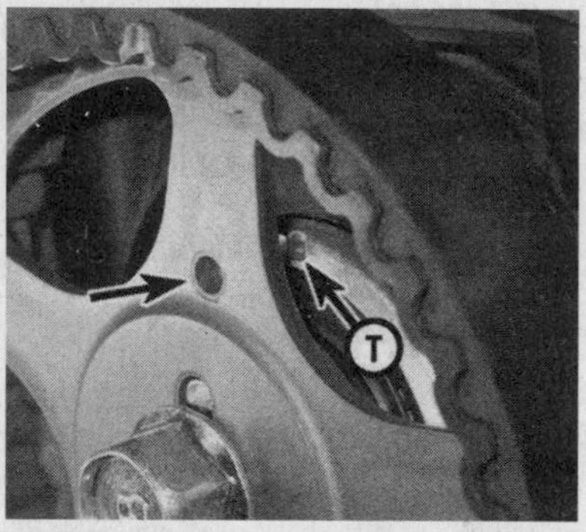

7.62a Make sure that the timing hole in the camshaft sprocket is aligned with the timing mark on the cylinder head . . .

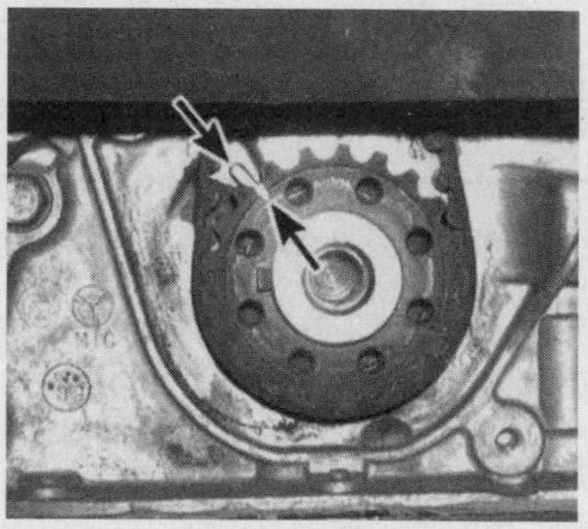

7.62b . . . and the mark on the crankshaft sprocket is aligned with the mark on the oil pump housing

2.0L DOHC ENGINE

✲✲ WARNING:

Wait until the engine is completely cool before beginning this procedure.

✲✲ CAUTION:

Do not rotate the crankshaft or the camshaft separately during this procedure with the timing belt removed as damage to valves may occur. Only rotate the camshaft a few degrees as necessary to align the camshaft sprocket marks with the marks on the rear timing cover.

Removal

➧ Refer to illustrations 7.60a, 7.60b, 7.61a, 7.61b, 7.62a, 7.62b, 7.63, 7.64, 7.66 and 7.67

✲✲ CAUTION:

The timing system is complex. Severe engine damage will occur if you make any mistakes. Do not attempt this procedure unless you are highly experienced with this type of repair. If you are at all unsure of your abilities, consult an expert. Double-check all your work and be sure everything is correct before you attempt to start the engine.

56 Disconnect the cable from the negative terminal of the battery (see Chapter 5).

57 Rotate the engine in the normal direction of rotation (clockwise) until the No.1 cylinder is located at TDC (see Section 3).

58 Remove the accessory drivebelts (see Chapter 1).

59 Loosen the water pump pulley bolts and remove the water pump pulley (see Chapter 3).

60 Using a chain wrench or a strap wrench to hold the crankshaft pulley, loosen the crank pulley bolt (see illustration), then remove the pulley bolt and the crank pulley. Make sure that you don't move the No. 1 cylinder from TDC while loosening the crank pulley bolt. After removing the crankshaft pulley, remove the timing belt retainer/guide flange (see illustration).

61 Remove the four upper timing belt cover bolts (see illustration) and remove the upper timing belt cover. Remove the lower timing belt cover bolts (see illustration).

62 Make sure that the camshaft sprocket timing mark is aligned with the mark on the cylinder head and the mark on the crankshaft sprocket is aligned with the mark on the oil pump housing (see illustrations).

63 If you're planning to re-use the timing belt, put a directional

7.63 If you're planning to re-use the timing belt, put a directional arrow, indicating the normal (clockwise) direction of rotation, on the belt

7.64 Remove the timing belt tensioner pulley bolt (arrow) and remove the tensioner pulley

7.66 Remove the timing belt idler pulley bolt (arrow) and remove the idler pulley

arrow, indicating the normal (clockwise) direction of rotation, on the belt (see illustration).

64 Remove the timing belt tensioner pulley bolt (see illustration), then remove the tensioner pulley.

65 Remove the timing belt.

66 Remove the timing belt idler pulley bolt (see illustration), then remove the idler pulley.

67 If the camshaft sprocket is damaged or must be removed to replace the camshaft seal or to strip the cylinder head for overhaul, use a wrench to hold the camshaft in place, then remove the sprocket retaining bolt (see illustration). Remove the camshaft sprocket from the end of the camshaft.

68 Remove the crankshaft timing belt sprocket.

Inspection

▶ Refer to illustration 7.70

❄ **CAUTION:**

Do not bend, twist or turn the timing belt inside out. Do not allow it to come in contact with oil, coolant or fuel. Do not turn the crankshaft or camshaft more than a few degrees (if necessary for tooth alignment) while the timing belt is removed.

---

69 Spin the idler pulley and the timing belt tensioner and check their bearings for smooth operation and excessive play. Inspect the timing belt sprocket teeth for any obvious damage. Replace all worn parts as necessary.

70 Examine the belt for evidence of contamination by coolant or lubricant. If this is the case, find the source of the contamination before progressing any further. Check the belt for signs of wear or damage, particularly around the leading edges of the belt teeth (see illustration).

❄ **CAUTION:**

If the belt appears to be in good condition and can be re-used, it is essential that it is reinstalled the same direction, otherwise accelerated wear will result leading to premature failure.

---

71 Replace the belt if its condition is in doubt; the cost of belt replacement is negligible compared with potential cost of the engine

7.67 To remove the camshaft sprocket, use a wrench to hold the camshaft in place while you loosen the camshaft sprocket retaining bolt, then remove the sprocket bolt and the cam sprocket

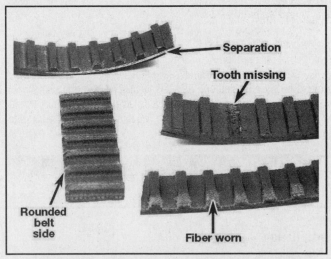

7.70 Inspect the timing belt for cracked and missing teeth; wear on one side of the belt indicates an alignment problem between the belt and the sprocket(s)

repairs should the belt fail in service. Similarly, if the belt is known to have covered more than 80,000 miles, it is prudent to replace it regardless of condition as a precautionary measure.

Installation

> **✳✳ CAUTION:**
>
> **Before starting the engine, carefully rotate the crankshaft by hand through at least two full revolutions (use a socket and breaker bar on the crankshaft pulley center bolt). If you feel any resistance, STOP! There is something wrong - most likely, valves are contacting the pistons. You must find the problem before proceeding. Check your work and see if any updated repair information is available.**

72   Verify that the No. 1 piston is still at TDC (see Section 3) and that the camshaft timing sprocket is still correctly aligned (see illustrations 7.62a and 7.62b). If the cam sprocket, idler pulley and/or crankshaft sprocket was removed for inspection or replacement, install it now. Be sure to tighten the camshaft sprocket retaining bolt and/or the idler pulley bolt to the torque listed in this Chapter's Specifications.

73   Loop the timing belt loosely under the crankshaft sprocket. If you're installing the old belt, don't forget to install it with the directional arrow facing in the correct direction.

74   Engage the timing belt teeth with the crankshaft sprocket, then maneuver it into position over the idler pulley and the camshaft sprocket. Make sure that the belt teeth are correctly seated on the sprockets, then install the belt around the timing belt tensioner.

➡**Note: Very slight adjustment of the position of the camshaft sprocket is permissible, if necessary, to get the belt teeth to lock into the teeth on the sprocket.**

75   Make sure that the front run of the belt (the side nearer the front of the vehicle) is taut, and that all belt slack is in the rear run (the part of the belt that is going to be tensioned by the tensioner pulley).

76   Tension the belt by turning the eccentrically-mounted tensioner counterclockwise, toward the water pump, then tighten the tensioner bolt to the torque listed in this Chapter's Specifications. The belt tension is correct if the belt can be deflected about 1/4-inch when pushed with about five pounds of pressure.

77   At this point, double check to make sure that the crankshaft is still set to TDC for the No. 1 cylinder (see Section 3) and the camshaft sprocket mark is aligned with the mark on the cylinder head (see illustration 7.62a). Also, make sure that the mark on the crankshaft timing belt sprocket is aligned with the stationary index mark on the oil pump housing (see illustration 7.62b).

78   Rotate the crankshaft through two complete revolutions. Reset the engine to TDC on No. 1 cylinder with reference to Section 3 and check the alignment marks again. Also re-check the timing belt tension and adjust it, if necessary (see Step 76).

79   Install the upper and lower timing belt covers, then tighten the timing belt cover bolts to the torque listed in this Chapter's Specifications.

80   Install the crankshaft pulley and, using a strap wrench or chain wrench to hold the pulley, tighten the crankshaft pulley bolt to the torque listed in this Chapter's Specifications.

81   Install the water pump pulley and tighten the pulley bolts as tightly as possible.

82   Install the accessory drivebelt (see Chapter 1).

83   Tighten the water pump pulley bolts to the torque listed in this Chapter's Specifications.

84   Reconnect the negative battery cable.

8   Camshaft oil seal(s) - replacement

ALL EXCEPT 2.0L DOHC ENGINE

Removal

▶ **Refer to illustration 8.2**

1   Remove the timing belt, the camshaft sprocket bolt(s) and sprocket(s) (see Section 7).

2   Carefully pry the camshaft seal out of the bore using a thin screwdriver (see illustration). An alternate method is to drill a small hole in the seal midway between the camshaft and cylinder head, thread a small screw into the seal with one or two threads and use the screw to pull the seal from the bore.

> **✳✳ CAUTION:**
>
> **DO NOT nick or scratch the camshaft or seal bore.**

Installation

3   Apply some clean engine oil to the lip of the new camshaft oil seal. Push the seal in slightly by hand.

4   Tap the seal into the bore using a seal driver or a socket with an outside diameter slightly smaller than the outside diameter of the oil seal, flush to the edge of the camshaft cap or into the cylinder head to the depth of the original seal.

5   Reinstall the remaining parts in the reverse order of removal.

6   Run the engine and check for proper operation.

2.0L DOHC ENGINE

▶ **Refer to illustrations 8.8 and 8.9**

7   Remove the timing cover, the timing belt and the camshaft timing belt sprocket (see Section 7).

8   Using a seal removal tool, carefully pry out the old camshaft seal (see illustration).

9   Clean the oil seal bore, lubricate the lip of the new camshaft oil seal with clean engine oil and slide it over the end of the camshaft. Gently push the seal onto the nose of the camshaft until it's positioned square to the seal bore. Using a socket with an outside diameter slightly smaller than the outside diameter of the seal, carefully drive the new seal into place with a hammer (see illustration). Make sure it's installed squarely and driven in to the same depth as the original. If a socket isn't available, a short section of pipe will also work.

10   Install the camshaft timing belt sprocket, the timing belt and the timing cover (see Section 7).

8.2 Carefully pry the camshaft seal out of the bore - DO NOT nick or scratch the camshaft or seal bore

8.8 Using a seal removal tool, carefully pry out the old camshaft seal

8.9 Using a socket with an outside diameter slightly smaller than the outside diameter of the seal, carefully drive the new seal into place with a hammer

9 Crankshaft pulley and front oil seal - removal and installation

ALL EXCEPT 2.0L DOHC ENGINE

▶ Refer to illustrations 9.7 and 9.9

1 Disconnect the cable from the negative battery terminal (see Chapter 5, Section 1).

2 Remove the engine splash shield (see Section 7).

3 Loosen the right front wheel lug nuts. Raise the front of the vehicle and support it securely on jackstands, then remove the wheel.

4 Remove the crankshaft pulley, timing belt covers, timing belt, and timing belt guide (see Section 7).

5 Remove the crankshaft sprocket using a special sprocket removal puller.

6 Cut the front oil seal lip with a razor knife.

7 Note how far the seal is seated in the bore and the direction the oil seal lip faces (the oil seal should be flush with the face of the oil pump body). Remove the front oil seal with a screwdriver taped or wrapped with a rag to protect the crankshaft surface and engine block (see illustration).

8 Clean the bore in the engine block and clean the crankshaft surface. Coat the outside of the new front oil seal with engine oil. Apply engine assembly lubricant or clean engine oil to the seal lip.

9 Press the oil seal in slightly by hand, with the oil seal lip facing the direction noted in Step 7. Using a seal driver or a socket with an outside diameter slightly smaller than the outside diameter of the oil seal, carefully tap the new seal into place with a hammer (see illustration) until the oil seal is flush with the face of the oil pump body. Make sure the oil seal is installed squarely.

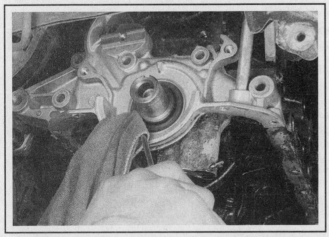

9.7 Before removal of the old oil seal, note how far the seal is seated in the bore and the direction the oil seal lip faces. Remove the front oil seal with a screwdriver taped or wrapped with a rag to protect the crankshaft surface and engine block - 1.6L SOHC engine shown

9.9 With the oil seal lips facing the correct direction as when removed, press the oil seal partially into place by hand. Using a large socket or seal driver, tap the seal into the bore until it is flush with the face of the oil pump body - 1.8L DOHC T8 engine shown

9.14a Carefully pry the crankshaft front oil seal out of the oil pump housing with a screwdriver or seal removal tool; be careful not to scratch, nick or gouge the crankshaft or the seal bore in the oil pump housing

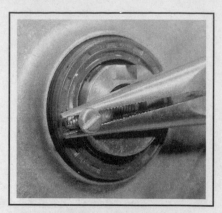

9.14b If a seal removal tool isn't available, remove the front seal by installing a pair of self-tapping screws and then, using the nose of the crank as a fulcrum, lever out the old seal with needle nose pliers as shown

9.16 Using a socket with an outside diameter slightly smaller than the outside diameter of the seal, carefully drive the new seal into place with a hammer

10 Reinstall the crankshaft timing belt sprocket and timing belt (see Section 7).

11 The remainder of the installation is the reverse of the removal procedure.

12 Run the engine and check for oil leaks at the front oil seal.

2.0L DOHC ENGINE

▶ Refer to illustrations 9.14a, 9.14b and 9.16

➡Note: The following procedure explains how to replace the front crank seal with the oil pump installed. If you're planning to remove the oil pump for inspection (see Section 12), the front crank seal is easier to replace with the pump removed.

13 Remove the timing belt cover, the timing belt and the crankshaft sprocket (see Section 5).

14 Note how far the seal is recessed in the bore, then carefully pry it out of the oil pump housing with a screwdriver or seal removal tool (see illustration). Don't scratch the housing bore or damage the crankshaft in the process (if the crankshaft is damaged, the new seal will end up leaking).

➡Note: If a seal removal tool is unavailable, you can thread two self tapping screws (180 degrees apart from one another) into the front seal to pry out the seal (see illustration).

15 Clean the bore in the housing and coat the outer edge of the new seal with engine oil or multi-purpose grease. Apply multi-purpose grease to the seal lip.

16 Using a socket with an outside diameter slightly smaller than the outside diameter of the seal, carefully drive the new seal into place with a hammer (see illustration). Make sure it's installed squarely and driven in to the same depth as the original. If a socket isn't available, a short section of large diameter pipe will also work. Check the seal after installation to make sure the spring didn't pop out of place.

17 Reinstall the crankshaft sprocket and timing belt (see Section 5).

18 Run the engine and check for oil leaks at the front seal.

10 Camshaft(s), lifters and rocker arms - removal, inspection, installation and adjustment

ALL EXCEPT 2.0L DOHC ENGINE

Removal

1 Position the engine at TDC for cylinder number 1 (see Section 3), then disconnect the cable from the negative terminal of the battery (see Chapter 5, Section 1). Remove the valve cover (see Section 4).

2 On 1994 through 1997 models, remove the distributor (see Chapter 5). On 1998 and later models, remove the camshaft position sensor (see Chapter 6).

3 Remove the timing belt covers, timing belt, and camshaft sprocket(s) (see Section 7).

4 Measure the thrust clearance (endplay) of the camshaft(s) with a dial indicator. If the clearance is greater than the value listed in this Chapter's Specifications, replace the camshaft thrust plate (SOHC models), camshaft, and/or the cylinder head depending on the type of engine and severity of thrust clearance.

SOHC engines

▶ Refer to Illustration 10.9

➡Note: The 1.6L SOHC engines use a rocker shaft and rocker arm with hydraulic lash adjusters. The hydraulic lash adjusters eliminate the need for valve lash adjusting screws or shims. After initial installation, no further valve adjustment is necessary.

5 Number or mark the components before removal to be sure that the parts will be reinstalled in the same location when reassembled. Be sure to keep things in order, as all components must be reinstalled in their original locations.

6 Loosen the rocker arm bolts, starting with the outer bolts and work to the center using a circular pattern.

7 Remove the rocker arm and rocker shaft assembly. Mark or otherwise store the rocker arms and springs for later reinstallation in the same locations from which they were removed.

10.9 Pull the camshaft straight out of the cylinder head (SOHC engine)

10.14 Mark up a cardboard box or a similar method to store the lifters/shims and bearing caps to relocate for reinstallation

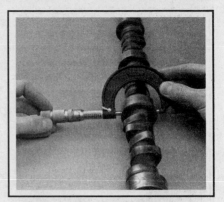

10.16a Measure each journal diameter with a micrometer (if any journal measures less than the specified limit, replace the camshaft)

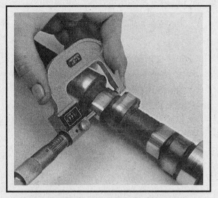

10.16b Measure the lobe heights on the camshaft(s) - if any lobe height is less than the minimum listed in this Chapter's Specifications, replace the camshaft

10.16c Measure the rocker arm shaft outer diameter

10.16d Measure the rocker arm inside diameter - subtract the shaft outside diameter from the rocker inside diameter to determine the oil clearance

8 In order to remove the camshaft without removing the cylinder head from the engine, remove the distributor, the air cleaner assembly and reposition the underhood fuse box.

9 Pull the camshaft straight out of the cylinder head (see illustration). Remove the camshaft oil seal.

DOHC engines

♦ **Refer to illustration 10.14**

➡**Note: The 1.6L and 1.8L DOHC engines use two overhead camshafts to directly-actuate hydraulic valve lifters, which are built into the lifter assemblies. After initial installation, no further valve adjustments are necessary. The hydraulic lifters eliminate the need for an adjusting shim. However, it is very important to properly mark or store parts for later reinstallation in the same locations.**

10 Remove the camshaft sprocket bolts (see Section 7) and remove the sprockets.

11 Loosen the camshaft bearing cap bolts a little at a time, equally, until they can be removed by hand.

✳✳ CAUTION:

It is important to make sure the camshaft rises from all of its bearing saddles equally, so it doesn't bind or become damaged.

12 Remove the camshaft bearing caps, marking or packaging to record their locations for correct reinstallation later. To further ensure correct reinstallation later, take note of the numbers and direction arrows stamped into the caps.

13 Mark the camshafts to ensure proper reinstallation later. Remove the camshafts. Remove the oil seals from the camshafts.

14 Using a magnet, lift out each valve lifter and set them in numbered boxes, plastic bags or other containers so they can be reinstalled in the same position during reassembly (see illustration).

➡**Note: Store the hydraulic lifter assemblies upside down in a pan filled with clean engine oil.**

Inspection

15 Examine all parts, looking for signs of pitting, scoring or scuffing.

SOHC engines

♦ **Refer to illustrations 10.16a, 10.16b, 10.16c and 10.16d**

16 Measure the camshaft journals and camshaft lobes. Measure each camshaft bore inside diameter and subtract the camshaft journal outside diameter measurement to determine the camshaft journal oil clearance. Measure the rocker arm shaft outside diameter and rocker arm inside diameter (see illustrations). Compare your measurements to the values listed in this Chapter's Specifications.

10.17a Lay a strip of Plastigage on each camshaft journal

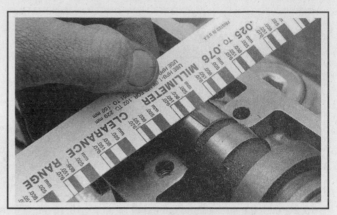

10.17b Compare the width of the crushed Plastigage to the scale on the envelope to determine the oil clearance

10.18 Wipe off the oil and inspect the lifter wall for wear and scuffing

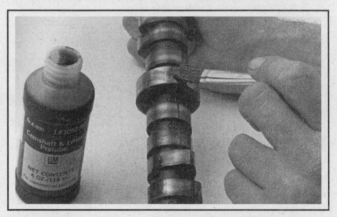

10.25 Coat the lobes and journals with camshaft and lifter prelube

DOHC engines

▶ **Refer to illustrations 10.17a, 10.17b and 10.18**

17 Check the oil clearance for each camshaft journal as follows:

a) *Clean the bearing caps and the camshaft journals with cleaning solvent and dry thoroughly.*

b) *Carefully lay the camshaft(s) in place in the head. Do not install the lifters and do not use any lubrication.*

c) *Lay a strip of Plastigage on each journal (see illustration).*

d) *Install the camshaft bearing caps in the proper locations as removed with the arrows pointing as removed.*

e) *Tighten the bolts a little at a time, equally, until the torque listed in this Chapter's Specifications is reached.*

➡ **Note: Do not turn the camshaft while the Plastigage is in place.**

f) *Remove the camshaft bearing cap bolts and detach the caps.*

g) *Compare the width of the crushed Plastigage (at its widest point) to the scale on the Plastigage envelope (see illustration).*

h) *If the clearance is greater than specified, replace the camshaft and/or cylinder head.*

i) *Scrape off the Plastigage with your fingernail or the edge of a credit card - do not scratch or nick the journals or bearing caps.*

18 Inspect each hydraulic lifter for scuffing and scoring marks (see illustration). Press the lifter plunger in by hand, checking for movement. If the lifter plunger moves, replace the lifter.

19 Measure the outside diameter of each lifter and measure the lifter bore diameter. Compare your measurements with the values listed in

this Chapter's Specifications. Replace any lifter that is worn excessively.

20 Visually examine the camshaft lobes and bearing journals for scoring marks, pitting, galling and evidence of overheating (blue, discolored areas). Look for flaking away of the hardened surface of each lobe.

21 Using a micrometer, measure the diameter of each camshaft journal (see illustration 10.16a). If the diameter of any one journal is less than specified, replace the camshaft.

22 Using a micrometer, measure the height of each lobe (see illustration 10.16b). If the height for any one lobe is less than the specified minimum, replace the camshaft.

23 Replace any parts that are worn beyond specifications.

Installation

SOHC engines

▶ **Refer to illustrations 10.25, 10.26 and 10.30**

24 Apply clean engine oil to the new camshaft oil seal and the cylinder head camshaft bore.

25 Apply camshaft assembly lubricant to the camshaft lobes and bearing journals (see illustration).

26 Install the camshaft in the cylinder head, then install the thrust plate (see illustration).

27 Install a new camshaft oil seal (see Section 8).

28 If the hydraulic lash adjusters were removed from the rocker arms, or are being replaced, fill the rocker arm cavity with clean engine

10.26 Installing the camshaft thrust plate

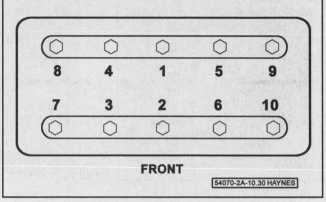

FRONT

54070-2A-10.30 HAYNES

10.30 Rocker arm bolt tightening sequence - (SOHC engines)

oil, coat the lash adjusters with clean engine oil, and install them into the rocker arm.

29 Assemble and install the rocker arm assembly as it was removed. Make sure that the rocker shaft oil holes face downward.

30 Tighten the rocker arm bolts to the torque listed in this Chapter's Specifications in several steps and in the recommended sequence (see Illustration).

31 Install the camshaft sprocket (see Section 7) and tighten the bolt to the torque listed in this Chapter's Specifications.

32 Install the timing belt (see Section 7).

33 The remainder of installation is the reverse of the removal procedure. Adjust the ignition timing (see Chapter 5).

DOHC engines

34 Apply engine assembly lubricant or clean engine oil to the hydraulic lifters and into the lifter bores, then install the lifters in their original locations. Check that the lifters travel smoothly in their bores.

35 Apply camshaft assembly lubricant to the camshaft lobes and bearing journals. Install the camshafts. Make sure the exhaust camshaft is reinstalled on the exhaust manifold side of the engine, and the intake camshaft is reinstalled on the intake manifold side of the engine.

36 Apply RTV sealant to the outside bearing cap surfaces along the perimeter of the cylinder head that are shared by the valve cover.

37 Install the camshaft bearing caps in the proper order as marked when removed, in the stamped numerical order with the arrows pointing as removed. Then tighten the cap bolts a little at a time, equally, until the torque listed in this Chapter's Specifications is reached.

✳ CAUTION:

It is important to make sure the camshaft stays level as the cap bolts are tightened, so it doesn't bind or bend.

38 Apply clean engine oil to the lips of the new camshaft oil seals and install the oil seals (see Section 8).

39 Install the camshaft sprockets on their correct camshafts (see Section 7).

40 Install the timing belt (see Section 7).

41 On 1995 through 1997 models, before reinstalling the distributor, install a new distributor O-ring. Apply grease to the O-ring and apply grease or engine assembly lubricant to the distributor drive lugs.

42 On 1995 through 1997 models, install the distributor and tighten the distributor timing adjustment bolt(s) hand-tight at this time. Connect the distributor electrical connector.

43 Reinstall the remaining parts in the reverse order of removal.

44 Run the engine and, on models equipped with a distributor, adjust the timing (see Chapter 5). Check the engine for proper operation.

2.0L DOHC ENGINE

➡**Note 1:** The camshaft and lifters should always be thoroughly inspected before installation and camshaft endplay should always be checked prior to camshaft removal.

➡**Note 2:** These models use the Constantly Variable Valve Timing (CVVT) system. This consists of a CVVT unit attached to the end of the exhaust camshaft that drives the intake camshaft with the timing chain. This increases performance by automatically changing the intake camshaft timing while running.

Removal

▶ **Refer to illustrations 10.47a, 10.47b, 10.49, 10.50 and 10.51**

45 Remove the valve cover (see Section 4).

46 Remove the timing cover, the timing belt and the camshaft timing belt sprocket (see Section 5).

47 Starting in the middle of the cylinder head, at bearing cap No. 3 on the intake camshaft or at cap No. 4 on the exhaust cam, loosen the camshaft bearing caps, working your way out toward the ends of the head in a criss-cross fashion (see illustration). Don't loosen two cap

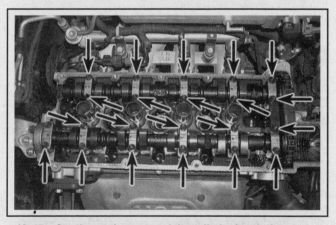

10.47a Starting at the center of the cylinder head, then working your way towards the ends of the head, gradually and evenly loosen the camshaft bearing cap bolts (arrows) in a criss-cross fashion

10.47b When you get to the bolts for the last two caps, remove the upper chain guide (arrow)

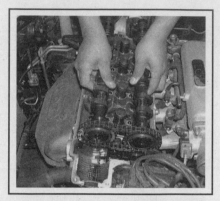

10.49 Remove the camshafts and the timing chain as a single assembly

10.50 To detach the lower timing chain guide, remove these two bolts

10.51 Wipe off the tops of the lifters and mark them with a marker (I-1, I-2, E-1, E-2, etc.), or mark strips of tape and affix them to the top of each lifter

10.57 Slide the new cam seal over the nose of the cam, place the cam in position in the head, then gently push the seal onto the nose of the cam until the chamfered edge around the face of the seal bore is exposed

bolts completely, then proceed to the next cap; this puts unnecessary stress on the camshafts. Instead, loosen the cap bolts gradually and evenly, in two or three passes. After removing the two inner bolts for the two rear caps, remove the upper chain guide (see illustration).

48 Remove the bearing caps. Keep the intake and exhaust cam caps separated. They must be installed at the same location from which they were removed. If you get them mixed up, the caps are marked "I" (intake) or "E" (exhaust) and are numbered (1, 2, 3, etc.).

49 Remove the intake and exhaust camshafts and the camshaft timing chain as a single assembly (see illustration). Remove the old camshaft seal from the exhaust cam and discard it.

50 Remove the lower chain guide (see illustration).

51 Wipe off the tops of the lifters and mark them with a marker (I-1, I-2, E-1, E-2, etc.), or mark strips of tape and affix them to the top of each lifter (see illustration).

52 Remove the lifters from the cylinder head. Keep the intake and exhaust lifters separated, and keep them in order.

53 Thoroughly clean the cam timing chain and the timing chain sprockets on the camshafts with fresh solvent and a stiff brush, then inspect the timing chain and the sprockets. Make sure that the bearing surfaces (the shiny parts) of the chain rollers are in good condition and that the chain isn't stiff. If the chain is excessively worn or damaged, replace it. Make sure that the teeth on the camshaft timing chain sprockets are in good condition. If any of the teeth are broken or excessively worn, replace the camshaft(s). Also inspect the timing chain

guides. Make sure that the friction surfaces of the guides are still in good condition. If either guide is excessively worn, replace it.

54 Inspect the camshafts and the lifters (see Chapter 2C).

Installation

▶ Refer to illustrations 10.57 and 10.58

55 Apply clean engine oil to the walls of the lifters, then insert the lifters into their respective bores in the cylinder head. Push down the lifters until they contact the valves, then lubricate the camshaft lobe contact surfaces (1996 through 2000 models) or the shims (2001 and later models).

56 Lubricate the camshaft and cylinder head bearing journals with clean engine oil.

57 Clean the oil seal bore and the sealing surface of the nose (forward end) of the camshaft, lubricate the lip of the new camshaft oil seal with clean engine oil and slide it over the nose. Place the camshaft in position in the cylinder head. Gently push the seal onto the nose of the cam until the chamfered edge around the face of the cam seal bore is visible (see illustration).

58 Install the camshaft timing chain on the camshaft sprockets. Make sure that the timing marks on the cam chain sprockets are aligned with the centers of the two dark side plates (see illustration).

59 Carefully lower the camshafts and timing chain into position on

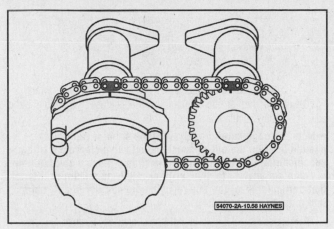

10.58 Make sure that the timing marks on the cam chain sprockets are aligned with the centers of the two dark side plates

10.67a Install the lifter tool as shown and squeeze the handles together to depress the lifter, then hold the lifter down with the smaller tool so the shim can be removed . . .

10.67b . . . keeping pressure on the lifter with the smaller tool and remove the shim with a small screwdriver . . .

10.67c . . . a pair of tweezers or a magnet as shown here

the cylinder head with the camshaft lobes for the No. 1 cylinder facing up (180 degrees from the cylinder head mating surface). Oil the upper surfaces of the camshaft bearing journals, then install the bearing caps over the camshafts. Working in a criss-cross fashion from the ends of the head toward the center, gradually and evenly tighten the cap retaining bolts to the torque listed in this Chapter's Specifications.

60 Install the timing belt sprocket on the exhaust camshaft (see Section 5).

61 Install the timing belt (see Section 5). When installing the timing belt, make sure the crankshaft is at TDC for the No. 1 cylinder (see Section 3), the camshaft sprocket mark is aligned with the upper edge of the cylinder head (see illustration 7.62a), and the crankshaft sprocket mark is aligned with the stationary index mark on the oil pump housing (see illustration 7.62b).

62 The remainder of installation is the reverse of removal.

Adjustment

▶ Refer to illustrations 10.67a, 10.67b, 10.67c and 10.68

➡Note 1: This procedure applies only to 2004 and later 2.0L engines.

➡Note 2: The following procedure requires the use of a special lifter tool. It is impossible to perform this task without it. The Kia part number is 09220-2D000; it is also available from automotive specialty tool outlets.

63 If you haven't already done so, refer to Section 4 and remove the valve cover.

64 Refer to Section 3 and position the number 1 piston at TDC on the compression stroke.

65 Measure the clearance of the valves of cylinder 1, the intake valves of cylinder 2 and the exhaust valves of cylinder 3 with a feeler gauge of the specified thickness.

➡Note: These valves should not have the camshaft contacting them in this position.

Record the clearance of each valve and note which are out of specification. This information will be used later to determine the required replacement shims.

66 Turn the crankshaft one complete revolution and realign the timing marks. Measure the remaining valves.

67 After measuring and recording the clearance of each valve, turn the crankshaft pulley until the camshaft lobe above the first valve which you intend to adjust is pointing upward, away from the shim. Position the notch in the lifter toward the spark plug. Depress the lifter with the special lifter tool (see illustration). Place the special lifter tool in position with the longer jaw of the tool gripping the lower edge of the cast lifter boss and the upper, shorter jaw gripping the upper edge of the lifter itself. Depress the lifter by squeezing the handles of the lifter tool together, then hold the lifter down with the smaller tool and remove the larger one. Remove the adjusting shim with a small screwdriver or a pair of tweezers (see illustrations). Note that the wire hook on the end of some lifter tool handles can be used to clamp both handles together to keep the lifter depressed while the shim is removed.

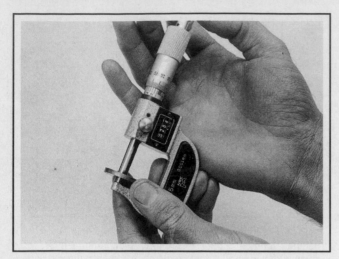

10.68 Measure the shim thickness with a micrometer

68 Measure the thickness of the shim with a micrometer (see illustration).

69 To calculate the correct thickness of a replacement shim or lifter that will place the valve clearance within the specified value, use the following formula:

$$N = T + A - V$$

Where:

T = thickness of the old shim or lifter
A = valve clearance measured
N = thickness of the new shim or lifter
V = desired valve clearance (see this Chapter's Specifications)

70 Select a shim or lifter with a thickness as close as possible to the valve clearance calculated.

➡**Note: Through careful analysis of the shim or lifter sizes needed to bring the out-of-specification valve clearance within specification, it is often possible to simply move a shim that has to come out anyway to another lifter requiring a shim or lifter of that particular size, thereby reducing the number of new shims that must be purchased.**

71 Place the special lifter tool in position with the longer jaw of the tool gripping the lower edge of the cast lifter boss and the upper, shorter jaw gripping the upper edge of the lifter itself, press down the lifter by squeezing the handles of the lifter tool together and install the new adjusting shim (note that the wire hook on the end of one lifter tool handle can be used to clamp the handles together to keep the lifter depressed while the shim is inserted). Measure the clearance with a feeler gauge to make sure that your calculations are correct.

72 Repeat this procedure until all the valves which are out of clearance have been corrected.

11 Cylinder head - removal and installation

❊❊ CAUTION:

The engine must be completely cool before beginning this procedure.

ALL EXCEPT 2.0L DOHC ENGINE

Removal

1 Relieve the fuel pressure (see Chapter 4).

2 Disconnect the cable from the negative battery terminal (see Chapter 5, Section 1).

3 Remove the spark plugs (see Chapter 1).

4 Drain the coolant from the engine block and radiator (see Chapter 1).

5 Drain the engine oil and remove the oil filter (see Chapter 1).

6 Remove the air intake duct and the air filter housing (see Chapter 4).

7 On 1994 through 1997 models, remove the distributor (see Chapter 5). On 1998 and later models, remove the camshaft position sensor (see Chapter 6).

8 Remove the intake manifold (see Section 5).

9 Remove the exhaust manifold (see Section 6).

10 Remove all electrical connectors and wiring harness connections to the cylinder head. Mark the connectors for later reinstallation.

11 Remove the thermostat and the water bypass tubing, if equipped (see Chapter 3).

12 Remove the drivebelts (see Chapter 1) and the water pump pulley (see Chapter 3).

13 Remove the timing belt covers and the timing belt (see Section 7).

14 Remove the valve cover (see Section 4).

15 Label and detach any remaining components that would interfere with cylinder head removal.

16 Remove the camshafts to access the head bolts (see Section 10).

17 Using a breaker bar and the appropriate socket or Allen-head driver, loosen the cylinder head bolts in 1/4-turn increments, loosening in the reverse of the tightening sequence (see illustration 11.29a and 11.29b) until they can be removed by hand.

18 Lift the cylinder head off the engine block. If it is stuck, very carefully pry up on a casting protrusion - NOT between the cylinder head and the engine block.

19 Set the cylinder head on wood blocks to prevent damage to the gasket sealing surfaces. Remove all external components from the head to allow for thorough cleaning and inspection by an automotive machine shop.

Installation

▶ **Refer to illustrations 11.23, 11.29a and 11.29b**

20 The mating surfaces of the cylinder head and block must be perfectly clean when the head is installed.

21 Use a gasket scraper to remove all traces of carbon and old gasket material, then clean the mating surfaces with lacquer thinner or acetone. If any oil residue is on the mating surfaces when the head is installed, the gasket may not seal correctly and leaks could develop. When working on the block, stuff the cylinders with clean shop rags to prevent the entry of debris. Use a vacuum cleaner to remove material that falls into the cylinders.

❊❊ CAUTION:

Be careful not to gouge the soft aluminum of the cylinder head.

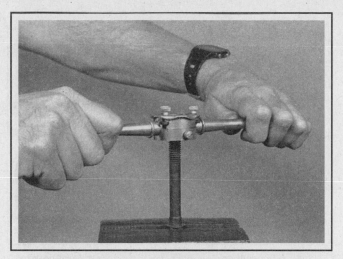

11.23 A die should be used to remove sealant and corrosion from the head bolt threads prior to installation

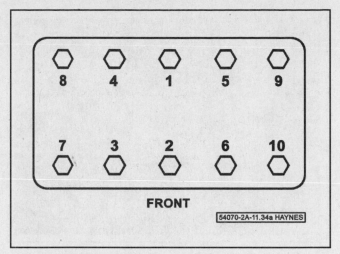

11.29a Cylinder head bolt TIGHTENING sequence on 1.6L SOHC engines

22 Check the block and head mating surfaces for nicks, deep scratches and other damage. If damage is slight, it can be removed with a file; if it's excessive, machining may be the only alternative.

23 Use a thread die of the correct thread size to chase (clean up) the head bolt threads (see illustration).

➡**Note: Cleaning up the threads using a thread die should not cut any metal from the threads. If you observe any metal cuttings while chasing the threads, stop and replace the bolt with a new bolt of the correct part number. Make sure the replacement bolt is an OEM (Original Equipment Manufacturer) replacement cylinder head bolt specifically designed for this engine, and is the correct length and thread type. Discard the defective bolt.**

Use a tap of the correct thread size to chase the threads in the head bolt holes, then clean the holes with compressed air - make sure that no residue such as dirt, corrosion, and sealant remains in the holes and the threads are not damaged as this will affect torque readings, which affects the quality of the head installation job.

❊❊ WARNING:

Wear eye protection when using compressed air!

24 Install the components that were removed from the head.

25 Position the new gasket over the dowel pins in the block. Check to see if there are any markings (such as "TOP") on the gasket to indicate how it is to be installed.

26 Carefully set the head on the block without disturbing the gasket.

27 Before installing the head bolts, apply a small amount of clean engine oil to the threads.

28 Install the bolts and tighten them finger tight.

29 Tighten the bolts following the recommended sequence in several steps to the torque listed in this Chapter's Specifications (see illustrations).

30 The remaining installation steps are the reverse of removal.

31 Refill the cooling system, install a new oil filter and add oil to the engine (see Chapter 1).

32 Run the engine and check for leaks. Set the ignition timing (models equipped with a distributor only; see Chapter 5) and road test the vehicle.

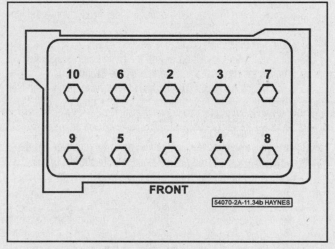

11.29b Cylinder head bolt TIGHTENING sequence on DOHC engines (except 2.0L DOHC)

33 Frequently recheck coolant level for the first few hundred miles to be sure that no leakage exists.

2.0L DOHC ENGINE

Removal

▶ **Refer to illustrations 11.43 and 11.44**

➡**Note: If you're only removing the cylinder head to replace the head gasket, or to service the cylinder block, the cylinder head can be removed with the intake and exhaust manifold attached. In this case, simply disregard any of the following steps that don't apply. However, if you're removing the head in order to overhaul it, or to have it overhauled, follow all of the steps below.**

34 Drain the engine coolant (see Chapter 1). Then disconnect the upper radiator hose and the other two coolant hoses from the thermostat housing (see Chapter 3).

35 Remove the spark plugs and the spark plug wires (see Chapter 1).

11.43 Cylinder head bolt loosening sequence
(2.0L DOHC engine)

11.44 If the cylinder head is stuck to the block, carefully pry
it loose at a casting protrusion

36 If you're going to disassemble the cylinder head, remove the ignition coil assembly (see Chapter 5).

37 Disconnect the valve cover (see Section 4).

38 Remove the timing belt cover and the timing belt (see Section 5).

39 Remove the camshafts and the lifters (see Section 6).

40 If you're going to disassemble the cylinder head, remove the fuel rail and the fuel injectors (see Chapter 4). If you're not going to disassemble the head, it's not necessary to remove the fuel rail and injectors; just unplug the electrical connectors, set the injector harness aside, disconnect the vacuum hose from the fuel pressure regulator and disconnect the fuel pressure and return lines (see Chapter 4).

41 Remove the power steering pump and then remove the pump bracket (see Chapter 10).

42 If you're going to disassemble the cylinder head for service, the intake manifold (see Section 8) and the exhaust manifold (see Section 9) will have to be removed, either now, or after the head is removed. If you're not going to disassemble the head, it's not necessary to remove the intake manifold or the exhaust manifold. In either case, it's not absolutely necessary that the manifolds be removed while the cylinder head is still installed on the block, but if you're going to lift off the head by yourself, removing the manifolds now will lighten the head considerably. On the other hand, if you have help, it's easier to remove the fasteners that secure the manifolds after the head has been removed.

43 Remove the cylinder head bolts in the sequence shown (see illustration). Progressively loosen the cylinder head bolts, by half a turn at a time, until all bolts can be unscrewed by hand. Discard the old head bolts; the head must be reinstalled with new bolts.

44 Verify that nothing is still connected to the cylinder head, then lift the head off the block. Get help if possible; the head is quite heavy, particularly if it's being removed with the manifolds still attached. If the head is stuck to the block, carefully pry it loose at a casting protrusion (see illustration).

✳✳ CAUTION:

Do NOT rotate the engine while the cylinder head is removed, unless absolutely necessary. If you do rotate the crankshaft, make sure that you put the piston in the No. 1 cylinder back to TDC before installing the cylinder head (see Section 3).

45 Remove the gasket from the top of the block, but don't discard it

yet; you'll need to compare the new head gasket to the old one to make sure that you've got the right gasket. Remove the dowel pins and put them in a plastic bag.

46 If the cylinder head is going to be serviced, separate the manifolds, if you haven't already done so (see Sections 8 and 9, but disregard the steps that don't apply). Then proceed to Chapter 2C for the cylinder head disassembly and overhaul procedures.

Installation

♦ Refer to illustrations 11.56a and 11.56b

47 The mating faces of the cylinder head and cylinder block must be perfectly clean before installing the head. Use a hard plastic or wood scraper to remove all traces of old gasket, sealing compound, scale and carbon deposits. Also clean the piston crowns. Use particular care when cleaning the head and the pistons; aluminum alloy is easily damaged. And make sure that no carbon or gasket material enters the oil or coolant passages; a chunk of carbon or gasket could block an oil or coolant passage, which would seriously damage the engine. To prevent debris from entering lubrication or coolant passages, use adhesive tape and paper to seal off all lubrication, coolant and cylinder-head-bolt holes in the block.

48 Inspect the mating surfaces of the cylinder block and the cylinder head for nicks, deep scratches and other damage. If they're slight, they may be removed carefully with abrasive paper.

49 If the cylinder head gasket surface is warped, or might be warped, use a straight-edge to check it for distortion (see Chapter 2C).

50 Install the intake and exhaust manifolds, if they were removed. You could also elect to install the manifolds later, after the head has been bolted to the block, but it's much easier to install the manifolds now, with the head removed, even though you'll probably need help when setting the head on the block.

51 To ensure that the cylinder head bolt holes are clean and dry before installing the head bolts, clean out the cylinder head bolt holes with a suitable tap, then blow them out with compressed air.

52 Make sure that the piston in the No. 1 cylinder is still at TDC (see Section 3).

53 Install the dowel pins in the cylinder block and position the new head gasket on the block. Make sure that the manufacturer's markings are facing up.

54 With the help of an assistant, place the cylinder head and mani-

11.56a Cylinder head bolt tightening sequence (2.0L DOHC engine)

11.56b Use an angle-measuring gauge to angle-torque the cylinder head bolts

folds on the cylinder block. Verify that the head gasket is still flat and correctly seated before allowing the full weight of the cylinder head to rest upon it. Make sure that the head is seated on the dowel pins.

➡**Note: If the cylinder head was disassembled for service, make sure that the camshaft lobes for the No. 1 cylinder are pointing upward.**

55 Oil the threads and the underside of the bolt heads, then carefully enter each bolt into its relevant hole and screw them in hand tight. Be sure to use NEW cylinder head bolts; the old bolts, which have already been stretched, cannot be correctly torqued.

56 Working progressively and in the sequence shown (see illustration), tighten the cylinder head bolts in three steps, first to the torque, then to the angle, listed in this Chapter's Specifications.

➡**Note: It is recommended that an angle-measuring gauge be used during the final stages of the tightening, to ensure accuracy (see illustration). If a gauge is not available, use white paint to make alignment marks between the bolt head and cylinder head prior to tightening; the marks can then be used to check the bolt has been rotated through the correct angle during tightening.**

57 Install the intake manifold (see Section 8) and the exhaust manifold (see Section 9), if they haven't already been installed.

58 Install the power steering pump bracket and the power steering pump (see Chapter 10).

59 Install the fuel rail and the fuel injectors (see Chapter 4), if they were removed.

60 Reconnect the fuel pressure line to the fuel rail and the fuel return line to the fuel pressure regulator, reconnect the vacuum hose to the pressure regulator and plug in the injector harness electrical connectors (see Chapter 4).

61 Install the camshafts and the lifters (see Section 6).

62 Install the timing belt and the timing belt cover (see Section 5).

63 Install the valve cover (see Section 4).

64 Install the ignition coil assembly, if it was removed (see Chapter 5).

65 Install the spark plugs, the spark plug wires and the spark plug wire cover (see Chapter 1).

66 Reconnect the upper radiator hose and the other two coolant hoses to the thermostat housing (see Chapter 3). Fill the engine cooling system with coolant (see Chapter 1).

67 Change the engine oil (see Chapter 1).

68 Run the engine and check for leaks.

12 Oil pan - removal and installation

REMOVAL

▸ **Refer to illustrations 12.7a, 12.7b, 12.7c, 12.7d and 12.8**

1 Disconnect the cable from the negative battery terminal (see Chapter 5, Section 1).

2 Set the parking brake and block the rear wheels. Raise the front of the vehicle and support it securely on jackstands.

3 Remove the engine splash shield(s) (see Section 7).

4 Drain the engine oil and remove the oil filter (see Chapter 1).

5 Disconnect the exhaust pipe from the exhaust manifold (see illustration 6.6) and the catalytic converter from the exhaust pipe.

6 Remove the oil pan bolts and the oil pan stiffener, if equipped.

➡**Note: Oil pan bolts may be of varying sizes. Store the oil pan bolts in such a way as to ensure that they will be reinstalled In their correct locations.**

7 On 1.6L SOHC models, the oil pan is protected by an oil pan stiffener at the transaxle end of the engine which attaches to the oil pan and transaxle. The 1.6L SOHC and the 1.8L DOHC BP engines are equipped with a main bearing support plate (MBSP) between the main bearings and the oil pan, attached at the main journals and the oil pan bolts. On the 1.6L SOHC models it will be necessary, first, to remove the oil pan stiffener bolts around the bottom of the transaxle and at the engine block, then remove the oil pan stiffener. On the 1.6L SOHC and 1.8L DOHC BP engines, remove all the oil pan bolts and then remove the oil pan. If the oil pan is stuck, carefully pry it loose by inserting

12.7a Carefully pry the oil pan loose, using a prybar between the pan and the "ears" at the transaxle end of the cylinder block

12.7b Remove the oil pickup tube/ screen assembly

12.7c Remove the MBSP bolts

12.7d Carefully pry the MBSP from the engine block by prying against a main bearing journal - DO NOT pry against a rod journal. If the mating surfaces are damaged, oil leaks could develop

12.8 On 2.0L DOHC engines, remove the exhaust pipe flange bolts (A) and exhaust pipe support bracket bolt (B) and remove the exhaust pipe from underneath the oil pan

a screwdriver or small pry bar at the engine block ears located at the transaxle end of the engine (see illustration). Do not pry along the oil pan lip and the main bearing support plate (MBSP). With the oil pan removed, detach the oil strainer from the main bearing support plate (MBSP) (see illustration). Then remove the MBSP bolts (see illustration), and very carefully pry the MBSP against the main bearing journal or at the corners of the MBSP (see illustration).

✳✳ CAUTION:

Do not insert the screwdriver or prying tool between the main bearing support plate (MBSP) and the engine block. Be very careful not to scratch, bend, or otherwise damage the mating surfaces of the oil pan, MBSP, and block or oil leaks could develop.

8   On 1.6L DOHC B6 and the 1.8L DOHC T8 models, remove the oil pan bolts (see illustration 12.17) and then remove the oil pan. If the oil pan is stuck, pry it loose very carefully by inserting a screwdriver or putty

knife at the engine block ears at the flywheel end of the engine block.

✳✳ CAUTION:

Do not insert the screwdriver or prying tool at any other area.

➡ Note 1: 1.6L DOHC B6 engines are equipped with an oil pan upper block between the oil pan and the crankshaft assembly. If it is necessary to remove the oil pan upper block, remove all the various size bolts, marking them for correct reassembly and follow the correct torque sequence (see illustration 12.15).

➡Note 2: On 1.8L DOHC T8 engines, the oil pan is attached to the transaxle with four large bolts. Also, there are two extra long bolts used to secure the bellhousing portion of the oil pan to the engine block. Make notes of the locations of the various bolts for proper reassembly.

➡Note 3: On 2.0L DOHC engines, remove the section of exhaust pipe that's routed underneath the oil pan (see illustration). Also remove the exhaust pipe support bracket.

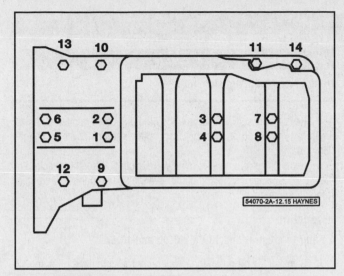

12.15 Tightening sequence for the oil pan upper block mounting bolts on the 1.6L DOHC B6 engine

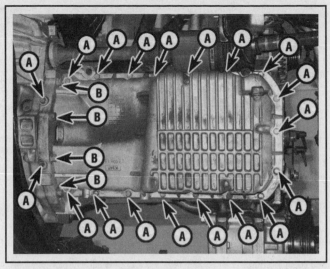

12.17 Location of the oil pan-to-engine block bolts (A) and the oil pan-to-transaxle bolts (B) on a 1.8L DOHC T8 engine

9 On all models, remove the oil pan bolts and then remove the oil pan. If the oil pan is stuck, pry it loose carefully by inserting a screwdriver or putty knife at the corners of the oil pan.

INSTALLATION

▸ **Refer to illustrations 12.15 and 12.17**

10 Use a scraper to remove all traces of old gasket material and sealant from the block, MBSP, and oil pan. Clean the mating surfaces with gasket cleaner or equivalent solvent, available at automotive parts stores.

✷✷ CAUTION:

Be very careful not to scratch, bend, or otherwise damage the mating surfaces of the pan and block or oil leaks could develop.

11 Make sure the threaded bolt holes in the block are clean. Also check the condition of the oil strainer.

12 Check the oil pan flange for cracks or distortion, particularly at the bolting flange.

13 On 1.6L SOHC, 1.6L DOHC B6 and 1.8L DOHC BP engines, apply RTV sealant where the main bearing caps meet the engine block. On 1.8L DOHC engines, apply RTV sealant where the front cover (oil pump) and rear main seal meet the engine block.

➡Note: This next step must be completed so that the MBSP on the 1.6L SOHC and 1.8L DOHC BP engines, can be installed within 5 minutes after the RTV sealant was applied.

14 On 1.6L SOHC and 1.8L DOHC BP engines, apply a continuous bead of RTV sealant to the bolting flange (lip) of the MBSP inside of the bolt holes. Install the MBSP bolts and tighten them to the torque listed in this Chapter's Specifications. Start with the inner bolts and work toward the outer bolts.

➡Note: The MBSP must be installed within 5 minutes of application of the sealant applied in Step 13.

15 On 1.6L DOHC B6 engines, install the oil pan upper block and tighten the bolts to the torque listed in this Chapter's Specifications. Follow the correct torque sequence (see illustration).

16 Apply a continuous bead of RTV sealant to the circumference of the oil pan bolting flange (lip) inside of the bolt holes.

17 Carefully position the oil pan on the engine block and install the bolts/nuts. Working from the center out, tighten them to the torque listed in this Chapter's Specifications in three or four steps (see illustration).

➡Note: The oil pan must be installed within 5 minutes of application of the sealant.

18 The remainder of installation is the reverse of removal. Be sure to add oil and install a new oil filter.

19 Let the RTV sealant set up approximately 12 hours before running the engine.

20 After sufficient time for the RTV sealant to set up, run the engine and check for oil leaks.

13 Oil pump - removal, inspection and installation

➡Note: If you are replacing the front oil seal only and not removing, inspecting, repairing or replacing the oil pump, the front oil seal can be replaced without oil pump removal as described in Section 9.

ALL EXCEPT 2.0L DOHC ENGINE

Removal

◆ Refer to illustration 13.2 and 13.3

1   Remove the timing belt and crankshaft sprocket (see Section 7).

2   Remove the oil pump mounting bolts (see illustration). Carefully pry the front cover off the engine block.

3   Place the oil pump on a workbench. Note how far the oil seal is seated in the bore. Using a seal removal tool or a screwdriver taped or wrapped with a rag to protect the pump bore, remove the oil seal from the housing (see illustration).

※※ CAUTION:

Do not scratch the housing bore.

4   Remove the screws that hold the oil pump cover (slotted plate) to the front cover/oil pump housing. Inspect the oil pump cover for distortion or damage.

5   Remove the oil pressure relief valve. Note or mark the direction of the components as installed, then remove the oil pump inner and outer rotors from the housing.

Inspection

◆ Refer to illustrations 13.6a, 13.6b and 13.6c

6   Reinstall the oil pump inner and outer rotors into the oil pump housing (see illustrations) and measure the clearance of:

a)   The driven rotor-to-pump housing.
b)   The drive rotor-to-oil pump driven rotor.
c)   The rotor set-to-oil pump housing endplay clearance.

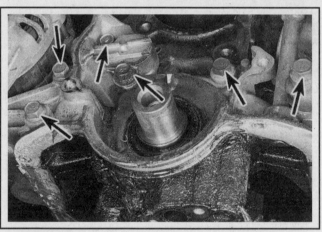

13.2 Remove the bolts and separate the oil pump from the engine block - 1.6L SOHC engine shown

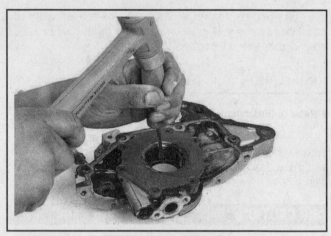

13.3 Remove the front oil seal using a screwdriver or punch - wrap the tool tip with tape to protect the oil pump bore - 1.6L SOHC engine shown

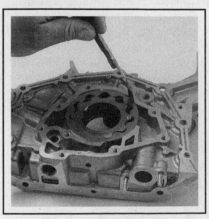

13.6a Measure the clearance between the oil pump driven rotor and the pump housing . . .

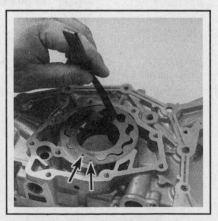

13.6b . . . then measure the clearance between the drive and driven rotor. . .

13.6c . . . and finally, use a straightedge and measure the endplay between the rotors and the pump housing

13.21 To detach the oil pump pick-up tube, remove these bolts (arrows)

13.23 Remove the oil pump-to-block bolts (arrows) and remove the oil pump assembly

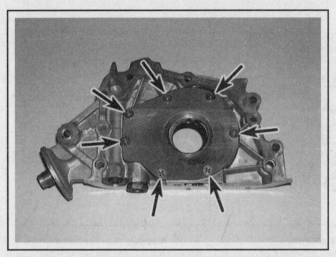

13.25 Remove the cover bolts (arrows) and remove the cover from the oil pump case

Compare your measurements to the clearance listed in this Chapter's Specifications.

7   Check the length of the oil pressure relief spring when removed from the oil pump. Compare the length measured with the free length listed in this Chapter's Specifications. Replace the spring if necessary.

8   Be sure the surfaces of the pump housing are clean and dry before reassembly.

9   Lightly coat the outer edge of a new oil seal with engine assembly lubricant or clean engine oil. Using a seal driver or a socket with an outside diameter slightly smaller than the outside diameter of the seal, carefully drive the new seal into place with a hammer. Make sure it's installed squarely and driven in to the same depth as the original. If a socket is not available, a short section of large diameter pipe will also work. Apply engine assembly lubricant to the seal lip surface that contacts the crankshaft.

10   Lubricate the oil pressure relief valve piston with clean engine oil and reinstall the valve components into the pump case. Tighten the plug to the torque listed in this Chapter's Specifications.

11   Lubricate the rotor set with clean engine oil. Reinstall the rotors.

12   Pack the pump cavities with petroleum jelly This will prime the pump and ensure good suction when the engine is started.

13   Install the cover and tighten the screws to the torque listed in this Chapter's Specifications.

14   It is a good idea to remove the oil pan and inspect the screen at the end of the oil pick-up tube (see Section 12) for any debris that might plug it. Either clean the tube and screen completely or replace it with a new one at this time.

Installation

15   Clean off all traces of old gasket and sealant from the mating surfaces of the pump and the engine block.

16   Install the oil pump onto the engine block, using a new gasket. Tighten the pump mounting bolts to the torque listed in this Chapter's Specifications.

17   Reinstall the remaining parts in the reverse order of removal.

18   Add oil (see Chapter 1), start the engine and check for oil pressure and leaks.

2.0L DOHC ENGINE

Removal

♦ **Refer to illustrations 13.21 and 13.23**

19   Remove the timing belt cover, the timing belt and the crankshaft drive sprocket (see Section 5).

20   Remove the oil pan (see Section 11).

21   Remove the oil pump pick-up tube bolts (see illustration) and remove the oil pump pick-up tube.

22   Inspect the crankshaft front oil seal. If it's leaking, replace it while the pump is removed (see below).

23   Remove the oil pump-to-block bolts (see illustration) and remove the oil pump assembly.

24   Remove the oil pump gasket.

Inspection

Disassembly

♦ **Refer to illustrations 13.25, 13.26, 13.27a, 13.27b and 13.28**

25   Clean off the pump assembly with solvent, remove the cover bolts (see illustration) and remove the cover from the oil pump case.

13.26 Note the mating marks on the inner and outer rotors (arrows), then remove the inner and outer gears from the pump case

13.27a Remove the plug . . .

13.27b . . . and remove the relief spring and the relief plunger from the pump case

13.28 Remove the old crankshaft front seal from the oil pump housing with a seal removal tool

13.32 Measure the clearance between the outer circumference of the outer rotor and the front case with a feeler gauge, then compare your measurement to the clearance listed in this Chapter's Specifications

13.33 Measure the clearance between the tip of the inner rotor and the inner circumference of the outer rotor, then compare your measurement to the clearance listed in this Chapter's Specifications

26 Note the mating marks on the inner and outer rotors (see illustration), then remove the inner and outer rotors from the pump case.

27 Remove the plug and remove the relief spring and the relief plunger from the pump case (see illustrations).

28 If you're going to replace the crankshaft front oil seal, carefully pry out the old seal with a seal removal tool or with a screwdriver (see illustration). Don't scratch or gouge the seal bore.

29 Clean all the parts in solvent and wipe them off with a clean shop rag.

Pick-up tube

30 Inspect the pick-up tube filter screen. Make sure that it's not clogged or damaged. If it's clogged, clean it with a wire brush. If it's damaged, replace the pick-up tube.

Pump case

31 Inspect the front case for cracks. If any damage is evident, replace the pump.

Oil pump rotors

▶ **Refer to illustrations 13.32, 13.33, 13.34 and 13.35**

32 Measure the clearance between the outer circumference of the outer rotor and the front case (see illustration) and compare your measurement to the clearance listed in this Chapter's Specifications.

33 Measure the clearance between the tip of the inner rotor and the inner circumference of the outer rotor (see illustration) and compare your measurement to the clearance listed in this Chapter's Specifications.

34 Measure the axial (side) clearance between the outer pump rotor and a straight edge (see illustration) and compare your measurement to the clearance listed in this Chapter's Specifications.

35 Measure the axial (side) clearance between the inner pump rotor and a straight edge (see illustration) and compare your measurement to the clearance listed in this Chapter's Specifications.

36 If any of the above clearances are excessive, replace the pump.

13.34 Measure the axial (side) clearance between the outer pump rotor and a straight edge, then compare your measurement to the clearance listed in this Chapter's Specifications

13.35 Measure the axial (side) clearance between the inner pump rotor and a straight edge, then compare your measurement to the clearance listed in this Chapter's Specifications

13.37 Measure the free height of the pressure relief spring, then compare your measurement to the spring free height listed in this Chapter's Specifications

13.39 Using a socket with an outside diameter slightly smaller than the outside diameter of the seal, install a new seal in the seal bore of the oil pump housing

Pressure relief spring and plunger

▶ **Refer to illustration 13.37**

37 Measure the free height of the pressure relief spring (see illustration). If the spring height is incorrect, replace the spring. Verify that the relief spring plunger moves freely in its bore. If it doesn't, inspect the walls of the bore and the plunger. If the plunger is damaged, replace it. If the bore is damaged, replace the pump.

Reassembly

▶ **Refer to illustration 13.39**

38 Make sure that the pump case is clean.

39 If you removed the old crankshaft front oil seal during disassembly, install a new seal now. Use a large socket with an outer diameter slightly smaller than the new seal. Make sure that the seal bore is clean, place the new seal in position over the seal bore and carefully tap it into the bore until it's correctly seated (see illustration).

40 Install the relief valve plunger and the pressure relief spring, then screw in the plug. Tighten the plug to the torque listed in this Chapter's Specifications.

13.44 Install a new oil pump gasket

41 Coat the inner and outer rotors with clean engine oil and install them in the case. Make sure that the mating marks are facing out (toward you) and that they're aligned (see illustration 12.26).

42 Install the cover, then install the cover bolts. Tighten the bolts to the torque listed in this Chapter's Specifications.

Installation

▶ **Refer to illustration 13.44**

43 Make sure that the gasket mating surface of the block is clean. Use a scraper to remove all traces of old gasket material from the engine block, then clean the mating surface thoroughly.

44 Install a new pump gasket (see illustration).

45 Install the pump assembly. Install the pump retaining bolts and tighten them to the torque listed in this Chapter's Specifications.

46 Install the oil pump pick-up tube assembly. Tighten the pick-up tube bolts to the torque listed in this Chapter's Specifications.

47 Install the oil pan (see Section 11).

48 Install the crankshaft timing belt sprocket, the timing belt and the timing belt cover (see Section 5).

49 Add oil, start the engine and check for oil pressure and leaks.

50 Turn off the engine, then recheck the engine oil level.

14 Flywheel/driveplate - removal and installation

REMOVAL

▶ **Refer to illustration 14.3**

1   Raise the vehicle and support it securely on jackstands, then refer to Chapter 7 and remove the transaxle.

2   If you're working on a model with a manual transaxle, remove the clutch cover and clutch disc (see Chapter 8). Now is a good time to check/replace the clutch components and pilot bearing.

3   Mark the relationship of the flywheel/driveplate and the rear plate or crankshaft to ensure correct reinstallation alignment later (see illustration).

4   Remove the bolts that secure the flywheel/driveplate to the crankshaft. If the crankshaft turns, wedge a screwdriver in the ring gear teeth to jam the flywheel.

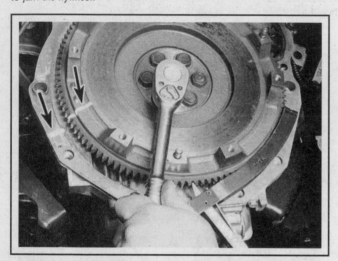

14.3 Marking the flywheel/driveplate and the rear plate will preserve the alignment of the flywheel and crankshaft as long as the crankshaft isn't turned; if you're going to turn the crankshaft, mark the flywheel/driveplate near one of the bolt holes

5   Remove the flywheel/driveplate from the crankshaft. On the automatic transaxle models, also remove the driveplate backing plate and adapter, taking note of which sides of the driveplate the adapter plates are mounted for correct reinstallation. Since the flywheel is fairly heavy, be sure to support it while removing the last bolt.

6   Clean the flywheel to remove grease and oil. Inspect the surface for cracks, rivet grooves, burned areas and score marks. Light scoring can be removed with emery cloth. Check for cracked and broken ring gear teeth. Lay the flywheel on a flat surface and use a straightedge to check for warpage. If necessary, take the flywheel to an automotive machine shop to have it resurfaced.

7   Clean and inspect the mating surfaces of the flywheel/driveplate and the crankshaft. If the crankshaft rear seal is leaking, replace it before reinstalling the flywheel/driveplate (see Section 15).

INSTALLATION

8   Remove any thread sealant from the crankshaft flywheel bolt holes and bolts.

☀☀ CAUTION:

If all the thread sealant cannot be removed from a bolt, replace that bolt. Do not apply new sealant when installing a new bolt.

9   For manual transaxle models, position the flywheel at the crankshaft. For automatic transaxle models, position the adapter, driveplate, and backing plate at the crankshaft. Be sure to align the marks made during removal. Before installing the bolts, apply thread sealant to the threads of any bolts except new bolts used.

10 Wedge a screwdriver in the ring gear teeth to keep the flywheel/driveplate from turning as you tighten the bolts to the torque listed in this Chapter's Specifications. Follow a criss-cross pattern and work up to the final torque in three or four steps.

11 The remainder of installation is the reverse of the removal procedure.

15 Rear main oil seal - replacement

▶ **Refer to illustrations 15.4 and 15.5**

1   The transaxle must be removed from the vehicle for this procedure (see Chapter 7).

2   Remove the flywheel/driveplate (see Section 14).

3   Cut the rear main oil seal lip with a razor knife.

4   Pry out the old seal with a screwdriver taped or wrapped in a rag, or use a seal removal tool to pry the seal out (see illustration).

5   Apply engine oil to the crankshaft seal journal and to the lip of the new seal. Carefully push the new seal part way into place by hand. Carefully tap into place using a seal driver, flat punch, large socket, or a suitable short pipe or tubing of the correct diameter until the oil seal is flush with the edge of the rear cover (see illustration).

6   Reinstall the flywheel/driveplate (see Section 14).

7   The remaining steps are the reverse of removal.

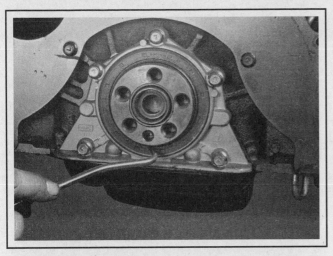

15.4 The quick way to replace the rear main oil seal is to simply pry the old one out . . .

15.5 . . . then lubricate the crankshaft journal and the lip of the new seal with engine oil and tap the new seal into place - the seal lip is stiff and can be easily damaged during installation if you are not careful

16 Engine mounts - check and replacement

CHECK

1   There are four engine/transaxle mounts on these models; the front engine mount, the passenger side engine mount (next to the timing belt upper cover), the rear lower engine mount (under the intake manifold) and the transaxle mount (under the air filter housing).

2   During the check, the engine must be raised slightly to remove the weight from the mounts.

3   Raise the vehicle and support it securely on jackstands, then position a jack under the engine oil pan. Place a large block of wood between the jack head and the oil pan, then carefully raise the engine just enough to take the weight off the mounts.

❈❈ WARNING:

DO NOT place any part of your body under the engine when it's supported only by a jack!

4   Check the mounts to see if the rubber is cracked, hardened or separated from the casing.

5   Check for relative movement between the mount plates and the engine or frame. Use a large screwdriver or prybar to attempt to move the mounts. If movement is noted, lower the engine and tighten the mount fasteners.

6   Rubber preservative should be applied to the mounts to slow deterioration.

7   Apply the parking brake, block the rear wheels, raise the front of the vehicle and support it securely on jackstands (if not already done).

REPLACEMENT

▶ **Refer to illustrations 16.9, 16.12, 16.16 and 16.21**

Right (passenger-side) mount

8   Use a floor jack under the engine to take the weight from the mount, or support the engine from above with an engine hoist or support fixture.

9   Remove the through-bolt from the mount (see illustration), then remove the fasteners holding the mount to the bracket.

16.9 Location of the right side (passenger's side) engine mount through-bolt on a 1.8L T8 engine

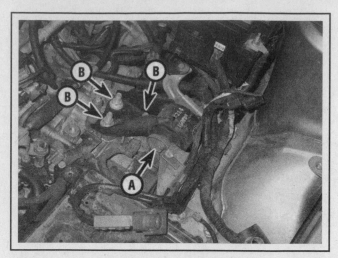

16.12 First remove the transaxle mount through-bolt (A) then remove the bracket-to-transaxle nuts (B)

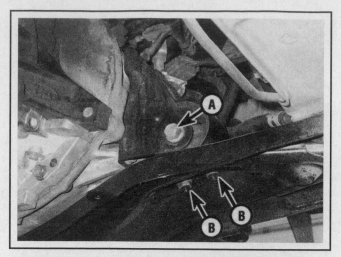

16.16 Location of the front engine mount through-bolt (A) and the retaining nuts (B)

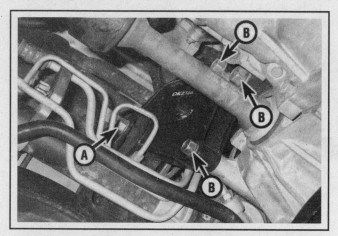

16.21 First remove the rear engine mount through-bolt (A), lift the engine/transaxle assembly slightly to gain access and remove the mount-to-transaxle bolts (B)

10 Installation is the reverse of removal.

➡**Note: Tighten the bolts securely only after the weight of the engine/transaxle is back onto the mount and the jack or support device is removed. Proceed to Step 25.**

Left (driver's-side) mount

11 The driver's-side mount is located under the air filter housing. For access to the transaxle mount, remove the air filter housing (see Chapter 4).

12 With the engine/transaxle supported, remove the through-bolt (see illustration).

13 Remove the nuts and detach the mount from the transaxle.

14 Installation is the reverse of removal.

➡**Note: Tighten the fasteners securely only after the weight of the engine/transaxle is back onto the mount and the jack or support device is removed. Proceed to Step 25.**

Front mount

15 The front mount is located between the engine and radiator.

16 With the engine/transaxle supported, remove the large through-bolt (see illustration).

17 Remove the nuts holding the mount to the crossmember.

18 Raise the engine enough for the front engine mount to clear the upper bracket and remove the mount.

19 Installation is the reverse of removal.

➡**Note: Tighten the fasteners securely only after the weight of the engine/transaxle is back onto the mount and the jack or support device is removed. Proceed to Step 25.**

Rear mount

20 The rear mount is positioned between the driveaxle and the intake manifold.

21 Remove the rear mount through-bolt (see illustration).

22 Remove the mount-to-transaxle bolts.

23 Remove the mount.

24 Installation is the reverse of removal.

➡**Note: Tighten the fasteners securely only after the weight of the engine/transaxle is back onto the mount and the jack or support device is removed. Proceed to Step 25.**

Final tightening, all mounts

25 To ensure maximum bushing life and prevent excessive noise and vibration, the vehicle should be level and the engine weight should be on the mounts during the final tightening stage.

➡**Note: Use non-hardening thread locking compound on the nuts/bolts.**

Ensure that the bushings are not twisted or offset. If you have replaced more than one mount, or when you are installing the engine, tighten the mounts in the following order: front, rear, passenger-side and driver's-side.

Specifications

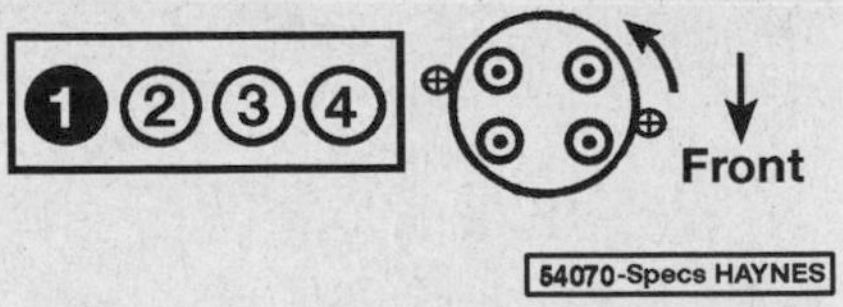

General

Firing order	1-3-4-2

Engine identification (eighth character of the Vehicle Identification Number)

Sephia/Spectra

VIN code 1 (1994 and 1995)	B6 1.6L Single Overhead Camshaft (SOHC)
VIN code 3, 4 (1995 through 1997)	B6 1.6L Double Overhead Camshaft (DOHC)
VIN code 5 (1995 through 1997)	BP 1.8L Double Overhead Camshaft (DOHC)
VIN code 1 (1998 through 2004)	T8 1.8L Double Overhead Camshaft (DOHC)
VIN code 1 (2004 and later)	2.0L Double Overhead Camshaft (DOHC)
VIN code 2 (2004 and later)	2.0L Double Overhead Camshaft (DOHC) SULEV

Sportage

VIN code 2	2.0L Double Overhead Camshaft (DOHC), Federal models
VIN code 4	2.0L Double Overhead Camshaft (DOHC), California models

①②③④

Front

54070-Specs HAYNES

Cylinder location and distributor rotation (1998 and later models do not have a distributor)

Timing belt

Tensioner spring free length

1.6L SOHC	2.52 inches (54.0 mm)
1.8L DOHC B6	2.31 inches (58.8 mm)
1.8L DOHC BP	2.33 inches (59.2 mm)
1.8L DOHC T8 and 2.0L DOHC	Not applicable

Timing belt deflection

1.6L SOHC	0.43 to 0.51 inches (11 to 13 mm)
1.6L DOHC B6, 1.8L DOHC BP, 1.8L DOHC T8	0.36 to 0.45 inches (9 to 11 mm)
2.0L DOHC	0.16 to 0.24 inches (4 to 6 mm)

Camshaft

1.6L SOHC

Lobe height

Two valve	1.4272 inches minimum (36.251 mm)

Four valve

Intake	1.4027 inches minimum (35.629 mm)
Exhaust	1.3960 inches minimum (35.459 mm)

Journal diameter

Two valve

Front and rear journals	1.7102 inches minimum (43.440 mm)
Center journals	1.7098 inches minimum (43.430 mm)

Four valve

Number 1, 5 journals	1.7102 inches minimum (43.440 mm)
Number 2, 4 journals	1.7096 inches minimum (43.425 mm)
Number 3 journal	1.7091 inches minimum (43.410 mm)
Out-of-round limit	0.002 inch maximum (0.05 mm)
Journal oil clearance	0.006 inch maximum (0.015 mm)
Endplay	0.008 inch maximum (0.203 mm)

1.6L DOHC B6

Lobe height

Intake	1.6019 inches minimum (40.688 mm)
Exhaust	1.7480 inches minimum (44.400 mm)

Camshaft (continued)

Journal diameter	1.0201 inches minimum (25.910 mm)
Out-of-round limit	0.002 inch maximum (0.05 mm)
Journal oil clearance	0.006 inch maximum (0.015 mm)
Endplay	0.008 inch maximum (0.203 mm)

1.8L DOHC BP

Lobe height	
Intake	1.7281 inches minimum (43.894 mm)
Exhaust	1.7480 inches minimum (44.400 mm)
Journal diameter	1.0201 inches minimum (25.910 mm)
Out-of-round limit	0.002 inch maximum (0.05 mm)
Journal oil clearance	0.006 inch maximum (0.015 mm)
Endplay	0.008 inch maximum (0.203 mm)

1.8L DOHC T8

Lobe height	
Intake	1.6415 inches minimum (41.695 mm)
Exhaust	1.6629 inches minimum (42.237 mm)
Journal diameter	1.0594 inches minimum (26.910 mm)
Out-of-round limit	0.002 inch maximum (0.05 mm)
Journal oil clearance	0.006 inch maximum (0.015 mm)
Endplay	0.008 inch maximum (0.203 mm)

2.0L DOHC

Lobe height	
Intake	1.7527 to 1.7605 inches (44.518 to 44.718 mm)
Exhaust	1.7487 to 1.7566 inches (44.418 to 44.618 mm)
Journal diameter	
2004 through 2007 models	1.1009 to 1.1016 inches (27.964 to 27.980 mm)
2008 and later models	1.1023 inches (28 mm)
Out-of-round limit	0.002 inch maximum (0.05 mm)
Journal oil clearance	0.0008 to 0.0024 inch (0.02 to 0.61 mm)
Endplay	0.0039 to 0.0079 inch (0.10 to 0.20 mm)

Oil pump

1.6L SOHC, 1.6L DOHC B6 and 1.8L DOHC BP

Rotor tooth-tip clearance	0.0079 inch maximum (0.20 mm)
Outer rotor-to-body clearance	0.0087 inch maximum (0.22 mm)
Rotor set-to-oil pump housing (side clearance)	0.0055 inch maximum (0.14 mm)

1.8L DOHC T8

Rotor tooth-tip clearance	0.007 inch maximum (0.180 mm)
Outer rotor-to-body clearance	0.015 inch maximum (0.376 mm)
Rotor set-to-oil pump housing (side clearance)	0.0035 inch maximum (0.090 mm)

2.0L DOHC

Rotor tooth-tip clearance	0.0010 to 0.0027 inch (0.025 to 0.069 mm)
Outer rotor-to-body clearance	0.0047 to 0.0073 inch (0.120 to 0.185 mm)
Rotor set-to-oil pump housing (side clearance)	
Inner rotor	0.0016 to 0.0033 inch (0.040 to 0.085 mm)
Outer rotor	0.0016 to 0.0035 inch (0.040 to 0.090 mm)

Rocker arm and shaft (SOHC)

1.6L SOHC

Outside diameter	
Two valve	0.7070 inch minimum (17.959 mm)
Four valve	0.7464 inch minimum (18.959 mm)

Rocker arm and shaft (SOHC) (continued)

Oil clearance	0.004 inch maximum (0.10 mm)
Rocker arm inside diameter	
Two valve	0.7097 inch maximum (18.027 mm)
Four valve	0.7493 inch maximum (19.033 mm)

Valve clearance (cold)

All engines (except 2.0L DOHC)	Zero lash (hydraulic, non-adjustable)
2.0L DOHC	
2004 through 2007 models	
Intake	0.0047 to 0.0110 inch (0.12 to 0.28 mm)
Exhaust	0.0079 to 0.0150 inch (0.20 to 0.38 mm)
2008 and later models	
Intake	0.0067 to 0.0091 inch (0.17 to 0.23 mm)
Exhaust	0.0098 to 0.0122 inch (0.25 to 0.31 mm)

Torque specifications	Ft-lbs (unless otherwise indicated)	Nm

➡**Note: One foot-pound (ft-lb) of torque is equivalent to 12 inch-pounds (in-lbs) of torque. Torque values below approximately 15 foot-pounds are expressed in inch-pounds, because most foot-pound torque wrenches are not accurate at these smaller values.**

Camshaft bearing cap bolts		
1.6L DOHC B6 and 1.8L DOHC BP	100 to 125 in-lbs	11 to 14
1.8L DOHC T8		
1998 through 2002	13 to 19.5	18 to 26.5
2003 and later	100 to 125 in-lbs	11 to 14
2.0L DOHC	121 to 130 in-lbs	13.5 to 14.5
Camshaft sprocket bolt		
All except 2.0L DOHC	37 to 44	50 to 60
2.0L DOHC	73 to 87	99 to 118
Camshaft thrust plate bolt (1.6L SOHC)	69 to 95 in-lbs	8 to 11
Crankshaft pulley bolts	109 to 152 in-lbs	12 to 17
Crankshaft sprocket bolt	116 to 123	157 to 167
Cylinder head bolts (see illustrations 11.34a and 11.34b)		
1.6L SOHC, 1.6L DOHC B6 and 1.8L DOHC BP	56 to 60	76 to 81
1.8L DOHC T8		
Step 1	36	49
Step 2	Loosen all bolts completely	
Step 3	28	39
Step 4	Tighten an additional 90 degrees	
Step 5	Tighten an additional 90 degrees	
2.0L DOHC		
Eight smaller diameter (M10) bolts		
Step 1	17 to 19	23 to 26
Step 2	Tighten an additional 60 to 65 degrees	
Step 3	Tighten an additional 60 to 65 degrees	
Two larger diameter (M12) bolts		
Step 1	21 to 23	28 to 31
Step 2	Tighten an additional 60 to 65 degrees	
Step 3	Tighten an additional 60 to 65 degrees	

Torque specifications	Ft-lbs (unless otherwise indicated)	Nm

➡**Note: One foot-pound (ft-lb) of torque is equivalent to 12 inch-pounds (in-lbs) of torque. Torque values below approximately 15 foot-pounds are expressed in inch-pounds, because most foot-pound torque wrenches are not accurate at these smaller values.**

Exhaust manifold nuts		
1.6L SOHC	12 to 17	16 to 23
1.6L DOHC B6, 1.8L DOHC BP and 1.8L DOHC T8	29 to 34	38 to 47
2.0L DOHC	31 to 40	42 to 54
Flywheel/driveplate bolts		
All except 2.0L DOHC	71 to 76	96 to 103
2.0L DOHC	87 to 94	118 to 128
Intake manifold bolts		
All except 2.0L DOHC	14 to 19	19 to 26
2.0L DOHC	13 to 17	17 to 23
Oil pan main bearing support plate (MBSP) bolts (1.6L SOHC		
and 1.8L DOHC BP engines)	12 to 15	18 to 21
Oil pan upper block (1.6L DOHC B6 engines) (see illustration 12.15)		
Bolts 1 through 8	12 to 15	16 to 20
Bolts 9 through 14	72 to 96 in-lbs	8 to 11
Oil pan stiffener bolts	27 to 38	37 to 52
Oil pan bolts		
1.6L SOHC, 1.8L DOHC BP	69 to 95 in-lbs	8 to 11
1.6L DOHC B6	14 to 18	19 to 25
1.8L DOHC T8 (see illustration 12.17)		
Bolts A	60 to 96 in-lbs	7 to 11.5
Bolts B	28 to 38	38 to 51
2.0L DOHC	86 to 104 in-lbs	9.5 to 11.5
Oil pump bolts	15 to 19	20 to 26
Rear main seal retainer bolts		
1.6L SOHC, 1.6L DOHC B6, 1.8L DOHC BP	69 to 104 in-lbs	8 to 11.5
1.8L DOHC T8		
Seal cover-to-engine block bolts	60 to 96 in-lbs	7 to 11
Oil pan-to-rear main seal cover	30 to 40	40 to 54
2.0L DOHC	86 to 104 in-lbs	9.5 to 11.5
Rocker arm shaft bolts (1.6L SOHC)	16 to 21	22 to 28
Tensioner pulley bolt		
1.6L SOHC	14 to 19	19 to 26
1.6L DOHC B6, 1.8L DOHC BP		
and 1.8L DOHC T8	28 to 38	38 to 51
2.0L DOHC	31 to 40	42 to 54
Timing belt idler pulley bolts		
1.6L SOHC	Not applicable	
1.6L DOHC B6, 1.8L DOHC BP		
and 1.8L DOHC T8	28 to 38	38 to 51
2.0L DOHC		
2004 through 2007 models	31 to 40	42 to 54
2008 and later models	17 to 21	23 to 28
Valve cover bolts		
1.6L SOHC, 1.6L DOHC B6, 1.8L DOHC BP	44 to 78 in-lbs	5 to 9
1.8L DOHC T8	66 to 88 in-lbs	8 to 10
2.0L DOHC	70 to 86 in-lbs	8 to 9.5
Water pump pulley	See Chapter 3	

2B
V6 ENGINES

Section

1   General information
2   Repair operations possible with the engine in the vehicle
3   Top Dead Center (TDC) for number one piston - locating
4   Valve covers - removal and installation
5   Intake manifold - removal and installation
6   Exhaust manifold/catalytic converter assemblies - removal and installation
7   Timing belt and sprockets - removal, inspection and installation
8   Oil seals - replacement
9   Camshafts and valvetrain - removal, inspection, installation and adjustment
10   Cylinder heads - removal, inspection and installation
11   Oil pan - removal and installation
12   Oil pump - removal, inspection and installation
13   Driveplate - removal and installation
14   Powertrain mounts - check and replacement

Reference to other Chapters

CHECK ENGINE light on - See Chapter 6
Crankshaft pulley - removal and installation - See Chapter 2A
Cylinder compression check - See Chapter 2C
Drivebelt check, adjustment and replacement - See Chapter 1
Engine - removal and installation - See Chapter 2C
Engine oil and filter change - See Chapter 1
Engine overhaul - general information - See Chapter 2C
Spark plug replacement - See Chapter 1
Water pump - removal and installation - See Chapter 3

1 General information

The 2.7L V6 is a DOHC (Dual OverHead Cam) engine with aluminum heads, four valves per cylinder and a two-piece oil pan.

This Part of Chapter 2 is devoted to in-vehicle repair procedures for the V6 engine. Information concerning engine removal and installation and engine overhaul can be found in Part C of this Chapter.

The following repair procedures are based on the assumption that the engine is installed in the vehicle. If the engine has been removed from the vehicle and mounted on a stand, many of the steps outlined in this Part of Chapter 2 will not apply.

2 Repair operations possible with the engine in the vehicle

Many major repair operations can be accomplished without removing the engine from the vehicle.

Clean the engine compartment and the exterior of the engine with some type of degreaser before any work is done. It will make the job easier and help keep dirt out of the internal areas of the engine.

Depending on the components involved, it may be helpful to remove the hood to improve access to the engine as repairs are performed (see Chapter 11 if necessary). Cover the fenders to prevent damage to the paint. Special pads are available, but an old bedspread or blanket will also work.

If vacuum, exhaust, oil or coolant leaks develop, indicating a need for gasket or seal replacement, the repairs can generally be made with the engine in the vehicle. The intake and exhaust manifold gaskets, oil pan gasket, crankshaft oil seals and cylinder head gaskets are all accessible with the engine in place.

Exterior engine components, such as the intake and exhaust manifolds, the oil pan, the oil pump, the water pump, the starter motor, the alternator, and the fuel system components can be removed for repair with the engine in place.

Since the cylinder heads can be removed without pulling the engine, valve component servicing can also be accomplished with the engine in the vehicle. Replacement of the camshafts, timing belt and sprockets is also possible with the engine in the vehicle.

3 Top Dead Center (TDC) for number one piston - locating

▶ **Refer to illustration 3.5**

1   Top Dead Center (TDC) is the highest point in the cylinder that each piston reaches as it travels up the cylinder bore. Each piston reaches TDC on the compression stroke and again on the exhaust stroke, but TDC generally refers to piston position on the compression stroke.

2   Positioning the piston(s) at TDC is an essential part of certain procedures such as camshaft and timing belt/sprocket removal.

3   Before beginning this procedure, be sure to place the transaxle in Neutral and apply the parking brake or block the rear wheels. Disable the fuel pump (see Chapter 4, Section 2). Disable the ignition system by disconnecting the electrical connector(s) from the coil(s).

4   In order to bring any piston to TDC, the crankshaft must be turned using one of the methods outlined below. When looking at the front of the engine, normal crankshaft rotation is clockwise.

    a) The preferred method is to turn the crankshaft clockwise with a socket and ratchet attached to the bolt threaded into the front of the crankshaft.

    b) A remote starter switch, which may save some time, can also be used. Follow the instructions included with the switch. Once the piston is close to TDC, use a socket and ratchet as described in the previous paragraph.

    c) If an assistant is available to turn the ignition switch to the Start position in short bursts, you can get the piston close to TDC without a remote starter switch. Make sure your assistant is out of the vehicle, away from the ignition switch, then use a socket and ratchet as described in Paragraph a) to complete the procedure.

5   Remove the spark plug and install a compression gauge in the number one spark plug hole. It should be a gauge with a screw-in fitting and a hose at least six inches long (see illustration).

3.5 A compression gauge can be used in the number one spark plug hole to assist in finding TDC

> ✳ **CAUTION:**
>
> It is possible to check the compression on cylinder number 1 on the V6 engine with the upper intake manifold and throttle body installed on the engine. The spark plugs can remain in the cylinder heads (except for number 1) if the ignition system and the fuel pump have been disabled.

6 Rotate the crankshaft using one of the methods described above while observing the compression gauge. When the compression stroke of the number one cylinder is reached, pressure will begin to show on the gauge; continue to rotate the crankshaft and align the notch on the crankshaft pulley with the 0 mark on the timing plate. If you go past the marks, release the gauge pressure and rotate the crankshaft around two more revolutions.

7 After the number one piston has been positioned at TDC on the compression stroke, TDC for the remaining cylinders can be located by turning the crankshaft 120-degrees (1/3-turn) at a time and following the firing order (see this Chapter's Specifications).

4 Valve covers - removal and installation

REMOVAL

♦ **Refer to illustrations 4.2, 4.6 and 4.7**

➡**Note: This procedure applies to both the front and rear valve covers.**

1 Disconnect the cable from the negative terminal of the battery (see Chapter 5).

2 Remove the engine cover (see illustration).

3 If you're removing the front valve cover, drain the engine coolant (see Chapter 1) and remove the upper radiator hose (see Chapter 3).

4 If you're removing the rear valve cover, remove the upper intake manifold (see Section 5). Depending on the year and model, there might be other brackets, supporting the upper intake manifold, that must be removed before you can remove the rear valve cover. If so, be sure to label them with respect to their location and keep them together with their fasteners.

5 Disconnect the spark plug wires and remove the spark plugs (see Chapter 1). Also disconnect the electrical connectors for all engine wiring harnesses that are routed over the top of the valve cover(s) and set them aside. To prevent confusion later, be sure to label everything as you disconnect it. Also remove any mounting brackets that prevent valve cover removal. Be sure to keep brackets and fasteners in order for reassembly.

6 Remove the valve cover retaining bolts (see illustration), then remove the valve cover. If a cover sticks to the head, bump the end with a wood block and a hammer to jar it loose. If that doesn't work, try to slip a flexible putty knife between the head and cover to break the seal.

※※ CAUTION:

Don't pry at the cover-to-head joint or damage to the sealing surfaces might occur, leading to oil leaks after the cover is reinstalled.

7 Remove and inspect the old valve cover seal type gasket and the spark plug hole seals (see illustration).

4.2 Engine cover bolts

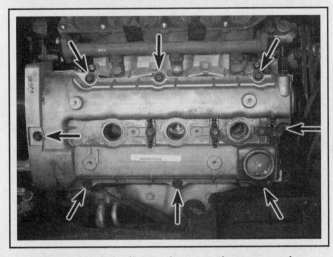

4.6 Valve cover bolts (front valve cover shown, rear valve cover identical)

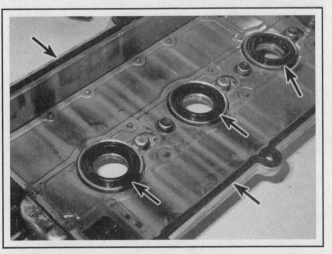

4.7 Valve cover seal type gasket and spark plug hole seals

INSTALLATION

8   The mating surfaces of the cylinder head and the valve cover must be clean when the cover is installed. Use a gasket scraper to remove all traces of sealant and old gasket material, then clean the mating surfaces with brake system cleaner. If there's residue or oil on the mating surfaces when the cover is installed, oil leaks may develop. If the valve cover gasket and spark plug hole seals are in good condition, they can be re-used.

9   Apply RTV sealant to the gasket/seal joints at the front and rear camshaft-to-head mounts and install the valve cover with a new gasket.

10 Install the valve cover bolts. Tighten the bolts evenly, a little at a time, to the torque listed in this Chapter's Specifications.

11 Installation is otherwise the reverse of removal. When you're done, be sure run the engine and check for oil leaks.

5   Intake manifold - removal and installation

❄❄ WARNING:

Wait until the engine is completely cool before beginning this procedure.

1   Disconnect the cable from the negative battery terminal (see Chapter 5), then drain the cooling system (see Chapter 1).

UPPER INTAKE MANIFOLD

▶ **Refer to illustration 5.11**

2   Remove the engine cover (see illustration 4.2) and the air intake duct assembly (see Chapter 4).

3   Disconnect the accelerator cable (see Chapter 4).

4   Disconnect the electrical connectors from the Throttle Position (TP) sensor, the Idle Speed Actuator (ISA), the Variable Intake Solenoid (VIS) actuator, the fuel injectors, the Purge Control Solenoid Valve (PCSV) and the Intake Air Temperature (IAT) sensor (see Chapter 6, if necessary). Label each connector using tape and a marker to ensure correct reassembly. Pull the wiring harnesses aside. The wiring and hoses vary from model to model - make sure that all interfering hoses and harnesses have been labeled, disconnected and pulled out of the way.

5   Disconnect the EVAP hose from the Purge Control Solenoid Valve (PCSV), the brake booster vacuum hose and the Positive Crankcase Ventilation (PCV) valve hose (see Chapter 6, if necessary).

6   Remove the ground strap bolt and disconnect the ground strap from the upper intake manifold.

7   Disconnect the coolant hoses from the throttle body (see Chapter 4).

➡ **Note: Clamp off the coolant hoses before detaching them, or plug them as soon as they are detached. Be prepared for coolant spillage.**

It's not necessary to remove the throttle body from the upper intake manifold in order to remove the manifold.

8   Unbolt and remove the upper intake manifold support bracket from the back of the manifold.

9   Remove the bolts mounting the upper intake manifold to the lower intake manifold, following the reverse of the tightening sequence (see illustration 5.11) and remove the upper intake manifold. Pull the manifold forward and detach the accelerator cable and cruise control cable from the cable bracket on the backside of the manifold (see illustration 10.1b in Chapter 4).

10 If you're replacing the upper intake manifold, you'll need to remove all components from it and install them on the new manifold. For information on the throttle body, refer to Chapter 4; for information on the other components, refer to Chapter 6.

11 Install the upper intake manifold on the lower manifold and tighten the fasteners in the correct sequence (see illustration). Installation is otherwise the reverse of removal.

LOWER INTAKE MANIFOLD

▶ **Refer to illustration 5.18**

12 Relieve the fuel system pressure (see Chapter 4).

13 Remove the upper intake manifold (see Steps 1 through 9).

14 Remove the fuel rail and injectors (see Chapter 4).

15 Remove the manifold bolts in the reverse order of the tightening sequence (see illustration 5.18), then detach the lower intake manifold from the engine. If the manifold is stuck, don't pry between the gasket mating surfaces or damage may result.

16 Check the lower manifold mating surface with a precision straightedge and compare your readings with those listed in this Chapter's Specifications. If the manifold is excessively warped, it must be resurfaced by an automotive machine shop.

17 Use a scraper to remove all traces of old gasket material and sealant from the lower manifold and cylinder heads, then clean the mating surfaces with brake system cleaner.

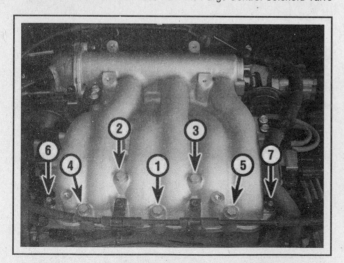

5.11 Upper intake manifold bolt tightening sequence

18 Install new gaskets, then position the lower intake manifold on the engine. Make sure the gaskets haven't shifted, and install the bolts. Tighten the bolts in three or four equal steps to the torque listed in this Chapter's Specifications. Tighten the bolts in the correct sequence (see illustration).

19 Install a new gasket between the lower intake manifold and the upper intake manifold. Place the upper intake manifold on the lower intake manifold. Install the bolts and tighten them, in the proper sequence (see illustration 5.11), to the torque listed in this Chapter's Specifications. Install or reconnect everything that you removed or disconnected from the upper intake manifold.

20 Check the coolant level (see Chapter 1). Reconnect the battery, then run the engine and check for fuel, vacuum and coolant leaks.

5.18 Lower intake manifold bolt tightening sequence (remove fasteners in reverse order)

6   Exhaust manifold/catalytic converter assemblies - removal and installation

▶ **Refer to illustrations 6.5 and 6.8**

✷✷ WARNING:

The engine must be completely cool before beginning this procedure.

➡ Note: **This procedure applies to both the front and the rear exhaust manifold/catalytic converter assemblies.**

1 Disconnect the cable from the negative terminal of the battery (see Chapter 5).

2 Raise the front of the vehicle and support it securely on jackstands, then remove the engine lower splash shield.

3 If you're removing the exhaust manifold/catalytic converter from the front cylinder head:

   a) Drain the coolant (see Chapter 1).
   b) Remove the coolant reservoir.
   c) Remove the radiator fan shroud and fan motor assembly (see Chapter 3).
   d) Remove the air conditioning compressor (see Chapter 3).

4 If you're removing the exhaust manifold/catalytic converter from the rear cylinder head:

   a) Remove the upper intake manifold (see Section 5).
   b) Remove the alternator (see Chapter 5).
   c) Remove the right driveaxle assembly (see Chapter 8).

5 Disconnect the upstream oxygen sensor electrical connector (see Chapter 6), then remove the upstream sensor from the manifold (see illustration).

6 Remove the heat shield fasteners and remove the heat shield from the exhaust manifold.

7 Spray penetrating oil on all upper and lower exhaust manifold fasteners and allow it to soak in.

8 Remove the front exhaust pipe fasteners (see illustration).

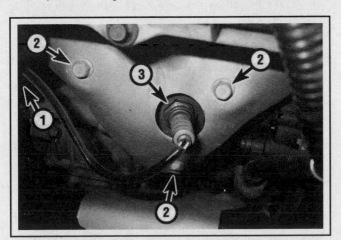

6.5 Exhaust manifold details (rear manifold shown, front similar):

1   Trace oxygen sensor electrical lead to connector and disconnect it
2   Heat shield fasteners
3   Oxygen sensor

6.8 Front exhaust pipe fasteners

9 Disconnect the downstream oxygen sensor electrical connector, then remove the downstream sensor from the manifold (see Chapter 6).

10 Unbolt the exhaust manifold(s) from the cylinder head(s), working from the ends toward the middle. Slip the manifold(s) off the mounting studs.

11 Carefully inspect the manifold(s) for cracks and damage.

12 Use a scraper to remove all traces of old gasket material and carbon deposits from the manifold and cylinder head mating surfaces. If the gasket was leaking, check the manifold for warpage on the cylinder head mounting surface by placing a straightedge over the surface and trying to insert a feeler gauge. If the clearance exceeds the limit listed in this Chapter's Specifications, have the manifold resurfaced at an automotive machine shop.

13 Position a new gasket over the cylinder head studs.

14 Install the manifold(s) and thread the mounting nuts into place.

15 Working from the center out tighten the exhaust manifold nuts to the torque listed in this Chapter's Specifications in three or four equal steps.

16 Reinstall the remaining parts in the reverse order of removal. Use new gaskets when connecting the front exhaust pipe.

17 Run the engine and check for exhaust leaks.

7   Timing belt and sprockets - removal, inspection and installation

✳✳ CAUTION:

The timing system is complex, and severe engine damage will occur if you make any mistakes. Do not attempt this procedure unless you are highly experienced with this type of repair. If you are at all unsure of your abilities, be sure to consult an expert. Double-check all your work and be sure everything is correct before you attempt to start the engine.

REMOVAL

▶ **Refer to illustrations 7.4a, 7.4b, 7.7 and 7.14**

1 Disconnect the cable from the negative terminal of the battery (see Chapter 5).

2 Remove the engine cover (see illustration 4.2).

3 Loosen the right front wheel lug nuts. Raise the front of the vehicle and place it securely on jackstands. Remove the engine under cover (see Section 6 in Chapter 1).

4 Remove the right front wheel, then remove the right engine cover (see illustrations).

5 Set the engine at TDC on the number one cylinder (see Section 3). Make absolutely sure that all of the timing marks are aligned.

6 Loosen the pulleys on the power steering pump, the idler pulley and the crankshaft pulley, then remove the drivebelt (see Chapter 1).

7 Remove the automatic tensioner for the drivebelt (see illustration).

8 Support the engine with a floor jack. Place a block of wood between the jack head and the engine to protect the engine. Remove the right engine mounting bracket.

9 Remove the power steering pump pulley, the idler pulley and the crankshaft pulley.

10 Remove the upper timing belt cover.

11 Remove the lower timing belt cover.

12 If you intend to reuse the timing belt, mark it with an arrow indicating direction of travel and put match marks from the belt to the sprockets so it can be realigned easily.

13 Remove the timing belt tensioner, then remove the timing belt.

✳✳ CAUTION:

Do not turn the crankshaft or the camshafts when the timing belt is removed.

14 To remove the camshaft sprockets, remove the valve covers (see Section 4) and hold the hex area of the camshaft securely with a wrench while removing the bolts (see illustration).

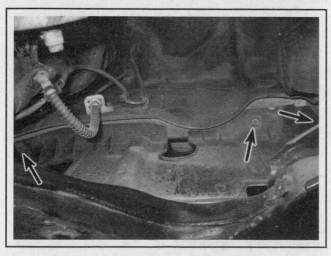

7.4a Right engine cover mounting bolt locations

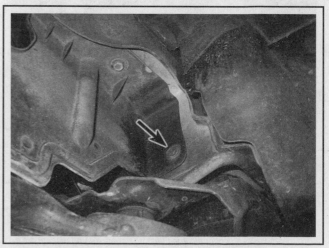

7.4b Right engine cover mounting bolt location

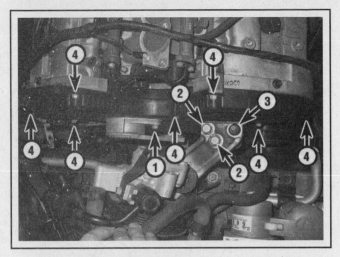

7.7 Upper timing belt cover details:

1   Automatic tensioner mounting bolt
2   Right engine mounting bracket bolts
3   Right engine mounting bracket nut (nut which secures bracket to vehicle body, not visible)
4   Upper timing belt cover mounting bolts

7.14 If the camshaft sprockets are to be removed, hold the hex portion of the camshaft with a wrench while removing the sprocket bolt

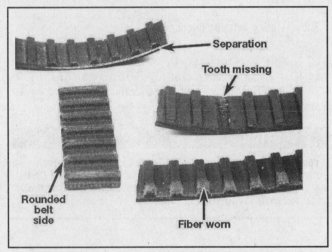

7.15 Check the timing belt for cracked or missing teeth - if the belt is cracked or worn, also check the sprockets and pulleys for nicks or burrs - wear on one side of the belt indicates sprocket misalignment problems

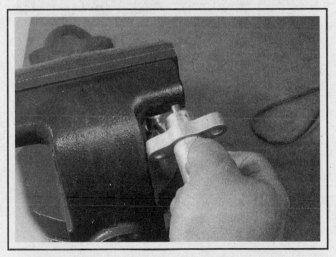

7.17 Check the tensioner for signs of leakage and test for leakdown by forcing it against an immovable object

INSPECTION

▶ **Refer to illustrations 7.15 and 7.17**

15   Check the belt for the presence of oil or dirt, and inspect for visible defects (see illustration).

16   Check the belt tensioner for visible oil leakage. If there's only a faint trace of oil on the pushrod side, the tensioner seal is in satisfactory condition.

17   Hold the tensioner in both hands and push it forcefully against an immovable object (see illustration). If the pushrod moves, replace the tensioner.

18   Check that the idler pulleys turn smoothly.

INSTALLATION

▶ **Refer to illustrations 7.23, 7.25a and 7.25b**

19   Remove all dirt, oil and grease from the timing belt area at the front of the engine.

20   Install the camshaft sprockets (if removed) on the camshaft. Align the pin hole in the sprocket with the pin in the end of the camshaft.

21   Install the camshaft sprocket bolts and tighten them to the torque listed in this Chapter's Specifications.

22   Carefully align all of the camshaft sprocket marks with the marks on the engine.

23   Using a press or vise compress the timing belt tensioner pushrod

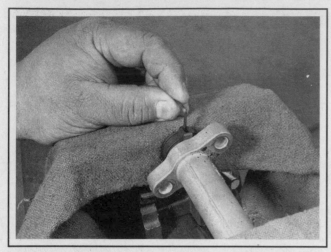

7.23 Restrain the tensioner pushrod by compressing the unit in a vise and inserting a pin approximately 0.060-inch (1.5 mm) in diameter

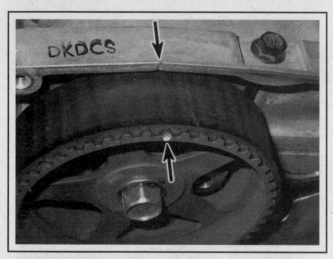

7.25b Timing belt alignment marks on intake camshafts (cam on front cylinder head shown, marks on other intake cam identical)

extremely slowly. Insert a metal pin, drill bit or Allen wrench through the holes in the pushrod and housing. Remove the tensioner from the press or vise (see illustration).

24 Install the timing belt tensioner and tighten the bolts to the torque listed in this Chapter's Specifications.

25 Make sure all of the timing marks are aligned and place the timing belt around the sprockets and pulleys in this order (see illustrations):
Crankshaft
Idler
Front cylinder head intake camshaft
Water pump
Rear cylinder head intake camshaft
Tensioner

26 Again verify that all timing marks are aligned, then pull the pin from the tensioner, allowing it to snap into position.

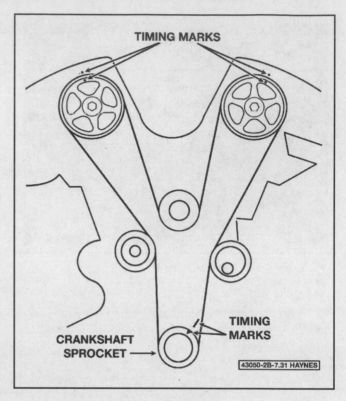

7.25a Timing belt alignment marks

27 Using a socket and breaker bar on the crankshaft pulley bolt, turn the crankshaft slowly (clockwise) through two complete revolutions (720-degrees) by hand (use a socket and breaker bar on the crankshaft pulley center-bolt).

❊❊ CAUTION:

If you feel any resistance, STOP! There is something wrong - most likely valves are contacting the pistons. You must find the problem before proceeding. Check your work and see if any updated repair information is available.

Recheck the timing marks.

❊❊ CAUTION:

If the timing marks are not aligned exactly as shown in illustrations 7.25a and 7.25b, repeat the timing belt installation procedure. DO NOT start the engine until you're absolutely certain that the timing belt is installed correctly. Serious and costly engine damage could occur if the belt is installed incorrectly. Stop turning the crankshaft immediately if you feel solid resistance; the valves could be contacting the pistons.

28 Let the engine sit for five minutes at TDC, then check the protrusion of the tensioner rod. Compare your measurement to that listed in this Chapter's Specifications. If it isn't correct, replace the tensioner or determine if there's another problem.

29 The remainder of installation is the reverse of removal.

8 Oil seals - replacement

CRANKSHAFT FRONT OIL SEAL

1 Remove the timing belt and crankshaft sprocket (see Section 7). Slip off the sensor ring and the spacer behind it.

2 Carefully pry the seal out with a screwdriver or seal removal tool. If you use a screwdriver, wrap tape around the tip - don't scratch the housing bore or damage the crankshaft (if the crankshaft is damaged, the new seal will end up leaking).

3 Clean the bore in the engine and coat the outer edge of the new seal with engine oil or multi-purpose grease. Apply the same grease to the seal lip.

4 Using a seal driver, carefully drive the new seal into place with a hammer. Make sure it's installed squarely and driven in to the same depth as the original. Check the seal after installation to make sure the spring didn't pop out of place.

5 Reinstall the components removed for access to the seal (refer to the appropriate Sections in this Chapter).

6 Run the engine and check for oil leaks at the front seal.

CRANKSHAFT REAR OIL SEAL

7 Refer to Chapter 2A, Section 15.

CAMSHAFT OIL SEALS

8 Remove the timing belt and camshaft sprockets (see Section 7).

9 Note how far the seals are installed in the bores, then pry them out with a seal removal tool or a screwdriver wrapped with tape. Don't scratch the bore or the camshaft; even a small scratch can cause a leak.

10 Clean the bores. Coat the outer edge of the new seals with oil or grease. Also apply grease to the lips of the seals.

11 Using a seal driver, carefully drive the new seals into place with a hammer. Make sure they're installed squarely and that they're driven in to the same depth as the originals.

12 Install all of the removed components, referring to the appropriate Sections in this Chapter to ensure that the belt and sprockets are correctly aligned. Clean carefully around the seals so you'll be able to detect any leaks later.

9 Camshafts and valvetrain - removal, inspection and installation

REMOVAL

1 Position the engine at TDC (see Section 3).

2 Remove the valve covers (see Section 4).

3 Remove the timing belt (see Section 7).

4 The following steps apply to the removal of each of the four camshafts. Make sure that the cam timing marks on the sprockets and engine are in alignment. The camshafts are not interchangeable. Mark them clearly to avoid confusion later.

5 Before you remove the camshaft bearing caps, note that each cap has a directional arrow on top indicating which way the cap must face when installed (all arrows must face toward the timing chain end of the cylinder head); and each cap is also numbered. So be sure to store the caps in the same order in which they're installed so that, when you install the caps, they will all be facing in the correct direction and will be in the same locations that they were in prior to disassembly and removal. Loosen the camshaft bearing cap bolts in a little at a time so the camshaft(s) rise from the head evenly.

6 The bearing caps are marked I and E (for intake and exhaust), and they should already be numbered. Mark the caps with your own numbers if necessary. Remove the bearing caps and gently lift out the camshaft.

➡Note: The camshafts in each head must be removed together because they are connected by a timing chain.

7 Store the bearing caps in the correct order. If necessary, the valve lifters can now be removed. Be sure to store all components in order so they can be reinstalled in their original locations.

INSPECTION

8 Refer to Chapter 2, Part A for the inspection procedures for the camshafts. Be sure to use the Specifications in this Part of Chapter 2 for the V6 engines.

INSTALLATION

⬧ **Refer to illustration 9.11**

9 Apply camshaft installation lubricant to the camshaft lobes and bearing journals.

10 Install the lifters in their original positions.

11 Install the timing chains around the sprockets of each pair of camshafts and set them in their journals. Make sure that the timing marks on the sprockets are aligned with the marks on the timing chains (see illustration).

12 Install the bearing caps in numerical order with the arrows pointing toward the drivebelt end of the engine.

13 Tighten the bearing cap bolts a little at a time to the torque listed in this Chapter's Specifications. Tighten them so that the camshafts are

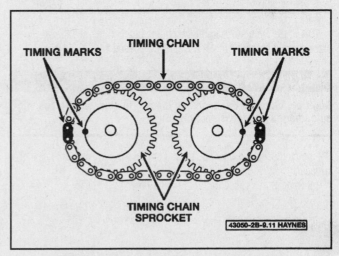

9.11 Camshaft sprocket/timing chain alignment marks

drawn into their bearing saddles evenly.

14 Install a new camshaft oil seal (if necessary) (see Section 9).

15 Reinstall the remaining components in the reverse order of removal.

16 The remainder of the installation is the reverse of the disassembly sequence.

10 Cylinder heads - removal, inspection and installation

✳ WARNING:

Wait until the engine is completely cool before beginning this procedure.

REMOVAL

1 Relieve the fuel system pressure (see Chapter 4), then disconnect the cable from the negative terminal of the battery (see Chapter 5).

2 Drain the cooling system (see Chapter 1). Remove the upper radiator hose.

3 Remove the upper and lower intake manifolds (see Section 5).

4 Remove the exhaust manifold(s) (see Section 6).

➡**Note: The exhaust manifolds can be left bolted to the cylinder heads if desired.**

5 Disconnect the timing belt from the camshaft sprocket(s) (see Section 7).

6 Disconnect the spark plug wires.

7 Disconnect all remaining sensors and hoses that interfere with removal.

8 Remove the camshafts (see Section 9).

9 Loosen the cylinder head bolts in 1/4-turn increments until they can be removed by hand, along with their hardened washers. Follow the reverse order of the recommended tightening sequence (see illustration 10.21).

✳ CAUTION:

Discard the cylinder head bolts and obtain new ones. The old head bolts must not be re-used.

10 Lift the cylinder head off the engine block. If the head is stuck, place a wood block against it and strike the wood with a hammer.

✳ CAUTION:

Don't pry between the head and block. The gasket surfaces may be damaged and leaks could result.

Set the cylinder head on wood blocks to prevent damage to the sealing surfaces.

11 Repeat the procedure for the other head if necessary.

✳ CAUTION:

Verify that all timing marks are aligned as shown in Section 7. Major engine damage can occur if they are not aligned.

17 Run the engine, then check for leaks and proper operation.

INSPECTION

12 Use a precision straightedge to check the gasket surfaces of each head. Try to insert a feeler gauge of the maximum specified size between the straightedge and the head surface. If the clearance is more than that listed in this Chapter's Specifications, the head must be resurfaced or replaced. Check the intake and exhaust manifold surfaces as well as the block surface.

13 Examine all areas of each head for signs of cracks and coolant leakage, especially around the valve seats.

INSTALLATION

▶ **Refer to illustrations 10.18 and 10.21**

14 The mating surfaces of the cylinder heads and block must be perfectly clean when the heads are installed.

15 Use a gasket scraper to remove all traces of carbon and old gasket material, then clean the mating surfaces with brake system cleaner. If there's oil on the mating surfaces when the head is installed, the gasket may not seal correctly and leaks could develop. When working on the block, stuff the cylinders with clean shop rags to keep out debris. Use a vacuum cleaner to remove material that falls into the cylinders.

16 Check the block and head mating surfaces for nicks, deep scratches and other damage. If damage is slight, it can be removed with a file; if it's excessive, machining may be the only alternative.

17 Use a tap of the correct size to chase the threads in the cylinder head bolt holes, then clean the holes with compressed air - make sure that nothing remains in the holes.

✳ WARNING:

Wear eye protection when using compressed air!

18 Position the new gaskets over the dowel pins in the block (see illustration). The side of the gasket with the identification mark must face upward. Apply a small dab of RTV sealant to the end of each leg of the gaskets.

19 Carefully set the head on the block without disturbing the gasket.

20 Before installing the head bolts, apply a small amount of clean engine oil to the threads and the underside of the bolt heads.

21 Install the NEW bolts and tighten them finger tight. Following the recommended sequence, tighten the bolts to the torque listed in this Chapter's Specifications (see illustration). If you don't have a torque angle gauge attachment, keep this in mind: 45-degrees equals 1/8-turn; 60-degrees equals the distance from one point of the bolt head to the next.

22 The remaining installation steps are the reverse of removal.

23 Refill the cooling system, change the oil and filter (see Chapter 1),

10.18 Be sure the new head gaskets are positioned right side up (check all holes and coolant passages for correct alignment) and over the block dowels

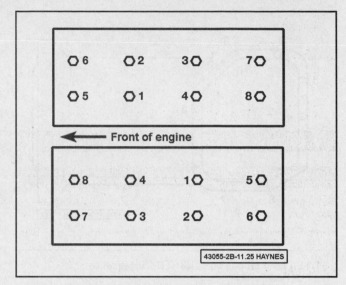

10.21 Cylinder head bolt TIGHTENING sequence

run the engine and check for leaks.

11 Oil pan - removal and installation

➡Note: The oil pan is a two-part assembly, with an aluminum casting attached to the cylinder block and transaxle, and a lower stamped-steel pan section at the bottom.

LOWER OIL PAN

Removal

▶ Refer to illustration 11.5

1   Disconnect the cable from the negative terminal of the battery (see Chapter 5).
2   Raise the vehicle and support it securely on jackstands
3   Remove the engine splash shield (see illustration 6.3 in Chapter 1).
4   Drain the engine oil (see Chapter 1).
5   Remove the lower pan mounting bolts (see illustration) and remove the lower pan. If it's stuck, pry it loose very carefully with a small screwdriver or putty knife. Don't damage the mating surfaces of the pan, or oil leaks could develop. Don't pry too much in one area, as you can bend the pan flange. Instead, drive in a putty knife and hammer it around the perimeter of the oil pan to break the seal.

Installation

▶ Refer to illustration 11.11

6   Use a scraper to remove all traces of old sealant from the block

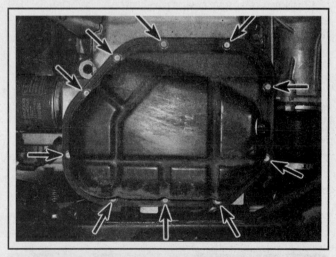

11.5 Lower oil pan mounting bolts

and oil pan. Clean the mating surfaces with brake system cleaner.
7   Make sure the threaded bolt holes in the block are clean.
8   Check the flange of the steel pan section for distortion, particularly around the bolt holes. If necessary, place the pan on a wood block and use a hammer to flatten and restore the gasket surface.
9   Clean the mating surfaces of the engine block and aluminum upper oil pan section, being careful not to gouge the soft metal, which could lead to leaks. Use brake system cleaner to remove all traces of

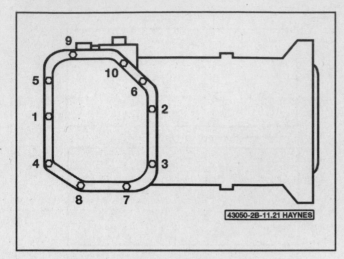

11.11 Lower oil pan bolt TIGHTENING sequence

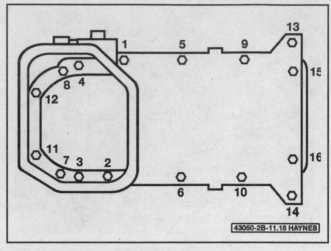

11.23 Upper oil pan bolt TIGHTENING sequence

oil.

10 Apply a continuous 1/8-inch bead of RTV sealant to the pan.

11 Install the pan within five minutes and tighten the bolts, a little at a time, in the specified sequence (see illustration) to the torque listed in this Chapter's Specifications. Allow the sealant to set for at least two hours before adding new oil and a new oil filter (see Chapter 1).

UPPER OIL PAN

Removal

12 Remove the lower oil pan (see Steps 1 through 5) and remove the oil filter (see Section 6 in Chapter 1).

13 Disconnect the front exhaust pipe from both exhaust manifolds and from the rest of the exhaust system (see illustration 6.8) and remove it.

14 Disconnect the electrical connectors for both downstream oxygen sensors (see Chapter 6).

15 Remove the starter motor (see Chapter 5).

16 Remove any other components that block access to the upper oil pan mounting bolts, or that will prevent you from dropping the pan.

17 Working through the hole where the lower oil pan was installed remove the lower baffle and the oil pump strainer/pickup.

18 Remove the upper oil pan fasteners including the ones inside of the pan (again, work through the hole for the lower pan) and those that

25 Run the engine and check for oil pressure and leaks.

12 Oil pump - removal, inspection and installa-

REMOVAL

1 Loosen the right front wheel lug nuts, then raise the front of the vehicle and place it securely on jackstands.

2 Drain the engine oil and remove the oil filter (see Section 6 in Chapter 1).

3 Remove the right front wheel, then remove the engine side cover

secure it to the transaxle, in the reverse order of the tightening sequence (see illustration 11.23).

19 Remove the upper oil pan by tapping it loose with a plastic hammer.

Installation

♦ **Refer to illustration 11.23**

20 Clean all sealing surfaces thoroughly with brake system cleaner to remove all traces of oil.

21 Inspect the oil pump pick-up/strainer assembly for cracks and a blocked strainer. Clean the pickup with solvent or thinner and install it now, using a new gasket. Tighten the fasteners to the torque listed in this Chapter's Specifications.

22 Apply a 3/16-inch wide bead of RTV sealant to the aluminum pan section.

➡**Note: The pan must be installed within five minutes after the sealant has been applied.**

23 Carefully position the pan on the engine block and install the bolts, tightening them to the torque listed in this Chapter's Specifications in three or four steps, in the specified tightening sequence (see illustration).

24 The remainder of installation is the reverse of removal. Allow the sealant to set for at least two hours before adding new oil and a new oil filter.

(see illustrations 7.4a and 7.4b).

4 Turn the crankshaft and align the white groove on the crankshaft pulley with the pointer on the lower cover.

5 Remove the front exhaust pipe (see illustration 6.8).

6 Remove the alternator (see Chapter 5).

7 Remove the timing belt (see Section 7).

8 Remove the crankshaft sprocket.

9 Remove the oil pan (see Section 11).

10 Remove the oil pump pick-up tube. Remove the oil pump housing mounting bolts and remove the oil pump from the front of the engine.

11 Place the oil pump housing on a clean workbench. Remove the

12.17a Measure the driven rotor-to-body clearance with a feeler gauge

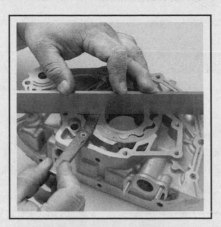

12.17b Measure the rotor side clearance with a precision straightedge and feeler gauge

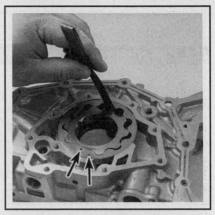

12.17c Measure the rotor tip clearance with a feeler gauge - note the rotor marks are facing out (when the pump body cover is installed, the marks will be against the cover)

oil pump cover screws, remove the cover from the oil pump and lift out the inner and outer gears.

12 Unscrew the cap for the oil pressure relief valve, remove the valve spring and remove the relief valve.

13 Use a scraper to remove all traces of sealant and old gasket material from the pump body and engine block, then clean the mating surfaces with brake system cleaner.

14 Clean all oil pump parts with solvent, then inspect them for wear and damage.

INSPECTION

◗ **Refer to illustrations 12.17a, 12.17b and 12.17c**

15 Inspect the oil pressure relief valve sliding surface. Coat the valve with clean engine oil and verify that it falls smoothly into its bore under its own weight; if it doesn't, replace it. If the bore itself is damaged, replace the front part of the oil pump case.

16 Inspect the condition of the spring for the oil pressure relief valve. If it's damaged, replace it.

➡**Note: The relief valve and spring are replaced as a set.**

17 Check the clearance of the following components with a feeler gauge and compare the measurements to this Chapter's Specifications (see illustrations):

a) Driven rotor-to-oil pump body clearance
b) Rotor side clearance
c) Rotor tip clearance

INSTALLATION

18 Pry out the old front crankshaft seal with a screwdriver.

19 Apply multi-purpose grease or engine oil to the outer edge of the new seal and carefully drive it into place with a seal driver and a hammer. Also apply multi-purpose grease to the seal lip.

20 Place the drive and driven rotors into the pump body.

21 Pack the pump cavities with petroleum jelly and install the cover using either a new gasket or RTV sealant. Tighten the screws securely following a criss-cross pattern to the torque listed in this Chapter's Specifications.

22 Lubricate the oil pressure relief valve with engine oil, install the valve and spring in the pump body and secure them with the cap. Be sure to tighten the cap securely.

23 Use brake cleaner and a clean rag to remove all traces of oil from the case gasket surfaces.

24 Install the oil pump case with a new gasket. Install the mounting bolts and tighten them gradually and evenly in a criss-cross pattern to the torque listed in this Chapter's Specifications.

25 Using a new gasket, install the oil pick-up tube and tighten the fasteners to the torque listed in this Chapter's Specifications.

26 Reinstall the remaining parts in the reverse order of removal.

27 Install a new oil filter and refill the engine with oil (see Chapter 1), start the engine and check for oil pressure and leaks.

28 Recheck the engine oil level.

13 Driveplate - removal and installation

Refer to Chapter 2, Part A for this procedure, but be sure to use the torque specifications in this Part of Chapter 2 for the V6 engine. On automatic transaxle vehicles, there is an adapter plate used on the rear of the driveplate.

14 Powertrain mounts - check and replacement

CHECK

1   Check the engine mounts on a V6 engine the same way that you would check them on a four-cylinder engine (see Section 16 in Chapter 2, Part A).

REPLACEMENT

▶ **Refer to illustrations 14.2a, 14.2b, 14.2c, 14.2d and 14.2e**

2   The V6 uses the same four engine mounts as a four-cylinder engine: a front roll-stopper between the engine subframe and the front of the engine block; a rear roll-stopper between the subframe and the back of the transaxle; a left mount between the vehicle body and the top of the transaxle; and a right mount between the vehicle body and the right (timing cover) end of the engine (see illustrations).

3   To remove any of these mounts, securely support the engine from

14.2a Front roll stopper and mounting bracket fasteners (as seen from left side)

14.2b Front roll stopper and mounting bracket (as seen from below)

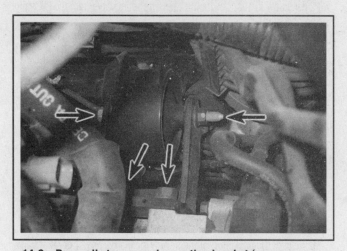

14.2c Rear roll stopper and mounting bracket (as seen from above)

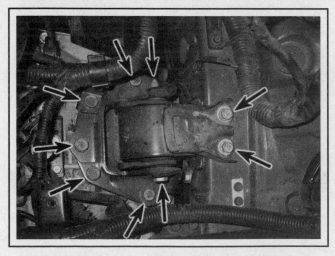

14.2d Left mount and bracket (transaxle side of engine)

14.2e Right mount and bracket (timing belt side of engine)

above, then remove the fasteners and remove the mount.

4   Installation is the reverse of removal. Be sure to tighten all fasteners securely.

Specifications

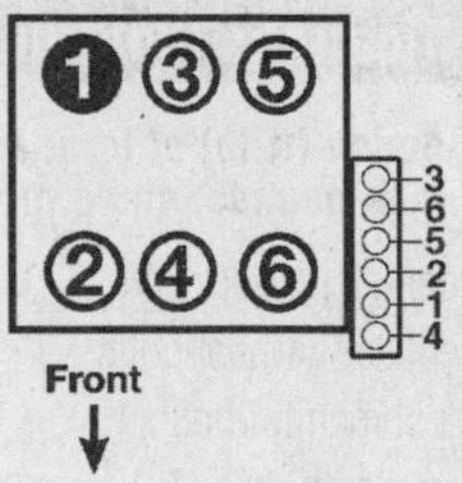

General

Engine identification	G6BA
Displacement	162 cubic inches (2,656 cc)
Cylinder numbers (timing belt or chain end-to-transaxle end)	
Right (firewall) side	1-3-5
Left (radiator) side	2-4-6
Firing order	1-2-3-4-5-6

V6 engines

Cylinder numbering

Cylinder head

Warpage limits	
Block surface	0.002 inch (0.05 mm)
Intake surface	0.006 inch (0.15 mm)
Exhaust surface	0.006 inch (0.15 mm)

Camshafts

Bearing journal diameter	1.022 to 1.023 inches (25.95 to 25.98 mm)
Bearing oil clearance	0.0007 to 0.0024 inch (0.02 to 0.06 mm)
Lobe height minimum allowable	1.711 inches (43.45 mm)
Thrust clearance (endplay) limit	0.005 inch (0.12 mm)

Intake manifold

Surface warpage limit	0.008 inch (0.2 mm)

Exhaust manifold

Surface warpage limit	0.012 inch (0.3 mm)

Oil pump

Driven rotor-to-pump body clearance	0.004 to 0.007 inch (0.10 to 0.18 mm)
Rotor side clearance	0.0016 to 0.0037 inch (0.040 to 0.096 mm)
Rotor tip clearance	0.0024 to 0.0071 inch (0.06 to 0.18 mm)

Timing belt tensioner

Tensioner rod protrusion (installed)	0.27 to 0.31 inch (7 to 9 mm)

Torque specifications

	Ft-lbs (unless otherwise indicated)	Nm

➡Note: One foot-pound (ft-lb) of torque is equivalent to 12 inch-pounds (in-lbs) of torque. Torque values below approximately 15 ft-lbs are expressed in inch-pounds, since most foot-pound torque wrenches are not accurate at these smaller values.

Camshaft bearing cap bolts		
38 mm bolts	84 to 108 in-lbs	9.5 to 12
50 mm bolts	120 to 144 in-lbs	13.5 to 16
Camshaft sprocket bolts	65 to 80	88 to 108
Crankshaft pulley bolt	130 to 138	176 to 187
Cylinder head bolts (cold engine, in sequence - see illustration 10.22)		
Step 1	18	24
Step 2	Tighten an additional 60 degrees	
Step 3	Tighten an additional 45 degrees	

Drivebelt automatic tensioner bolt	25 to 40	34 to 54
Drivebelt idler pulley bolt	25 to 40	34 to 54

Torque specifications (continued)	Ft-lbs (unless otherwise indicated)	Nm

➡**Note: One foot-pound (ft-lb) of torque is equivalent to 12 inch-pounds (in-lbs) of torque. Torque values below approximately 15 ft-lbs are expressed in inch-pounds, since most foot-pound torque wrenches are not accurate at these smaller values.**

Drivebelt tensioner bolt	25 to 40	34 to 54
Driveplate/flywheel bolts	53 to 56	72 to 76
Exhaust manifold nuts	22 to 26	30 to 35
Idler pulley bolt	25 to 40	34 to 54
Intake manifold bolts/nuts		
Upper manifold	132 to 168 in-lbs	15 to 19
Lower manifold	14 to 15	19 to 20
Oil pan bolts		
Lower oil pan	84 to 108 in-lbs	9.5 to 12
Upper oil pan		
10 mm X 38 mm	22 to 30	30 to 40
8 mm X 22 mm	14 to 20	19 to 27
Long bolts	48 to 60 in-lbs	5.5 to 7
Oil pump case bolt	108 to 132 in-lbs	12 to 15
Oil pump cover screw	108 in-lbs	12
Oil relief valve plug	29 to 36	39 to 49
Oil pick-up tube mounting bolts	72 in-lbs	8
Timing belt idler pulley bolt	36 to 43	49 to 58
Timing belt tensioner bolts	14 to 20	19 to 27
Rear main oil seal retainer mounting bolts	84 to 96 in-lbs	9.5 to 11
Valve cover bolts	72 to 84 in-lbs	8 to 9.5

Section

1   General information - engine overhaul
2   Oil pressure check
3   Cylinder compression check
4   Vacuum gauge diagnostic checks
5   Engine rebuilding alternatives
6   Engine removal - methods and precautions
7   Engine - removal and installation
8   Engine overhaul - disassembly sequence
9   Pistons and connecting rods - removal and installation
10 Crankshaft - removal and installation
11 Engine overhaul - reassembly sequence
12 Initial start-up and break-in after overhaul

Reference to other Chapters

CHECK ENGINE light on - See Chapter 6

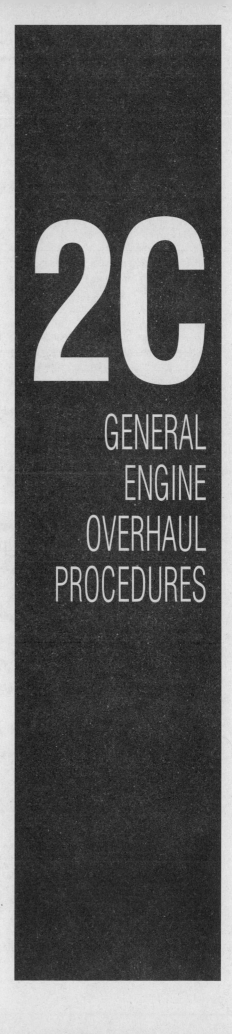

2C

GENERAL
ENGINE
OVERHAUL
PROCEDURES

1   General information - engine overhaul

◆ **Refer to illustrations 1.1, 1.2, 1.3, 1.4, 1.5 and 1.6**

Included in this portion of Chapter 2 are general information and diagnostic testing procedures for determining the overall mechanical condition of your engine.

The information ranges from advice concerning preparation for an overhaul and the purchase of replacement parts and/or components to detailed, step-by-step procedures covering removal and installation.

The following Sections have been written to help you determine whether your engine needs to be overhauled and how to remove and install it once you've determined it needs to be rebuilt. For information concerning in-vehicle engine repair, see Chapter 2A or 2B.

It's not always easy to determine when, or if, an engine should be completely overhauled, because a number of factors must be considered.

High mileage is not necessarily an indication that an overhaul is needed, while low mileage doesn't preclude the need for an overhaul. Frequency of servicing is probably the most important consideration. An engine that's had regular and frequent oil and filter changes, as well as other required maintenance, will most likely give many thousands of miles of reliable service. Conversely, a neglected engine may require an overhaul very early in its service life.

Excessive oil consumption is an indication that piston rings, valve seals and/or valve guides are in need of attention. Make sure that oil leaks aren't responsible before deciding that the rings and/or guides are bad. Perform a cylinder compression check to determine the extent of the work required (see Section 3). Also check the vacuum readings under various conditions (see Section 4).

Check the oil pressure with a gauge installed in place of the oil pressure sending unit and compare it to this Chapter's Specifications (see Section 2). If it's extremely low, the bearings and/or oil pump are probably worn out.

Loss of power, rough running, knocking or metallic engine noises, excessive valve train noise and high fuel consumption rates may also point to the need for an overhaul, especially if they're all present at the same time. If a complete tune-up doesn't remedy the situation, major mechanical work is the only solution.

An engine overhaul involves restoring the internal parts to the specifications of a new engine. During an overhaul, the piston rings are replaced and the cylinder walls are reconditioned (rebored and/or honed) (see illustrations 1.1 and 1.2). If a rebore is done by an automotive machine shop, new oversize pistons will also be installed. The main

1.1 An engine block being bored - an engine rebuilder will use special machinery to recondition the cylinder bores

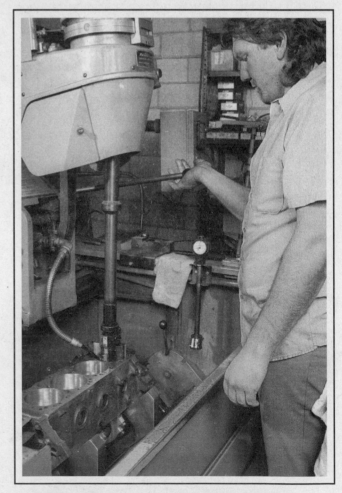

1.2 If the cylinders are bored, the machine shop will normally hone the engine on a machine like this

1.3 A crankshaft having a main bearing journal ground

1.4 A machinist checks for a bent connecting rod, using specialized equipment

1.5 A bore gauge being used to check the main bearing bore

1.6 Uneven piston wear like this indicates a bent connecting rod

bearings and connecting rod bearings are generally replaced with new ones and, if necessary, the crankshaft may be reground to restore the journals (see illustration 1.3). Generally, the valves are serviced as well, since they're usually in less-than-perfect condition at this point. While the engine is being overhauled, other components, such as the starter and alternator, can be rebuilt as well. The end result should be a like-new engine that will give many trouble-free miles.

➡**Note: Critical cooling system components such as the hoses, drivebelts, thermostat and water pump should be replaced with new parts when an engine is overhauled. The radiator should be checked carefully to ensure that it isn't clogged or leaking (see Chapter 3). If you purchase a rebuilt engine or short block, some rebuilders will not warranty their engines unless the radiator has been professionally flushed. Also, we don't recommend overhauling the oil pump - always install a new one when an engine is rebuilt.**

Overhauling the internal components on today's engines is a difficult and time-consuming task that requires a significant amount of specialty tools and is best left to a professional engine rebuilder (see illustrations 1.4, 1.5 and 1.6). A competent engine rebuilder will handle the inspection of your old parts and offer advice concerning the reconditioning or replacement of the original engine. Never purchase parts or have machine work done on other components until the block has been thoroughly inspected by a professional machine shop. As a general rule, time is the primary cost of an overhaul, especially since the vehicle may be tied up for a minimum of two weeks or more. Be aware that some engine builders only have the capability to rebuild the engine you bring them while other rebuilders have a large inventory of rebuilt exchange engines in stock. Also be aware that many machine shops could take as much as two weeks time to completely rebuild your engine depending on shop workload. Sometimes it makes more sense to simply exchange your engine for another engine that's already rebuilt to save time.

2   Oil pressure check

▶ **Refer to illustrations 2.2a, 2.2b, 2.2c and 2.2d**

1   Low engine oil pressure can be a sign of an engine in need of rebuilding. A "low oil pressure" indicator (often called an "idiot light") is not a test of the oiling system. Such indicators only come on when the oil pressure is dangerously low. Even a factory oil pressure gauge in the instrument panel is only a relative indication, although much better for driver information than a warning light. A better test is with a mechanical (not electrical) oil pressure gauge.

2   Locate the oil pressure sending unit on the engine block:
   a) On 1.6L SOHC, 1.6L DOHC B6 and 1.8L DOHC BP engines, the oil pressure sending unit is located next to the oil filter and behind the intake manifold bracket (see illustration).
   b) On 1.8L DOHC T8 engines, the oil pressure sending unit is located next to the oil filter behind the alternator on the rear of the engine block (see illustration).
   c) On 2.0L DOHC engines, the oil pressure sending unit is mounted on the front of the engine block (see illustration).
   d) On 2.7L V6 engines, the oil pressure sending unit is located below the air conditioning compressor, next to the oil filter (see illustration).

3   On 1.6L SOHC, 1.6L DOHC B6 and 1.8L DOHC BP engines, remove the intake manifold bracket (see Chapter 2A).

4   Unscrew and remove the oil pressure sending unit and screw in the hose for your oil pressure gauge. If necessary, install an adapter fitting. Use Teflon tape or thread sealant on the threads of the adapter and/ or the fitting on the end of your gauge's hose.

5   Connect an accurate tachometer to the engine, according to the tachometer manufacturer's instructions.

6   Check the oil pressure with the engine running (normal operating temperature) at the specified engine speed, and compare it to this Chapter's Specifications. If it's extremely low, the bearings and/or oil pump are probably worn out.

2.2a Location of the oil pressure sending unit on a 1.6L SOHC engine - the intake manifold support bracket is removed for access

2.2b Location of the oil pressure sending unit on a 1.8L DOHC T8 engine

2.2c Location of the oil pressure sending unit on a 2.0L DOHC engine

2.2d Location of the oil pressure sending unit on the V6 engine

3   Cylinder compression check

▶ **Refer to illustration 3.6**

1   A compression check will tell you what mechanical condition the upper end of your engine (pistons, rings, valves, head gaskets) is in. Specifically, it can tell you if the compression is down due to leakage caused by worn piston rings, defective valves and seats or a blown head gasket.

➡**Note: The engine must be at normal operating temperature and the battery must be fully charged for this check.**

2   Disable the ignition system by unplugging the primary electrical connector from the distributor (1994 through 1997 models) or the electrical connector(s) from the ignition coils (1998 and later models) (see Chapter 5). Also, disable the fuel system by disconnecting the fuel pump electrical connector (see Chapter 4).

3   Clean the area around the spark plugs before you remove them (compressed air should be used, if available). The idea is to prevent dirt from getting into the cylinders as the compression check is being done.

4   Remove all of the spark plugs from the engine (see Chapter 1).

5 Block the throttle wide open.

6 Install a compression gauge in the spark plug hole (see illustration).

7 Crank the engine over at least seven compression strokes and watch the gauge. The compression should build up quickly in a healthy engine. Low compression on the first stroke, followed by gradually increasing pressure on successive strokes, indicates worn piston rings. A low compression reading on the first stroke, which doesn't build up during successive strokes, indicates leaking valves or a blown head gasket (a cracked head could also be the cause). Deposits on the undersides of the valve heads can also cause low compression. Record the highest gauge reading obtained.

8 Repeat the procedure for the remaining cylinders and compare the results to this Chapter's Specifications.

9 Add some engine oil (about three squirts from a plunger-type oil can) to each cylinder, through the spark plug hole, and repeat the test.

10 If the compression increases after the oil is added, the piston rings are definitely worn. If the compression doesn't increase significantly, the leakage is occurring at the valves or head gasket. Leakage past the valves may be caused by burned valve seats and/or faces or warped, cracked or bent valves.

11 If two adjacent cylinders have equally low compression, there's a strong possibility that the head gasket between them is blown. The appearance of coolant in the combustion chambers or the crankcase would verify this condition.

12 If one cylinder is slightly lower than the others, and the engine has a slightly rough idle, a worn lobe on the camshaft could be the cause.

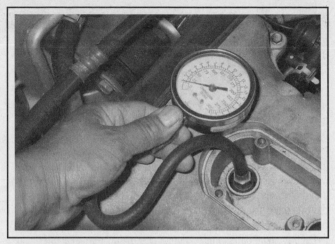

3.6 Use a compression gauge with a threaded fitting for the spark plug hole, not the type that requires hand pressure to maintain the seal

13 If the compression is unusually high, the combustion chambers are probably coated with carbon deposits. If that's the case, the cylinder head(s) should be removed and decarbonized.

14 If compression is way down or varies greatly between cylinders, it would be a good idea to have a leak-down test performed by an automotive repair shop. This test will pinpoint exactly where the leakage is occurring and how severe it is.

4 Vacuum gauge diagnostic checks

♦ **Refer to illustrations 4.4 and 4.6**

1 A vacuum gauge provides inexpensive but valuable information about what is going on in the engine. You can check for worn rings or cylinder walls, leaking head or intake manifold gaskets, restricted exhaust, stuck or burned valves, weak valve springs, improper ignition or valve timing and ignition problems.

2 Unfortunately, vacuum gauge readings are easy to misinterpret, so they should be used in conjunction with other tests to confirm the diagnosis.

3 Both the absolute readings and the rate of needle movement are important for accurate interpretation. Most gauges measure vacuum in inches of mercury (in-Hg). The following references to vacuum assume the diagnosis is being performed at sea level. As elevation increases (or atmospheric pressure decreases), the reading will decrease. For every 1,000-foot increase in elevation above approximately 2000 feet, the gauge readings will decrease about one inch of mercury.

4 Connect the vacuum gauge directly to the intake manifold vacuum, not to ported (throttle body) vacuum (see illustration). Be sure no hoses are left disconnected during the test or false readings will result.

5 Before you begin the test, allow the engine to warm up completely. Block the wheels and set the parking brake. With the transmission in Park, start the engine and allow it to run at normal idle speed.

4.4 A simple vacuum gauge can be handy in diagnosing engine condition and performance

6   Read the vacuum gauge; an average, healthy engine should normally produce about 17 to 22 in-Hg with a fairly steady needle (see illustration). Refer to the following vacuum gauge readings and what they indicate about the engine's condition:

7   A low steady reading usually indicates a leaking gasket between the intake manifold and cylinder head(s) or throttle body, a leaky vacuum hose, late ignition timing or incorrect camshaft timing. Check ignition timing with a timing light and eliminate all other possible causes, utilizing the tests provided in this Chapter before you remove the timing belt cover to check the timing marks.

8   If the reading is three to eight inches below normal and it fluctuates at that low reading, suspect an intake manifold gasket leak at an intake port or a faulty fuel injector.

9   If the needle has regular drops of about two-to-four inches at a steady rate, the valves are probably leaking. Perform a compression check or leak-down test to confirm this.

10   An irregular drop or down-flick of the needle can be caused by a sticking valve or an ignition misfire. Perform a compression check or leak-down test and read the spark plugs.

11   A rapid vibration of about four in-Hg variation at idle combined with exhaust smoke indicates worn valve guides. Perform a leak-down test to confirm this. If the rapid vibration occurs with an increase in engine speed, check for a leaking intake manifold gasket or head gasket, weak valve springs, burned valves or ignition misfire.

12   A slight fluctuation, say one inch up and down, may mean ignition problems. Check all the usual tune-up items and, if necessary, run the engine on an ignition analyzer.

13   If there is a large fluctuation, perform a compression or leak-down test to look for a weak or dead cylinder or a blown head gasket.

14   If the needle moves slowly through a wide range, check for a clogged PCV system, incorrect idle fuel mixture, throttle body or intake manifold gasket leaks.

15   Check for a slow return after revving the engine by quickly snapping the throttle open until the engine reaches about 2,500 rpm and let it shut. Normally the reading should drop to near zero, rise above normal idle reading (about 5 in-Hg over) and then return to the previous idle reading. If the vacuum returns slowly and doesn't peak when the throttle is snapped shut, the rings may be worn. If there is a long delay, look for a restricted exhaust system (often the muffler or catalytic converter). An easy way to check this is to temporarily disconnect the exhaust ahead of the suspected part and redo the test.

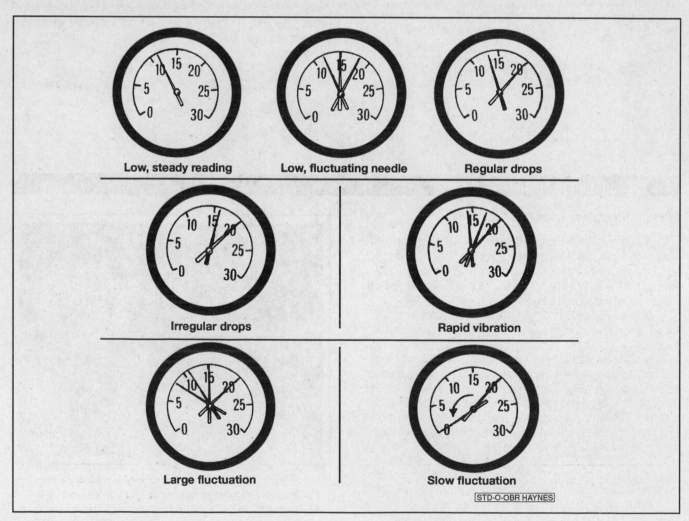

4.6 Typical vacuum gauge readings

5   Engine rebuilding alternatives

The do-it-yourselfer is faced with a number of options when purchasing a rebuilt engine. The major considerations are cost, warranty, parts availability and the time required for the rebuilder to complete the project. The decision to replace the engine block, piston/connecting rod assemblies and crankshaft depends on the final inspection results of your engine. Only then can you make a cost effective decision whether to have your engine overhauled or simply purchase an exchange engine for your vehicle.

Some of the rebuilding alternatives include:

Individual parts - If the inspection procedures reveal that the engine block and most engine components are in reusable condition, purchasing individual parts and having a rebuilder rebuild your engine may be the most economical alternative. The block, crankshaft and piston/connecting rod assemblies should all be inspected carefully by a machine shop first.

Short block - A short block consists of an engine block with a crankshaft and piston/connecting rod assemblies already installed. All new bearings are incorporated and all clearances will be correct. The existing camshafts, valve train components, cylinder head and external

parts can be bolted to the short block with little or no machine shop work necessary.

Long block - A long block consists of a short block plus an oil pump, oil pan, cylinder head, valve cover, camshaft and valve train components, timing sprockets and belt or gears and timing cover. All components are installed with new bearings, seals and gaskets incorporated throughout. The installation of manifolds and external parts is all that's necessary.

Low mileage used engines - Some companies now offer low mileage used engines that are a very cost effective way to get your vehicle up and running again. These engines often come from vehicles that have been in totaled in accidents or come from other countries that have a higher vehicle turn over rate. A low mileage used engine also usually has a similar warranty like the newly remanufactured engines.

Give careful thought to which alternative is best for you and discuss the situation with local automotive machine shops, auto parts dealers and experienced rebuilders before ordering or purchasing replacement parts.

6   Engine removal - methods and precautions

▶ **Refer to illustrations 6.1, 6.2, 6.3 and 6.4**

If you've decided that an engine must be removed for overhaul or major repair work, several preliminary steps should be taken. Read all removal and installation procedures carefully prior to committing to this job.

Locating a suitable place to work is extremely important. Adequate work space, along with storage space for the vehicle, will be needed. If a shop or garage isn't available, at the very least a flat, level, clean work surface made of concrete or asphalt is required.

Cleaning the engine compartment and engine before beginning the

removal procedure will help keep tools clean and organized (see illustrations 6.1 and 6.2).

An engine hoist will also be necessary. Make sure the hoist is rated in excess of the combined weight of the engine and transaxle. Safety is of primary importance, considering the potential hazards involved in removing the engine from the vehicle.

If you're a novice at engine removal, get at least one helper. One person cannot easily do all the things you need to do to remove a big heavy engine and transaxle assembly from the engine compartment. Also helpful is to seek advice and assistance from someone who's experienced in engine removal.

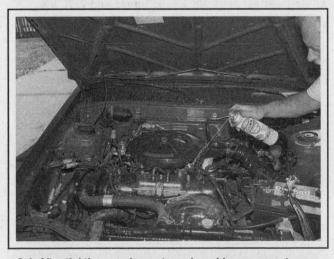

6.1 After tightly wrapping water-vulnerable components, use a spray cleaner on everything, with particular concentration on the greasiest areas, usually around the valve cover and lower edges of the block. If one section dries out, apply more cleaner

6.2 Depending on how dirty the engine is, let the cleaner soak in according to the directions and hose off the grime and cleaner. Get the rinse water down into every area you can get at; then dry important components with a hair dryer or paper towels

Plan the operation ahead of time. Arrange for or obtain all of the tools and equipment you'll need prior to beginning the job (see illustrations 6.3 and 6.4). Some of the equipment necessary to perform engine removal and installation safely and with relative ease are (in addition to a vehicle hoist) a heavy duty floor jack (preferably fitted with a transaxle jack head adapter), complete sets of wrenches and sockets as described in the front of this manual, wooden blocks, plenty of rags and cleaning solvent for mopping up spilled oil, coolant and gasoline.

Plan for the vehicle to be out of use for quite a while. A machine shop can do the work that is beyond the scope of the home mechanic. Machine shops often have a busy schedule, so before removing the engine, consult the shop for an estimate of how long it will take to rebuild or repair the components that may need work.

6.3 Get an engine stand sturdy enough to firmly support the engine while you're working on it. Stay away from three-wheeled models; they have a tendency to tip over more easily, so get a four-wheeled unit.

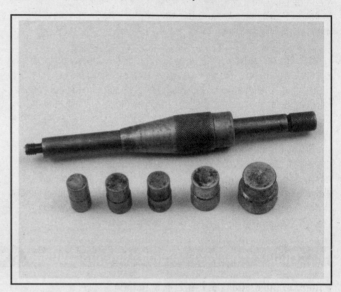

6.4 A clutch alignment tool is necessary if you plan to install a rebuilt engine mated to a manual transaxle

7 Engine - removal and installation

✻✻ WARNING 1:

Gasoline is extremely flammable, so take extra precautions when you work on any part of the fuel system. Don't smoke or allow open flames or bare light bulbs near the work area, and don't work in a garage where a gas-type appliance (such as a water heater or clothes dryer) is present. Since gasoline is carcinogenic, wear fuel-resistant gloves when there's a possibility of being exposed to fuel, and, if you spill any fuel on your skin, rinse it off immediately with soap and water. Mop up any spills immediately and do not store fuel-soaked rags where they could ignite. The fuel system is under constant pressure, so, if any fuel lines are to be disconnected, the fuel pressure in the system must be relieved first (see Chapter 4 for more information). When you perform any kind of work on the fuel system, wear safety glasses and have a Class B type fire extinguisher on hand.

✻✻ WARNING 2:

The engine must be completely cool before beginning this procedure.

➡**Note: Read through the entire sequence before beginning this procedure. The engine and transaxle must be removed as a unit, to be separated afterward on the garage floor.**

REMOVAL

All engines except 2.0L four-cylinder and 2.7L V6

▶ **Refer to illustrations 7.7 and 7.27**

1   Relieve the fuel system pressure (see Chapter 4).

2   Disconnect the cable from the negative battery terminal (see Chapter 5, Section 1). Next, disconnect the positive battery cable.

3   Place protective covers on the fenders and cowl and remove the hood (see Chapter 11).

4   Remove the battery and battery tray (see Chapter 5).

5   Remove the air filter housing (see Chapter 4).

6   Disconnect the throttle valve cable, if equipped (see Chapter 7B). Remove the accelerator cable and the cruise control actuator cable from the throttle body, if equipped (see Chapter 4).

7   Clearly label and disconnect all vacuum lines, coolant and emissions hoses, electrical connectors, ground straps and fuel lines (for fuel line removal see Chapter 4). Masking tape and/or a touch up paint applicator work well for marking items (see illustration). Take instant photos or sketch the locations of components and brackets, if necessary.

8   Remove the Data Link Connector (DLC) next to the Mass Airflow (MAF) sensor (if applicable) and position it off to the side.

9   If you're working on a model with an automatic transaxle, discon-

nect the shift cables from the transaxle (see Chapter 7B).

10 On automatic transaxle models, disconnect the transmission fluid cooler lines from their pipes at the transaxle. Plug the lines and hoses.

11 Remove the drivebelts (see Chapter 1).

12 Unbolt the power steering pump (see Chapter 10). Tie the pump aside without disconnecting the hoses.

13 Loosen the front wheel lug nuts. Raise the vehicle and support it securely on jackstands.

➡**Note: Don't raise the vehicle any higher than necessary to perform the following steps.**

14 Remove the engine splash shields (see Chapter 2A).

15 Drain the cooling system and engine oil (see Chapter 1).

16 Disconnect the heater hoses at the firewall (see Chapter 3).

17 Remove the engine cooling fan(s), shroud and radiator (see Chapter 3).

18 Drain the transaxle fluid (see Chapter 1).

19 Remove the starter (see Chapter 5).

20 On air-conditioned models, unbolt the compressor and set it aside (see Chapter 3).

✳✳ WARNING:

Do not disconnect the refrigerant hoses.

21 Unbolt the exhaust pipe from the exhaust manifold(s) (see Chapter 2A). Also detach the pipe bracket from the engine block.

22 Remove the driveaxles (see Chapter 8).

23 On manual transaxle models, remove the clutch release cylinder (see Chapter 8).

24 On manual transaxle models, detach the shift rod and extension bar from the transaxle (see Chapter 7A).

25 On automatic transaxle models, detach the torque converter cover from the lower bellhousing (see Chapter 7B). Mark the relationship of the torque converter to the driveplate.

26 On automatic transaxle models, remove the torque converter-to-driveplate fasteners (see Chapter 7B) and push the converter back slightly into the bellhousing.

27 Support the engine/transaxle assembly from above with a hoist. Attach the hoist chain to the lifting brackets (see illustration). If no lifting brackets or hooks are present, lifting hooks may be available from your local auto parts store or dealer parts department. If not, you will have to fasten the chains to some substantial parts of the engine - ones

that are strong enough to take the weight, but in locations that will provide good balance. If you're attaching a chain to a stud on the engine, or are using a bolt passing through the chain and into a threaded hole, place a washer between the nut or bolt head and the chain and tighten the nut or bolt securely. Raise the hoist slightly to take up the slack in the chain.

✳✳ WARNING:

Do not place any part of your body under the engine/transaxle when it's supported only by a hoist or other lifting device.

28 Recheck to be sure nothing except the mounts are still connecting the engine/transaxle to the vehicle. Disconnect anything still remaining on the engine and transaxle (see Chapter 7A).

29 Remove the front and rear engine/transaxle mounts (see Chapter 2A).

30 Remove the through-bolt from the right engine mount and the left transaxle mount (see Chapter 2A). Disconnect the ground strap from the transaxle.

31 Slowly raise the engine/transaxle assembly out of the vehicle. It may be necessary to tilt the engine up at the front (right side).

32 Move the engine/transaxle assembly away from the vehicle and carefully lower the hoist until the engine/transaxle assembly is on the floor, supported by wood blocks.

33 Remove the transaxle-to-engine mounting bolts and separate the engine from the transaxle. Remove the flywheel or driveplate and mount the engine on an engine stand.

2.0L four-cylinder and 2.7L V6 models

▸ **Refer to illustration 7.56**

✳✳ WARNING:

The engine must be removed from the underside of the engine compartment on 2.0L four-cylinder and 2.7L V6 models. First, you must remove the engine/transaxle/subframe assembly from below, then separate the engine and transaxle from the subframe. This procedure requires the use of a vehicle hoist; it's impossible, using only a floor jack and jackstands, to safely raise the vehicle high enough to slide the engine/transaxle/subframe assembly out from under the vehicle. Do not attempt to remove the engine without the necessary equipment.

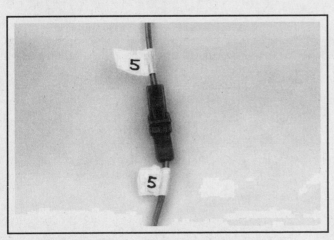

7.7 Label both ends of each wire and hose before disconnecting it

7.27 Attach the hoist chain to the engine lifting brackets

➡Note: Carefully read this entire Section before beginning this procedure.

34 Remove the hood (see Chapter 11).

35 Remove the engine cover.

36 Remove the fresh air inlet duct, the air filter housing and the air intake duct (see Chapter 4).

37 Disconnect and remove the battery (see Chapter 5). Remove the battery tray.

38 Drain the engine coolant (see Chapter 1).

39 Disconnect and remove the upper and lower radiator hoses (see Chapter 3).

40 Disconnect and remove the heater hoses.

41 Disconnect and set aside the accelerator and cruise control cables (see Chapter 4).

42 Disconnect all engine wiring harness connectors and ground cables and set the harnesses aside.

43 Disconnect and remove all EVAP, PCV and vacuum hoses (see Chapter 6). Disconnect and remove the power brake booster vacuum hose.

44 Disconnect and set aside the fuel supply hose (see Chapter 4).

45 Disconnect, plug and set aside the power steering hoses (see Chapter 10).

46 Disconnect all transaxle wiring harness connectors and ground cables and set the harnesses aside.

47 Disconnect the shift control cable from the transaxle (see Chapter 7A or 7B).

48 Loosen the front wheel lug nuts. Raise the vehicle on a vehicle hoist. Remove the front wheel lug nuts and remove the front wheels.

49 Remove the engine under cover/splash shield.

50 On vehicles with an automatic transaxle, disconnect and plug the transaxle oil cooler hoses (see Chapter 7B).

51 Remove the front exhaust pipe (see Chapter 2A or 2B). On 4WD models, remove the driveshaft (see Chapter 8).

52 Remove the driveaxles (see Chapter 8).

53 Under the dash, remove the cover over the steering column U-joint, remove the U-joint bolt and separate the steering shaft from the steering gear.

54 Lower the vehicle as far as possible so that it's low enough for an engine lift to clear the fender. Support the engine/transaxle assembly with an engine hoist.

55 Remove the left and right engine/transaxle mounting brackets (see Chapter 2A or 2B).

56 Remove the subframe mounting bolts (see illustration).

57 Raise the vehicle on the vehicle hoist just high enough to verify

7.56 Before removing the subframe fasteners, be sure to remove the front exhaust pipe (A) and, on 4WD models, the driveshaft (B) (2.7L V6 Sportage model shown)

that everything between the chassis and the engine/transaxle/subframe assembly is now disconnected.

58 Lower the engine/transaxle/subframe assembly to the ground. Make sure there is nothing still connected.

59 Disconnect the engine hoist from the engine/transaxle/subframe assembly, then raise the vehicle high enough to clear the engine/transaxle/subframe assembly. Reconnect the engine hoist, then detach the engine/transaxle assembly from the subframe.

60 Unbolt the transaxle from the engine.

INSTALLATION

61 Installation is the reverse of removal, noting the following points:

a) *Check the engine/transaxle mounts. If they're worn or damaged, replace them.*

b) *Attach the transaxle to the engine following the procedure described in Chapter 7.*

c) *Add coolant, oil, power steering and transaxle fluids as needed (see Chapter 1).*

d) *Reconnect the battery (see Chapter 5, Section 1).*

e) *Run the engine and check for proper operation and leaks. Shut off the engine and recheck fluid levels.*

8 Engine overhaul - disassembly sequence

1 It's much easier to remove the external components if the engine is mounted on a portable engine stand. A stand can often be rented quite cheaply from an equipment rental yard. Before the engine is mounted on a stand, the flywheel/driveplate should be removed from the engine.

2 If a stand isn't available, it's possible to remove the external engine components with it blocked up on the floor. Be extra careful not to tip or drop the engine when working without a stand.

3 If you're going to obtain a rebuilt engine, all external components must come off first, to be transferred to the replacement engine. These components include:

Clutch and flywheel (models with manual transaxle)
Driveplate (models with automatic transaxle)
Ignition system components
Emissions-related components
Engine mounts and mount brackets
Flywheel plate (spacer plate between flywheel/driveplate and engine block)
Intake/exhaust manifolds
Fuel injection components
Oil filter
Ignition coils and spark plugs
Thermostat and housing assembly
Water pump

➡Note: When removing the external components from the engine, pay close attention to details that may be helpful or important during installation. Note the installed position of gaskets, seals, spacers, pins, brackets, washers, bolts and other small items.

4   If you're going to obtain a short block (assembled engine block,

crankshaft, pistons and connecting rods), then remove the timing chain or belt, cylinder head(s), oil pan, oil pump pick-up tube, oil pump and water pump from your engine so that you can turn in your old short block to the rebuilder as a core. See *Engine rebuilding alternatives* for additional information regarding the different possibilities to be considered.

---

9   Pistons and connecting rods - removal and installation

REMOVAL

▸ **Refer to illustrations 9.1, 9.3 and 9.4**

➡Note: Prior to removing the piston/connecting rod assemblies, remove the cylinder head(s)and oil pan (see Chapter 2A or 2B).

1   Use your fingernail to feel if a ridge has formed at the upper limit of ring travel (about 1/4-inch down from the top of each cylinder). If carbon deposits or cylinder wear have produced ridges, they must be completely removed with a special tool (see illustration). Follow the manufacturer's instructions provided with the tool. Failure to remove the ridges before attempting to remove the piston/connecting rod assemblies may result in piston breakage.

2   After the cylinder ridges have been removed, turn the engine so the crankshaft is facing up.

3   Before the connecting rods are removed, check the connecting rod endplay with feeler gauges. Slide them between the first connecting rod and the crankshaft throw until the play is removed (see illustration). Repeat this procedure for each connecting rod. The endplay is equal to

the thickness of the feeler gauge(s). Check with an automotive machine shop for the endplay service limit (a typical endplay limit should measure between 0.005 to 0.015 inch [0.127 to 0.369 mm]). If the play exceeds the service limit, new connecting rods will be required. If new rods (or a new crankshaft) are installed, the endplay may fall under the minimum allowable. If it does, the rods will have to be machined to restore it. If necessary, consult an automotive machine shop for advice.

4   Check the connecting rods and caps for identification marks. If they aren't plainly marked, use paint or marker to clearly identify each rod and cap (1, 2, 3, etc., depending on the cylinder they're associated with) (see illustration).

5   Remove the connecting rod cap nuts or bolts from the number one connecting rod.

✳✳ CAUTION:

On models that use connecting rod bolts, obtain new bolts (the old ones have stretched and can't be re-used). Save the old bolts for the oil clearance checking procedure.

9.1 Before you try to remove the pistons, use a ridge reamer to remove the raised material (ridge) from the top of the cylinders

9.3 Checking the connecting rod endplay (side clearance)

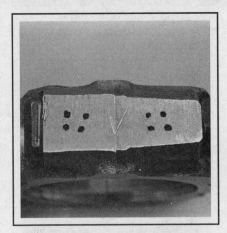

9.4 If the connecting rods and caps are not marked, mark the caps to the rods by cylinder number (for example, this would be the No. 4 connecting rod)

6   Remove the number one connecting rod cap and bearing insert. Don't drop the bearing insert out of the cap.

7   Remove the bearing insert and push the connecting rod/piston assembly out through the top of the engine. Use a wooden dowel to push on the connecting rod. If resistance is felt, double-check to make sure that all of the ridge was removed from the cylinder.

8   Repeat the procedure for the remaining cylinders.

9   After removal, reassemble the connecting rod caps and bearing inserts in their respective connecting rods and install the cap nuts finger tight. Leaving the old bearing inserts in place until reassembly will help prevent the connecting rod bearing surfaces from being accidentally nicked or gouged.

10   The pistons and connecting rods are now ready for inspection and overhaul at an automotive machine shop.

PISTON RING INSTALLATION

♦ **Refer to illustrations 9.13, 9.14, 9.15, 9.19a, 9.19b and 9.22**

11   Before installing the new piston rings, the ring end gaps must be checked. It's assumed that the piston ring side clearance has been checked and verified correct.

12   Lay out the piston/connecting rod assemblies and the new ring sets so the ring sets will be matched with the same piston and cylinder during the end gap measurement and engine assembly.

13   Insert the top (number one) ring into the first cylinder and square it up with the cylinder walls by pushing it in with the top of the piston (see illustration). The ring should be near the bottom of the cylinder, at the lower limit of ring travel.

14   To measure the end gap, slip feeler gauges between the ends of the ring until a gauge equal to the gap width is found (see illustration). The feeler gauge should slide between the ring ends with a slight amount of drag. A typical ring gap should fall between 0.010 and 0.020 inch [0.25 to 0.50 mm] for compression rings and up to 0.030 inch [0.76 mm] for the oil ring steel rails. If the gap is larger or smaller than specified, double-check to make sure you have the correct rings before proceeding.

15   If the gap is too small, it must be enlarged or the ring ends may come in contact with each other during engine operation, which can cause serious damage to the engine. If necessary, increase the end gaps by filing the ring ends very carefully with a fine file. Mount the file in a vise equipped with soft jaws, slip the ring over the file with the ends contacting the file face and slowly move the ring to remove material from the ends. When performing this operation, file only by pushing the ring from the outside end of the file towards the vise (see illustration).

16   Excess end gap isn't critical unless it's greater than 0.040 inch (1.01 mm). Again, double-check to make sure you have the correct ring type.

17   Repeat the procedure for each ring that will be installed in the first cylinder and for each ring in the remaining cylinders. Remember to keep rings, pistons and cylinders matched up.

18   Once the ring end gaps have been checked/corrected, the rings can be installed on the pistons.

19   The oil control ring (lowest one on the piston) is usually installed first. It's composed of three separate components. Slip the spacer/expander into the groove (see illustration). If an anti-rotation tang is used, make sure it's inserted into the drilled hole in the ring groove. Next, install the upper side rail in the same manner (see illustration). Don't use a piston ring installation tool on the oil ring side rails, as they may be damaged. Instead, place one end of the side rail into the groove between the spacer/expander and the ring land, hold it firmly in place and slide a finger around the piston while pushing the rail into the groove. Finally, install the lower side rail.

20   After the three oil ring components have been installed, check to make sure that both the upper and lower side rails can be rotated smoothly inside the ring grooves.

21   The number two (middle) ring is installed next. It's usually stamped with a mark which must face up, toward the top of the piston. Do not mix up the top and middle rings, as they have different cross-sections.

➡ **Note: Always follow the instructions printed on the ring package or box - different manufacturers may require different approaches.**

22   Use a piston ring installation tool and make sure the identification mark is facing the top of the piston, then slip the ring into the middle groove on the piston (see illustration). Don't expand the ring any more than necessary to slide it over the piston.

23   Install the number one (top) ring in the same manner. Make sure the mark is facing up. Be careful not to confuse the number one and number two rings.

24   Repeat the procedure for the remaining pistons and rings.

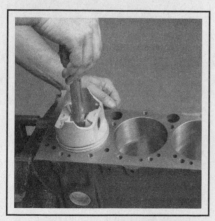

9.13   Install the piston ring into the cylinder then push it down into position using a piston so the ring will be square in the cylinder

9.14   With the ring square in the cylinder, measure the ring end gap with a feeler gauge

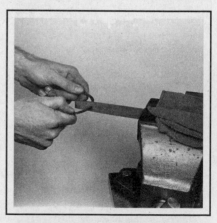

9.15   If the ring end gap is too small, clamp a file in a vise as shown and file the piston ring ends - be sure to remove all raised material

9.19a Installing the spacer/expander in the oil ring groove

9.19b DO NOT use a piston ring installation tool when installing the oil control side rails

9.22 Use a piston ring installation tool to install the number 2 and the number 1 (top) rings - be sure the directional mark on the piston ring(s) is facing toward the top of the piston

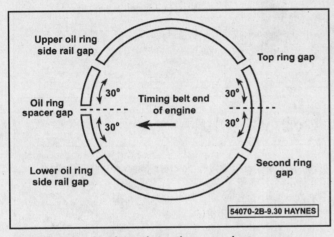

9.30 Position the piston ring end gaps as shown

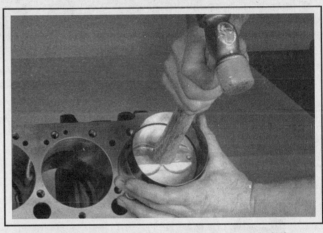

9.35 Use a plastic or wooden hammer handle to push the piston into the cylinder

INSTALLATION

25 Before installing the piston/connecting rod assemblies, the cylinder walls must be perfectly clean, the top edge of each cylinder bore must be chamfered, and the crankshaft must be in place.

26 Remove the cap from the end of the number one connecting rod (refer to the marks made during removal). Remove the original bearing inserts and wipe the bearing surfaces of the connecting rod and cap with a clean, lint-free cloth. They must be kept spotlessly clean.

Connecting rod bearing oil clearance check

▸ **Refer to illustrations 9.30, 9.35, 9.37 and 9.41**

27 Clean the back side of the new upper bearing insert, then lay it in place in the connecting rod.

28 Make sure the tab on the bearing fits into the recess in the rod. Don't hammer the bearing insert into place and be very careful not to nick or gouge the bearing face. Don't lubricate the bearing at this time.

29 Clean the back side of the other bearing insert and install it in the rod cap. Again, make sure the tab on the bearing fits into the recess in the cap, and don't apply any lubricant. It's critically important that the mating surfaces of the bearing and connecting rod are perfectly clean and oil free when they're assembled.

30 Position the piston ring gaps at the specified intervals around the piston as shown (see illustration).

31 Lubricate the piston and rings with clean engine oil and attach a piston ring compressor to the piston. Leave the skirt protruding about 1/4-inch to guide the piston into the cylinder. The rings must be compressed until they're flush with the piston.

32 Rotate the crankshaft until the number one connecting rod journal is at BDC (bottom dead center) and apply a liberal coat of engine oil to the cylinder walls.

33 With the arrow on top of the piston facing the front (timing belt end) of the engine, gently insert the piston/connecting rod assembly into the number one cylinder bore and rest the bottom edge of the ring compressor on the engine block. Install the pistons with the cavity mark(s) or arrow facing toward the timing belt end of the engine.

34 Tap the top edge of the ring compressor to make sure it's contacting the block around its entire circumference.

35 Gently tap on the top of the piston with the end of a wooden or plastic hammer handle (see illustration) while guiding the end of the connecting rod into place on the crankshaft journal (a pair of wooden dowels would be helpful for this). The piston rings may try to pop out of the ring compressor just before entering the cylinder bore, so keep some downward pressure on the ring compressor. Work slowly, and if any resistance is felt as the piston enters the cylinder, stop immediately.

ENGINE BEARING ANALYSIS

Debris

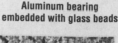

Babbitt bearing embedded with debris from machinings

Microscopic detail of debris

Microscopic detail of gouges

Overplated copper alloy bearing gouged by cast iron debris

Aluminum bearing embedded with glass beads

Microscopic detail of glass beads

Damaged lining caused by dirt left on the bearing back

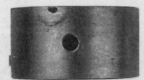

Misassembly

Result of a lower half assembled as an upper - blocking the oil flow

Excessive oil clearance is indicated by a short contact arc

Polished and oil-stained backs are a result of a poor fit in the housing bore

Result of a wrong, reversed, or shifted cap

Overloading

Damage from excessive idling which resulted in an oil film unable to support the load imposed

Damaged upper connecting rod bearings caused by engine lugging; the lower main bearings (not shown) were similarly affected

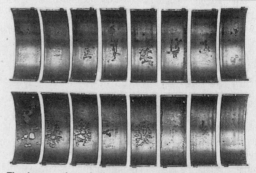

The damage shown in these upper and lower connecting rod bearings was caused by engine operation at a higher-than-rated speed under load

Misalignment

A warped crankshaft caused this pattern of severe wear in the center, diminishing toward the ends

A poorly finished crankshaft caused the equally spaced scoring shown

A tapered housing bore caused the damage along one edge of this pair

A bent connecting rod led to the damage in the "V" pattern

Corrosion

Microscopic detail of corrosion

Corrosion is an acid attack on the bearing lining generally caused by inadequate maintenance, extremely hot or cold operation, or inferior oils or fuels

Lubrication

Result of dry start: The bearings on the left, farthest from the oil pump, show more damage

Microscopic detail of cavitation

Example of cavitation - a surface erosion caused by pressure changes in the oil film

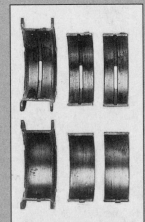

Result of a low oil supply or oil starvation

Severe wear as a result of inadequate oil clearance

Damage from excessive thrust or insufficient axial clearance

Bearing affected by oil dilution caused by excessive blow-by or a rich mixture

Find out what's hanging up and fix it before proceeding. Do not, for any reason, force the piston into the cylinder - you might break a ring and/or the piston.

36 Once the piston/connecting rod assembly is installed, the connecting rod bearing oil clearance must be checked before the rod cap is permanently installed.

37 Cut a piece of the appropriate size Plastigage slightly shorter than the width of the connecting rod bearing and lay it in place on the number one connecting rod journal, parallel with the journal axis (see illustration).

38 Clean the connecting rod cap bearing face and install the rod cap. Make sure the mating mark on the cap is on the same side as the mark on the connecting rod (see illustration 9.4).

39 Install the rod cap nuts or bolts, and tighten them to the torque listed in this Chapter's Specifications.

➡ Note: Use a thin-wall socket to avoid erroneous torque readings that can result if the socket is wedged between the rod cap and the nut. If the socket tends to wedge itself between the fastener and the cap, lift up on it slightly until it no longer contacts the cap. DO NOT rotate the crankshaft at any time during this operation.

➡ Note: On models that use connecting rod bolts, use the old bolts for this check (save the new bolts for final installation).

40 Remove the fasteners and detach the rod cap, being very careful not to disturb the Plastigage.

41 Compare the width of the crushed Plastigage to the scale printed on the Plastigage envelope to obtain the oil clearance (see illustration). The connecting rod oil clearance is usually about 0.001 to 0.002 inch (0.025 to 0.05 mm). Consult an automotive machine shop for the clearance specified for the rod bearings on your engine.

42 If the clearance is not as specified, the bearing inserts may be the wrong size (which means different ones will be required). Before deciding that different inserts are needed, make sure that no dirt or oil was between the bearing inserts and the connecting rod or cap when the clearance was measured. Also, recheck the journal diameter. If the Plastigage was wider at one end than the other, the journal may be tapered. If the clearance still exceeds the limit specified, the bearing will have to be replaced with an undersize bearing.

✳✳ CAUTION:

When installing a new crankshaft always use a standard size bearing.

Final installation

43 Carefully scrape all traces of the Plastigage material off the rod journal and/or bearing face. Be very careful not to scratch the bearing - use your fingernail or the edge of a plastic card.

44 Make sure the bearing faces are perfectly clean, then apply a uniform layer of clean moly-base grease or engine assembly lube to both of them. You'll have to push the piston into the cylinder to expose the face of the bearing insert in the connecting rod.

45 Slide the connecting rod back into place on the journal, install the rod cap, install the nuts and tighten them to the torque listed in this Chapter's Specifications.

46 Repeat the entire procedure for the remaining pistons/connecting rods.

47 The important points to remember are:

a) Keep the back sides of the bearing inserts and the insides of the connecting rods and caps perfectly clean when assembling them.
b) Make sure you have the correct piston/rod assembly for each cylinder.
c) The arrow or mark on the piston must face the front (timing belt) of the engine.
d) Lubricate the cylinder walls liberally with clean oil.
e) Lubricate the bearing faces when installing the rod caps after the oil clearance has been checked.

48 After all the piston/connecting rod assemblies have been correctly installed, rotate the crankshaft a number of times by hand to check for any obvious binding.

49 As a final step, check the connecting rod endplay, as described in Step 3. If it was correct before disassembly and the original crankshaft and rods were reinstalled, it should still be correct. If new rods or a new crankshaft were installed, the endplay may be inadequate. If so, the rods will have to be removed and taken to an automotive machine shop for resizing.

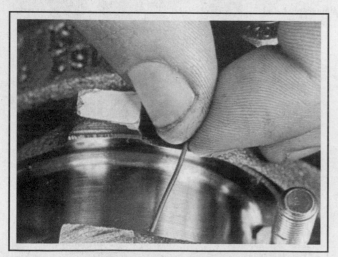

9.37 Place Plastigage on each connecting rod bearing journal parallel to the crankshaft centerline

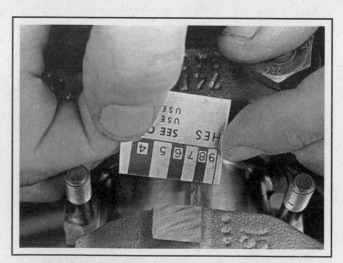

9.41 Use the scale on the Plastigage package to determine the bearing oil clearance - be sure to measure the widest part of the Plastigage and use the correct scale; it comes with both standard and metric scales

10 Crankshaft - removal and installation

REMOVAL

◆ **Refer to illustrations 10.1 and 10.3**

➡**Note: The crankshaft can be removed only after the engine has been removed from the vehicle. It's assumed that the flywheel or driveplate, crankshaft pulley, timing belt or timing chain, oil pan, oil pump body, oil filter and piston/connecting rod assemblies have already been removed. The rear main oil seal retainer must be unbolted and separated from the block before proceeding with crankshaft removal.**

1 Before the crankshaft is removed, measure the endplay. Mount a dial indicator with the indicator in line with the crankshaft and touching the end of the crankshaft as shown (see illustration).

2 Pry the crankshaft all the way to the rear and zero the dial indicator. Next, pry the crankshaft to the front as far as possible and check the reading on the dial indicator. The distance traveled is the endplay. A typical crankshaft endplay will fall between 0.003 to 0.010 inch (0.076 to 0.254 mm). If it is greater than that, check the crankshaft thrust surfaces for wear after it's removed. If no wear is evident, new main bearings should correct the endplay.

3 If a dial indicator isn't available, feeler gauges can be used. Gently pry the crankshaft all the way to the front of the engine. Slip feeler gauges between the crankshaft and the front face of the thrust bearing or washer to determine the clearance (see illustration).

4 Loosen the main bearing cap bolts 1/4-turn at a time each, until they can be removed by hand. Follow the reverse of the tightening sequence (see illustration 10.19a or 10.19b).

> ❉❉ **CAUTION:**
>
> **On models that use main bearing cap bolts, obtain new bolts (the old ones have stretched and can't be re-used). Save the old bolts for the oil clearance checking procedure.**

5 Remove the main bearing caps from the engine block.

6 Carefully lift the crankshaft out of the engine. It may be a good idea to have an assistant available, since the crankshaft is quite heavy and awkward to handle.

INSTALLATION

7 Crankshaft installation is the first step in engine reassembly. It's assumed at this point that the engine block and crankshaft have been cleaned, inspected and repaired or reconditioned.

8 Position the engine block with the bottom facing up.

9 Remove the original bearing inserts from the main bearing caps.

10 If they're still in place, remove the original bearing inserts from the block. Wipe the bearing surfaces of the block and main bearing caps with a clean, lint-free cloth. They must be kept spotlessly clean. This is critical for determining the correct bearing oil clearance.

Main bearing oil clearance check

◆ **Refer to illustrations 10.17, 10.19a, 10.19b and 10.21**

11 Without mixing them up, clean the back sides of the new upper main bearing inserts (with grooves and oil holes) and lay one in each main bearing saddle in the engine block. Each upper bearing (engine block) has an oil groove and oil hole in it.

> ❉❉ **CAUTION:**
>
> **The oil holes in the block must line up with the oil holes in the engine block inserts. The thrust washers must be installed in the correct location.**

➡**Note: The thrust washers on the 1.6L SOHC are located on the 4th journal in the engine block (counting from the front). The thrust washers on the 1.6L DOHC B6, the 1.8L DOHC BP and the 1.8L T8 DOHC engines are located on the 3rd journal in the engine block.**

Clean the back sides of the lower main bearing inserts and lay them in the corresponding location in the main bearing caps. Make sure the tab on the bearing insert fits into the recess in the block.

> ❉❉ **CAUTION:**
>
> **Do not hammer the bearing insert into place and don't nick or gouge the bearing faces. DO NOT apply any lubrication at this time.**

12 Clean the faces of the bearing inserts in the block and the crankshaft main bearing journals with a clean, lint-free cloth.

10.1 Checking crankshaft endplay with a dial indicator

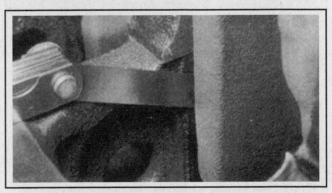

10.3 Checking the crankshaft endplay with feeler gauges at the thrust bearing journal

13 Check or clean the oil holes in the crankshaft, as any dirt here can go only one way - straight through the new bearings.

14 Once you're certain the crankshaft is clean, carefully lay it in position in the cylinder block.

15 Before the crankshaft can be permanently installed, the main bearing oil clearance must be checked.

16 Cut several strips of the appropriate size of Plastigage. They must be slightly shorter than the width of the main bearing journal.

17 Place one piece on each crankshaft main bearing journal, parallel with the journal axis as shown (see illustration).

18 Clean the faces of the bearing inserts in the engine block and main bearing caps. Hold the bearing inserts in place and install the main bearing caps onto the crankshaft and cylinder block. DO NOT disturb the Plastigage.

19 Apply clean engine oil to all bolt threads prior to installation, then install all bolts finger-tight.

➡Note: Use the old bolts for this check (save the new bolts for final installation). Tighten the main bearing cap bolts in the sequence shown (see illustrations) progressing in steps, to the torque listed in this Chapter's Specifications. DO NOT rotate the crankshaft at any time during this operation.

20 Remove the bolts in the reverse order of the tightening sequence and carefully lift the main bearing bridge straight up and off the block. Do not disturb the Plastigage or rotate the crankshaft.

21 Compare the width of the crushed Plastigage on each journal to the scale printed on the Plastigage envelope to determine the main bearing oil clearance (see illustration). Check with an automotive machine shop for the oil clearance for your engine.

22 If the clearance is not as specified, the bearing inserts may be the wrong size (which means different ones will be required). Before deciding if different inserts are needed, make sure that no dirt or oil was between the bearing inserts and the caps or block when the clearance was measured. If the Plastigage was wider at one end than the other, the crankshaft journal may be tapered. If the clearance still exceeds the limit specified, the bearing insert(s) will have to be replaced with an undersize bearing insert(s).

✳✳ CAUTION:

When installing a new crankshaft always install a standard bearing insert set.

10.17 Place the Plastigage onto the crankshaft bearing journal as shown

10.19a Main bearing cap bolt tightening sequence - four-cylinder engines

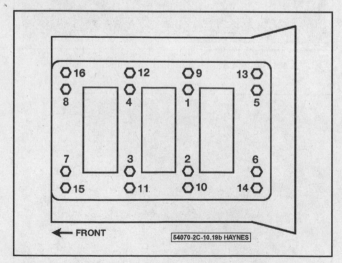

10.19b Main bearing cap bolt tightening sequence - V6 engines

10.21 Use the scale on the Plastigage package to determine the bearing oil clearance - be sure to measure the widest part of the Plastigage and use the correct scale; it comes with both standard and metric scales

23 Carefully scrape all traces of the Plastigage material off the main bearing journals and/or the bearing insert faces. Be sure to remove all residue from the oil holes. Use your fingernail or the edge of a plastic card - don't nick or scratch the bearing faces.

Final installation

24 Carefully lift the crankshaft out of the cylinder block.

25 Clean the bearing insert faces in the cylinder block, then apply a thin, uniform layer of moly-base grease or engine assembly lube to each of the bearing surfaces. Be sure to coat the thrust faces as well as the journal face of the thrust bearing.

26 Make sure the crankshaft journals are clean, then lay the crankshaft back in place in the cylinder block.

27 Clean the bearing insert faces and apply the same lubricant to them. Clean the engine block and the mating surface of the bearing caps thoroughly. The surfaces must be free of oil residue.

28 Prior to installation, apply clean engine oil to the NEW bolt threads, wiping off any excess, then install all bolts finger-tight.

29 Tighten the bolts to the torque listed in this Chapter's Specifications following the correct torque sequence (see illustration 10.19a or 10.19b).

30 Recheck the crankshaft endplay with a feeler gauge or a dial indicator. The endplay should be correct if the crankshaft thrust faces aren't worn or damaged and if new bearings have been installed.

31 Rotate the crankshaft a number of times by hand to check for any obvious binding. It should rotate with a running torque of 50 in-lbs or less. If the running torque is too high, correct the problem at this time.

32 Install the new rear main oil seal (see Chapter 2A or 2B).

11 Engine overhaul - reassembly sequence

1 Before beginning engine reassembly, make sure you have all the necessary new parts, gaskets and seals as well as the following items on hand:

   Common hand tools
   A 1/2-inch drive torque wrench
   New engine oil
   Gasket sealant
   Thread locking compound

2 If you obtained a short block it will be necessary to install the cylinder heads, the oil pump and pick-up tube, the oil pan, the water pump, the timing belt and timing cover, and the valve covers (see Chapter 2A or 2B). In order to save time and avoid problems, the external components must be installed in the following general order:

   Thermostat and housing cover
   Water pump
   Intake and exhaust manifolds
   Fuel injection components
   Emission control components
   Spark plug wires and spark plugs
   Ignition distributor or coils
   Oil filter
   Engine mounts and mount brackets
   Clutch and flywheel (manual transaxle)
   Driveplate (automatic transaxle)

12 Initial start-up and break-in after overhaul

✱✱ WARNING:

Have a fire extinguisher handy when starting the engine for the first time.

1 Once the engine has been installed in the vehicle, double-check the engine oil and coolant levels.

2 With the spark plugs out of the engine and the ignition system and fuel pump disabled, crank the engine until oil pressure registers on the gauge or the light goes out.

3 Install the spark plugs, hook up the plug wires and restore the ignition system and fuel pump functions.

4 Start the engine. It may take a few moments for the fuel system to build up pressure, but the engine should start without a great deal of effort.

5 After the engine starts, it should be allowed to warm up to normal operating temperature. While the engine is warming up, make a thorough check for fuel, oil and coolant leaks.

6 Shut the engine off and recheck the engine oil and coolant levels.

7 Drive the vehicle to an area with minimum traffic, accelerate from 30 to 50 mph, then allow the vehicle to slow to 30 mph with the throttle closed. Repeat the procedure 10 or 12 times. This will load the piston rings and cause them to seat properly against the cylinder walls. Check again for oil and coolant leaks.

8 Drive the vehicle gently for the first 500 miles (no sustained high speeds) and keep a constant check on the oil level. It is not unusual for an engine to use oil during the break-in period.

9 At approximately 500 to 600 miles, change the oil and filter.

10 For the next few hundred miles, drive the vehicle normally. Do not pamper it or abuse it.

11 After 2,000 miles, change the oil and filter again and consider the engine broken in.

GLOSSARY

B

Backlash - The amount of play between two parts. Usually refers to how much one gear can be moved back and forth without moving the gear with which it's meshed.

Bearing Caps - The caps held in place by nuts or bolts which, in turn, hold the bearing surface. This space is for lubricating oil to enter.

Bearing clearance - The amount of space left between shaft and bearing surface. This space is for lubricating oil to enter.

Bearing crush - The additional height which is purposely manufactured into each bearing half to ensure complete contact of the bearing back with the housing bore when the engine is assembled.

Bearing knock - The noise created by movement of a part in a loose or worn bearing.

Blueprinting - Dismantling an engine and reassembling it to EXACT specifications.

Bore - An engine cylinder, or any cylindrical hole; also used to describe the process of enlarging or accurately refinishing a hole with a cutting tool, as to bore an engine cylinder. The bore size is the diameter of the hole.

Boring - Renewing the cylinders by cutting them out to a specified size. A boring bar is used to make the cut.

Bottom end - A term which refers collectively to the engine block, crankshaft, main bearings and the big ends of the connecting rods.

Break-in - The period of operation between installation of new or rebuilt parts and time in which parts are worn to the correct fit. Driving at reduced and varying speed for a specified mileage to permit parts to wear to the correct fit.

Bushing - A one-piece sleeve placed in a bore to serve as a bearing surface for shaft, piston pin, etc. Usually replaceable.

C

Camshaft - The shaft in the engine, on which a series of lobes are located for operating the valve mechanisms. The camshaft is driven by gears or sprockets and a timing chain. Usually referred to simply as the cam.

Carbon - Hard, or soft, black deposits found in combustion chamber, on plugs, under rings, on and under valve heads.

Cast iron - An alloy of iron and more than two percent carbon, used for engine blocks and heads because it's relatively inexpensive and easy to mold into complex shapes.

Chamfer - To bevel across (or a bevel on) the sharp edge of an object.

Chase - To repair damaged threads with a tap or die.

Combustion chamber - The space between the piston and the cylinder head, with the piston at top dead center, in which air-fuel mixture is burned.

Compression ratio - The relationship between cylinder volume (clearance volume) when the piston is at top dead center and cylinder volume when the piston is at bottom dead center.

Connecting rod - The rod that connects the crank on the crankshaft with the piston. Sometimes called a con rod.

Connecting rod cap - The part of the connecting rod assembly that attaches the rod to the crankpin.

Core plug - Soft metal plug used to plug the casting holes for the coolant passages in the block.

Crankcase - The lower part of the engine in which the crankshaft rotates; includes the lower section of the cylinder block and the oil pan.

Crank kit - A reground or reconditioned crankshaft and new main and connecting rod bearings.

Crankpin - The part of a crankshaft to which a connecting rod is attached.

Crankshaft - The main rotating member, or shaft, running the length of the crankcase, with offset throws to which the connecting rods are attached; changes the reciprocating motion of the pistons into rotating motion.

Cylinder sleeve - A replaceable sleeve, or liner, pressed into the cylinder block to form the cylinder bore.

D

Deburring - Removing the burrs (rough edges or areas) from a bearing.

Deglazer - A tool, rotated by an electric motor, used to remove glaze from cylinder walls so a new set of rings will seat.

E

Endplay - The amount of lengthwise movement between two parts. As applied to a crankshaft, the distance that the crankshaft can move forward and back in the cylinder block.

F

Face - A machinist's term that refers to removing metal from the end of a shaft or the face of a larger part, such as a flywheel.

Fatigue - A breakdown of material through a large number of loading and unloading cycles. The first signs are cracks followed shortly by breaks.

Feeler gauge - A thin strip of hardened steel, ground to an exact thickness, used to check clearances between parts.

Free height - The unloaded length or height of a spring.

Freeplay - The looseness in a linkage, or an assembly of parts, between the initial application of force and actual movement. Usually perceived as slop or slight delay.

Freeze plug - See Core plug.

G

Gallery - A large passage in the block that forms a reservoir for engine oil pressure.

Glaze - The very smooth, glassy finish that develops on cylinder walls while an engine is in service.

H

Heli-Coil - A rethreading device used when threads are worn or damaged. The device is installed in a retapped hole to reduce the thread size to the original size.

I

Installed height - The spring's measured length or height, as installed on the cylinder head. Installed height is measured from the spring seat to the underside of the spring retainer.

J

Journal - The surface of a rotating shaft which turns in a bearing.

K

Keeper - The split lock that holds the valve spring retainer in position on the valve stem.

Key - A small piece of metal inserted into matching grooves machined into two parts fitted together - such as a gear pressed onto a shaft - which prevents slippage between the two parts.

Knock - The heavy metallic engine sound, produced in the combustion chamber as a result of abnormal combustion - usually detonation. Knock is usually caused by a loose or worn bearing. Also referred to as detonation, pinging and spark knock. Connecting rod or main bearing knocks are created by too much oil clearance or insufficient lubrication.

L

Lands - The portions of metal between the piston ring grooves.

Lapping the valves - Grinding a valve face and its seat together with lapping compound.

Lash - The amount of free motion in a gear train, between gears, or in a mechanical assembly, that occurs before movement can begin. Usually refers to the lash in a valve train.

Lifter - The part that rides against the cam to transfer motion to the rest of the valve train.

M

Machining - The process of using a machine to remove metal from a metal part.

Main bearings - The plain, or babbitt, bearings that support the crankshaft.

Main bearing caps - The cast iron caps, bolted to the bottom of the block, that support the main bearings.

O

O.D. - Outside diameter.

Oil gallery - A pipe or drilled passageway in the engine used to carry engine oil from one area to another.

Oil ring - The lower ring, or rings, of a piston; designed to prevent excessive amounts of oil from working up the cylinder walls and into the combustion chamber. Also called an oil-control ring.

Oil seal - A seal which keeps oil from leaking out of a compartment. Usually refers to a dynamic seal around a rotating shaft or other moving part.

O-ring - A type of sealing ring made of a special rubberlike material; in use, the O-ring is compressed into a groove to provide the sealing action.

Overhaul - To completely disassemble a unit, clean and inspect all parts, reassemble it with the original or new parts and make all adjustments necessary for proper operation.

P

Pilot bearing - A small bearing installed in the center of the flywheel (or the rear end of the crankshaft) to support the front end of the input shaft of the transmission.

Pip mark - A little dot or indentation which indicates the top side of a compression ring.

Piston - The cylindrical part, attached to the connecting rod, that moves up and down in the cylinder as the crankshaft rotates. When the fuel charge is fired, the piston transfers the force of the explosion to the connecting rod, then to the crankshaft.

Piston pin (or wrist pin) - The cylindrical and usually hollow steel pin that passes through the piston. The piston pin fastens the piston to the upper end of the connecting rod.

Piston ring - The split ring fitted to the groove in a piston. The ring contacts the sides of the ring groove and also rubs against the cylinder wall, thus sealing space between piston and wall. There are two types of rings: Compression rings seal the compression pressure in the combustion chamber; oil rings scrape excessive oil off the cylinder wall.

Piston ring groove - The slots or grooves cut in piston heads to hold piston rings in position.

Piston skirt - The portion of the piston below the rings and the piston pin hole.

Plastigage - A thin strip of plastic thread, available in different sizes, used for measuring clearances. For example, a strip of plastigage is laid across a bearing journal and mashed as parts are assembled. Then parts are disassembled and the width of the strip is measured to determine clearance between journal and bearing. Commonly used to measure crankshaft main-bearing and connecting rod bearing clearances.

Press-fit - A tight fit between two parts that requires pressure to force the parts together. Also referred to as drive, or force, fit.

Prussian blue - A blue pigment; in solution, useful in determining the area of contact between two surfaces. Prussian blue is commonly used to determine the width and location of the contact area between the valve face and the valve seat.

R

Race (bearing) - The inner or outer ring that provides a contact surface for balls or rollers in bearing.

Ream - To size, enlarge or smooth a hole by using a round cutting tool with fluted edges.

Ring job - The process of reconditioning the cylinders and installing new rings.

Runout - Wobble. The amount a shaft rotates out-of-true.

S

Saddle - The upper main bearing seat.

Scored - Scratched or grooved, as a cylinder wall may be scored by abrasive particles moved up and down by the piston rings.

Scuffing - A type of wear in which there's a transfer of material between parts moving against each other; shows up as pits or grooves in the mating surfaces.

Seat - The surface upon which another part rests or seats. For example, the valve seat is the matched surface upon which the valve face rests. Also used to refer to wearing into a good fit; for example, piston rings seat after a few miles of driving.

Short block - An engine block complete with crankshaft and piston and, usually, camshaft assemblies.

Static balance - The balance of an object while it's stationary.

Step - The wear on the lower portion of a ring land caused by excessive side and back-clearance. The height of the step indicates the ring's extra side clearance and the length of the step projecting from the back wall of the groove represents the ring's back clearance.

Stroke - The distance the piston moves when traveling from top dead center to bottom dead center, or from bottom dead center to top dead center.

Stud - A metal rod with threads on both ends.

T

Tang - A lip on the end of a plain bearing used to align the bearing during assembly.

Tap - To cut threads in a hole. Also refers to the fluted tool used to cut threads.

Taper - A gradual reduction in the width of a shaft or hole; in an engine cylinder, taper usually takes the form of uneven wear, more pronounced at the top than at the bottom.

Throws - The offset portions of the crankshaft to which the connecting rods are affixed.

Thrust bearing - The main bearing that has thrust faces to prevent excessive endplay, or forward and backward movement of the crankshaft.

Thrust washer - A bronze or hardened steel washer placed between two moving parts. The washer prevents longitudinal movement and provides a bearing surface for thrust surfaces of parts.

Tolerance - The amount of variation permitted from an exact size of measurement. Actual amount from smallest acceptable dimension to largest acceptable dimension.

U

Umbrella - An oil deflector placed near the valve tip to throw oil from the valve stem area.

Undercut - A machined groove below the normal surface.

Undersize bearings - Smaller diameter bearings used with re-ground crankshaft journals.

V

Valve grinding - Refacing a valve in a valve-refacing machine.

Valve train - The valve-operating mechanism of an engine; includes all components from the camshaft to the valve.

Vibration damper - A cylindrical weight attached to the front of the crankshaft to minimize torsional vibration (the twist-untwist actions of the crankshaft caused by the cylinder firing impulses). Also called a harmonic balancer.

W

Water jacket - The spaces around the cylinders, between the inner and outer shells of the cylinder block or head, through which coolant circulates.

Web - A supporting structure across a cavity.

Woodruff key - A key with a radiused backside (viewed from the side).

Specifications

General

Engine identification (8th character of the Vehicle Identification Number)

Sephia/Spectra

VIN code 1 (1994 and 1995)	B6 1.6L Single Overhead Camshaft (SOHC)
VIN code 3, 4 (1995 through 1997)	B6 1.6L Double Overhead Camshaft (DOHC)
VIN code 5 (1995 through 1997)	BP 1.8L Double Overhead Camshaft (DOHC)
VIN code 1 (1998 through 2004)	T8 1.8L Double Overhead Camshaft (DOHC)
VIN code 1 (2004 and later)	2.0L Double Overhead Camshaft (DOHC)

Sportage

VIN code 2 (Federal)	2.0L Double Overhead Camshaft (DOHC)
VIN code 4 (California)	2.0L Double Overhead Camshaft (DOHC)
VIN code 3	2.7L Double Overhead Camshaft (DOHC) V6

Displacement

1.6L SOHC	97.4 cubic inches
1.6L DOHC B6	97.4 cubic inches
1.8L DOHC BP	112.0 cubic inches
1.8L DOHC T8	109.4 cubic inches
2.0L DOHC	120.5 cubic inches
V6 engine	162 cubic inches

Bore and Stroke

1.6L SOHC	3.07 x 3.29 inches (78.0 x 83.6 mm)
1.6L DOHC B6	3.07 x 3.29 inches (78.0 x 83.6 mm)
1.8L DOHC BP	3.27 x 3.35 inches (83.0 x 85.0 mm)
1.8L DOHC T8	3.19 x 3.43 inches (81.0 x 87.0 mm)
2.0L DOHC	3.23 x 3.68 inches (82.0 x 93.5 mm)
V6 engine	3.41 x 2.95 inches (86.7 x 75 mm)

Cylinder compression

1.6L SOHC

2-valve cylinder heads	192 psi (1,324 kPa)
4-valve cylinder heads	186 psi (1,275 kPa)
1.6L DOHC B6 and 1.8L DOHC BP	Lowest reading cylinder must be within 75 percent of the highest reading cylinder
1.8L DOHC T8	193 psi (1,333 kPa)
2.0L DOHC	206 psi (1,422 kPa)
V6 engine	140 psi (965 kPa) or more

Oil pressure (engine at operating temperature)

All four-cylinder engines except 2.0L DOHC

Idle speed	28 to 43 psi (196 to 294 kPa)
3,000 rpm	43 to 57 psi (294 to 392 kPa)

2.0L DOHC

2004 through 2007 models (at idle)	22.8 psi (157 kPa)
2008 and later models (at 1500 rpm)	35.5 psi (245 kPa)
V6 engine (at idle)	7 psi (48 kPa) or more

Torque specifications	Ft-lbs (unless otherwise indicated)	Nm

→Note: One foot-pound (ft-lb) of torque is equivalent to 12 inch-pounds (in-lbs) of torque. Torque values below approximately 15 ft-lbs are expressed in inch-pounds, since most foot-pound torque wrenches are not accurate at these smaller values.

Sephia/Spectra

Connecting rod bearing cap nuts/bolts		
All 2003 and earlier models,		
and 2004 1.8L models)	37	50
2004 and later 2.0L models*		
Step 1	15	20
Step 2	Tighten an additional 90-degrees	
Main bearing cap bolts		
1997 and earlier models	40 to 43	54 to 59
1998 through 2003 models*		
Step 1	29	39
Step 2	Loosen all bolts	
Step 3	15	20
Step 4	Tighten an additional 90-degrees	
Step 5	Tighten an additional 60-degrees	
2004 and later models*		
Step 1	20 to 23	27.5 to 31
Step 2	Tighten an additional 60-degrees	

* Bolts must be replaced with new ones

Sportage

Connecting rod bearing cap nuts/bolts*		
Step 1	15	20
Step 2	Tighten an additional 90-degrees	
Main bearing cap bolts*		
Four-cylinder engines		
Step 1	20 to 23	27.5 to 31
Step 2	Tighten an additional 60-degrees	
V6 engine		
M8 bolts		
Step 1	144 inch-pounds	16
Step 2	Tighten an additional 90-degrees	
M10 bolt		
Step 1	22	30
Step 2	Tighten an additional 90-degrees	

* Bolts must be replaced with new ones

Notes

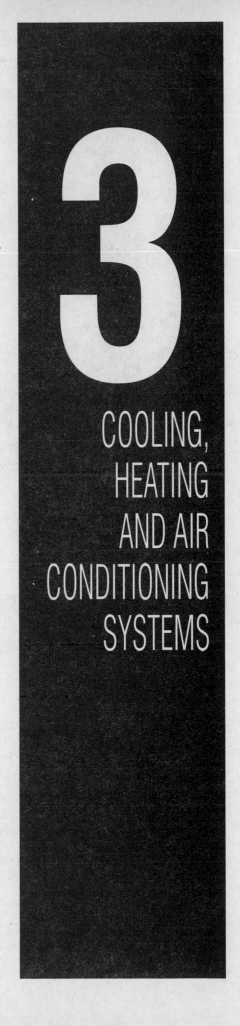

3

COOLING, HEATING AND AIR CONDITIONING SYSTEMS

Section

1   General information
2   Antifreeze - general information
3   Thermostat - check and replacement
4   Engine cooling fans and switch - check and replacement
5   Coolant reservoir - removal and installation
6   Radiator - removal and installation
7   Water pump - check
8   Water pump - replacement
9   Coolant temperature sending unit - check and replacement
10   Blower motor resistor and blower motor - replacement
11   Heater/air conditioning control assembly - removal and installation
12   Heater core - replacement
13   Air conditioning and heating system - check and maintenance
14   Air conditioning compressor - removal and installation
15   Air conditioning receiver-drier - removal and installation
16   Air conditioning condenser - removal and installation
17   Air conditioning pressure switch - replacement

Reference to other Chapters

CHECK ENGINE or MIL light on - See Chapter 6
Coolant level check - See Chapter 1
Cooling system check - See Chapter 1
Cooling system servicing (draining, flushing and refilling) - See Chapter 1
Drivebelts - check, replacement and adjustment - See Chapter 1
Underhood hose check and replacement - See Chapter 1

1.1 Underhood cooling and air conditioning components (DOHC four-cylinder engine shown, others similar)

1	Air conditioning line service port (high side)	3	Air conditioning line service port (low side)	6	Thermostat
2	Receiver-drier and pressure switch (location varies by year)	4	Radiator	7	Coolant reservoir (location varies by year)
		5	Radiator cap	8	Fuse and relay box

1 General information

ENGINE COOLING SYSTEM

Refer to illustrations 1.1 and 1.2

All vehicles covered by this manual employ a pressurized engine cooling system with thermostatically controlled coolant circulation (see illustration). An impeller-type water pump mounted on the engine block pumps coolant through the engine. The coolant flows around each cylinder and toward the rear of the engine. Cast-in coolant passages direct coolant around the intake and exhaust ports, near the spark plug areas and in close proximity to the exhaust valve guides.

A wax-pellet type thermostat controls engine coolant temperature. During warm up, the closed thermostat prevents coolant from circulating through the radiator. As the engine nears normal operating temperature, the thermostat opens and allows hot coolant to travel through the radiator, where it's cooled before returning to the engine (see illustration).

The cooling system is sealed by a pressure-type radiator cap, which raises the boiling point of the coolant and increases the cooling efficiency of the radiator. If the system pressure exceeds the cap pressure relief value, the excess pressure in the system forces the spring-loaded valve inside the cap off its seat and allows the coolant to escape through the overflow tube into a coolant reservoir. When the system cools the excess coolant is automatically drawn from the reservoir back into the radiator.

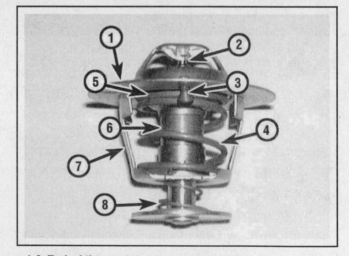

1.2 Typical thermostat

1	Flange	5	Valve seat
2	Piston	6	Valve
3	Jiggle valve	7	Frame
4	Main coil spring	8	Secondary coil spring

The coolant reservoir serves as both the point at which fresh coolant is added to the cooling system to maintain the proper fluid level and as a holding tank for overheated coolant.

This type of cooling system is known as a closed design because coolant that escapes past the pressure cap is saved and reused.

ENGINE COOLING FAN(S)

All vehicles covered by this manual are equipped with either one or two electric cooling fans; a radiator fan and a condenser fan (on models equipped with air conditioning). The fans are controlled electronically. The radiator and condenser fan relays are located in the fuse and relay boxes found in the engine compartment or under the dash. An ECT (engine coolant temperature) fan switch is used on 1994 and 1995 SOHC engines only and is mounted in the thermostat housing cover. All other years and models (covered in this manual) utilize ECT sensors and work with the onboard computer to control the cooling fans.

HEATING SYSTEM

The heating system consists of a blower fan and heater core located in the heater box, the hoses connecting the heater core to the engine cooling system and the heater/air conditioning control head on the dashboard. Hot engine coolant is circulated through the heater core. When the heater mode is activated, a flap door opens to expose the heater box to the passenger compartment. A fan switch on the control head activates the blower motor, which forces air through the core, heating the air.

AIR CONDITIONING SYSTEM

The air conditioning system consists of a condenser mounted in front of the radiator, an evaporator mounted adjacent to the heater core, a compressor mounted on the engine, a receiver-drier mounted in front of the condenser, behind the radiator grille (early models) or along the right side of the engine compartment (later models) and the plumbing connecting all of the above components.

A blower fan forces the warmer air of the passenger compartment through the evaporator core (sort of a radiator-in-reverse), transferring the heat from the air to the refrigerant. The liquid refrigerant boils off into low pressure vapor, taking the heat with it when it leaves the evaporator.

2   Antifreeze - general information

▶ **Refer to illustration 2.4**

✳✳ WARNING:

Do not allow antifreeze to come in contact with your skin or painted surfaces of the vehicle. Rinse off spills immediately with plenty of water. Antifreeze is highly toxic if ingested. Never leave antifreeze lying around in an open container or in puddles on the floor; children and pets are attracted by its sweet smell and may drink it. Check with local authorities about disposing of used antifreeze. Many communities have collection centers which will see that antifreeze is disposed of safely. Never dump used antifreeze on the ground or pour it into drains.

The cooling system should be filled with a water/ethylene glycol based antifreeze solution, which will prevent freezing down to at least -20-degrees F (even lower in cold climates). It also provides protection against corrosion and increases the coolant boiling point. The engines in these vehicles have aluminum cylinder heads. The manufacturer recommends that the correct type of coolant be used and strongly urges that coolant types not be mixed (see the Chapter 1 Specifications).

Drain, flush and refill the cooling system at least every other year (see Chapter 1). The use of antifreeze solutions for periods of longer than two years is likely to cause damage and encourage the formation of rust and scale in the system.

2.4 Use an antifreeze hydrometer (available at most auto parts stores) to test the condition of your coolant

Before adding antifreeze to the system, inspect all hose connections. Antifreeze can leak through very minute openings.

Hydrometers are available at most auto parts stores to test the coolant (see illustration). Use antifreeze that meets factory specifications (see Chapter 1).

3 Thermostat - check and replacement

CHECK

1 Before assuming the thermostat is to blame for a cooling system problem, check the coolant level and temperature gauge operation.

2 If the engine seems to be taking a long time to warm up, based on heater output or temperature gauge operation, the thermostat is probably stuck open. Replace the thermostat with a new one.

3 If the engine runs hot, use your hand to check the temperature of the upper radiator hose. If the hose isn't hot, but the engine is, the thermostat is probably stuck closed, preventing the coolant inside the engine from escaping to the radiator. Replace the thermostat.

❊❊ CAUTION:

Don't drive the vehicle without a thermostat. The computer may stay in open loop and emissions and fuel economy will suffer.

4 If the upper radiator hose is hot, it means that the coolant is flowing and the thermostat is open. Consult the *Troubleshooting* Section at the front of this manual for cooling system diagnosis.

REPLACEMENT

▶ Refer to illustrations 3.9a, 3.9b and 3.12

❊❊ WARNING:

Do not remove the radiator cap, drain the coolant or replace the thermostat until the engine has cooled completely.

5 Disconnect the cable from the negative battery terminal (see Chapter 5, Section 1).

6 Drain the cooling system (see Chapter 1). If the coolant is relatively new or in good condition, save it and reuse it. Read the **Warning** in Section 2.

7 Follow the upper radiator hose to the engine to locate the thermostat housing cover.

8 Loosen the hose clamp, then detach the hose from the fitting. If it's stuck, grasp it near the end with a pair of adjustable pliers and twist it to break the seal, then pull it off. If the hose is old or deteriorated, cut it off and install a new one.

➡**Note 1: If the outer surface of the large fitting that mates with the hose is deteriorated (corroded, pitted, etc.), it may be damaged further by hose removal. If it is, the thermostat housing cover will have to be replaced.**

➡**Note 2: On some models it isn't necessary to remove the hose from the housing cover. Just unbolt the housing cover and swing it out of the way with the hose attached.**

9 Remove the thermostat housing cover fasteners and cover. If the cover is stuck, tap it with a soft-face hammer to jar it loose. Be prepared for some coolant to spill as the seal is broken (see illustrations).

10 Take note of how the thermostat and gasket are installed. Also, note the orientation of the jiggle pin and then remove the thermostat.

➡**Note: On 1997 and earlier models, the thermostat has two valves instead of one.**

11 Remove all traces of the old gasket from the mating surfaces and clean them thoroughly.

12 Install the new thermostat, with the jiggle pin in the 12 o'clock position (see illustration), and the spring end directed into the engine.

13 Install a new gasket, making sure that it is oriented in the same way as the original.

➡**Note: It is standard practice to use RTV sealant when installing flat replacement gaskets. However, if the gasket is designed with a raised, crushable sealing surface (not flat), no RTV sealant is necessary.**

14 Install the thermostat housing cover, tightening the fasteners to the torque listed in this Chapter's Specifications.

15 Reattach the hose and tighten the hose clamp securely. Install all components that were previously removed.

16 Reconnect the battery (see Chapter 5, Section 1).

17 Refill the cooling system (see Chapter 1).

18 Start the engine and allow it to reach normal operating temperature, then check for leaks and proper thermostat operation (as described in Steps 2 through 4).

3.9a Thermostat mounting fasteners (1.8L DOHC engine shown, other four-cylinder engines similar)

3.9b Thermostat mounting fasteners (V6 engines)

3.12 Make sure that the thermostat is installed like this, with the jiggle pin at the 12 o'clock position

4 Engine cooling fans and switch - check and replacement

✳✳ WARNING:

To avoid possible injury or damage, DO NOT operate the engine with a damaged fan. Do not attempt to repair fan blades - replace a damaged fan with a new one.

➡Note: All air-conditioned models have two fans.

CHECK

◆ Refer to illustrations 4.1a, 4.1b and 4.3

1 If the engine is overheating and the cooling fan is not coming on when the engine temperature rises to an excessive level, unplug the fan motor electrical connector (see illustrations) and then connect the motor directly to the battery with a fused jumper wire on terminal A. Use another jumper wire to ground terminal B. If the fan motor doesn't come on, replace the motor. Models with air conditioning are equipped with two fans. If the radiator fan motor checks out okay, be sure to test the condenser fan motor as well.

➡Note: On 1997 and earlier models, the condenser fan is mounted in front of the condenser. Remove the radiator grille to gain access to the fan connector if necessary.

✳✳ CAUTION:

Do not apply battery power to the vehicle harness side of the connector.

2 If the radiator fan motor is okay, but it isn't coming on when the engine gets hot, the fan relay(s) might be defective.

3 Locate the fan relays in the engine compartment fuse/relay box (see illustration).

➡Note: The condenser fan relay on 1997 and earlier models is externally mounted near the lower left corner of the engine compartment.

4 Test the relay(s) (see Chapter 12).

5 If the relay(s) are okay, test the radiator fan switch.

➡Note: The 1994 and 1995 models with SOHC engines are the only models that utilize a fan switch. On later models the fan is controlled by the PCM, via a signal from the Engine Coolant Temperature (ECT) sensor (see Chapter 6 for information on the ECT sensor).

The radiator fan switch controls the operation of the fans based on temperature. The fan switch is mounted in the thermostat housing cover. The switch can be tested with an ohmmeter. When the temperature is below 194-degrees F (90-degrees C), the switch should be open (no continuity across the switch terminals). When the temperature is above 207-degrees F (97-degrees C), the switch should be closed (continuity exists across the switch terminals).

6 If the relay(s) and the fan switch are okay, check all wiring and connections to the fan motors. Any further checking should be directed to a qualified repair facility.

REPLACEMENT

Sephia and Spectra models

Cooling fans

◆ Refer to illustrations 4.15a, 4.15b, 4.15c, 4.17 and 4.18

✳✳ WARNING:

Wait until the engine is completely cool before beginning this procedure.

7 Disconnect the cable from the negative battery terminal (see Chapter 5, Section 1).

8 Set the parking brake and block the rear wheels to prevent the vehicle from rolling. Raise the front of the vehicle and support it securely on jackstands.

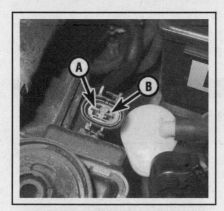

4.1a To test the radiator fan motor, disconnect the electrical connector and use jumper wires to connect the fan directly to battery positive (on terminal A) and ground (on terminal B) - if the fan still doesn't work, replace the motor

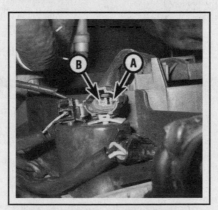

4.1b To test the condenser fan motor, disconnect the electrical connector and use jumper wires to connect the fan directly to battery positive (on terminal A) and ground (on terminal B) - if the fan still doesn't work, replace the motor

4.3 Location of the radiator fan relay (A) and the condenser fan relay (B) (see the fusebox cover for locations on early models)

4.15a Use pliers to expand the upper radiator hose clamp (A) and slide it back on the hose, then remove the radiator fan assembly upper mounting bolts (B)

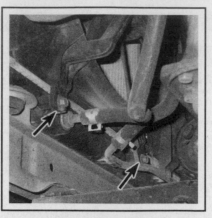

4.15b The radiator fan assembly lower mounting bolts

4.15c The condenser fan assembly lower and side mounting bolts

4.17 Remove the C-clip (arrow), then pull the fan blade from the motor shaft

4.18 Fan motor mounting screws

9   Remove the lower splash shield from under the radiator.

10 Drain the cooling system (see Chapter 1). If the coolant is relatively new or in good condition, save it and reuse it. Read the **Warning** in Section 2.

11 On some later models, remove the fresh air inlet duct if necessary (see Chapter 4).

12 Remove the coolant reservoir (see Section 5).

13 Disconnect the fan electrical connectors (see illustrations 4.1a and 4.1b).

14 Remove any wiring harness clamps or anything else connected to the fan shrouds.

15 Disconnect the upper radiator hose from the radiator and move it aside, then unbolt the engine cooling fan assembly from the radiator (see illustrations).

➡Note: On 1997 and earlier models, the condenser fan is mounted in front of the condenser. To remove the condenser fan, remove the radiator grill to gain access to the fan shroud assembly bolts.

16 Carefully remove the fan shroud assembly.

17 To detach the fan from the motor, remove the C-clip from the end of the motor shaft (see illustration).

18 To detach the fan motor from the shroud, remove the mounting

screws (see illustration).

19 Installation is the reverse of removal.

20 Refill the cooling system (see Chapter 1).

21 Reconnect the battery (see Chapter 5, Section 1).

Cooling fan switch (1994 and 1995 SOHC models only)

❊❊❊ WARNING:

Wait until the engine is completely cool before beginning this procedure.

22 Drain the cooling system (see Chapter 1).

23 Locate the fan switch at the thermostat housing cover and then disconnect the electrical connector.

24 Unscrew the switch from the thermostat housing cover.

25 Installation is the reverse of removal, noting the following points:

a) *Use a new O-ring when installing the switch. Lightly coat the O-ring with engine coolant.*

b) *Refill the cooling system (see Chapter 1).*

c) *Start the engine and allow it to reach normal operating temperature, then verify proper fan operation.*

Sportage models

▶ Refer to illustration 4.30

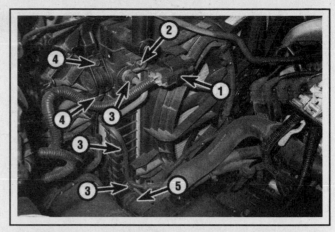

❊❊ WARNING:

Wait until the engine is completely cool before beginning this procedure.

26 Drain the cooling system (see Chapter 1).

27 Remove the fresh air inlet duct (see *Air filter housing - removal and installation* in Chapter 4).

28 Remove the battery and the battery tray (see Chapter 5).

29 Remove the coolant reservoir (see Section 5), then detach the upper radiator hose from the radiator.

30 Disconnect the electrical connector for the fan motor (see illustration).

31 Remove the fan shroud mounting bolts.

32 Remove the fan shroud assembly from the engine compartment.

33 Installation is the reverse of removal.

34 Refill the cooling system (see Chapter 1).

4.30 Fan shroud and radiator details (left side) - Sportage models

1   Fan motor electrical connector
2   Transaxle cooler hoses (vehicles with an automatic transaxle)
3   Left fan shroud mounting bolt
4   Automatic transaxle cooler lines
5   Lower radiator hose

5   Coolant reservoir - removal and installation

▶ Refer to illustrations 5.3, 5.4a and 5.4b

❊❊ WARNING:

Wait until the engine is completely cool before beginning this procedure.

1   Disconnect the reservoir hose from the radiator filler neck. Plug the hose to prevent leakage.

SEPHIA AND SPECTRA MODELS

2   Set the parking brake and block the rear wheels. Raise the front of the vehicle and support it securely on jackstands. Remove the left-side engine splash shield (see illustration 7.3b in Chapter 2A).

3   Remove the upper mounting bolts (see illustration).

4   Remove the lower mounting bolt and then remove the reservoir from the bottom of the engine compartment (see illustrations).

SPORTAGE MODELS

5   Remove the mounting bolts and lift out the reservoir (see illustration).

6   Clean out the tank with soapy water and a brush to remove any deposits inside. Inspect the reservoir carefully for cracks. If you find a crack, replace the reservoir.

7   Installation is the reverse of removal. Fill the reservoir with the proper type and amount of coolant (see Chapter 1).

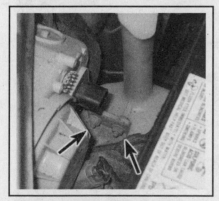

5.3 The coolant reservoir upper mounting bolts (Sephia and Spectra models)

5.4a The coolant reservoir lower mounting bolt (Sephia and Spectra models)

5.4b Coolant reservoir (Sportage models):

1   Overflow hose
2   Mounting bolt (left bolt, at other end of reservoir, not visible)

6   Radiator - removal and installation

⁕⁕ WARNING:

Wait until the engine is completely cool before beginning this procedure.

REMOVAL

Sephia and Spectra models

▸ **Refer to illustrations 6.5, 6.6 and 6.10**

1   Disconnect the cable from the negative battery terminal (see Chapter 5, Section 1). On 2004 models with a 2.0L DOHC engine and on all 2005 and later models, remove the battery and battery tray (see Chapter 5).

2   Set the parking brake and block the rear wheels. Raise the front of the vehicle and support it securely on jackstands. Remove the engine

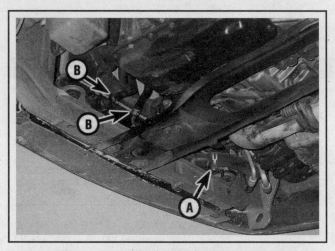

6.5 The lower radiator hose (A) and transaxle cooling lines (B) (typical)

6.6 Typical radiator mounting bracket bolts

splash shields (see illustrations 7.3a and 7.3b in Chapter 2A).

3   Drain the cooling system (see Chapter 1). If the coolant is relatively new or in good condition, save it and reuse it. Read the **Warning** in Section 2.

4   On 1998 and later models, remove the fresh air inlet duct (see Chapter 4). On some models, it's easier to remove the radiator if you remove the cooling fans that are mounted between the radiator and engine (see Section 4). Even if you determine that it's not necessary to remove the fans and fan shrouds at this time, disconnect the fan motor electrical connectors on all models.

5   Disconnect the lower radiator hose and the transaxle fluid cooling lines (if equipped) from the radiator (see illustration).

➡**Note: Plug the ends of the transaxle cooling lines to minimize fluid loss and contamination.**

6   Remove the radiator brackets (see illustration).

7   Carefully lift out the radiator. Don't spill coolant on the vehicle or scratch the paint.

8   Inspect the radiator for leaks and damage. If it needs repair, have a radiator shop or dealer service department perform the work as special techniques are required.

9   Bugs and dirt can be removed from the radiator by spraying it with a garden hose nozzle from the back side. The radiator should be flushed out with a garden hose before reinstallation.

10   Check the radiator mounts (see illustration) for deterioration and replace them if necessary.

Sportage models

▸ **Refer to illustration 6.12**

11   Remove the fan shroud (see Section 4). Detach the automatic transaxle fluid cooler lines from the left side of the radiator.

12   Remove the radiator mounting bolts and brackets (see illustration 4.30 and accompanying illustration).

13   Remove the condenser mounting bolts (see illustration 16.12).

14   Lift up the condenser just far enough to disengage the locator tabs at the bottom (see illustration 16.12), then reposition the condenser forward, away from the radiator.

6.10 Typical radiator rubber mounts (lower)

15 Remove the radiator from the engine compartment by lifting it straight up.

16 When installing the radiator, make sure that the lower insulators are seated securely in their mounting holes (see illustration 6.10).

INSTALLATION

17 Installation is the reverse of the removal procedure. Guide the radiator into the mounts until it seats completely.

18 Install the radiator upper mounting brackets and tighten the bolts securely.

19 After installation, fill the cooling system with the proper coolant (see Chapter 1).

20 Reconnect the battery (see Chapter 5, Section 1).

21 Start the engine and check for leaks. Allow the engine to reach normal operating temperature, indicated by the upper radiator hose becoming hot. Recheck the coolant level and add more if required.

22 Check and add transaxle fluid as needed (see Chapter 1).

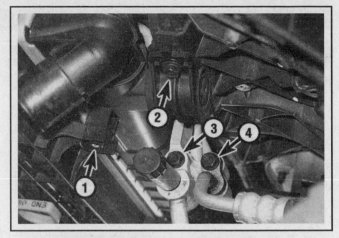

6.12 Radiator and condenser details (right side) - Sportage models

1 *Right fan shroud mounting bolt*
2 *Right radiator mounting bolt and bracket*
3 *High-pressure refrigerant line connection*
4 *Low-pressure refrigerant line connection*

---

7 Water pump - check

▶ **Refer to illustration 7.2**

1 A failure in the water pump can cause serious engine damage due to overheating.

2 If a failure occurs at the pump seal, coolant will leak from the weep hole(s) on the water pump (see illustration).

3 Using a flashlight, look for traces of coolant residue or dried coolant tracks around the weep hole(s). If the seal has leaked, it should be very apparent.

4 If the water pump shaft bearings fail, there may be a howling sound near the water pump while it's running. With the engine off, shaft wear can be felt if the water pump pulley is rocked up-and-down. Don't mistake drivebelt slippage, which causes a squealing sound, for water pump bearing failure.

5 A quick water pump performance check can be done by doing the following:

   a) *Make certain that the coolant level in the system is full.*
   b) *Start the vehicle and warm it up fully.*
   c) *Turn the heater on in the passenger compartment.*
   d) *Check for little or no heat output. If this is the case, the water pump may be failing because coolant flow does not appear to be going through the heater core.*

7.2 Typical water pump weep hole

6 A water pump may still be due for replacement even if it's not leaking or making any noise. The only sure way to tell if replacement is necessary is to remove the pump and examine it closely. A loose or corroded impeller, a leaking shaft seal or a worn shaft bearing are all causes for replacement.

8   Water pump - replacement

Wait until the engine is completely cool before beginning this procedure.

1   Disconnect the cable from the negative battery terminal (see Chapter 5, Section 1).

2   Drain the cooling system (see Chapter 1). If the coolant is relatively new or in good condition, save it and reuse it. Read the **Warning** in Section 2.

FOUR-CYLINDER MODELS

◗ **Refer to illustrations 8.3, 8.7, 8.8a, 8.8b and 8.13**

3   Loosen the water pump pulley bolts, remove the drivebelt (see Chapter 1) and then the water pump pulley (see illustration).

4   Remove the timing belt, timing belt tensioner and idler pulleys (see Chapter 2A).

➡**Note: 1995 and earlier SOHC engines do not have an idler pulley.**

5   On 1997 and earlier models, remove the water inlet pipe bolts and separate it from the water pump.

6   On 2004 models with a 2.0L DOHC engine and on all 2005 and later models, remove the power steering pump and the power steering pump bracket (see Chapter 10).

7   On all models except those with a 2.0L DOHC engine, remove the water pump bolts (see illustration) and remove the water pump.

8   On 2004 models with a 2.0L DOHC engine and on all 2005 and later models, remove the alternator (see Chapter 5) and alternator support bracket (see illustration), then remove the rest of the water pump bolts (see illustration) and remove the pump.

9   Check the impeller on the backside for evidence of corrosion or missing fins. If the pump is in good shape, proceed to the next Step. If the pump is damaged or corroded, replace it before proceeding.

8.3 Typical water pump pulley bolts (four-cylinder engines)

8.7 Water pump mounting bolts (four-cylinder engines, except 2.0L DOHC engine)

8.8a Alternator support bracket bolts and upper water pump bolt (2004 models with a 2.0L DOHC engine and all 2005 and later four-cylinder models)

8.8b Lower water pump mounting bolts (2.0L DOHC engine)

8.13 On 1997 and earlier 1.6L engines, use a little gasket adhesive to ensure that the gasket doesn't fall off or become pinched when you install the pump

10 Remove all traces of the old gasket material from the engine mounting surface and clean it thoroughly.

11 Make sure the bolt threads and the threaded holes in the engine are clear of corrosion.

12 Compare the new pump to the old one to make sure they're identical.

13 On 1997 and earlier models, apply a thin layer of RTV sealant to both sides of the new gasket and install the gasket on the water pump (see illustration). On 1998 and later models, apply a small amount of sealant to hold the gasket seal in the groove of the new water pump. Do not apply sealant on the mating surfaces.

14 Apply a small amount of RTV sealant to the threads of each mounting bolt.

15 Carefully move the water pump into position while keeping the gasket (or seal) in place. Install the mounting bolts finger tight making certain that the water pump and gasket are aligned correctly on the engine.

16 Tighten the bolts to the torque listed in this Chapter's Specifications in 1/4-turn increments. Don't over-tighten the bolts or the pump may become distorted and leak.

17 The remainder of the installation procedure is the reverse of removal. On 1997 and earlier models, be sure to use a new gasket when attaching the water inlet pipe to the water pump and a new O-ring for the bypass pipe.

18 Reinstall all parts removed for access to the pump.

V6 ENGINES (SPORTAGE MODELS)

♦ **Refer to illustration 8.24**

19 Remove the drivebelt (see Chapter 1).

20 Remove the timing belt covers, the timing belt and the timing belt idler pulley (see Chapter 2B).

21 Remove the water pump mounting bolts and remove the water pump.

22 Inspect the pump for cracks, damage and/or wear. Check the pump bearing for damage, noise and/or rotational resistance. Replace

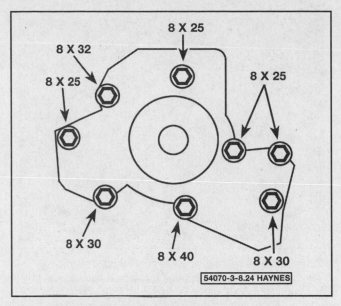

8.24 Water pump bolt locations (V6 models)

the pump if any damage or wear is evident.

23 Before installing the pump, make sure that the gasket surfaces are clean.

24 Install the pump mounting bolts. Note that the mounting bolts are four different bolt lengths. Make sure that you install the bolts in the correct holes (see illustration). Tighten the bolts to the torque listed in this Chapter's Specifications.

ALL MODELS

25 Refill the cooling system and check the drivebelt tension (see Chapter 1).

26 Reconnect the battery (see Chapter 5, Section 1). Run the engine and check for leaks.

---

9 Coolant temperature sending unit - check and replacement

➡**Note: This Section applies only to 2004 and earlier models. 2005 and later models use the Engine Coolant Temperature (ECT) sensor to send a signal to both the Powertrain Control Module (PCM) and to the temperature gauge.**

CHECK

♦ **Refer to illustrations 9.3a and 9.3b**

1 If the coolant temperature gauge is inoperative, check the fuses first (see Chapter 12).

2 If the temperature gauge indicates excessive temperature after running awhile, see the *Troubleshooting* section in the front of the manual.

3 If the temperature gauge indicates HOT as soon as the engine is started cold, disconnect the electrical connector at the coolant gauge sending unit (see illustrations). If the gauge reading drops, replace the

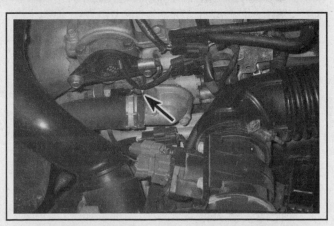

9.3a The sending unit is threaded into the cylinder head, just inboard of the thermostat housing cover (1999 shown, other models are similar)

9.3b On 2.0L DOHC engines, the coolant temperature sending unit is threaded into the thermostat housing just in front of the Engine Coolant Temperature (ECT) sensor

sending unit. If the reading remains high, the wire to the gauge may be shorted to ground or the gauge is faulty.

4   If the coolant temperature gauge fails to show any indication after the engine has been warmed up, (approximately 10 minutes) and the fuses are good, shut off the engine. Disconnect the electrical connector at the sending unit and, using a jumper wire, connect the wire to a clean ground on the engine. Briefly turn on the ignition without starting the engine. If the gauge now indicates HOT, replace the sending unit.

5   If the gauge fails to respond, the circuit may be open or the temperature gauge may he faulty.

REPLACEMENT

> **✳✳ WARNING:**
>
> **Do not start this procedure until the engine is completely cool.**

6   Drain the coolant (see Chapter 1).

7   Disconnect the electrical connector for the sending unit.

8   Using a deep socket or a wrench, remove the sending unit.

9   Install the new sending unit, and tighten it securely. Do not use thread sealant as it may electrically insulate the sending unit. Connect the electrical connector.

10   Refill the cooling system and check for coolant leakage and proper gauge operation.

---

10 Blower motor resistor and blower motor - replacement

> **✳✳ WARNING:**
>
> **The models covered by this manual are equipped with Supplemental Restraint systems (SRS), more commonly known as airbags. Always disable the airbag system before working in the vicinity of any airbag system component to avoid the possibility of accidental deployment of the airbag, which could cause personal injury (see Chapter 12).**

BLOWER MOTOR RESISTOR (2004 AND EARLIER MODELS)

▸ Refer to illustration 10.1

1   Disconnect the cable from the negative battery terminal (see Chapter 5, Section 1). Working in the passenger compartment under the glove box, disconnect the electrical connector from the blower motor resistor (see illustration).

2   Remove the blower motor resistor mounting screws and remove it from the housing.

3   Installation is the reverse of removal.

4   Reconnect the battery (see Chapter 5, Section 1).

10.1 Typical blower motor and resistor details

1   Blower motor resistor electrical connector
2   Blower motor resistor mounting screws
3   Blower motor electrical connector
4   Blower motor mounting screws

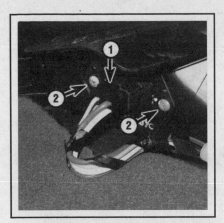

10.5 Power MOSFET details (2005 and later models)

1 *Electrical connector*
2 *Mounting screws*

10.8 Blower motor details (Sportage models)

1 *Electrical connector*
2 *Blower motor mounting screws (third screw not visible)*

10.10 To separate the fan from the motor shaft, remove this retaining clip (typical)

POWER MOSFET (2005 AND LATER MODELS)

▶ **Refer to illustration 10.5**

➡**Note: These models use a power MOSFET (Metal Oxide Semiconductor Field-Effect Transistor) instead of a conventional blower motor resistor. The power MOSFET is located under the right part of the instrument panel, to the left of the blower motor.**

5 Disconnect the electrical connector from the power MOSFET (see illustration).
6 Remove the MOSFET mounting screws and remove the MOSFET.
7 Installation is the reverse of removal.

BLOWER MOTOR

▶ **Refer to illustrations 10.8 and 10.10**

8 Disconnect the cable from the negative battery terminal (see Chapter 5, Section 1). Working in the passenger compartment under the glove box, disconnect the electrical connector from the blower motor (Sephia and Spectra models, see illustration 10.1, Sportage models, see illustration).
9 Remove the blower motor mounting screws and then remove the blower motor assembly.
10 Remove the circlip (see illustration) from the blower motor shaft to release the fan from the motor.
11 Installation is the reverse of removal.
12 Reconnect the battery (see Chapter 5, Section 1).

11 Heater/air conditioning control assembly - removal and installation

▶ **Refer to illustrations 11.3 and 11.4**

✳✳ WARNING:

The models covered by this manual are equipped with Supplemental Restraint systems (SRS), more commonly known as airbags. Always disable the airbag system before working in the vicinity of any airbag system component to avoid the possibility of accidental deployment of the airbag, which could cause personal injury (see Chapter 12).

1 Disconnect the cable from the negative battery terminal (see Chapter 5, Section 1).
2 Remove the center instrument panel bezel (see Chapter 11).

SEPHIA AND SPECTRA MODELS

3 Remove the mounting screws for the control assembly (see illustration).

11.3 Typical control assembly mounting screws

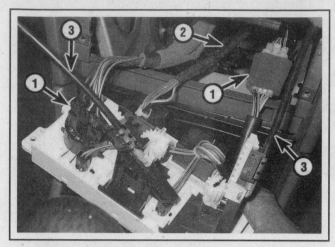

11.4 Typical control assembly details (backside)

1 Electrical connectors
2 Electrical connector harness (connector not visible in this photo)
3 Control cables

4   Disconnect the electrical connectors and control cables and then remove the unit (see illustration).

➡**Note: Follow each harness to its connector to locate it. Also, it's possible to detach either end of the control cables to remove the control assembly; from either the heater/air conditioning unit or the control assembly.**

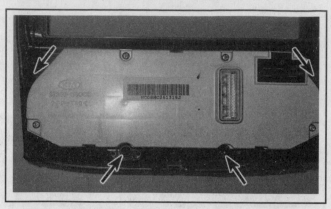

11.6 Heater/air conditioning control assembly mounting screws (Sportage models)

SPORTAGE MODELS

▶ **Refer to illustration 11.6**

5   Remove the center trim panel (see *Dashboard trim panels - removal and installation* in Chapter 11).
6   Remove the heater/air conditioning control assembly mounting screws (see illustration) and remove the unit.

ALL MODELS

7   Installation is the reverse of removal.
8   Reconnect the battery (see Chapter 5, Section 1).

12   Heater core - replacement

▶ **Refer to illustrations 12.4, 12.5, 12.8, 12.9, 12.10 and 12.11**

❊❊ **WARNING:**

The models covered by this manual are equipped with Supplemental Restraint systems (SRS), more commonly known as airbags. Always disable the airbag system before working in the vicinity of any airbag system component to avoid the possibility of accidental deployment of the airbag, which could cause personal injury (see Chapter 12).

❊❊ **WARNING:**

The air conditioning system is under high pressure. DO NOT loosen any fittings or remove any components until after the system has been discharged. Air conditioning refrigerant must be properly discharged into an EPA-approved container at a dealer service department or an automotive air conditioning repair facility. Always wear eye protection when disconnecting air conditioning system fittings.

❊❊ **WARNING:**

Wait until the engine is completely cool before beginning this procedure.

➡**Note: The photos accompanying this Section depict a typical heater core replacement procedure. The shape of the blower, evaporator and heater housings, and the location of the fasteners securing these housings, might vary somewhat from the photos that you see here, but the procedure itself is similar on all models.**

1   If so equipped, have the air conditioning system refrigerant discharged and recovered by an air conditioning technician.
2   Disconnect the cable from the negative battery terminal (see Chapter 5, Section 1).
3   Drain the cooling system (see Chapter 1).
4   Disconnect the air conditioning evaporator lines and note the drain tube at the firewall (see illustration).

➡**Note: Plug the ends of line fittings going to the rest of the A/C system to prevent dirt or moisture from getting into it.**

5   Disconnect the heater hoses from the heater core tubes at the firewall (see illustration).
6   Remove the instrument panel (see Chapter 11).
7   Disconnect and remove any harnesses fastened to the heater/air conditioning unit that would prevent it from being removed.
8   Remove the mounting fasteners for the blower and evaporator housing (see illustration) and then lift that section of the heater/air conditioning unit out of the vehicle.

➡**Note: When removing this part of the unit, be careful not to damage the seals for the condenser lines and the evaporator drain tube.**

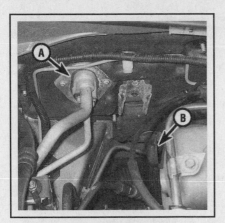

12.4 Disconnect the line fittings for the evaporator (A) and note the location of the evaporator housing drain tube (B) (typical)

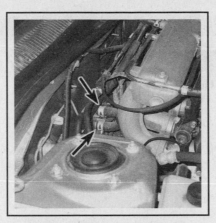

12.5 Expand the hose clamps with pliers, slide them back on the hoses and disconnect the heater hoses from the heater core tubes at the firewall (typical)

12.8 Typical blower and evaporator housing fastener locations

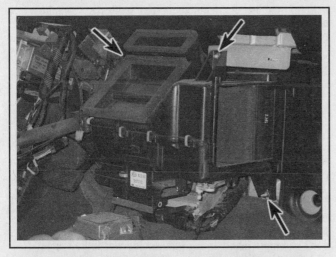

12.9 Typical heater core housing fastener locations (lower left-side nut not visible)

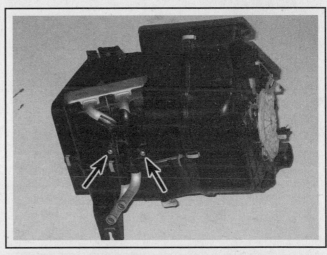

12.10 Remove these screws and detach the heater core tube cover . . .

9 Remove the mounting fasteners for the remaining section of the heater/air conditioning unit and then lift it out of the vehicle (see illustration).

10 Remove the cover that secures the heater core tubes (see illustration).

11 Remove the heater core (see illustration).

12 Installation is the reverse of removal, noting the following points:

a) When reinstalling the heater/air conditioning unit, make certain that the evaporator drain tube is placed correctly through the hole in the firewall.

b) Be sure to connect all electrical connectors on the heater/air conditioning unit before reinstalling the instrument panel.

c) Reconnect the heater hoses in the engine compartment.

13 Reconnect the battery (see Chapter 5, Section 1).

14 Refill the cooling system (see Chapter 1).

15 If equipped with A/C, have the system evacuated, recharged and leak tested by the shop that discharged it.

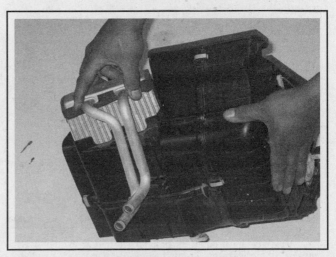

12.11 . . . then pull the heater core out of the housing (typical)

13 Air conditioning and heating system - check and maintenance

✳✳ WARNING:

The air conditioning system is under high pressure. DO NOT loosen any fittings or remove any components until after the system has been discharged. Air conditioning refrigerant must be properly discharged Into an EPA-approved container at a dealer service department or an automotive air conditioning repair facility. Always wear eye protection when disconnecting air conditioning system fittings.

1   The following maintenance checks should be performed on a regular basis to ensure the air conditioner continues to operate at peak efficiency.

a) *Check the compressor drivebelt. If it's worn or deteriorated, replace it (see Chapter 1).*

b) *Check the drivebelt tension and, if necessary, adjust it (see Chapter 1).*

c) *Check the system hoses. Look for cracks, bubbles, hard spots and deterioration. Inspect the hoses and all fittings for oil bubbles and seepage. If there's any evidence of wear, damage or leaks, replace the hose(s).*

d) *Inspect the condenser fins for leaves, bugs and other debris. Use a fin comb or compressed air to clean the condenser.*

e) *Make sure the system has the correct refrigerant charge.*

f) *Check the evaporator housing drain tube (see illustration 12.4) for blockage.*

2   It's a good idea to operate the system for about 10 minutes at least once a month, particularly during the winter. Long term non-use can cause hardening, and subsequent failure, of the seals.

3   Because of the complexity of the air conditioning system and the special equipment necessary to service it, in-depth troubleshooting and repairs are not included in this manual. However, simple checks and component replacement procedures are provided in this Chapter.

4   The most common cause of poor cooling is simply a low system refrigerant charge. If a noticeable drop in cool air output occurs, the following quick check will help you determine if the refrigerant level is low.

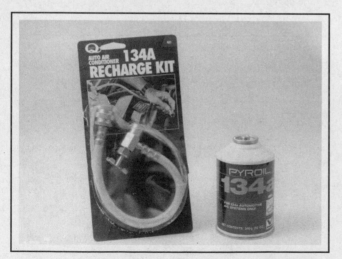

13.9 A basic charging kit for R-134a systems is available at most auto parts stores - it must say R-134a (not R-12) and so should the can of refrigerant

CHECKING THE REFRIGERANT CHARGE

5   Warm the engine up to normal operating temperature.

6   Place the air conditioning temperature selector at the coldest setting and the blower at the highest setting. Open the vehicle doors (to make sure the air conditioning system doesn't cycle off as soon as it cools the passenger compartment).

7   With the compressor engaged - the clutch will make an audible click and the center of the clutch will rotate - feel the evaporator inlet and outlet lines at the firewall. The inlet (small diameter) line should feel somewhat warm and the outlet (large diameter) line should feel cold. If so, the system charge is probably adequate.

8   Place a thermometer in the dashboard vent nearest the evaporator and operate the system until the indicated temperature is around 40 to 45-degrees F. If the ambient (outside) air temperature is very high, say 110-degrees F, the duct air temperature may be as high as 60-degrees F, but generally the air conditioning is 30 to 40-degrees F cooler than the ambient air.

➡**Note: Humidity of the ambient air also affects the cooling capacity of the system. Higher ambient humidity lowers the effectiveness of the air conditioning system.**

ADDING REFRIGERANT

◆ **Refer to illustrations 13.9, 13.12, and 13.15**

9   Buy an automotive charging kit at an auto parts store (see illustration). A charging kit includes a can of refrigerant, a tap valve and a short section of hose that can be attached between the tap valve and the system low side service valve.

✳✳ CAUTION:

Although the system will hold more than one can of refrigerant, don't add more than one can (you could overfill the system).

✳✳ CAUTION:

There are two types of refrigerant used in automotive systems; R-12, which has been widely used on earlier models, and the more environmentally-friendly R-134a used in all models covered by this manual. These two refrigerants (and their appropriate refrigerant oils) are not compatible and must never be mixed or components will be damaged. Use only R-134a refrigerant in the models covered by this manual.

10 Hook up the charging kit by following the manufacturer's instructions.

✳✳ WARNING:

DO NOT hook the charging kit hose to the system high side! The fittings on the charging kit are designed to fit only on the low side of the system.

11 Back off the valve handle on the charging kit and screw the kit onto the refrigerant can, making sure first that the O-ring or rubber seal

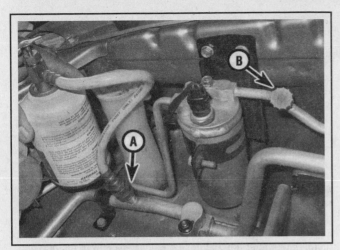

13.12 Attach the kit's quick-connect fitting to the low side service port (A) to administer R-134a into the air conditioning system - the high side service port (B) is not used for recharging with the kit (1999 shown, other models are similar)

13.15 Insert a thermometer in the center vent, turn on the air conditioning system and wait for it to cool down; depending on the humidity, the output air should be 30 to 40-degrees cooler than the ambient air temperature

inside the threaded portion of the kit is in place.

❊❊ WARNING:

Wear protective eyewear when dealing with pressurized refrigerant cans.

12 Locate the low-side service port in the engine compartment and unscrew the dust cap. Attach the quick-connect fitting to the service port (see illustration).

13 Warm up the engine and turn on the air conditioner. Keep the charging kit hose away from the fan and other moving parts.

➡Note: The charging process requires the compressor to be running. Your compressor may cycle off if the pressure is low due to a low charge. If the clutch cycles off, you can pull the low-pressure cycling switch plug (mounted on the receiver-drier) (see illustration 15.3) and attach a jumper wire across the terminals of the electrical connector (on the harness side). This will keep the compressor ON.

14 Turn the valve handle on the kit until the stem pierces the can, then back the handle out to release the refrigerant. You should be able to hear the rush of gas. Add refrigerant to the low side of the system until the temperature of the evaporator inlet and outlet lines is as described in Step 7. Allow stabilization time between each addition.

15 If you have an accurate thermometer, place it in the center air conditioning vent (see illustration) and note the temperature of the air coming out of the vent. A fully charged system which is working correctly should cool down to about 40-degrees F. Generally, an air conditioning system will put out air that is 30 to 40-degrees F cooler than the ambient air. For example, if the ambient (outside) air temperature is very high (over 100degrees F), the temperature of air coming out of the registers should be 60 to 70-degrees F.

16 When the can is empty, turn the valve handle to the closed position and release the connection from the low-side port. Replace the dust cap.

17 Remove the charging kit from the can and store the kit for future use with the piercing valve in the UP position, to prevent inadvertently piercing the can on the next use.

HEATING SYSTEMS

18 If the carpet under the heater core is damp, or if antifreeze vapor or steam is coming through the vents, the heater core is leaking. Remove it (see Section 12) and install a new unit (most radiator shops will not repair a leaking heater core).

19 If the air coming out of the heater vents isn't hot, the problem could stem from any of the following causes:

a) *The thermostat is stuck open, preventing the engine coolant from warming up enough to carry heat to the heater core. Replace the thermostat (see Section 3).*

b) *There is a blockage in the system, preventing the flow of coolant through the heater core. Feel both heater hoses at the firewall. They should be hot. If one of them is cool, there is an obstruction in one of the hoses or in the heater core. Detach the hoses and back flush the heater core with a water hose. If the heater core is clear but circulation is impeded, remove the two hoses and flush them out with a water hose.*

c) *If flushing fails to remove the blockage from the heater core, the core must be replaced (see Section 12).*

ELIMINATING AIR CONDITIONING ODORS

▶ **Refer to illustration 13.23**

➡Note: 2001 and earlier models do not utilize an interior ventilation air filter.

20 Unpleasant odors that often develop in air conditioning systems are caused by the growth of a fungus, usually on the surface of the evaporator core. The warm, humid environment there is a perfect breeding ground for mildew to develop.

21 The evaporator core on most vehicles is difficult to access, and dealerships have a lengthy, expensive process for eliminating the fungus by opening up the evaporator case and using a powerful disinfectant and rinse on the core until the fungus is gone. You can service your own system at home, but it takes something much stronger than basic household germ-killers or deodorizers.

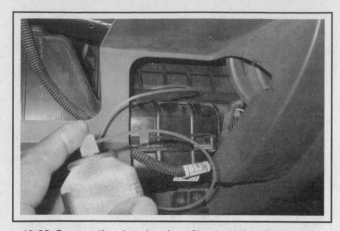

13.23 Remove the glove box (see Chapter 11) and place the disinfectant nozzle into the evaporator housing through the edge of the cabin recirculation door

22 Aerosol disinfectants for automotive air conditioning systems are available in most auto parts stores, but remember when shopping for them that the most effective treatments are also the most expensive. The basic procedure for using these sprays is to start by running the system in the RECIRC mode for ten minutes with the blower on its highest speed. Use the highest heat mode to dry out the system and keep the compressor from engaging by disconnecting the wiring connector at the compressor (see Section 14).

23 Make sure that the disinfectant can comes with a long spray hose. Guide the hose through the door just above the blower motor so that it protrudes just inside the housing (see illustration), turn on the A/C and set the blower on high and then spray according to the manufacturer's recommendations. Follow the manufacturer's recommendations for the length of spray and waiting time between applications.

> ❋❋ **WARNING:**
>
> **Do not place more than two inches of hose into the housing because the blower motor fan blades are just beneath the cabin recirculation door and the hose could get caught in the blades.**

24 Once the evaporator has been cleaned, the best way to prevent the mildew from coming back again is to make sure your evaporator housing drain tube is clear (see illustration 12.4).

14 Air conditioning compressor - removal and installation

> ❋❋ **WARNING:**
>
> **The air conditioning system is under high pressure. Do not loosen any hose fittings or remove any components until after the system has been discharged. Air conditioning refrigerant must be properly discharged into an EPA-approved recovery/recycling unit at a dealer service department or an automotive air conditioning repair facility. Always wear eye protection when disconnecting air conditioning system fittings.**

> ❋❋ **CAUTION:**
>
> **When replacing entire components, additional refrigerant oil should be added equal to the amount that is removed with the component being replaced. Be sure to read the can before adding any oil to the system, to make sure it is compatible with the R-134a system.**

➡ Note: The receiver-drier should be replaced whenever the compressor is replaced.

REMOVAL

🔸 **Refer to illustrations 14.6 and 14.7**

1 Have the air conditioning system refrigerant discharged and recovered by an air conditioning technician.

2 Disconnect the cable from the negative battery terminal (see

14.6 The compressor clutch electrical connector (shown detached from the fan shroud assembly)

Chapter 5, Section 1).

3 Remove the A/C compressor drivebelt (see Chapter 1).

4 Set the parking brake, block the rear wheels and raise the front of the vehicle, supporting it securely on jackstands.

5 Remove the splash shield from under the engine compartment (see Chapter 2A).

6 Disconnect the compressor clutch electrical connector (see illustration).

7   Disconnect the refrigerant lines from the compressor. Plug the open fittings immediately to prevent entry of dirt and moisture (see illustration).

8   Remove the compressor mounting bolts (see illustration 14.7).

9   Carefully guide the compressor out of the engine compartment from below.

INSTALLATION

10   If a new compressor is being installed, follow the accompanying directions on draining the excess oil from it prior to installation.

11   The clutch may have to be transferred from the old compressor to the new unit.

12   Installation is the reverse of removal. Use new O-rings (lightly coated with fresh refrigerant oil) at the line fittings.

➡**Note: Only use O-rings that are designed specifically for A/C system applications.**

13   Have the system evacuated, recharged and leak tested by an air conditioning technician.

14   Reconnect the battery (see Chapter 5, Section 1).

14.7 Typical air conditioning compressor details

1   Refrigerant line fittings   *2   Mounting bolts*

---

15 Air conditioning receiver-drier - removal and installation

▶ **Refer to illustration 15.3**

✳ WARNING:

The air conditioning system is under high pressure. Do not loosen any hose fittings or remove any components until after the system has been discharged. Air conditioning refrigerant must be properly discharged into an EPA-approved recovery/recycling unit at a dealer service department or an automotive air conditioning repair facility. Always wear eye protection when disconnecting air conditioning system fittings.

✳ CAUTION:

When replacing entire components, additional refrigerant oil should be added equal to the amount that is removed with the component being replaced. Be sure to read the can before adding any oil to the system, to make sure it is compatible with the R-134a system.

1   Have the refrigerant discharged and recovered by an air conditioning technician.

RECEIVER-DRIER MOUNTED SEPARATELY FROM THE CONDENSER

2   On 1997 and earlier models, remove the radiator grille.

➡**Note: On 1997 and earlier models, the receiver drier is mounted in front of the condenser and the grill must be removed for access.**

3   Remove the refrigerant lines from the receiver-drier and cap them immediately to prevent the entry of dirt or moisture into the system (see

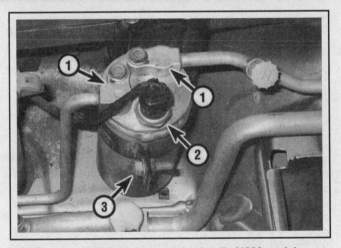

15.3 Air conditioning receiver-drier details (1999 model shown, others are similar)

1   Refrigerant line fittings   *3   Bracket bolt*
2   Pressure switch

illustration). Discard the O-ring seals.

4   Remove the bracket bolt that secures the receiver-drier and remove the unit from its bracket (see illustration 15.3).

5   Installation is the reverse of removal. Be sure to install new O-rings onto the line fittings and lightly coat them with refrigerant oil.

➡**Note: Only use O-rings that are designed specifically for A/C system applications.**

If you are replacing the receiver-drier with a new unit, add 1/3-ounce (10 ml) of refrigerant oil to the replacement.

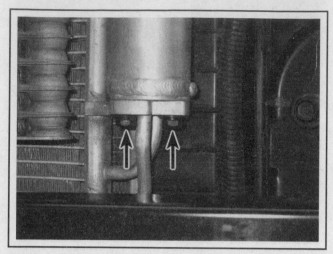

15.7 Receiver-drier mounting nuts (models with a receiver-drier mounted integrally with condenser)

RECEIVER-DRIERS INTEGRAL WITH CONDENSER

▶ Refer to illustration 15.7

➡Note: On later models the receiver-drier is mounted integrally with the condenser, at the left end of the condenser. On these models you must remove the condenser to replace the receiver-drier.

6 Remove the condenser (see Section 16).

7 Remove the two nuts that secure the receiver-drier to the condenser (see illustration) and remove the receiver-drier.

8 Remove and discard the old O-rings, coat the new O-rings with a thin coat of refrigerant oil and install the new O-rings. If you're installing a new receiver-drier, be sure to add ND-OIL8 refrigerant oil.

9 Installation is the reverse of removal. Be sure to tighten the mounting nuts securely.

ALL MODELS

10 Have the system evacuated, charged and leak tested by the shop that discharged it.

16 Air conditioning condenser - removal and installation

✳ **WARNING:**

The air conditioning system is under high pressure. Do not loosen any hose fittings or remove any components until after the system has been discharged. Air conditioning refrigerant must be properly discharged into an EPA-approved recovery/recycling unit at a dealer service department or an automotive air conditioning repair facility. Always wear eye protection when disconnecting air conditioning system fittings.

✳ **CAUTION:**

When replacing entire components, additional refrigerant oil should be added equal to the amount that is removed with the component being replaced. Be sure to read the can before adding any oil to the system, to make sure it is compatible with the R-134a system.

➡Note: The receiver-drier should be replaced whenever the condenser is replaced.

REMOVAL

▶ Refer to illustrations 16.7 and 16.8

1 Have the refrigerant discharged and recovered by an air conditioning technician.

2 Disconnect the cable from the negative battery terminal (see Chapter 5, Section 1).

Sephia and Spectra models

3 On 1997 and earlier models, remove the radiator grille and the condenser fan (see Section 4).

16.7 Typical refrigerant line fittings for the condenser

4 On 1997 and earlier models, remove the receiver-drier (see Section 15) and disconnect the refrigerant line on the right side of the condenser and cap it immediately to prevent dirt or moisture from entering the system.

5 On 1998 and later models, remove the front bumper cover (see Chapter 11).

6 Remove the hood latch support brace.

7 On 1998 and later models, disconnect the refrigerant line fittings to the condenser (see illustration).

8 Remove the condenser bracket bolts (see illustration) and carefully lift the condenser from its lower mounts to remove it.

16.8 The condenser mounting bolts and brackets (A) and hood latch support brace bolt locations (B) (typical)

16.13 Condenser details; right side shown, left side identical (Sportage models)

1   Right mounting bolt   2   Right mounting tab/bracket

Sportage models

▶ **Refer to illustration 16.13**

9   Detach the coolant reservoir (see Section 5) and set it aside. Don't disconnect the hose that connects the reservoir to the radiator.

10 On vehicles with an automatic transaxle, remove the transaxle oil cooler (see Chapter 7B).

11 Remove the left and right radiator mounting bolts and brackets (see illustrations 4.30 and 6.12).

12 Disconnect the high and low-side refrigerant lines at the right side of the radiator (see illustration 6.12), then pull the radiator back a little.

13 Remove the condenser mounting bolts (see illustration).

14 Disengage the lower mounting tabs from their brackets and lift the condenser up and out.

INSTALLATION (ALL MODELS)

▶ **Refer to illustration 16.15**

15 If you're going to reuse the old condenser, straighten any bent condenser fins with a fin comb (see illustration), then blow out the debris with compressed air.

❊❊ CAUTION:

Use a face shield and goggles when using compressed air to clean the condenser.

16.15 Straighten and clean bent condenser fins with a fin comb (available at most auto parts stores)

16 Installation is the reverse of removal. Assemble all connections with new O-rings, lightly lubricated with R-134a refrigerant oil.

➡**Note: Only use O-rings that are designed specifically for A/C system applications. If a new condenser was installed, add 2/3-ounce (20 ml) of fresh refrigerant oil.**

17 Reconnect the battery (see Chapter 5, Section 1).

18 Have the system evacuated, charged and leak tested by the shop that discharged it.

17 Air conditioning pressure switch - replacement

❋❋ WARNING:

The air conditioning system is under high pressure. Do not loosen any hose fittings or remove any components until after the system has been discharged. Air conditioning refrigerant must be properly discharged into an EPA-approved recovery/ recycling unit at a dealer service department or an automotive air conditioning repair facility. Always wear eye protection when disconnecting air conditioning system fittings.

➡Note: The air conditioning pressure switch detects low and high system pressure and shuts the system off if the pressure is too low or too high.

1 Have the refrigerant discharged and recovered by an air conditioning technician.

2 Unplug the electrical connector from the air conditioning pressure switch (see illustration 15.3).

3 Unscrew the pressure switch from the receiver-drier.

➡Note: It's best to plug the opening or have the replacement switch ready to install so the system does not get contaminated.

4 Lubricate the O-ring on the switch with clean refrigerant oil of the correct type.

5 Screw the new switch in place until hand tight, then tighten it securely.

6 Reconnect the electrical connector.

7 Have the system evacuated, charged and leak tested by the shop that discharged it.

Specifications

General

Radiator cap pressure rating	14 to 18 psi (93 to 123 kPa)
Thermostat rating (opening to fully open temperature range)	182 to 212-degrees F (87 to 100-degrees C)
Cooling system capacity	See Chapter 1
Refrigerant type	R-134a
Refrigerant capacity	Refer to HVAC specification tag

Torque specifications

➡Note: One foot-pound (ft-lb) of torque is equivalent to 12 inch-pounds (in-lbs) of torque. Torque values below approximately 15 foot-pounds are expressed in inch-pounds, because most foot-pound torque wrenches are not accurate at these smaller values.

	Ft-lbs (unless otherwise indicated)	Nm
Condenser inlet and outlet nuts/bolts	86 in-lbs	9.5
Thermostat housing cover bolts		
All four-cylinder engines except 2.0L DOHC	19	26
2.0L DOHC	11 to 15	15 to 20
2.7L V6	13 to 14	17 to 20
Water pump pulley bolts		
All four-cylinder engines except 2.0L DOHC	144 in-lbs	16
2.0L DOHC	72 to 84 in-lbs	8 to 9.5
2.7L V6	N/A	
Water pump mounting bolts		
All four-cylinder engines except 2.0L DOHC	19	26
2.0L DOHC	108 to 132 in-lbs	12 to 15
2.7L V6	120 to 192 in-lbs	13.5 to 21.5

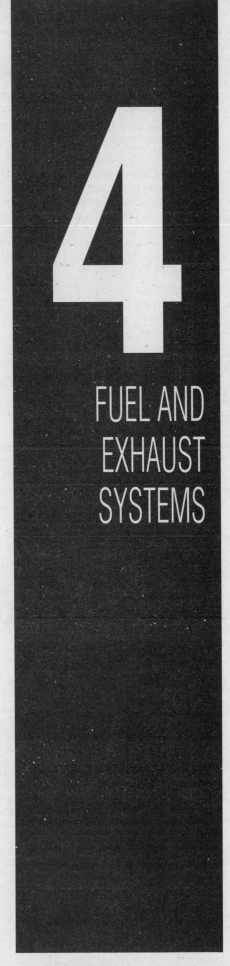

4

FUEL AND EXHAUST SYSTEMS

Section

1   General information
2   Fuel pressure relief procedure
3   Fuel pump/fuel pressure - check
4   Fuel lines and fittings - general information
5   Fuel pump/fuel gauge sending unit - removal and installation
6   Fuel pump/fuel gauge sending unit - component replacement
7   Fuel tank - removal and installation
8   Fuel tank cleaning and repair - general information
9   Air filter housing - removal and installation
10 Accelerator cable - removal, installation and adjustment
11 Multiport Fuel Injection (MFI) system - general information
12 Fuel injection system - check
13 Throttle body - removal and installation
14 Fuel pressure regulator - removal and installation
15 Fuel pulsation damper - removal and installation
16 Fuel rail and injectors - removal and installation
17 Exhaust system servicing - general information

Reference to other Chapters

Air filter replacement - See Chapter 1
CHECK ENGINE light on - See Chapter 6
Exhaust manifold - removal and installation - See Chapter 2A or 2B
Exhaust system check - See Chapter 1
Fuel system check - See Chapter 1
Intake manifold - removal and installation - See Chapter 1
Underhood hose check and replacement - See Chapter 1

1 General information

AIR INDUCTION SYSTEM

The air induction system consists of the air filter housing, the air intake duct, the throttle body, the accelerator cable and the intake manifold.

The throttle body contains a throttle plate that regulates the amount of air entering the intake manifold. The throttle plate is opened and closed by the accelerator cable. The throttle body is also the location of the Throttle Position (TP) sensor, a potentiometer that monitors the opening angle of the throttle plate and sends a variable voltage signal to the Powertrain Control Module (PCM). Another information sensor, the Intake Air Temperature (IAT) sensor, is located either inside the Mass Air Flow (MAF) sensor (1994 through 1997 models) or on the air filter housing (1998 and later models).

All of the air induction components (air filter housing, air intake duct, accelerator cable and throttle body) are covered in this Chapter except for the intake manifold, which is covered in Chapter 2A, and the information sensors, which are covered in Chapter 6.

FUEL SYSTEM

The fuel system consists of the fuel tank, an electric fuel pump/fuel gauge sending unit assembly inside the tank, the fuel filter, the fuel pulsation damper (1998 and later models), the fuel rail, the fuel injectors and the fuel lines and fittings connecting all of these components. The pulsation damper, which is located on the fuel rail, is a hydraulic accumulator (reservoir) that dampens the pressure pulses of the fuel pump.

All models are also equipped with a fuel pressure regulator, which maintains system operating fuel pressure within the range specified by the manufacturer. On 1994 through 1997 models, the fuel pressure regulator is located on the fuel rail. These models are equipped with a conventional fuel system, i.e. there is a fuel supply line from the fuel pump

in the tank to the fuel rail on the engine, and a fuel return line from the fuel rail back to the fuel tank. On 1998 and later models, the pressure regulator is an integral component of the fuel pump/fuel gauge sending unit. These models are equipped with a returnless system. There is an additional line coming out of the outlet side of the fuel filter that's routed back to the fuel pressure regulator. When the fuel pressure is excessive, the fuel pressure regulator opens, and fuel is diverted through the regulator and back into the fuel tank until the pressure is within the normal operating range, at which time the regulator closes.

The Multiport Fuel Injection (MFI) system is a sequential multiport system, which means that the fuel injectors deliver fuel directly into the intake ports of the cylinders in firing order sequence (1-3-4-2). Sequential multiport systems provide much better control of the air/fuel mixture ratio than earlier fuel injection systems, and are therefore able to produce more power, better mileage and lower emissions.

If you're looking for the fuel filter, refer to Chapter 1. Changing the fuel filter is a scheduled maintenance item. For more information about the MFI system, see Section 11. For more information about the PCM and the information sensors, refer to Chapter 6.

EXHAUST SYSTEM

The exhaust system consists of the exhaust manifold, the catalytic converter(s), the muffler, the tailpipe and the various sections of exhaust pipe connecting these components. On 1994 and 1995 B6 SOHC models and on 1995 through 1997 BP DOHC models there is one Three-Way Catalyst (TWC) underneath the vehicle. On 1995 through 1997 B6 DOHC models and on all 1998 through 2001 models there are two catalysts: a Warm-Up Three-Way Catalyst (WU-TWC) and the same TWC underneath the vehicle that's used on the other models. The exhaust manifolds are covered in Chapter 2A and the catalytic converters are in Chapter 6. The information in this Chapter covers maintenance, inspection and service for the rest of the exhaust system.

2 Fuel pressure relief procedure

◆ **Refer to illustration 2.3**

1   Remove the rear seat cushion (see Chapter 11).
2   Start the engine.
3   Disconnect the fuel pump electrical connector (see illustration).

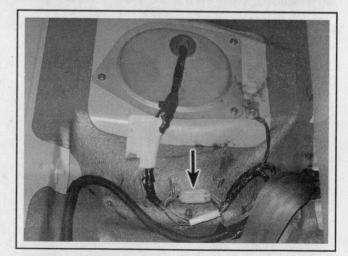

2.3 To disable the fuel pump, disconnect the fuel pump/fuel gauge sending unit electrical connector

The engine will stall immediately. Turn the ignition key to OFF or LOCK. The system fuel pressure is now relieved, but there is still fuel in the lines, so be sure to have some rags handy to wipe up any spilled fuel when disconnecting fuel lines.

4   Remove the fuel filler neck cap to relieve the pressure inside the fuel tank.

5   Disconnect the cable from the negative terminal of the battery (see Chapter 5, Section 1). It's now safe to work on the fuel system.

3   Fuel pump/fuel pressure - check

✳✳ WARNING:

Gasoline is extremely flammable, so take extra precautions when you work on any part of the fuel system. See the Warning in Section 2.

GENERAL CHECKS

1   Verify that there is fuel in the fuel tank.

2   Verify that the fuel pump actually runs. Turn the ignition switch to ON - you should hear a brief whirring noise for about two seconds as the pump comes on and pressurizes the system. If you can't hear the pump from inside the vehicle, open the fuel filler neck cap, then have an assistant turn the ignition switch to ON while you listen to the pump through the fuel filler neck.

MODELS WITHOUT A SCHRADER VALVE

▶ **Refer to illustrations 3.3, 3.5a, 3.5b and 3.6**

3   There are no service ports on these models, so you'll need to obtain a fuel pressure gauge (see illustration) capable of reading at least 60 psi (414 kPa), a tee-fitting, three short sections of approved fuel hose and the appropriate hose clamps to secure everything together. You'll also need a short section of approved fuel pipe to connect your inlet test hose to the fuel supply hose. Fuel pressure gauges, fuel hose and fuel pipes are available at most auto parts stores.

4   Relieve the system fuel pressure (see Section 2), then disconnect the cable from the negative battery terminal (see Chapter 5, Section 1).

5   On Sephia and Spectra models, locate the fuel filter on the firewall, then trace the hose from the fuel filter to the fuel rail. This is the fuel supply hose (see illustration). Loosen the hose clamp and disconnect the fuel supply hose from the fuel rail. On Sportage models, locate the supply line at the left end of the front fuel rail (see illustration 16.30), then trace the supply hose back to the threaded fitting below the brake master cylinder (see illustration). Unscrew the fitting and tee into the system here.

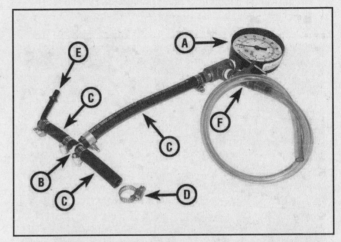

3.3 Fuel pressure gauge setup for checking fuel pressure on models without a Schrader valve

A . *Fuel pressure gauge*	D *Hose clamps*
B *T-fitting*	E *Short section of fuel pipe*
C *Fuel hose*	F *Bleeder valve (optional)*

3.5a Loosen the hose clamp (A) for the fuel supply hose and disconnect the supply hose from the fuel rail. The other hose (B) is the fuel return hose - don't disconnect this hose unless you're removing the fuel rail

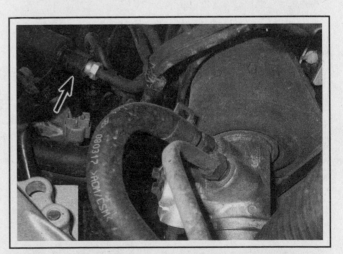

3.5b On Sportage models, the threaded fuel line fitting is located below the brake master cylinder (this view is as seen looking through the left wheel housing, but you can access the fitting from the engine compartment)

3.6 To measure the fuel pressure on a model without a Schrader valve, tee into the fuel system between the fuel supply hose and the fuel rail

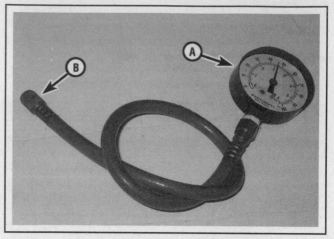

3.11 Fuel pressure gauge setup for checking fuel pressure on models with a Schrader valve

A   *Fuel pressure gauge*
B   *Hose with Schrader valve fitting*

the pressure does not increase, replace the fuel filter (see Chapter 1) and recheck the pressure. If it's still low, check the fuel supply hose and line for a restriction. If there is no restriction, replace the fuel pump (see Section 6).

➡**Note: As the fuel pump is removed, check the inlet strainer on the bottom of the pump for clogging.**

9   To check the operation of the fuel pressure regulator, disconnect the vacuum hose from the regulator with the engine idling and watch the fuel pressure gauge - the fuel pressure should increase 3 to 10 psi as soon as the hose is disconnected. If it doesn't, check for vacuum at the hose (see Step 8a). If vacuum is present, replace the fuel pressure regulator.

10 Relieve the system fuel pressure (see Section 2), then disconnect the cable from the negative battery terminal (see Chapter 5, Section 1). Remove the fuel pressure gauge and test hoses, then reconnect the fuel supply hose to the fuel rail. Reconnect the cable to the negative battery terminal (see Chapter 5, Section 1), then start the engine and check for leaks.

MODELS WITH A SCHRADER VALVE

▶ **Refer to illustrations 3.11 and 3.13**

11 To measure the fuel pressure, you'll need a fuel pressure gauge capable of reading up to 60 psi (414 kPa), some fuel hose and an adapter suitable for connecting the gauge to the Schrader valve-type service port on the fuel rail (see illustration). Fuel pressure gauges and adapters are available at most auto parts stores.

12 Relieve the system fuel pressure (see Section 2), then disconnect the cable from the negative battery terminal (see Chapter 5, Section 1).

13 Locate the Schrader valve test port on the fuel rail, unscrew the cap and connect the fuel pressure gauge to the test port (see illustration).

14 Reconnect the cable to the negative battery terminal (see Chapter 5, Section 1).

15 Turn the ignition switch to ON (don't start the engine yet). The fuel pump should run for about two seconds - pressure should register on the gauge and should hold steady.

3.13 To measure the fuel pressure on models with a Schrader valve, locate the Schrader valve test port on the fuel rail, unscrew the cap and connect the fuel pressure gauge to the test port

6   Using your tee fitting, hose clamps and short sections of hose, install the fuel pressure gauge between the disconnected fuel supply hose and the fuel rail (see illustration).

7   Reconnect the cable to the negative battery terminal (see Chapter 5, Section 1), then turn the ignition key to ON (don't start the engine yet). The fuel pump should run for about two seconds and the gauge should indicate pressure and hold steady.

8   Turn on the engine, allow it to warm up to its normal operating temperature, then measure the fuel pressure and compare your readings to the system pressure listed in this Chapter's Specifications.

   a) *If the pressure is high, disconnect the vacuum hose from the fuel pressure regulator and connect a vacuum gauge to it. Make sure there is 12 in-Hg or more vacuum present at the hose. If there isn't, check the hose for a restriction or leak.*

   b) *If there is adequate vacuum to the regulator but the pressure is high, check for a restricted fuel return hose or line. If the return hose and line are clear, replace the pressure regulator (see Section 14).*

   c) *If the pressure is low, pinch the fuel return hose. If the pressure goes up, replace the fuel pressure regulator (see Section 14). If*

16 Start the engine and let it warm up until it's idling at its normal operating temperature, then measure the fuel pressure and compare your reading to the fuel pressure listed in this Chapter's Specifications.

  a) *If the indicated fuel pressure is low, inspect the fuel supply hose and line for an obstruction. If the hose and line are clear, replace the fuel filter, then recheck the fuel pressure. If the indicated fuel pressure is still low, replace the fuel pressure regulator, then recheck the fuel pressure. If the fuel pressure is still low, replace the fuel pump.*

  b) *If the indicated fuel pressure is high, replace the fuel pressure regulator (see Section 6), then recheck the fuel pressure. If the fuel pressure is still high, have the fuel system diagnosed by a dealer service department or other qualified repair shop.*

17 After the test is complete, relieve the system fuel pressure (see Section 2), then disconnect the cable from the negative battery terminal (see Chapter 5, Section 1).

18 Remove the fuel pressure gauge.

19 Reconnect the cable to the negative battery terminal (see Chapter 5, Section 1).

20 Start the engine and check for fuel leaks.

4 Fuel lines and fittings - general information

✳✳ WARNING:

Gasoline is extremely flammable, so take extra precautions when you work on any part of the fuel system. See the Warning in Section 2.

1 Always relieve the fuel pressure before servicing fuel lines or fittings (see Section 2), then disconnect the cable from the negative battery terminal (see Chapter 5, Section 1) before proceeding.

2 Whenever you're working under the vehicle, be sure to inspect all fuel and evaporative emission lines for leaks, kinks, dents and other damage. Always replace a damaged fuel or EVAP line immediately. Leaking fuel and EVAP lines will result in loss of fuel and excessive air pollution (leaking raw fuel emits unburned hydrocarbon vapors into the atmosphere).

3 All fuel and EVAP lines are secured to the underbody with small plastic or metal brackets attached to the vehicle floorpan. To detach a metal fuel/EVAP bracket from the pan, simply remove the bracket retaining bolt, then pull the bracket down and disengage it from the lines. If any of the brackets feel loose after installation, remove them and replace them with new brackets.

4 If you find signs of dirt in the lines during disassembly, disconnect all lines and blow them out with compressed air. Inspect the fuel strainer on the fuel pump pick-up unit (see Sections 5 and 6) for damage and deterioration. And inspect the fuel pump's inlet filter, which is an integral component of the fuel pump/fuel gauge sending unit module (see Section 6).

STEEL TUBING

5 Because fuel lines used on fuel-injected vehicles are under fairly high pressure, it is critical that they be replaced with lines of equivalent specification. If you have to replace a fuel line, use only steel tubing that meets the manufacturer's specifications. Don't use copper or aluminum tubing to replace steel tubing. These materials cannot withstand normal vehicle vibration.

6 Some steel fuel lines have threaded fittings. When loosening these fittings to service or replace components:

  a) *Always hold the stationary fitting with a wrench while turning the tube nut (this will prevent the line from twisting).*

  b) *If you're going to replace one of these fittings, use original equipment parts or parts that meet original equipment standards.*

PLASTIC TUBING

7 Some fuel lines - between the fuel supply and return pipes of the fuel pump and the front of the fuel tank, for example - are plastic. If you ever have to replace either line, use only the original equipment plastic tubing.

✳✳ CAUTION:

When removing or installing plastic fuel line tubing, be careful not to bend or twist it too much, which can damage it. And damaged fuel lines MUST be replaced! Also, be aware that the plastic fuel tubing is NOT heat resistant, so keep it away from excessive heat. Nor is it acid-proof, so don't wipe it off with a shop rag that has been used to wipe off battery electrolyte. If you accidentally spill or wipe electrolyte on plastic fuel tubing, replace the tubing.

FLEXIBLE HOSES

✳✳ WARNING:

Use only original equipment replacement hoses or their equivalent. Unapproved hoses might fail when subjected to the high operating pressures of the fuel system.

8 Don't route fuel hoses (or metal lines) within four inches of the exhaust system or within ten inches of the catalytic converter. Make sure that no rubber hoses are installed directly against the vehicle, particularly in places where there is any vibration. If allowed to touch some vibrating part of the vehicle, a hose can easily become chafed and it might start leaking. A good rule of thumb is to maintain a minimum of 1/4-inch clearance around a hose (or metal line) to prevent contact with the vehicle underbody.

DISCONNECTING AND RECONNECTING FUEL SYSTEM FITTINGS

Spring-type hose clamps (1994 through 1997 models)

9 On these models, flexible fuel hoses are secured to metal fuel

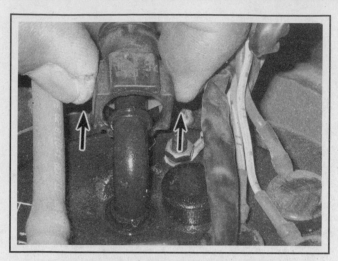

4.12 To disconnect the quick-connect fitting from the fuel pump outlet pipe, depress the two release buttons on the sides of the fitting (this disengages the locking mechanism inside the fitting from the raised ridge on the pipe), and pull off the fitting

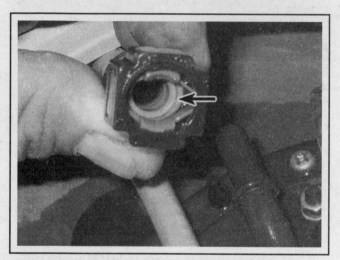

4.13 After disconnecting the quick-connect fitting from the fuel pump outlet pipe, inspect the condition of the O-ring inside the fitting. If it's cracked, torn or otherwise deteriorated, replace it

lines by spring-type hose clamps. This type of hose clamp relies on spring pressure - think of a small, short coil spring - to secure the hose tightly to the metal line. Once this type of clamp has been loosened, it might not pinch down the end of the hose as tightly when it's installed again. So it's a good idea to discard the old clamp and replace it with a new one when disconnecting one of these fittings.

10 After disconnecting a flexible hose from a metal fuel line, note the bulge at the end of the metal line, and the ridge around the circumference of the line, above an inch or so from the bulge at the end. When reconnecting the hose to the metal line, slide a new spring-type clamp onto the hose, then push the hose over the bulge and onto the metal line far enough so that the end of the hose is positioned at or near the smaller ridge. Then slide the new spring-type hose clamp into place about midway between the ridge and the bulge.

Quick-connect fittings (1998 and later models)

▶ **Refer to illustrations 4.12 and 4.13**

⁂ CAUTION:

When disconnecting or reconnecting quick-connect fittings, be careful not to bend or twist them excessively, or they will be damaged and will have to be replaced. Also, be aware that the quick-connect fittings are NOT heat resistant, so keep them away from excessive heat. Nor are they acid-proof, so don't wipe them off with a shop rag that has been used to wipe off battery electrolyte. If you accidentally spill or wipe electrolyte on quick-connect fittings, replace them.

---

11 Quick-connect fittings are used to connect the fuel supply and bypass lines to the fuel pump, the fuel filter and the fuel rail. The fittings at the fuel pump and fuel filter look slightly different from the fitting at the fuel rail, but both types are disconnected and reconnected in a similar fashion. Before disconnecting any fuel line fittings, relieve the fuel system pressure (see Section 2), then remove the fuel filler neck cap to relieve any pressure inside the fuel tank.

12 Depress the two buttons on the sides of the fittings and pull off the fitting far enough to release it from the ridge on the pipe (see illustration).

13 Inspect the old O-ring inside the bore of the fitting (see illustration). If it's cracked, torn or otherwise damaged, replace it.

14 To reconnect the fitting, push it onto the pipe until the locking mechanism in the fitting snaps over the ridge on the pipe.

15 Verify that the fitting is secure by trying to pull it off the pipe.

---

5 Fuel pump/fuel gauge sending unit - removal and installation

⁂ WARNING:

Gasoline is extremely flammable, so take extra precautions when you work on any part of the fuel system. See the Warning in Section 2.

1 Relieve the fuel system pressure (see Section 2), then remove the fuel filler neck cap to relieve any pressure inside the fuel tank.

2 Disconnect the cable from the negative battery terminal (see Chapter 5, Section 1).

3 Remove the rear seat cushion (see Chapter 11).

1994 THROUGH 1997 MODELS

▶ **Refer to illustrations 5.4, 5.5, 5.7 and 5.8**

4 Disconnect the electrical connector for the harness that runs through the fuel pump access cover, then remove the access cover screws (see illustration) and remove the cover.

5 Disconnect the fuel pump electrical connector and the ground

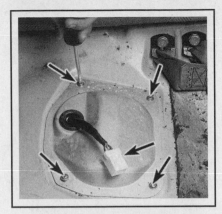

5.4 Disconnect the electrical connector for the fuel pump/fuel gauge sending unit harness, then remove these four screws and lift off the cover. Be careful not to damage the connector and harness when removing the cover (1994 through 1997 models)

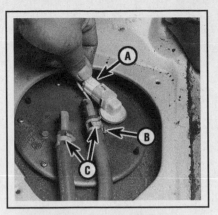

5.5 Disconnect the electrical connector from the fuel pump (A), remove the ground wire nut and disconnect the ground wire (B), then disconnect the fuel hoses from the pump (C) (1994 through 1997 models)

5.7 To detach the fuel pump from the fuel tank, remove these screws . . .

5.8 . . . then lift the fuel pump assembly out of the tank at an angle so that you don't bend the float arm on the fuel gauge sending unit

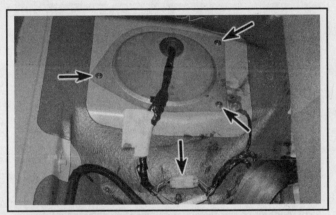

5.11 Disconnect the two electrical connectors for the harness that runs through the fuel pump access cover, then remove the cover screws and remove the cover (typical 1998 and later model)

wire attached to the top of the fuel pump (see illustration).

6   Disconnect the fuel supply and return hoses from the pump (see illustration).

7   Remove the fuel pump retaining screws (see illustration).

8   Carefully lift the fuel pump assembly out of the fuel tank (see illustration). Inspect the seal for cracks, tears and deterioration. If it's damaged, replace it.

9   Installation is the reverse of removal.

10   Connect the cable to the negative battery terminal (see Chapter 5, Section 1), start the engine and look for leaks.

1998 AND LATER MODELS (EXCEPT SPORTAGE)

Refer to illustrations 5.11, 5.12, 5.14, 5.16a and 5.16b

11   Disconnect the two electrical connectors for the harness that runs through the fuel pump access cover, then remove the fuel pump access cover screws (see illustration) and remove the access cover.

12   After removing the fuel pump access cover, disconnect the electrical connector for the EVAP canister close valve (see illustration).

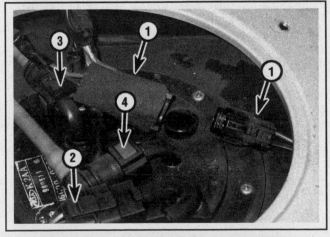

5.12 Disconnect the electrical connector for the EVAP canister close valve (1) and the fuel tank pressure sensor (2), then disconnect the quick-connect fittings for the fuel supply line (3) and the fuel bypass line (4) (typical 1998 and later model)

5.14 To remove the pump/sending unit, remove these screws and this nut (A) (typical 1998 and later model)

5.16a Lift the fuel pump assembly out of the tank at an angle so that you don't bend the float arm on the fuel gauge sending unit (typical 1998 and later model)

5.16b After removing the pump, be sure to remove the sealing ring from the underside of the pump mounting flange and inspect the ring for cracks, tears and deterioration. If it's damaged or worn, replace it (typical 1998 and later model)

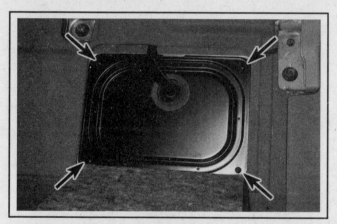

5.19 Fuel pump access cover screws (Sportage models)

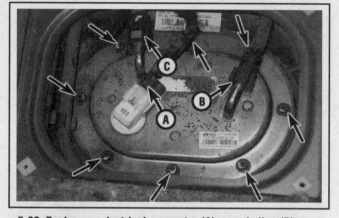

5.20 Fuel pump electrical connector (A), supply line (B), suction line from right side of tank (C) and mounting flange bolts (Sportage models)

13 Disconnect the quick-connect fittings for the fuel supply line and for the fuel bypass line and set the supply and bypass lines aside. If you're not familiar with quick-connect fittings, refer to Section 4 for an illustrated step-by-step disconnection and reconnection procedure. Note that the release buttons on the fuel supply line quick-connect fitting are green and the buttons on the fuel bypass line fitting are red. Make sure that you mark the two pipes protruding from the top of the fuel pump/fuel gauge sending unit assembly accordingly. Each fitting must be reconnected to the same pipe to which it was connected prior to disconnection.

14 If the vehicle is equipped with a fuel tank pressure sensor (see illustration), and if you're replacing the fuel pump assembly - not simply the fuel gauge sending unit, pump or regulator - then you'll need to remove this sensor and install it on top of the new pump assembly. Remove the sensor retaining nut and remove the sensor from the pump assembly.

15 Remove the fuel pump/fuel gauge sending unit assembly mounting screws.

16 Remove the fuel pump/fuel gauge sending unit assembly from the tank (see illustration). When removing the pump/sending unit from the tank, carefully angle the module to protect the float arm and float from damage. After removing the pump/sending unit module, inspect the

seal (see illustration) for cracks, tears and deterioration. If it's damaged, replace it.

17 Installation is the reverse of removal.

18 Connect the cable to the negative battery terminal (see Chapter 5, Section 1), start the engine and look for leaks.

SPORTAGE MODELS

♦ **Refer to illustrations 5.19 and 5.20**

➡ **Note: On these models, the fuel pump assembly is located on the left side of the fuel tank (rectangular access cover). This assembly includes the fuel filter, the fuel pump, the fuel pressure regulator and the fuel gauge sending unit. A second fuel gauge sending unit is located on the right side of the tank (square access cover); if you're going to replace this component, refer to Section 6.**

19 Remove the access cover screws (see illustration) and remove the cover.

20 Disconnect the electrical connector from the fuel pump (see illustration).

21 Disconnect the fuel supply line and suction line quick-connect fittings from the pump.

22 Remove the bolts from the fuel pump mounting flange and remove the pump assembly from the fuel tank.

23 If you're replacing the fuel pressure regulator or the fuel gauge sending unit, refer to Section 6. If you're replacing the fuel pump or the integral fuel filter, no further disassembly is possible.

24 Installation is the reverse of removal.

25 Connect the cable to the negative battery terminal (see Chapter 5, Section 1), start the engine and check for leaks.

6 · Fuel pump/fuel gauge sending unit - component replacement

❊❊ WARNING:

Gasoline is extremely flammable, so take extra precautions when you work on any part of the fuel system. See the Warning in Section 2.

1994 THROUGH 1997 MODELS

1 Remove the fuel pump/fuel gauge sending unit (see Section 5) and place the pump/sending unit assembly on a clean workbench.

Fuel pump

♦ **Refer to illustration 6.2**

2 Disconnect the fuel pump electrical connector (see illustration).

3 Loosen the two springs clamps and slide them off the short section of hose connecting the pump outlet pipe to the pipe on the underside of the pump assembly mounting flange. Discard these two spring clamps and replace them with new ones.

4 Remove the retainer that secures the fuel pump's inlet filter to the small bracket at the bottom of the pump and remove the inlet filter. Carefully wash the inlet filter in clean solvent, blow it dry with low-pressure compressed air, then inspect it for holes, tears and obstructions. If the inlet filter is damaged or worn, replace it.

5 Remove the screw that secures the small bracket at the bottom of the pump to the main pump bracket, then remove the small bracket.

6 Remove the rubber mount located between the small bracket and the bottom of the pump. Inspect the condition of the rubber mount. If it's cracked, torn or otherwise deteriorated, replace it.

7 Remove the large rubber band that secures the pump to the main bracket and remove the pump. Inspect the condition of the rubber band. If it's cracked, torn or otherwise deteriorated, replace it.

8 Remove the short section of hose from the old pump's outlet pipe. When you disconnect this hose, you'll see an O-ring, cap and spacer. Remove all three and replace them with a new O-ring set.

9 Discard the old pump assembly sealing ring and replace it with new ring.

10 After installing the rubber mount and small bracket, pull the pump down so that it is seated tightly against the rubber mount. When the pump is secured, slide the new hose clamps into position on the outlet hose.

11 Installation is otherwise the reverse of removal.

Fuel gauge sending unit

♦ **Refer to illustrations 6.12 and 6.13**

12 Disconnect the fuel gauge sending unit electrical connector (see illustration).

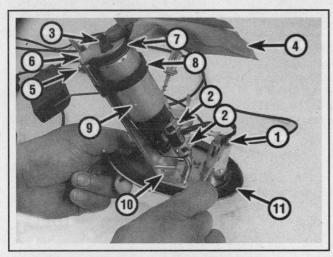

6.2 Fuel pump replacement details (1994 through 1997 models)

1 *Fuel pump electrical connector*
2 *Hose clamps*
3 *Fuel pump inlet filter retainer*
4 *Fuel pump inlet filter*
5 *Fuel pump small mounting bracket screw*
6 *Fuel pump small mounting bracket*
7 *Rubber mount*
8 *Large rubber band*
9 *Fuel pump*
10 *Fuel pump main mounting bracket*
11 *Sealing ring*

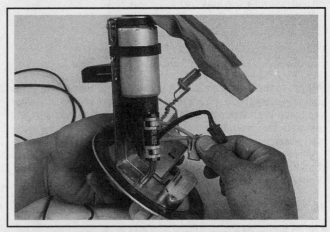

6.12 Disconnect the fuel gauge sending unit electrical connector (1994 through 1997 models)

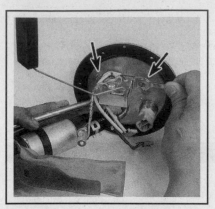

6.13 To detach the fuel gauge sending unit from the fuel pump assembly, remove these two nuts (1994 through 1997 models)

6.15a Pry the fuel gauge sending unit loose from these two retainers . . .

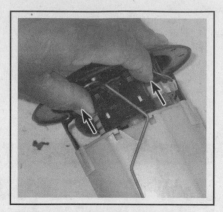

6.15b . . . then slide it up and carefully remove it and set it next to the pump assembly (typical 1998 and later model)

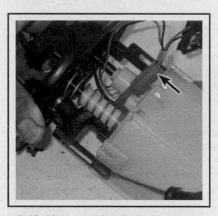

6.16 After removing the fuel gauge sending unit, disconnect the sending unit electrical connector. If you're going to disassemble the pump assembly further, pry loose the retainers for the upper part of the pump assembly (typical 1998 and later model)

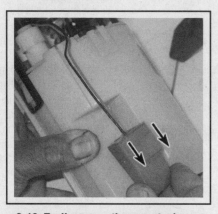

6.18 To disengage the receptacle locator pin from the mounting hole, slide the pin toward the larger part of the hole, then pull it out. Carefully set the ground wire receptacle aside (typical 1998 and later model)

6.21 To disconnect the fuel pump electrical connector, press this release tab and pull off the connector (typical 1998 and later model)

13 Remove the two nuts (see illustration) that secure the fuel gauge sending unit bracket to the fuel pump assembly and separate the sending unit from the pump assembly.

14 Installation is the reverse of removal.

1998 AND LATER MODELS (EXCEPT SPORTAGE)

➡Note: At the time of writing, it was possible to purchase a new fuel gauge sending unit or a new fuel pressure regulator, but the fuel pump itself was available from Kia dealers only as part of a complete fuel pump/fuel gauge sending unit/fuel pressure regulator assembly. However, by the time you need to replace the pump, you might be able to purchase a new aftermarket pump at an auto parts store even if it's still unavailable from dealer service departments as a separate component.

Fuel gauge sending unit

♦ Refer to illustrations 6.15a, 6.15b and 6.16

15 Pry the two mounting tabs for the fuel gauge sending unit loose from their plastic retainers (see illustration), then slide the sending unit up (see illustration) and remove it from the fuel pump assembly.

16 Disconnect the fuel gauge sending unit electrical connector (see illustration).

17 Installation is the reverse of removal.

Fuel pump

♦ Refer to illustrations 6.18, 6.21, 6.22, 6.26, 6.27 and 6.29

18 Disengage the ground wire receptacle from the side of the fuel pump assembly (see illustration). (The receptacle is secured to the side of the pump assembly by a locator pin pushed into one of those holes that's smaller at one end and wider at the other. To disengage the locator pin from the hole, slide it to the wider part of the hole and pull it out.)

19 Remove the fuel gauge sending unit (see Steps 15 and 16).

20 Disengage the retainers for the upper part of the fuel pump assembly from the lower part of the pump assembly (see illustration 6.16).

21 Disconnect the fuel pump electrical connector (see illustration).

22 Disconnect the fuel pump outlet hose from the outlet pipe on the

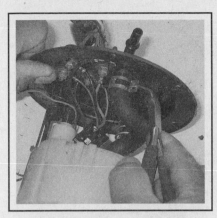

6.22 To disconnect the fuel pump outlet hose from the outlet pipe on the upper part of the fuel pump assembly, loosen this spring-type hose clamp, slide it down the hose and pull the hose off the pipe (typical 1998 and later model)

6.26 Pry the cover retainers loose from the lower part of the fuel pump assembly with a small screwdriver, then carefully pull off the cover (typical 1998 and later model)

6.27 Carefully pull the fuel pump out of the pump assembly cover (typical 1998 and later model)

6.29 To detach the fuel pump inlet filter from the pump, pry off the retainer. Discard the retainer; be sure to use a new retainer when installing the filter again (typical 1998 and later model)

6.32 Remove the fuel pressure regulator from the fuel pump cover (typical 1998 and later model)

6.33 Even if you're planning to install the old fuel pressure regulator, be sure remove and discard the old O-rings and install new ones. If you're installing a new pressure regulator, be sure to install new O-rings (don't swap the old O-ring from the old pressure regulator onto the new regulator!) (typical 1998 and later model)

upper part of the pump assembly (see illustration).

23 Detach the wiring harness clip from the lower part of the pump assembly.

24 Pull the two halves of the fuel pump assembly apart.

25 Disconnect the fuel pump outlet hose from the fuel pump outlet pipe.

26 Remove the cover from the lower part of the fuel pump assembly (see illustration).

27 Pull the pump out of the cover (see illustration).

28 Remove the rubber insulators from both ends of the pump. Inspect the insulators for cracks, tears and deterioration and replace them if they're damaged or worn

29 Remove the fuel pump inlet filter from the pump (see illustration). Carefully wash the filter in clean solvent, then blow it dry with low-pressure compressed air, then inspect it for tears, deterioration and obstructions. If the filter is damaged or worn, replace it.

30 Installation is the reverse of removal.

Fuel pressure regulator

▶ **Refer to illustrations 6.32 and 6.33**

31 Disassemble the fuel pump assembly as described in Steps 18 through 28.

32 Remove the fuel pressure regulator from the pump cover (see illustration).

33 Install new O-rings on the fuel pressure regulator (see illustration).

34 Installation is the reverse of removal.

SPORTAGE MODELS

Fuel filter, fuel pressure regulator or fuel gauge sending unit

→Note: The fuel pump assembly includes the fuel filter, the fuel pump, the fuel pressure regulator and the fuel gauge sending unit.

35 Remove the fuel pump assembly (see Section 5).
36 Remove the old fuel filter, fuel pressure regulator or fuel gauge sending unit.
37 Install the new filter, regulator or sending unit on the fuel pump.
38 Install the fuel pump assembly (see Section 5).

Sub fuel sender

Refer to illustration 6.40

→Note: The sub fuel sender (the fuel gauge sending unit for the right half of the fuel tank) is located under the right (square) access cover on top of the right half of the fuel tank.

39 Remove the rear seat cushion and the carpeting underneath (see Chapter 11).
40 Remove the access cover screws and the access cover (see illustration).

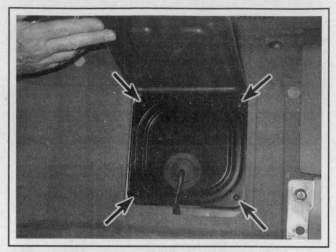

6.40 Sub fuel sender access cover screws (Sportage models)

41 Disconnect the electrical connector and disconnect the quick-connect fitting for the suction line.
42 Remove the sub fuel sender mounting flange bolts and remove the sub fuel sender from the fuel tank.
43 Installation is the reverse of removal.

7 Fuel tank - removal and installation

※ WARNING:

Gasoline is extremely flammable, so take extra precautions when you work on any part of the fuel system. See the Warning in Section 2.

※ CAUTION:

The following procedure is much easier to perform if the fuel tank is empty. The tank has no drain plug, so the fuel must be siphoned from the tank with a siphoning kit, which is available at most auto parts stores. NEVER try to start the siphoning action with your mouth!

1 Relieve the fuel system pressure (see Section 2).
2 Disconnect the cable from the negative battery terminal (see Chapter 5, Section 1).
3 Raise the vehicle and support it securely on jackstands.
4 Disconnect the fuel supply and return lines from the fuel pump/ fuel gauge sending unit (see Section 5). If the fuel tank is empty or nearly empty, it's not necessary to siphon the remaining fuel from the tank. But if there is a lot of fuel in the tank, remove the fuel pump/fuel gauge sending unit (see Section 5) and siphon any residual fuel out of the tank through the mounting hole for the fuel pump/fuel gauge sending unit.

※ WARNING:

Always siphon fuel into an approved gasoline container. Also, never start the siphoning action by mouth - use a siphoning pump (available at most auto parts stores).

5 Disconnect the hoses and electrical connectors at the fuel pump (see Section 5). On 4WD Sportage models, also disconnect the electrical connector and the fuel suction line quick-connect fitting from the sub-fuel sender (the sending unit for the right part of the tank).
6 Support the fuel tank with a transmission jack or with a floor jack. If you're going to use a floor jack, place a sturdy board between the jack head and the fuel tank to protect the tank.

SEPHIA AND SPECTRA MODELS

1994 through 1997 models

▸ **Refer to illustrations 7.7a, 7.7b and 7.8**

7 Disconnect the fuel lines and the evaporative hoses at the tank (see illustrations).

→Note: Be sure to plug the hoses to prevent leakage and contamination of the fuel system.

8 Remove the bolt from the rear end of each of the two fuel tank retaining straps (see illustration). Carefully lower the fuel tank.
9 If you need to remove the fuel pump/fuel gauge sending unit, but haven't yet done so, refer to Section 5. If you're going to have the fuel tank cleaned, refer to Section 8.
10 Installation is the reverse of removal. Reconnect the cable to the negative battery terminal (see Chapter 5, Section 1), then start the engine and check for fuel leaks.

1998 and later models

▸ **Refer to illustrations 7.11, 7.12, 7.13 and 7.14**

11 Disconnect the EVAP hose from the On-Board Refueling Vapor

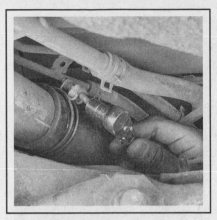

7.7a Loosen the hose clamp screw, slide the clamp down the hose and disconnect the fuel filler neck hose . . .

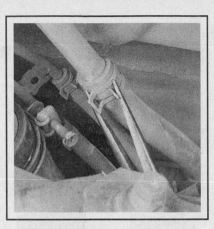

7.7b . . . then loosen the spring-type hose clamps, slide the clamps down the hoses and disconnect the three EVAP hoses (1994 through 1997 models)

7.8 Remove the fuel tank strap bolts (one bolt at the rear end of each strap - the straps are hinged at the front), then swing down the straps (1994 through 1997 models)

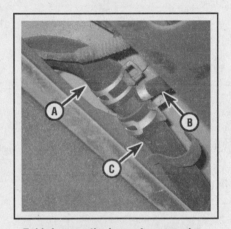

7.11 Loosen the hose clamps and disconnect the On-Board Refueling Vapor Recovery hose (A) and the rollover valve hose (B) from the EVAP canister hose (C) (typical 1998 and later model)

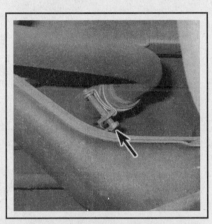

7.12 To disconnect the fuel filler neck hose, loosen this hose clamp screw, slide the clamp up the hose and pull off the hose from the fuel filler neck pipe (typical 1998 and later model)

7.13 To detach the exhaust pipe heat shield from the underside of the fuel tank, remove these three bolts (typical 1998 and later model)

Recovery (ORVR) hose and from the rollover valve hose (see illustration). Inspect these hoses for cracks, tears and other deterioration. If a hose is damaged or worn, replace it.

12 Disconnect the fuel filler neck hose from the fuel tank filler pipe (see illustration). Inspect the fuel filler neck hose for cracks, tears and other deterioration. If the filler neck hose is damaged or worn, replace it.

13 Remove the exhaust pipe (see Section 17), then remove the heat shield (see illustration).

14 Remove the fuel tank retaining strap bolts (see illustration) and allow the straps to swing down (they're hinged at the other end) or remove them.

15 Carefully lower the fuel tank.

16 If you need to remove the fuel pump/fuel gauge sending unit, but haven't yet done so, refer to Section 5. If you're going to have the fuel tank cleaned, refer to Section 8.

17 Installation is the reverse of removal. Reconnect the cable to the negative battery terminal (see Chapter 5, Section 1), then start the engine and check for fuel leaks.

7.14 To detach the fuel tank from the vehicle, remove these two bolts, then swing down the fuel tank straps (they're hinged at the other end) or remove the straps (typical 1998 and later model)

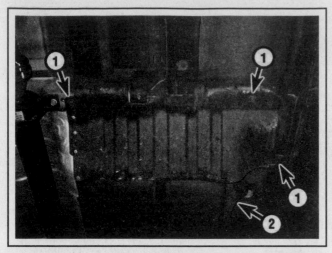

7.18 Fuel tank details, front (left front side shown, right front side identical) (Sportage models)

1 Rock shield fasteners 2 Parking brake cable bracket

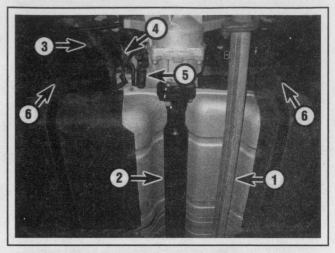

7.22 Fuel tank details, rear (Sportage models)

1	Exhaust pipe	5	EVAP system ventilation
2	Driveshaft (4WD models)		hose
3	Fuel filler neck hose	6	Fuel tank strap bolts
4	Fuel leveling hose		

SPORTAGE MODELS

▶ **Refer to illustrations 7.18 and 7.22**

18 On 4WD models, remove the left and right rock shields from the front end of the fuel tank (see illustration).

19 Remove the bolts that secure the parking brake cable brackets and push the cables aside.

20 Remove the exhaust system (see Section 17).

21 On 4WD models, remove the driveshaft (see Chapter 8).

22 Loosen the hose clamps that secure the fuel filler neck hose, the fuel leveling hose and the EVAP ventilation hose (see illustration) and disconnect all three hoses.

23 Support the fuel tank securely.

24 Remove the fuel tank strap bolts and the straps, then carefully lower the tank a little, verify that nothing is connected to the tank or in the way, then fully lower the tank.

25 Installation is the reverse of removal.

8 Fuel tank cleaning and repair - general information

1 Any repairs to the fuel tank or filler neck should be carried out by a professional who has experience in this critical and potentially dangerous work. Even after cleaning and flushing of the fuel system, explosive fumes can remain and ignite during repair of the tank.

2 If the fuel tank is removed from the vehicle, it should not be placed in an area where sparks or open flames could ignite the fumes coming out of the tank. Be especially careful inside garages where a gas-type appliance is located, because it could cause an explosion.

9 Air filter housing - removal and installation

1994 THROUGH 1997 MODELS

Air intake duct

▶ **Refer to illustrations 9.1, 9.2 and 9.3**

1 Disconnect the PCV fresh air inlet hose from the valve cover (see illustration).

2 Loosen the air intake duct hose clamp at the throttle body and disconnect the intake duct from the throttle body (see illustration).

3 Loosen the air intake duct hose clamp at the resonance chamber and disconnect the intake duct from the resonance chamber (see illustration).

4 Installation is the reverse of removal.

Resonance chamber

▶ **Refer to illustrations 9.6 and 9.7**

5 Remove the air intake duct (see Steps 1 through 3).

6 Using needle-nose pliers, loosen the spring-type hose clamp that secures the small hose to the underside of the resonance chamber (see illustration) and disconnect the hose from the resonance chamber.

7 Loosen the hose clamp at the air cleaner housing and remove the resonance chamber (see illustration).

8 Installation is the reverse of removal.

9.1 Using a pair of needle-nose pliers, loosen the spring-type hose clamp and disconnect the PCV fresh air inlet hose from the valve cover (1994 through 1997 models)

9.2 Loosen this hose clamp screw, then pull the air intake duct off the mouth of the throttle body (1994 through 1997 models)

9.3 Loosen this hose clamp screw, then pull the air intake duct off the resonance chamber (1994 through 1997 models)

9.6 Use a pair of needle-nose pliers to loosen the spring-type clamp that secures the hose to the underside of the resonance chamber, then disconnect the hose from the chamber (1994 through 1997 models)

9.7 Loosen this hose clamp screw and disconnect the resonance chamber from the Mass Air Flow (MAF) sensor (1994 through 1997 models)

9.10 Use a small screwdriver to pry loose the connector retainer, then disconnect the electrical connector from the Mass Air Flow (MAF) sensor (1994 through 1997 models)

Air filter housing

▶ Refer to illustrations 9.10 and 9.11

9   Remove the air intake duct (see Steps 1 through 3) and, if necessary, the resonance chamber (see Steps 6 and 7). (If you're simply removing the air filter housing to service some other component, it's not absolutely necessary to remove the resonance chamber, although you must still disconnect the hose that's connected to the resonance chamber before you can remove the air filter housing.)

10 Disconnect the electrical connector from the MAF sensor (see illustration).

11 Remove the air filter housing mounting bolts (see illustration) and remove the air filter housing.

12 Installation is the reverse of removal.

9.11 To detach the air filter housing from the vehicle, remove these mounting bolts (1994 through 1997 models)

**9.13 To remove the air intake duct from a 1998 and
later model, loosen the hose clamp screws at both ends,
disconnect the duct from the air filter housing and from the
throttle body and remove it**

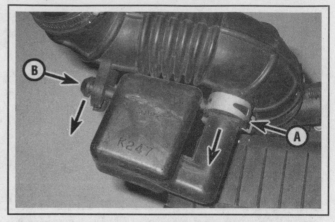

**9.14 To detach the resonator from the air intake duct, loosen
the hose clamp (A) and slide it down, then pull the resonator
tube out of the air intake duct and disengage the resonator
locator pin (B) from its mounting bracket by pulling it straight
down (typical 1998 and later model)**

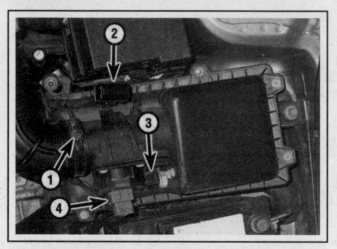

**9.17 Typical air filter housing removal details (1998 and
later models):**

1   *Loosen hose clamp and disconnect air intake duct/resonator from
    air filter housing*
2   *Detach diagnostic connector from mounting bracket on air filter
    housing*
3   *Disconnect the electrical connector from the Intake Air Temperature
    (IAT) sensor*
4   *Disconnect the electrical connector from the Mass Air Flow
    (MAF) sensor*

1998 AND LATER MODELS (EXCEPT SPORTAGE)

Air intake duct/resonator

▶ **Refer to illustrations 9.13 and 9.14**

13 Loosen the hose clamps at both ends of the air intake duct (see
illustration) and disconnect the air intake duct from the air filter housing
and from the throttle body.

14 The resonator (see illustration) is located on the underside of the
air intake duct. If you wish to remove the resonator from the air intake
duct, loosen the big hose clamp and pull off the resonator.

15 Installation is the reverse of removal.

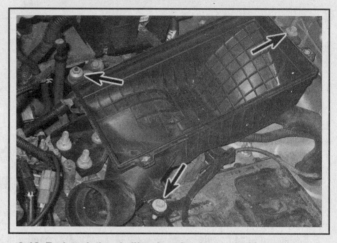

**9.18 To detach the air filter housing from a 1998 or later
model, remove these bolts/nuts**

Air filter housing

Refer to illustrations 9.17 and 9.18

✳✳ WARNING:

**Wait until the engine is completely cool before beginning this
procedure.**

16 Remove the air intake duct/resonator (see Step 13).

17 Detach the diagnostic connector from the air filter housing and
disconnect the electrical connectors from the Intake Air Temperature
(IAT) sensor and from the Mass Air Flow (MAF) sensor (see illustration).

18 Remove the air filter housing mounting nut and bolts (see illustration) and remove the air filter housing.

19 While the air filter housing assembly is removed, inspect the rubber insulator grommets at the three mounting points. If they're cracked,
torn or otherwise deteriorated, replace them.

20 Installation is the reverse of removal.

Ambient air intake box

◗ Refer to illustration 9.23

➡Note: The ambient (outside) air inlet box is located at the lower left front corner of the vehicle, behind the front bumper cover and ahead of the left inner fender splash shield. The purpose of this box is to provide a source of cooler outside air to the air filter housing. Not much can go wrong with the box, but if it's ever damaged in an accident you might have to replace it.

21 Loosen the lug nuts for the left front wheel, raise the front of the vehicle, place it securely on jackstands and remove the left front wheel.

22 Remove the left front inner fender splash shield (see Chapter 11).

23 Remove the ambient air inlet box mounting bolts (see illustration) and remove the box.

24 Installation is the reverse of removal.

SPORTAGE MODELS

Air intake duct

◗ Refer to illustration 9.25

25 Disconnect the electrical connector from the MAF sensor (see illustration).

9.23 To detach the ambient (outside) air inlet box, remove these two bolts

26 Disconnect the PCV fresh air inlet hose from the air intake duct.

27 Loosen the hose clamps that secure the air intake duct to the air filter housing and the throttle body and remove the duct.

28 Installation is the reverse of removal.

Air filter housing

◗ Refer to illustrations 9.31a, 9.31b and 9.32

29 Remove the air intake duct (see Steps 25 through 27).

30 Remove the air filter housing cover and the air filter element (see *Air filter replacement* in Chapter 1).

31 Remove the fresh air inlet duct (see illustrations).

32 Remove the air filter housing bolts (see illustration) and remove the filter housing.

33 Installation is the reverse of removal.

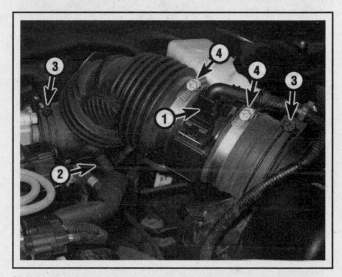

9.25 Air intake duct details (Sportage models):

1 Mass Air Flow (MAF) sensor electrical connector
2 PCV fresh air inlet hose
3 Air intake duct hose clamps
4 MAF sensor hose clamps (loosen only to replace the air intake duct or the MAF sensor)

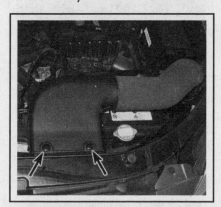

9.31a Fresh air inlet duct fasteners (Sportage models)

9.31b To disconnect the fresh air inlet duct from the lower part of the air filter housing, pull it straight up (Sportage models)

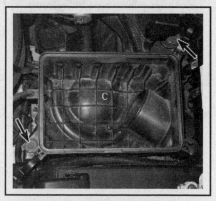

9.32 Air filter housing mounting bolts (Sportage models)

10 Accelerator cable - removal, installation and adjustment

◆ **Refer to illustrations 10.1a, 10.1b, 10.2, 10.3, 10.4, 10.5 and 10.8**

1   Remove the engine cover, if equipped. Back off the adjustment nut and disengage the accelerator cable from the cable bracket on the intake manifold (see illustrations).

2   Slide the cable end plug out of its slot in the throttle cam (see illustration).

3   Note the routing of the accelerator cable, then trace the cable back to the firewall and detach it from any clips or brackets (see illustration).

4   Using a flashlight so that you can see underneath the dash, locate the cable connection at the top of the accelerator pedal, push the upper end of the pedal forward and disengage the cable from the pedal arm (see illustration).

10.1a Using a back-up wrench to hold the locknut, back off the adjustment nut, then disengage the accelerator cable from the cable bracket (four-cylinder models)

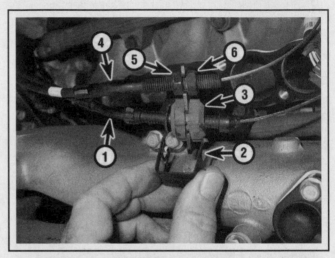

10.1b Cruise control cable and accelerator cable mounting bracket details (V6 models) (upper intake manifold unbolted and moved forward for clarity):

1	Cruise control cable	4	Accelerator cable
2	Retaining clip	5	Adjustment nut
3	Grommet	6	Locknut

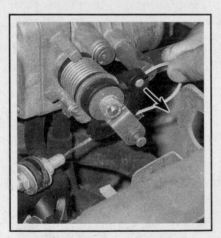

10.2 To disengage the cable end plug from the throttle cam, simply slide it sideways out of its slot

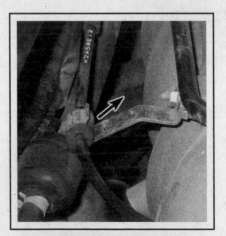

10.3 Trace the accelerator cable back to the firewall and detach it from any clips or brackets, such as this bracket on the backside of the intake manifold

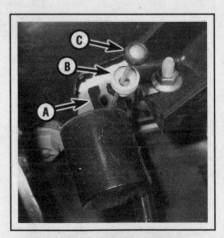

10.4 To disengage the accelerator cable from the accelerator pedal, push the upper end of the pedal (A) forward, pull the cable bushing (B) and the cable end plug (C) out of the hole in the top of the pedal, then slide the cable out the slot above the hole

10.5 To detach the accelerator cable from the firewall, carefully pry this grommet out of the firewall

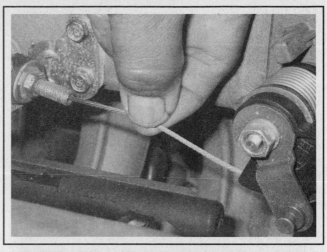

10.8 To measure accelerator cable freeplay, pull up on the cable between the cable bracket and the throttle cam. The cable freeplay is the distance that the cable moves before it begins to move the throttle cam

5   Carefully pry the accelerator cable grommet out of the firewall (see illustration), then pull cable out from the engine compartment side.

6   Installation is the reverse of removal. When you're done installing the cable, be sure to adjust it.

7   Fully depress the accelerator pedal and verify that the throttle is fully opened.

8   Measure the cable freeplay (see illustration) and compare your measurement to the cable freeplay listed in this Chapter's Specifications.

9   If the throttle doesn't fully open or if the freeplay is incorrect, loosen the locknut, and adjust the cable (see illustration 10.1a or 10.1b).

10 Tighten the locknut and recheck the adjustment. Make sure the throttle closes fully when the pedal is released.

11 Multiport Fuel Injection (MFI) system - general information

The fuel injection system is a sequential multiport system. This means that there is a fuel injector in each intake port, and that these fuel injectors inject fuel into the intake ports in the cylinder firing order (1-3-4-2). The injectors are turned on and off by the Powertrain Control Module (PCM). When the engine is running, the PCM constantly monitors engine operating conditions with an array of information sensors, calculates the correct amount of fuel, then varies the interval of time during which the injectors are open. Sequential multiport systems provide much better control of the air/fuel mixture ratio than earlier fuel injection systems, and are therefore able to produce more power, better mileage and lower emissions.

The fuel injection system uses the PCM and an array of information sensors to determine and deliver the correct air/fuel ratio under all operating conditions. The fuel injection system consists of three sub-systems: air induction, electronic control and fuel delivery. The fuel injection system is also closely interrelated with PCM-controlled emission control systems. For additional information about the PCM, the information sensors and the emission control systems, refer to Chapter 6.

AIR INDUCTION SYSTEM

The air induction system consists of the air filter housing assembly, the Mass Air Flow (MAF) sensor, the air intake duct (which also includes a resonator on some models), the throttle body and the intake manifold. Removal and installation procedures for all of the air induction components (air filter housing, air intake duct and throttle body) are covered in this Chapter, except for the intake manifold, which is covered in Chapter 2A. Replacement procedures for the information sensors are covered in Chapter 6.

The MAF sensor measures the mass (volume) of intake air entering the engine. The term "mass" refers to the amount of air that can be pumped into each cylinder. Mass flow is proportional to air density (how much oxygen is in the air). And air density is proportional to the temperature of the air. The cooler the air, the greater the air density. And the greater the density of the air, the greater its mass. For information about replacing the MAF sensor, refer to Chapter 6.

The single-barrel, cast aluminum throttle body contains a throttle plate that regulates the amount of air entering the intake manifold. The throttle plate is opened and closed by the accelerator cable. The lower part of the throttle body is heated by engine coolant to prevent icing in cold weather. The throttle body is also the location of the Throttle Position (TP) sensor, a potentiometer that monitors the opening angle of the throttle plate and sends a variable voltage signal to the Powertrain Control Module (PCM).

Another information sensor, the Intake Air Temperature (IAT) sensor, sends a voltage signal to the PCM that varies in accordance with the temperature of the incoming air in the manifold. The PCM uses this data to calculate how rich or lean the air/fuel mixture should be. On 1994 through 1997 models, the IAT sensor is an integral part of the MAF sensor. On 1998 and later models, the IAT sensor is located on the air filter housing.

When the engine is idling, the Idle Air Control (IAC) system maintains the correct idle speed by regulating the amount of air that bypasses the (closed) throttle plate in response to a command from the Powertrain Control Module (PCM). The IAC system consists of the IAC valve (located on the throttle body), the PCM, and several information sensors, including the Engine Coolant Temperature (ECT) sensor and the IAT sensor. The IAC valve is activated and controlled by the PCM in response to the running conditions of the engine (cold or warm running, power steering pressure high or low, air conditioning system on or off, etc.). As the PCM receives data from the information sensors (vehicle speed, coolant temperature, air conditioning and/or power steering load, etc.) it adjusts the idle according to the demands of the engine and driver.

ELECTRONIC CONTROL SYSTEM

For more information about the electronic control system, i.e. the PCM, its information sensors and output actuators, refer to Chapter 6.

FUEL DELIVERY SYSTEM

The fuel delivery system consists of the fuel pump, the fuel filter, the fuel pressure regulator, the fuel pulsation damper (1998 and later models), the fuel rail and fuel injectors, and the lines and fittings that carry fuel between all of these components.

The fuel pump is an in-tank design, and it can be removed from the top of the fuel tank without removing the tank. Fuel is drawn through a sock (or strainer) at the pump inlet, then pumped out the other end of the pump and through a fuel filter located in front of the fuel tank. After the pressurized fuel has been filtered, it's pumped through the supply line to the fuel rail in the engine compartment.

The fuel pressure regulator maintains the fuel pressure within the specified operating range. When the fuel pressure is too high on 1994 through 1997 models, the fuel pressure regulator on the fuel rail opens and sends excess fuel back to the fuel tank through a fuel return line. On 1998 and later models, the fuel pressure regulator is located on the fuel pump and there is no fuel return line between the fuel rail and the fuel tank. On these models, a short fuel bypass line is plumbed into the supply line at the outlet side of the fuel filter. When the engine is operating, this bypass line is filled with pressurized fuel. When the fuel pressure is too high on these models, the fuel pressure regulator opens and allows fuel from the bypass line to dump back into the fuel tank.

Right before the fuel reaches the fuel rail on 1998 and later models, it's pumped through a fuel pulsation damper, which is located near the fuel rail. The pulsation damper lessens the hydraulic and acoustic noise produced by the fuel pump when it's operating. The fuel rail, which is bolted to the intake manifold, functions as a reservoir for pressurized fuel so that there's always enough fuel available for acceleration and high speed operation. The fuel rail also houses the upper end of each fuel injector (the lower end of each injector is inserted into the intake manifold).

Each fuel injector is a solenoid-actuated, pintle-type design consisting of a solenoid, plunger, needle valve and housing. When the engine is running, there is always voltage on the hot side of each injector terminal. The PCM turns the injectors on and off by switching their ground paths on and off. When the ground path for an injector is closed by the PCM, current flows through the solenoid coil, the needle valve raises and pressurized fuel inside the injector housing squirts out the nozzle. The quantity of fuel injected each time an injector opens is determined by the pulse width, which is the interval of time during which the valve is open.

12 Fuel injection system - check

‣ **Refer to illustrations 12.7 and 12.9**

✲✲ WARNING:

Gasoline is extremely flammable, so take extra precautions when you work on any part of the fuel system. See the Warning in Section 2.

➡**Note: The following procedure is based on the assumption that the fuel pump is working and the fuel pressure is adequate (see Section 3).**

1 Check all electrical connectors that are related to the system. Check the ground wire connections for tightness. Loose connectors and poor grounds can cause many problems that resemble more serious malfunctions.

2 Verify that the battery is fully charged. The Powertrain Control Module (PCM), information sensors and output actuators (the fuel injectors are output actuators) depend on a stable voltage supply in order to meter fuel correctly.

3 Inspect the air filter element (see Chapter 1). A dirty or partially blocked filter will severely impede performance and economy.

4 Check all fuses related to the fuel system (see Chapter 12). If you find a blown fuse, replace it and see if it blows again. If it does, look for a wire shorted to ground in the circuit(s) protected by that fuse.

5 Check the air induction system between the throttle body and the intake manifold for air leaks, which will cause a lean air/fuel mixture ratio. (When the mixture ratio becomes excessively lean, the engine will misfire.) Also inspect the condition of all vacuum hoses connected to the intake manifold and to the throttle body. A loose or broken vacuum hose will allow false (unmetered) air into the intake manifold. The Manifold Absolute Pressure (MAP) sensor and the PCM can compensate for some false air, but if it's excessive, especially at idle and during other high-intake-manifold-vacuum conditions, the engine will misfire.

6 Remove the air intake duct from the throttle body and look for dirt, carbon, varnish, or other residue in the throttle body, particularly around the throttle plate. If it's dirty, clean it with carb cleaner, a toothbrush and a clean shop towel.

7 With the engine running, place an automotive stethoscope against each injector, one at a time, and listen for a clicking sound that indi-

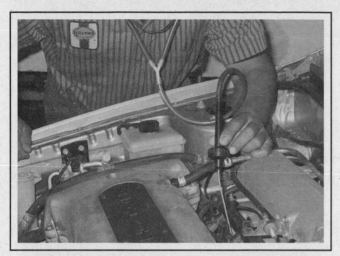

12.7 Use an automotive stethoscope to listen to each fuel injector while the engine is operating. If an injector is operating correctly, it should make a soft clicking sound that rises and falls with engine speed

12.9 If an injector isn't working (it's not making a clicking sound), turn off the engine, disconnect the injector electrical connector and use an ohmmeter to measure the resistance across the two injector electrical terminals

cates operation (see illustration). If you don't have a stethoscope, touch the tip of a long screwdriver against each injector and listen through the handle.

8   If you can hear the injectors operating, but the engine is misfiring, then the electrical circuits are functioning correctly, but the injectors might be dirty or clogged. Try a commercial injector cleaning product (available at auto parts stores). If cleaning the injectors doesn't help, the injectors probably need to be replaced.

9   If an injector is not operating (it makes no clicking sound), dis-

connect the injector electrical connector and measure the resistance across the injector terminals with an ohmmeter (see illustration). Compare your measurement with the resistance value listed in this Chapter's Specifications. Replace any injector whose resistance value does not fall within the specifications.

10 If the injector is not operating, but the resistance reading is within specifications, the PCM or the circuit between the PCM and the injector might be faulty.

13 Throttle body - removal and installation

✳✳ WARNING:

Wait until the engine is completely cool before beginning this procedure.

1994 THROUGH 1997 MODELS

▶ Refer to illustrations 13.3a, 13.3b, 13.4 and 13.7

1   Remove the air intake duct (see Section 9).

2   Clearly label any vacuum hoses connected to the throttle body, then disconnect them. Plug the vacuum hoses to keep out dirt and moisture.

3   Disconnect the electrical connectors from the Throttle Position (TP) sensor and from the Idle Air Control (IAC) valve (see illustrations).

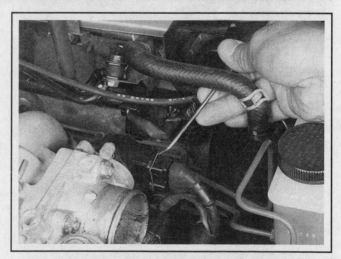

13.3a To release the TP sensor electrical connector, remove this wire retainer (but don't lose it! - you'll need it to secure the connector during reassembly)

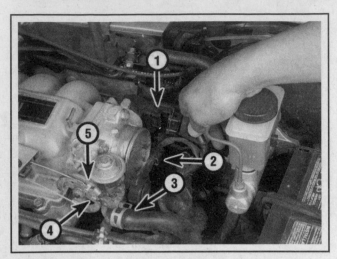

13.3b Throttle body removal details (1994 through 1997 models):

1   Disconnect the TP sensor electrical connector
2   Disconnect the IAC valve electrical connector
3   Disconnect the coolant hoses from the IAC valve (other hose not visible in this photo)
4   Disconnect the accelerator cable (see Section 10)
5   Disconnect the throttle valve cable (see next illustration)

13.7 To detach the throttle body from the intake manifold, remove these two bolts and two nuts (1994 through 1997 models)

4   If the vehicle is equipped with an automatic transmission, detach the throttle valve cable from the cable bracket and from the throttle cam (see illustration), then set the cable aside.

5   Disconnect the accelerator cable from the throttle body (see Section 10).

6   Clamp off the coolant hoses connected to the throttle body, then detach the hoses. Be prepared for a little coolant spillage.

7   Remove the throttle body mounting fasteners (see illustration), then remove the throttle body and gasket from the intake manifold.

8   If you want to remove the Idle Air Control (IAC) valve (SOHC models) or the Bypass Air Control (BAC) valve (DOHC models) from the throttle body, refer to "Idle Air Control (IAC) system - component replacement" in Chapter 6.

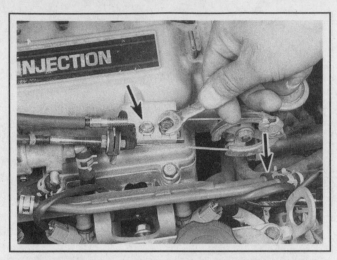

13.4 To detach the throttle valve cable (if equipped) from the throttle body, remove these two nuts and disengage the cable from the cable bracket, then slide the cable end plug sideways to disengage it from the throttle cam (1994 through 1997 models)

9   Using a soft brush and carburetor cleaner, thoroughly clean the throttle body casting, then blow out all passages with compressed air.

✳✳ CAUTION:

Do not clean the TP sensor with solvent. Just wipe it off carefully with a clean, soft cloth.

10   Installation is the reverse of removal. Be sure to tighten the throttle body mounting bolts to the torque listed in this Chapter's Specifications. Proceed to Step 21.

1998 AND LATER MODELS

▸ **Refer to illustrations 13.12a, 13.12b, 13.13, 13.16, 13.17 and 13.19**

11   Remove the air intake duct/resonator (see Section 9).

12   Disconnect the electrical connectors from the Throttle Position (TP) sensor and the Idle Air Control (IAC) valve (see illustrations).

13   On Spectra models, disconnect the Positive Crankcase Ventilation (PCV) fresh air inlet hose from the throttle body (see illustration). On Sportage models, disconnect the EVAP canister purge control solenoid valve hose from the throttle body.

14   Clamp off the two coolant hoses connected to the underside of the throttle body (see illustration 13.13), then loosen the spring-type hose clamps and disconnect both hoses. Be prepared for some coolant spillage.

15   Disconnect the accelerator cable from the throttle body (see Section 10).

16   Remove the throttle body mounting fasteners (see illustration) and remove the throttle body.

17   Remove the old throttle body gasket (see illustration) and discard it. Be sure to remove all traces of old gasket material from the gasket mating surfaces of the throttle body and the intake manifold.

18   If you want to remove the Idle Air Control (IAC) valve from the throttle body, refer to "Idle Air Control (IAC) system - component

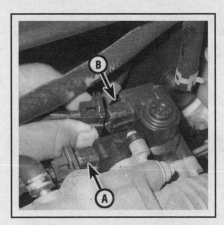

13.12a Depress the wire retainer and disconnect the electrical connector from the Throttle Position (TP) sensor, then disconnect the connector from the Idle Air Control (IAC) valve (typical 1998 and later Spectra model)

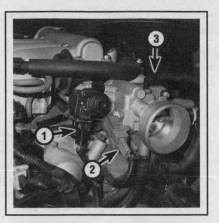

13.12b Throttle body details (V6 Sportage)

1 *Idle Speed Control Actuator (ISCA) electrical connector*
2 *Throttle Position (TP) sensor electrical connector*
3 *EVAP canister purge control solenoid valve hose*

13.13 Disconnect the Positive Crankcase Ventilation (PCV) fresh air inlet hose (1) from the throttle body, then loosen the hose clamps and disconnect the two coolant hoses (2) from the underside of the throttle body (typical 1998 and later model)

13.16 To detach the throttle body from the intake manifold, remove these four nuts (typical 1998 and later model)

13.17 Be sure to remove the old gasket and all traces of gasket material from the gasket mating surfaces of both the throttle body and the intake manifold (typical 1998 and later model)

13.19 Using carb cleaner and a clean shop rag, carefully and thoroughly clean off any carbon deposits from the area behind the throttle plate (typical 1998 and later model)

replacement" in Chapter 6.

19 Before installing the old throttle body (if you're installing the old unit), spray the bore with carburetor cleaner or some other suitable solvent and thoroughly clean the bore, particularly the area below the throttle valve, by wiping off the oily residue, varnish and/or carbon deposits with a clean shop rag (see illustration).

✳ CAUTION:

Make sure that you don't spray any sensor with carb cleaner. Solvent will damage the plastic housings for these units and might even damage the delicate electronics inside them.

20 Installation is the reverse of removal. Be sure to use new gaskets and tighten the throttle body mounting fasteners to the torque listed in this Chapter's Specifications. Proceed to the next Step

ALL MODELS

21 When you're done, check the coolant level and top it up if necessary (see Chapter 1).

22 Check the accelerator cable adjustment and adjust it if necessary (see Section 10).

23 Start the engine and check for air and coolant leaks.

14 Fuel pressure regulator - replacement

❊❊ WARNING:

Gasoline is extremely flammable, so take extra precautions when you work on any part of the fuel system. See the Warning in Section 2.

1994 THROUGH 1997 MODELS

▸ **Refer to illustrations 14.3 and 14.6**

1 Relieve the system fuel pressure (see Section 2), then remove the fuel filler neck cap to relieve any pressure inside the fuel tank.
2 Disconnect the cable from the negative battery terminal (see Chapter 5, Section 1).
3 Disconnect the vacuum hose from the fuel pressure regulator (see illustration).
4 Put a small metal pan or shop towel under the fuel return hose.
5 Loosen the spring-type hose clamp (see illustration 14.3), slide it down the fuel return hose and disconnect the fuel return hose from the pressure regulator.
6 Remove the pressure regulator mounting bolts (see illustration)

and detach the pressure regulator from the fuel rail.
7 Remove and discard the old fuel pressure regulator O-ring.
8 Install a new O-ring on the regulator. Coat the new O-ring with a little clean engine oil to protect it from damage when installing the pressure regulator.

❊❊ WARNING:

When installing the regulator on the end of the fuel rail, make sure that it's installed square to the bore of the pipe on the fuel rail. If the regulator is cocked, fuel will leak out, which could cause a fire.

9 The remainder of installation is the reverse of removal. Tighten the bolts to the torque listed in this Chapter's Specifications.
10 Start the engine and check for fuel leakage at the regulator.

1998 AND LATER MODELS

11 On these models, the fuel pressure regulator is an integral component of the fuel pump/fuel gauge sending unit. To replace the fuel pressure regulator, refer to Section 6.

14.3 Disconnect the vacuum hose (1) and the fuel return hose (2) from the fuel pressure regulator (1994 through 1997 models)

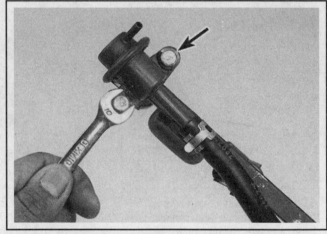

14.6 To detach the fuel pressure regulator from the fuel rail, remove these two bolts (fuel rail removed for clarity) (1994 through 1997 models)

15 Fuel pulsation damper - removal and installation

SPECTRA MODELS

▸ **Refer to illustrations 15.3 and 15.5**

➡**Note: This procedure applies only to 1998 and later models. 1994 through 1997 models are not equipped with a fuel pulsation damper.**

1 Relieve the system fuel pressure (see Section 2).
2 Disconnect the cable from the negative battery terminal (see Chapter 5, Section 1).

3 Disconnect the fuel supply line quick-connect fitting from the fuel pulsation damper (see illustration). If you're unfamiliar with quick-connect fittings, refer to Section 4.
4 Remove the pulsation damper mounting bolts (see illustration 15.3) and remove the pulsation damper from the fuel rail.
5 Remove and discard the old pulsation damper O-ring (see illustration).
6 Install a new O-ring on the pulsation damper. Use a little clean engine oil to protect the O-ring when installing the damper on the fuel rail.

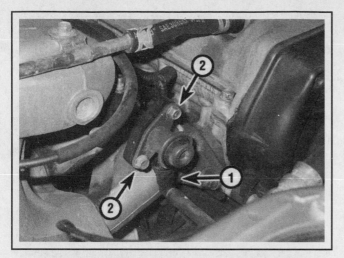

15.3 To detach the fuel pulsation damper from the fuel rail on 1998 and later models, disconnect the quick-connect fitting (1) for the fuel supply line (see Section 4), then remove the damper mounting bolts (2)

15.5 Be sure to remove and discard the old pulsation damper O-ring. Whether you plan to reuse the old pulsation damper or a new unit, always use a new O-ring when installing the pulsation damper

7 Installation is the reverse of removal. Be sure to tighten the damper mounting bolts securely.

SPORTAGE MODELS

Refer to illustration 15.11

8 Relieve the system fuel pressure (see Section 2).
9 Disconnect the cable from the negative battery terminal.
10 Remove the engine cover, if equipped.
11 Using a large open-end wrench, unscrew the fuel pulsation damper. On V6 models the damper is located at the left end of the rear fuel rail (see illustration).
12 Installation is the reverse of removal. Be sure to use a new sealing washer and tighten the damper securely.

ALL MODELS

13 Reconnect the cable to the negative battery terminal, then start the engine and check for leaks around the pulsation damper.

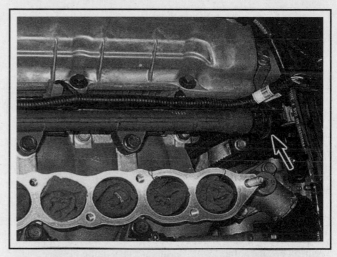

15.11 On Sportage models, the fuel pulsation damper is screwed into the end of the fuel rail (V6 engine shown, four-cylinder similar; upper intake manifold removed for clarity)

16 Fuel rail and injectors - removal and installation

✳ WARNING:

Gasoline is extremely flammable, so take extra precautions when you work on any part of the fuel system. See the Warning in Section 2.

1 Relieve the fuel pressure (see Section 2).
2 Disconnect the cable from the negative terminal of the battery (see Chapter 5, Section 1).

1994 THROUGH 1997 MODELS

▸ **Refer to illustrations 16.5a, 16.5b, 16.8, 16.9, 16.10, 16.11a, 16.11b and 16.11c**

3 Disconnect the Positive Crankcase Ventilation (PCV) valve from the valve cover, trace the PCV hose back to its pipe on the intake manifold, disconnect the hose from the manifold and set the PCV valve and hose aside (see "Positive Crankcase Ventilation (PCV) system" in Chapter 6).

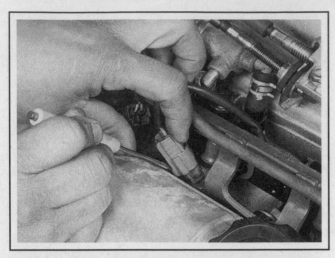

16.5a To disconnect each injector electrical connector, use a small screwdriver to release the connector lock lever while simultaneously pulling on the connector (1994 through 1997 models)

4   On SOHC models, remove the hose clamps from the air valve, then remove the air valve from the side of the intake plenum (see "Idle Air Control [IAC] system - component replacement" in Chapter 6).

5   Mark each injector electrical connector with a felt pen or paint (1, 2, etc.). Using a small flat-blade screwdriver to release the connector lock lever while gently pulling the connector, disconnect each injector electrical connector (see illustration). Then carefully detach the two injector harness clips (see illustration). When all the injector connectors have been disconnected, set the wire harness aside.

6   Disconnect the vacuum hose from the fuel pressure regulator (see illustration 14.3).

7   Disconnect the fuel lines from the fuel rail (see illustration 3.5).

8   Remove the fuel rail mounting bolts (see illustration).

9   Remove the fuel rail and the fuel injectors as a single assembly (see illustration).

10   Remove the fuel injectors from the fuel rail (see illustration). If one of the injector seals sticks during removal, gently wiggle the injector from side-to-side and keep pulling. Set the injectors aside in a clearly labeled storage container.

11   Remove and discard the old injector grommets, O-rings and insulators (see illustrations). Whether you intend to install new injectors

16.5b Using a pair of needle-nose pliers, detach the injector wiring harness clips, then set the harness aside (1994 through 1997 models)

16.8 To detach the fuel rail from the intake manifold, remove these two bolts (1994 through 1997 models)

16.9 Carefully lift the fuel rail and the injectors as a single assembly. Be prepared for some fuel to drip out of the pressure regulator and the fuel rail (1994 through 1997 models)

16.10 Carefully pull on each injector to remove it from the fuel rail. If the injector is stuck, gently wiggle it from side-to-side as you work it out of the fuel rail (1994 through 1997 models)

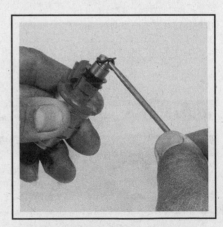

16.11a Remove the old O-ring from the upper end of each injector . . .

or reuse the old injectors, be sure to install new grommets, O-rings and insulators.

12 Coat the new upper injector grommets and O-rings with clean engine oil, then insert each injector into its corresponding bore in the fuel rail.

13 Coat each new injector lower insulator with clean engine oil and press it into that injector's bore in the intake manifold.

14 Installation is the reverse of removal. Be sure to tighten the fuel rail mounting bolts securely.

15 Reconnect the cable to the negative battery terminal (see Chapter 5, Section 1), then proceed to Step 36.

1998 AND LATER FOUR-CYLINDER MODELS

▶ **Refer to illustrations 16.16, 16.18, 16.19, 16.20, 16.21, 16.22 and 16.23**

16 Disconnect the PCV crankcase ventilation hose from the valve cover and from the PCV pipe that's bolted to the intake manifold (see illustration).

17 Disconnect the electrical connectors from the fuel injectors (see illustration 16.16).

18 Disconnect the fuel supply line quick-connect fitting from the fuel pulsation damper (see illustration). If you're unfamiliar with quick-connect fittings, refer to Section 4.

19 Detach the accelerator cable bracket from the intake manifold (see illustration).

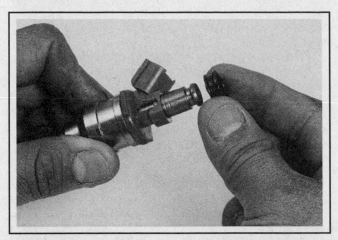

16.11b . . . then remove the grommet from the injector (1994 through 1997 models)

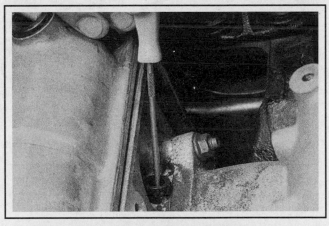

16.11c Also be sure to remove the insulator from each injector bore in the intake manifold (1994 through 1997 models)

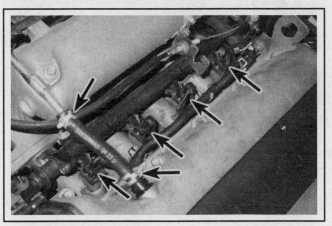

16.16 Loosen the two hose clamps and remove the PCV hose, then disconnect the electrical connectors from the four fuel injectors (typical)

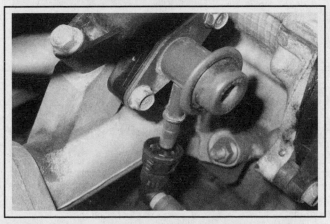

16.18 Disconnect the fuel supply line quick-connect fitting from the fuel pulsation damper (typical)

16.19 To detach the accelerator cable bracket from the intake manifold plenum, remove these bolts (typical)

20 Remove the two fuel rail mounting bolts (see illustration).

21 Remove the fuel rail and the injectors as a single assembly (see illustration). If any of the injectors stick in their bores, gently wiggle the fuel rail from side-to-side and keep pulling up.

22 Place the fuel rail/fuel injector assembly on a clean work bench, then remove the injectors from the fuel rail. To remove each injector, remove the retainer clip (see illustration), then pull the injector out of its bore in the fuel rail.

23 Remove and discard the old upper and lower O-rings from each injector (see illustration), discard them and install new O-rings. Coat each new O-ring with clean engine oil to make it easier to slide the O-ring into place on the injector. Repeat this procedure for each injector.

➡Note: Even if you only removed the fuel rail assembly to replace a single injector or a leaking O-ring, it's a good idea to remove all of the injectors from the fuel rail and replace all the injector O-rings at the same time.

24 Coat the new upper injector O-rings with clean engine oil, then insert each injector into its corresponding bore in the fuel rail.

25 Coat each new lower injector O-ring with clean engine oil and press it into that injector's bore in the intake manifold.

26 Once the fuel rail assembly is in place, with all four injectors fully seated in their respective bores, install the fuel rail mounting bolts and tighten them securely.

27 The remainder of installation is the reverse of removal.

28 Reconnect the cable to the negative battery terminal (see Chapter 5, Section 1), then proceed to Step 36.

2005 AND LATER V6 MODELS

▶ **Refer to illustrations 16.30 and 16.32**

29 Remove the upper intake manifold (see Chapter 2B).

30 Remove the two bolts and disconnect the fuel supply line fitting from the fuel rail (see illustration).

16.20 To detach the fuel rail assembly from the intake manifold, remove these two bolts (typical)

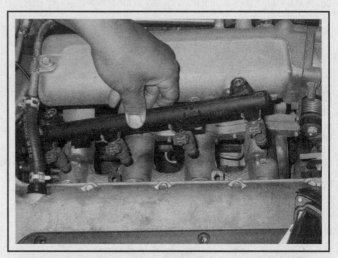

16.21 Carefully remove the fuel rail and injectors as a single assembly. If any of the injectors stick in their bores, wiggle the fuel rail from side-to-side and keep pulling (typical)

16.22 To release each injector from the fuel rail, carefully pry off this retainer (typical 1998 and later model)

16.23 Remove and discard the old injector O-rings. Whether you plan to re-use the old injectors or install new ones, always use new O-rings when installing the injectors (typical 1998 and later model)

16.30 Fuel supply line fitting nuts (Sportage V6 models)

31 Disconnect the electrical connectors from the fuel injectors.

32 Remove the fuel rail mounting bolts (see illustration).

33 Remove the fuel rail and injectors as a single assembly. If any of the injectors stick in their bores, gently wiggle them from side-to-side while pulling.

34 For the injector removal and installation procedure, refer to Steps 22 through 25.

35 Install the fuel rail and injectors as a single assembly and tighten the fuel rail mounting bolts securely. The remainder of installation is the reverse of removal.

ALL MODELS

36 Turn the ignition switch to ON to activate the fuel pump and build up fuel pressure in the fuel lines and the fuel rail, but DON'T operate the starter yet. Repeat this step two or three times, then check the fuel lines, fuel rails and injectors for fuel leaks.

37 Once you're confident that there are no leaks, start the engine and verify that the injectors are working and there are no fuel leaks.

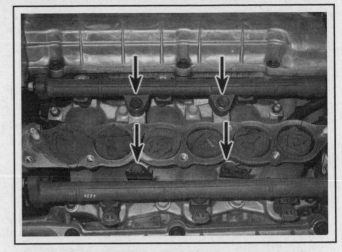

16.32 Fuel rail mounting bolts (Sportage V6 models)

17 Exhaust system servicing - general information

▶ **Refer to illustrations 17.1a, 17.1b and 17.2**

❊❊ WARNING:

Inspect and repair exhaust system components only after enough time has elapsed after driving the vehicle to allow the system components to cool completely. Also, when working under the vehicle, make sure it is securely supported on jackstands.

1 The exhaust system consists of the exhaust manifold, the catalytic converter, the muffler, the tailpipe and all connecting pipes, flanges and clamps. The exhaust system is isolated from the vehicle body and from chassis components by a series of rubber hangers (see illustrations). Periodically inspect these hangers for cracks or other signs of deterioration, replacing them as necessary.

2 Ever wondered why your muffler seems to rust out? Because when the engine is running, the catalytic converter produces a good

17.1a A pair of typical exhaust system rubber hangers. Every time you raise the vehicle to inspect or service anything underneath, carefully inspect all rubber exhaust hangers for cracks, tears and deterioration. If a rubber hanger is damaged or worn, replace it immediately

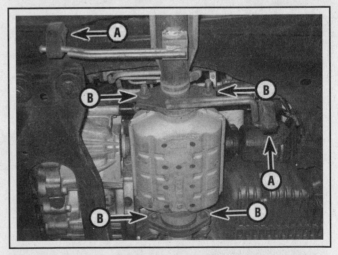

17.1b The manufacturer puts these rubber exhaust hangers (A) at the end of long support rods to protect them from the intense heat of the catalytic converter. The fasteners (B) for the catalyst mounting flanges also get very hot, so spray them with a liberal amount of penetrating oil and give it half an hour to soak in before attempting to loosen these fasteners

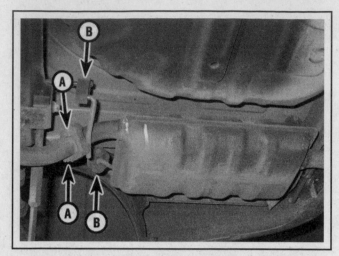

17.2 Inspect the muffler regularly for corrosion. If you find any holes in the muffler, replace it immediately. Be sure to use a liberal amount of penetrant to loosen up the muffler

deal of water vapor that is emitted harmlessly into the atmosphere. But when the engine is turned off, the exhaust system cools off and this water vapor condenses and mixes with more toxic substances such as sulfur, producing a corrosive mix that settles in the muffler and slowly eats its way through the floor of the muffler. Conduct regular inspections of the exhaust system, particularly the muffler (see illustration), to keep the system safe and quiet. Look for any damaged or bent parts, open seams, holes, loose connections, corrosion or other defects which could allow exhaust fumes to enter the vehicle. Do not repair deteriorated exhaust system components; replace them with new parts.

3   If the exhaust system components are extremely corroded, or rusted together, you'll need welding equipment and a cutting torch to remove them. The convenient strategy at this point is to have a muffler repair shop remove the corroded sections with a cutting torch. If you want to save money by doing it yourself, but you don't have a welding outfit and cutting torch, simply cut off the old components with a hacksaw. If you have compressed air, there are special pneumatic cutting chisels (available from specialty tool manufacturers) that can also be used. If you decide to tackle the job at home, be sure to wear safety goggles to protect your eyes from metal chips and wear work gloves to protect your hands.

4   Here are some simple guidelines to follow when repairing the exhaust system:

a)   *Work from the back to the front when removing exhaust system components.*

b)   *Apply penetrating oil to the exhaust system component fasteners to make them easier to remove.*

c)   *Use new gaskets and clamps when installing exhaust systems components.*

d)   *Apply anti-seize compound to the threads of all exhaust system fasteners during reassembly.*

e)   *Be sure to allow sufficient clearance between newly installed parts and all points on the underbody to avoid overheating the floor pan and possibly damaging the interior carpet and insulation. Pay particularly close attention to the catalytic converter and heat shield.*

Specifications

Accelerator cable freeplay	3/64 to 1/8 inch (1 to 3 mm)
Fuel system pressure	
1994 through 1997	
B6 SOHC	38 to 46 psi (265 to 314 kPa)
B6 DOHC and BP DOHC	41 to 50 psi (284 to 343 kPa)
1998 and later (except Sportage)	46 to 51 psi (320 to 350 kPa)
Sportage (2.0L DOHC and 2.7L V6)	50 psi (343 kPa)
Injector resistance (approximate)	
1994 through 1997	12 to 16 ohms
1998 and later (except Sportage)	14.5 ohms
Sportage (2.0L DOHC and 2.7L V6)	13.8 to 15.2 ohms

Torque specifications

	Ft-lbs (unless otherwise indicated)	Nm

➡ **Note: One foot-pound (ft-lb) of torque is equivalent to 12 inch-pounds (in-lbs) of torque. Torque values below approximately 15 foot-pounds are expressed in inch-pounds, because most foot-pound torque wrenches are not accurate at these smaller values.**

	Ft-lbs (unless otherwise indicated)	Nm
Throttle body mounting bolts/nuts	18	24
Fuel pressure regulator mounting bolts		
(1994 through 1997)	69 to 95 in-lbs	8 to 10.5

Notes

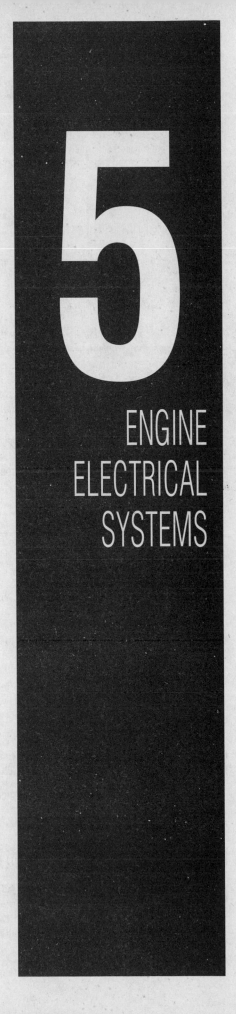

5

ENGINE ELECTRICAL SYSTEMS

Section

1   General information, precautions and battery disconnection
2   Battery - emergency jump starting
3   Battery - check and replacement
4   Battery cables - check and replacement
5   Ignition system - general information
6   Ignition system - check
7   Ignition control module - replacement
8   Ignition coil - check and replacement
9   Distributor (1997 and earlier models) - removal and installation
10   Ignition timing - check and adjustment
11   Charging system - general information and precautions
12   Charging system - check
13   Alternator - removal and installation
14   Starting system - general information and precautions
15   Starter motor and circuit - check
16   Starter motor - removal and installation

Reference to other Chapters

CHECK ENGINE light on - See Chapter 6

1 General information, precautions and battery disconnection

The engine electrical systems include all ignition, charging and starting components. Because of their engine-related functions, these components are covered separately from body electrical devices such as the lights, the instruments, etc. (which you'll find in Chapter 12).

PRECAUTIONS

Always observe the following precautions when working on the electrical system:

a) *Be extremely careful when servicing engine electrical components. They are easily damaged if checked, connected or handled improperly.*

b) *Never leave the ignition switched on for long periods of time when the engine is not running.*

c) *Never disconnect the battery cables while the engine is running.*

d) *Maintain correct polarity when connecting battery cables from another vehicle during jump starting - see the "Booster battery (jump) starting" Section at the front of this manual.*

e) *Always disconnect the cable from the negative battery terminal before working on the electrical system, but read the following battery disconnection procedure first.*

It's also a good idea to review the safety-related information regarding the engine electrical systems located in the "Safety first!" Section at the front of this manual, before beginning any operation included in this Chapter.

BATTERY DISCONNECTION

Some systems on the vehicle require battery power to be available at all times, either to maintain continuous operation (alarm system, power door locks, etc.), or to maintain control unit memory (radio station presets, Powertrain Control Module and other control units). When the battery is disconnected, the power that maintains these systems is cut.

Devices known as "memory-savers" can be used to avoid some of these problems. Precise details vary according to the device used. The typical memory saver is plugged into the cigarette lighter and is connected to a spare battery. Then the vehicle battery can be disconnected from the electrical system. The memory saver will provide sufficient current to maintain audio unit security codes, PCM memory, etc. and will provide power to always-hot circuits such as the clock and radio memory circuits.

✳✳ WARNING:

Some memory savers deliver a considerable amount of current in order to keep vehicle systems operational after the main battery is disconnected. If you're using a memory saver, make sure that the circuit concerned is actually open before servicing it.

✳✳ WARNING:

If you're going to work near any of the airbag system components, the battery MUST be disconnected and a memory saver must NOT be used. If a memory saver is used, power will be supplied to the airbag control unit, which means that it could accidentally deploy the airbag(s) and cause serious personal injury.

If you are planning to disconnect the battery or remove the radio on a 1994 through 1997 model, read Theft Deterrent System below before proceeding. To disconnect the battery for service procedures requiring power to be cut from the vehicle, loosen the cable clamp nut and disconnect the cable from the negative battery post. Isolate the cable end to prevent it from coming into accidental contact with the battery post.

Theft Deterrent System (1994 through 1997 models)

If someone tries to start one of these models without using the ignition key, i.e. if someone tries to "hot wire" it, the horn will sound and the exterior lights will flash for about three minutes. The Theft Deterrent System will also activate if the battery cables are disconnected from the battery or if the radio is removed. So, before disconnecting the battery or removing the radio on one of these models, be sure to disarm the Theft Deterrent System by inserting the ignition key into the key lock cylinder and turning it to the ACC position. If you leave the key in the ACC position while the battery is disconnected or the radio is removed, the Theft Deterrent System won't come on when the battery cables are reconnected. But it WILL come on when you remove the key! So re-insert the key into the key lock cylinder and turn it to the ACC position again to disarm the system.

2 Battery - emergency jump starting

Refer to the *Booster battery (jump) starting* procedure at the front of this manual.

3 Battery - check and replacement

✳✳ WARNING:

Always disconnect the cable from the negative battery terminal FIRST and hook it up LAST or the battery may be shorted by the tool being used to loosen the cable clamps.

CHECK

♦ **Refer to illustrations 3.2 and 3.3**

1 Disconnect the negative battery cable, then the positive cable from the battery.

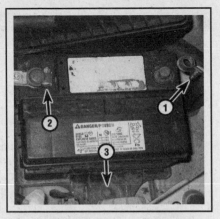

3.2 To test the open circuit voltage of the battery, touch the black probe of the voltmeter to the negative terminal and the red probe to the positive terminal of the battery; a fully charged battery should be about 12.6 volts

3.3 Some battery load testers (like this one) are equipped with an ammeter that allows you to vary the amount of the load on the battery (less expensive testers only have a load switch that puts the battery under a fixed load)

3.4 Typical battery mounting details

1. *Negative cable clamp (always disconnect this one first, and hook it up last)*
2. *Positive cable clamp*
3. *Hold-down clamp bolt*

2   Check the battery state of charge. Visually inspect the indicator eye on the top of the battery; if the indicator eye is black in color charge the battery as described in Chapter 1. Next perform an open-circuit voltage test with a multimeter (see illustration).

➡Note: The battery's surface charge must be removed before accurate voltage measurements can be made. Turn on the high beams for ten seconds, then turn them off and let the vehicle stand for two minutes.

With the engine and all accessories Off, touch the negative probe of the voltmeter to the negative terminal of the battery and the positive probe to the positive terminal of the battery. The battery voltage should be about 12.4 volts or slightly higher. If the battery is less than the specified voltage, charge the battery before proceeding to the next test. Do not proceed with the battery load test unless the battery charge is correct.

3   Perform a battery load test. An accurate check of the battery condition can only be performed with a load tester (available at most auto parts stores). This test evaluates the ability of the battery to operate the starter and other accessories during periods of high current draw. Hook up a special load tester to the battery terminals (see illustration). Load test the battery according to the manufacturer's instructions. This tool utilizes a carbon-pile-type variable resistor to increase the load demand (current draw) on the battery. Maintain the load on the battery for 15 seconds or less and observe that the battery voltage does not drop below 9.6 volts. If the battery condition is weak or defective, the tool will indicate this condition immediately.

➡Note: Cold temperatures will cause the minimum voltage requirements to drop slightly. Follow the chart given in the manufacturer's instructions to compensate for cold climates. Minimum load voltage for freezing temperatures (32-degrees F) should be approximately 9.1 volts.

REPLACEMENT

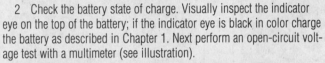

◆ Refer to illustrations 3.4 and 3.8

4   Disconnect the cable from the negative battery terminal first, then (and only then!) disconnect the cable from the positive battery terminal

3.8 To remove the battery tray from the engine compartment, remove these bolts (typical)

(see illustration).

5   Remove the battery hold-down clamp bolt (see illustration 3.4) and remove the hold-down clamp.

6   Lift out the battery. Be careful - it's heavy.

➡Note: Battery straps and handlers are available at most auto parts stores for a reasonable price. They make it easier to remove and carry the battery.

7   While the battery is out, inspect the battery tray for corrosion.

8   If there's corrosion on the battery tray, remove the tray's mounting bolts (see illustration) and remove the tray from the engine compartment. Clean the deposits from the metal to prevent the battery tray from further corrosion.

9   If you are replacing the battery, make sure you get one that's identical, with the same dimensions, amperage rating, cold cranking rating, etc.

10   Installation is the reverse of removal. Be sure to connect the positive cable first and the negative cable last.

11   Disarm the Theft Deterrent System if you're servicing a 1994 through 1997 model (see Section 1).

4 Battery cables - check and replacement

▶ **Refer to illustrations 4.4a, 4.4b, 4.4c and 4.4d**

1 Periodically inspect the entire length of each battery cable for damage, cracked or burned insulation and corrosion. Poor battery cable connections can cause starting problems and decreased engine performance.

2 Inspect the cable-to-terminal connections at the ends of the cables for cracks, loose wire strands and corrosion. The presence of white, fluffy deposits under the insulation at the cable terminal connection means that the cable is corroded and should be replaced. Also inspect the battery posts for distortion and corrosion. If they're corroded, clean them up.

3 When removing the cables, always disconnect the cable from the negative battery terminal first and hook it up last, or you might accidentally short out the battery with the tool you're using to loosen the cable clamps. Even if you're only replacing the cable for the positive terminal, be sure to disconnect the negative cable from the battery first (see Section 1).

4 Disconnect the old cables from the battery, then trace each cable to its opposite end and disconnect it (see illustrations). Be sure to note the routing of each cable before disconnecting it to ensure correct installation. Starter cable replacement isn't entirely straightforward on the vehicles covered in this manual because the starter cable disappears into a thicket of harnesses and emerges from the other end down at the starter solenoid. What you must do is carefully remove all of the old electrical tape, remove the conduit surrounding each harness, then separate the starter cable from the other wiring. Then, after you've installed the new starter cable, carefully bunch the wiring - including the starter cable - back together again, tape it to hold it together tightly, re-cover it with the conduit, then finish taping all exposed wiring.

4.4a The battery ground cable bolt is located on the left inner fender, between the air filter housing and the battery tray. To access it, remove the battery (typical)

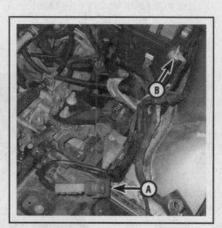

4.4b There are two positive battery cables bundled together. Both of them are connected to the positive battery terminal at A (battery removed for clarity) and the shorter of the two cables terminates at a stud-type terminal (B)

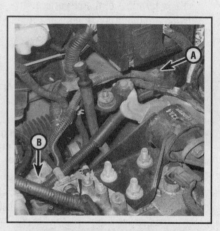

4.4c The other positive battery cable is secured by a clip (A) bolted to the fender below the fuse and relay box. This cable terminates at a ground bolt (B) screwed into the transaxle housing

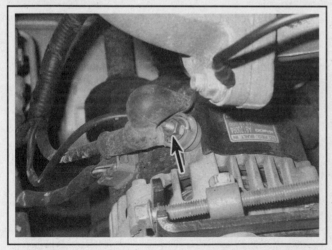

4.4d One branch of the positive cable harness terminates at the alternator's B+ terminal

4.4e Another branch of the positive cable harness terminates at the starter motor solenoid terminal

5 When purchasing battery cables, take the old one(s) with you when buying new cables. It is vitally important that you replace the cables with identical parts.

6 Clean the threads of the solenoid or ground connection with a wire brush to remove rust and corrosion. Apply a light coat of battery terminal corrosion inhibitor or petroleum jelly to the threads to prevent future corrosion.

7 Attach the cable to the solenoid or ground connection and tighten the mounting nut/bolt securely.

8 Before connecting a new cable to the battery make sure that it reaches the battery post without having to be stretched.

9 Connect the cable to the positive battery terminal first, then connect the ground cable to the negative battery terminal (see Section 1).

5 Ignition system - general information

WARNING:

Because of the high voltage generated by the ignition system, be extremely careful when performing any procedure involving ignition components.

1 On 1994 through 1997 models, the electronic ignition system consists of the ignition control module, the ignition coil, the distributor, the spark plug wires and the spark plugs. On 1994 and 1995 models, the ignition coil and the ignition control module (Kia refers to the control module as the "igniter" on 1994 models) are separate components located on the left side of the engine compartment. On 1996 and 1997 models, the ignition coil and the ignition control module are integral components of the distributor assembly. If either component is defective on one of these models, you must replace the distributor assembly.

2 On 1998 and later models, the electronic ignition system consists of the Powertrain Control Module (PCM), the Camshaft Position (CMP) sensor, the Crankshaft Position (CKP) sensor, two coil-over-plug type ignition coils and the spark plugs. The coils are located over the No. 2 and No. 4 spark plugs and are connected to their companion cylinders' spark plugs by short spark plug wires. During start-ups, the PCM uses the signal from the CMP sensor to determine when the piston in the No. 1 cylinder is at Top Dead Center (TDC). The PCM alters ignition timing in accordance with engine speed. It calculates engine speed from the signal that it receives from the CKP sensor. The PCM also uses the CKP sensor to detect misfires. The CKP sensor enables the PCM to detect variations in the angular velocity of the crankshaft during every power stroke. When all four cylinders are firing evenly, the crankshaft speeds up evenly with each power stroke. When a misfire occurs, the angular velocity of the crankshaft is no longer uniform, and the PCM interprets this change as a misfire. For more information about the CMP and CKP sensors, refer to Chapter 6.

6 Ignition system - check

Refer to illustrations 6.3 and 6.4

WARNING:

Because of the high voltage generated by the ignition system, use extreme care when performing a procedure involving ignition components.

Note: For the following test, you'll need to obtain a calibrated spark tester, which is available at most auto parts stores.

1 If a malfunction occurs in the ignition system, check the following items:

- a) *Make sure that the cable clamps at the battery terminals are clean and tight.*
- b) *Test the condition of the battery (see Section 3). If it doesn't pass all the tests, replace it.*
- c) *Check the ignition coil connections.*
- d) *Check any relevant fuses in the engine compartment fuse and relay box (see Chapter 12). If they're burned, determine the cause and repair the circuit.*

2 If the engine turns over but won't start, disconnect the spark plug wire from each spark plug on 1994 through 1997 models (see Chapter 1) or remove the two ignition coils on 1998 through 2004 models, except models with a 2.0L DOHC engine (see Section 8).

3 On 1994 through 1997 models, and on 2004 and later models with a 2.0L DOHC engine, install a calibrated spark tester inline between the spark plug wire for the No. 1 cylinder and a good ground (see illustration). Then crank the engine and see if the tester sparks or flashes (depending on the type of tester being used). Be sure to check the ignition spark from each spark plug wire.

6.3 To use this type of spark tester on a 1994 through 1997 model or a 2004 and later model with a 2.0L DOHC engine, remove the plug wire from the spark plug for the No. 1 cylinder, insert the tester into the spark plug boot, clip the tester to a good ground and crank the engine (repeat this test for each cylinder)

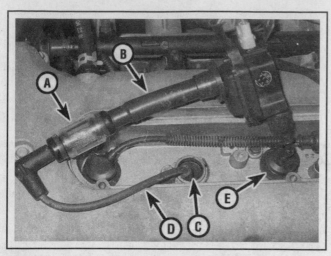

6.4 To use this type of spark tester on 1998 through 2004 models (except models with 2.0L DOHC engines), insert the tester (A) into the boot (B) on the bottom of the coil, push the boot (C) on the end of the tester lead (D) onto the plug and crank the engine. After that, reinstall the coil and repeat the test on the companion cylinder spark plug boot (E)

4   On 1998 through 2004 models, except models with a 2.0L DOHC engine, install a calibrated spark tester inline between the coil high-tension terminal and the spark plug (see illustration). Then crank the engine and see if the tester sparks or flashes (depending on the type of tester being used). Be sure to check the spark from the high-tension terminal and from the spark plug wire of each ignition coil.

5   If sparks occur during cranking, sufficient voltage is reaching the plug to fire it. Repeat this test for each cylinder to verify that there is spark at each cylinder. However, be aware that even if the ignition coil(s) is/are able to fire the spark tester, the plugs themselves might be fouled, so remove and inspect the plugs too (see Chapter 1).

6   If no sparks occur during cranking at one cylinder, inspect the primary wire connection at the coil. Make sure that it's clean and tight.

7   If no sparks or intermittent sparks occur during cranking at all cylinders, the ignition control module (1994 through 1997 models) or the crankshaft position sensor or PCM (1998 and later models) may be defective.

➡ **Note: Testing the ignition control module or PCM is beyond the scope of the do-it-yourselfer.**

8   If all of the spark plugs are in good shape, check the ignition coil(s) (see Section 8).

9   Any further testing of the ignition system should be done by a dealer service department or other qualified repair shop equipped with the right tools.

7   Ignition control module - replacement

▸ **Refer to illustration 7.2**

➡ **Note: This procedure applies only to 1994 and 1995 models with a B6 SOHC engine. The ignition control module is located on the left side of the engine compartment, below the ignition coil. If you have to replace the ignition control module, be aware that Kia refers to the module as the "igniter" on 1994 models.**

1   Disconnect the cable from the negative battery terminal (see Section 1).

2   Disconnect the electrical connector from the ignition control module (see illustration).

3   Remove the ignition control module mounting screws and remove the module.

4   Installation is the reverse of removal.

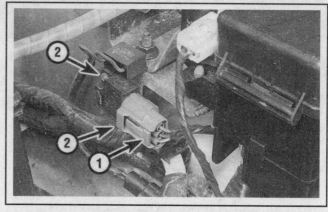

7.2 To remove the ignition control module from a 1994 or 1995 model with an SOHC engine, depress the release tab (1) and disconnect the electrical connector, then remove the two mounting screws (2)

8   Ignition coil - check and replacement

1994 AND 1995 MODELS

Check

▸ **Refer to illustrations 8.2 and 8.3**

1   Remove the ignition coil (see *Replacement* below).

2   Using an ohmmeter, measure the resistance of the coil primary winding (see illustration) and compare the indicated resistance to the resistance listed in this Chapter's Specifications.

3   Measure the resistance of the coil secondary winding (see illustration) and compare the indicated resistance to the resistance listed in this Chapter's Specifications.

4   If the indicated resistance is within the specified range of resistance for both of the above tests, the coil is okay.

5   If the indicated resistance is outside the range of resistance for either of the above tests, replace the ignition coil.

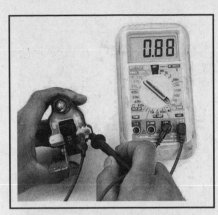

8.2 To measure the primary coil resistance, connect the leads of an ohmmeter to the two terminals of the ignition coil electrical connector

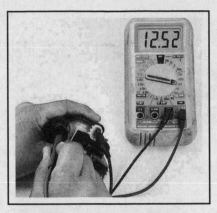

8.3 To measure the secondary coil resistance, connect one lead of the ohmmeter to one of the two coil primary terminals and connect the other lead to the coil high-tension terminal

8.7 To remove the ignition coil from a 1994 or 1995 model:

1   *Disconnect the primary voltage electrical connector from the coil*
2   *Disconnect the cable from the coil high-tension terminal*
3   *Remove the coil mounting nuts*

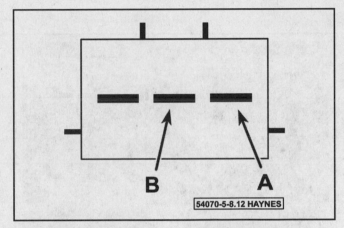

8.12 Ignition coil terminal guide (1996 and 1997 models)

Replacement

▸ **Refer to illustration 8.7**

6   Disconnect the cable from the negative battery terminal (see Section 1).

7   Disconnect the primary voltage electrical connector from the ignition coil (see illustration).

8   Disconnect the high-tension cable from the ignition coil.

9   Remove the ignition coil mounting nuts and remove the coil assembly.

10   Installation is the reverse of removal.

1996 AND 1997 MODELS

Check

▸ **Refer to illustration 8.12**

11   Disconnect the electrical connector from the distributor (see illustration 9.4).

12   Using an ohmmeter, measure the coil primary resistance between terminals A and B (see illustration) and compare the indicated resistance to the resistance listed in this Chapter's Specifications.

8.17 To measure the coil primary resistance on a 1998 through 2004 models (except models with a 2.0L DOHC engine) ignition coil, connect the leads of an ohmmeter to the two coil primary voltage terminals

13   Measure the coil secondary resistance between terminal A and the distributor body.

14   If the indicated resistance is within the specified range of resistance for both of the above tests, the coil is okay.

15   If the indicated resistance is outside the range of resistance for either of the above tests, replace the distributor (see Section 9).

1998 THROUGH 2004 MODELS

➡ **Note: This Section does not apply to 2004 models with a 2.0L DOHC engine. Refer to Steps 26 through 31.**

Check

▸ **Refer to illustrations 8.17 and 8.18**

16   Remove the ignition coil (see below).

17   Using an ohmmeter, measure the coil primary resistance between the two coil primary terminals (see illustration) and compare the indicated resistance to the resistance listed in this Chapter's Specifications.

8.18 To measure the coil secondary resistance on a 1998 through 2004 model (except models with a 2.0L DOHC engine) ignition coil, connect the leads of an ohmmeter to the high-tension terminals

8.21 To remove the ignition coil cover, remove these six screws (1998 through 2004 models, except models with a 2.0L DOHC engine)

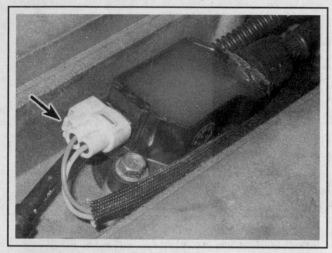

8.22 To disconnect the electrical connector from the ignition coil on a 1998 through 2004 model, except models with a 2.0L DOHC engine, depress this release tab and pull off the connector

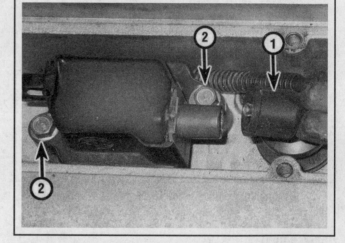

8.23 Disconnect the spark plug wire boot (1) from the coil high-tension terminal and remove the coil mounting bolts (2) . . .

18 Measure the coil secondary resistance between the secondary (high-tension) terminals (see illustration) and compare the indicated resistance to the resistance listed in this Chapter's Specifications.

19 If the indicated resistance is within the specified range of resistance for both of the above tests, the coil is okay.

20 If the indicated resistance is outside the range of resistance for either of the above tests, replace the distributor (see Section 9).

Replacement

▶ **Refer to illustrations 8.21, 8.22, 8.23 and 8.24**

21 Remove the ignition coil cover (see illustration).

22 Disconnect the electrical connector from the ignition coil (see illustration).

23 Disconnect the spark plug wire from the coil high-tension terminal (see illustration).

24 Remove the ignition coil mounting bolts, then pull the ignition coil straight up to disconnect it from the spark plug (see illustration).

25 Installation is the reverse of removal. Be sure to tighten the ignition coil mounting bolts securely.

2004 AND LATER MODELS (2.0L DOHC ENGINE)

▶ **Refer to illustration 8.29**

26 Disconnect the cable from the negative terminal of the battery (see Section 1).

27 Unplug the coil electrical connector.

28 Unplug the spark plug wires from the coils (see Chapter 1).

29 Remove the coil mounting fasteners (see illustration).

30 Remove the coil assembly.

31 Installation is the reverse of removal.

8.24 . . . then grasp the coil body firmly and pull it straight up (1998 through 2004 models, except models with a 2.0L DOHC engine)

8.29 To detach the coil assembly from a 2.0L DOHC engine, remove these two fasteners

2.7L V6 SPORTAGE MODELS

▶ **Refer to illustration 8.33**

32 Disconnect the spark plug cables (see Chapter 1).

33 Disconnect the electrical connector from the ignition coil (see illustration).

34 Remove the ignition coil mounting bolts and remove the coil.

35 Installation is the reverse of removal.

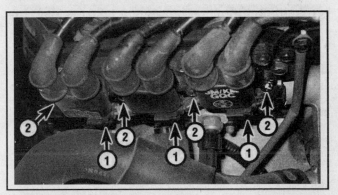

8.33 Ignition coil details (2.7L V6):

1 *Electrical connectors*   2 *Mounting screws*

---

9 Distributor (1997 and earlier models) - removal and installation

▶ **Refer to illustration 9.4**

1 Detach the cable from the negative battery terminal (see Section 1).

2 Look for a raised "1" on the distributor cap. This marks the location for the number one cylinder spark plug wire terminal. If the cap does not have a mark for the number one terminal, locate the number one spark plug and trace the wire back to the terminal on the cap.

3 Remove the distributor cap (see Chapter 1) and turn the engine over until the rotor is pointing toward the number one spark plug terminal (see the Top Dead Center locating procedure in Chapter 2A).

4 Disconnect the electrical connector from the distributor (see illustration).

5 Make a mark on the edge of the distributor base directly below the rotor tip and in line with it. Also, mark the distributor base and the cylinder head block to ensure that the distributor is installed correctly.

6 Remove the distributor hold-down bolt, then pull the distributor straight out to remove it.

✳✳ CAUTION:

DO NOT turn the crankshaft while the distributor is out of the engine, or your alignment marks will be useless, and you'll have to realign everything before installing the distributor.

7 Remove the old distributor O-ring.

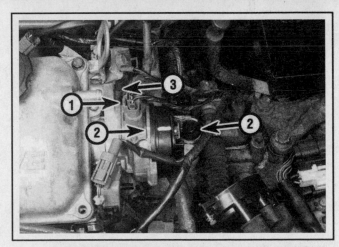

9.4 Distributor removal details (1994 through 1997 models):

1 *Disconnect the electrical connector*

2 *With the engine set at TDC for the No. 1 cylinder, mark the distributor base directly below the rotor tip and make a mark across the split line between the distributor base and the cylinder head*

3 *Remove the distributor hold-down bolt (bolt already removed in this photo)*

INSTALLATION

➡ **Note: If the crankshaft has been moved while the distributor is out, locate Top Dead Center (TDC) for the piston in cylinder No. 1 (see Chapter 2A) and position the distributor and the rotor accordingly.**

8   Install a new O-ring onto the distributor housing.

9   Align the cut-out portion of the coupling with the groove in the housing, then insert the distributor into the engine in exactly the same relationship to the cylinder head that it was in when removed.

10 If the distributor does not seat completely, recheck the alignment marks between the distributor base and the block to verify that the distributor is in the same position it was in before removal. Also check the rotor to see if it's aligned with the mark you made on the edge of the distributor base.

11 Loosely install the distributor hold-down bolt.

12 Install the distributor cap and reconnect the distributor electrical connector.

13 Check the ignition timing (see Section 10), then tighten the distributor hold-down bolt securely.

10 Ignition timing - check and adjustment

◆ **Refer to illustrations 10.2 and 10.4**

➡ **Note: The adjustment portion of this procedure applies only to 1994 through 1997 models. You can check the ignition timing on 1998 and later models but you can't adjust it. If the ignition timing is incorrect on a later model, it could be caused by a defective Camshaft Position (CMP) sensor, Crankshaft Position (CKP) sensor, PCM or by a misalignment between the crankshaft and the camshaft, i.e. an incorrectly installed timing belt.**

1   Hook up a tachometer in accordance with the manufacturer's instructions.

2   Locate the Data Link Connector (DLC) on the firewall. Open the DLC's protective lid and install a jumper wire between the ENGINE TEST and GROUND terminals (see illustration).

3   With the ignition key turned to OFF, hook up a timing light in accordance with the tool manufacturer's instructions.

4   Locate the timing marks on the stationary index pointer adjacent to the crankshaft pulley and locate the single notch in the outer face of the pulley (see illustration).

5   Start the engine, allow it to warm up to its normal operating temperature (the upper radiator hose is hot). Make sure that all electrical accessories, including the air conditioning system, are turned off.

6   Once the engine is warmed up and idling normally, aim the timing light at the index pointer. The notch on the crankshaft pulley should be aligned with the timing mark.

7   If the notch on the crankshaft pulley isn't aligned with the timing mark, loosen the distributor hold-down bolt and slowly rotate the distributor until the notch is aligned with the timing mark.

8   When the timing marks are aligned, tighten the distributor hold-down bolt and recheck the timing.

9   Remove the jumper wire from the DLC and verify that the ignition timing advances 9 to 11 degrees BTDC.

10 Turn off the engine and disconnect the timing light and tachometer.

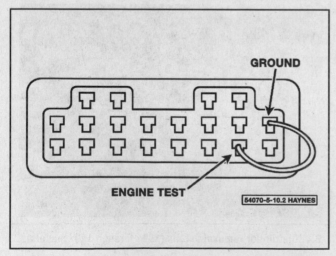

10.2 To check ignition timing on 1994 through 1997 models, you must remove all ignition advance. To do so, you must temporarily take the ignition control module out of the loop by jumping the ENGINE TEST and GROUND terminals in the Data Link Connector (DLC)

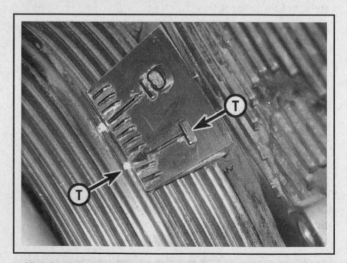

10.4 Look for the stationary pointer with ignition timing and advance marks on it. The timing mark that you want to use for this test is a "T" with an arrow on it (T). Now look for the timing mark (a notch) in the edge of the crankshaft pulley (T). When you put the timing light on these marks with the engine at idle and the DLC's ENGINE TEST and GROUND terminals jumped, these two marks should be aligned as shown

11 Charging system - general information and precautions

The charging system includes the alternator (with an integral voltage regulator inside), the battery, a charge indicator light (on the instrument cluster) and the wiring connecting all of these components. The charging system supplies electrical power for the ignition system, the lights, the radio, etc. The alternator is belt-driven by the crankshaft. The alternator's voltage output is controlled by a conventional internal voltage regulator, which keeps charging output within a range of about 14.1 to 14.7 volts.

The charging system doesn't ordinarily require periodic maintenance. However, the drivebelt, battery and wires and connections should be inspected at the intervals outlined in Chapter 1.

The dashboard warning light should come on when the ignition key is turned to ON, but it should go off immediately after the engine is started. If it remains on, there is a malfunction in the charging system (see Section 12).

Be very careful when making electrical circuit connections to a vehicle equipped with an alternator and note the following:

a) *When reconnecting wires to the alternator from the battery, be sure to note the polarity.*

b) *Before using arc-welding equipment to repair any part of the vehicle, disconnect the wires from the alternator and the battery terminals.*

c) *Never start the engine with a battery charger connected.*

d) *Always disconnect both battery leads before using a battery charger.*

e) *The alternator is turned by an engine drivebelt that could cause serious injury if your hands, hair or clothes become entangled in it with the engine running.*

f) *Because the alternator is connected directly to the battery, it could arc or cause a fire if overloaded or shorted out.*

g) *Wrap a plastic bag over the alternator and secure it with rubber bands before steam cleaning the engine.*

12 Charging system - check

1   If a malfunction occurs in the charging circuit, do not immediately assume that the alternator is causing the problem. First, check the following items:

a) *Make sure the battery cable clamps, where they connect to the battery, are clean and tight.*

b) *Test the condition of the battery (see Section 3). If it does not pass all the tests, replace it with a new battery.*

c) *Check the external alternator wiring and connections.*

d) *Check the drivebelt condition and tension (see Chapter 1).*

e) *Check the alternator mounting bolts for tightness.*

f) *Run the engine and check the alternator for abnormal noise.*

g) *Check the charging system warning light on the dash. It should illuminate when the ignition key is turned to ON (engine not running). If it doesn't come on, disconnect the electrical connector and the ground wire from the alternator. The charge light should now come on (because by opening the charging circuit, you have eliminated all charging voltage). If the light still doesn't illuminate, check the METER fuse, which is located in the left (driver's side) passenger compartment fuse and relay box in the left kick panel. If the METER fuse is blown, troubleshoot and repair the charging system warning light circuit and then replace the fuse (15-amp fuse on 1994 through 1997 models and 10-amp fuse on 1998 and later models). If the charging system warning light still doesn't come on, check the bulb (see "Bulb replacement" in Chapter 12). If it's blown, replace it.*

2   With the ignition key turned to the OFF position, check the open-circuit battery voltage (see illustration 3.2). Make sure that all electrical accessories - blower fan, radio, cigarette lighter, cooling fan, etc. - are turned off. It should be at least 12.6 volts (it might be slightly higher if the engine has been turned off for less than an hour). If the open-circuit voltage is below 12.6 volts, try quick-charging the battery for two hours, then recheck it. If the battery is still below 12.6 volts, replace it.

3   Check the charging voltage with the engine running. Start the engine, raise the engine rpm to 1500 and check the battery voltage again. It should now be approximately 14.1 to 14.7 volts.

4   Load the battery and observe the charging voltage. Turn on the high beam headlights, turn the A/C blower to HIGH and turn on the windshield wipers and the radio. The voltage should drop and then come back up as each accessory is selected. If the charging system is working properly the voltage should stay above 14 volts. If the voltage drops below 14 volts, the charging system is defective.

5   Lower the engine rpm back to idle and observe the charging voltage. The charging voltage should not drop below 14 volts with the decrease in engine rpm. Apply the brakes and observe the charging voltage at idle. It should remain above 14 volts.

6   Turn off all the electrical loads (high beam headlights, the A/C blower on HIGH, the windshield wipers and the radio), run the engine at 1600 rpm and watch the charging voltage rise. It should not rise above 14.7 volts.

7   If the charging voltage does not change in response to changes in engine speed and/or changes in accessory loads, the voltage regulator is defective. If the charging voltages are low and the drivebelts and battery are all in good condition, the alternator or the regulator, or both, are defective. Replace the alternator (the voltage regulator is an integral component of the alternator and cannot be serviced separately).

13 Alternator - removal and installation

1   Disconnect the cable from the negative battery terminal (see Section 1).

2   Remove the alternator drivebelt (see Chapter 1).

1994 THROUGH 1997 MODELS

♦ **Refer to illustration 13.3**

3   Flip open the cap that protects the B+ terminal (see illustration), remove the nut that attaches the alternator output cable to the B+ terminal stud and disconnect the battery output cable from the stud. Then disconnect the electrical connector from the alternator. Set the alternator harnesses aside.

4   Remove the alternator adjusting bolt and pivot bolt and remove the alternator.

1998 AND LATER MODELS

♦ **Refer to illustration 13.5a, 13.5b, 13.6a, 13.6b, 13.7a and 13.7b**

5   Remove the rubber cover from the B+ terminal (see illustrations), remove the nut that attaches the alternator output cable to the B+ terminal stud and disconnect the battery output cable from the stud. Then disconnect the electrical connector from the alternator and set the alternator wiring harnesses aside.

6   On four-cylinder models, remove the tensioner mounting bolt and the tensioner adjusting bolt (see illustration). Loosen the tensioner bracket bolt and flip up the tensioner bracket to provide enough clearance to remove the alternator. From underneath the alternator, remove the alternator pivot bolt (see illustration) and remove the alternator.

7   On Sportage V6 models, loosen the right front wheel lug nuts, raise the front of the vehicle and place it securely on jackstands. Remove the right front wheel, then remove the right engine cover (see illustrations 7.4a and 7.4b in Chapter 2B). Remove the upper and lower alternator mounting bracket bolts (see illustrations) and remove the alternator.

ALL MODELS

8   If you're replacing the alternator, take the old one with you when purchasing the replacement unit. Make sure that the new/rebuilt unit looks identical to the old alternator. Look at the terminals - they should be the same in number, size and location as the terminals on the old alternator. Finally, look at the identification numbers - they will be stamped into the housing or printed on a tag attached to the housing. Make sure the numbers are the same on both alternators.

9   Many new/rebuilt alternators DO NOT have a pulley installed, so you might have to swap the pulley from the old unit to the new/rebuilt one. When buying an alternator, find out the store's policy regarding

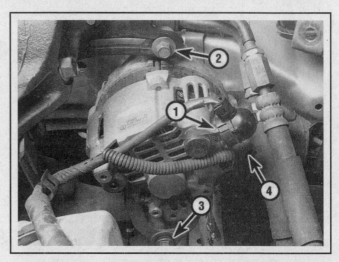

13.3 Alternator mounting details (1994 through 1997 models; SOHC model shown, DOHC model has a belt-tension adjusting setup similar to 1998 and later models)

1	Output cable	3	Pivot bolt
2	Drivebelt adjusting bolt	4	Electrical connector

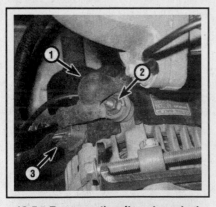

13.5a To access the alternator output cable on 1998 and later four-cylinder models, peel back the rubber weather protector (1), remove the nut (2) and disconnect the output cable from the B+ terminal stud. Then disconnect the electrical connector (3)

13.5b Alternator connectors (Sportage 2.7L V6 models):

1   *Alternator output cable connection (B+ terminal)*
2   *Electrical connector*
3   *Oxygen sensor harness clip*

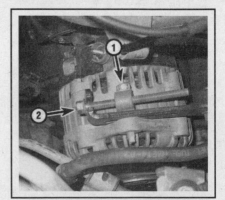

13.6a To remove the belt tensioner assembly from a 1998 and later model, remove the tensioner mounting bolt (1), remove the tensioner adjusting bolt (2) from the bracket, loosen the tensioner bracket bolt (3) and flip up the tensioner bracket to make room to remove the alternator

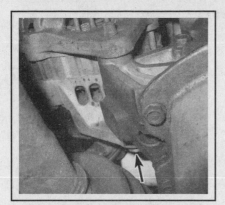

13.6b To remove the alternator assembly from a 1998 and later model, remove this pivot bolt from underneath, then lift the alternator out from above

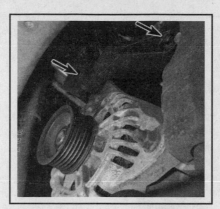

13.7a Upper alternator mounting bracket bolts (Sportage V6 models)

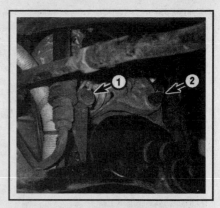

13.7b Lower alternator mounting bracket fasteners (Sportage V6 models):

1   *Mounting bracket bolt*
2   *Mounting bracket nut and through-bolt*

pulley swaps. Some stores perform this service free of charge. If your local auto parts store doesn't offer this service, you'll have to purchase a puller for removing the pulley and do it yourself.

10 Installation is the reverse of removal. Be sure to tighten the alter-nator adjusting and mounting bolts securely.

11 Reconnect the cable to the negative terminal of the battery (see Section 1). When you're done, check the charging voltage (see Section 12) to verify that the alternator is operating correctly.

14 Starting system - general information and precautions

The starting system consists of the battery, an 80 amp fuse, the ignition switch, the clutch start switch (manual transaxle) or the transaxle range switch (automatic transaxle), the starter solenoid and starter motor assembly, and the wires connecting these components. The solenoid is mounted directly on the starter motor. The solenoid/starter motor assembly is located on the backside of the engine, at the flywheel/driveplate end of the engine, on all models.

When the ignition key is turned to the START position, the starter solenoid is actuated through the starter control circuit. The starter solenoid then connects the battery to the starter. The battery supplies the electrical energy to the starter motor, which does the actual work of cranking the engine.

On models with a manual transaxle, the starter can only be oper-ated when the clutch pedal is depressed. On models with an automatic transaxle, the starter can only be operated when the shift lever is in PARK or NEUTRAL.

Always observe the following precautions when working on the starting system:

a) *Excessive cranking of the starter motor can overheat it and cause serious damage. Never operate the starter motor for more than 15 seconds at a time without pausing to allow it to cool for at least two minutes.*
b) *The starter is connected directly to the battery and could arc or cause a fire if mishandled, overloaded or shorted out.*
c) *Always detach the cable from the negative terminal of the battery before working on the starting system.*

15 Starter motor and circuit - check

▶ **Refer to illustrations 15.3 and 15.4**

1   If a malfunction occurs in the starting circuit, do not immediately assume that the starter is causing the problem. First, check the follow-ing items:

a) *Make sure that the clutch pedal is depressed (manual transaxle) or the shift lever is in PARK or NEUTRAL (automatic transaxle).*
b) *Make sure the battery cable clamps, where they connect to the battery, are clean and tight.*
c) *Check the condition of the battery cables (see Section 4). Replace any defective battery cables with new ones.*
d) *Test the condition of the battery (see Section 3). If it does not pass all the tests, replace it with a new battery.*

e) *Check the starter solenoid wiring and connections. Refer to the wiring diagrams at the end of Chapter 12.*
f) *Check the starter mounting bolts for tightness.*
g) *Check the fuses in the engine compartment fuse and relay box (see Chapter 12). If they're burned, determine the cause and repair the circuit. Also, check the ignition switch circuit for correct operation (see the wiring diagrams at the end of Chapter 12).*
h) *The clutch start switch circuit (manual transaxle) or transaxle range switch circuit (automatic transaxle) directs battery voltage to the starter solenoid (see the wiring diagrams at the end of Chapter 12). Verify that the clutch start switch circuit (manual transaxle) or the transaxle range switch circuit (automatic transaxle) is operat-ing correctly.*

15.3 To use an inductive ammeter, simply hold the ammeter over the positive or negative battery cable (whichever cable has better clearance)

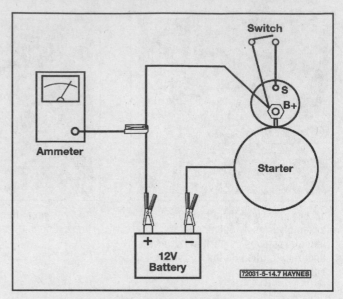

15.4 Starter motor bench testing details

2   If the starter does not activate when the ignition switch is turned to the start position, check for battery voltage to the solenoid. This will determine if the solenoid is receiving the correct voltage signal from the ignition switch. Connect a voltmeter to the starter solenoid "S" terminal. Then note the indicated voltage when an assistant turns the ignition switch to the START position. It should be about the same as battery voltage. If there's no voltage at the S terminal, refer to the wiring diagrams at the end of Chapter 12 and check the ignition switch/starter circuit fuse(s), which is/are located inside the engine compartment fuse and relay box. On 1994 through 1997 models, there is one 10-amp fuse for the starter/ignition switch circuit. On 1998 and 1999 models, there are two fuses (10-amp and 25-amp). On 2000 and later models, there are three fuses (10-amp, 20-amp and 30-amp). If voltage is available but the starter motor doesn't engage and crank the engine over, remove the starter from the engine (see Section 16) and bench test the starter (see Step 4).

3   If the starter turns over slowly, check the starter cranking voltage and the current draw from the battery. This test must be performed with the starter assembly on the engine. Crank the engine over (for 10 seconds or less) and observe the battery voltage. It should not drop below 8.5 volts. Also, observe the current draw using an ammeter (see illustration). It should not exceed 380 amps. If the starter motor exceeds these values, replace it. Several conditions might affect the starter's

cranking power. The battery must be in good condition and the battery cold-cranking rating must not be under-rated for the application. Be sure to check the battery specifications carefully. The battery terminals and cables must be clean and not corroded. Also, in cases of extremely cold temperatures, make sure the battery and/or engine block is warmed before performing the tests.

4   If the starter is receiving voltage but does not activate, remove and check the starter/solenoid assembly on the bench. Most likely the solenoid is defective. In some rare cases, the engine may be seized, so be sure to try and rotate the crankshaft pulley (see Chapter 2) before proceeding. With the starter/solenoid assembly mounted in a vise on the bench, install one jumper cable from the negative terminal (-) to the body of the starter. Install another jumper cable from the positive terminal (+) on the battery to the B+ terminal on the starter (see illustration). Install a starter switch and apply battery voltage to the solenoid S terminal (for 10 seconds or less) and observe the solenoid plunger, shift lever and overrunning clutch extend and rotate the pinion drive. If the pinion drive extends but does not rotate, the solenoid is operating but the starter motor is defective. If there is no movement but the solenoid clicks, the solenoid and/or the starter motor is defective. If the solenoid plunger extends and rotates the pinion drive, the starter/solenoid assembly is working properly.

16   Starter motor - removal and installation

FOUR-CYLINDER MODELS

▸ **Refer to illustrations 16.2, 16.3, 16.4 and 16.5**

1   Disconnect the cable from the negative battery terminal (see Section 1).

2   Remove the bolts from the upper end of the intake manifold support bracket (see illustration).

3   Raise the vehicle and place it securely on jackstands, then

remove the bolt from the lower end of the intake manifold support bracket.

4   Disconnect the battery cable and the starter wire from their respective terminals on the starter motor solenoid (see illustration).

5   Remove the starter mounting bolts (see illustration) and detach the starter.

6   Installation is the reverse of removal. Be sure to tighten the starter mounting bolts securely.

7   When you're done, reconnect the cable to the negative terminal of the battery (see Section 1).

V6 (SPORTAGE) MODELS

♦ **Refer to illustrations 16.11, 16.12 and 16.13**

8   Disconnect the cable from the negative battery terminal (see Section 1).

9   Raise the front of the vehicle and place it securely on jackstands. Remove the engine under cover/splash shield (see illustration 6.3 in Chapter 1).

10   Remove the front exhaust pipe (see illustration 6.8 in Chapter 2B).

11   Remove the starter motor heat shield (see illustration).

12   Disconnect the electrical connector and the battery cable from the starter motor (see illustration).

13   Remove the starter motor mounting bolts (see illustration) and remove the starter motor.

14   Installation is the reverse of removal. Be sure to tighten the starter motor mounting bolts securely.

15   Reconnect the cable to the negative battery terminal (see Section 1).

16.2   To detach the upper end of the intake manifold support bracket from the intake manifold on a 1998 and later model, remove these two bolts (on 1994 through 1997 models, this bracket is attached to the intake manifold by a single nut)

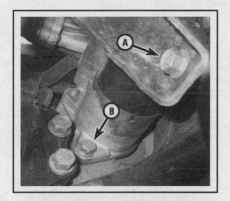

16.3   To detach the lower end of the intake manifold support bracket from the engine block on a 1998 and later model, remove this bolt (A) (on 1994 through 1997 models, this bracket is attached to the block by two bolts). To detach the lower part of the starter, remove this bolt (B)

16.4   Remove the nut (1) and disconnect the battery cable lead from the starter solenoid, then disconnect the starter wire (2) from the solenoid

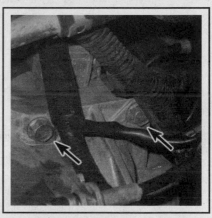

16.5   To detach the starter motor, remove these two upper bolts and the lower bolt (see illustration 16.3)

16.11   Starter motor heat shield bolts (Sportage V6 models)

16.12   Starter motor electrical connector (A) and battery cable terminal (B) (Sportage V6 models)

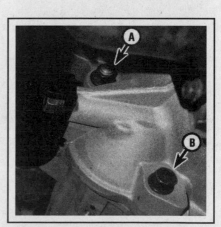

16.13   Starter motor upper mounting nut and stud (A) and lower mounting bolt (B) (Sportage V6 models)

General

Battery voltage	
Engine off	12 to 12.5 volts
Engine running	ApproxImately 13.5 volts
Firing order	
Four-cylinder engines	1-3-4-2
V6 engines	1-2-3-4-5-6
Ignition coil resistance	
1994 and 1995	
Primary resistance	0.81 to 0.99 ohms
Secondary resistance	10 to 16 k-ohms
1996 and 1997	
Primary resistance	0.49 to 0.73 ohms
Secondary resistance	20 to 31 k-ohms
1998 through 2004 (except 2.0L DOHC)	
Primary resistance	0.45 to 0.55 ohms
Secondary resistance	13 to 15 k-ohms
2.0L DOHC (except Sportage)	
Primary resistance	0.52 to 0.64 ohms
Secondary resistance	7.92 to 9.68 k-ohms
Sportage	
2.0L DOHC	
Primary resistance	0.48 to 0.68 ohms
Secondary resistance	7.48 to 10.12 k-ohms
2.7L V6	
Primary resistance	0.86 to 1.06 ohms
Secondary resistance	10.63 to 14.38 k-ohms

6

EMISSIONS
AND ENGINE
CONTROL
SYSTEMS

Section

1   General information
2   CHECK ENGINE light on/On-Board Diagnostic (OBD) system
     and trouble codes
3   Camshaft Position (CMP) sensor - replacement
4   Chassis acceleration sensor - replacement
5   Clutch pedal position switch - replacement
6   Crankshaft Position (CKP) sensor - replacement
7   Engine Coolant Temperature (ECT) sensor - replacement
8   Fuel tank pressure sensor - replacement
9   Input shaft and output shaft speed sensors - replacement
10   Intake Air Temperature (IAT) sensor - replacement
11   Knock sensor - replacement
12   Mass Air Flow (MAF) sensor - replacement
13   Neutral position switch - replacement
14   Oxygen sensors - replacement
15   Power Steering Pressure (PSP) switch - replacement
16   Throttle Position (TP) sensor - replacement
17   Transmission Range (TR) switch - replacement and adjustment
18   Vehicle Speed Sensor (VSS) - replacement
19   Volume Air Flow (VAF) sensor - replacement
20   Powertrain Control Module (PCM) - removal and installation
21   Catalytic converter - general description, check and replacement
22   Dashpot - replacement
23   Idle air control system - component replacement
24   Evaporative Emissions Control (EVAP) system - general
     description and component replacement
25   Exhaust Gas Recirculation (EGR) system - general description
     and component replacement
26   Positive Crankcase Ventilation (PCV) system - general
     description and component replacement
27   Continuously Variable Valve Timing (CVVT) system - description
     and component replacement
28   Variable Induction Control system (Sportage V6 models) -
     description and component replacement

1   General information

To prevent pollution of the atmosphere from incompletely burned and evaporating gases, and to maintain good driveability and fuel economy, a number of emission control systems are incorporated. They include the:

Catalytic converter
Evaporative Emissions Control (EVAP) system
Exhaust Gas Recirculation (EGR) system
Multiport Fuel Injection (MFI) system (the electronic engine control system)
On-Board Diagnostic-II (OBD-II) system
Positive Crankcase Ventilation (PCV) system

This Chapter includes general descriptions of these and other emissions-related devices and component replacement procedures (when possible) for each of the systems listed above. Before assuming that an emissions control system is malfunctioning, check the fuel and ignition systems carefully. The diagnosis of some emission control devices requires specialized tools, equipment and training. If a procedure is beyond your ability, consult a dealer service department or other repair shop. Remember, the most frequent cause of emissions problems is simply a loose or broken wire or vacuum hose, so always check all hose and wiring connections first.

➡**Note: Because of a Federally mandated extended warranty which covers the emissions control system components, check with your dealer about warranty coverage before working on any emissions-related systems. Once the warranty has expired, you may wish to perform some of the component checks and/or replacement procedures in this Chapter to save money.**

Pay close attention to any special precautions outlined in this Chapter. It should be noted that the illustrations of the various systems might not exactly match the system installed on your vehicle because of changes made by the manufacturer during production.

A Vehicle Emissions Control Information (VECI) label is located in the engine compartment, either on the underside of the hood or attached to the radiator support or one of the strut towers. This label specifies the important emissions systems on the vehicle and it provides the important specifications for tune-ups. Part of the VECI label, the Vacuum Hose Routing Diagram, provides a vacuum hose schematic with emissions components identified. When servicing the engine or emissions systems, the VECI label and the vacuum hose routing diagram should always be checked for up-to-date information.

2   On-Board Diagnostic (OBD) system and trouble codes

SCAN TOOL INFORMATION

◆ **Refer to illustration 2.1**

1   Hand-held scanners are the most powerful and versatile tools for analyzing engine management systems used on later model vehicles (see illustration). Early model scanners handle codes and some diagnostics for many systems. Each brand scan tool must be examined carefully to match the year, make and model of the vehicle you are working on. Often, interchangeable cartridges are available to access the particular manufacturer (Chrysler, Ford, GM, Honda, Toyota etc.). Some manufacturers will specify by continent (Asia, Europe, USA, etc.). Note: An aftermarket generic scanner should work with any model covered by this manual. Before purchasing a generic scan tool, contact the manufacturer of the scanner you're planning to buy and verify that it will work properly with the system you want to scan. If necessary, of course, you can always have the codes extracted by a dealer service department or an independent repair shop with a professional scan tool.

OBD SYSTEM GENERAL DESCRIPTION

2   All models are equipped with an On-Board Diagnostic (OBD) system. This system consists of an on-board computer known as the Powertrain Control Module (PCM), and information sensors, which monitor various functions of the engine and send data to the PCM. This system incorporates a series of diagnostic monitors that detect and identify fuel injection and emissions control systems faults and store the information in the computer memory. This updated system also tests sensors and output actuators, diagnoses drive cycles, freezes data and clears codes.

3   The PCM is the brain of the electronically controlled fuel and emissions system. It receives data from a number of sensors and other electronic components (switches, relays, etc.). Based on the information it receives, the PCM generates output signals to control various relays, solenoids (i.e. fuel injectors) and other actuators. The PCM is specifically calibrated to optimize the emissions, fuel economy and driveability of the vehicle.

4   It isn't a good idea to attempt diagnosis or replacement of the PCM or emission control components at home while the vehicle is under warranty. Because of a Federally mandated warranty which covers the emissions system components and because any owner-induced damage to the PCM, the sensors and/or the control devices may void this warranty, take the vehicle to a dealer service department if the PCM or a system component malfunctions.

2.1 Scanners like these from Actron and AutoXray are powerful diagnostic aids - they can tell you just about anything that you want to know about your engine management system

INFORMATION SENSORS

→Note: Not all sensors apply to all models.

5 **Brake pedal position switch** - The brake pedal position switch (also referred to as the "brake light switch" or the "stop light switch") is located on a bracket near the top of the brake pedal. It's a normally open switch that closes when the brake pedal is applied and sends a signal to the Transmission Control Module (TCM) and/or the PCM, which interprets this signal as its cue to disengage the torque converter clutch. The brake pedal switch is also used to disengage the cruise control system and the automatic transaxle shift interlock system. For information regarding the replacement and adjustment of the brake pedal position switch, refer to Chapter 9.

6 **Camshaft Position (CMP) sensor** - The CMP sensor produces a signal that the PCM uses to identify the number 1 cylinder and to time the firing sequence of the fuel injectors. On 1994 through 1997 models, the CMP sensor is located in the distributor. (On these models, you cannot replace the CMP sensor separately; if it's defective you must replace the distributor assembly.) On 1998 and later models, the CMP sensor is located on the left end of the cylinder head, near the left end of the exhaust camshaft.

7 **Chassis acceleration sensor** - The chassis acceleration sensor, which is used on 1998 and later models, is located in the right rear corner of the engine compartment, right below and behind the right strut tower. The chassis acceleration sensor detects vertical chassis movement on rough terrain and sends a signal to the PCM, which uses this signal to rule out a false misfire signal from the crankshaft position sensor caused by rough roads rather than by an actual misfire condition.

8 **Clutch pedal position switch** - The clutch pedal position switch is located at the top of the clutch pedal. (Don't confuse the clutch pedal position switch with the clutch start switch. The clutch pedal position switch is secured to its mounting bracket by a locknut, which is also used to adjust it. The clutch start switch is secured to its mounting bracket by a pair of nuts.) The clutch pedal position switch, which is normally open, closes the circuit when the clutch pedal is depressed, sending a voltage signal to the PCM.

9 **Crankshaft Position (CKP) sensor** - The CKP sensor produces a signal that the PCM uses to determine the speed and position of the crankshaft. It is also used to detect a misfire condition on OBD-II models. On 1996 and 1997 models the CKP sensor is located on the front edge of the timing belt cover, adjacent to the crankshaft pulley. On 1998 and later models the CKP sensor is located on the front of the transaxle bellhousing, near the flywheel or driveplate.

10 **Engine Coolant Temperature (ECT) sensor** - The ECT sensor is a thermistor (temperature-sensitive variable resistor) that sends a voltage signal to the PCM, which uses this data to determine the temperature of the engine coolant. The ECT sensor helps the PCM control the air/fuel mixture ratio and ignition timing, and it also helps the PCM determine when to turn the Exhaust Gas Recirculation (EGR) system on and off. The ECT sensor is located on the intake manifold.

11 **Fuel tank pressure sensor** - The fuel tank pressure sensor measures the fuel tank pressure when the PCM tests the EVAP system, and it's also used to control fuel tank pressure by signaling the EVAP system to purge the tank when the pressure becomes excessive. The fuel tank pressure sensor is located on top of the fuel pump/fuel gauge sending unit assembly, which is located in the upper part of the fuel tank.

12 **Input shaft speed sensor** - The input shaft speed sensor is a magnetic pick-up coil located on top of the automatic transaxle, underneath the air filter housing assembly (you'll have to remove the air filter housing to access the input shaft speed sensor. On OBD-II vehicles, the PCM compares the signal from the input shaft speed sensor with the signal from the output shaft speed sensor to calculate whether slippage (i.e. wear) is occurring inside the transaxle.

13 **Intake Air Temperature (IAT) sensor** - The IAT sensor monitors the temperature of the air entering the engine and sends a signal to the PCM. On 1994 through 1997 models, the IAT sensor is an integral component of the Mass Air Flow (MAF) sensor, which is located on the air filter housing. On 1998 and later models, the IAT sensor is located on the air filter housing.

14 **Knock sensor** - The knock sensor is a piezoelectric crystal that oscillates in proportion to engine vibration. The term piezoelectric refers to the property of certain crystals that produce a voltage output when subjected to a mechanical stress. This voltage output is proportional to the intensity of the stress. The knock sensor's voltage output is monitored by the PCM, which retards the ignition timing when the oscillation exceeds a certain threshold. When the engine is operating normally, the knock sensor oscillates consistently and its voltage signal is steady. When detonation occurs, engine vibration increases, and the oscillation of the knock sensor exceeds a design threshold. (Detonation is an uncontrolled explosion, after the spark occurs at the spark plug, which spontaneously combusts the remaining air/fuel mixture, resulting in a pinging or slapping sound.) If allowed to continue, detonation could damage the engine.

15 **Mass Air Flow (MAF) sensor** - The MAF sensor is a device used by the PCM to measure the amount of intake air drawn into the engine. It uses a hot-wire sensing element to measure the amount of air entering the engine. The wire is constantly maintained at a specified temperature above the ambient temperature of the incoming air by electrical current. As intake air passes through the MAF sensor and over the hot wire, it cools the wire, and the control system immediately corrects the temperature back to its constant value. The current required to maintain the constant value is used by the PCM to determine the amount of air flowing through the MAF sensor. The MAF sensor is located at the air filter housing on all models with a MAF sensor. On 1995 through 1997 DOHC models, the MAF sensor also includes an integral Intake Air Temperature (IAT) sensor. On these models the two components cannot be serviced separately. If either sensor is defective, replace the MAF/IAT sensor. 1994 models and 1995 B6 SOHC models use a Volume Air Flow (VAF) sensor instead of a MAF sensor (see Step 23). On 1998 and later models, the MAF sensor and the IAT sensor are separate components.

16 **Neutral position switch** - The neutral position switch, which is located on the transaxle, is used only on 1994 and 1995 B6 SOHC models and on 1995 through 1997 B6 DOHC models with a manual transaxle. When the transaxle is any gear other than Neutral, the neutral position switch circuit is open and there is no signal to the PCM. When the transaxle is shifted into Neutral, the neutral position switch closes the circuit and sends a voltage signal to the PCM, which leans out (decreases the pulse width of) the fuel injectors.

17 **Output shaft speed sensor** - The output shaft speed sensor is a magnetic pick-up coil, which is located on top of the transaxle differential, below the throttle body. The output shaft speed sensor provides the Powertrain Control Module (PCM) with information about the rotational speed of the output shaft in the transmission. The PCM uses this information to control the torque converter and to calculate speed scheduling and the correct operating pressure for the transaxle. On OBD-II vehicles, the PCM compares the signal from the input shaft speed sensor with the signal from the output shaft speed sensor to calculate whether slippage (i.e. wear) is occurring inside the transaxle.

18 Oxygen sensors - An oxygen sensor is a galvanic battery that generates a small variable voltage signal in proportion to the difference between the oxygen content in the exhaust stream and the oxygen content in the ambient air. The PCM uses the voltage signal from the upstream oxygen sensor to maintain a stoichiometric air/fuel ratio of 14.7:1 by constantly adjusting the on-time of the fuel injectors. On all 1994 models and on 1995 models with a B6 SOHC engine, there is one oxygen sensor, which is located on the exhaust manifold, near the manifold-exhaust pipe flange. On 1995 models with BP DOHC engines and on all 1996 and later models, there are two oxygen sensors: one upstream sensor (in the exhaust manifold, right above the flange between the manifold and the warm-up catalyst) and a downstream oxygen sensor (in the exhaust pipe right below the warm-up catalyst's lower flange).

19 Power Steering Pressure (PSP) switch - The PSP switch, which is used on 1994 through 1997 models, monitors the pressure inside the power steering system. When the pressure exceeds a certain threshold at idle or during low speed maneuvers, the switch sends a voltage signal to the PCM, which raises the idle slightly to compensate for the extra load on the engine. The PSP switch is located on the power steering pump, which is located at the lower right end of the engine.

20 Throttle Position (TP) sensor - The TP sensor is a potentiometer that receives a constant voltage input from the PCM and sends back a voltage signal that varies in relation to the opening angle of the throttle plate inside the throttle body. This voltage signal tells the PCM when the throttle is closed, half-open, wide open or anywhere in between. The PCM uses this data, along with information from other sensors, to calculate injector pulse width (the interval of time during which an injector solenoid is energized by the PCM). The TP sensor is located on the throttle body, on the end of the throttle plate shaft. On 1994 through 1997 models, the TP sensor is serviceable separately from the throttle body. On 1998 and later models, the TP sensor is not removable; if it's defective, you must replace the throttle body.

21 Transmission Range (TR) switch - The transmission range switch, which is used only on models with an automatic transaxle, functions like a conventional Park/Neutral Position (PNP) switch: it prevents the engine from starting in any gear other than Park or Neutral, and it closes the circuit for the back-up lights when the shift lever is moved to Reverse. The PCM also sends a voltage signal to the transmission range switch, which uses a series of step-down resistors that act as a voltage divider. The PCM monitors the voltage output signal from the switch, which corresponds to the position of the manual lever. Thus the PCM is able to determine the gear selected and is able to determine the correct pressure for the electronic pressure control system of the transaxle. The transmission range switch is located on top of the forward part of the transaxle.

22 Vehicle Speed Sensor (VSS) - The VSS is a Hall Effect type switch that is driven by the differential. The VSS receives a 5-volt reference signal from the PCM and generates a pulsed output that the PCM uses to determine vehicle speed (the number of pulses per minute rises and falls in proportion to the speed). The VSS is used on all manual transaxles. The VSS is located on top of the transaxle, right above the differential.

23 Volume Air Flow (VAF) sensor - The VAF sensor, which is used only on 1994 models and on 1995 B6 SOHC models, is located on the air filter housing. The VAF sensor uses a spring-loaded, hinged trap door to measure the volume of air entering the engine. The trap door is connected to a potentiometer. As the volume of air entering the engine increases, the trap door opens, moving a conductor that sweeps across the potentiometer, altering the output voltage signal to the PCM. The PCM interprets this variable voltage signal to determine how much air is entering the engine, then adjusts the pulse width of the fuel injectors accordingly.

OUTPUT ACTUATORS

➡**Note: Not all output actuators apply to all models.**

24 EVAP canister purge valve - The EVAP canister purge valve is normally closed. But when ordered to do so by the PCM, it allows the fuel vapors that are stored in the EVAP canister to be drawn into the intake manifold, where they're mixed with intake air, then burned along with the normal air/fuel mixture, under certain operating conditions. The EVAP canister purge solenoid is located in front of the firewall, behind the intake manifold.

25 EVAP canister close valve - The EVAP canister close valve is located underneath the vehicle, right behind the fuel tank. The canister close valve prevents excessive vacuum in the fuel tank by allowing filtered ambient (outside) air into the canister and the fuel tank while the EVAP system is being purged, and anytime that there's a relative vacuum inside the fuel tank. To prevent vapors from escaping into the atmosphere, the PCM closes the EVAP canister close valve during leak tests of the fuel tank and the EVAP system, and anytime that the fuel tank pressure sensor detects a positive pressure inside the fuel tank.

26 Exhaust Gas Recirculation (EGR) valve - An EGR system is used only on 1995 through 1997 B6 DOHC and BP DOHC models. When the engine is put under a load (hard acceleration, passing, going up a steep hill, pulling a trailer, etc.), combustion chamber temperature increases. When combustion chamber temperature exceeds 2500 degrees, excessive amounts of oxides of nitrogen (NOx) are produced. NOx is a precursor of photochemical smog. When combined with hydrocarbons (HC), other reactive organic compounds (ROCs) and sunlight, it forms ozone, nitrogen dioxide and nitrogen nitrate and other nasty stuff. The PCM-controlled EGR valve allows exhaust gases to be recirculated back to the intake manifold where they dilute the incoming air/fuel mixture, which lowers the combustion chamber temperature and decreases the amount of NOx produced during high-load conditions.

27 Fuel injectors - The fuel injectors, which spray a fine mist of fuel into the intake ports, where it is mixed with incoming air, are inductive coils under PCM control. For more information about the injectors, see Chapter 4.

28 Idle Air Control (IAC) valve - The IAC valve controls the amount of air allowed to bypass the throttle plate when the throttle plate is at its (nearly closed) idle position. The IAC valve is controlled by the PCM. When the engine is placed under an additional load at idle (high power steering pressure or running the air conditioning compressor during low-speed maneuvers, for example), the engine can run roughly, stumble and even stall. To prevent this from happening, the PCM opens the IAC valve to increase the idle speed enough to overcome the extra load imposed on the engine. On 1994 through 1997 models, the IAC valve is mounted on the underside of the throttle body. On 1998 and later models, it's mounted on the side of the throttle body.

29 Ignition coils - On 1994 and 1995 models, the ignition coil and the ignition control module (Kia refers to the control module as the "igniter" on 1994 models) are separate components located on the left side of the engine compartment. On 1996 and 1997 models, the ignition coil and the ignition control module are integral components of the distributor assembly; if either component is defective on one of these models, you must replace the distributor assembly. 1998 and later models are equipped with two PCM-controlled "coil-over-plug" style coils, located on top of the valve cover, directly over the spark plugs for cylinder Nos. 2 and 4. Each of these coils fires two spark plugs: the coil

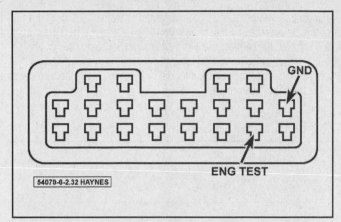

54070-6-2.32 HAYNES

2.32 On 1994 models and on 1995 B6 SOHC and B6 DOHC models, the Data Link Connector (DLC) is located in a small black plastic box located behind the intake manifold, in the center of the upper firewall area. To command the PCM to display any stored DTC(s), use a jumper wire to bridge the ENG TEST and GND terminals

directly over cylinder No. 4 fires cylinder No. 1 (its companion cylinder) and cylinder No. 4; the coil directly over cylinder No. 2 fires cylinder No. 3 (its companion cylinder) and cylinder No. 2. These ignition coils are under the control of the Powertrain Control Module (PCM). There is no separate ignition control module. Instead, coil drivers inside the PCM turn the primary side of the coils on and off. For more information about the ignition coils, see Chapter 5.

OBTAINING AND CLEARING DIAGNOSTIC TROUBLE CODES (DTCS)

30 All models covered by this manual are equipped with on-board diagnostics. When the PCM recognizes a malfunction in a monitored emission control system, component or circuit, it turns on the Malfunction Indicator Light (MIL) on the dash. The PCM will continue to display the MIL until the problem is fixed and the Diagnostic Trouble Code (DTC) is cleared from the PCM's memory.

31 Before outputting any DTCs stored in the PCM, thoroughly inspect ALL electrical connectors and hoses. Make sure that all electrical connections are tight, clean and free of corrosion. And make sure that all hoses are correctly connected, fit tightly and are in good condition (no cracks or tears). Also, make sure that the engine is tuned up. A poorly running engine is probably one of the biggest causes of emission-related malfunctions. Often, simply giving the engine a good tune-up will correct the problem.

Accessing the DTCs on all 1994 models and 1995 B6 SOHC and B6 DOHC models

▶ Refer to illustration 2.32

32 These models are equipped with On-Board Diagnostic (OBD) systems, but not with OBD-II, the Data Link Connector (DLC) is located in the engine compartment, behind the intake manifold, in front of the upper center of the firewall. The DLC, which is housed inside a small black plastic box, is protected by a hinged cover. It will say something like "DIAGNOSIS" on top of the cover. Open the cover and, using a jumper wire, bridge the ENG TEST and GND terminals (see illustration).

33 Turn the ignition switch to ON (but don't start the engine).

2.39 On 1995 BP DOHC models and all 1996 and later models, the Data Link Connector (DLC) is located under the left part of the dash

34 Start the engine and allow it to warm up to its normal operating temperature, then run it at 2000 rpm for three minutes.

35 Any stored DTC(s) will be displayed by the Malfunction Indicator Light (MIL) (also known as the Check Engine light) on the instrument cluster. The MIL displays each DTC as a series of flashes. For example, DTC 02 would be expressed as two flashes, DTC 08 would be displayed as eight flashes, etc. If there is only one DTC stored in the PCM, the MIL will pause a little longer between each displayed DTC, then repeat. If there is more than one DTC stored, the PCM will display each DTC, in ascending numerical order, until all stored DTCs have been displayed, then it will start over again. There is a slightly longer pause between the completion of one DTC display and the beginning of the next DTC display.

36 Write down each displayed DTC, then refer to the accompanying DTC chart.

37 After you have repaired or replaced the source of the problem, erase the DTC(s) from the PCM. To clear the DTC(s) from the PCM, turn the ignition switch to OFF, then disconnect the cable from the negative battery terminal for at least 20 seconds.

38 Disconnect the jumper wire from the DLC and reconnect the cable the negative battery terminal.

Accessing the DTCs on OBD-II vehicles

▶ Refer to illustration 2.39

39 On 1995 BP DOHC models and on all 1996 and later models, all of which are equipped with On-Board Diagnostic II (OBD-II) systems, the Diagnostic Trouble Codes (DTCs) can only be accessed with a scan tool. Professional scan tools are expensive, but relatively inexpensive generic scan tools (see illustration 2.1) are available at most auto parts stores. Simply plug the connector of the scan tool into the Data Link Connector (DLC), which is located under the lower edge of the dash (see illustration). Then follow the instructions included with the scan tool to extract the DTCs.

40 Once you have outputted all of the stored DTCs, look them up on the accompanying DTC chart.

41 After troubleshooting the source of each DTC make any necessary repairs or replace the defective component(s).

Clearing the DTCs

42 Clear the DTCs with the scan tool in accordance with the instructions provided by the scan tool's manufacturer.

DIAGNOSTIC TROUBLE CODES

43 The accompanying tables are a list of the Diagnostic Trouble Codes (DTCs) that can be accessed by a do-it-yourselfer working at home (there are many, many more DTCs available to professional mechanics with proprietary scan tools and software, but those codes cannot be accessed by a generic scan tool). If, after you have checked and repaired the connectors, wire harness and vacuum hoses (if applicable) for an emission-related system, component or circuit, the problem persists, have the vehicle checked by a dealer service department or other qualified repair shop.

OBD TROUBLE CODES (1994 MODELS AND 1995 B6 SOHC AND B6 DOHC MODELS)

➡Note: Not all trouble codes apply to all models.

Code	Probable cause
02	No Ne signal from distributor
03	No G signal from distributor (4-valve models only)
08	Mass Air Flow (MAF) sensor, open or short circuit
08	Volume Air Flow (VAF) sensor, open or short circuit
09	Engine Coolant Temperature (ECT) sensor, open or short circuit
10	Intake Air Temperature (IAT) sensor, open or short circuit
12	Throttle Position (TP) sensor, open or short circuit
14	Barometric pressure sensor (inside PCM), open or short circuit
15	Oxygen sensor output below 0.55 volt 95 seconds after engine starts
17	Feedback system, sensor output unchanged 50 seconds after engine exceeds 1500 rpm
25	Pressure regulator control solenoid valve, open or short circuit
26	Purge control solenoid valve, open or short circuit
34	Idle speed control solenoid valve, open or short circuit

OBD-II TROUBLE CODES (1995 BP DOHC MODELS AND ALL 1996 AND LATER MODELS)

➡Note: Not all trouble codes apply to all models.

Code	Probable cause
P0011	"A" Camshaft position - timing - over-advanced (bank 1)
P0016	Crankshaft position/camshaft position (bank 1, sensor A)
P0030	Upstream oxygen sensor, heater circuit malfunction (bank 1, sensor 1)
P0031	Upstream oxygen sensor heater circuit, low voltage input (bank 1, sensor 1)
P0032	Upstream oxygen sensor heater circuit, high voltage input (bank 1, sensor 1)
P0036	Downstream oxygen sensor, heater circuit malfunction (bank 1, sensor 2)
P0037	Downstream oxygen sensor heater circuit, low voltage input (bank 1, sensor 2)
P0038	Downstream oxygen sensor heater circuit, high voltage input (bank 1, sensor 2)
P0050	Upstream oxygen sensor, heater circuit malfunction (bank 2, sensor 1)
P0051	Upstream oxygen sensor heater circuit, low voltage input (bank 2, sensor 1)
P0052	Upstream oxygen sensor heater circuit, high voltage input (bank 2, sensor 1)

Code	Probable cause
P0056	Downstream oxygen sensor, heater circuit malfunction (bank 2, sensor 2)
P0057	Downstream oxygen sensor heater circuit, low voltage input (bank 2, sensor 2)
P0058	Downstream oxygen sensor heater circuit, high voltage input (bank 2, sensor 2)
P0076	Intake valve control solenoid circuit low (bank 1)
P0077	Intake valve control solenoid circuit high (bank 1)
P0100	Mass Air Flow (MAF) sensor, circuit malfunction
P0101	Mass Air Flow (MAF) sensor circuit, range or performance problem
P0102	Mass Air Flow (MAF) sensor circuit, low input voltage
P0103	Mass Air Flow (MAF) sensor circuit, high input voltage
P0106	Manifold absolute pressure or barometric pressure circuit, range or performance problem
P0107	Manifold absolute pressure or barometric pressure circuit, low input
P0108	Manifold absolute pressure or barometric pressure circuit, high input
P0110	Intake Air Temperature (IAT) sensor, circuit malfunction
P0111	Intake Air Temperature (IAT) sensor, range or performance problem
P0112	Intake Air Temperature (IAT) sensor, low input voltage
P0113	Intake Air Temperature (IAT) sensor, high input voltage
P0115	Engine Coolant Temperature (ECT) sensor, circuit malfunction
P0116	Engine Coolant Temperature (ECT) sensor circuit, range or performance problem
P0117	Engine Coolant Temperature (ECT) sensor circuit, low input voltage
P0118	Engine Coolant Temperature (ECT) sensor circuit, high input voltage
P0119	Engine Coolant Temperature (ECT) sensor circuit, intermittent
P0120	Throttle Position (TP) sensor, circuit malfunction
P0121	Throttle Position (TP) sensor circuit, range or performance problem
P0122	Throttle Position (TP) sensor circuit, low input voltage
P0123	Throttle Position (TP) sensor circuit, high input voltage
P0125	Insufficient coolant temperature for closed loop fuel control
P0126	Insufficient coolant temperature for stable operation
P0128	Engine Coolant Temperature (ECT) sensor circuit, insufficient coolant temperature for closed loop
P0128	Coolant thermostat (coolant temperature below thermostat regulating temperature)
P0130	Upstream oxygen sensor, circuit malfunction (bank 1, sensor 1)
P0131	Upstream oxygen sensor circuit, low voltage input (bank 1, sensor 1)
P0132	Upstream oxygen sensor circuit, high voltage input (bank 1, sensor 1)
P0133	Upstream oxygen sensor circuit, slow response (bank 1, sensor 1)
P0134	Upstream oxygen sensor circuit, no activity detected (bank 1, sensor 1)
P0135	Upstream oxygen sensor heater, circuit malfunction (bank 1, sensor 1)

OBD-II TROUBLE CODES (1995 BP DOHC MODELS AND ALL 1996 AND LATER MODELS) (CONTINUED)

➡**Note: Not all trouble codes apply to all models.**

Code	Probable cause
P0136	Downstream oxygen sensor, circuit malfunction (bank 1, sensor 2)
P0137	Downstream oxygen sensor circuit, low voltage input (bank 1, sensor 2)
P0138	Downstream oxygen sensor circuit, high voltage input (bank 1, sensor 2)
P0139	Downstream oxygen sensor circuit, slow response (bank 1, sensor 2)
P0140	Downstream oxygen sensor circuit, no activity detected (bank 1, sensor 2)
P0141	Downstream oxygen sensor heater, circuit malfunction (bank 1, sensor 2)
P0150	Upstream oxygen sensor, circuit malfunction (bank 2, sensor 1)
P0151	Upstream oxygen sensor circuit, low voltage input (bank 2, sensor 1)
P0152	Upstream oxygen sensor circuit, high voltage input (bank 2, sensor 1)
P0153	Upstream oxygen sensor circuit, slow response (bank 2, sensor 1)
P0154	Upstream oxygen sensor circuit, no activity detected (bank 2, sensor 1)
P0156	Downstream oxygen sensor, circuit malfunction (bank 2, sensor 2)
P0157	Downstream oxygen sensor circuit, low voltage input (bank 2, sensor 2)
P0158	Downstream oxygen sensor circuit, high voltage input (bank 2, sensor 2)
P0159	Downstream oxygen sensor circuit, slow response (bank 2, sensor 2)
P0160	Downstream oxygen sensor circuit, no activity detected (bank 2, sensor 2)
P0170	Fuel trim malfunction (bank 1)
P0171	Fuel system too lean (bank 1)
P0172	Fuel system too rich (bank 1)
P0173	Fuel trim malfunction (bank 2)
P0174	Fuel system too lean (bank 2)
P0175	Fuel system too rich (bank 2)
P0196	Fuel rail pressure sensor circuit, range or performance problem
P0197	Fuel rail pressure sensor circuit, low input
P0198	Fuel rail pressure sensor circuit, high input
P0201	Cylinder No. 1 fuel injector, circuit malfunction
P0202	Cylinder No. 2 fuel injector, circuit malfunction
P0203	Cylinder No. 3 fuel injector, circuit malfunction
P0204	Cylinder No. 4 fuel injector, circuit malfunction
P0230	Fuel pump circuit malfunction
P0261	Cylinder No. 1 fuel injector circuit, low voltage input
P0262	Cylinder No. 1 fuel injector circuit, high voltage input

Code	Probable cause
P0264	Cylinder No. 2 fuel injector circuit, low voltage input
P0265	Cylinder No. 2 fuel injector circuit, high voltage input
P0267	Cylinder No. 3 fuel injector circuit, low voltage input
P0268	Cylinder No. 3 fuel injector circuit, high voltage input
P0270	Cylinder No. 4 fuel injector circuit, low voltage input
P0271	Cylinder No. 4 fuel injector circuit, high voltage input
P0273	Cylinder No. 5 fuel injector circuit, low voltage input
P0274	Cylinder No. 5 fuel injector circuit, high voltage input
P0276	Cylinder No. 6 fuel injector circuit, low voltage input
P0277	Cylinder No. 6 fuel injector circuit, high voltage input
P0300	Random or multiple cylinder misfire detected
P0301	Cylinder No. 1 misfire detected
P0302	Cylinder No. 2 misfire detected
P0303	Cylinder No. 3 misfire detected
P0304	Cylinder No. 4 misfire detected
P0305	Cylinder No. 5 misfire detected
P0306	Cylinder No. 5 misfire detected
P0315	Crankshaft position system - variation not learned
P0325	Knock sensor circuit malfunction
P0326	Knock sensor circuit, range or performance problem
P0330	Knock sensor 2 circuit, range or performance problem
P0335	Crankshaft Position (CKP) sensor, circuit malfunction
P0336	Crankshaft Position (CKP) sensor circuit, range or performance problem
P0340	Camshaft Position (CMP) sensor, circuit malfunction
P0342	Camshaft Position (CMP) sensor circuit, low input
P0343	Camshaft Position (CMP) sensor circuit, high input
P0350	Ignition coil primary or secondary circuit malfunction
P0351	Ignition coil A primary or secondary circuit malfunction
P0352	Ignition coil B primary or secondary circuit malfunction
P0353	Ignition coil C primary or secondary circuit malfunction
P0354	Ignition coil D primary or secondary circuit malfunction
P0355	Ignition coil E primary or secondary circuit malfunction
P0356	Ignition coil F primary or secondary circuit malfunction
P0400	Exhaust Gas Recirculation (EGR) system, insufficient flow
P0420	Catalyst system efficiency below threshold

OBD-II TROUBLE CODES (1995 BP DOHC MODELS AND ALL 1996 AND LATER MODELS) (CONTINUED)

➡Note: Not all trouble codes apply to all models.

Code	Probable cause
P0422	Evaporative Emission Control (EVAP) system, small leak detected (pre-1998)
P0422	Main catalyst efficiency below threshold (1998 and later, bank 1)
P0430	Main catalyst efficiency below threshold (2005 and later, bank 2)
P0440	Evaporative Emission Control (EVAP) system malfunction
P0441	Evaporative Emission Control (EVAP) system, incorrect purge flow (pre-2002)
P0441	Evaporative Emission Control (EVAP) system purge control valve stuck open (2002 and later)
P0442	Evaporative Emission Control (EVAP) system, small leak detected
P0443	Evaporative Emission Control (EVAP) system purge control valve, circuit malfunction
P0444	Evaporative Emission Control (EVAP) system, purge control valve circuit open
P0445	Evaporative Emission Control (EVAP) system, purge control valve circuit shorted
P0446	EVAP system vent control circuit malfunction
P0447	Evaporative emission control system, open vent control circuit
P0448	Evaporative emission control system, shorted vent control circuit
P0449	Evaporative emission control system, vent valve/solenoid circuit malfunction
P0450	EVAP system pressure sensor, circuit malfunction
P0451	Fuel tank pressure sensor circuit, range or performance problem
P0452	Fuel tank pressure sensor circuit, low input
P0453	Fuel tank pressure sensor circuit, high input
P0454	Evaporative emission control system, pressure sensor intermittent
P0455	Evaporative Emission Control (EVAP) system, large leak detected
P0456	Evaporative emission (EVAP) control system leak detected (very small leak)
P0460	Fuel level sensor circuit malfunction
P0461	Fuel level sensor circuit, range or performance problem
P0462	Fuel level sensor, stuck in Low position
P0463	Fuel level sensor, stuck in High position
P0464	Fuel level sensor circuit intermittent
P0470	Exhaust Gas Recirculation (EGR) pressure sensor, circuit malfunction
P0500	Vehicle Speed Sensor (VSS), circuit malfunction
P0501	Vehicle Speed Sensor (VSS) circuit, range or performance problem
P0505	Idle control system malfunction
P0506	Idle control system rpm lower than expected
P0507	Idle control system rpm higher than expected

Code	Probable cause
P0510	Closed throttle position switch malfunction
P0551	Power Steering Pressure (PSP) switch circuit, range or performance problem
P0560	System voltage malfunction
P0561	System voltage unstable
P0562	System voltage, low input
P0563	System voltage, high input
P0601	Powertrain Control Module (PCM), memory checksum error
P0604	PCM Random Access Memory (RAM) error
P0605	Powertrain Control Module (PCM) malfunction
P0625	Generator field terminal – circuit low
P0626	Generator field terminal – circuit high
P0630	VIN not programmed or incompatible with Powertrain Control Module (PCM)
P0650	Malfunction Indicator Light (MIL) circuit malfunction
P0661	Intake manifold tuning valve control circuit, low voltage (bank 1)
P0662	Intake manifold tuning valve control circuit, high voltage (bank 1)
P0663	Intake manifold tuning valve control circuit, low voltage (bank 2)
P0664	Intake manifold tuning valve control circuit, high voltage (bank 2)
P0700	Transmission control system malfunction
P0703	Brake pedal switch, circuit malfunction
P0705	Transmission Range (TR) sensor, circuit malfunction
P0706	Transmission Range (TR) switch, open circuit
P0707	Transaxle Range (TR) sensor, low voltage
P0708	Transaxle Range (TR) sensor, high voltage
P0710	Automatic Transmission Fluid (ATF) temperature sensor
P0711	Transaxle fluid temperature sensor output jumps, or sticks on high or low temperature
P0712	Transmission temperature sensor, low input
P0713	Transmission temperature sensor, high input
P0715	Input Shaft Speed (ISS) sensor or ISS circuit malfunction
P0716	Input/turbine speed sensor, range/performance
P0717	Input/turbine speed sensor, no signal
P0720	Output Shaft Speed (OSS) sensor or OSS circuit malfunction
P0726	Engine speed input circuit range/performance
P0727	Engine speed input circuit, no signal
P0731	Gear No. 1, incorrect ratio
P0732	Gear No. 2, incorrect ratio

OBD-II TROUBLE CODES (1995 BP DOHC MODELS AND ALL 1996 AND LATER MODELS) (CONTINUED)

➡ Note: Not all trouble codes apply to all models.

Code	Probable cause
P0733	Gear No. 3, incorrect ratio
P0734	Gear No. 4, incorrect ratio
P0740	Torque converter clutch circuit malfunction
P0743	Torque converter clutch solenoid, electrical problem
P0748	Line pressure control solenoid, electrical problem
P0750	Shift control solenoid valve A, circuit malfunction
P0753	Shift control solenoid A, electrical problem
P0755	Shift control solenoid valve B, circuit malfunction
P0758	Shift control solenoid B, electrical problem
P0760	Shift control solenoid valve C, circuit malfunction
P0763	Shift control solenoid C, electrical problem
P0765	Shift control solenoid valve D, circuit malfunction
P0885	Automatic transaxle relay circuit malfunction

3 Camshaft Position (CMP) sensor - replacement

1996 AND 1997 MODELS

1   On these models, the CMP sensor is an integral component of the distributor. To replace the CMP sensor you must replace the distributor (see Chapter 5).

1998 AND LATER MODELS

▶ Refer to illustrations 3.2a and 3.2b

➡ Note: On four-cylinder engines (except 2.0L DOHC), the CMP sensor is located on the left end of the cylinder head, adjacent to the left end of the exhaust camshaft. On 2.0L DOHC engines, the CMP sensor is located on the right rear corner of the cylinder head, adjacent to the right end of the intake camshaft. On 2.7L V6 engines, the CMP sensor is located at the left end of the rear cylinder head.

2   Disconnect the CMP sensor electrical connector (see illustrations).

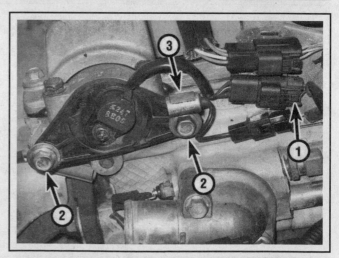

3.2a To disconnect the CMP sensor electrical connector, depress the release tab (1) and pull off the connector. To detach the CMP sensor from the cylinder head, remove the two sensor mounting bolts (2), set the noise suppressor (3) aside and remove the sensor (1.8L DOHC four-cylinder engines)

3   Remove the CMP sensor mounting bolts, set the noise suppressor aside and remove the CMP sensor. It may be necessary to carefully pry the sensor out of its bore. Once the sensor has been removed, check the condition of the O-ring, replacing it if it is hardened or damaged.

4   Installation is the reverse of removal. Don't forget to secure the noise suppressor to the cylinder head with the rear CMP sensor mounting bolt and be sure to tighten the CMP sensor mounting bolts securely.

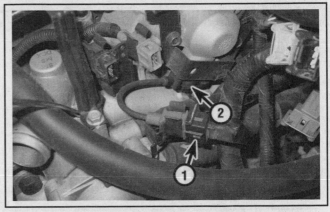

3.2b CMP sensor details (2.7L V6 engines)

1   Electrical connector   *2   CMP sensor*

4   Chassis acceleration sensor - replacement

♦ **Refer to illustrations 4.1 and 4.2**

➡ **Note: The chassis acceleration sensor, which is used on 1998 and later models, is located in the right rear corner of the engine compartment, behind the right strut tower.**

1   Disconnect the electrical connector from the chassis acceleration

sensor (see illustration).

2   Remove the chassis acceleration sensor mounting bolts (see illustration).

3   Installation is the reverse of removal. Be sure to tighten the chassis acceleration sensor mounting bolts securely.

4.1 To disconnect the electrical connector from the chassis acceleration sensor, depress this wire retainer with your thumb and simultaneously pull off the connector

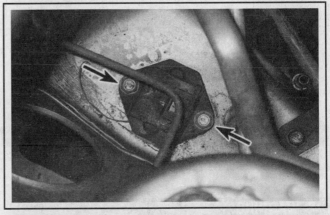

4.2 To detach the chassis acceleration sensor, remove these two mounting bolts

5   Clutch pedal position switch - replacement

➡ **Note: The clutch pedal position switch is located near the top of the clutch pedal assembly.**

1   Working under the dash with a flashlight, locate the clutch pedal position switch at the upper end of the clutch pedal.

➡ **Note: There are actually two switches at the top of the clutch pedal. Don't confuse the clutch pedal position switch (which is an information sensor for the PCM) with the clutch start switch (which prevents the vehicle from being started unless the clutch pedal is depressed). The clutch start switch is on the left and the clutch pedal position switch is on the right. The clutch start switch is secured to its mounting bracket by a pair of nuts and**

is not adjustable. The clutch pedal position switch is secured to its mounting bracket by a single nut, which also serves as the adjustment nut for the clutch pedal position switch and for clutch pedal height.

2   Disconnect the electrical connector from the clutch pedal position switch.

3   Remove the clutch pedal position switch locknut/adjustment nut and remove the switch.

4   Installation is the reverse of removal.

5   Adjust the clutch pedal height (see "Clutch pedal adjustment" in Chapter 8).

6 Crankshaft Position (CKP) sensor - replacement

1996 AND 1997 MODELS

➡Note: The CKP sensor is located on the front edge of the timing belt cover, adjacent to the crankshaft pulley.

1   Raise the front of the vehicle and place it securely on jackstands.
2   Disconnect the electrical connector from the CKP sensor.
3   Remove the CKP sensor mounting bolt and remove the sensor.
4   Installation is the reverse of removal. Be sure to tighten the CKP sensor mounting bolt securely.

6.5 To disconnect the CKP sensor electrical connector on a 1998 and later model, depress this wire retainer with your thumb and pull off the connector

1998 AND LATER MODELS

▶ Refer to illustrations 6.5 and 6.6

➡Note: The CKP sensor is located on the front of the transaxle bellhousing, adjacent to the flywheel/driveplate.

5   Locate the CKP sensor on the front of the transaxle bellhousing, trace the sensor electrical lead up to the connector, which is located on a small bracket at the left end of the cylinder head, then disconnect the CKP sensor electrical connector (see illustration).
6   Remove the CKP sensor mounting bolt (see illustration) and remove the CKP sensor.
7   Installation is the reverse of removal. Be sure to tighten the CKP sensor mounting bolt securely.

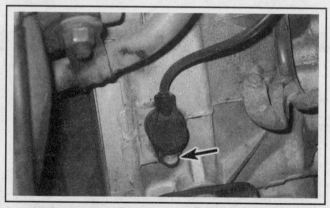

6.6 To detach the CKP sensor from the transaxle bellhousing, remove this bolt

7 Engine Coolant Temperature (ECT) sensor - replacement

▶ Refer to illustrations 7.2a, 7.2b, 7.2c and 7.3

❊❊ WARNING:

Wait until the engine has cooled completely before beginning this procedure.

➡Note: On 1994 through 1997 four-cylinder models, the ECT sensor is located at the left end of the cylinder head, right behind the distributor. On 1998 and later four-cylinder models (except 2.0L DOHC models), it's in the same location, except that there is no distributor. On 2.0L DOHC models, the ECT sensor is located at the left front corner of the cylinder head. On 2.7L V6 models, it's located below the ignition coil pack on the left end of the front cylinder head.

1   Partially drain the engine coolant so that it's below the level of the cylinder head (see Chapter 1). (If you don't want to drain the coolant, be prepared for some coolant to run out when you remove the ECT sensor.)
2   Disconnect the electrical connector from the ECT sensor (see illustrations).

7.2a On 1994 through 1997 models, the ECT sensor is located right behind the distributor (1994 and 1995 SOHC model shown, 1995 through 1997 DOHC models similar). To disconnect the electrical connector, carefully pry this retainer wire loose, then pull off the connector

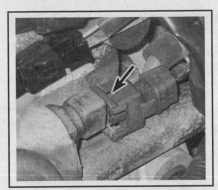

7.2b On 1998 and later four-cylinder models, the ECT sensor is located at the left end of the cylinder head, facing toward the firewall. To disconnect the electrical connector, carefully pry the retainer wire loose, then pull off the connector

7.2c On 2.7L V6 engines, the ECT sensor is located just below the ignition coil pack

7.3 After unscrewing the ECT sensor, remove and discard the old sensor sealing washer (a new one should be used during installation)

3   Unscrew the ECT sensor and remove and discard the old ECT sensor sealing washer (see illustration).

✳✳ CAUTION:

If you're planning to reuse the old ECT sensor, handle it with care. Damage to the ECT sensor will adversely affect the operation of the fuel injection system.

4   Installation is the reverse of removal. Be sure to use a new sealing washer and tighten the ECT sensor to the torque listed in this Chapter's Specifications.
5   Refill the cooling system (see Chapter 1)

8   Fuel tank pressure sensor - replacement

✳✳ WARNING:

Gasoline is extremely flammable, so take extra precautions when you work on any part of the fuel system. Don't smoke or allow open flames or bare light bulbs near the work area, and don't work in a garage where a gas-type appliance (such as a water heater or a clothes dryer) is present. Since gasoline is carcinogenic, wear fuel resistent gloves when there's a possibility of being exposed to fuel, and, if you spill any fuel on your skin, rinse it off immediately with soap and water. Mop up any spills immediately and do not store fuel-soaked rags where they could ignite. The fuel system is under constant pressure, so, if any fuel lines are to be disconnected, the fuel pressure in the system must be relieved first. When you perform any kind of work on the fuel system, wear safety glasses and have a Class B type fire extinguisher on hand.

➡Note: The fuel tank pressure sensor is used on 1998 and later models. It is located on the top of the fuel pump/fuel gauge sending unit.

ALL MODELS (EXCEPT SPORTAGE)

▸ **Refer to illustration 8.4**

1   Disconnect the cable from the negative battery terminal (see Chapter 5, Section 1).
2   Remove the rear seat cushion (see Chapter 11).
3   Remove the fuel pump/fuel gauge sending unit access cover.
4   Disconnect the electrical connector from the fuel tank pressure

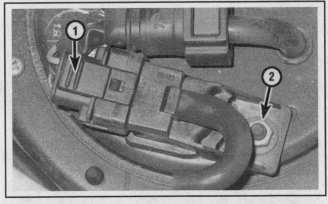

8.4 Depress the release tab (1) and disconnect the electrical connector from the fuel tank pressure sensor, then unscrew the retaining nut (2) and remove the sensor from the fuel pump/fuel gauge sending unit

sensor (see illustration).
5   Remove the fuel tank pressure sensor retaining nut and remove the sensor.
6   Installation is the reverse of removal.

SPORTAGE MODELS

7   Raise the vehicle and place it securely on jackstands.
8   Remove the EVAP canister (see Section 24).
9   Remove the fuel tank pressure sensor from the EVAP canister.
10 Installation is the reverse of removal.

9   Input shaft and output shaft speed sensors - replacement

INPUT SHAFT SPEED SENSOR

◗ **Refer to illustrations 9.2 and 9.4**

➡**Note: This section applies only to models with an automatic transaxle. If you have to replace an input shaft speed sensor, a Kia parts department might refer to it as a "pulse generator" (1994 models) or an "input/turbine speed sensor" (1995 and later models). We simply refer to this sensor as the input shaft speed sensor for all years. The input shaft speed sensor is located on top of the transaxle, near the left end of the transaxle case, directly below the air filter housing.**

9.2 Depress this release tab (1) and disconnect the electrical connector, then unscrew the input shaft speed sensor mounting bolt (2) and remove the sensor from the transaxle

1   Remove the air intake duct and the air filter housing (see "Air filter housing - removal and installation" in Chapter 4).

2   Disconnect the electrical connector from the input shaft speed sensor (see illustration).

3   Remove the input shaft speed sensor mounting bolt (see illustration 9.2) and remove the sensor.

4   Remove and discard the old sensor O-ring (see illustration).

5   Installation is the reverse of removal. Be sure to use a new O-ring and tighten the sensor mounting bolt securely.

OUTPUT SHAFT SPEED SENSOR

◗ **Refer to illustrations 9.7 and 9.9**

➡**Note: This procedure applies only to models with an automatic transaxle. If you have to replace an output shaft speed sensor, a Kia parts department might refer to it as a "vehicle speed sensor." In order to distinguish this sensor from the vehicle speed sensor used on models with a manual transaxle, we refer to this sensor as the "output shaft speed sensor." The output shaft speed sensor is located on top of the transaxle differential, behind the input shaft sensor.**

6   Remove the air intake duct and the air filter housing (see "Air filter housing - removal and installation" in Chapter 4).

7   Disconnect the electrical connector from the output shaft speed sensor (see illustration).

8   Remove the output shaft speed sensor mounting bolt and remove the sensor.

9   Remove and discard the sensor O-ring (see illustration).

10 Installation is the reverse of removal. Be sure to use a new O-ring and tighten the sensor mounting bolt securely.

9.4 Be sure to remove and discard the old input shaft speed sensor O-ring. Always use a new O-ring when installing the input shaft speed sensor whether you're installing the old sensor or a new unit

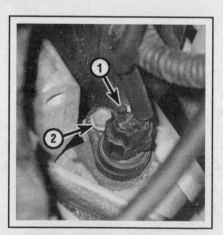

9.7 Depress this release tab (1) and disconnect the electrical connector, then unscrew the output shaft speed sensor mounting bolt (2) and remove the sensor from the transaxle differential

9.9 Be sure to remove and discard the old output shaft speed sensor O-ring. Always use a new O-ring when installing the output shaft speed sensor whether you're installing the old sensor or a new unit

10 Intake Air Temperature (IAT) sensor - replacement

1994 THROUGH 1997 MODELS AND ALL SPORTAGE MODELS

1 The IAT sensor is an integral component of the Mass Air Flow (MAF) sensor. To replace the IAT sensor, you must replace the MAF sensor (see Section 12).

1998 AND LATER MODELS (EXCEPT SPORTAGE)

▶ Refer to illustrations 10.2

➥Note: The IAT sensor is located on the air filter housing.

2 Disconnect the electrical connector from the IAT sensor (see illustration).

3 Unscrew the IAT sensor from the air filter housing.

4 Remove the old IAT sensor sealing washer and discard it.

5 Installation is the reverse of removal. Be sure to use a new sealing washer and tighten the IAT sensor securely.

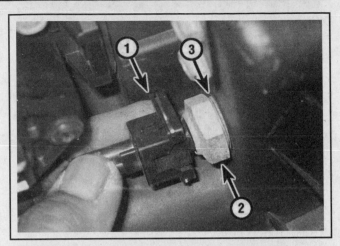

10.2 Depress this wire retainer (1) and disconnect the electrical connector from the IAT sensor (2), then unscrew the sensor and remove and discard the old sensor sealing washer (3)

11 Knock sensor - replacement

➥Note: A knock sensor is used on some 1998 and later models. On 1.8L and 2.0L DOHC engines, the knock sensor is located on the right rear side of the engine block. On 2.7L V6 engines, there are two knock sensors, one for each cylinder; they're located in the valley between the cylinder heads, under the intake manifold.

FOUR-CYLINDER MODELS

1 Raise the front of the vehicle and place it securely on jackstands.

2 On 1.8L DOHC engines, remove the intake manifold support bracket (see illustration 5.10 in Chapter 2A).

3 Disconnect the electrical connector from the knock sensor.

4 Remove the knock sensor retaining bolt and detach the sensor.

5 Installation is the reverse of removal. Be sure to tighten the knock sensor retaining bolt securely.

V6 MODELS

6 Remove the upper and lower intake manifolds (see Chapter 2B).

7 Disconnect the knock sensor electrical connectors.

8 Remove the knock sensor mounting bolts and remove the knock sensors.

9 When installing either knock sensor, be sure to tighten the knock sensor mounting bolt to the torque listed in this Chapter's Specifications.

10 The remainder of installation is the reverse of removal.

12 Mass Air Flow (MAF) sensor - replacement

▶ Refer to illustrations 12.1a, 12.1b and 12.2

1 Disconnect the electrical connector from the MAF sensor (see illustrations).

2 Disconnect the air intake duct from the MAF sensor (see illustration).

3 Remove the DIAGNOSIS connector from its mounting tab on the MAF sensor support bracket (see illustration 12.2).

4 Remove the two bolts that secure the MAF sensor to the sensor support bracket (see illustration 12.2).

5 Pull the MAF sensor assembly out of the air filter housing.

6 Installation is the reverse of removal.

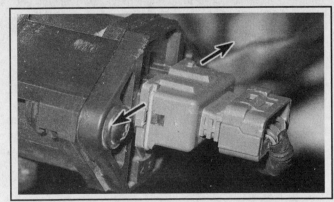

12.1a To disconnect the electrical connector from the MAF sensor, spread the ends of the wire retainer apart and pull off the connector

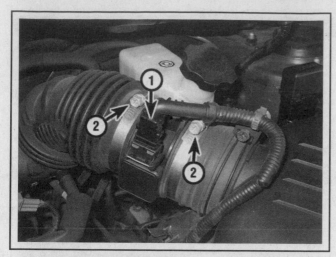

12.1b Mass Air Flow (MAF) sensor details (Sportage V6 models)

1 Electrical connector	2 Hose clamp screws

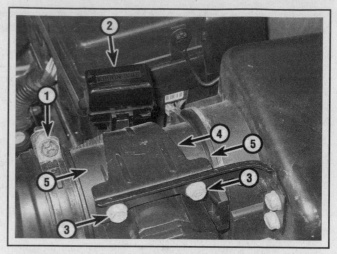

12.2 MAF sensor removal details (except Sportage):

1   Loosen this hose clamp screw and disconnect the air intake duct from the MAF sensor
2   Pull the DIAGNOSIS connector straight up to remove it from its mounting tab
3   Remove the bolts that secure the MAF sensor to the sensor support bracket
4   Two-piece MAF sensor support bracket
5   Pull the MAF sensor straight out of the air filter housing (it's not screwed in)

13 Neutral position switch - replacement

➡Note: The neutral position switch is used on 1994 and 1995 B6 SOHC and 1995 through 1997 B6 DOHC models with a manual transaxle. The neutral position switch is located on top of the transaxle.

1   Disconnect the electrical connector from the neutral position switch.

2   Unscrew the neutral position switch from the transaxle case.
3   Remove and discard the old neutral position switch O-ring.
4   Installation is the reverse of removal. Be sure to use a new O-ring and tighten the switch securely.

14 Oxygen sensors - replacement

➡Note: Because it is installed in the exhaust manifold or pipe, both of which contract when cool, an oxygen sensor might be very difficult to loosen when the engine is cold. Rather than risk damage to the sensor or its mounting threads, start and run the engine for a minute or two, then shut it off. Be careful not to burn yourself during the following procedure.

1   Remove the key from the ignition key lock cylinder. Raise the vehicle and place it securely on jackstands.
2   Special care must be taken whenever a sensor is serviced.

a) Oxygen sensors have a permanently attached pigtail and an electrical connector that cannot be removed. Damaging or removing the pigtail or electrical connector will render the sensor useless.
b) Keep grease, dirt and other contaminants away from the electrical connector and the louvered end of the sensor.
c) Do not use cleaning solvents of any kind on an oxygen sensor.
d) Oxygen sensors are extremely delicate. Do not drop a sensor, throw it around or handle it roughly.
e) Make sure the silicone boot on the sensor is installed in the correct position. Otherwise, the boot might melt and it might prevent the sensor from operating correctly.

1994 MODELS AND 1995 B6 SOHC MODELS

▶ Refer to illustration 14.3

➡Note: On these models, there is one oxygen sensor, which is located on the exhaust manifold.

3   Locate the oxygen sensor in the exhaust manifold (see illustration), trace the electrical lead up from the sensor to the electrical connector and disconnect the connector.
4   Using an oxygen sensor socket, unscrew the oxygen sensor from the exhaust manifold (see illustration 14.8).
5   If you're going to install the old oxygen sensor, be sure to coat the threads of the sensor with anti-seize compound to facilitate future removal. If you're going to install a new sensor, the threads will already be coated with anti-seize compound.
6   Installation is otherwise the reverse of removal. Be sure to tighten the oxygen sensor to the torque listed in this Chapter's Specifications.

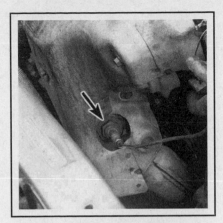

14.3 To remove the oxygen sensor from the exhaust manifold, trace the electrical lead up to the electrical connector and disconnect the connector, then use an oxygen sensor socket to unscrew the sensor from the manifold (1994 models and 1995 B6 SOHC models)

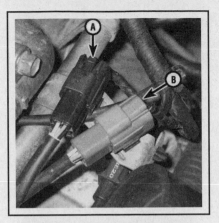

14.7 On 1995 BP DOHC models and all 1996 and later models, the oxygen sensor electrical connectors are located to the left of the cylinder head, above the transaxle

A   Upstream oxygen sensor electrical connector
B   Downstream oxygen sensor electrical connector

14.8 Use an oxygen sensor socket to unscrew the upstream oxygen sensor from the exhaust manifold

1995 BP DOHC MODELS AND ALL 1996 AND LATER FOUR-CYLINDER MODELS

Upstream oxygen sensor

▸ Refer to illustrations 14.7 and 14.8

➡Note: The upstream oxygen sensor is located on the exhaust manifold.

7   Disconnect the upstream oxygen sensor electrical connector (see illustration).

8   Remove the upstream oxygen sensor with an oxygen sensor socket (see illustration).

9   If you're going to install the old sensor, apply anti-seize compound to the threads of the sensor to facilitate future removal. If you're going to install a new oxygen sensor, it's not necessary to apply anti-seize compound to the threads. The threads on new sensors already have anti-seize compound on them.

10 Installation is the reverse of removal. Be sure to tighten the upstream oxygen sensor to the torque listed in this Chapter's Specifications.

Downstream oxygen sensor

▸ Refer to illustration 14.13

➡Note: The downstream oxygen sensor is located in the exhaust pipe right below the exhaust manifold/catalytic converter flange.

11 Disconnect the downstream oxygen sensor electrical connector (see illustration 14.7).

12 Raise the front of the vehicle and support it securely on jackstands.

13 Using an oxygen sensor socket, unscrew the downstream oxygen sensor (see illustration).

14 If you're going to install the old sensor, apply anti-seize compound to the threads of the sensor to facilitate future removal. If you're

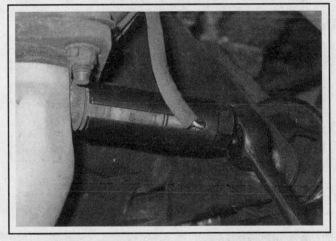

14.13 The downstream oxygen sensor is located in the exhaust pipe, right below the catalytic converter (1995 BP DOHC models and all 1996 and later models)

going to install a new oxygen sensor, it's not necessary to apply anti-seize compound to the threads. The threads on new sensors already have anti-seize compound on them.

15 Installation is the reverse of removal. Be sure to tighten the downstream oxygen sensor to the torque listed in this Chapter's Specifications.

SPORTAGE V6 MODELS

Upstream oxygen sensors

▸ Refer to illustrations 14.18a and 14.18b

16 If you're replacing the upstream oxygen sensor for the front cylinder head, remove the coolant reservoir (see Chapter 3).

14.18a Front upstream oxygen sensor (Sportage V6 models)

14.18b Rear upstream oxygen sensor (Sportage V6 models)

14.22a Front downstream oxygen sensor (Sportage V6 models; front exhaust pipe removed for clarity)

17 If you're replacing the upstream oxygen sensor for the rear cylinder head, remove the upper intake manifold (see Chapter 2B).

18 Locate the upstream oxygen sensor (see illustrations), trace the sensor electrical harness to its connector and disconnect it, then unscrew the sensor with an oxygen sensor wrench (see illustration 14.8).

19 If you're going to install the old sensor, see Step 9.

20 Installation is the reverse of removal. Be sure to tighten the oxygen sensor to the torque listed in this Chapter's Specifications.

Downstream oxygen sensors

▶ **Refer to illustrations 14.22a and 14.22b**

21 Raise the front of the vehicle and place it securely on jackstands. Remove the engine under cover/splash shield (see illustration 6.3 in Chapter 1).

22 Locate the downstream oxygen sensor (see illustrations), trace the sensor electrical harness to its connector and disconnect it, then unscrew the sensor with an oxygen sensor wrench (see illustration 14.8).

23 If you're going to install the old sensor, see Step 9.

24 Installation is the reverse of removal. Be sure to tighten the oxygen sensor to the torque listed in this Chapter's Specifications.

14.22b Rear downstream oxygen sensor (Sportage V6 models; front exhaust pipe removed for clarity)

15 Power Steering Pressure (PSP) switch - replacement

▶ **Refer to illustration 15.1**

➡**Note: On 1994 through 1997 models, the PSP switch is located on top of the power steering pump. This procedure does not apply to 1998 and later models.**

1 Find the power steering pressure switch (see illustration), which is located on top of the power steering pump.

2 Trace the electrical lead from the power steering switch up to the electrical connector and disconnect the switch connector.

3 Unscrew the PSP switch from the power steering pump.

4 Installation is the reverse of removal. Be sure to tighten the PSP switch to the torque listed in this Chapter's Specifications.

5 Check the power steering fluid level, adding as necessary (see Chapter 1).

15.1 On 1994 through 1997 models, the PSP switch is located on top of the power steering pump. To remove the PSP switch, disconnect the electrical connector and unscrew the switch from the pump

16 Throttle Position (TP) sensor - replacement

1994 THROUGH 1997 MODELS

Removal and installation

▶ Refer to illustration 16.2

1   Disconnect the electrical connector from the TP sensor (see illustrations 13.3a and 13.3b in Chapter 4).

2   Remove the TP sensor mounting screws (see illustration) and remove the TP sensor from the throttle body.

3   Look at the two tangs on the end of the throttle plate shaft: Note that each tang has a flat side; this is the drive side of the tang. Now look at the two tabs on the (backside of) the TP sensor: Note that each tab has a slot in one side, but no slot in the other side. The side of each tab without a slot is the driven side of the tab. When installing a new (or old) TP sensor, open the throttle plate slightly and install the TP sensor so that the drive side of each tang on the end of the throttle shaft engages the non-slotted side of each tab on the TP sensor. Then push the TP sensor into place and hand tighten the TP sensor mounting screws. Don't tighten the TP sensor mounting screws until the TP sensor has been correctly adjusted.

4   With the TP sensor installed, the TP sensor mounting screws loose and the TP sensor electrical connector still disconnected, proceed to the appropriate TP sensor adjustment procedure below.

Adjustment

1994 and 1995 B6 SOHC models and 1995 B6 DOHC models

▶ Refer to illustrations 16.5 and 16.6

5   Connect an ohmmeter to TP sensor terminals IDL and E (see illustration).

6   On B6 SOHC models with a manual transaxle, insert a 0.016-inch (0.4 mm) feeler gauge between the throttle stop screw and the stop lever (see illustration). On B6 SOHC models with an automatic transaxle, insert a 0.010-inch (0.25 mm) feeler gauge between the throttle stop

screw and the stop lever. On B6 DOHC models, insert a 0.012-inch (0.30 mm) feeler gauge between the throttle stop screw and the stop lever.

7   Rotate the TP sensor clockwise about 30-degrees, then rotate it counterclockwise until there is continuity.

8   On B6 SOHC models with a manual transaxle, remove the 0.016-inch (0.4 mm) feeler gauge, insert a 0.027-inch feeler gauge and verify that no continuity exists. On B6 SOHC models with an automatic transact, remove the 0.010-inch (0.25 mm) feeler gauge, insert a 0.016-inch (0.4 mm) feeler gauge and verify that no continuity exists. On B6 DOHC models, remove the 0.012-inch (0.30 mm) feeler gauge, insert a 0.016-inch (0.4 mm) feeler gauge and verify that no continuity exists.

9   If there is continuity, repeat Steps 5 through 8.

10 Tighten the TP sensor screws securely and connect the electrical connector to the TP sensor.

16.2 To detach the TP sensor from the throttle body, remove these two screws (throttle body removed for clarity)

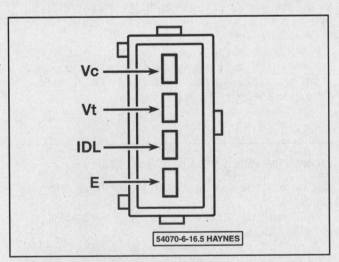

16.5 TP sensor terminal guide (all 1994 and 1995 B6 SOHC models and 1995 B6 DOHC models)

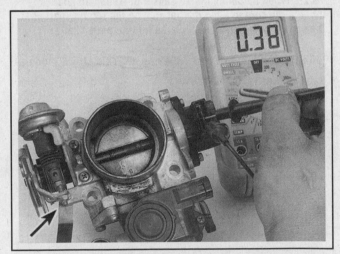

16.6 Insert a feeler gauge of the appropriate thickness (see text) between the throttle stop screw and the stop lever (all 1994 models, 1995 SOHC models with a manual transaxle, 1995 B6 SOHC models with an automatic transaxle and 1995 B6 DOHC models)

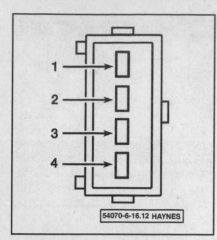

16.12 TP sensor terminal guide (1996 and 1997 B6 DOHC models and 1995 through 1997 BP DOHC models)

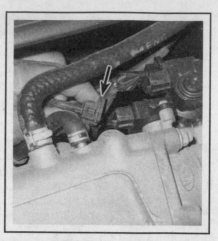

16.26 To disconnect the electrical connector from the TP sensor on 1998 and later models, depress this wire retainer with your finger and pull off the connector

16.27 To detach the TP sensor from the throttle body on 1998 and later models, remove these two screws

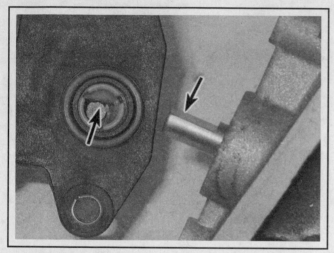

16.28 When installing the TP sensor on 1998 and later models, be sure to align the flat spot on the rotating part of the sensor with the flat spot on the throttle plate shaft

1995 BP DOHC models and 1996 and 1997 B6 DOHC models

▶ **Refer to illustration 16.12**

11 Verify that the throttle plate is closed.

12 Using an ohmmeter, check for continuity between TP sensor terminals 1 and 2 (see illustration).

13 Insert a 0.006-inch (0.15 mm) feeler gauge between the throttle adjusting screw and the throttle lever (see illustration 16.6) and verify that there's continuity.

14 If there's no continuity, adjust the TP sensor until there is continuity.

15 Remove the 0.006-inch (0.15 mm) feeler gauge, insert a 0.020-inch (0.5mm) feeler gauge between the throttle adjusting screw and the throttle lever and verify that there is no continuity.

16 If there is continuity, adjust the TP sensor (with the feeler gauge still in place).

17 Repeat Steps 11 through 16 until the continuity is as specified with each feeler gauge.

18 When continuity is as specified with each feeler gauge, tighten the TP sensor screws securely, then connect the electrical connector to the TP sensor.

19 If the TP sensor cannot be adjusted to the specified continuity with each feeler gauge, replace it.

1996 and 1997 BP DOHC models

20 Turn the ignition switch to the ON position.

21 Reconnect the electrical connector to the TP sensor.

22 Using a digital voltmeter or multimeter, backprobe between the light green and white wire from terminal 3 (see illustration 16.12) and ground.

23 Measure the voltage with the throttle valve fully closed. It should be 0.58 to 0.61 volts (1996 models) or 0.40 to 0.60 volts (1997 models).

24 If the indicated voltage is out of range, rotate the TP sensor until the voltage reading is within the specified range. When the indicated voltage is within the specified range, tighten the TP sensor mounting screws securely.

25 Slowly open the throttle plate and verify that the indicated voltage increases smoothly as the opening angle of the throttle plate increases. At wide-open-throttle (WOT), the indicated voltage should be 3.65 volts (1996 models) or 3.5 to 4.3 volts (1997 models).

1998 AND LATER MODELS

▶ **Refer to illustrations 16.26, 16.27 and 16.28**

26 Disconnect the electrical connector from the TP sensor (see illustration).

27 Remove the TP sensor mounting screws (see illustration) and remove the TP sensor.

28 When installing the TP sensor, make sure that the flat spot on the rotating part of the sensor is aligned with the flat spot on the throttle plate shaft (see illustration).

29 Installation is otherwise the reverse of removal.

17 Transmission Range (TR) switch - replacement and adjustment

REPLACEMENT

▶ Refer to illustration 17.3

➡Note: The TR switch, which is used only on automatic transaxles, is located on top of the transaxle.

1 Place the shift lever in the Neutral position.
2 Remove the air intake duct (see *Air filter housing - removal and installation* in Chapter 4). On Sportage models, also remove the air filter housing (see Chapter 4) and the battery and battery tray (see Chapter 5).

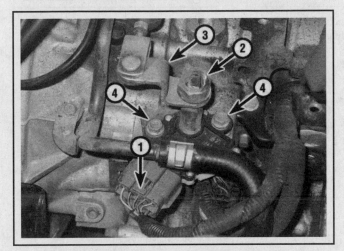

17.3 To remove the TR switch from the transaxle:

1 *Disconnect the electrical connector from the TR switch*
2 *Remove the nut that secures the selector lever to the manual shaft*
3 *Remove the selector lever and set the lever and shift cable aside*
4 *Remove the TR switch mounting bolts, then pull the switch straight up to remove it from the manual shaft*

3 Disconnect the electrical connector from the TR switch (see illustration).
4 Remove the big nut that connects the selector lever to the manual shaft and disconnect the selector lever from the manual shaft.
5 Remove the TR switch mounting bolts and remove the switch.

✳✳ CAUTION:

While the TR switch is removed, do NOT rotate the manual shaft on the transaxle.

6 Make sure that the TR switch is still in the Neutral position. You'll hear/feel a click when you put the switch into Neutral.
7 If for some reason the manual shaft has moved from the Neutral position, rotate the manual shaft in a clockwise direction until it stops. As you rotate the shaft, it clicks into each gear position. Rotate it counterclockwise to the third position (third click), which is Neutral.
8 Install the TR switch and loosely install the switch mounting bolts. Don't tighten the bolts until after you've adjusted the TR switch.

ADJUSTMENT

1994 through 2003 models

▶ Refer to illustrations 17.9a, 17.9b, 17.9c, 17.9d and 17.9e

9 Hook up the leads of an ohmmeter to the indicated terminals of the TR switch (see illustrations), then rotate the switch until there's continuity between the indicated terminals.
10 When there is continuity between the indicated terminals, tighten the TR switch mounting bolts to the torque listed in this Chapter's Specifications.

➡Note: Be careful not to move the TR switch while tightening the switch mounting bolts.

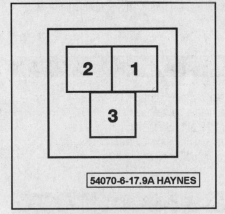

17.9a On 1994 models there should be continuity between terminals 2 and 3 when the TR switch is correctly adjusted. On 1995 B6 SOHC models and on B6 DOHC models without a shift pattern indicator there should be continuity between terminals 1 and 2 when the TR switch is correctly adjusted

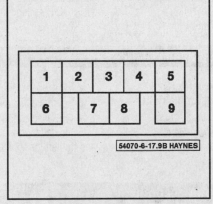

17.9b On 1995 models there should be continuity between terminals 5 and 7 when the TR switch is correctly adjusted

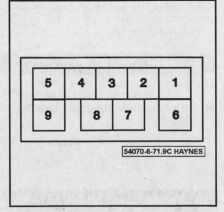

17.9c On 1996 and 1997 models, there should be continuity between terminals 5 and 7 when the TR switch is correctly adjusted

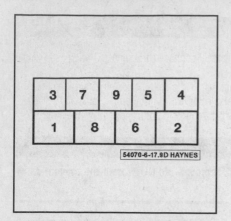

17.9d On 1998 through 2000 models, there should be continuity between terminals 5 and 7 when the TR switch is correctly adjusted

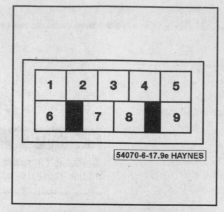

17.9e On 2001 through 2003 models, there should be continuity between terminals 5 and 7 when the TR switch is correctly adjusted

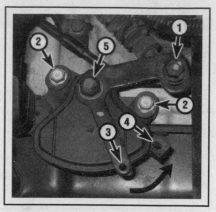

17.12 Transmission Range (TR) switch details (2004 and later models):

1   *Shift cable nut*
2   *TR switch mounting bolts*
3   *Manual control lever alignment hole*
4   *TR switch alignment hole*
5   *Manual control lever nut*

2004 and later models

▶ **Refer to illustration 17.12**

11 Put the shift lever (inside the vehicle) in the NEUTRAL position.

12 Loosen the nut that secures the shift control cable to the manual control lever (see illustration).

13 Put the manual control lever (on the transaxle) in the NEUTRAL position.

➡**Note: When you click the manual control lever through the gears - Park, Reverse, Neutral, Drive - the Neutral position will be the one that is closest to the alignment hole in the TR switch flange.**

14 Loosen the TR switch mounting bolts, then turn the TR switch body so that the hole in the end of the manual control lever is aligned with the hole in the TR switch flange.

15 Tighten the TR switch mounting bolts securely, then verify that the TR switch didn't move (make sure the two holes are still aligned).

16 Gently pull the slack out of the shift control cable and tighten the nut that secures the cable to the manual control lever.

17 Verify that the shift lever (inside the vehicle) is still in the NEUTRAL position; if it isn't, repeat this procedure.

All models

18 The remainder of installation is the reverse of removal.

19 Turn the ignition switch to ON, move the shift lever through all the gears and verify that the TR switch is correctly synchronized with the gear position indicator on the instrument cluster. Then verify that the engine will NOT start in any gear position other than Park or Neutral, and that the back-up lights come on when the shift lever is in the Reverse position. If the vehicle fails to meet any of these criteria, readjust the TR switch.

18 Vehicle Speed Sensor (VSS) - replacement

➡**Note: The VSS, which is used on manual transaxles, is located on top of the transaxle, near the CV joint for the right driveaxle.**

1 Remove the air intake duct (see *Air filter housing - removal and installation* in Chapter 4).

2 Disconnect the electrical connector from the VSS.

3 Remove the VSS mounting bolt and remove the VSS.

4 Remove and discard the old VSS O-ring.

5 Installation is the reverse of removal. Be sure to use a new O-ring and tighten the VSS mounting bolt securely.

19 Volume Air Flow (VAF) sensor - replacement

▶ **Refer to illustrations 19.1a, 19.1b, 19.3 and 19.4**

➡**Note: The VAF sensor, which is used on 1994 models and on 1995 B6 SOHC models, is located on the air filter housing.**

1 Disconnect the electrical connector from the VAF sensor (see illustrations).

2 Disconnect the air intake duct from the resonance chamber and remove the resonance chamber from the air filter housing (see Section 9 in Chapter 4).

3 Disconnect the upper part of the air filter housing from the lower half (see illustration).

4 Remove the upper part of the air filter housing and the VAF sensor as a single assembly (see illustration).

5 Remove the nuts that secure the VAF sensor to the upper part of the air filter housing and separate the two components.

6 Installation is the reverse of removal.

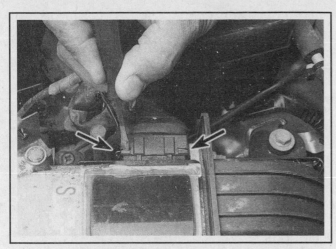

19.1a To release the electrical connector from the VAF sensor, carefully pry both ends of the wire retainer away from the sides of the connector . . .

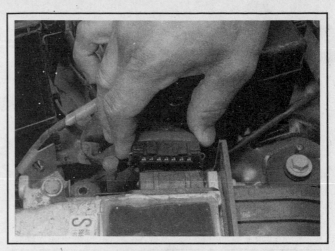

19.1b . . . and pull off the connector

19.3 To detach the upper part of the air filter housing from the lower part, remove these fasteners

19.4 Remove the upper part of the air filter housing and the VAF sensor as a single assembly, then remove the four nuts that secure the VAF sensor to the air filter's upper half and separate the sensor

20 Powertrain Control Module (PCM) - removal and installation

✳✳ WARNING:

All models covered by this manual are equipped with a Supplemental Restraint System (SRS), more commonly known as airbags. Always disarm the airbag system before working in the vicinity of any airbag system component to avoid the possibility of accidental deployment of the airbag, which could cause personal injury (see Chapter 12).

✳✳ CAUTION:

To avoid electrostatic discharge damage to the PCM, handle the PCM only by its case. Do not touch the electrical terminals during removal and installation. If available, ground yourself to the vehicle with a anti-static ground strap, available at computer supply stores.

➡Note: The PCM is a component of the immobilizer (vehicle security) system. If a new PCM is installed in the vehicle, the immobilizer code must be programmed into the new PCM by a dealership service department before the engine will start. The dealer will need the vehicle, the new PCM unit and all of the vehicle keys to program the new PCM unit. So if you're planning to replace the old PCM with a new unit, a dealer service department must perform the following procedure (unless you want to have the vehicle towed to the dealer after you have installed the new PCM!).

1   Disconnect the cable from the negative battery terminal (see Chapter 5, Section 1).

2   Disable the airbag system (see Chapter 12).

20.4 On 1994 models and 1995 B6 SOHC and B6 DOHC models, the PCM is located up inside the dash, ahead of the center console. After removing the center console, disconnect the electrical connectors (1) from the PCM, remove the PCM mounting screws (2), then disengage the PCM from its mounting bracket in the center of the dash, carefully pull it down and remove it

20.7 On 1995 BP DOHC models and on all 1996 and later models, the PCM is located on the floor, under the center of the dash, at the extreme forward end, up against the firewall

1994 MODELS AND 1995 B6 SOHC AND B6 DOHC MODELS

♦ Refer to illustration 20.4

➡Note: The PCM is located under the center of the dash, ahead of the center console.

3 Remove the center console (see Chapter 11).
4 Disconnect the electrical connectors from the PCM (see illustration).
5 Remove the PCM mounting bolts and remove the PCM.
6 Installation is the reverse of removal.

1995 BP DOHC MODELS AND 1996 THROUGH 2004 MODELS

♦ Refer to illustrations 20.7, 20.8a, 20.8b, 20.9, 20.10a and 20.10b

➡Note: The PCM is located on the floor, under the center of the dash, ahead of the center console.

7 Using a flashlight, locate the PCM ahead of the center console, in the void located at the extreme front end of the tunnel, up against the firewall (see illustration).
8 On the left side, remove the PCM mounting bolt and, on the right side, remove the two mounting nuts (see illustrations), then carefully work the PCM out from under the dash from the right side.

❊❊ CAUTION:

Avoid any static electricity damage to the computer by grounding yourself to the body before touching the PCM and using a special anti-static pad to store the PCM on once it is removed.

9 Disconnect the electrical connector from the PCM (see illustration).
10 When reconnecting the big electrical connector, make sure that the dimples on the end of the two arms are locked into the detents on the side of the connector (see illustrations).
11 Installation is otherwise the reverse of removal.

20.8a To detach the PCM from the floor, remove this bolt from the left side . . .

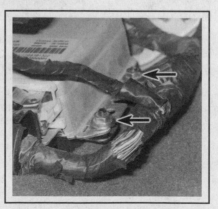

20.8b . . . and remove these two nuts from the right side

20.9 To release the electrical connector from the PCM, swing this locking retainer up and pull off the connector

2005 AND LATER SPECTRA AND SPORTAGE MODELS

▶ **Refer to illustration 20.13**

➡ **Note: On all 2005 and later Spectra and Sportage models, a new replacement PCM or Transmission Control Module (TCM) (models with an automatic transaxle), must be reprogrammed with a factory scan tool and software before the new unit will work properly. It's okay to simply remove either of these modules to access or replace some other component, but if you decide to replace either module at home you will have to tow the vehicle to a dealer to have the PCM or TCM reprogrammed.**

12 Disconnect the cable from the negative battery terminal (see Chapter 5).

13 Locate the Powertrain Control Module (PCM) and the Transmission Control Module (TCM) under the left end of the dash (see illustration).

�֎ CAUTION:

Before you decide to replace either the PCM or the TCM at home, please read the Note above.

14 Disconnect the electrical connectors from the PCM or TCM, then remove the module mounting bracket fasteners and remove the module.

15 Installation is the reverse of removal.

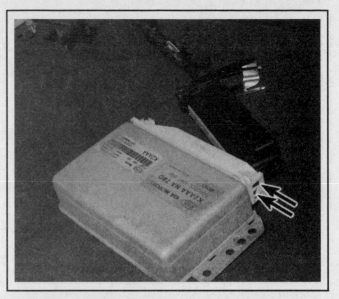

20.10a When connecting the electrical connector to the PCM, make sure that the two tabs on the end of the connector are correctly engaged with these slots . . .

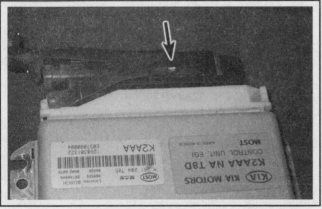

20.10b . . . and the dimples on the end of the two arms are locked into the detents on the side of the connector

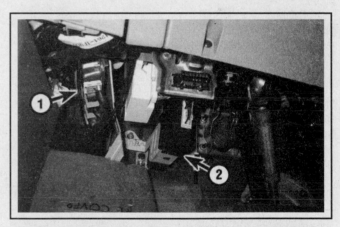

20.13 Powertrain Control Module (PCM) and Transmission Control Module (TCM) locations (2005 and later Sportage model shown)

1 Powertrain Control Module (PCM)
2 Transmission Control Module (TCM) (automatic transaxles)

21 Catalytic converter - general description, check and replacement

➡ **Note: Because of a Federally mandated extended warranty that covers emissions-related components such as the catalytic converter, check with a dealer service department before replacing the converter at your own expense.**

GENERAL DESCRIPTION

1 A catalytic converter (or catalyst) is an emission control device in the exhaust system that reduces certain pollutants in the exhaust gas stream. There are two types of converters: oxidation converters and reduction converters.

2 Oxidation converters contain a monolithic substrate (a ceramic honeycomb) coated with the semi-precious metals platinum and palladium. An oxidation catalyst reduces unburned hydrocarbons (HC) and carbon monoxide (CO) by adding oxygen to the exhaust stream as it passes through the substrate, which in the presence of high temperature and the catalyst materials converts the HC and CO to water vapor (H_2O) and carbon dioxide (CO_2).

21.10 If the catalytic converter fasteners are rusted and frozen up, spray them with penetrating oil before attempting to loosen them

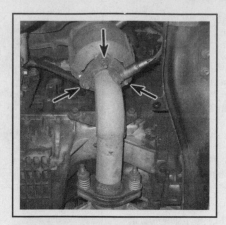

21.14 To disconnect the lower flange of the catalytic converter from the exhaust pipe flange, remove these three nuts

21.15 To disconnect the upper mounting flange of the catalytic converter from the exhaust manifold flange, remove these five nuts

3   Reduction converters contain a monolithic substrate coated with platinum and rhodium. A reduction catalyst reduces oxides of nitrogen (NOx) by removing oxygen, which in the presence of high temperature and the catalyst material produces nitrogen (N) and carbon dioxide (CO2).

4   Catalytic converters that combine both types of catalysts in one assembly are known as three-way catalysts or TWCs. A TWC can reduce all three pollutants. All catalysts used by the vehicles covered in this manual are equipped with three-way catalysts.

5   On 1994 and 1995 B6 SOHC models and on 1995 through 1997 BP DOHC models, there is one Three-Way Catalyst (TWC) underneath the vehicle. On 1995 through 1997 B6 DOHC models and on all 1998 and later models, there are two catalysts: a Warm-Up Three-Way Catalyst (WU-TWC) and the same TWC underneath the vehicle that's used on earlier models. In this manual, these catalysts are simply referred to as the upstream and downstream catalytic converters.

CHECK

6   The test equipment for a catalytic converter (a loaded-mode dynamometer and a 5-gas analyzer) is expensive. If you suspect that the converter on your vehicle is malfunctioning, take it to a dealer or authorized emission inspection facility for diagnosis and repair.

7   Whenever you raise the vehicle to service underbody components, inspect the converter assembly for leaks, corrosion, dents and other damage. Carefully inspect the welds and/or flange bolts and nuts that attach the front and rear ends of the converter to the exhaust system. If you note any damage, replace the converter.

8   Although catalytic converters don't break too often, they can become clogged or even plugged up. The easiest way to check for a restricted converter is to use a vacuum gauge to diagnose the effect of a blocked exhaust on intake vacuum.

   a)   *Connect a vacuum gauge to any intake manifold vacuum source (any pipe on the intake manifold with a vacuum hose connected to it will provide the necessary intake manifold vacuum).*

   b)   *Warm the engine to operating temperature, place the transaxle in Park (automatic models) or Neutral (manual models) and apply the parking brake.*

   c)   *Note the vacuum reading at idle and write it down.*

   d)   *Quickly open the throttle to near its wide-open position and then quickly get off the throttle and allow it to close. Note the vacuum reading and jot it down.*

   e)   *Do this test three more times, recording your measurement after each test.*

   f)   *If your fourth reading is more than one in-Hg lower than the reading that you noted at idle, the exhaust system might be restricted (the catalytic converter could be plugged, OR an exhaust pipe or muffler could be restricted).*

REPLACEMENT

Four-cylinder models

1994 and 1995 B6 SOHC models

◗ **Refer to illustration 21.10**

9   Raise the vehicle and place it securely on jackstands.

10   Remove the fasteners from the flanges at each end of the converter (see illustration) and remove the catalytic converter.

11   Installation is the reverse of removal. If the rear flange of the catalyst is connected to the exhaust pipe flange with nuts, springs and studs, make sure that the springs are in place before installing the nuts. Also be sure to replace any rusted or damaged fasteners with new ones.

1995 through 1997 B6 DOHC models and all 1998 and later models

◗ **Refer to illustrations 21.14 and 21.15**

➡ **Note: The following procedure describes the replacement procedure for the "upstream" Warm-Up Three-Way Catalyst on 1995 through 1997 B6 DOHC models and on all 1998 and later models. For the "downstream" converter replacement procedures on these models, refer to Steps 9 through 11.**

12   Raise the front of the vehicle and place it securely on jackstands.

13   Remove the upstream and downstream oxygen sensors (see Section 14).

14   Unbolt the exhaust pipe from the catalytic converter (see illustration).

15   Remove the exhaust manifold heat shield, then unbolt the cata-

lytic converter from the exhaust manifold (see illustration).

16 Disconnect the two forward rubber hangers, pull down the exhaust pipe and remove the catalyst.

17 Installation is the reverse of removal. Be sure to replace any rusted or damaged fasteners with new ones.

V6 models

18 There are two catalytic converters, one for each cylinder bank; they are integral components of the exhaust manifolds (see Chapter 2B).

22 Dashpot - check, replacement and adjustment

➡**Note: The dashpot, which is used only on 1994 and 1995 B6 SOHC models, is a spring-loaded sealed diaphragm that prevents the throttle valve from closing too abruptly. The dashpot is located on the throttle body.**

CHECK

▶ **Refer to illustration 22.2**

1 Remove the air intake duct (see *Air filter housing - removal and installation* in Chapter 4).

2 Locate the dashpot (see illustration) on the front side of the throttle body.

3 Open the throttle plate all the way to move the adjustment screw out of the way and hold it there while pushing the dashpot pushrod up into the dashpot, then release the pushrod and verify that it quickly protrudes down from the dashpot.

4 If the dashpot pushrod doesn't operate as described, replace the dashpot.

REPLACEMENT

5 Remove the two dashpot mounting screws (see illustration 22.2)

and remove the dashpot.

6 Installation is the reverse of removal. Be sure to tighten the dashpot mounting screws securely.

ADJUSTMENT

▶ **Refer to illustration 22.8**

7 Warm up the engine until it's fully warmed up and idling smoothly.

8 Locate the diagnostic connector, which is located right behind the intake manifold. Connect a tachometer to the diagnostic connector's IG terminal (see illustration).

9 Increase the engine speed to 4000 rpm.

10 Slowly decrease the engine speed and verify that the dashpot adjustment screw on the throttle lever contacts the dashpot pushrod at about 3000 rpm.

11 If the adjustment screw contacts the pushrod above or below 3000 rpm, loosen the locknut (see illustration 22.2), turn the adjustment screw in or out as necessary, tighten the locknut, increase the engine speed to 4000 rpm again, slowly decrease the engine speed and recheck. Continue adjusting the screw until it contacts the dashpot pushrod at 3000 rpm.

22.2 Dashpot assembly check, replacement and adjustment details (1994 and 1995 B6 SOHC models only):

A	Dashpot	*D*	Adjustment screw locknut
B	Dashpot pushrod	*E*	Dashpot mounting screws
C	Adjustment screw		

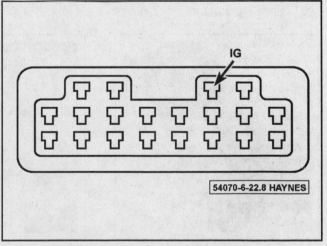

22.8 To adjust the dashpot, connect a tachometer to the diagnostic connector's IG terminal, increase the engine speed to 4000 rpm, slowly decrease the engine speed and verify that the dashpot adjustment screw on the throttle lever contacts the dashpot pushrod at about 3000 rpm

54070-6-22.8 HAYNES

23 Idle air control system - component replacement

⁂ WARNING:

Wait until the engine is completely cool before beginning this procedure.

1994 THROUGH 1997 MODELS

1994 and 1995 B6 SOHC models

Idle Speed Control (ISC) solenoid valve

♦ **Refer to illustration 23.2**

➡**Note: The ISC solenoid valve is located on the underside of the throttle body.**

1 Remove the throttle body (see Chapter 4).

2 Remove the ISC solenoid valve mounting screws (see illustration) and remove the solenoid valve from the throttle body.

3 Remove and discard the old ISC solenoid valve gasket.

4 Thoroughly clean off any old gasket residue from the gasket mating surface of the throttle body and, if you're reusing the old ISC solenoid valve, from the mating surface of the ISC solenoid valve itself.

5 Installation is the reverse of removal. Be sure to use a new gasket and tighten the ISC solenoid valve mounting screws securely.

Air valve

♦ **Refer to illustrations 23.6 and 23.7**

➡**Note: The air valve is located on the front of the intake manifold plenum.**

6 Loosen the spring-type hose clamps and disconnect the hoses from the air valve (see illustration).

7 Remove the air valve mounting bolts (see illustration) and remove the air valve.

8 Remove and discard the old air valve gasket.

9 Thoroughly clean off any old gasket residue from the gasket mating surface of the intake manifold plenum and, if you're reusing the old air valve, from the mating surface of the air valve itself.

10 Installation is the reverse of removal. Be sure to use a new gasket and tighten the air valve mounting screws securely.

1995 B6 DOHC and BP DOHC and all 1996 and 1997 models

➡**Note: The Idle Air Control (IAC) valve is located on the underside of the throttle body.**

11 Remove the throttle body (see Chapter 4).

12 Remove the IAC valve mounting screws and remove the IAC valve from the throttle body.

13 Remove and discard the old IAC valve gasket.

14 Thoroughly clean off any old gasket residue from the gasket mating surface of the throttle body and, if you're reusing the old IAC valve, from the mating surface of the IAC valve itself.

15 Installation is the reverse of removal. Be sure to use a new gasket and tighten the IAC valve mounting screws securely.

1998 THROUGH 2004 MODELS (EXCEPT 2.0L DOHC ENGINE)

♦ **Refer to illustrations 23.16, 23.17 and 23.18**

➡**Note: The Idle Air Control (IAC) valve is located on the backside of the throttle body.**

16 Disconnect the electrical connector from the IAC valve (see illustration).

17 Remove the IAC valve mounting screws (see illustration) and remove the IAC valve.

18 Remove the old IAC valve gasket (see illustration) and discard it.

19 Thoroughly clean off any old gasket residue from the gasket mating surface of the throttle body and, if you're reusing the old IAC valve, from the mating surface of the IAC valve itself.

23.2 To detach the Idle Speed Control (ISC) solenoid valve from the throttle body, remove these three screws

23.6 Loosen the spring-type hose clamps with a pair of needle-nose pliers, slide the clamps down the hoses and disconnect the hoses from the pipes on the air valve (1994 models and 1995 B6 SOHC and B6 DOHC models)

23.7 To detach the air valve from the intake manifold plenum, remove these four mounting bolts (1994 models and 1995 B6 SOHC and B6 DOHC models)

20 Installation is the reverse of removal. Be sure to use a new gasket and tighten the IAC valve mounting screws securely.

2004 AND LATER MODELS (2.0L DOHC ENGINE)

▶ **Refer to illustrations 23.22a and 23.22b**

21 Remove the engine cover, if equipped.
22 Disconnect the electrical connector from the Idle Speed Control Actuator (ISCA) (see illustrations).
23 Remove the ISCA mounting screws.
24 Remove the ISCA from the intake manifold.
25 Installation is the reverse of removal.

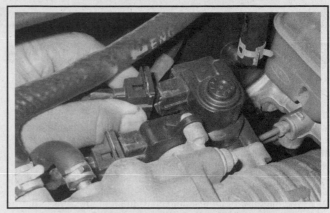

23.16 To disconnect the electrical connector from the IAC valve, depress the retainer wire and pull off the connector (1998 and later models)

23.17 To detach the IAC valve from the throttle body on 1998 and later models, remove these two screws (throttle body removed for clarity)

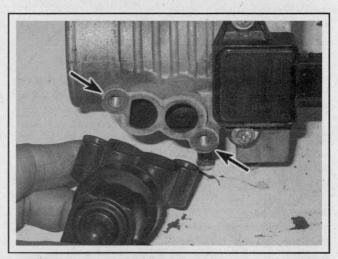

23.18 Be sure to remove and discard the old IAC valve gasket, which might be stuck to the IAC valve mating surface on the throttle body, like the one shown here (1998 and later models)

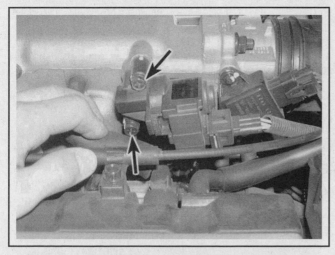

23.22a On 2.0L DOHC engines, the Idle Speed Control (ISC) actuator is mounted on the front of the intake plenum

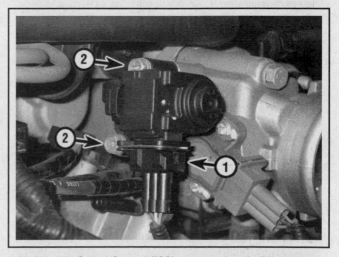

23.22b Idle Speed Control (ISC) actuator details (V6 engine):

1   Electrical connector   2   Mounting screws

24 Evaporative Emissions Control (EVAP) system - general description and component replacement

> ❄❄ **WARNING:**
>
> Gasoline is extremely flammable, so take extra precautions when you work on any part of the fuel system. Don't smoke or allow open flames or bare light bulbs near the work area, and don't work in a garage where a gas-type appliance (such as a water heater or a clothes dryer) is present. Since gasoline is carcinogenic, wear fuel resistent gloves when there's a possibility of being exposed to fuel, and, if you spill any fuel on your skin, rinse it off immediately with soap and water. Mop up any spills immediately and do not store fuel-soaked rags where they could ignite. The fuel system is under constant pressure, so, if any fuel lines are to be disconnected, the fuel pressure in the system must be relieved first. When you perform any kind of work on the fuel system, wear safety glasses and have a Class B type fire extinguisher on hand.

GENERAL DESCRIPTION

1 The Evaporative Emissions Control (EVAP) system prevents fuel system vapors (which contain unburned hydrocarbons) from escaping into the atmosphere. On warm days, vapors trapped inside the fuel tank expand until the pressure reaches a certain threshold. Then the fuel vapors are routed from the fuel tank through the EVAP two-way valve to the EVAP canister, where they're stored temporarily until the next time the vehicle is operated. When the conditions are right (engine warmed up, vehicle up to speed, moderate or heavy load on the engine, etc.) the PCM opens the canister purge valve, which allows fuel vapors to be drawn from the canister into the intake manifold. Once in the intake manifold, the fuel vapors mix with incoming air before drawn through the intake ports into the combustion chambers where they're burned up with the rest of the air/fuel mixture. The EVAP system is complex and virtually impossible to troubleshoot without the right tools and training. However, the following description should give you a good idea of how it works:

2 On 1994 and 1995 SOHC models and on 1995 through 1997 B6 DOHC models, the EVAP canister is located in the right rear corner of the engine compartment (on later vehicles, there's a "canister" at this location, but it's actually an EVAP system filter). On 1995 through 1997 BP DOHC models and on all 1998 and later models, the EVAP canister is located under the vehicle, on the right side of the fuel tank. The canister, which contains activated carbon, is a repository for storing fuel vapors. On models with the canister underneath the vehicle, you'll have to raise the vehicle to inspect or replace the canister, or any other part of the EVAP system, except for the canister purge valve (which is located in the engine compartment). But the canister is designed to be maintenance-free and should last the life of the vehicle. There are several other important components located on or near the canister: the air filter, the canister vent shut valve, the two-way valve/bypass solenoid valve assembly and the fuel tank pressure sensor.

3 The EVAP canister filter (1998 and later models) is an integral part of the canister close valve. When the canister is purged, fresh air is drawn through the filter before passing through the canister. The filter prevents dust and dirt particles from entering the EVAP canister and the EVAP system.

4 The canister close valve is mounted on the crossmember behind the fuel tank. The canister close valve is normally closed, but it opens to allow fresh air from the filter to enter the EVAP canister when the canister is being purged.

5 The fuel tank pressure sensor is located on top of the fuel pump/fuel gauge sending unit assembly. The fuel tank pressure sensor monitors the pressure inside the fuel tank, converts fuel tank absolute pressure into a variable voltage signal and transmits this data to the PCM. To replace the fuel tank pressure sensor, refer to Section 8.

6 The EVAP canister purge valve, which is under the control of the Powertrain Control Module (PCM), regulates the flow of vapors being purged from the EVAP canister into the intake manifold. The canister purge valve is always closed unless the engine coolant is at its normal operating temperature; during this period, intake manifold vacuum is blocked from drawing vapors from the EVAP canister. Once the coolant is warmed up, the PCM opens or closes the purge valve in accordance with data from various information sensor inputs. The purge valve is located in the engine compartment, behind the intake manifold.

General system checks

7 The most common symptom of a faulty EVAP system is a strong fuel odor (particularly during hot weather). If you smell fuel while driving or (more likely) right after you park the vehicle and turn off the engine, check the fuel filler cap first. Make sure that it's screwed onto the fuel filler neck all the way. If the odor persists, inspect all EVAP hose connections, both in the engine compartment and under the vehicle. You'll have to raise the vehicle and place it securely on jackstands to inspect most of the EVAP system, since it's located under the vehicle. Be sure to inspect each hose attached to the canister for damage and leakage along its entire length. Repair or replace as necessary. Inspect the canister for damage and look for fuel leaking from the bottom. If fuel is leaking or the canister is otherwise damaged, replace it.

8 Poor idle, stalling, and poor driveability can be caused by a defective fuel vapor vent valve or canister purge valve, a damaged canister, cracked hoses, or hoses connected to the wrong tubes. Fuel loss or fuel odor can be caused by fuel leaking from fuel lines or hoses, a cracked or damaged canister, or a defective vapor valve.

9 To check for excessive fuel vapor pressure in the fuel tank, remove the gas cap and listen for the sound of pressure release If the fuel tank emits a whooshing sound when you open the filler cap, fuel tank vapor pressure is excessive. Inspect the canister vapor hoses and the canister inlet port for blockage or collapsed hoses. Also inspect the vapor vent valve.

10 Further testing requires the use of a proprietary scan tool, which will run a series of checks using the fuel tank pressure sensor and other output actuators to detect excessive pressure. You'll have to take the vehicle to a dealer service department or other qualified repair shop to have the EVAP system professionally diagnosed.

COMPONENT REPLACEMENT

EVAP canister purge valve

▸ **Refer to illustration 24.11**

➡**Note: The EVAP canister purge valve is located in the engine compartment, behind the intake manifold and the throttle body.**

11 Disconnect the electrical connector from the EVAP canister purge valve (see illustration).

12 Disconnect the EVAP hoses from the canister purge valve.

13 Installation is the reverse of removal. When installing the canister

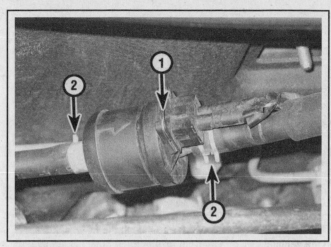

24.11 To remove the EVAP canister purge valve, depress the wire retainer (1) and pull off the electrical connector, then loosen the two spring-type hose clamps (2), slide them back and pull off the EVAP hoses. Note the directional arrow on the valve

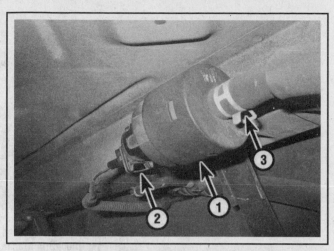

24.15 On 2003 and earlier models, the EVAP canister close valve (1) is located on the crossmember behind the fuel tank. Depress the wire retainer (2) and pull off the electrical connector, then loosen the spring-type hose clamp (3), slide it back and disconnect the EVAP hose

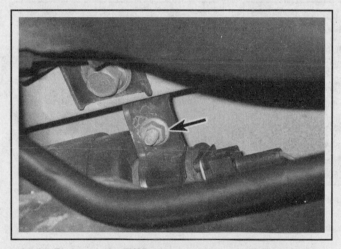

24.17 To detach the EVAP canister close valve from its mounting bracket, remove this nut (2003 and earlier models)

24.20 To remove the EVAP canister from 1994 and 1995 B6 SOHC models and from 1995 through 1997 B6 DOHC models, label and disconnect the EVAP hoses, then detach the canister from its mounting bracket

purge valve, make sure that the directional arrow points in the direction of the intake manifold.

EVAP canister close valve

▶ Refer to illustrations 24.15 and 24.17

➡Note: On 2003 and earlier models, the EVAP canister close valve is located right behind the crossmember behind the fuel tank. On 2004 and later models, the canister close valve is located on the EVAP canister (see Step 28).

14 Raise the vehicle and place it securely on jackstands.

15 Disconnect the electrical connector from the canister close valve (see illustration).

16 Disconnect the EVAP hose from the canister close valve.

17 Remove the canister close valve mounting nut (see illustration) and remove the valve.

18 Installation is the reverse of removal.

EVAP fuel tank pressure sensor

19 To replace the fuel tank pressure sensor, refer to Section 8.

EVAP canister

1994 and 1995 B6 SOHC models and 1995 through 1997 B6 DOHC models

▶ Refer to illustration 24.20

➡Note: The EVAP canister is located in the right rear corner of the engine compartment.

20 Disconnect the EVAP hoses from the EVAP canister (see illustration).

21 Remove the EVAP canister from its mounting bracket.

22 Installation is the reverse of removal.

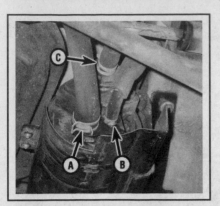

24.24 Disconnect these three EVAP hoses from the EVAP canister:

A   From rollover valve and On-Board Refueling Vapor Recovery (ORVR) system (on top of fuel tank)
B   To EVAP canister purge valve (in engine compartment)
C   From canister close valve

24.25 To detach the EVAP canister mounting bracket from the vehicle, remove these three bolts

24.26 To detach the EVAP canister from its mounting bracket, remove these two bolts

24.30 EVAP canister hose details (2004 and later models, Sportage model shown):

1   EVAP canister-to-fuel tank hose
2   EVAP canister-to-intake manifold purge hose
3   EVAP canister-to-atmosphere hose (via fuel tank air filter)

24.31 EVAP canister electrical details (2004 and later models, Sportage model shown):

1   Fuel Tank Pressure Sensor (FTPS) electrical connector
2   Canister Close Valve (CCV) electrical connector

24.32 EVAP canister details (2004 and later models, Sportage model shown):

1   EVAP canister mounting bracket bolts (one bolt not visible in this photo)
2   EVAP canister-to-mounting bracket nuts (do not remove until after canister and bracket are removed from vehicle)

1995 through 1997 BP DOHC models and all 1998 through 2003 models

♦ Refer to illustrations 24.24, 24.25 and 24.26

➥Note: The EVAP canister is located under the vehicle, on the right side of the fuel tank.

23 Raise the vehicle and place it securely on jackstands.
24 Disconnect the vapor hoses from the EVAP canister (see illustration).
25 Remove the EVAP canister mounting bracket bolts (see illustration), then lower the canister and mounting bracket as a single assembly.
26 Detach the EVAP canister from its mounting bracket (see illustration).
27 Installation is the reverse of removal.

2004 AND LATER MODELS

♦ Refer to illustrations 24.30, 24.31 and 24.32

28 Raise the vehicle and place it securely on jackstands.
29 Locate the EVAP canister behind the fuel tank.
30 Disconnect the EVAP hoses (see illustration) from the EVAP canister.
31 Disconnect the electrical connectors from the Fuel Tank Pressure Sensor (FTPS) and the Canister Close Valve (CCV) (see illustration).
32 Remove the bolts that secure the EVAP canister mounting bracket to the underside of the vehicle (see illustration) and remove the canister and bracket as a single assembly.
33 Remove the nuts that secure the EVAP canister to its mounting bracket and remove the canister from the bracket.
34 Installation is the reverse of removal.

25 Exhaust Gas Recirculation (EGR) system - general description and component replacement

GENERAL DESCRIPTION

➡**Note: Only 1995 through 1997 B6 DOHC and BP DOHC models are equipped with an EGR system.**

1   Oxides of nitrogen (or simply NOx) is a compound that is formed in the combustion chambers when the oxygen and nitrogen in the incoming air mix together. NOx is a natural byproduct of high combustion chamber temperatures. When NOx is emitted from the tailpipe, it mixes with reactive organic compounds (ROCs), hydrocarbons (HC) and sunlight to form ozone and photochemical smog. The Exhaust Gas Recirculation (EGR) system reduces oxides of nitrogen by recirculating exhaust gases from the exhaust manifold, through the EGR valve and intake manifold, then back to the combustion chambers, where it mixes with the incoming air/fuel mixture before being consumed. These recirculated exhaust gases dilute the incoming air/fuel mixture, which cools the combustion chambers, thereby reducing NOx emissions.

2   The EGR system consists of the Powertrain Control Module (PCM), the EGR valve, a pair of EGR solenoid valves (one for venting and one for vacuum), the EGR valve, the EGR valve position sensor (an integral part of the EGR valve) and various other information sensors (CMP sensor, ECT sensor, MAF sensor, TP sensor and VSS) that the PCM uses to determine when to open the EGR valve. The degree to which the EGR valve is opened is referred to as "EGR valve lift." The PCM is programmed to produce the ideal EGR valve lift for varying operating conditions. The EGR valve position sensor, which is an integral part of the EGR valve, detects the amount of EGR valve lift and sends this information to the PCM. The PCM then compares it with the appropriate EGR valve lift for the operating conditions. The PCM increases current flow to the EGR valve to increase valve lift and reduces the current to reduce the amount of lift. If EGR flow is inappropriate to the operating conditions (idle, cold engine, etc.) the PCM simply cuts the current to the EGR valve and the valve closes.

EGR VALVE REPLACEMENT

➡**Note: The EGR valve is located below the throttle body.**

3   Disconnect the electrical connector from the EGR valve.
4   Remove the two EGR valve mounting bolts and remove the EGR valve from the coolant housing.
5   Remove and discard the old EGR valve gasket.
6   Installation is the reverse of removal. Be sure to use a new EGR valve gasket, and tighten the EGR valve mounting bolts to the torque listed in this Chapter's Specifications.

26 Positive Crankcase Ventilation (PCV) system - general description and component replacement

➡**Note: If you're looking for PCV valve check and replacement procedures, see Chapter 1.**

GENERAL DESCRIPTION

1   The Positive Crankcase Ventilation (PCV) system reduces hydrocarbon emissions by scavenging crankcase vapors. It does this by circulating fresh air from the air intake duct into and through the crankcase, where it mixes with blow-by gases before being drawn by intake manifold vacuum through a PCV valve to the intake manifold.

2   The main components of the PCV system are the PCV valve and a pair of hoses. The fresh air inlet hose draws fresh air from the air intake duct (1994 through 1997 models) or from the throttle body (1998 and later models), through a pipe on the valve cover, then into the crankcase, where it mixes with blow-by gases. This mixture of fresh air and crankcase vapors is drawn from the crankcase into the intake manifold by intake manifold vacuum through the PCV valve and the crankcase ventilation hose, which connects a pipe on the valve cover to the intake manifold.

3   To maintain idle quality, the PCV valve restricts the flow of crankcase vapors into the intake manifold when intake manifold vacuum is high, and allows full flow when intake manifold decreases.

COMPONENT REPLACEMENT

➡**Note: The following procedures do not include PCV valve replacement because it's a regularly scheduled maintenance item. To replace the PCV valve, refer to Chapter 1.**

Four-cylinder models

Fresh air inlet hose

◗ **Refer to illustrations 26.4a and 26.4b**

4   On 1994 through 1997 models, disconnect the fresh air inlet hose from the air intake duct and from the valve cover (see illustration).

26.4a To disconnect the fresh air inlet hose from 1994 through 1997 models, pull the hose off the pipe on the air intake duct, then slide back the spring-type hose clamp at the other end and disconnect the hose from the valve cover

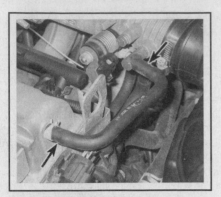

26.4b To disconnect the fresh air inlet hose from 1998 and later models, pull the hose off the pipe on the throttle body, then slide back the spring-type hose clamp at the other end and disconnect the hose from the valve cover

26.6a To disconnect the crankcase ventilation hose from 1994 through 1997 models, loosen the spring type hose clamp at each end of the hose, slide them back and pull off the hose (intake manifold end of hose not shown)

26.6b To disconnect the crankcase ventilation hose from 1998 and later models, loosen the spring-type hose clamp at each end of the hose, slide them back and pull off the hose

On 1998 and later models, disconnect the fresh air inlet hose from the throttle body and from the valve cover (see illustration). Simply loosen the hose clamps at both ends of the hose, slide them back and disconnect the hose from the air intake duct or the throttle body and from the valve cover.

5   Installation is the reverse of removal. Make sure that both hose clamps are in good shape. If either one is loose, replace it.

Crankcase ventilation hose (PCV hose)

◆ **Refer to illustrations 26.6a and 26.6b**

6   On 1994 through 1997 models, disconnect the crankcase ventilation hose from the PCV valve, which is installed in the right rear corner of the valve cover (see illustration). On 1998 and later models, disconnect the crankcase ventilation hose from the PCV valve, which is installed in the right rear corner of the valve cover, and from the metal pipe that routes PCV vapors to the intake manifold (see illustration).

7   Loosen the hose clamps at both ends of the crankcase ventilation hose, then disconnect the hose from the PCV valve and from the intake manifold.

8   Installation is the reverse of removal. Make sure that both hose clamps are in good shape. If either one is loose, replace it.

Sportage V6 models

Fresh air inlet hose

◆ **Refer to illustration 26.9**

9   Loosen the hose clamps at both ends of the fresh air inlet hose (see illustration) and remove the hose.

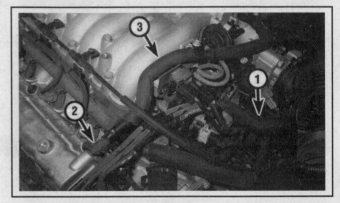

26.9 Positive Crankcase Ventilation (PCV) system details (Sportage V6 models):

1 PCV fresh air inlet hose	3 Crankcase ventilation hose
2 PCV valve	(PCV hose)

10 Installation is the reverse of removal.

Crankcase ventilation hose (PCV hose)

11 Loosen the hose clamps at both ends of the crankcase ventilation hose (see illustration 26.9) and remove the hose.

12 Installation is the reverse of removal.

PCV valve

13 Disconnect the crankcase ventilation hose from the PCV valve.

14 Unscrew the PCV valve from the front valve cover.

15 Installation is the reverse of removal.

---

27 Continuously Variable Valve Timing (CVVT) system - description and component replacement

DESCRIPTION

1   The CVVT system improves fuel efficiency and reduces nitrogen oxide (NOx) emissions by continuously altering the phase of the intake camshaft and, therefore, valve overlap. The CVVT system makes continuous changes to intake valve timing in response to changing operating conditions:

During light-load conditions, intake valve timing is retarded for stable combustion.
During part-load conditions, intake valve timing is advanced, enhancing fuel economy and lowering exhaust emissions.
During high-load/low rpm conditions, intake valve timing is advanced, increasing torque.
During high-load/high rpm conditions, intake valve timing is retarded, improving power.

2   The CVVT system consists of the Camshaft Position (CMP) sensor, the oil temperature sensor, various other sensors, the Powertrain Control Module (PCM), the oil control valve and the CVVT assembly itself, which is mounted on the end of the exhaust camshaft.

3   The PCM monitors various inputs, including oil pressure and temperature, camshaft and crankshaft position, vehicle speed and other variables, processes this data and responds by sending commands to open and close the OCV. The OCV responds to these PCM commands by either sending oil through the retard or advance chamber inside the CVVT assembly, or by cutting off the oil flow through the CVVT assembly, which puts the assembly in a "hold" state (neither retarded nor advanced).

4   Diagnosis of the CVVT system is beyond the scope of the home mechanic. However, there are components that you can replace at home.

5   The component replacement procedure for the CVVT assembly is in Chapter 2A. The replacement procedure for the OCV and the OCV filter are in this Section. The replacement procedures for various other sensors are located elsewhere in this Chapter.

COMPONENT REPLACEMENT

Oil Control Valve (OCV)

➡ **Note: The OCV is located at the front left corner of the cylinder head, to the left of the intake manifold.**

6   Remove the engine cover.
7   Disconnect the electrical connector from the OCV.
8   Remove the OCV retaining bolt and remove the OCV.
9   Installation is the reverse of removal.

Oil Control Valve (OCV) filter

➡ **Note: The OCV filter is located below the OCV and is screwed into the left end of the cylinder head.**

10 Remove the engine cover.
11 Unscrew the OCV filter.
12 Remove and discard the old OCV filter gasket.
13 Installation is the reverse of removal. Be sure to use a filter gasket and tighten the OCV filter securely.

CVVT Oil Temperature sensor

❋❋ **CAUTION:**

Make sure that the engine is cool before doing this procedure.

➡ **Note: This sensor is below the oil control valve at the front of the engine.**

14 Place rags beneath the sensor to catch oil spillage.
15 Disconnect the wiring from the sensor, then remove it.

❋❋ **CAUTION:**

Use a wrench only on the hex flats of the sensor to avoid damaging it.

16 Installation is the reverse of removal.

---

28 Variable Induction Control system (Sportage V6 models) - description and component replacement

DESCRIPTION

▸ **Refer to illustration 28.2**

1   Sportage V6 models are equipped with a variable induction control system, which changes the length of the intake manifold runners to optimize power and torque and to improve fuel efficiency across the range of engine operation.

2   The variable induction control system consists of two intake manifold control solenoids (Kia calls them intake manifold tuning valves) and two vacuum-operated diaphragms (which Kia calls vacuum valves) (see illustration).

3   The two PCM-controlled intake manifold tuning valves control vacuum to the two vacuum valves. Each vacuum valve actuates a bell crank connected to the valve by a linkage rod. In proportional response to the absence or presence of a given vacuum signal, the vacuum valve actuates the bell crank by pushing or pulling the link rod. Each bell crank is mounted on the end of a long shaft inside the intake manifold that opens and closes butterfly valves that open, restrict or close off passages inside the manifold, effectively altering the length of the intake tracts.

28.2 Variable induction control system details (Sportage V6 models):

1   Intake manifold control solenoid for plenum-side vacuum operated diaphragm
2   Plenum-side vacuum-operated diaphragm
3   Intake manifold control solenoid for intake-manifold-runner-side vacuum-operated diaphragm
4   Intake-manifold-runner-side vacuum-operated diaphragm

4   One vacuum valve controls the flow of air through the air intake plenum (Kia calls it the surge tank) and the other vacuum valve controls the flow of air through the intake manifold runners.

COMPONENT REPLACEMENT

Intake manifold control solenoid (intake manifold tuning valves)

▶ **Refer to illustration 28.5**

➡**Note: This procedure applies to either solenoid.**

5   Disconnect the electrical connector from the solenoid (see illustration).

6   Disconnect the vacuum hose from the solenoid.

7   Remove the solenoid mounting screws and remove the solenoid.

8   Installation is the reverse of removal.

Vacuum-operated diaphragms (vacuum valves)

➡**Note: This procedure applies to either diaphragm.**

9   Disconnect the vacuum hose from the diaphragm.

10 Pop the end of the link rod loose from the spherical bearing on the end of the bell crank rod.

11 Remove the diaphragm mounting screws and remove the diaphragm.

12 Installation is the reverse of removal.

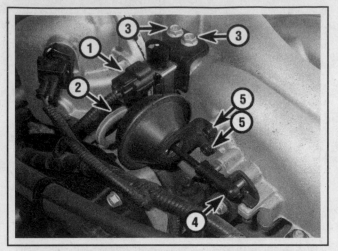

28.5 Intake manifold control solenoid and vacuum-operated diaphragm (intake manifold runner side shown, intake plenum setup similar):

1   *Solenoid electrical connector*
2   *Solenoid-to-diaphragm vacuum hose*
3   *Solenoid mounting bolts*
4   *Link rod-to-bellcrank connection (pulls off)*
5   *Diaphragm mounting screws*

Torque specifications	Ft-lbs (unless otherwise indicated)	Nm

➡ **Note: One foot-pound (ft-lb) of torque is equivalent to 12 inch-pounds (in-lbs) of torque. Torque values below approximately 15 foot-pounds are expressed in inch-pounds, because most foot-pound torque wrenches are not accurate at these smaller values.**

Engine Coolant Temperature (ECT) sensor		
1994 through 2004 (except 2.0L DOHC)	18 to 22	24 to 30
2.0L DOHC	11 to 15	15 to 20
2.7L V6	14 to 29	20 to 40
Exhaust Gas Recirculation (EGR) valve mounting bolts	168 to 192 in-lbs	19 to 21.5
Knock sensor mounting bolt (all knock sensors,		
all engines)	15 to 18	20 to 25
Oxygen sensors		
1994 through 2004 (except 2.0L DOHC)	22 to 36	30 to 49
2.0L DOHC and 2.7L V6 (all sensors)	36 to 43	49 to 59
Power Steering Pressure (PSP) switch*	19 to 21	26 to 28
Oil Control Valve (OCV) filter	86 to 104 in-lbs	9.5 to 11.5

    Does not apply to 2.0L DOHC and 2.7L V6 models.

Notes

Section

1 General information
2 Driveaxle oil seals - replacement
3 Shift lever - removal and installation
4 Back-up light switch - check and replacement
5 Manual transaxle - removal and installation
6 Manual transaxle overhaul - general information

Reference to other Chapters

Lubricant change - See Chapter 1
Lubricant level check - See Chapter 1
Transaxle mount - check and replacement - See Chapter 2A
Transfer case - See Chapter 8

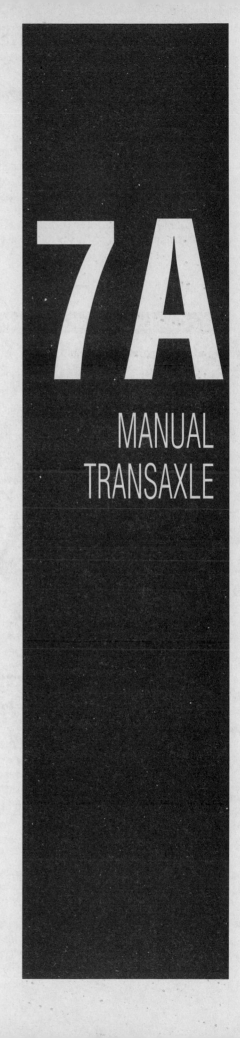

7A

MANUAL
TRANSAXLE

1 General information

The vehicles covered by this manual are equipped with a 5-speed manual transaxle or 4-speed automatic transaxle. Information on the manual transaxle is included in this Part of Chapter 7. Service procedures for the automatic transaxle are contained in Chapter 7, Part B.

The manual transaxle is a compact, two-piece, lightweight aluminum alloy housing containing both the transmission and differential assemblies. A F5M-R transaxle is used with the 1.6L SOHC engines and a G25M-R unit is used with the 1.8L DOHC BP engine. A F25M-R manual transaxle is used on the 1.6L DOHC B6 engine and 1.8L DOHC

T8 engines. All transaxles are virtually identical except for different gear ratios.

Because of the complexity, unavailability of replacement parts and special tools necessary, internal repair procedures for the manual transaxle are beyond the scope of this manual. For readers who wish to tackle a transaxle rebuild, a brief Manual transaxle overhaul, general information Section is provided. The bulk of information in this Chapter is devoted to removal and installation procedures.

2 Driveaxle oil seals - replacement

♦ **Refer to illustrations 2.4 and 2.6**

1   Oil leaks frequently occur due to wear of the driveaxle oil seals. Replacement of these seals is relatively easy, since the repair can be performed without removing the transaxle from the vehicle.

2   Driveaxle oil seals are located at the sides of the transaxle, where the driveaxles are attached. If leakage at the seal is suspected, raise the vehicle and support it securely on jackstands. If the seal is leaking, lubricant will be found on the sides of the transaxle, below the seals.

3   Refer to Chapter 8 and remove the driveaxle(s).

4   Use a screwdriver or prybar to carefully pry the oil seal out of the

transaxle bore (see illustration).

5   If the oil seal cannot be removed with a screwdriver or prybar, a special oil seal removal tool (available at auto parts stores) will be required.

6   Using a seal driver or a large deep socket (slightly smaller than the outside diameter of the seal) as a drift, install the new oil seal (see illustration). Drive it into the bore squarely and make sure it's completely seated. Coat the seal lip with transaxle lubricant.

7   Install the driveaxle(s). Be careful not to damage the lip of the new seal.

2.4 Carefully pry out the driveaxle oil seal with a seal removal tool or a large screwdriver. Make sure you don't damage the seal bore or the new seal may leak

2.6 Use a seal installer or a large socket to install the new seal

3 Shift lever - removal and installation

1   Remove the center console (see Chapter 11) and the rubber boot.

2   Raise the vehicle and support it securely on jackstands.

3   Working under the vehicle, disconnect the control rod from the shift lever and remove the bushings from the lever foot.

4   Working inside the vehicle, remove the hooked part of the spring

from the bracket groove, then remove the spring and upper ball seat.

5   Remove the shift lever.

6   Installation is the reverse of removal. Be sure to lubricate the bushings and ball seats with multi-purpose grease.

4   Back-up light switch - check and replacement

CHECK

1   The back-up light switch is located on the front side of the transaxle, near the bottom of the transaxle case.

2   Turn the ignition key to the On position and move the shift lever to the Reverse position. The switch should close the back-up light circuit and turn on the back-up lights.

3   If it doesn't, check the back-up light fuse (see Chapter 12).

4   If the fuse is okay, verify that there's voltage available on the battery side of the switch (ignition ON, engine not running).

5   If there's no voltage on the battery side of the switch, check the wire between the fuse and the switch; if there is voltage, put the shift lever in reverse and see if there's voltage on the ground side of the switch.

6   If there's no voltage on the ground side of the switch, replace the switch (see below); if there is voltage, note whether one or both back-up lights are out.

7   If only one bulb is out, replace it; if they're both out, the bulbs could be the problem, but it's more likely that the wire between the switch and the bulbs has an open somewhere.

REPLACEMENT

8   Unplug the electrical connector in the harness to the back-up light switch.

9   Unscrew and remove the old switch.

10   To test the new switch before installation, simply check continuity across the switch terminals: With the plunger depressed, there should be continuity; with the plunger free, there should be no continuity.

11   Screw in the new switch and tighten it securely.

12   Connect the electrical connector.

13   Check the switch to ensure that the circuit is working properly.

5   Manual transaxle - removal and installation

REMOVAL

1   Remove the battery and the battery tray (see Chapter 5).

2   Remove the air intake duct and the air filter housing (see Chapter 4).

3   Clearly label and disconnect all vacuum lines, emissions hoses and wiring harness connectors that may interfere with the transaxle removal. Use masking tape and/or a touch up paint applicator work well for marking items. Take instant photos or sketch the locations of components and brackets.

4   On early models, disconnect the speedometer cable.

5   Support the engine with an engine support fixture or an engine hoist (an engine support fixture is recommended, as it doesn't have legs that extend under the vehicle that would get in the way). Connect the sling or chain to the lifting eye attached to the left (driver's side) end of the cylinder head.

6   Remove the transaxle mount (see Chapter 2A).

7   Remove the transaxle-to-engine bolts accessible from the top.

8   Loosen the front wheel lug nuts, then raise the vehicle and support it on jackstands. Remove the front wheels.

9   Remove the engine splash shields (see Chapter 2A), the inner fender splash shields and the hood (see Chapter 11). Cover the fenders and cowl using special pads. An old bedspread or blanket will also work.

10   Drain the transaxle lubricant (see Chapter 1). Be sure to use a new sealing washer when you reinstall the drain plug.

11   Remove the starter (see Chapter 5).

12   Remove the clutch release cylinder without disconnecting the hydraulic fluid line (see Chapter 8). Position the release cylinder off to the side.

❊❊ CAUTION:

Do not depress the clutch pedal while the release cylinder is removed.

13   Remove the exhaust pipe from the exhaust manifold to the catalytic converter (see Chapter 4).

14   Disconnect the shifter extension bar and the shifter control rod from the transaxle and support them with wire.

15   On 2001 and earlier models, disconnect the stabilizer bar links (see Chapter 10).

16   Remove the driveaxles (see Chapter 8).

❊❊ CAUTION:

Install a special tool into each side of the transaxle to prevent the transaxle side gears from becoming misaligned. Check with your local auto parts store or specialty tool dealer for tool availability.

17   Remove the through-bolts from the front and rear engine mounts (see Chapter 2A), then remove the engine crossmember.

18   Remove the oil pan-to-transaxle bolts or the engine stiffener bolts (see Chapter 2A), if equipped.

19   Support the transaxle with a jack (preferably a special jack made for this purpose). Safety chains will help steady the transaxle on the jack.

20   Remove the transaxle-to-engine bolts accessible from below.

21   Make a final check that all wires and hoses have been disconnected from the transaxle.

22   Move the transaxle back to disengage it from the engine block dowel pins. Once the input shaft is clear of the splines in the clutch hub, lower the transaxle and remove it from under the vehicle.

➡**Note: It may be necessary to slowly lower the engine a little while the transaxle is being lowered. This will provide more clearance between the transaxle and the body.**

23   The clutch components can now be inspected (see Chapter 8). In most cases, new clutch components should be routinely installed whenever the transaxle is removed.

INSTALLATION

24 If removed, install clutch components (see Chapter 8). Lightly lubricate the splines of the transaxle input shaft with high-temperature grease.

25 With the transaxle secured to the jack as on removal, raise it into position and then carefully slide it forward, engaging the input shaft with the splines in the clutch hub. Do not use excessive force to install the transaxle - if the input shaft does not slide into place, readjust the angle of the transaxle so it is level and/or turn the input shaft so the splines engage properly with the clutch.

26 Install the transaxle-to-engine bolts. Tighten the bolts to the torque listed in this Chapter's Specifications.

✳✳ CAUTION:

Don't use the bolts to force the transaxle and engine together. If the transaxle doesn't slide easily up against the engine, find out why before you tighten the bolts.

27 Install the engine crossmember and tighten the bolts to the torque listed in this Chapter's Specifications.

28 Remove the transaxle support jack.

29 The remainder of installation is the reverse of removal.

30 Refill the transaxle with the recommended lubricant (see Chapter 1).

31 Road test the vehicle and check for fluid leaks.

6 Manual transaxle overhaul - general information

1 Overhauling a manual transaxle is a difficult job for the do-it-yourselfer. It involves the disassembly and reassembly of many small parts. Numerous clearances must be precisely measured and, if necessary, changed with select-fit spacers and snap-rings. As a result, if transaxle problems arise, it can be removed and installed by a competent do-it-yourselfer, but overhaul should be left to a transmission repair shop. Rebuilt transaxles may be available - check with your dealer parts department and auto parts stores. At any rate, the time and money involved in an overhaul is almost sure to exceed the cost of a rebuilt unit.

2 Nevertheless, it's not impossible for an inexperienced mechanic to rebuild a transaxle if the special tools are available and the job is done in a deliberate step-by-step manner so nothing is overlooked.

3 The tools necessary for an overhaul include internal and external snap-ring pliers, a bearing puller, a slide hammer, a set of pin punches, a dial indicator and possibly a hydraulic press. In addition, a large, sturdy workbench and a vise or transaxle stand will be required.

4 During disassembly of the transaxle, make careful notes of how each piece comes off, where it fits in relation to other pieces and what holds it in place.

5 Before taking the transaxle apart for repair, it will help if you have some idea what area of the transaxle is malfunctioning. Certain problems can be closely tied to specific areas in the transaxle, which can make component examination and replacement easier. Refer to the *Troubleshooting* section at the front of this manual for information regarding possible sources of trouble.

Torque specifications	Ft-lbs	Nm
Transaxle mounting bolts		
1994 through 1997		
Transaxle-to-engine bolts	48 to 65	65 to 88
Oil pan-to-transaxle bolts	28 to 38	38 to 52
1998 through 2004 models (except 2.0L DOHC)		
Three upper bolts	66 to 86	89 to 117
Five lower bolts	28 to 38	38 to 52
2.0L DOHC engine	32 to 41	43 to 56

7B

AUTOMATIC TRANSAXLE

Section

1 General information
2 Diagnosis - general
3 Throttle valve cable (1994 through 1997 models) - check, adjustment and replacement
4 Shift cable - removal, installation and adjustment
5 Shift lever - removal and installation
6 Shift interlock system - description and component replacement
7 Automatic transaxle - removal and installation
8 Automatic transaxle overhaul - general information
9 Transaxle oil cooler - removal and installation

Reference to other Chapters

Automatic transaxle fluid and filter change - See Chapter 1
Automatic transaxle fluid level check - See Chapter 1
Driveaxle oil seal replacement - See Chapter 7A
Transaxle mount replacement - See Chapter 2A
Transaxle range switch replacement - See Chapter 6
Transfer case - See Chapter 8

1 General information

All vehicles covered in this manual are equipped with either a 5-speed manual transaxle or a 4-speed automatic transaxle. All information on the automatic transaxle is included in this Part of Chapter 7. Information for the manual transaxle can be found in Part A of this Chapter.

The 4-speed automatic transaxle is electronically controlled with fourth gear being an overdrive gear. Shifts are attained by the use of shift solenoids, which are controlled by the Powertrain Control Module. The transaxles utilize a lock-up torque converter.

Because of the complexity of the automatic transaxles and the specialized equipment necessary to perform most service operations, this Chapter contains only those procedures related to general diagnosis, routine maintenance, adjustment and removal and installation.

If the transaxle requires major repair work, it should be left to a dealer service department or an automotive or transmission repair shop. You can, however, remove and install the transaxle yourself and save the expense, even if the repair work is done by a transmission shop (but be sure a proper diagnosis has been made before removing the transaxle).

2 Diagnosis - general

1   Automatic transaxle malfunctions may be caused by five general conditions:

   a) *Poor engine performance*
   b) *Improper adjustments*
   c) *Hydraulic malfunctions*
   d) *Mechanical malfunctions*
   e) *Malfunctions in the computer or its signal network*

2   Diagnosis of these problems should always begin with a check of the easily repaired items: fluid level and condition (see Chapter 1), shift cable adjustment and shift lever installation. Next, perform a road test to determine if the problem has been corrected or if more diagnosis is necessary. If the problem persists after the preliminary tests and corrections are completed, additional diagnosis should be performed by a dealer service department or other qualified transmission repair shop. Refer to the *Troubleshooting* section at the front of this manual for information on symptoms of transaxle problems.

PRELIMINARY CHECKS

3   Drive the vehicle to warm the transaxle to normal operating temperature.

4   Check the fluid level as described in Chapter 1:

   a) *If the fluid level is unusually low, add enough fluid to bring the level within the designated area of the dipstick, then check for external leaks (see below).*
   b) *If the fluid level is abnormally high, drain off the excess, then check the drained fluid for contamination by coolant. The presence of engine coolant in the automatic transmission fluid indicates that a failure has occurred in the internal radiator walls that separate the coolant from the transmission fluid (see Chapter 3).*
   c) *If the fluid is foaming, drain it and refill the transaxle, then check for coolant in the fluid, or a high fluid level.*

5   Make sure the engine idle speed is correct. If the idle speed is incorrect, have it adjusted by a dealer service department or other qualified repair shop before proceeding.

6   On 1994 through 1997 models, check the throttle valve cable for freedom of movement. Adjust it if necessary (see Section 3).

➡**Note: The throttle valve cable may function properly when the engine is shut off and cold, but it may malfunction once the engine is hot. Check it cold and at normal engine operating temperature.**

7   Inspect the shift cable. Make sure that it's properly adjusted and operates smoothly (see Section 3).

FLUID LEAK DIAGNOSIS

8   Most fluid leaks are easy to locate visually. Repair usually consists of replacing a seal or gasket. If a leak is difficult to find, the following procedure may help.

9   Identify the fluid. Make sure it's transmission fluid and not engine oil or brake fluid (automatic transmission fluid is a deep, red color).

10   Try to pinpoint the source of the leak. Drive the vehicle several miles, then park it over a large sheet of cardboard. After a minute or two, you should be able to locate the leak by determining the source of the fluid dripping onto the cardboard.

11   Make a careful visual inspection of the suspected component and the area immediately around it. Pay particular attention to gasket mating surfaces. A mirror is often helpful for finding leaks in areas that are hard to see.

12   If the leak still cannot be found, clean the suspected area thoroughly with a degreaser or solvent, then dry it.

13   Drive the vehicle for several miles at normal operating temperature and varying speeds. After driving the vehicle, visually inspect the suspected component again.

14   Once the leak has been located, the cause must be determined before it can be properly repaired. If a gasket is replaced but the sealing flange is bent, the new gasket will not stop the leak. The bent flange must be straightened.

15   Before attempting to repair a leak, check to make sure that the following conditions are corrected or they may cause another leak.

➡**Note: Some of the following conditions cannot be fixed without highly specialized tools and expertise. Such problems must be referred to a transmission shop or a dealer service department.**

Seal leaks

16   If a transaxle seal is leaking, the fluid level or pressure may be too high, the vent may be plugged, the seal bore may be damaged, the seal itself may be damaged or improperly installed, the surface of the shaft protruding through the seal may be damaged or a loose bearing may be causing excessive shaft movement.

17   Make sure the dipstick tube seal is in good condition and the tube is properly seated. Periodically check the area around the speedometer gear or sensor for leakage. If transmission fluid is evident, check the O-ring for damage.

Case leaks

18 If the case itself appears to be leaking, the casting is porous and will have to be repaired or replaced.

19 Make sure the oil cooler hose fittings are tight and in good condition.

Fluid comes out vent pipe or fill tube

20 If this condition occurs, the transaxle is overfilled, there is coolant in the fluid, the case is porous, the dipstick is incorrect, the vent is plugged or the drain-back holes are plugged.

---

3   Throttle valve cable (1994 through 1997 models) - check, adjustment and replacement

CHECK

1 Check the cable and housing for damage.

2 Actuate the accelerator through its full range of travel and ensure it doesn't bind, and that it returns rapidly and completely.

3 Replace the throttle valve cable if it doesn't operate smoothly.

ADJUSTMENT

◆ **Refer to illustrations 3.7 and 3.10**

4 Remove the square-head plug on the front of the transaxle and install an oil pressure gauge (capable of reading up to 100 psi) in the test port.

5 With the shift lever in the Park (P) position, start the engine and let it warm up to normal operating temperature.

6 Check the idle speed adjustment (see Chapter 1) and ensure that it is adjusted correctly.

7 Loosen the bolts securing the throttle cable to the bracket on the front side of the throttle body assembly.

➡**Note: First loosen the bolt on the driver's side (left side; closest to the throttle valve) (see illustration) and then the bolt on the right side.**

8 Check and ensure that the throttle valve lever on the throttle body is in the closed position.

9 Tighten the left cable bolt (see illustration 3.7) securely.

10 Pull the throttle cable toward the right side of the vehicle (see illustration) until the line pressure exceeds the specified pressure range listed in this Chapter's Specifications.

11 Push the throttle cable toward the left side of the vehicle until the line pressure decreases to the adjustment pressure listed in this Chapter's Specifications.

✳✳ CAUTION:

If the line pressure will not decrease to the adjustment pressure, tighten the right side bolt with the line pressure at the closest reading to the adjustment pressure.

12 Tighten the right side bolt securely.

13 Stop the engine and ensure that the throttle cable moves smoothly.

14 Restart the engine and accelerate it slightly, then let it run at idle speed.

15 Verify that the line pressure is within the specified pressure range listed in this Chapter's Specifications.

16 If the line pressure is not correct, repeat the adjustment procedure.

17 Turn off the engine, remove the pressure gauge and install the square-head plug.

➡**Note: Wrap the threads of the plug with Teflon tape to prevent leakage.**

3.7 Loosen the cable mounting bolt on the driver's side first and then the bolt on the right side

3.10 Pull the throttle cable toward the right side (arrow direction) of the vehicle

3.26 Disconnect the solenoid connectors

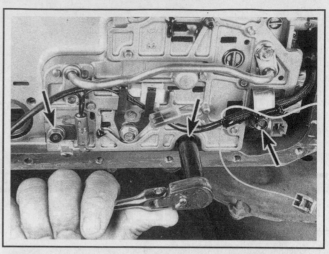

3.27 Loosen then remove the control valve body mounting bolts (there are nine of them - arrows point to three)

3.28 Remove the cable from the throttle cam in the transaxle

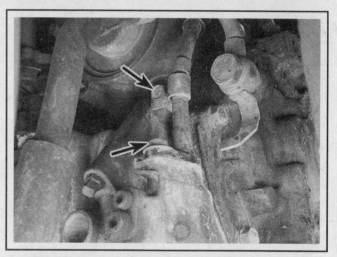

3.29 Remove the cable-to-transaxle mounting bolts

REPLACEMENT

▶ **Refer to illustrations 3.26, 3.27, 3.28 and 3.29**

18 Remove the battery and battery tray (see Chapter 5, Section 1).

19 Loosen and remove the bolts securing the throttle valve cable to the bracket on the front side of the throttle body assembly.

➡**Note: First loosen the bolt on the driver's side (left side; closest to the throttle valve) (see illustration 3.7) and then the bolt on the right side.**

20 Remove the throttle valve cable from the throttle lever on the throttle body.

21 Loosen the left front wheel lug nuts, then raise the vehicle and support it securely on jackstands. Remove the wheel and the engine splash shield.

22 Drain the transaxle lubricant into a suitable container (see Chapter 1).

23 Support the engine from above by using an engine hoist or support fixture.

➡**Note: Although after the next Step the engine and transaxle will still be connected to the chassis by the mounts at the timing belt end of the engine and at the transaxle, supporting the powertrain from above will give an added measure of safety and prevent the engine/transaxle from tipping forward or backward, which could damage surrounding components.**

24 Remove the front and rear engine mount through-bolts (NOT the mount at the timing belt end of the engine or the one connected to the transaxle), then remove the engine crossmember.

25 Remove the transaxle oil pan and gasket (see Chapter 1).

26 Disconnect the solenoid connectors (see illustration).

27 Remove the control valve body mounting bolts (see illustration) and lower the valve body from the transaxle.

28 Remove the throttle valve cable from the throttle cam in the transaxle (see illustration).

29 Remove the mounting bolts and throttle cable from the transaxle (see illustration).

30 Install a new throttle valve cable to the throttle cam in the transaxle.

31 Connect the throttle valve cable to the throttle lever on the throttle body.

32 Attach the throttle cable to the transaxle using new bolts and tighten the bolts securely.

33 Install the control valve body, tightening the bolts to the torque listed in this Chapter's Specifications.

⁂ CAUTION:

There are two bolt lengths; installing the long bolts in the wrong position could cause severe damage.

34 Reconnect the solenoid connectors.
35 Install the transaxle oil pan (see Chapter 1).

36 Install the engine crossmember. Tighten the bolts to the torque listed in this Chapter's Specifications.

37 Remove the engine support fixture or hoist.

38 Reinstall the battery and battery tray (see Chapter 5, Section 1).

⁂ WARNING:

When connecting the battery cables always attach the positive cable first.

39 Fill the transaxle with the proper type and amount of fluid (see Chapter 1).

40 Adjust the throttle valve cable as described in Steps 4 through 17.

4   Shift cable - removal, installation and adjustment

⁂ WARNING:

The models covered by this manual are equipped with Supplemental Restraint systems (SRS), more commonly known as airbags. Always disable the airbag system before working in the vicinity of any airbag system component to avoid the possibility of accidental deployment of the airbag, which could cause personal injury (see Chapter 12). Do not use a memory saving device to preserve the PCM's memory when working on or near airbag system components.

REMOVAL AND INSTALLATION

◆ **Refer to illustrations 4.3a, 4.3b, 4.3c, 4.5, 4.7 and 4.8**

1 Disconnect the cable from the negative terminal of the battery (see Chapter 5, Section 1).

2 Remove the air filter housing (see Chapter 4) to access the top of the transaxle where the shift cable is attached.

3 Move the shift lever to the Park (P) position. Disconnect the shift cable end from the transaxle (see illustrations).

4 Remove the center console (see Chapter 11).

5 Remove the nut securing the shift cable to the shift lever (see illustration) and pull the cable end from the lever.

➡Note: With the console removed you will see two cables coming into the front of the shift mechanism. The shift cable is on the left (driver's side) and the shift interlock cable is on the right (passenger's side).

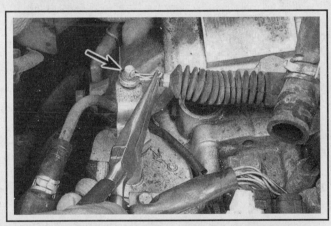

4.3a On early models, remove the retaining clip and detach the shift cable from the shift lever on the transaxle

4.3b On later models (without a retaining clip), unscrew the nut and detach the lever, which is permanently attached to the cable end, from the transaxle shift shaft

4.3c Remove the bracket clip and lift the shift cable off the bracket

4.5 Remove the nut securing the cable end to the shift lever (A), then remove the bolts securing the cable casing (B)

4.7 Remove the nuts and position the airbag control unit off to the side (radio and climate control head removed for clarity)

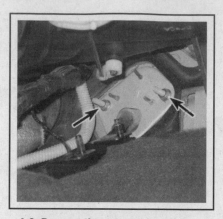

4.8 Remove these two nuts and detach the grommet plate from the firewall

4.13 Shift cable measurement points (1994 through 2004 models, except 2.0L DOHC models)

6   Remove the bolts securing the shift cable to the shift lever assembly (see illustration 4.5).

7   Unbolt the airbag control unit from the floor pan, but don't disconnect the electrical connector (see illustration). Also unbolt the Powertrain Control Module (PCM) and position it off to the side (see Chapter 6).

8   Follow the cable up to the firewall and remove the two nuts that retain the grommet plate (see illustration). Lift the cable clear of the shift lever assembly and pull the cable into the interior of the vehicle.

9   Installation is the reverse of removal. Proceed to adjust the shift cable.

ADJUSTMENT

1994 through 2004 models (except 2.0L DOHC models)

♦ Refer to illustration 4.13

10 Move the shift lever to the Park (P) position.

11 Loosen the two shift cable mounting bolts, if they're not already loose (see illustration 4.5).

12 While holding the shift lever forward against the stop, tighten the

shift cable mounting bolts securely.

13 Move the shift lever to the Neutral (N) position. Measure the distance between the indicated points (see illustration). Compare the measurement to the distance listed in this Chapter's Specifications.

14 If the distance is incorrect, loosen the two shift cable bolts and adjust the shift cable to achieve the specified distance between the measurement points.

15 Check the operation of the transaxle in each shift lever position. Try to start the engine in each gear. The starter should operate in the Park and Neutral positions only.

2004 and later (2.0L DOHC) models

16 Put the shift lever in the Neutral position.

17 Put the transmission manual control lever (on the Transmission Range switch) in the Neutral position.

18 Loosen the cable adjusting nut on the manual control lever.

19 Push the cable toward the manual control lever to eliminate freeplay, then tighten the cable adjusting nut.

20 Have an assistant move the shift lever inside the vehicle through its range of gear positions and verify that the manual control lever moves freely.

5   Shift lever - removal and installation

♦ Refer to illustrations 5.3, 5.6 and 5.7

❋❋ WARNING:

The models covered by this manual are equipped with Supplemental Restraint Systems (SRS), more commonly known as airbags. Always disable the airbag system before working in the vicinity of any airbag system component to avoid the possibility of accidental deployment of the airbag, which could cause personal injury (see Chapter 12). Do not use a memory saving device to preserve the PCM's memory when working on or near airbag system components.

1   Disconnect the cable from the negative battery terminal (see Chapter 5, Section 1).

2   Remove the aunter console (see Chapter 11).

3   Remove the knob from the shift lever (see illustration).

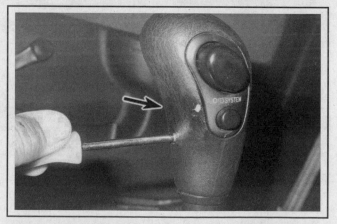

5.3 Remove the screws from the shift knob (one hidden from view) and separate the shift knob from the shift lever

5.6 Unplug the electrical connectors at the rear of the shifter assembly

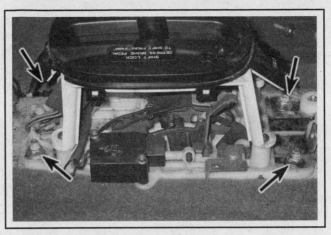

5.7 Remove the shifter mounting nuts

4   Remove the shift cable from the shift lever assembly (see Section 4).

5   Remove the shift interlock cable from the shift lever base (see Section 6).

6   Disconnect the electrical connectors (see illustration).

7   Remove the four nuts that secure the shifter assembly to the floor pan (see illustrations).

8   Lift the shift assembly clear of the mounting studs.

9   Installation is the reverse of removal.

10 Adjust the shift cable (see Section 4).

---

6   Shift interlock system - description and component replacement

DESCRIPTION

1   Vehicles equipped with an automatic transaxle have an interlock system to prevent unintentional shifting out of the Park position. The interlock system consists of two subsystems: a shift lock system and a key interlock system.

Shift lock system

▶ **Refer to illustration 6.2**

2   The shift lock system prevents the shift lever from moving from the Park position unless the brake pedal is depressed. In the event of a system malfunction, you can release the shift lever by removing the cover and inserting a screwdriver into the slot on the right front of the shift indicator panel (see illustration).

Key interlock system

3   The key interlock system prevents the ignition key from being turned to the Lock position or removed from the ignition switch unless the shift lever is in the Park position. It is actuated by a cable between the shift lever assembly and the ignition key lock cylinder.

COMPONENT REPLACEMENT

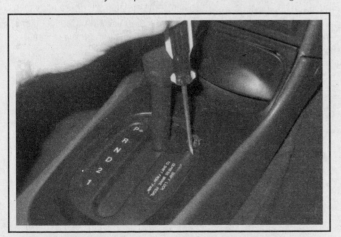

6.2 If the shift interlock system malfunctions, remove the cover and insert a screwdriver into the hole (this will manually release the shifter lock and allow the shifter to be moved from the Park position)

> ❋❋ **WARNING:**
>
> **The models covered by this manual are equipped with Supplemental Restraint systems (SRS), more commonly known as airbags. Always disable the airbag system before working in the vicinity of any airbag system component to avoid the possibility of accidental deployment of the airbag, which could cause personal injury (see Chapter 12). Do not use a memory saving device to preserve the PCM's memory when working on or near airbag system components.**

Key interlock cable

▶ **Refer to illustrations 6.6 and 6.7**

4   Remove the center console, the steering column covers and the driver's knee bolster (see Chapter 11).

6.6 Loosen this nut and detach the interlock cable from the shift lever base

6.7 Remove the bolt (A) that secures the key interlock cable to the ignition lock cylinder, then detach the cable end from the pin on the interlock mechanism (B)

6.13 Remove the shift interlock solenoid mounting nuts, then lift the solenoid off the studs and detach the plunger from the post

5 Unbolt the airbag control unit from the floor pan, but don't disconnect the electrical connector (see illustration 4.7).

6 Loosen the nut on the key interlock cable and detach the cable from the shift lever base (see illustration).

7 Remove the bolt securing the cable to the ignition lock cylinder, then detach the cable end from the pin on the interlock mechanism (see illustration).

8 Note how the cable is routed, then detach the cable from any clips and remove it.

9 Installation is the reverse of removal.

Shift lock solenoid

Refer to illustration 6.13

10 Remove the center console (see Chapter 11).

11 Move the shift lever to the Park position.

12 Follow the wiring harness from the solenoid to the electrical connector, then unplug the connector.

13 Remove the mounting nuts from the shift interlock solenoid (see illustration). Lift the solenoid off the studs and detach the plunger from the post.

14 Installation is the reverse of removal.

7   Automatic transaxle - removal and installation

✳✳ WARNING:

The models covered by this manual are equipped with Supplemental Restraint systems (SRS), more commonly known as airbags. Always disable the airbag system before working in the vicinity of any airbag system component to avoid the possibility of accidental deployment of the airbag, which could cause personal injury (see Chapter 12). Do not use a memory saving device to preserve the PCM's memory when working on or near airbag system components.

REMOVAL

▶ **Refer to illustrations 7.13, 7.19, 7.21 and 7.22**

1 Remove the battery and the battery tray (see Chapter 5).

2 Remove the air intake duct and the air filter housing (see Chapter 4).

3 Clearly label and disconnect all vacuum lines, emissions hoses and wiring harness connectors that may interfere with the transaxle removal. Masking tape and/or a touch up paint applicator work well for marking items. Take instant photos or sketch the locations of components and brackets.

4 Disconnect the transaxle shift cable (see Section 4).

5 Disconnect the transaxle throttle valve cable, if equipped (see Section 3).

6 Support the engine with an engine support fixture or an engine hoist (an engine support fixture is recommended, as it doesn't have legs that extend under the vehicle that would get in the way). Connect the sling or chain to the lifting eye attached to the left end (driver's side) end of the cylinder head.

7 Remove the transaxle mount (see Chapter 2A).

8 Remove the transaxle-to-engine bolts accessible from the top.

9 Disconnect the automatic transaxle fluid cooler lines from the transaxle. Be sure to position a pan to catch excess fluid. Plug the lines to prevent leakage.

10 Loosen the front wheel lug nuts, then raise the vehicle and support it on jackstands. Remove the front wheels.

11 Remove the engine splash shields (see Chapter 2A), the inner fender splash shields and the hood (see Chapter 11). Cover the fenders and cowl using special pads. An old bedspread or blanket will also work.

12 Drain the transaxle fluid (see Chapter 1). Be sure to use a new sealing washer when you reinstall the drain plug.

13 On early models, disconnect the speedometer cable (see illustration).

14 Remove the starter (see Chapter 5).

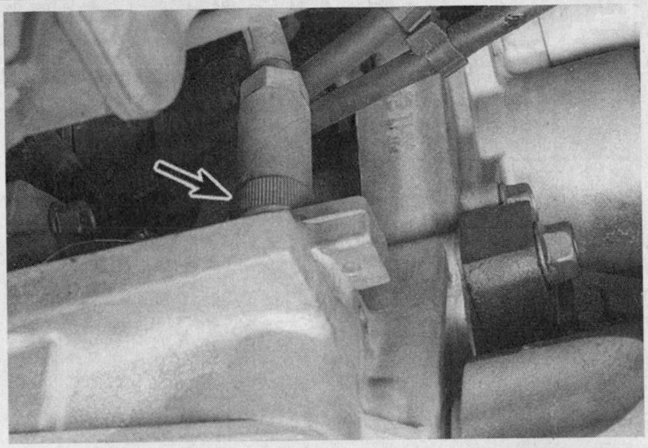

7.13 Location of the speedometer cable on early models

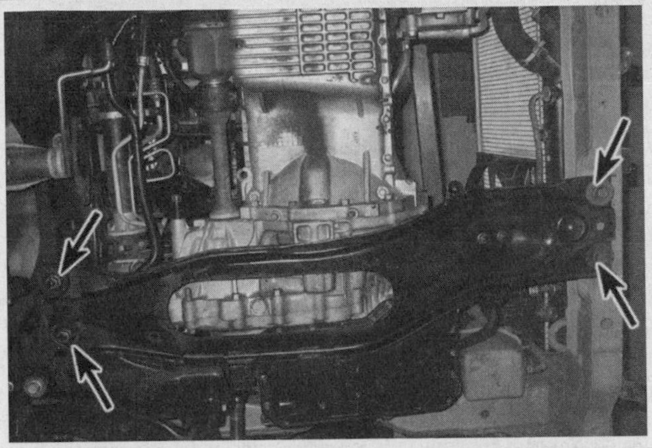

7.19 Location of the transaxle crossmember mounting fasteners

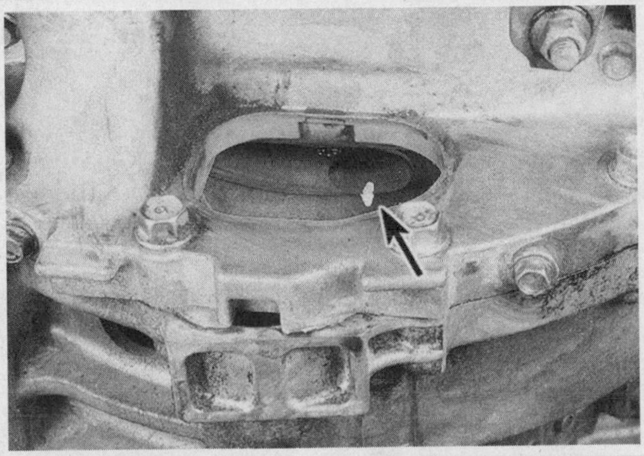

7.21 Mark the relationship of the torque converter to the driveplate to ensure proper dynamic balance when it's reattached . . .

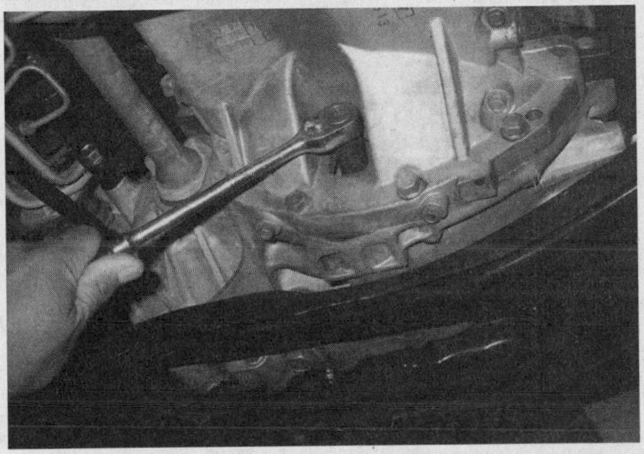

7.22 . . . then remove the torque converter bolts by rotating the crankshaft to bring each bolt to the bottom

15 Remove the exhaust pipe from the exhaust manifold to the catalytic converter (see Chapter 4).

16 Disconnect the shifter extension bar and the shifter control rod from the transaxle and support them with wire.

17 On 2001 and earlier models, disconnect the stabilizer bar links (see Chapter 10).

18 Remove the driveaxles (see Chapter 8).

CAUTION:

Install a special tool into each side of the transaxle to prevent the transaxle side gears from becoming misaligned. Check with your local auto parts store or specialty tool dealer for tool availability.

19 Remove the through-bolts from the front and rear engine mounts (see Chapter 2A), then remove the engine crossmember (see illustration).

20 Remove the driveplate inspection cover, if equipped.

Note: Some models are equipped with a driveplate cover, while other models are equipped with an access hole in the oil pan stiffener.

21 Mark the relationship of the torque converter to the driveplate so that they can be reinstalled in the same relationship to one another (see illustration).

22 Remove the torque converter or flywheel-to-driveplate bolts one at a time by rotating the crankshaft pulley for access to each bolt (see illustration).

23 Support the transaxle with a jack (preferably a special jack made for this purpose). Safety chains will help steady the transaxle on the jack.

24 Remove the transaxle-to-engine bolts accessible from below.

25 Make a final check that all wires and hoses have been disconnected from the transaxle.

26 Move the transaxle back to disengage it from the engine block dowel pins, and make sure the torque converter is detached from the driveplate. Lower the transaxle and remove it from under the vehicle. It's a good idea to clamp a pair of locking pliers on the transaxle case to prevent the torque converter from falling out.

Note: It may be necessary to slowly lower the engine a little while the transaxle is being lowered. This will provide more clearance between the transaxle and the body.

INSTALLATION

27 Flush the transaxle cooler lines thoroughly and make sure no solvent remains in the lines or cooler (radiator) after flushing. It's a good idea to repeat the flushing procedure with clean automatic transmission fluid to ensure that no solvent remains in the lines or cooler.

28 Prior to installation, make sure that the torque converter hub is securely engaged in the pump. With the transaxle secured to the jack, raise it into position. Be sure to keep it level so the torque converter does not slide out.

29 Turn the torque converter to line it up with the driveplate. The marks you made on the torque converter and the driveplate must line up.

30 Make sure the dowel pins are still installed, then move the transaxle forward carefully until the dowel pins and the torque converter are engaged.

31 Install the transaxle-to-engine bolts and the oil pan-to-transaxle bolts, if equipped. Tighten the bolts evenly to the torque listed in this Chapter's Specifications.

✳✳ CAUTION:

Don't use the bolts to force the transaxle and engine together. If the transaxle doesn't slide easily up against the engine, find out why before you tighten the bolts.

32 Install the oil pan stiffener, if equipped (see Chapter 2A).

33 The remainder of installation is the reverse of removal.

34 Refill the transaxle with fluid to the specified level (see Chapter 1). Note that the transaxle may require more fluid than in a normal fluid and filter change, since the torque converter may be empty (the converter is not drained during a fluid change).

35 Start the engine, set the parking brake and shift the transaxle through all gears three times. Make sure the shift cable is working properly (see Section 4).

36 Allow the engine to reach its proper operating temperature, then check the fluid level (see Chapter 1).

37 Road test the vehicle and check for fluid leaks.

8   Automatic transaxle overhaul - general information

In the event of a problem occurring, it will be necessary to establish whether the fault is electrical, mechanical or hydraulic in nature, before repair work can be contemplated. Diagnosis requires detailed knowledge of the transaxle's operation and construction, as well as access to specialized test equipment, and so is deemed to be beyond the scope of this manual. It is therefore essential that problems with the automatic transaxle are referred to a dealer service department or other qualified repair facility for assessment.

Note that a faulty transaxle should not be removed before the vehicle has been diagnosed by a knowledgeable technician equipped with the proper tools, as troubleshooting must be performed with the transaxle installed in the vehicle.

9   Transaxle oil cooler - removal and installation

▶ **Refer to illustration 9.2**

➡**Note: The transaxle oil cooler is located in front of the left part of the air conditioning condenser, which is located in front of the radiator.**

1   Remove the bumper cover (see Chapter 11).

2   Loosen the hose clamps and disconnect both hoses from the cooler (see illustration). Plug the hoses immediately to prevent transaxle fluid from running out.

3   Remove the oil cooler mounting bolts and remove the cooler.

4   Installation is the reverse of removal.

5   Check the fluid level in the transaxle and add transmission fluid as necessary (see Chapter 1).

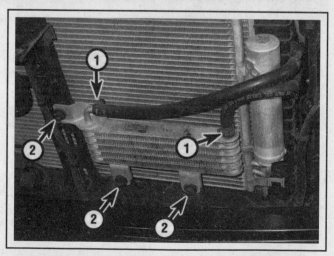

9.2 Automatic transaxle oil cooler details (Sportage models with an automatic transaxle)

1   *Cooler line hose clamps*   2   *Oil cooler mounting bolts*

Specifications

Throttle valve cable adjustment (1994 through 1997 models)

Specified pressure (engine idling)
    1.6L SOHC models
        2-valve   51 to 64 psi (353 to 441 kPa)
        4-valve   61 to 81 psi (422 to 559 kPa)
    1.6L DOHC B6 and 1.8L DOHC BP models   61 to 81 psi (422 to 559 kPa)
Adjustment pressure (engine idling)
    1.6L SOHC models
        2-valve   60 psi (410 kPa)
        4-valve   74 psi (510 kPa)
    1.6L DOHC B6 models   74 psi (510 kPa)
    1.8L DOHC BP models   71 psi (490 kPa)

Shift cable adjustment

Distance "A"
    1994 through 1997 (see illustration 4.13)   3.12 inches (79.3 mm)
    1998 through 2004 (except 2.0L DOHC)   3.66 inches (93.0 mm)

Torque specifications	Ft-lbs (unless otherwise indicated)	Nm

➡**Note: One foot-pound (ft-lb) of torque is equivalent to 12 inch-pounds (in-lbs) of torque. Torque values below approximately 15 foot-pounds are expressed in inch-pounds, because most foot-pound torque wrenches are not accurate at these smaller values.**

	Ft-lbs	Nm
Torque converter-to-driveplate bolts	26 to 36	34 to 49
Transaxle-to-engine bolts		
1994 through 1997 models	48 to 65	65 to 88
1998 and later models	65 to 86	89 to 118
Engine oil pan-to-transaxle bolts	See Chapter 2A	
Control valve body bolts	70 to 94 in-lbs	8 to 11
Engine crossmember-to-vehicle frame bolts	48 to 65	65 to 88

Notes

8

CLUTCH AND DRIVELINE

Section

1   General information

2   Clutch - description and check

3   Clutch master cylinder - removal and installation

4   Clutch release cylinder - removal and installation

5   Clutch hydraulic system - bleeding

6   Clutch components - removal, inspection and installation

7   Clutch release bearing and lever - removal, inspection and installation

8   Clutch pedal adjustment

9   Clutch start switch - check and replacement

10   Driveaxles - removal and installation

11   Driveaxle boot - replacement

12   Universal joint (4WD models) - general information and check

13   Driveshaft (4WD models) - check, removal and installation

14   Universal joint (4WD models) - replacement

15   Rear driveaxle oil seal (4WD models) - replacement

16   Rear differential (4WD models) - removal and installation

17   Transfer case (4WD models) - removal and installation

1   General information

The information in this Chapter deals with the components from the rear of the engine to the front wheels, except for the transaxle, which is dealt with in the previous Chapter. For the purposes of this Chapter, these components are grouped into two categories - clutch and driveline. Separate Sections within this Chapter offer general descriptions and checking procedures for components in each of the two groups.

Since nearly all the procedures covered in this Chapter involve working under the vehicle, make sure it's securely supported on sturdy jackstands or on a hoist where the vehicle can be easily raised and lowered.

2   Clutch - description and check

1   All vehicles with a manual transaxle use a single dry-plate, diaphragm-spring type clutch. The clutch disc has a splined hub which allows it to slide along the splines of the transaxle input shaft. The clutch and pressure plate are held in contact by spring pressure exerted by the diaphragm in the pressure plate.

2   The clutch release system is operated by hydraulic pressure. The hydraulic release system consists of the clutch pedal, a master cylinder and fluid reservoir, the hydraulic line, a release (or slave) cylinder which actuates the clutch release lever and the clutch release (or throwout) bearing.

3   When pressure is applied to the clutch pedal to release the clutch, hydraulic pressure is exerted against the outer end of the clutch release lever. As the lever pivots the shaft fingers push against the release bearing. The bearing pushes against the fingers of the diaphragm spring of the pressure plate assembly, which in turn releases the clutch plate.

4   Terminology can be a problem when discussing the clutch components because common names are in some cases different from those used by the manufacturer. For example, the driven plate is also called the clutch plate or disc, the clutch release bearing is sometimes called a throwout bearing, the release cylinder is sometimes called the operating or slave cylinder.

5   Other than to replace components with obvious damage, some preliminary checks should be performed to diagnose clutch problems. These checks assume that the transaxle is in good working condition.

a) The first check should be of the fluid level in the clutch master cylinder reservoir (see Chapter 1). If the fluid level is low, add fluid as necessary and inspect the hydraulic system for leaks. If the master cylinder reservoir has run dry, bleed the system as described in Section 5 and retest the clutch operation.

b) To check clutch spin-down time, run the engine at normal idle speed with the transaxle in Neutral (clutch pedal up - engaged). Disengage the clutch (pedal down), wait several seconds and shift the transaxle into Reverse. No grinding noise should be heard. A grinding noise would most likely indicate a problem in the pressure plate or the clutch disc.

c) To check for complete clutch release, run the engine (with the parking brake applied to prevent movement) and hold the clutch pedal approximately 1/2-inch from the floor. Shift the transaxle between 1st gear and Reverse several times. If the shift is rough, component failure is indicated. Check the release cylinder pushrod travel. With the clutch pedal depressed completely, the release cylinder pushrod should extend substantially. If it doesn't, check the fluid level in the clutch master cylinder.

d) Visually inspect the pivot bushing at the top of the clutch pedal to make sure there is no binding or excessive play.

e) Crawl under the vehicle and make sure the clutch release lever is solidly mounted on the ball stud.

3   Clutch master cylinder - removal and installation

✳✳ CAUTION:

Don't allow brake fluid to come into contact with the paint, as it will damage the finish.

REMOVAL

1   If you're working on a 1998 or later model, clamp a pair of locking pliers onto the clutch fluid feed hose, a couple of inches downstream of the reservoir. The pliers should be just tight enough to prevent fluid flow when the hose is disconnected. Loosen the fluid feed hose clamp and detach the hose from the cylinder. Have rags handy as some fluid will be lost as the line is removed.

2   Disconnect the hydraulic line at the cylinder. Cap or plug the ends of the lines (and/or hose) to prevent fluid leakage and the entry of contaminants.

3   Working under the dashboard, remove the cotter pin or spring clip from the master cylinder pushrod clevis. Pull out the clevis pin to disconnect the pushrod from the pedal. Unscrew the two clutch master cylinder retaining nuts and remove the cylinder.

INSTALLATION

4   Installation is the reverse of removal, noting the following points:

a) Use a new gasket between the master cylinder and the firewall. Tighten the master cylinder mounting nuts securely.

b) Fill the clutch master cylinder reservoir with brake fluid conforming to DOT 3 specifications and bleed the clutch system as described in Section 5.

4   Clutch release cylinder - removal and installation

REMOVAL

1   Raise the front of the vehicle and support it securely on jackstands. Remove the engine splash shield (see Chapter 2A).

2   Disconnect the hydraulic line at the cylinder. Cap or plug the end of the line to prevent fluid leakage and the entry of contaminants. Have a small can and rags handy - some fluid will be spilled as the line is removed.

3   Remove the two release cylinder mounting bolts and remove the release cylinder.

INSTALLATION

4   Lightly lubricate the release cylinder pushrod and the release fork pocket with high temperature grease. Install the release cylinder on the clutch housing. Make sure the pushrod is seated in the release fork pocket, then tighten the mounting bolts to the torque listed in this Chapter's Specifications.

5   Connect the hydraulic line to the release cylinder.

6   The remainder of installation is the reverse of removal, noting the following points:

    a) *Fill the clutch master cylinder with brake fluid conforming to DOT 3 specifications.*

    b) *Bleed the system as described in Section 5.*

5   Clutch hydraulic system - bleeding

1   Bleed the hydraulic system whenever any part of the system has been removed or the fluid level has fallen so low that air has been drawn into the master cylinder. The bleeding procedure is very similar to bleeding a brake system.

2   Fill the clutch master cylinder reservoir with new brake fluid conforming to DOT 3 specifications.

✻✻ CAUTION:

Do not re-use any of the fluid coming from the system during the bleeding operation or use fluid which has been inside an open container for an extended period of time.

3   Working at the release cylinder, remove the dust cap which fits over the bleeder valve and push a length of plastic hose over the valve.

Place the other end of the hose into a clear container with about two inches of brake fluid. The hose end must be in the fluid at the bottom of the container.

4   Have an assistant depress the clutch pedal and hold it. Open the bleeder valve on the release cylinder, allowing fluid to flow through the hose. Close the bleeder valve when the flow of fluid (and bubbles) ceases. Once closed, have your assistant release the pedal.

5   Continue this process until all air is evacuated from the system, indicated by a solid stream of fluid being ejected from the bleeder valve each time with no air bubbles in the hose or container. Keep a close watch on the fluid level inside the clutch master cylinder reservoir - if the level drops too far, air will get into the system and you'll have to start all over again.

6   Check carefully for proper operation before placing the vehicle into normal service.

6   Clutch components - removal, inspection and installation

✻✻ WARNING:

Dust produced by clutch wear is hazardous to your health. DO NOT blow it out with compressed air and DO NOT inhale it. DO NOT use gasoline or petroleum-based solvents to remove the dust. Brake system cleaner should be used to flush the dust into a drain pan. After the clutch components are wiped clean with a rag, dispose of the contaminated rags and cleaner in a covered, marked container.

REMOVAL

▶ **Refer to illustration 6.5**

1   Access to the clutch components is normally accomplished by removing the transaxle, leaving the engine in the vehicle. If the engine is being removed for major overhaul, check the clutch for wear and replace worn components as necessary. However, the relatively low cost of the clutch components compared to the time and trouble spent gaining access to them warrants their replacement anytime the engine or transaxle is removed, unless they are new or in near-perfect condition. The following procedures are based on the assumption the engine will stay in place.

2   Remove the transaxle from the vehicle (see Chapter 7, Part A).

3   The clutch fork and release bearing can remain attached to the transaxle housing for the time being.

Clutch disc and pressure plate

4   To support the clutch disc during removal, install a clutch alignment tool through the clutch disc hub.

5   Carefully inspect the flywheel and pressure plate for indexing marks. The marks are usually an X, an O or a white letter. If they cannot be found, scribe or paint marks yourself so the pressure plate and the fly-

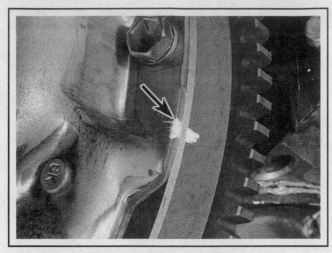

6.5 Mark the relationship of the pressure plate to the flywheel (if you're planning to re-use the old pressure plate)

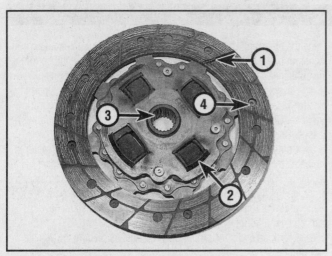

6.9 The clutch disc

1   *Lining - this will wear down in use*
2   *Springs or dampers - check for cracking and deformation*
3   *Splined hub - the splines must not be worn and should slide smoothly on the transaxle input shaft splines*
4   *Rivets - these secure the lining and will damage the flywheel or pressure plate if allowed to contact the surfaces*

wheel will be in the same alignment during installation (see illustration).

6   Turning each bolt a little at a time, loosen the pressure plate-to-flywheel bolts. Work in a criss-cross pattern until all spring pressure is relieved. Then hold the pressure plate securely and completely remove the bolts, followed by the pressure plate and clutch disc.

Pilot bearing

➡**Note: Because of the amount of work involved in gaining access to the clutch components, it is recommended that the pilot bearing be replaced whenever the clutch components are replaced. The release bearing should also be replaced at this time (see Section 7).**

7   Use a slide hammer with an internal puller attachment to remove the pilot bearing from the flywheel.

INSPECTION

◆ **Refer to illustrations 6.9, 6.10a and 6.10b**

➡**Note: Ordinarily, when a problem occurs in the clutch, it can be attributed to wear of the clutch driven plate assembly (clutch disc). However, all components should be inspected at this time.**

8   Inspect the flywheel for cracks, heat checking, grooves and other obvious defects. If the imperfections are slight, a machine shop can machine the surface flat and smooth, which is highly recommended regardless of the surface appearance. Refer to Chapter 2 for the flywheel removal and installation procedure.

9   Inspect the lining on the clutch disc. There should be at least 1/16-inch of lining above the rivet heads. Check for loose rivets, distortion, cracks, broken springs and other obvious damage (see illustration). As mentioned above, ordinarily the clutch disc is routinely replaced, so if in doubt about the condition, replace it with a new one.

10 Check the machined surfaces and the diaphragm spring fingers of the pressure plate (see illustrations). If the surface is grooved or otherwise damaged, replace the pressure plate. Also check for obvious damage, distortion, cracking, etc. Light glazing can be removed with emery cloth or sandpaper. If a new pressure plate is required, new and re-manufactured units are available.

INSTALLATION

◆ **Refer to illustration 6.13**

11 Before installation, clean the flywheel and pressure plate machined surfaces with brake cleaner, lacquer thinner or acetone. It's

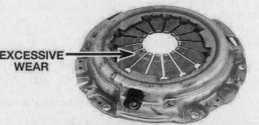

NORMAL FINGER WEAR   **EXCESSIVE FINGER WEAR**   **BROKEN OR BENT FINGERS**

EXCESSIVE WEAR

6.10a Replace the pressure plate if excessive wear or damage are noted

6.10b Inspect the pressure plate surface for excessive score marks, cracks and signs of overheating

6.13 Center the clutch disc in the pressure plate with a clutch alignment tool

important that no oil or grease is on these surfaces or the lining of the clutch disc. Handle the parts only with clean hands.

12 Drive the new pilot bearing into the bore in the flywheel until it is flush with the hub of the flywheel (on the friction surface side).

13 Position the clutch disc and pressure plate against the flywheel with the clutch held in place with an alignment tool (see illustration). Make sure the disc is installed properly (most replacement clutch discs will be marked "flywheel side" or something similar - if not marked, install the clutch disc with the damper springs toward the transaxle).

14 Tighten the pressure plate-to-flywheel bolts only finger tight, working around the pressure plate.

15 Center the clutch disc by ensuring the alignment tool extends through the splined hub and into the pilot bearing. Wiggle the tool up, down or side-to-side as needed to center the disc. Tighten the pressure plate-to-flywheel bolts a little at a time, working in a criss-cross pattern to prevent distorting the cover. After all of the bolts are snug, tighten them to the torque listed in this Chapter's Specifications. Remove the alignment tool.

16 Using high-temperature grease, lubricate the inner groove of the release bearing (see Section 7). Also place a small amount of grease on the release lever contact areas and the transaxle input shaft bearing retainer.

17 Install the clutch release bearing (see Section 7).

18 Install the transaxle and all components removed previously.

7   Clutch release bearing and lever - removal, inspection and installation

❋❋ WARNING:

Dust produced by clutch wear is hazardous to your health. DO NOT blow it out with compressed air and DO NOT inhale it. DO NOT use gasoline or petroleum-based solvents to remove the dust. Brake system cleaner should be used to flush the dust into a drain pan. After the clutch components are wiped clean with a rag, dispose of the contaminated rags and cleaner in a covered, marked container.

REMOVAL

1 Remove the transaxle (see Chapter 7A).

2 Pull the clutch release fork off the ballstud and slide the release bearing off the input shaft along with the release fork.

INSPECTION

▸ **Refer to illustration 7.4**

3 Wipe off the bearing with a clean rag and inspect it for damage, wear and cracks. Don't immerse the bearing in solvent - it's sealed for life and immersion in solvent will ruin it.

4 Hold the center of the bearing and rotate the outer portion while applying pressure (see illustration). If the bearing doesn't turn smoothly or if it's noisy or rough, replace it.

➡**Note: Considering the difficulty involved with replacing the release bearing, we recommend replacing the release bearing whenever the clutch components are replaced.**

INSTALLATION

5 Lightly lubricate the friction surfaces of the release bearing, ballstud and the input shaft bearing retainer with high-temperature grease.

6 Install the release lever and bearing onto the input shaft.

7 The remainder of installation is the reverse of removal.

7.4 Hold the bearing by the outer race and rotate the inner race while applying force - if the bearing doesn't turn smoothly or if it's noisy, replace the bearing

8   Clutch pedal adjustment

PEDAL HEIGHT

◗ **Refer to illustration 8.1**

1   The height of the clutch pedal is the distance the pedal sits off the floor (see illustration). If the pedal height is not within the specified range, it must be adjusted.

2   To adjust the clutch pedal, loosen the locknut on the clutch pedal position switch (the switch near the top of the pedal, and to the rear of it) and back the switch out until the pedal is at the correct height, then tighten the locknut.

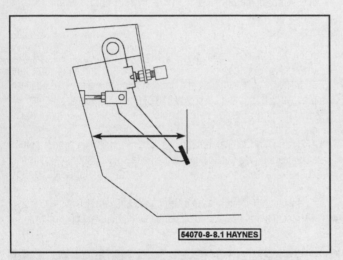

8.1 Pedal height is the distance between the pedal and the floor

PEDAL FREEPLAY

◗ **Refer to illustration 8.3**

3   The freeplay is the pedal slack, or the distance the pedal can be depressed before it begins to have any effect on the clutch system (see illustration). If the pedal freeplay is not within the specified range, it must be adjusted.

4   To adjust the pedal freeplay, loosen the locknut on the clutch pushrod. Then back off the pushrod to adjust the pedal freeplay to the specified range and retighten the locknut.

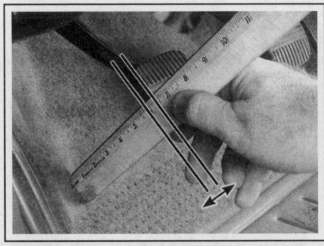

8.3 Pedal freeplay is the distance the pedal travels before resistance is felt

9   Clutch start switch - check and replacement

CHECK

1   Verify that the engine will not start when the clutch pedal is released.

2   Verify that the engine will start when the clutch pedal is depressed all the way.

3   If the engine won't start with the pedal depressed, or starts with the pedal released, unplug the electrical connector to the switch. The clutch start switch is located on the clutch pedal bracket, forward of the pedal, and is secured by two nuts. Check continuity between the connector terminals with the clutch pedal depressed.

4   If there's continuity between the terminals with the pedal

depressed, the switch is okay; if there's no continuity between the terminals with the pedal depressed, replace the switch. If there's continuity between the terminals when the clutch pedal is released, replace the switch.

REPLACEMENT

5   Unplug the switch electrical connector, if you haven't already done so.

6   Remove the nuts, and detach the switch from the clutch pedal bracket.

7   Installation is the reverse of removal.

10 Driveaxles - removal and installation

FRONT

Driveaxle

Removal

▶ **Refer to illustrations 10.2, 10.3, 10.6a and 10.6b**

1   Loosen the front wheel lug nuts, raise the vehicle and support it securely on jackstands. Remove the wheel.

2   Unstake the driveaxle/hub nut with a punch or chisel (see illustration).

3   Loosen the driveaxle/hub nut with a large socket and breaker bar (see illustration), then remove the driveaxle/hub nut from the axle and discard it.

4   Separate the lower control arm from the steering knuckle (see Chapter 10).

5   Swing the knuckle/hub assembly out (away from the vehicle) until the end of the driveaxle is free of the hub..

➡**Note: If the driveaxle splines stick in the hub, tap on the end of the driveaxle with a plastic hammer.**

Support the outer end of the driveaxle with a piece of wire to avoid unnecessary strain on the inner CV joint.

6   Pry the inner CV joint out of the transaxle or, on models so equipped, off of the intermediate shaft, using a large screwdriver or prybar (see illustrations).

7   Support the CV joints and carefully remove the driveaxle from the vehicle.

Installation

▶ **Refer to illustrations 10.8a and 10.8b**

8   Pry the old spring clip from the inner end of the driveaxle or, on models so equipped, the outer end of the intermediate shaft and install a new one (see illustrations).

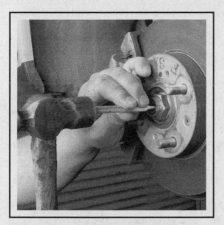

10.2 Use a punch or chisel and unstake the driveaxle/hub nut

10.3 To prevent the hub from turning while you're loosening the driveaxle/ hub nut, wedge a prybar between two of the wheel studs

10.6a Use a large screwdriver or a prybar to pop the inner end of the drlveaxle from the transaxle . . .

10.6b . . . or, if you're removing a driveaxle from a vehicle equipped with an intermediate shaft, insert the prybar between the intermediate shaft bearing and the driveaxle to pop it loose

10.8a Pry the old spring clip from the inner end of the driveaxle with a small screwdriver or awl

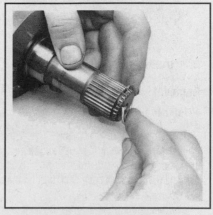

10.8b To install the new spring clip, start one end in the groove and work the clip over the shaft end, into the groove

10.11 Intermediate shaft bearing support bolts

9   Installation is the reverse of removal, but with the following additional points:

a)   *Apply a film of multi-purpose grease around the splines of the stub shafts*

b)   *When installing the driveaxle, hold the driveaxle straight out, then push it in sharply to seat the driveaxle spring clip.*

➡**Note: To ease insertion and seating of the retaining ring, position the gap in the ring facing downward (6 o'clock position).**

c)   *Clean all foreign matter from the driveaxle outer CV joint threads and coat the splines with multi-purpose grease. Guide the driveaxle into the hub splines and install the new driveaxle/hub nut. Tighten the nut securely but not to the specified torque at this time.*

d)   *Reconnect the control arm, then tighten the suspension fasteners to the torque listed in the Chapter 10 Specifications.*

e)   *Tighten the driveaxle/hub nut to the torque listed in this Chapter's Specifications. Stake the nut into the groove in the end of the driveaxle.*

f)   *Install the wheel and lug nuts, then lower the vehicle.*

g)   *Tighten the wheel lug nuts to the torque listed in the Chapter 1 Specifications.*

h)   *Add transaxle lubricant if it was drained or if any fluid spilled out (see Chapter 1).*

Intermediate shaft

Removal

◆ **Refer to illustration 10.11**

10   Remove the driveaxle (see Steps 1 through 7).

11   Remove the bearing support mounting bolts (see illustration), then slide the intermediate shaft out of the transaxle. Be careful not to damage the transaxle seal when pulling the shaft out.

12   Check the support bearing for smooth operation by turning the shaft while holding the bearing. If you feel any roughness, take the intermediate shaft to an automotive machine shop or other qualified repair facility to have a new bearing installed.

Installation

13   Lubricate the lips of the transaxle seal with multi-purpose grease. Carefully guide the intermediate shaft into the transaxle side gear, then install the mounting bolts for the bearing support. Tighten the bolts to the torque listed in this Chapter's Specifications.

14   The remainder of installation is the reverse of removal.

REAR (4WD SPORTAGE MODELS)

Removal

15   Loosen the rear wheel lug nuts, raise the rear of the vehicle and support it securely on jackstands, then remove the wheel.

16   Loosen the rear driveaxle/hub nut (see illustration 10.3).

17   Detach the trailing arm and the lateral arms from the rear knuckle (see Chapter 10, Section 11).

18   Pull out on the rear knuckle and separate the driveaxle from the hub.

➡**Note: If the driveaxle splines stick in the hub, tap on the end of the driveaxle with a soft-faced hammer.**

Support the outer end of the driveaxle with wire to avoid unnecessary strain on the inner CV joint.

19   Pry the inner CV joint out of the rear differential using a large screwdriver or prybar.

Installation

20   Pry the old spring clip from the inner end of the driveaxle or, on models so equipped, the outer end of the intermediate shaft and install a new one (see illustrations 10.8a and 10.8b).

21   Installation is the reverse of removal, but with the following additional points:

a)   *Apply a film of multi-purpose grease around the splines of the stub shafts.*

b)   *When installing the driveaxle, hold the driveaxle straight out, then push it in sharply to seat the driveaxle spring clip.*

➡**Note: To ease insertion and seating of the retaining ring, position the gap in the ring facing downward (6 o'clock position).**

c)   *Clean all foreign matter from the driveaxle outer CV joint threads and coat the splines with multi-purpose grease. Guide the driveaxle into the hub splines and install the new driveaxle/hub nut. Tighten the nut securely but not to the specified torque at this time.*

d)   *Reconnect the rear suspension arms to the knuckle. Raise the knuckle with a floor jack to simulate normal ride height, then tighten the fasteners to the torque listed in the Chapter 10 Specifications.*

e)   *Tighten the driveaxle/hub nut to the torque listed in this Chapter's Specifications. Stake the nut into the groove in the end of the driveaxle.*

f)   *Install the wheel and lug nuts, then lower the vehicle.*

g)   *Tighten the wheel lug nuts to the torque listed in the Chapter 1 Specifications.*

h)   *Add differential lubricant if it was drained or if any spilled out (see Chapter 1).*

11 Driveaxle boot - replacement

➡**Note 1: Complete rebuilt driveaxles are available on an exchange basis, which eliminates much time and work.**

➡**Note 2: Some auto parts stores carry "split" type replacement boots, which can be installed without removing the driveaxle from the vehicle. This is a convenient alternative; however, the driveaxle should be removed and the CV joint disassembled and cleaned to ensure the joint is free from contaminants such as moisture and dirt which will accelerate CV joint wear.**

1 Remove the driveaxle from the vehicle (see Section 10).
2 Mount the driveaxle in a vise. The jaws of the vise should be lined with wood or rags to prevent damage to the driveaxle.

INNER CV JOINT - TRI-POT TYPE

Disassembly

◆ **Refer to illustrations 11.3a, 11.3b and 11.6**

3 If you have any doubts about the condition of the outer boot this would be a good time to replace it as well. Cut off both boot clamps and slide the boot towards the center of the driveaxle (see illustrations).
4 Scribe or paint alignment marks on the outer race and the tri-pot bearing assembly so they can be returned to their original position, then slide the outer race off the tri-pot bearing assembly.
5 Remove the snap-ring from the end of the axleshaft.

6 Secure the bearing rollers with tape, then remove the tri-pot bearing assembly from the axleshaft with a brass drift and a hammer (see illustration). Remove the tape, but don't let the rollers fall off and get mixed up.
7 Slide the old boot off the driveaxle and discard it.

Inspection

8 Clean the old grease from the outer race and the tri-pot bearing assembly. Carefully disassemble each section of the tri-pot assembly, one at a time so as not to mix up the parts, and clean the needle bearings with solvent.
9 Inspect the rollers, tri-pot, bearings and outer race for scoring, pitting or other signs of abnormal wear, which will warrant the replacement of the inner CV joint.

Reassembly

◆ **Refer to illustrations 11.10a, 11.10b, 11.12, 11.13, 11.14, 11.16, 11.17a, 11.17b 11.17c, 11.17d and 11.17e**

10 Wrap the splines of the axleshaft with tape to avoid damaging the new boot, then slide the boot onto the axleshaft (see illustration). Remove the tape and slide the inner stop-ring (if equipped) into place (see illustration).
11 Slide the tri-pot assembly onto the axleshaft.
12 Install the outer snap-ring (see illustration).

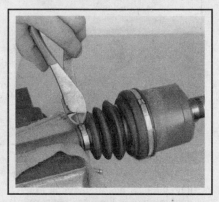

11.3a Cut off the boot clamps and discard them - don't try to re-use old clamps

11.3b Slide the boot down the driveaxle, out of the way

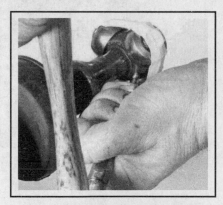

11.6 Secure the bearing rollers with tape and drive the tri-pot off the shaft with a hammer and brass drift, then remove the stop-ring

11.10a Wrap the splined area of the axleshaft with tape to prevent damage to the boot when installing it

11.10b If equipped, install the stop-ring on the axleshaft, making sure it seats in its groove

11.12 Install the tri-pot assembly on the axleshaft, then install the snap-ring

11.13 Use plenty of CV joint grease to hold the needle bearings in place when you install the roller assemblies on the tri-pot, and make sure you put each roller in its original position

11.14 Pack the outer race with grease and slide it over the tri-pot assembly - make sure the match marks on the outer race and tri-pot line up

11.16 Equalize the pressure inside the boot by inserting a small, dull screwdriver between the boot and the outer race

11.17a To install fold-over type clamps, bend the tang down . . .

11.17b . . . and flatten the tabs to hold it in place

11.17c You'll need a special tightening tool to install "band" type boot clamps: Install the band with its end pointing in the direction of axle rotation and tighten it securely . . .

13 Apply a coat of CV joint grease to the inner bearing surfaces to hold the needle bearings in place when reassembling the tri-pot assembly (see illustration). Make sure each roller is installed on the same post as before.

14 Pack the outer race with half of the grease furnished with the new boot and place the remainder in the boot. Install the outer race (see illustration). Make sure the marks you made on the tri-pot assembly and the outer race are aligned.

15 Seat the boot in the grooves in the outer race and the axleshaft, then position the CV joint midway through its (in-and-out) travel.

16 Equalize the pressure in the boot by inserting a blunt screwdriver between the boot and the outer race (see illustration). Don't damage the boot with the tool.

17 Install and tighten the new boot clamps (see illustrations).

18 Install the driveaxle assembly (see Section 10).

INNER CV JOINT - BALL-AND-CAGE TYPE

▶ **Refer to illustrations 11.21, 11.22 and 11.24**

19 Remove the driveaxle (see Section 10).

20 Remove the clamps from the boot and discard them.

21 Slide the boot back on the axleshaft and pry the wire ring ball retainer from the outer race (see illustration).

22 Pull the outer race off the inner bearing assembly (see illustration).

23 Wipe as much grease as possible off the inner bearing.

24 Remove the snap-ring from the end of the axleshaft (see illustration).

25 Slide the inner bearing assembly off the axleshaft.

26 The manufacturer recommends against any further disassembly.

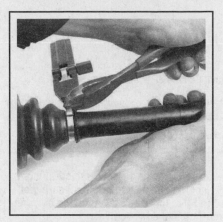

11.17d . . . bend back the end of the clamp, cut off the excess, then place a dimple in the center of the folded-over portion with a hammer and center punch

11.17e If you're installing crimp-type boot clamps, you'll need a pair of special crimping pliers (available at most auto parts stores)

11.21 Pry the wire retainer ring from the CV joint housing with a small screwdriver

11.22 With the retainer removed, the outer race can be pulled off the bearing assembly

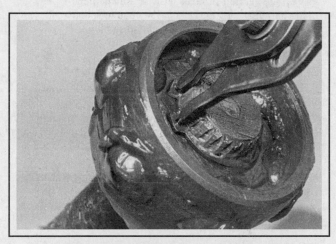

11.24 Remove the snap-ring from the end of the axleshaft

Inspection

27 Clean the components with solvent to remove all traces of grease. Inspect the cage and races for pitting, score marks, cracks and other signs of wear and damage. Shiny, polished spots are normal and will not adversely affect CV joint performance. If the outer CV joint boot is torn or damaged, now is the time to set aside the inner CV joint parts, remove the outer boot, and clean and inspect the outer CV joint.

Reassembly

28 Wrap the axleshaft splines with tape to avoid damaging the boot (see illustration 11.10a).

29 Slide the small boot clamp and boot onto the axleshaft, then remove the tape.

30 Install the inner race and cage assembly on the axleshaft.

31 Install the snap-ring.

32 Fill the boot with CV joint grease (normally included with the new boot kit).

33 Pack the inner race and cage assembly with grease, by hand, until grease is worked completely into the assembly.

34 Slide the outer race down onto the inner race and install the wire ring retainer.

35 Wipe any excess grease from the axle boot groove on the outer race. Seat the small diameter of the boot in the recessed area on the axleshaft and install the clamp. Push the other end of the boot onto the outer CV joint housing and seat it into the recessed area on the housing.

36 Position the CV joint mid-way through its travel, then equalize the pressure in the boot by inserting a dull screwdriver between the boot and the outer race (see illustration 11.16). Don't damage the boot with the tool.

37 Install the boot clamps (see illustrations 11.17a through 11.17e).

38 Install the driveaxle assembly (see Section 1).

OUTER CV JOINT AND BOOT

Disassembly

39 Following Steps 3 through 7, remove the inner CV joint from the driveaxle and disassemble it.

40 If the driveaxle is equipped with a dynamic damper, scribe or

11.43 After the old grease has been rinsed away and the solvent has been blown out with compressed air, rotate the outer joint assembly through its full range of motion and inspect the bearing surfaces for wear and damage - if any of the ball bearings, the race or the cage look damaged, replace the driveaxle and outer joint assembly

paint a location mark on the axleshaft along the outer edge of the damper (the side facing the outer CV joint), cut the retaining clamp and slide the damper off.

➡Note: If you're planning to replace the axleshaft and outer CV joint assembly, measure the distance between the inner CV joint boot and the dynamic damper so the damper can be placed in the proper position on the new driveaxle.

41 Cut the boot clamps from the outer CV joint. Slide the boot off the shaft.

➡Note: The outer CV joint can't be disassembled or removed from the shaft.

Inspection

◗ **Refer to illustration 11.43**

42 Thoroughly wash the inner and outer CV joints in clean solvent and blow them dry with compressed air, if available.

✳✳ WARNING:

Wear eye protection when using compressed air.

➡Note: Because the outer joint can't be disassembled, it is difficult to wash away all the old grease and to rid the bearing of solvent once it's clean. But it is imperative that the job be done thoroughly, so take your time and do it right.

43 Bend the outer CV joint housing at an angle to the axleshaft to expose the bearings, inner race and cage (see illustration). Inspect the bearing surfaces for signs of wear. If the bearings are damaged or worn, replace the driveaxle.

Reassembly

44 Slide the new outer boot onto the axleshaft. It's a good idea to wrap tape around the splines of the shaft to prevent damage to the boot (see illustration 11.10a). When the boot is in position, add the specified amount of grease (included in the boot replacement kit) to the outer joint and the boot (pack the joint with as much grease as it will hold and put the rest into the boot). Slide the boot on the rest of the way and install the new clamps (see illustrations 11.17a through 11.17e).

45 Slide the dynamic damper, if equipped, onto the shaft. Make sure its outer edge is aligned with the previously applied mark.

➡Note: If you're using a new axleshaft and outer CV joint assembly, install the damper on the shaft to the distance from the inner CV joint boot measured in Step 20.

Install a new retaining clamp.

46 Clean and reassemble the inner CV joint by following Steps 8 through 17, then install the driveaxle as outlined in Section 10.

12 Universal joint (4WD models) - general information and check

1   Universal joints are mechanical couplings which connect two rotating components that meet each other at different angles.

2   These joints are composed of a yoke on each side connected by a crosspiece called a trunnion. Cups at each end of the trunnion contain needle bearings which provide smooth transfer of the torque load. Snap-rings, either inside or outside of the bearing cups, hold the assembly together.

3   Wear in the needle roller bearings is characterized by vibration in the driveline, noise during acceleration, and in extreme cases of lack of lubrication, metallic squeaking and ultimately grating and shrieking sounds as the bearings disintegrate.

4   It is easy to check if the needle bearings are worn with the driveshaft in position, by trying to turn the shaft with one hand, the

other hand holding the rear axle flange when the rear universal joint is being checked, and the front half coupling when the front universal joint is being checked. Any movement between the driveshaft and the front half couplings, and around the rear half couplings, is indicative of considerable wear. Another method of checking for universal joint wear is to use a pry bar inserted into the gap between the universal joint and the driveshaft or flange. Leave the vehicle in gear and try to pry the joint both radially and axially. Any looseness should be apparent with this method. A final test for wear is to attempt to lift the shaft and note any movement between the yokes of the joints.

5   If any of the above conditions exist, replace the universal joints with new ones.

13 Driveshaft (4WD models) - check, removal and installation

CHECK

1   Release the parking brake and put the transaxle in Neutral. Raise the vehicle and place it securely on jackstands.

2   Crawl under the vehicle and visually inspect the driveshaft. Look for dents, bends and cracks in the driveshaft tubing. If you find any damage, replace the driveshaft.

3   Inspect the front and rear ends of the driveshaft for signs of oil leakage. Leakage at the front end of the driveshaft indicates a leaking transfer case output shaft seal; leakage at the rear end of the driveshaft indicates a leaking differential pinion seal (see Section 15).

4   While you're still under the vehicle, have an assistant rotate a rear wheel to rotate the driveshaft. As the driveshaft rotates, verify that the universal joint and the rear rubber coupling are operating properly, without binding, noise or looseness. Listen carefully for any noise from the center bearing; if the center bearing is making noise, it's worn or damaged. Finally, inspect the rubber part of the center bearing for cracks and any other damage.

5   You can also inspect the universal joint with the driveshaft sta-tionary by gripping your hands on both sides of the joint and trying to twist the joint. Any freeplay is a sign of considerable wear; replace the universal joint.

REMOVAL AND INSTALLATION

▶ **Refer to illustrations 13.6a, 13.6b and 13.8**

6   Mark the relationship of the driveshaft flange at the front end of the driveshaft and the rubber coupling at the rear end in relation to their corresponding companion mounting flanges at the transfer case and at the rear differential (see illustrations).

7   Remove the bolts that secure the rubber coupling to the rear differential companion flange.

8   Remove the center support bearing bracket mounting bolts (see illustration).

9   Remove the bolts that secure the driveshaft yoke to the transfer case companion flange and remove the driveshaft assembly.

10 Installation is the reverse of removal.

13.6a Driveshaft universal joint bolts and nuts (other two bolts/nuts not visible) at the transfer case (Sportage 4WD models)

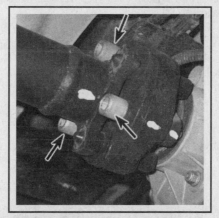

13.6b Driveshaft rubber coupling bolts at the differential (Sportage 4WD models)

13.8 Driveshaft center support bearing bracket bolts (Sportage 4WD models)

14 Universal joint (4WD models) - replacement

▶ **Refer to illustrations 14.2, 14.4 and 14.9**

➡ **Note: A large vise or a press is required for this procedure. It may be advisable to take the driveshaft to a dealer service department, service station or machine shop where the universal joints can be replaced for you.**

1   Refer to Section 13 and remove the driveshaft.

2   Use pliers to remove the snap-rings from the spider (see illustration).

3   While supporting the driveshaft, place it in position on a work-bench equipped with a vise.

4   Place a piece of pipe or a large socket, with an inside diameter slightly larger than the outside diameter of the bearing caps, over one of the bearing caps. Position a socket with an outside diameter slightly smaller than that of the opposite bearing cap over that cap, and use

14.2 Use needle-nose pliers to remove the universal joint snap-rings

14.4 To press the universal joint out of the driveshaft yoke, set it up in a vise, with the small socket pushing the joint and bearing cap into the larger socket

14.9 If the snap-ring won't seat in its groove, strike the yoke with a brass hammer; this relieves the tension in the yoke and slightly springs the yoke ears (also do this if the joint feels tight when assembled)

the vise or press to force the bearing cap out (inside the pipe or large socket) (see illustration). Use the vise or large pliers to work the bearing cap the rest of the way out.

5   Transfer the sockets to the opposite sides and press the other bearing cap out in the same manner.

6   Pack the new joints with grease. Usually, specific instructions will be included with the universal joint kit. Follow them carefully.

7   Position the spider into the yoke and partially install one bearing cap in the yoke.

8   Start the spider into the bearing cap, then partially install the other bearing cap. Press the bearing caps into place, keeping the spider

correctly centered as you do so. Be careful to avoid damaging the dust seals.

9   Use the smaller socket to press the caps fully into place. Install the snap-rings. If you have difficulty in seating them, strike the driveshaft yoke sharply with a hammer. This will spring the yoke ears slightly and allow the snap-rings to seat in their grooves (see illustration).

10   If the universal joint has a grease fitting, install it now and add grease using a grease gun.

11   Install the driveshaft.

15   Rear driveaxle oil seal (4WD models) - replacement

1   Raise the rear of the vehicle and support it securely on jackstands. Block the front wheels to prevent the vehicle from rolling. Place the transmission in Neutral with the parking brake off.

2   Remove the driveaxles (see Section 10).

3   Carefully pry out the side gear shaft oil seal with a seal removal tool or a large screwdriver; make sure you don't scratch the seal bore.

4   Using a seal installer or a large deep socket as a drift, install the

new oil seal. Drive it into the bore squarely and make sure it's completely seated.

5   Lubricate the lip of the new seal with multi-purpose grease, then install the driveaxles (see Section 10). Be careful not to damage the lip of the new seal.

6   Check the differential lubricant level and add some, if necessary, to bring it to the appropriate level (see Chapter 1).

16   Rear differential (4WD models) - removal and installation

▶ **Refer to illustrations 16.3 and 16.6**

1   Raise the rear of the vehicle and support it securely on jackstands. Block the front wheels to prevent the vehicle from rolling. Place the transmission in Neutral with the parking brake off. Remove the spare wheel.

2   Drain the differential lubricant (see Chapter 1).

3   Disconnect the speed sensor from the differential (see illustration).

4   Remove the rear part of the exhaust system (see Chapter 4).

5   Remove the driveaxles (see Section 10) and disconnect the driveshaft from the differential (see Section 13).

6   Support the differential, then remove the three mounting bolts (see illustration) and slowly lower the jack.

7   Installation is the reverse of removal.

8   Refill the differential with the specified type and amount of lubricant (see Chapter 1).

16.3 Disconnect the electrical connector (A) from the speed sensor and pull off the harness locator clip (B) from the differential

16.6 Rear differential details (4WD Sportage models):

1	Exhaust pipe	3	Driveaxles
2	Driveshaft	4	Differential mounting bolts

17 Transfer case (4WD models) - removal and installation

1   Raise the vehicle and place it securely on jackstands.
2   Remove the driveshaft (see Section 13).
3   Remove the front exhaust pipe (see Chapter 4).
4   Drain the transfer case lubricant (see Chapter 1).
5   Support the transfer case securely.

6   Remove the transfer case mounting bolts and remove the transfer case.
7   Installation is the reverse of removal. Be sure to tighten the transfer case mounting bolts securely.
8   Refill the transfer case with the specified type and amount of lubricant (see Chapter 1).

Specifications

Clutch

Fluid type	See Chapter 1
Pedal height	
1997 and earlier models	7.72 to 8.03 inches (196 to 204 mm)
1998 through 2004, except 2.0L DOHC models	7.83 to 8.15 inches (199 to 207 mm)
2.0L DOHC	6.57 inches (166.9 mm)
Pedal freeplay	
1997 and earlier models	0.12 to 0.35 inch (3 to 9 mm)
1998 through 2004, except 2.0L DOHC models	0.12 to 0.20 inch (3 to 5 mm)
2.0L DOHC	0.24 to 0.51 inch (6 to 13 mm)

Torque specifications	Ft-lbs	Nm
Clutch pressure plate-to-flywheel bolts		
1994 through 2004 except 2.0L DOHC	13 to 20	18 to 27
2.0L DOHC	10 to 16	13 to 22
Clutch release cylinder mounting bolts		
1994 through 2004 except 2.0L DOHC	14 to 17	19 to 23
2.0L DOHC	11 to 16	15 to 22
Driveaxle/hub nut		
1994 through 2004 except 2.0L DOHC	155 to 205	210 to 278
2.0L DOHC	145 to 188	196 to 255
Intermediate shaft support bracket bolts	32 to 45	42 to 62
Driveshaft rubber coupling bolts		
(4WD Sportage models)	73 to 86	100 to 120
Driveshaft-to-transfer case flange bolts		
(4WD Sportage models)	Not available	
Wheel lug nuts	See Chapter 1	

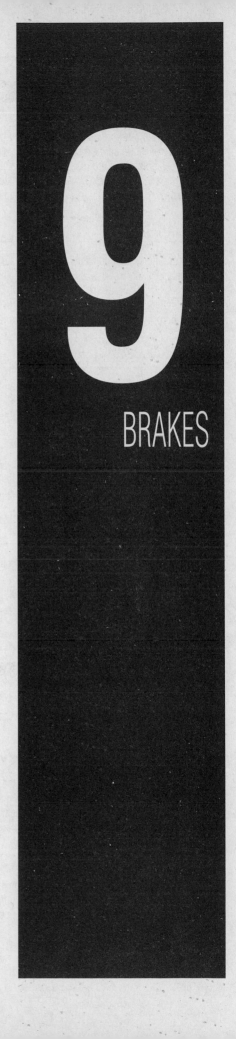

9

BRAKES

Section

1   General information
2   Anti-lock Brake System (ABS) - general information
3   Disc brake pads - replacement
4   Disc brake caliper - removal and installation
5   Brake disc - inspection, removal and installation
6   Drum brake shoes/parking brake shoes - replacement
7   Wheel cylinder - removal and installation
8   Master cylinder - removal and installation
9   Brake hoses and lines - inspection and replacement
10   Brake hydraulic system - bleeding
11   Power brake booster - removal and installation
12   Parking brake - adjustment
13   Brake light switch - replacement
14   Brake pedal - adjustment

Reference to other Chapters

Brake check - See Chapter 1
Brake fluid level check - See Chapter 1

1 General information

The vehicles covered by this manual are equipped with hydraulically operated front and rear brake systems. The front brakes are disc type and the rear brakes are either disc or drum type. Both the front and rear brakes are self adjusting. The disc brakes automatically compensate for pad wear, while the drum brakes incorporate an adjustment mechanism which is activated as the parking brake is applied.

HYDRAULIC SYSTEM

The hydraulic system consists of two separate circuits. The master cylinder has separate reservoir chambers for the two circuits, and, in the event of a leak or failure in one hydraulic circuit, the other circuit will remain operative. A dual proportioning valve provides brake balance between the front and rear brakes.

POWER BRAKE BOOSTER

The power brake booster - which utilizes engine manifold vacuum and atmospheric pressure to provide assistance to the hydraulically operated brakes - is mounted on the firewall in the engine compartment.

PARKING BRAKE

The parking brake operates the rear brakes only, through cable actuation. It's activated by a lever mounted in the center console.

SERVICE

After completing any operation involving disassembly of any part of the brake system, always test drive the vehicle to check for proper braking performance before resuming normal driving. When testing the brakes, perform the tests on a clean, dry, flat surface. Conditions other than these can lead to inaccurate test results.

Test the brakes at various speeds with both light and heavy pedal pressure. The vehicle should stop evenly without pulling to one side or the other. Avoid locking the brakes, because this slides the tires and diminishes braking efficiency and control of the vehicle.

Tires, vehicle load and wheel alignment are factors which also affect braking performance.

PRECAUTIONS

There are some general cautions and warnings involving the brake system on this vehicle:

a) *Use only brake fluid conforming to DOT 3 specifications.*

b) *The brake pads and linings contain fibers which are hazardous to your health if inhaled. Whenever you work on brake system components, clean all parts with brake system cleaner. Do not allow the fine dust to become airborne. Also, wear an approved filtering mask.*

c) *Safety should be paramount whenever any servicing of the brake components is performed. Do not use parts or fasteners which are not in perfect condition, and be sure that all clearances and torque specifications are adhered to. If you are at all unsure about a certain procedure, seek professional advice. Upon completion of any brake system work, test the brakes carefully in a controlled area before putting the vehicle into normal service. If a problem is suspected in the brake system, don't drive the vehicle until it's fixed.*

2 Anti-lock Brake System (ABS) - general information

GENERAL INFORMATION

1   The anti-lock brake system is designed to maintain vehicle steerability, directional stability and optimum deceleration under severe braking conditions on most road surfaces. It does so by monitoring the rotational speed of each wheel and controlling the brake line pressure to each wheel during braking. This prevents the wheels from locking up.

2   The ABS system has three main components - the wheel speed sensors, the electronic control unit (ECU) and the hydraulic unit. Four wheel speed sensors - one at each wheel - send a variable voltage signal to the control unit, which monitors these signals, compares them to its program and determines whether a wheel is about to lock up. When a wheel is about to lock up, the control unit signals the hydraulic unit to reduce hydraulic pressure (or not increase it further) at that wheel's brake caliper. Pressure modulation is handled by electrically-operated solenoid valves.

3   If a problem develops within the system, an "ABS" warning light will glow on the dashboard. Sometimes, a visual inspection of the ABS system can help you locate the problem. Carefully inspect the ABS wiring harness. Pay particularly close attention to the harness and connections near each wheel. Look for signs of chafing and other damage caused by incorrectly routed wires. If a wheel sensor harness is damaged, the sensor must be replaced.

✳✳ WARNING:

Do NOT try to repair an ABS wiring harness. The ABS system is sensitive to even the smallest changes in resistance. Repairing the harness could alter resistance values and cause the system to malfunction. If the ABS wiring harness is damaged in any way, it must be replaced.

✳✳ CAUTION:

Make sure the ignition is turned off before unplugging or reattaching any electrical connections.

DIAGNOSIS AND REPAIR

4   If a dashboard warning light comes on and stays on while the vehicle is in operation, the ABS system requires attention. Although special electronic ABS diagnostic testing tools are necessary to properly diagnose the system, you can perform a few preliminary checks before taking the vehicle to a dealer service department.

 a) *Check the brake fluid level in the reservoir.*
 b) *Verify that the computer electrical connectors are securely connected.*
 c) *Check the electrical connectors at the hydraulic control unit.*
 d) *Check the fuses.*
 e) *Follow the wiring harness to each wheel and verify that all connections are secure and that the wiring is undamaged.*

5   If the above preliminary checks do not rectify the problem, the vehicle should be diagnosed by a dealer service department or other qualified repair shop. Due to the complex nature of this system, all actual repair work must be done by a qualified automotive technician.

3   Disc brake pads - replacement

✳✳ WARNING:

Disc brake pads must be replaced on both front and rear wheels at the same time - never replace the pads on only one side. Also, the dust created by the brake system is harmful to your health. Never blow it out with compressed air and don't inhale any of it. An approved filtering mask should be worn when working on the brakes. Do not, under any circumstances, use petroleum-based solvents to clean brake parts. Use brake system cleaner only!

➡️**Note: This procedure applies to front and rear disc brakes.**

1   Remove the cap from the brake fluid reservoir.
2   Loosen the wheel lug nuts, raise the front, or rear, of the vehicle and support it securely on jackstands.
3   Remove the front, or rear, wheels. Work on one brake assembly at a time, using the assembled brake for reference if necessary.
4   Inspect the brake disc carefully as outlined in Section 5. If

WHEEL SPEED SENSOR - REMOVAL AND INSTALLATION

6   Loosen the wheel lug nuts, raise the vehicle and support it securely on jackstands. Remove the wheel.
7   Make sure the ignition key is turned to the Off position.
8   Trace the wiring back from the sensor, detaching all brackets and clips while noting its correct routing, then disconnect the electrical connector.
9   Remove the mounting bolt and carefully pull the sensor out from the knuckle.
10 Installation is the reverse of the removal procedure. Tighten the mounting bolt securely.
11 Install the wheel and lug nuts, tightening them securely. Lower the vehicle and tighten the lug nuts to the torque listed in the Chapter 1 Specifications.

machining is necessary, follow the information in that Section to remove the disc, at which time the calipers and pads can be removed as well.

FRONT PADS

2004 and earlier models

▶ **Refer to illustrations 3.5 and 3.6a through 3.6l**

5   Push the piston back into the bore to provide room for the new brake pads. A C-clamp can be used to accomplish this (see illustration). As the piston is depressed to the bottom of the caliper bore, the fluid in the master cylinder will rise. Make sure it doesn't overflow. If necessary, siphon off some of the fluid.
6   Follow the accompanying illustrations (beginning with illustration 3.6a) for the actual pad replacement procedure. Be sure to stay in order and read the caption under each illustration. Once you have installed the new pads, proceed to Step 28.

3.5 Using a large C-clamp, push the piston back into the caliper - note that one end of the clamp is on the back side of the caliper and the other end (screw end) is pressing on the outer brake pad (1994 through 2004 models)

3.6a Before removing anything, spray the assembly with brake system cleaner to remove the dust produced by brake pad wear - DO NOT blow the dust off with compressed air! (1994 through 2004 models)

3.6b Remove the anti-rattle spring clip (if equipped) (1994 through 2004 models)

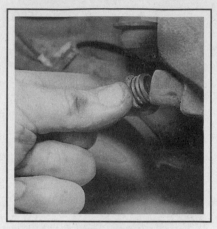

3.6c Remove the caliper guide pin covers . . .

3.6d . . . then remove the caliper guide pins (1994 through 2004 models)

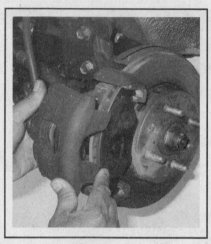

3.6e Remove the caliper . . .

3.6f . . . and hang it from the strut with a piece of wire (1994 through 2004 models)

3.6g Remove the inner brake pad by pushing it away from the piston (1994 through 2004 models)

3.6h Remove the outer brake pad from the caliper mounting bracket (1994 through 2004 models)

3.6i Install the new outer brake pad (1994 through 2004 models)

3.6j Install the new inner brake pad by pushing the clip's prongs into the piston (1994 through 2004 models)

2005 and later models

▶ **Refer to illustrations 3.8a through 3.8k**

7   Using a C-clamp, push the piston back into the caliper bore to provide room for the new brake pads (see illustration 3.5). As you depress the piston, the brake fluid in the master cylinder reservoir will rise. Make sure that it doesn't overflow. If necessary, siphon off some of the fluid. Also clean the brake with brake system cleaner (see illustration 3.6a).

8   Follow illustrations 3.8a through 3.8k for the brake pad replacement procedure. Be sure to stay in order and read the caption under each illustration. Once you've installed the new pads, proceed to Step 28.

REAR PADS

9   Wash the brake assembly with brake system cleaner (see illustration 3.6a).

1997 and earlier models

10   Using a punch, drive out the upper pad retaining pin and partially drive out the lower one - just enough to unseat it.

11   Remove the anti-rattle spring and then remove the lower pad retaining pin.

12   Pull the inner pad from the caliper with a pair of pliers. Using a screwdriver or prybar push the piston back into its bore to make room for the new pad. As the piston is depressed to the bottom of the caliper bore, the fluid in the master cylinder will rise. Make sure it doesn't overflow. If necessary, siphon off some of the fluid.

13   Install the new inner pad, then repeat the previous step to replace the outer pad.

14   Install the pad retaining pins going from the inboard side of the caliper until they are fully seated. Proceed to Step 28.

1998 and later Sephia and Spectra models

15   Remove the caliper mounting bolts and the caliper from its mounting bracket. Hang the caliper out of the way with a piece of wire. Don't let the caliper hang by the brake hose.

3.6k Position the caliper on the mounting bracket, clean the guide pins and lubricate them with high temperature grease and then install them (keep grease away from other brake parts) (1994 through 2004 models)

3.6l Tighten the guide pins to the torque listed in this Chapter's Specifications, then install the anti-rattle spring clip (If equipped) (1994 through 2004 models)

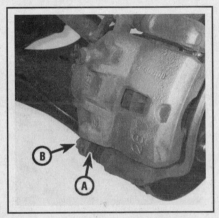

3.8a Using a back-up wrench to hold the guide pin (A), remove the lower guide pin bolt (B) . . .

3.8b . . . then swing the caliper up on its upper guide pin and secure it to the strut coil spring with a piece of wire (2005 and later models)

3.8c Remove the inner brake pad and shim . . .

3.8d . . . and the outer pad and shim (2005 and later models)

3.8e Remove and inspect the upper and lower pad retainers (2005 and later models)

3.8f Remove the caliper and hang it from the strut coil spring so you can lubricate the guide pins and inspect the rubber boots

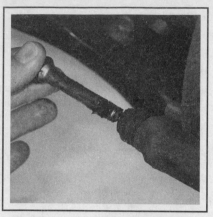

3.8g Inspect the guide pins, then remove and inspect the rubber boots. If a guide pin is dirty, clean it and lubricate it with high-temperature brake grease. If a boot is damaged, replace it (2005 and later models)

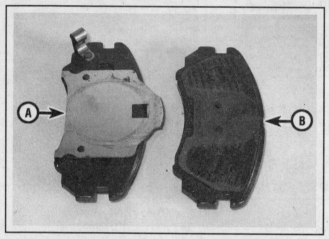

3.8h Remove the shims from the old pads and inspect them for dirt, oil, etc. The shims must be clean and undamaged before installing them on the new inner (A) and outer (B) pads (2005 and later models)

3.8i Install the pad retainers; make sure that they're fully seated (2005 and later models)

3.8j Install the inner and outer pads and shims (the pad with the wear indicator is the inner pad) (2005 and later models)

3.8k Install the caliper over the pads, install the guide pin bolt and tighten it to the torque listed in this Chapter's Specifications (2005 and later models)

➡Note: Detach the parking brake cable if necessary.

16 Remove the outer brake pad and shim.

17 Remove the inner brake pad and shim(s).

18 Remove and inspect the upper and lower pad retainer clips.

19 Install the pad retainer clips. They should fit snugly in the caliper mounting bracket; if they don't, replace them. Apply a thin film of high-temperature grease to the retainer.

20 Apply a small amount of high-temperature grease to both sides of the shims.

21 Install the new inner pad and shim(s). Make sure the "ears" on the upper and lower ends of the pad are fully engaged with their respective grooves and the pad retainer clips

22 Install the new outer pad and shim.

23 Before installing the caliper, remove the caliper pin dust boots and inspect them for tears and cracks; if they're damaged, replace them.

24 Retract the piston by engaging the tips of a pair of needle-nose pliers with two of the grooves or holes in the face of the piston and turning it until it bottoms in the bore. Now, rotate the piston out until one of its grooves or holes is aligned with the tab on the inner brake pad when you install the caliper. You may have to adjust the piston position by turning it back and forth to fit the tab in the groove. If the piston dust boot becomes distorted when the piston is turned, turn the piston in the opposite direction to restore the shape of the boot, but make sure the groove is aligned properly.

➡Note: If the piston is difficult to turn with needle-nose pliers, special caliper piston tools are available at auto parts stores.

25 Install the caliper mounting bolts and tighten them to the torque listed in this Chapter's Specifications. Proceed to Step 28.

Sportage models

▶ Refer to illustrations 3.27a through 3.27k

26 Using a C-clamp, push the piston back into the caliper bore to provide room for the new brake pads (see illustration 3.5). As you depress the piston, the brake fluid in the master cylinder reservoir will rise. Make sure that it doesn't overflow. If necessary, siphon off some of the fluid.

27 Follow illustrations 3.27a through 3.8k for the brake pad replacement procedure. Be sure to stay in order and read the caption under each illustration. Once you've installed the new pads, proceed to Step 28.

FRONT OR REAR PADS

28 Install the wheels and lug nuts, lower the vehicle and tighten the lug nuts to the torque listed in the Chapter 1 Specifications.

29 Apply and release the brake pedal several times to bring the pads into contact with the brake discs.

30 Check the brake fluid level and add fluid, if necessary (see Chapter 1). Check the operation of the brakes in an isolated area before driving the vehicle in traffic.

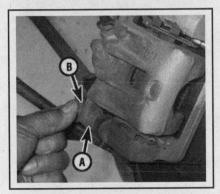

3.27a Using a back-up wrench to hold the guide pin (A), remove the lower guide pin bolt (B) . . .

3.27b . . . then swing the caliper up on its upper guide pin (Sportage models)

3.27c Remove the inner brake pad and shim . . .

3.27d . . . and the outer pad and shim (Sportage models)

3.27e Remove and inspect the pad retainers (Sportage models)

3.27f Inspect the guide pins and boots. If a guide pin is dirty, clean it and lubricate it with high-temperature brake grease. If a boot is damaged, replace it (Sportage models)

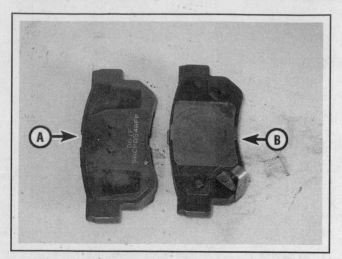

3.27g Remove the shims from the old pads and inspect the shims for dirt, oil, etc. The shims must be clean and undamaged before installing them on the new outer (A) and inner (B) pads (Sportage models)

3.27h Install the pad retainers; make sure that they're fully seated (Sportage models)

3.27i Install the outer brake pad and shim . . .

3.27j . . . and the inner pad and shim (the inner pad is the one with the wear indicator) (Sportage models)

3.27k Install the caliper over the pads, install the guide pin bolt and tighten it to the torque listed in this Chapter's Specifications (Sportage models)

4   Disc brake caliper - removal and installation

✳✳ WARNING:

The dust created by the brake system is harmful to your health. Never blow it out with compressed air and don't inhale any of it. An approved filtering mask should be worn when working on the brakes. Do not, under any circumstances, use petroleum-based solvents to clean brake parts. Use brake system cleaner only!

➡Note: Always replace the calipers in pairs (front/front, rear/rear) - never replace just one of them.

FRONT

➡Note: The following procedure describes caliper removal on models without a brake hose-to-caliper banjo fitting. On models with a banjo fitting, refer to Steps 13 through 20.

Removal

▶ Refer to illustration 4.2

1   Loosen - but don't remove - the lug nuts on the front wheels. Raise the front of the vehicle and place it securely on jackstands. Remove the front wheels.

2 Break loose the brake hose fitting (but don't try to unscrew it yet), then remove the caliper guide pins (see illustration). Lift the caliper off its mounting bracket, then unscrew it from the brake hose. Plug the hose to keep contaminants out of the brake system and to prevent losing any more brake fluid than necessary.

➡**Note: If you're simply removing the caliper for access to other components, don't disconnect the hose. Do not let the caliper hang by the brake hose.**

3 Remove the inner brake pad from the caliper (see illustration 3.6g).

Installation

4 Install the caliper by reversing the removal procedure. Tighten the caliper guide pins to the torque listed in this Chapter's Specifications, then tighten the brake hose securely. Make sure the hose is not twisted or kinked.

5 Bleed the brake system if the brake line was disconnected (see Section 10).

6 Install the wheels and lug nuts and lower the vehicle. Tighten the lug nuts to the torque listed in the Chapter 1 Specifications.

REAR

1997 and earlier models

Removal

7 Remove the rear brake pads (see Section 3).

8 Disconnect the brake line from the caliper. Use a flare-nut wrench, if available, to prevent rounding-off the corners of the fitting. Plug the fitting to prevent fluid loss and contamination.

9 Remove the caliper mounting bolts and then remove the caliper.

Installation

10 Install the caliper by reversing the removal procedure. Refer to Section 3 for brake pad installation. Tighten the caliper mounting bolts to the torque listed in this Chapter's Specifications.

11 Bleed the brake system (see Section 10).

12 Install the wheels and lug nuts. Lower the vehicle and tighten the lug nuts to the torque listed in the Chapter 1 Specifications.

1998 and later models

Removal

13 Loosen - but don't remove - the lug nuts on the wheels. Raise the vehicle and place it securely on jackstands. Remove the wheels.

4.2 Front brake caliper details:

1 Brake line fitting
2 Caliper guide pins (dust covers removed)
3 Caliper bracket mounting bolts

14 Unscrew the banjo bolt and detach the brake line from the caliper. Plug the fitting to prevent fluid loss and contamination.

➡**Note: If you're simply removing the caliper for access to other components, don't disconnect the hose.**

Discard the sealing washers (new ones should be used during reassembly).

15 Remove the caliper mounting bolts.

16 Remove the clip securing the parking brake cable and then separate the cable from the caliper.

17 Detach the caliper from its mounting bracket.

Installation

18 Install the caliper by reversing the removal procedure. Remember to replace the sealing washers on either side of the brake line fitting with new ones. Tighten the caliper mounting bolts and the banjo fitting bolt to the torque listed in this Chapter's Specifications.

19 Bleed the brake system (see Section 10).

20 Install the wheels and lug nuts. Lower the vehicle and tighten the lug nuts to the torque listed in the Chapter 1 Specifications.

5 Brake disc - inspection, removal and installation

❋❋ WARNING:

The dust created by the brake system is harmful to your health. Never blow it out with compressed air and don't inhale any of it. An approved filtering mask should be worn when working on the brakes. Do not, under any circumstances, use petroleum-based solvents to clean brake parts. Use brake system cleaner only!

INSPECTION

▸ **Refer to illustrations 5.2, 5.3, 5.4a, 5.4b and 5.5**

1 Loosen the wheel lug nuts, raise the vehicle and support it securely on jackstands. Remove the wheel and install the lug nuts to hold the disc in place against the hub flange.

➡**Note: If the lug nuts don't contact the disc when screwed on all the way, install washers under them. If you're checking the rear disc, release the parking brake.**

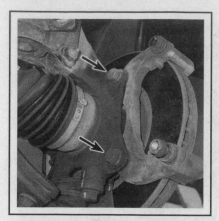

5.2 Typical caliper bracket bolts (Sportage model shown, other models similar)

5.3 The brake pads on this vehicle were obviously neglected, as they wore down completely and cut deep grooves into the disc - wear this severe means the disc must be replaced

5.4a To check disc runout, mount a dial indicator as shown and rotate the disc

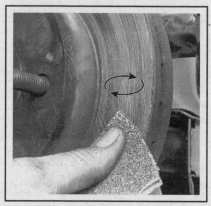

5.4b Using a swirling motion, remove the glaze from the disc surface with sandpaper or emery cloth

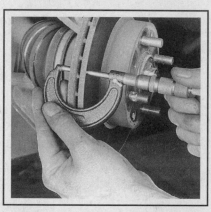

5.5 Use a micrometer to measure disc thickness

5.6a If the disc retaining screws are stuck, use an impact screwdriver to loosen them

2   Remove the brake caliper as outlined in Section 4. It isn't necessary to disconnect the brake hose. After removing the caliper bolts, suspend the caliper out of the way with a piece of wire. Remove the two caliper mounting bracket-to-steering knuckle bolts (see illustration) or, on rear calipers, the bracket-to-knuckle bolts and remove the mounting bracket.

3   Visually inspect the disc surface for score marks and other damage. Light scratches and shallow grooves are normal after use and may not always be detrimental to brake operation, but deep scoring requires disc removal and refinishing by an automotive machine shop. Be sure to check both sides of the disc (see illustration). If pulsating has been noticed during application of the brakes, suspect disc runout.

4   To check disc runout, place a dial indicator at a point about 1/2-inch from the outer edge of the disc (see illustration). Set the indicator to zero and turn the disc. The indicator reading should not exceed the specified allowable runout limit. If it does, the disc should be refinished by an automotive machine shop.

➡Note: The discs should be resurfaced regardless of the dial indicator reading, as this will impart a smooth finish and ensure a perfectly flat surface, eliminating any brake pedal pulsation or other undesirable symptoms related to questionable discs.

At the very least, if you elect not to have the discs resurfaced, remove the glaze from the surface with emery cloth or sandpaper, using a swirling motion (see illustration).

5   It's absolutely critical that the disc not be machined to a thickness under the specified minimum thickness. The minimum (or discard) thickness is cast or stamped into the disc. The disc thickness can be checked with a micrometer (see illustration).

REMOVAL

▸ **Refer to illustrations 5.6a and 5.6b**

6   Remove the lug nuts which were installed to hold the disc in place, or remove the two disc retaining screws (see illustration) and remove the disc from the hub. If the disc is stuck to the hub and won't come off, thread two bolts into the holes provided (see illustration) and tighten them. Alternate between the bolts, turning them a couple of turns at a time, until the disc is free. Remove the disc from the hub.

➡Note: Discs that only have one threaded hole to install a bolt into work similarly.

INSTALLATION

7   Place the disc in position over the threaded studs. Install the disc retaining screws and tighten them securely.

8   Install the caliper mounting bracket and caliper, tightening the bolts to the torque values listed in this Chapter's Specifications.

9   Install the wheel, then lower the vehicle to the ground. Tighten the lug nuts to the torque listed in the Chapter 1 Specifications. Depress the brake pedal a few times to bring the brake pads into contact with the disc. Bleeding won't be necessary unless the brake hose was disconnected from the caliper. Check the operation of the brakes carefully before driving the vehicle.

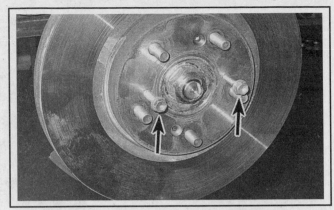

5.6b If the disc is stuck, thread two 8 mm bolts into the threaded holes in the disc and tighten them to force the disc off the hub

6   Drum brake shoes/parking brake shoes - replacement

✳✳ WARNING:

Drum brake shoes must be replaced on both wheels at the same time - never replace the shoes on only one wheel. Also, the dust created by the brake system is harmful to your health. Never blow it out with compressed air and don't inhale any of it. An approved filtering mask should be worn when working on the brakes. Do not, under any circumstances, use petroleum-based solvents to clean brake parts. Use brake system cleaner only!

✳✳ CAUTION:

Whenever the brake shoes are replaced, the return and hold-down springs should also be replaced. Due to the continuous heating/cooling cycle the springs are subjected to, they can lose tension over a period of time and may allow the shoes to drag on the drum and wear at a much faster rate than normal.

6.2 If the drum is hard to pull off, thread a pair of 8 mm bolts into the holes provided to force the drum off

DRUM BRAKE SHOES

▶ **Refer to illustrations 6.2, 6.4a through 6.4s and 6.5**

1   Loosen the rear wheel lug nuts, raise the rear of the vehicle and support it securely on jackstands. Block the front wheels to keep the vehicle from rolling. Remove the rear wheels. Release the parking brake.

2   Remove the brake drum. It should simply pull straight off the hub. If the drum won't come off, tap it carefully with a soft-faced mallet, or screw a couple of 8.0 mm bolts into the tapped holes (see illustration).

3   Replacing the shoes is a lot easier if you remove the rear hub and wheel bearing assembly (see Chapter 10).

4   Follow illustrations 6.4a through 6.4s for the inspection and replacement of the brake shoes. Be sure to stay in order and read the caption under each illustration. All four rear brake shoes must be replaced at the same time, but to avoid mixing up parts, work on one brake assembly at a time.

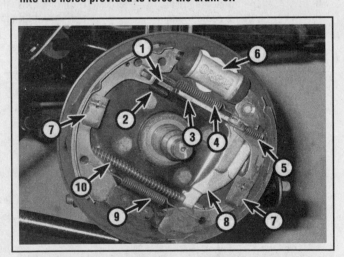

6.4a Details of the rear drum brake assembly

1	Self-adjuster cam	6	Wheel cylinder
2	Self-adjuster spring	7	Shoe retainer spring
3	Adjuster assembly	8	Parking brake lever
4	Upper return spring	9	Lower return spring
5	Anti-rattle spring	10	Parking brake cable

6.4b Before removing anything, clean the brake assembly with brake cleaner and allow it to dry - position a drain pan under the brake assembly to catch the residue - DO NOT USE COMPRESSED AIR TO BLOW BRAKE DUST OFF THE PARTS!

6.4c Use a small screwdriver to move the self-adjuster cam inward so that the adjuster assembly is at its minimum setting

6.4d Pull the upper return spring back and unhook it . . .

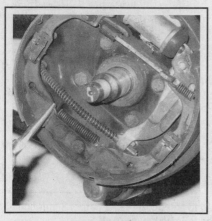

6.4e . . . then detach the lower return spring in the same manner

6.4f Compress the shoe retainer spring and turn the pin to match the slot in the spring to remove it (repeat this on the other shoe)

6.4g Remove the leading shoe

6.4h Remove the anti-rattle spring from the adjuster assembly and the trailing shoe and then remove the adjuster

6.4i Remove the parking brake lever retaining clip; be careful not to lose the wave washer that is under the clip

6.4j Remove the retaining spring from the trailing shoe and then remove the shoe (the parking brake lever will remain attached to the parking brake cable and will hang freely out of the way)

6.4k Clean the backing plate, then lubricate the brake shoe contact areas on the backing plate with high-temperature grease

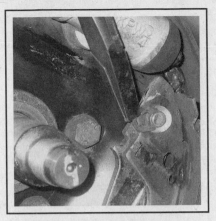

6.4l Assemble the new trailing shoe and the parking brake lever, place the wave washer over the pin and then install the retaining clip

6.4m Install the trailing shoe retainer spring and tension pin

6.4n Set the self adjuster cam on the assembly to the minimum setting (if it slips out of adjustment during the following steps, it can be easily reset again)

6.4o Install the anti-rattle spring to the trailing shoe and then install the adjuster assembly by hooking the spring and moving the adjuster into place on the shoe and parking lever

6.4p Engage the leading shoe with the self-adjuster cam . . .

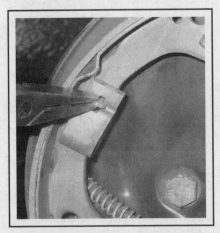

6.4q . . . and install the leading shoe retainer spring

6.4r Install the lower return spring. . .

6.4s . . . and the upper return spring, making sure the adjuster is still set to the minimum setting

5 Before reinstalling the drum it should be checked for cracks, score marks, deep scratches and hard spots, which will appear as small discolored areas. If the hard spots cannot be removed with fine emery cloth or if any of the other conditions listed above exist, the drum must be taken to an automotive machine shop to have it machined.

➡Note: Professionals recommend resurfacing the drums whenever a brake job is done. Resurfacing will eliminate the possibility of out-of-round drums. If the drums are worn so much that they can't be resurfaced without exceeding the maximum allowable diameter (stamped into the drum) (see illustration), then new ones will be required. At the very least, if you elect not to have the drums resurfaced, remove the glazing from the surface with sandpaper or emery cloth using a swirling motion.

6 If previously removed, reinstall the hub and wheel bearing assembly (see Chapter 10). Tighten the hub retaining nut to the torque listed in the Chapter 10 Specifications.

7 Install the brake drum.

8 Mount the wheel, install the lug nuts, then lower the vehicle. Tighten the lug nuts to the torque listed in the Chapter 1 Specifications.

9 Depress the brake pedal several times and then operate the parking brake a few times. Drive the vehicle in reverse and press the brake pedal several times. This will bring the shoes into the proper adjustment.

10 Check brake operation before driving the vehicle in traffic.

✳ WARNING:

Do not operate the vehicle if you are in doubt about the effectiveness of the brake system.

PARKING BRAKE SHOES

◆ Refer to illustrations 6.15a through 6.15v, 6.16a and 6.16b

✳ WARNING:

The dust created by the brake system is harmful to your health. Never blow it out with compressed air and don't inhale any of it. An approved filtering mask should be worn when working on the brakes. Do not, under any circumstances, use petroleum-based solvents to clean brake parts. Use brake system cleaner only!

➡Note: Do one side at a time so that you'll have the other side as a reference.

11 Loosen the rear wheel lug nuts, raise the rear of the vehicle and support it securely on jackstands. Block the front wheels and remove the rear wheels. Release the parking brake.

➡Note: All four parking brake shoes must be replaced at the same time, but to avoid mixing up parts, work on only one brake assembly at a time.

12 Remove the rear brake calipers (see Section 4) and the rear brake discs (see Section 5).

13 Inspect the thickness of the lining material on the shoes. If the lining has worn down to 1/32-inch or less, the shoes must be replaced.

14 To simplify this procedure, you can remove the hub and bearing assembly (see Chapter 10).

➡Note: It's not impossible to do this job without removing the hub and bearing assembly, but it's more difficult.

6.5 The maximum allowable diameter is cast into the drum (typical)

6.15a Before disassembling the parking brake assembly, be sure to wash it with brake cleaner

6.15b Remove the upper return springs. Note: Removing the hub will make this job easier, but isn't absolutely necessary

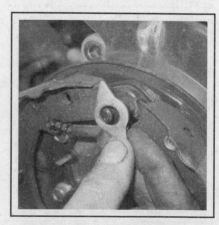

6.15c Lift off the retainer plate

6.15d Spread the shoes and remove the strut

6.15e Remove the star-wheel mechanism, noting which end is facing forward

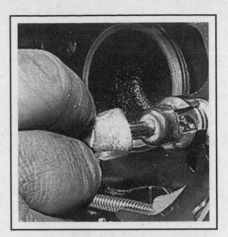

6.15f Remove the shoe hold-down springs and retainers

6.15g Remove the lower spring

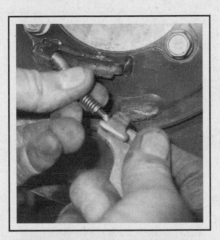

6.15h Disconnect the shoe from the parking brake cable and set all the components aside for cleaning

6.15i Apply brake lubricant to the backing plates at the raised areas that support the shoes

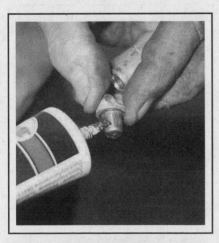

6.15j Lightly lubricate the star-wheel threads and friction surfaces

6.15k Install the front shoe . . .

6.15l . . . followed by the hold-down spring and retainer

6.15m Install the rear shoe, hold-down spring and retainer

6.15n Install the star-wheel with the correct (threaded) end facing forward

6.15o Install the lower spring

6.15p Install the strut with its spring on the forward end

6.15q Install the upper retainer

6.15r Install the front spring . . .

6.15s . . . and the rear spring

6.15t The upper section should now look like this

6.15u This is how the complete parking brake assembly should look when you're done

6.15v If removed, tighten the hub nut to the torque listed in the Chapter 10 Specifications, then stake the nut to the spindle. It might be necessary to shorten the adjuster to install the brake disc

6.16a To adjust the parking brake shoes, remove this plug from the adjuster hole in the brake disc . . .

6.16b . . . position the hole at 6 o'clock, insert a small screwdriver or brake adjuster tool through the hole and rotate the adjuster wheel as necessary until the shoes contact the disc and the disc cannot be turned, then back off the adjuster five notches and install the hole plugs. Turn the disc and make sure the shoes don't drag

15 Wash off the brake parts with brake system cleaner (see illustration), then follow illustrations 6.15b through 6.15v for the brake shoe replacement procedure. Be sure to stay in order and read the caption under each illustration.

16 Adjust the parking brake shoe clearance: Install the brake disc, thread the wheel lug nuts onto the studs to hold the disc in place, then remove the hole plug from the brake disc (see illustration). To adjust the parking brake shoes, turn the adjuster star wheel with a brake adjusting

tool or screwdriver (see illustration) until the shoes contact the disc and the disc cannot be turned, then back off the adjuster five notches and install the hole plugs.

17 Installation is otherwise the reverse of removal. When you're done with one side, repeat this procedure for the other parking brake shoe assembly.

18 Install the rear wheels, lower the vehicle, then adjust the parking brake lever (see Section 12).

7   Wheel cylinder - removal and installation

❋❋ WARNING:

The dust created by the brake system is harmful to your health. Never blow it out with compressed air and don't inhale any of it. An approved filtering mask should be worn when working on the brakes. Do not, under any circumstances, use petroleum-based solvents to clean brake parts. Use brake system cleaner only!

➡ Note: If replacement is indicated (usually because of fluid leakage or sticky operation), it is recommended that the wheel cylinders be replaced, not overhauled. Always replace the wheel cylinders in pairs - never replace just one of them.

REMOVAL

▸ **Refer to illustration 7.4**

1   Raise the rear of the vehicle and support it securely on jackstands. Block the front wheels to keep the vehicle from rolling.

2   Remove the brake shoe assembly (see Section 6).

3   Remove all dirt and foreign material from around the wheel cylinder.

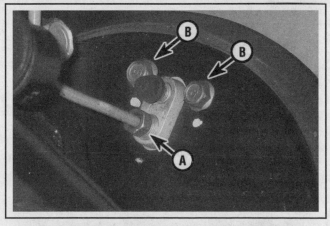

7.4 Disconnect the brake line (A), then remove the wheel cylinder mounting bolts (B)

4   Unscrew the brake line fitting, using a flare-nut wrench, if available, to prevent rounding-off the corners of the fitting (see illustration). Don't pull the brake line away from the wheel cylinder.

5   Remove the wheel cylinder mounting bolts.
6   Detach the wheel cylinder from the brake backing plate and immediately plug the brake line to prevent fluid loss and contamination.

INSTALLATION

7   Apply a small amount of RTV sealant between the backing plate and wheel cylinder, then place the wheel cylinder in position and install the bolts finger tight. Connect the brake line to the cylinder, being careful not to cross-thread the fitting. Tighten the wheel cylinder mounting bolts to the torque listed in this Chapter's Specifications, and tighten the brake line fitting securely.
8   Install the brake shoe assembly (see Section 6).
9   Bleed the brakes (see Section 10).
10 Check the operation of the brakes carefully before driving the vehicle.

8   Master cylinder - removal and installation

REMOVAL

▶ **Refer to illustration 8.3**

1   The master cylinder is located in the engine compartment, mounted to the power brake booster.
2   Using a large syringe or equivalent, siphon the brake fluid from the master cylinder reservoir and dispose of it properly.

❋❋ CAUTION:

Brake fluid will damage paint. Cover all painted surfaces and avoid spilling fluid during this procedure.

3   Disconnect the electrical connector from the fluid level warning switch (see illustration).
4   Place rags under the fluid fittings and prepare caps or plastic bags to cover the ends of the lines once they are disconnected. Loosen the fittings at the ends of the brake lines where they enter the master cylinder. To prevent rounding off the corners on these nuts, the use of a flare-nut wrench, which wraps around the nut, is preferred. Pull the brake lines slightly away from the master cylinder and plug the ends to prevent contamination.

5   Remove the nuts attaching the master cylinder to the power booster. Pull the master cylinder off the studs and out of the engine compartment. Again, be careful not to spill the fluid as this is done.
6   If a new master cylinder is being installed and is not equipped with a reservoir, transfer the reservoir from the old master cylinder to the new one using new seals. Remove the reservoir retaining screw and carefully pry the reservoir away from the old master cylinder. Use clean brake fluid to ease installation of the new seals and reservoir.

INSTALLATION

▶ **Refer to illustration 8.9**

7   If a new master cylinder is being installed, the booster pushrod-to-master cylinder clearance must be checked and, if necessary, adjusted. Refer to Section 11 of this Chapter for the check and adjustment procedures.
8   Bench bleed the new master cylinder before installing it. Mount the master cylinder in a vise, with the jaws of the vise clamping on the mounting flange.
9   Attach a pair of master cylinder bleeder tubes to the outlet ports of the master cylinder (see illustration).
10 Fill the reservoir with brake fluid of the recommended type (see Chapter 1).

8.3 Typical master cylinder mounting details

1	*Electrical connector*	*3 Mounting nuts*
2	*Brake line fittings*	

8.9 The best way to bleed air from the master cylinder before installing it on the vehicle is with a pair of bleeder tubes that direct brake fluid back into the reservoir during bleeding

11 Slowly push the pistons into the master cylinder (a large Phillips screwdriver can be used for this) - air will be expelled from the pressure chambers and into the reservoir. Because the tubes are submerged in fluid, air can't be drawn back into the master cylinder when you release the pistons.

12 Repeat the procedure until no more air bubbles are present.

13 Remove the bleed tubes, one at a time, and install plugs in the open ports to prevent fluid leakage and air from entering. Install the reservoir cap.

14 Install the master cylinder over the studs on the power brake booster and tighten the attaching nuts only finger tight at this time.

15 Thread the brake line fittings into the master cylinder. Since the master cylinder is still a bit loose, it can be moved slightly in order for the fittings to thread in easily. Be careful not to cross-thread or strip the fittings as they are installed.

16 Fully tighten the mounting nuts, then the brake line fittings. Tighten the nuts to the torque listed in this Chapter's Specifications.

17 Fill the master cylinder reservoir with fluid, then bleed the master cylinder and the brake system as described in Section 10. To bleed the cylinder on the vehicle, have an assistant depress the brake pedal and hold the pedal to the floor. Loosen the fitting just enough to allow air and fluid to escape then tighten it lightly. Repeat this procedure on both fittings until the fluid is clear of air bubbles and then tighten the fittings securely.

✳✳ CAUTION:

Have plenty of rags on hand to catch the fluid - brake fluid will ruin painted surfaces. After the bleeding procedure is completed, rinse the area under the master cylinder with clean water.

18 The remainder of installation is the reverse of removal. Test the operation of the brake system carefully before placing the vehicle into normal service.

✳✳ WARNING:

Do not operate the vehicle if you are in doubt about the effectiveness of the brake system. On models equipped with ABS, it is possible for air to become trapped in the anti-lock brake system hydraulic control unit, so, if the pedal continues to feel spongy after repeated bleedings or the BRAKE or ANTI-LOCK light stays on, have the vehicle towed to a dealer service department or other qualified shop to be bled with the aid of a scan tool.

9   Brake hoses and lines - inspection and replacement

1   About every six months, with the vehicle raised and placed securely on jackstands, the flexible hoses which connect the steel brake lines with the front and rear brake assemblies should be inspected for cracks, chafing of the outer cover, leaks, blisters and other damage. These are important and vulnerable parts of the brake system and inspection should be complete. A light and mirror will be needed for a thorough check. If a hose exhibits any of the above defects, replace it with a new one.

FLEXIBLE HOSES

▶ Refer to illustration 9.3

2   Clean all dirt away from the ends of the hose.

3   To disconnect a brake hose from the brake line, unscrew the metal tube nut with a flare nut wrench, remove the U-clip from the female fitting at the frame bracket and then remove the hose from that bracket and the bracket on the strut (see illustration).

4   Disconnect the hose from the caliper.

➡Note: Some models have brake lines that use sealing washers with a banjo fitting. Discard the sealing washers (new ones should be used during installation.

5   Attach the new brake hose to the caliper (with new sealing washers if equipped). Tighten the fitting securely or tighten the brake hose banjo bolt (if equipped) to the torque listed in this Chapter's Specifications.

6   To reattach a brake hose to the metal line, insert the end of the hose through the frame bracket, make sure the hose isn't twisted, then attach the metal line by tightening the tube nut fitting securely. Install

9.3 Unscrew the brake line threaded fitting with a flare-nut wrench to protect the fitting corners from being rounded off (A), then pull off the U-clip (B) with a pair of pliers and remove the brake line from the bracket on the frame and the bracket on the strut (C)

the U-clip at the frame bracket and guide the hose into the bracket on the strut.

7   Carefully check to make sure the suspension or steering components don't make contact with the hose. Have an assistant push down on the vehicle and also turn the steering wheel lock-to-lock during inspection.

8   Bleed the brake system (see Section 10).

METAL BRAKE LINES

9 When replacing brake lines, be sure to use the correct parts. Don't use copper tubing for any brake system components. Purchase steel brake lines from a dealer parts department or auto parts store.

10 Prefabricated brake line, with the tube ends already flared and fittings installed, is available at some auto parts stores and dealer parts departments. These lines can be bent to the proper shapes using a tub-ing bender.

11 When installing the new line make sure it's well supported in the brackets and has plenty of clearance between moving or hot components.

12 After installation, check the master cylinder fluid level and add fluid as necessary. Bleed the brake system as outlined in Section 10 and test the brakes carefully before placing the vehicle into normal operation.

10 Brake hydraulic system - bleeding

▶ **Refer to illustration 10.8**

❋❋ **WARNING:**

If air has found its way into the hydraulic control unit on models with ABS, the system must be bled with the use of a scan tool. If the brake pedal feels "spongy" even after bleeding the brakes, or the ABS light on the instrument panel does not go off, or if you have any doubts whatsoever about the effectiveness of the brake system, have the vehicle towed to a dealer service department or other repair shop equipped with the necessary tools for bleeding the system.

❋❋ **WARNING:**

Wear eye protection when bleeding the brake system. If the fluid comes in contact with your eyes, immediately rinse them with water and seek medical attention.

➡**Note: Bleeding the brake system is necessary to remove any air that's trapped in the system when it's opened during removal and installation of a hose, line, caliper, wheel cylinder or master cylinder.**

1 It will probably be necessary to bleed the system at all four brakes if air has entered the system due to low fluid level, or if the brake lines have been disconnected at the master cylinder.

2 If a brake line was disconnected only at a wheel, then only that caliper or wheel cylinder must be bled.

3 If a brake line is disconnected at a fitting located between the master cylinder and any of the brakes, that part of the system served by the disconnected line must be bled.

4 Remove any residual vacuum (or hydraulic pressure) from the brake power booster by applying the brake several times with the engine off.

5 Remove the master cylinder reservoir cap and fill the reservoir with brake fluid. Reinstall the cap.

➡**Note: Check the fluid level often during the bleeding operation and add fluid as necessary to prevent the fluid level from falling low enough to allow air bubbles into the master cylinder.**

6 Have an assistant on hand, as well as a supply of new brake fluid, an empty clear plastic container, a length of plastic, rubber or vinyl tubing to fit over the bleeder valve and a wrench to open and close the bleeder valve.

7 Beginning at the right rear wheel, loosen the bleeder screw slightly, then tighten it to a point where it's snug but can still be loosened quickly and easily.

8 Place one end of the tubing over the bleeder screw fitting and submerge the other end in brake fluid in a container (see illustration).

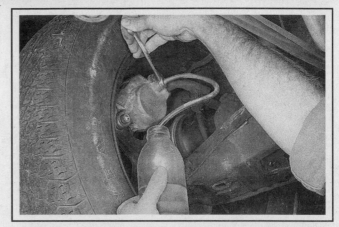

10.8 When bleeding the brakes, a hose is connected to the bleed screw at the caliper and submerged in brake fluid - air will be seen as bubbles in the tube and container (all air must be expelled before moving to the next wheel)

9 Have the assistant slowly depress the brake pedal and hold it in the depressed position.

10 While the pedal is held depressed, open the bleeder screw just enough to allow a flow of fluid to leave the valve. Watch for air bubbles to exit the submerged end of the tube. When the fluid flow slows after a couple of seconds, tighten the screw and have your assistant release the pedal.

11 Repeat Steps 9 and 10 until no more air is seen leaving the tube, then tighten the bleeder screw and proceed to the left rear wheel, the right front wheel and the left front wheel, in that order, and perform the same procedure. Be sure to check the fluid in the master cylinder reservoir frequently.

12 Always use fresh brake fluid when bleeding the brake system. Old brake fluid contains moisture which can boil and disable the brake system.

13 Refill the master cylinder with fluid at the end of the operation.

14 Check the operation of the brakes. The pedal should feel solid when depressed, with no sponginess. If necessary, repeat the entire process.

❋❋ **WARNING:**

Do not operate the vehicle if you are in doubt about the effectiveness of the brake system. On models equipped with ABS, it's possible for air to become trapped in the anti-lock brake system hydraulic control unit, so, if the pedal continues to feel spongy after repeated bleedings or the BRAKE or ANTI-LOCK light stays on, have the vehicle towed to a dealer service department or other qualified shop to be bled with the aid of a scan tool.

11 Power brake booster - removal and installation

OPERATING CHECK

1   Depress the brake pedal several times with the engine off until there is no change in the pedal reserve distance (the distance between the pedal and the floor).

2   Depress the pedal and start the engine. If the pedal goes down slightly, operation is normal.

AIRTIGHTNESS CHECK

3   Start the engine and turn it off after one or two minutes. Depress the brake pedal several times slowly. If the pedal goes down farther the first time but gradually rises after the second or third depression, the booster is airtight.

4   Depress the brake pedal while the engine is running, then stop the engine with the pedal depressed. If there is no change in the pedal reserve travel after holding the pedal for 30 seconds, the booster is airtight.

REMOVAL

▶ **Refer to illustration 11.8**

5   Power brake booster units should not be disassembled. They require special tools not normally found in most automotive repair stations or shops. They are fairly complex and because of their critical relationship to brake performance it is best to replace a defective booster unit with a new or rebuilt one.

6   To remove the booster, first remove the brake master cylinder as described in Section 8.

7   Disconnect the hose leading from the engine to the booster. Be careful not to damage the hose when removing it from the booster fitting.

8   Working inside the vehicle, locate the pushrod clevis pin connecting the booster to the brake pedal (see illustration). Remove the clevis pin retaining clip with pliers and pull out the pin.

9   Remove the four nuts holding the brake booster to the firewall.

10   Slide the booster straight out from the firewall until the studs clear the holes, then pull the booster and gaskets from the engine compartment area.

INSTALLATION

▶ **Refer to illustrations 11.13a, 11.13b, 11.13c and 11.14**

11   If a new booster is being installed, adjust the clevis on the booster's input rod to roughly match the old one.

➡**Note: This adjustment affects pedal freeplay so a refined adjustment will be completed after installation.**

12   Installation procedures are the reverse of those for removal. Tighten the booster mounting nuts to the torque listed in this Chapter's Specifications. Also, be sure to use a new cotter pin on the clevis pin.

13   If a new power brake booster unit is being installed, the booster pushrod-to-master cylinder clearance must be at zero - if there is interference between the two, the brakes may drag; if there is too much clearance, there will be excessive brake pedal travel. Check the pushrod clearance as follows:

   a) *Using a hand-held vacuum pump, apply a vacuum of 20 in-Hg to the booster. Measure the distance that the pushrod protrudes from the master cylinder mounting surface on the front of the power brake booster, including the gasket (if used). Write down this measurement (see illustration). This is "dimension A."*

   b) *Measure the distance from the mounting flange to the end of the master cylinder (see illustration). Write down this measurement. This is "dimension B."*

   c) *Measure the distance from the end of the master cylinder to the bottom of the pocket in the piston (see illustration). Write down this measurement. This is "dimension C."*

   d) *Subtract measurement B from measurement C, then subtract measurement A from the difference between B and C. This the pushrod clearance.*

   e) *The pushrod clearance should be at zero. If necessary, adjust the pushrod length to achieve the correct clearance (see the next Step).*

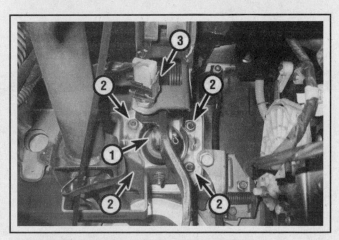

11.8 Brake component details (under the dash)

  1   Pushrod clevis pin
  2   Power booster mounting nuts (one hidden in photo)
  3   Brake light switch

11.13a Measure the distance that the pushrod protrudes from the brake booster at the master cylinder mounting surface (including the gasket, if equipped)

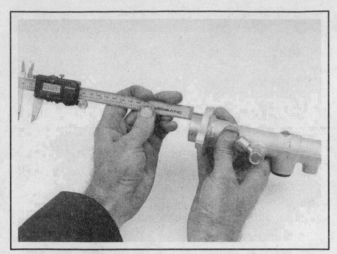

11.13b Measure the distance from the mounting flange to the end of the master cylinder

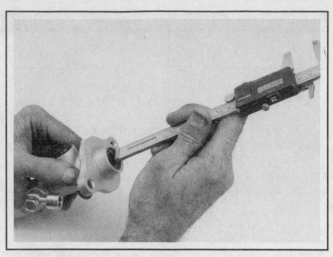

11.13c Measure the distance from the piston pocket to the end of the master cylinder

11.14 To adjust the length of the booster pushrod, hold the serrated portion of the rod with a pair of pliers and turn the adjusting screw

14 Use the adjuster on the end of the power booster pushrod to change its length (see illustration). Recheck the clearance and repeat this step as often as necessary until a zero clearance is met.

15 After the final installation of the master cylinder and brake hoses and lines, adjust the brake pedal freeplay (see Section 14) and then bleed the brakes as described in Section 10.

12 Parking brake - adjustment

◆ **Refer to illustrations 12.6a and 12.6b**

1 The travel on the parking brake lever should be as listed in the Chapter 1 Specifications when properly adjusted. If it travels less than specified, there's a chance the parking brake might not be releasing completely and might be dragging on the drum or disc. If the lever can be pulled more than specified, the parking brake may not hold adequately on an incline, allowing the car to roll.

2 Drive the vehicle in reverse and press the brake pedal several times.

3 On 1995 through 1997 models with rear disc brakes, and on all Sportage models, adjust the (rear) parking brake shoes (see Section 6).

4 On Sportage models, remove the center console (see Chapter 11).

5 Block the front wheels, raise the rear of the vehicle and support it securely on jackstands. Apply the parking brake lever until you hear one click.

6 On Sephia/Spectra models, tighten the adjusting nut on the parking brake lever (see illustration). On Sportage models, tighten the adjusting nut on the parking brake cable equalizer (see illustration). On all models, tighten the adjusting nut in small increments and rotate the rear wheels. Stop turning the nut when the brakes just start to drag on the rear wheels.

7 Release the parking brake lever and check to see that the brakes don't drag when the rear wheels are turned.

8 Lower the vehicle and confirm proper parking brake operation and adjustment.

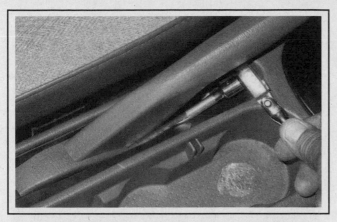

12.6a The parking brake adjusting nut is on the side of the lever assembly (Sephia and Spectra models)

12.6b Parking brake cable adjusting nut (Sportage models)

13 Brake light switch - replacement

1 Disconnect the electrical connector from the brake light switch (see illustration 11.8).

2 Remove the switch by removing the nut that is closest to the brake pedal stop (see illustration 14.2).

3 Install the new switch by rotating it until the plunger (on the switch) is completely compressed and the end of the switch is just against the brake pedal stop.

4 Tighten the switch mounting nuts securely.

5 Check and adjust the brake pedal height and freeplay (see Section 14).

6 Connect the electrical connector to the switch and then check the brake lights for proper operation.

14 Brake pedal - adjustment

BRAKE PEDAL HEIGHT

▶ **Refer to illustrations 14.1 and 14.2**

1 Measure the brake pedal height (see illustration). If the measurement differs from the one listed in this Chapter's Specifications, it must be adjusted.

2 Disconnect the brake light switch, loosen the adjustment and lock nuts and rotate it away from the brake pedal stop (see illustration).

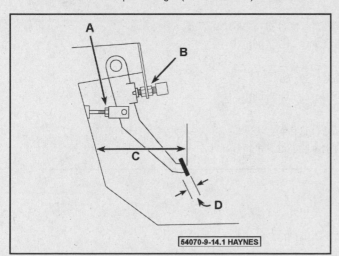

14.1 Brake pedal height and freeplay measuring and adjustment points

A Clevis locknut
B Brake light switch adjusting nut/locknut
C Pedal height measurement point
D Freeplay measurement point

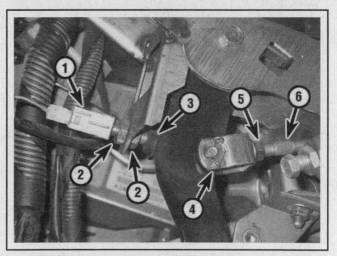

14.2 Brake pedal adjustment details

1 Brake light switch and connector
2 Brake light switch mounting nuts
3 Brake pedal stop
4 Clevis
5 Clevis locknut
6 Power brake booster input (push) rod

3 Loosen the clevis locknut on the booster input rod (see illustration 14.2).

4 Turn the booster input rod until the pedal height is correct.

➡**Note: It may be necessary to move the brake pedal switch further away from the brake pedal stop if more clearance for adjustment is required.**

5 Tighten the clevis locknut securely.

6 Rotate the brake light switch until the plunger (on the switch) is completely compressed and the end of the switch is against the brake pedal stop.

7 Tighten the brake light switch mounting nuts securely.

8 After adjusting the pedal height, check the brake pedal freeplay (see illustration 14.1).

BRAKE PEDAL FREEPLAY

9 With the engine off, depress the brake pedal several times until it becomes firm.

10 Gently press the pedal by hand until resistance is felt. This measured amount of travel is considered brake pedal freeplay (see illustration 14.1).

11 Compare the measurement to the specifications in this Chapter.

12 If adjustment is required, loosen the clevis locknut on the booster input rod (see illustration 14.2).

➡**Note: Also check the clevis, clevis pin and the hole in the brake pedal arm for excessive wear as these will affect pedal freeplay as well.**

13 Turn the booster input rod until the pedal freeplay measurement is correct (see illustration 14.2).

14 Tighten the clevis locknut securely and confirm that the brake pedal freeplay is within specification.

Specifications

General

Brake fluid type	See Chapter 1
Brake pedal	
1994 through 2004 (except 2.0L DOHC)	
Height	7.60 to 7.72 inches (193 to 196 mm)
Freeplay	0.16 to 0.28 inch (4 to 7 mm)
2.0L DOHC	
Height	7.24 inches (189 mm)
Freeplay	0.11 to 0.31 inch (3 to 8 mm)
2005 and later models (all)	
Height	6.42 inches (163 mm)
Freeplay	0.11 to 0.31 inch (3 to 8 mm)

Disc brakes

Brake pad minimum thickness	See Chapter 1
Disc lateral runout limit (front and rear)	
1994 through 2004 (except 2.0L DOHC)	0.004 inch (0.10 mm)
2.0L DOHC and 2.7L V6	0.0012 inch (0.03 mm)
Disc minimum thickness	Cast into disc

Drum brakes

Maximum drum diameter	Cast into drum
Shoe lining minimum thickness	See Chapter 1

Torque specifications	Ft-lbs (unless otherwise indicated)	Nm

➡ Note: One foot-pound (ft-lb) of torque is equivalent to 12 inch-pounds (in-lbs) of torque. Torque values below approximately 15 foot-pounds are expressed in inch-pounds, because most foot-pound torque wrenches are not accurate at these smaller values.

Brake hose banjo fitting bolt	20	27
Caliper mounting bracket bolts		
1997 and earlier models	24	32
1998 through 2004 models (except 2.0L DOHC)	49	66
2.0L DOHC	51 to 54	69 to 73
2005 and later models (all)		
Front	58 to 73	78 to 98
Rear	36 to 44	49 to 59
Caliper mounting guide pins/bolts		
1994 through 2004 (except 2.0L DOHC)		
Front	21	28
Rear	29	39
2.0L DOHC and 2.7L V6 (front and rear)	16 to 23	22 to 32
Master cylinder mounting nuts		
1994 through 2004 (except 2.0L DOHC)	144 in-lbs	16
2.0L DOHC and 2.7L V6	72 to 108 in-lbs	8 to 12
Power brake booster mounting nuts		
1994 through 2004 (except 2.0L DOHC)	19	26
2.0L DOHC and 2.7L V6	120 to 144 in-lbs	13.5 to 16
Wheel cylinder mounting bolts		
1994 through 2004 (except 2.0L DOHC)	108 in-lbs	12
2.0L DOHC	48 to 96 in-lbs	5.5 to 11
Wheel lug nuts	See Chapter 1	

Notes

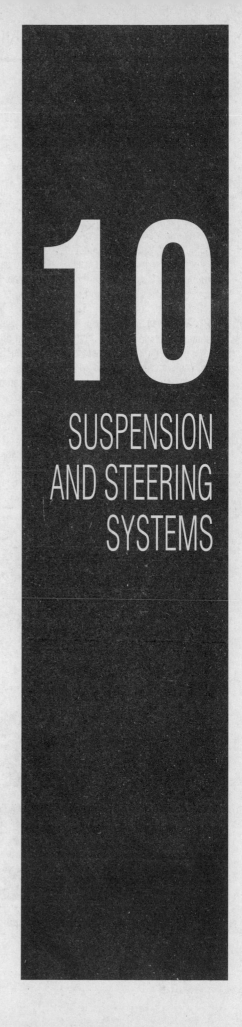

10

SUSPENSION AND STEERING SYSTEMS

Section

1 General information
2 Strut assembly (front) - removal, inspection and installation
3 Strut/coil spring - replacement
4 Stabilizer bar bushings and links (front) - removal and installation
5 Control arm - removal, inspection and installation
6 Balljoints - replacement
7 Steering knuckle and hub (front) - removal and installation
8 Hub and wheel bearing assembly (front) - replacement
9 Strut assembly (rear) - removal, inspection and installation
10 Rear knuckle - removal and installation
11 Suspension arms (rear) - removal and installation
12 Hub and wheel bearing assembly (rear) - replacement
13 Stabilizer bar, bushings and links (rear) - removal and installation
14 Steering wheel - removal and installation
15 Steering column - removal and installation
16 Tie-rod ends - removal and installation
17 Steering gear boots - removal and installation
18 Steering gear - removal and installation
19 Power steering pump - removal and installation
20 Power steering system - bleeding
21 Wheels and tires - general information
22 Wheel alignment - general information

1   General information

◗ **Refer to illustrations 1.1a, 1.1b, 1.2a and 1.2b**

The front suspension is a MacPherson strut design. The upper end of each strut is attached to the vehicle's body strut support. The lower end of the strut is connected to the upper end of the steering knuckle. The steering knuckle is attached to a balljoint mounted on the outer end of the suspension control arm. A stabilizer bar connected to each side of the suspension reduces body roll during cornering (see illustrations).

The rear suspension employs a trailing arm, two lateral arms, and strut/coil spring assemblies all connected to a rear knuckle. As with the front suspension, a stabilizer bar is connected to each side of the suspension to reduce body roll during cornering (see illustrations).

The power-assisted rack-and-pinion steering gear is attached to a front suspension crossmember. The steering gear actuates the tie-rods, which are attached to the steering knuckles.

Frequently, when working on the suspension or steering system components, you may come across fasteners which seem impossible to loosen. These fasteners on the underside of the vehicle are continually subjected to water, road grime, mud, etc., and can become rusted or "frozen" in place, making them extremely difficult to remove. In order to unscrew these stubborn fasteners without damaging them (or other components), be sure to use lots of penetrating oil and allow it to soak in for a while. Using a wire brush to clean exposed threads will also ease removal of the nut or bolt and prevent damage to the threads. Sometimes a sharp blow with a hammer and punch will break the bond between a nut and bolt threads, but care must be taken to prevent the punch from slipping off the fastener and ruining the threads. Heating the stuck fastener and surrounding area with a torch sometimes helps too, but isn't recommended because of the obvious dangers associated with fire. Long breaker bars and extension, or "cheater," pipes will increase leverage, but never use an extension pipe on a ratchet - the ratcheting mechanism could be damaged. Sometimes tightening the nut or bolt first will help to break it loose. Fasteners that require drastic measures to remove should always be replaced with new ones.

Since most of the procedures dealt with in this Chapter involve jacking up the vehicle and working underneath it, a good pair of jackstands will be needed. A hydraulic floor jack is the preferred type of jack to lift the vehicle, and it can also be used to support certain components during various operations.

❊❊ WARNING:

Never, under any circumstances, rely on a jack to support the vehicle while working on it. Whenever any of the suspension or steering fasteners are loosened or removed they must be inspected and, if necessary, replaced with new ones of the same part number or of original equipment quality and design. Torque specifications must be followed for proper reassembly and component retention. Never attempt to heat or straighten any suspension or steering components. Instead, replace any bent or damaged part with a new one.

1.1a   Front suspension and steering components (Sephia and Spectra models)

1	Control arm	3	Steering knuckle	5	Stabilizer bar link
2	Tie-rod end	4	Balljoint	6	Stabilizer bar

1.1b Front suspension and steering components (Sportage models)

1	Control arm	*3*	Steering knuckle	*5*	Stabilizer bar
2	Tie-rod end	*4*	Balljoint		

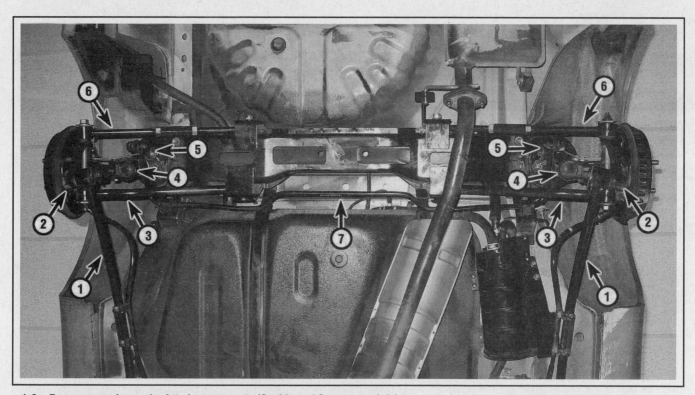

1.2a Rear suspension and related components (Sephia and Spectra models)

1	Trailing arm	*4*	Strut	*6*	Rear lateral arm
2	Rear knuckle	*5*	Stabilizer bar link	*7*	Stabilizer bar
3	Front lateral arm				

1.2b Rear suspension and steering components (Sportage models)

1	*Trailing arm*	*3*	*Front lateral arm*	*5*	*Rear lateral arm*
2	*Rear knuckle*	*4*	*Toe adjuster*	*6*	*Strut*

2   Strut assembly (front) - removal, inspection and installation

❋❋ WARNING:

Struts and/or coil springs must be replaced in pairs - never replace just one of them.

REMOVAL

▶ **Refer to illustrations 2.3, 2.5 and 2.6**

1   Loosen the wheel lug nuts, raise the front of the vehicle and support it securely on jackstands. Apply the parking brake and block the rear wheels to keep the vehicle from rolling off the jackstands. Remove the wheels.

2   Remove the brake hose from the strut's brake hose bracket. On models equipped with ABS, remove the ABS harness from its bracket (see Chapter 9).

➥**Note: On 2002 and later models, disconnect the stabilizer bar link from the strut.**

3   Remove the strut-to-knuckle nuts and then remove the bolts (see illustration).

➥**Note: Use a hammer and punch to remove bolts that are stuck.**

4   Separate the strut from the steering knuckle. Support the steering knuckle from falling outward and overextending the inner CV joint or

causing damage to the brake line.

5   Mark the relationship of the strut mount (top) to the strut tower (see illustration).

❋❋ CAUTION:

Wheel alignment will be adversely affected if the strut mount is not placed back in its original position in the strut tower.

6   Remove the mounting nuts (see illustration 2.5 or accompanying illustration) and then remove the assembly from the fenderwell.

➥**Note: An assistant would be helpful with this step because the strut is heavy and awkward and must be held while the mounting nuts are removed.**

INSPECTION

7   Check the strut body for leaking fluid, dents, cracks and other obvious damage that would warrant repair or replacement.

8   Check the coil spring for chips or cracks in the spring coating (this can cause premature spring failure due to corrosion). Inspect the spring seat for cuts, hardness and general deterioration.

9   If any undesirable conditions exist, proceed to the strut disassembly procedure (see Section 3).

2.3 Remove the strut-to-steering knuckle fasteners

2.5 Strut upper mounting nuts and alignment marks for reinstallation (Sephia and Spectra models)

2.6 Strut upper mounting nuts (Sportage models)

INSTALLATION

10 Guide the strut assembly up into the fenderwell and insert the strut mount studs through the holes in the shock tower. Once seated, install the nuts so the strut won't fall back through and then tighten the nuts to the torque listed in this Chapter's Specifications.

➡**Note: An assistant would be helpful with this step because the strut is heavy and awkward and should be held while the mounting nuts are installed.**

11 Slide the steering knuckle into the strut flange and insert the two bolts. Install the nuts and then tighten them to the torque listed in this Chapter's Specifications.

12 Reattach the brake hose and the ABS harness (if equipped) to the strut bracket

13 Install the wheel and lug nuts, then lower the vehicle and tighten the lug nuts to the torque listed in the Chapter 1 Specifications.

14 Have the front wheel alignment checked and, if necessary, adjusted.

3 Strut/coil spring - replacement

❋❋ WARNING:

Struts and/or coil springs must be replaced in pairs - never replace just one of them.

➡**Note: You'll need a spring compressor for this procedure. Spring compressors are available on a daily rental basis at most auto parts stores or equipment yards.**

1 If the struts or coil springs exhibit the telltale signs of wear (leaking fluid, loss of damping capability, chipped, sagging or cracked coil springs) explore all options before beginning any work. The strut/coil spring assemblies are not serviceable and must be replaced if a problem develops. However, strut assemblies complete with springs may be available on an exchange basis, which eliminates much time and work. Whichever route you choose to take, check on the cost and availability of parts before disassembling your vehicle.

❋❋ WARNING:

Disassembling a strut is potentially dangerous and utmost attention must be directed to the job, or serious injury may result. Use only a high-quality spring compressor and carefully follow the manufacturer's instructions furnished with the tool. After removing the coil spring from the strut assembly, set it aside in a safe, isolated area.

DISASSEMBLY

▸ **Refer to illustrations 3.3, 3.5, 3.6 and 3.7**

2 Remove the strut and spring assembly (see Section 2). Mount the assembly in a vise. Line the vise jaws with wood or rags to prevent damage to the unit and don't tighten the vise excessively.

3.3 Install the spring compressor following the tool manufacturer's instructions; compress the spring until all pressure is relieved from the upper spring seat (you can verify this by wiggling the spring)

3.5 Lift the upper mount off the damper rod

3.6 Remove the upper spring seat and insulator from the damper rod

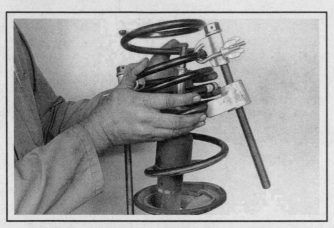

3.7 Carefully remove the compressed spring from the strut

3.10 When installing the spring, make sure the end rests against the raised stop

3   Following the tool manufacturer's instructions, install the spring compressor (which can be obtained at most auto parts stores or equipment yards on a daily rental basis) on the spring and compress it sufficiently to relieve all pressure from the upper spring seat (see illustration). This can be verified by wiggling the spring.

4   Hold the damper shaft from turning with a socket, and unscrew the damper shaft nut with a box-end wrench.

5   Remove the nut and upper mount (see illustration). Lay the parts out in the exact order in which they are removed. Check the rubber portion of the upper mount for cracking and general deterioration. If there is any separation of the rubber, replace it.

6   Remove the upper spring seat from the damper shaft (see illustration). Check the rubber portion of the spring seat for cracking and hardness; replace it if necessary. Inspect the bearing in the spring seat for smooth operation. If it doesn't turn smoothly, replace it.

7   Carefully lift the compressed spring from the assembly (see illustration) and set it in a safe place.

✳✳ WARNING:

When removing the compressed spring, lift it off carefully and set it in a safe place. Keep the ends of the spring away from your body.

➡**Note: If you are disassembling both struts, mark the springs LEFT and RIGHT so you don't mix them up (they're different).**

8   Remove the dust cover and bump stop from the shaft. Check them for cracking or deterioration and replace accordingly.

REASSEMBLY

▶ **Refer to illustration 3.10**

9   Extend the damper rod to its full length and install the rubber bump stop and dust cover.

10   Carefully place the compressed coil spring onto the lower seat of the damper, with the end of the spring resting against the raised stop (see illustration).

11   Install the upper insulator and spring seat.

12   Install the upper mount and mounting nut, then tighten it to the torque listed in this Chapter's Specifications. Remove the spring compressor tool.

13   Install the strut/spring assembly (see Section 2).

---

4   Stabilizer bar bushings and links (front) - removal and installation

▶ Refer to illustrations 4.2 and 4.3

➡Note: Stabilizer bar removal involves lowering the suspension crossmember, removing the stabilizer bar from behind it, and if one becomes damaged it is most likely the result of an accident that was severe enough to damage other major components (such as the crossmember itself). Damage this severe will require the services of an auto body shop. For this reason, front stabilizer bar removal and installation is not covered in this manual.

1   Loosen the wheel lug nuts, raise the front of the vehicle and support it securely on jackstands. Apply the parking brake and block the rear wheels to keep the vehicle from rolling off the jackstands. Remove the wheels.

SEPHIA AND SPECTRA MODELS

2   Detach the links from the lower control arm (or strut) by holding the ballstud with an Allen wrench and removing the nut (see illustration).

➡Note: On 1997 and earlier models, the links are mounted to the lower control arms with a bolt as the link. On 2002 and later models, the links are attached to the front struts and are similar in design as the one illustrated.

3   Remove the stabilizer bar brackets and then the bushings (see illustration).

4   Inspect the bushings for cracks and tears. If either bushing is damaged, replace them both. If the ballstuds on the links are loose, replace the links.

➡Note: On 1997 and earlier models, inspect the link bushings and replace them accordingly.

5   Clean the bushings and the stabilizer bar where the bushings secure it. Lubricate the bushings sparingly with silicone type lubricant and install them onto the bar. Vegetable oil will serve as an alternative lubricant.

✳✳ **CAUTION:**

Use of petroleum or mineral-based lubricants will cause the bushings to deteriorate.

6   Install the brackets and bolts, tightening them to the torque values listed in this Chapter's Specifications.

7   Install the links, tightening the link nuts to the torque listed in this Chapter's Specifications.

SPORTAGE MODELS

▶ Refer to illustrations 4.8, 4.17a and 4.17b

✳✳ **CAUTION:**

This procedure is tricky and potentially dangerous, because you must detach and lower the engine/transaxle subframe in order to remove the stabilizer bar. If you lack the skills and/or the tools for this job, have it done by a professional.

8   Remove the nuts that secure the stabilizer link rods to the stabilizer bar and to the strut housing (see illustration) and remove the link rods.

9   Remove the two bolts that secure the lower control arm balljoint (see Section 6).

10 Remove the front exhaust pipe (see illustration 6.8 in Chapter 2B).

11 On 4WD models, remove the driveshaft (see Chapter 8).

12 Drain the oil from the transfer case (see Chapter 1).

13 Unbolt the rear flange assembly from the transfer case.

14 Separate the intermediate shaft from the steering gear (see Section 10).

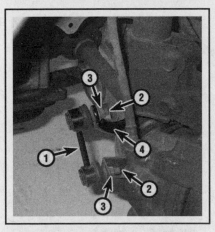

4.2 Stabilizer bar link details (1999 model shown)

1   Stabilizer link
2   Ballstud
3   Nut
4   Stabilizer bar

4.3 Stabilizer bar bracket and mounting bolt

4.8 Stabilizer bar link rod nuts (Sportage models)

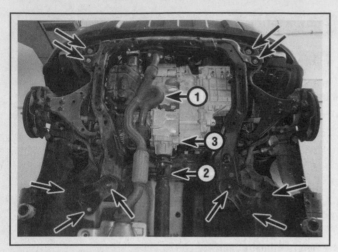

4.17a Remove the subframe fasteners and lower the subframe after removing these components

1   *Front exhaust pipe (see Chapter 2B)*
2   *Driveshaft (4WD models, see Chapter 8)*
3   *Transfer case rear flange assembly*

15 Drain the power steering fluid. Disconnect the power steering pressure line fittings.
16 Support the engine/transaxle assembly with an engine support fixture. Support the subframe assembly with a pair of hydraulic floor jacks (one per side).
17 Remove the engine mounting bolts (see Chapter 2B) and the subframe mounting bolts (see illustration), then lower the subframe assembly just enough to remove the stabilizer bar clamp bolts (see illustration).
18 Remove the stabilizer bar assembly.

4.17b Stabilizer bar bushing clamp and bolts (Sportage models)

19 Remove and inspect the stabilizer bar clamp bushings. If they're cracked, torn or deteriorated, replace them.
20 Installation is the reverse of removal. Be sure to tighten all fasteners securely.

ALL MODELS

21 Install the wheel and lug nuts, lower the vehicle and tighten the lug nuts to the torque listed in the Chapter 1 Specifications.

5   Control arm - removal, inspection and installation

REMOVAL

1   Loosen the front wheel lug nuts, raise the front of the vehicle and support it securely on jackstands. Apply the parking brake and block the rear wheels to keep the vehicle from rolling off the jackstands. Remove the front wheels.

Sephia and Spectra models

▶ **Refer to illustrations 5.3a and 5.3b**

2   On 2001 and earlier models, separate the stabilizer bar link from the control arm (see Section 4).
3   Remove the pinch bolt and nut securing the balljoint to the steering knuckle. Carefully pry the lower control arm (and balljoint) away from the steering knuckle to separate them (see illustrations).
4   Remove the bolts that attach the control arm to the crossmember and then remove the arm (see illustration 5.3a).

Sportage models

▶ **Refer to illustration 5.5**

5   Remove the balljoint-to-steering knuckle bolts (see illustration).

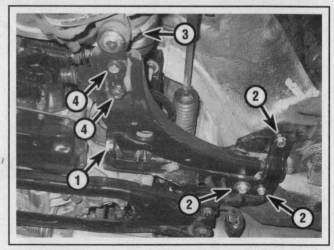

5.3a Control arm details (1999 model shown, other models similar)

1	*Pivot bolt*	3	*Pinch bolt and nut*
2	*Rear bushing mounting bolts*	4	*Balljoint mounting fasteners*

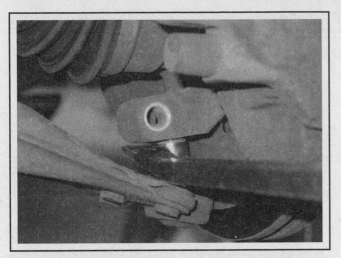

5.3b Separating the balljoint from the steering knuckle using a prybar (Sephia and Spectra models)

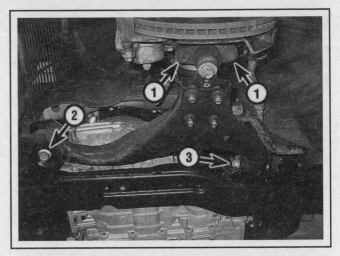

5.5 Control arm details (Sportage models)

1   *Balljoint-to-steering knuckle bolts*
2   *Front control arm mounting bolt*
3   *Rear control arm mounting bolt*

6   Remove the control arm mounting bolts and remove the control arm.

INSPECTION

7   Check the control arm for distortion and the bushings for wear, replacing parts as necessary. Do not attempt to straighten a bent control arm. If the front bushing is worn or cracked, take the control arm to an automotive machine shop and have the bushing replaced. If the rear bushing is in need of replacement, the nut and washer can be removed, the bushing slid off, and the new one installed in its place.

➡ **Note: Make certain that replacement bushings are available before having any work done.**

INSTALLATION

8   Installation is the reverse of removal. Tighten all of the fasteners to the torque values listed in this Chapter's Specifications.
9   Install the wheel and lug nuts, lower the vehicle and tighten the lug nuts to the torque listed in the Chapter 1 Specifications.
10 It's a good idea to have the front wheel alignment checked and, if necessary, adjusted.

6   Balljoints - replacement

♦ **Refer to illustration 6.4**

1   Loosen the wheel lug nuts, raise the front of the vehicle and support it securely on jackstands. Apply the parking brake and block the rear wheels to keep the vehicle from rolling off the jackstands. Remove the wheels.
2   Separate the balljoint from the steering knuckle (see Section 5).
3   On Sephia and Spectra models, remove the fasteners that attach the balljoint to the control arm (see illustration 5.3b).

➡ **Note: The balljoint boot can be replaced if it is damaged but a special tool is required to install a new one. You can take the balljoint to a qualified repair shop for service.**

4   On Sportage models, remove the balljoint cotter pin and nut (see illustration), then remove the balljoint mounting fasteners and remove the balljoint.
5   Installation is the reverse of removal, tighten all of the fasteners to the torque values listed in this Chapter's Specifications.
6   Install the wheel and lug nuts, lower the vehicle and tighten the lug nuts to the torque listed in the Chapter 1 Specifications.

6.4 Balljoint removal details (Sportage models)

1   *Cotter pin*
2   *Balljoint nut*
3   *Balljoint-to-steering knuckle bolts*

7 Steering knuckle and hub (front) - removal and installation

※※ WARNING:

Dust created by the brake system is harmful to your health. Never blow it out with compressed air and don't inhale any of it. Do not, under any circumstances, use petroleum-based solvents to clean brake parts. Use brake system cleaner only.

REMOVAL

1   Loosen the wheel lug nuts and the driveaxle/hub nut, then raise the front of the vehicle and support it securely on jackstands. Apply the parking brake and block the rear wheels to keep the vehicle from rolling off the jackstands. Remove the wheels.

2   Remove the brake caliper and support it with a piece of wire as described in Chapter 9. Remove the caliper mounting bracket, then remove the brake disc from the hub. If the vehicle is equipped with ABS, remove the wheel speed sensor (see Chapter 9).

3   Loosen, but do not remove the strut-to-steering knuckle bolts (see illustration 2.3).

4   Separate the tie-rod end from the steering knuckle arm (see Section 16).

5   Separate the balljoint from the steering knuckle (see Section 5).

6   Remove the driveaxle/hub nut and push the driveaxle from the hub as described in Chapter 8. Support the end of the driveaxle with wire.

7   The strut-to-knuckle bolts can now be removed.

8   Carefully separate the steering knuckle from the strut.

INSTALLATION

9   Guide the knuckle and hub assembly into position, inserting the driveaxle into the hub.

10 Push the knuckle into the strut flange and install the bolts and nuts, but don't tighten them yet.

11 Connect the balljoint to the knuckle and tighten the pinch bolt/nut to the torque listed in this Chapter's Specifications.

12 Attach the tie-rod to the steering knuckle arm (see Section 16). Tighten the strut bolt nuts and the tie-rod nut to the torque values listed in this Chapter's Specifications.

13 Place the brake disc on the hub and install the caliper mounting bracket and caliper as outlined in Chapter 9.

14 Install a new driveaxle/hub nut and tighten it securely (final tightening will be carried out when the vehicle is lowered).

15 Install the wheel and lug nuts.

16 Lower the vehicle and tighten the lug nuts to the torque listed in the Chapter 1 Specifications. Tighten the driveaxle/hub nut to the torque listed in the Chapter 8 Specifications.

17 Have the front-end alignment checked and, if necessary, adjusted.

8 Hub and wheel bearing assembly (front) - replacement

Due to the special tools and expertise required to press the hub and bearing from the steering knuckle, this job should be left to a professional mechanic. However, the steering knuckle and hub may be removed and the assembly taken to an automotive machine shop or other qualified repair facility equipped with the necessary tools. See Section 7 for the steering knuckle and hub removal procedure.

9 Strut assembly (rear) - removal, inspection and installation

※※ WARNING:

Always replace the struts and/or coil springs in pairs - never replace just one of them.

REMOVAL

▶ **Refer to illustrations 9.5, 9.7 and 9.9**

1   Loosen the rear wheel lug nuts, raise the rear of the vehicle and support it securely on jackstands. Block the front wheels to prevent the vehicle from rolling off the jackstands. Remove the wheels.

2   On 1998 and later models, detach the stabilizer bar link from the strut (see Section 13).

3   Remove any brake lines or ABS harnesses that may be attached to the strut.

4   Place a floor jack under the rear knuckle to support it.

5   On Sephia and Spectra models, remove the rear shelf trim panel inside the vehicle (see Chapter 11) to access the upper strut mounting nuts. On Sportage models, remove the trim cover (see illustration) to access the upper strut mounting nuts.

6   On models equipped with ABS, detach the rear wheel speed sensor harness bracket from the strut. On Sportage models, disconnect the rear stabilizer bar link rod from the strut (see Section 13).

7   Remove the strut upper mounting nuts (see illustration).

8   Carefully lower the rear knuckle to separate the strut from the body. Also, support the knuckle from falling outward.

9   Remove the strut-to-knuckle fasteners (see illustration) and carefully separate and remove the strut from the knuckle.

➡**Note: An assistant would be helpful with this procedure because the strut is heavy and awkward and should be held while the mounting fasteners are removed.**

9.5 To access the upper strut mounting nuts on Sportage models, remove this trim cover

9.7 Rear strut upper mounting nuts (Sephia and Spectra models)

9.9 Rear strut-to-knuckle mounting bolts

INSPECTION

10 Refer to Section 2 of this Chapter for inspection procedures.

INSTALLATION

11 Installation is the reverse of removal. Be sure to tighten all fasteners to the torque values listed in this Chapter's Specifications.

12 Tighten the wheel lug nuts to the torque listed in the Chapter 1 Specifications.

10 Rear knuckle - removal and installation

REMOVAL

1 Loosen the rear wheel lug nuts, raise the rear of the vehicle and support it securely on jackstands. Block the front wheels to prevent the vehicle from rolling off the jackstands. Remove the rear wheels.

Disc brake models

♦ **Refer to illustration 10.3**

2 Unbolt the brake hose bracket from the knuckle. Unbolt the brake caliper, hang it out of the way with a piece of wire, then remove the caliper mounting bracket (see Chapter 9).

3 On models equipped with an Anti-Lock Brake System (ABS), detach the bracket(s) for the ABS wheel speed sensor electrical harness from the strut, then remove the bolt that secures the ABS wheel speed sensor to the knuckle (see illustration) and remove the sensor from the knuckle.

4 Remove the two screws that retain the brake disc to the hub. Remove the brake disc (see Chapter 9). Also remove the brake disc splash guard.

5 Remove the hub and bearing assembly from the knuckle (see Section 12).

Drum brake models

♦ **Refer to illustration 10.8**

6 Disconnect the brake line from the wheel cylinder and plug or cap the line and the wheel cylinder (see Chapter 9).

7 Remove the hub and bearing assembly from the knuckle (see Section 12).

8 Remove the bolts that retain the brake backing plate to the

10.3 ABS wheel speed sensor details (Sportage model shown)

1 *ABS wheel speed sensor harness bracket bolt (other harness bracket bolt, on front of strut, not visible)*
2 *ABS wheel speed sensor mounting bolt*

knuckle (see illustration).

All models

9 Detach the lower end of the strut from the knuckle (see Section 9).

10 Unbolt the suspension arms from the knuckle (see Section 11).

11 Remove the knuckle from the suspension arms.

10.8 Mounting bolts for the brake backing plate (rear drum brake models)

12 If the wheel bearing is in need of replacement, replace the hub and bearing assembly as a single unit.

INSTALLATION

13 Connect the suspension arms to the knuckle (see Section 11).

14 Connect the lower end of the strut to the knuckle (see Section 9).

15 Install the hub and bearing assembly (see Section 12).

16 Tighten all of the suspension fasteners to the torque values listed in this Chapter's Specifications.

17 Install the brake components (see Chapter 9). If you're working on a model with rear drum brakes, bleed the brake system (see Chapter 9).

18 Install the wheel and lug nuts, lower the vehicle and tighten the lug nuts to the torque listed in the Chapter 1 Specifications.

11 Suspension arms (rear) - removal and installation

▶ **Refer to illustration 11.3**

1 Loosen the rear wheel lug nuts, raise the rear of the vehicle and support it securely on jackstands. Block the front wheels to prevent the vehicle from rolling off the jackstands. Remove the wheels.

2 Support the rear knuckle with a floor jack.

3 Remove the front or rear lateral arm mounting fasteners from the rear knuckle and the crossmember (see illustration).

➡**Note: On 1997 and earlier models, the inboard end of the lateral arms share the same mounting bolt just like the outboard end on all models.**

➡**Note: There is no need to change the adjustment of the rear lateral arm for removal. Changing this adjustment will adversely affect the rear wheel alignment. If this arm is being replaced, attempt to match the length of the new arm to the old one as closely as possible, and have the vehicle's wheel alignment adjusted after reassembly.**

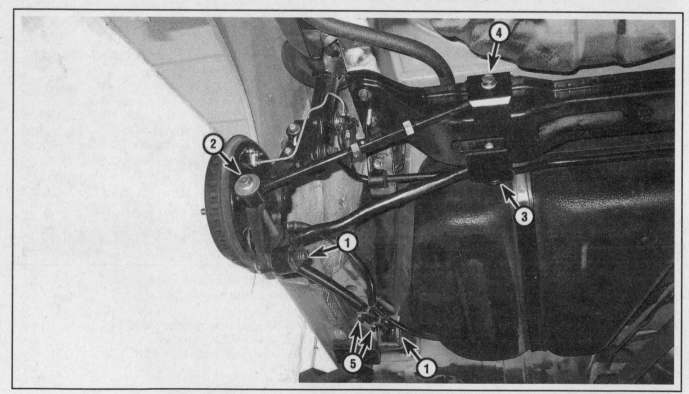

11.3 Rear suspension arm details (1999 model shown, other models similar)

| 1 | Trailing arm mounting bolts | 3 | Front lateral arm mounting bolt (inboard) | 5 | Parking brake cable bracket |
| 2 | Front and rear lateral arm mounting bolt (outboard) | 4 | Rear lateral arm mounting bolt (inboard) | | |

4   Remove the front or rear lateral arm.

5   For trailing arm removal, remove the parking brake cable bracket from the arm (see illustration 11.3).

6   Remove the bolts from each end of the trailing arm, then remove the arm.

7   Inspect the bushings on the arm(s) for wear and deterioration. If replacement is needed, take the arm(s) to an automotive machine shop to have the bushings replaced.

➡Note: Make certain that replacement bushings are available before having any work done.

8   Installation is the reverse of removal. Tighten the fasteners to the torque listed in this Chapter's Specifications.

9   Install the wheel and lug nuts. Lower the vehicle and tighten the lug nuts to the torque listed in the Chapter 1 Specifications.

10 Have the rear wheel alignment checked and, if necessary, adjusted.

12 Hub and wheel bearing assembly (rear) - replacement

♦ Refer to illustrations 12.3a, 12.3b and 12.5

✳✳ WARNING:

Dust created by the brake system is harmful to your health. Never blow it out with compressed air and don't inhale any of it. Do not, under any circumstances, use petroleum-based solvents to clean brake parts. Use brake system cleaner only.

➡Note: The rear hub and bearing are combined into a single assembly. The bearing is sealed for life and requires no lubrication or attention. If the bearing is worn or damaged, replace the entire hub and bearing assembly.

1   Loosen the rear wheel lug nuts, raise the rear of the vehicle and support it securely on jackstands. Block the front wheels to prevent the vehicle from rolling off the jackstands. Remove the wheels.

2   Remove the brake drum or disc (see Chapter 9).

3   Remove the dust cover then unstake and remove the hub retaining nut (see illustrations).

4   Remove the hub and bearing assembly from the spindle.

5   Installation is the reverse of removal, noting the following points:

a) Install a new hub retaining nut and tighten it to the torque listed in this Chapter's Specifications. Stake the new hub nut in place (see illustration).

➡Note: Apply a little clean engine oil to the seating surface of the hub retaining nut before installing it.

b) Install the dust cover by tapping lightly around the edge until it is seated.

c) On models with rear disc brakes, tighten the caliper bolts to the torque listed in the Chapter 9 Specifications.

d) Install the wheel and lug nuts. Lower the vehicle and tighten the lug nuts to the torque listed in the Chapter 1 Specifications.

12.3a Using a hammer and chisel to remove the dust cover

12.3b Using a punch to unstake the hub locknut

12.5 Using a punch to stake the new hub locknut

13 Stabilizer bar, bushings and links (rear) - removal and installation

▶ **Refer to illustrations 13.2 and 13.4**

1   Loosen the rear wheel lug nuts, raise the rear of the vehicle and support it securely on jackstands. Block the front wheels to prevent the vehicle from rolling off the jackstands. Remove the wheels.

2   Detach the link from the stabilizer bar by holding the ballstud with an Allen wrench and removing the nut (see illustration).

➡**Note: On 1997 and earlier models, the links are mounted to the front lateral link (see Section 11) with a long bolt serving as the link.**

3   On 1998 and later models, detach the stabilizer bar links from the rear struts (see illustration 13.2).

4   Unbolt the bushing bracket from each side of the stabilizer bar, then remove the bar (see illustration).

5   Pull the bushings off the bar and inspect them for cracks or other damage. If the bushings are damaged, replace them. On 1998 and later models, also check the stabilizer bar links for loose balljoints and other damage, replacing them as necessary.

➡**Note: On 1997 and earlier models, inspect the link bushings and replace them accordingly.**

6   Clean the bushings and the stabilizer bar where the bushings secure it. Lubricate the bushings sparingly with silicone type lubricant and install them onto the bar. Vegetable oil will serve as an alternative lubricant.

❊❊ **CAUTION:**

Use of petroleum or mineral-based lubricants will cause the bushings to deteriorate.

7   Installation is the reverse of removal. Be sure to tighten all fasteners to the torque values listed in this Chapter's Specifications.

➡**Note: On 1997 and earlier models, use new self-locking nuts to attach the stabilizer bar links.**

8   Tighten the wheel lug nuts to the torque listed in the Chapter 1 Specifications

13.2 Stabilizer bar link nuts

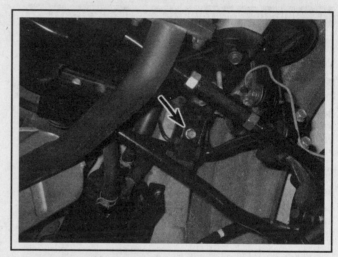

13.4 Stabilizer bar bracket and mounting bolt

14 Steering wheel - removal and installation

❊❊ **WARNING:**

Most of these models are equipped with a Supplemental Restraint System (SRS), more commonly known as airbags. Always disable the airbag system before working in the vicinity of any airbag system component to avoid the possibility of accidental deployment of the airbag(s), which could cause personal injury (see Chapter 12).

❊❊ **WARNING:**

Do not use a memory saving device to preserve the PCM or radio memory when working on or near airbag system components.

REMOVAL

▶ **Refer to illustrations 14.3, 14.4, 14.6 and 14.8**

1   Park the vehicle with the wheels pointing straight ahead. Disconnect the cable from the negative terminal of the battery (see Chapter 5, Section 1).

2   Disable the airbag system (see Chapter 12).

3   Remove the bolts on the back of the steering wheel that mount the airbag module to the steering wheel (see illustration).

4   Carefully lift the airbag module away from the steering wheel and disconnect the electrical connectors (see illustration).

➡**Note: These connectors (like most) have release tabs or some kind of release mechanism that must be dislocated in order to separate them.**

14.3 Airbag module mounting bolts (typical)

14.4 Lifting the airbag module away exposes the electrical connectors

14.6 Use a steering wheel puller to remove the steering wheel

5   Remove the airbag module and store it in a safe location.

✳✳ WARNING:

Carry the airbag module with the trim (upholstered) side facing away from you, and set the airbag module down with the trim side facing up. Don't place anything on top of the airbag module.

6   Remove the steering wheel retaining nut, then mark the relationship of the steering wheel hub to the steering shaft (the index mark will help ensure that the steering wheel is installed in its original position on the steering shaft). Remove the steering wheel using a steering wheel puller (see illustration). The puller screw must be in contact with the steering shaft.

✳✳ CAUTION:

Don't thread the bolts of the puller into the steering wheel too far, as they could contact the airbag clockspring and damage it.

7   Disconnect any remaining electrical connectors and lift the steering wheel off the shaft, feeding the wiring harness through the hole in the wheel.

✳✳ CAUTION:

Do not turn the clockspring, steering shaft or front wheels while the steering wheel is removed. The airbag clockspring could be damaged if the steering wheel is reinstalled with these components misaligned. If one of the components is turned, perform the alignment procedures found later in this section.

8   If it is necessary to remove the clockspring, remove the steering column covers (see Chapter 11), unplug its electrical connectors and then detach it from the combination switch (see illustration).

➡Note: The electrical connector can be found by following the wires on the clockspring down the steering column.

INSTALLATION

9   With the wheels pointing straight ahead, make absolutely sure

14.8 Clockspring mounting screws and alignment marks

that the airbag clockspring is centered. This shouldn't be a problem as long as you have not turned the steering shaft while the wheel was removed. If for some reason the shaft was turned, center the clockspring as follows:

a) *Rotate the clockspring clockwise until it stops (don't apply too much force, though).*

b) *Rotate the clockspring counterclockwise about 2-3/4 turns until the small arrows on the clockspring align at the top (see illustration 14.8).*

10 Installation is the reverse of removal, noting the following points:

a) *Make sure the airbag clockspring is centered before installing the steering wheel.*

b) *When installing the steering wheel, engage the pins on the clockspring with the slots on the steering wheel hub while also noting the alignment marks on the steering shaft and the steering wheel hub.*

c) *Tighten the steering wheel nut to the torque listed in this Chapter's Specifications.*

d) *Carefully install the airbag module on the steering wheel, making certain all electrical connectors are properly connected and tightening the mounting bolts to the torque values listed in this Chapter's Specifications.*

e) *Enable the airbag system (see Chapter 12).*

15 Steering column - removal and installation

✳✳ WARNING::

Most of these models are equipped with a Supplemental Restraint System (SRS), more commonly known as airbags. Always disable the airbag system before working in the vicinity of any airbag system component to avoid the possibility of accidental deployment of the airbag(s), which could cause personal injury (see Chapter 12).

✳✳ WARNING:

Do not use a memory saving device to preserve the PCM or radio memory when working on or near airbag system components.

REMOVAL

▶ Refer to illustrations 15.7 and 15.9

1 Park the vehicle with the wheels in the straight-ahead position. Disconnect the cable from the negative terminal of the battery (see Chapter 5, Section 1). Disable the airbag system (see Chapter 12).

2 Remove the steering wheel (see Section 14).

3 Remove the steering column covers (see Chapter 11).

4 Remove the lower instrument panel trim (under the steering column) (see Chapter 11).

5 Remove the combination switch (see Chapter 12) and the airbag clockspring.

➡Note: The clockspring is mounted to the combination switch. They can be removed together by removing the combination switch. Make sure to disconnect the electrical connectors for the clockspring.

6 Detach the cable for the shift interlock near the ignition lock cylinder.

7 Mark the relationship of the steering column shaft U-joint to the intermediate shaft, then remove the pinch bolt (see illustration).

8 Mark and disconnect any electrical connectors that would interfere with removal.

9 Remove the steering column mounting fasteners, then guide the column out from the instrument panel (see illustration 15.7 and the accompanying illustration).

INSTALLATION

10 Guide the column into position, connecting the steering shaft U-joint with the intermediate shaft. Be sure to align the marks made in Step 7.

11 Install the mounting fasteners, tightening them to the torque listed in this Chapter's Specifications.

12 Install the pinch bolt and tighten it to the torque listed in this Chapter's Specifications.

13 The remainder of installation is the reverse of the removal procedure. Refer to Section 14 for the clockspring, steering wheel and airbag module installation details.

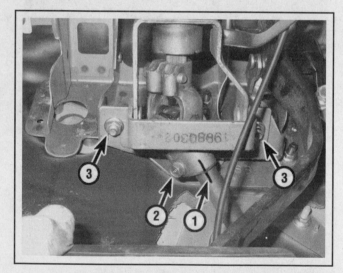

15.7 Steering column shaft to intermediate shaft details (typical):

1   Mark on steering column shaft U-joint to intermediate shaft
2   Steering column shaft U-joint pinch bolt
3   Steering column mounting fasteners (lower)

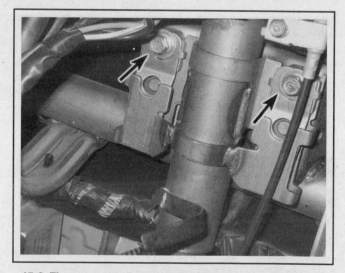

15.9 The upper steering column fasteners

16 Tie-rod ends - removal and installation

REMOVAL

▶ **Refer to illustrations 16.2, 16.3 and 16.4**

1   Loosen the wheel lug nuts, raise the front of the vehicle and support it securely on jackstands. Apply the parking brake and block the rear wheels to keep the vehicle from rolling off the jackstands. Remove the wheels.

2   Loosen the tie-rod end jam nut (see illustration).

3   Mark the relationship of the tie-rod end to the threaded portion of the tie-rod. This will ensure the toe-in setting is restored when reassembled (see illustration).

4   Remove the cotter pin and loosen the nut from the tie-rod end ballstud a few turns. Disconnect the tie-rod end ballstud from the steering knuckle arm with a puller (see illustration).

5   Remove the nut from the ballstud, separate the tie-rod end from the steering knuckle, then unscrew the tie-rod end from the tie-rod.

INSTALLATION

6   Thread the tie-rod end onto the tie-rod to the marked position and connect the tie-rod end to the steering arm. Install the nut on the ballstud and tighten it to the torque listed in this Chapter's Specifications. Install a new cotter pin.

➡**Note: If necessary, tighten the nut a little more to allow insertion of the cotter pin. Never loosen the nut to align the cotter pin holes.**

7   Tighten the jam nut securely and install the wheel. Lower the vehicle and tighten the lug nuts to the torque listed in the Chapter 1 Specifications.

8   Have the front end alignment checked and, if necessary, adjusted.

16.2 Hold the tie-rod end with one wrench and loosen the jam nut with another

16.3 Mark the position of the tie-rod end in relation to the threads

16.4 Disconnect the tie-rod end from the steering knuckle arm with a puller

17 Steering gear boots - removal and installation

▶ **Refer to illustration 17.3**

1   Loosen the wheel lug nuts, raise the front of the vehicle and support it securely on jackstands. Apply the parking brake and block the rear wheels to keep the vehicle from rolling off the jackstands. Remove the wheels.

2   Remove the tie-rod end and jam nut (see Section 16).

3   Remove the outer steering gear boot clamp with a pair of pliers. Cut off the inner boot clamp with a pair of diagonal cutters and slide off the boot (see illustration).

4   Before installing the new boot, wrap the threads on the end of the steering rod with a layer of tape so the small end of the new boot isn't damaged.

5   Slide the new boot into position on the steering gear until it seats in the groove in the steering rod and install new clamps.

➡**Note: Some replacement clamps require special tools for installation. These tools are typically available at most auto parts stores.**

6   Remove the tape and install the tie-rod end (see Section 16).

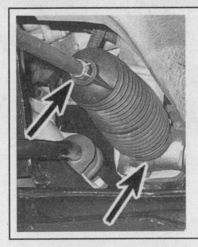

17.3 Remove the clamps from the steering gear boot

7   Install the wheel and lug nuts. Lower the vehicle and tighten the lug nuts to the torque listed in the Chapter 1 Specifications.

8   Have the front end alignment checked and, if necessary, adjusted.

18 Steering gear - removal and installation

✳✳ WARNING:

Make sure the steering shaft is not turned while the steering gear is removed or you could damage the airbag clockspring. To prevent the shaft from turning, place the ignition key in the lock position or thread the seatbelt through the steering wheel and clip it into place.

REMOVAL

Sephia and Spectra models (except 2.0L models)

♦ **Refer to illustrations 18.5, 18.9 and 18.10**

1 Park the vehicle with the front wheels pointing straight ahead. Loosen the front wheel lug nuts, raise the front of the vehicle and support it securely on jackstands. Apply the parking brake and block the rear wheels to keep the vehicle from rolling off the jackstands. Remove the front wheels.

2 Disconnect the cable from the negative battery terminal (see Chapter 5, Section 1).

3 Drain the power steering fluid from the remote power steering reservoir. Use a large syringe, or disconnect the fluid hose, and drain the fluid into a container.

4 Remove the splash shield under the engine compartment (see Chapter 2A).

5 From inside the vehicle under the dashboard, mark the relationship of the intermediate shaft U-joint to the steering gear input shaft, then remove the pinch bolt securing the U-joint to the steering gear input shaft (see illustration).

6 Remove the nuts that secure the sealing cover and leave the cover loose around the steering gear input shaft see illustration 18.5).

7 Detach the tie-rod ends from the steering knuckles (see Section 16).

8 On models with a manual transaxle, disconnect the shift control and extension rods from the transaxle (see Chapter 7A).

9 Place a drain pan under the steering gear and detach the power steering pressure and return lines (see illustration). Cap the ends to prevent excessive fluid loss and contamination.

10 Remove the bracket that supports the pressure and return lines to the steering gear (see illustration).

2.0L models (except Sportage)

11 Remove the front portion of the exhaust system, including the catalytic converter (see Chapter 4).

12 Remove the bolts securing the engine mount to the rear of the subframe, between the engine and the firewall (see Chapter 2A).

13 Support the rear of the subframe with a floor jack. Remove the rear subframe mounting nuts and the control arm rear bushing bracket bolts (see illustration 5.3a). Slowly lower the subframe just enough to allow steering gear removal.

All models

♦ **Refer to illustrations 18.14a and 18.14b**

14 Remove the fasteners from the steering gear mounting brackets (see illustrations).

15 Carefully lower the steering gear to separate the gear's input shaft from the intermediate shaft U-joint (inside the vehicle) and then guide the steering gear out the right side of the vehicle.

➡ **Note: Be careful not to damage the sealing cover while removing the steering gear.**

Sportage models

16 Lower the subframe (see Steps 8 through 17 in Section 4).

17 Remove the two steering gear mounting bolts (left side) and the steering gear clamp bolts (right side) and remove the steering gear from the subframe.

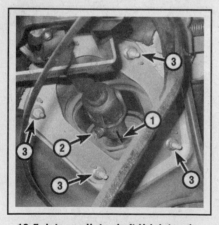

18.5 Intermediate shaft U-joint and steering gear details:

1   Mark on intermediate shaft U-joint to steering input shaft
2   Intermediate shaft U-joint pinch bolt
3   Sealing cover mounting fasteners

18.9 Use a flare-nut wrench to remove the two larger lines from the steering gear

18.10 Steering gear line bracket and fasteners

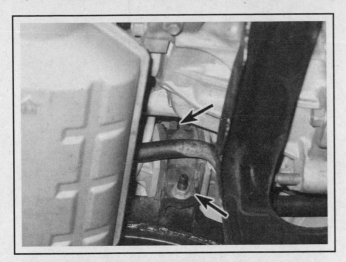

18.14a Steering gear left-side mounting bracket and fasteners

18.14b Steering gear right-side mounting bracket and fasteners

INSTALLATION

18 Installation is the reverse of removal, noting the following points:

a) When placing the steering gear in position, be sure to align the marks on the gear's input shaft with the intermediate shaft U-joint.

➡ Note: Make sure that the tie rods are even on both sides of the steering gear (centered).

b) Tighten the mounting bracket bolts to the torque listed in this Chapter's Specifications.

c) On 2.0L models and all Sportage models, tighten the subframe nuts and the control arm rear mounting bolts to the torque listed in this Chapter's Specifications. Tighten the engine mount bolts securely.

d) Fill the power steering pump with the recommended fluid (see Chapter 1), bleed the system (see Section 20) and recheck the fluid level. Check for leaks.

e) Run the engine and check for proper operation and leaks. Shut off the engine and recheck fluid levels.

f) Reconnect the negative battery cable (see Chapter 5, Section 1).

g) Have the front end alignment checked and, if necessary, adjusted.

19 Power steering pump - removal and installation

1 Disconnect the cable from the negative battery terminal (see Chapter 5, Section 1).

2 Place a drain pan under the vehicle to catch any fluid spills when the hoses are disconnected.

FOUR-CYLINDER MODELS

▶ **Refer to illustrations 19.3 and 19.4**

3 Clamp the feed hose shut, then disconnect it (see illustration). Also unscrew the banjo fitting and disconnect the pressure line from the pump.

➡ Note: Cap or plug the hoses and lines to prevent contamination or leakage while they are disconnected.

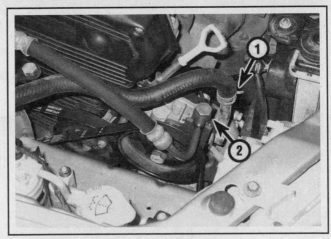

19.3 Power steering pump hose and line (four-cylinder models)

1 Feed hose and clamp
2 Pressure line (with banjo fitting)

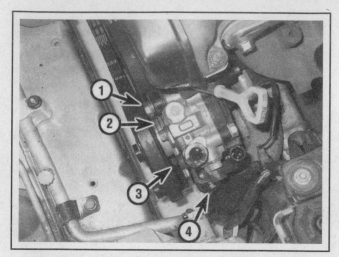

**19.4 Power steering pump mounting fasteners
(four-cylinder models)**

1 Pivot bolt (accessible through the slot in the pulley)
2 Mounting bracket bolt
3 Mounting locknut
4 Adjusting bolt

4   Loosen the mounting and adjusting fasteners to remove the
drivebelt (see Chapter 1), then remove the fasteners to detach the pump
(see illustration).

V6 MODELS

▶ **Refer to illustration 19.5**

5   Disconnect the Power Steering Pressure (PSP) switch (see illustration) from the power steering pump.
6   Remove the banjo bolt and disconnect the power steering high-
pressure line from the pump.
7   Loosen the hose clamp and disconnect the suction hose from the
pump.
8   Remove the power steering pump support bracket bolts and

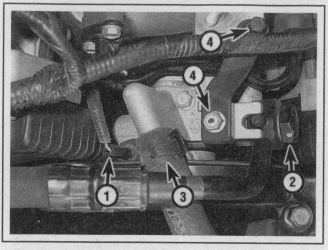

19.5 Power steering pump details (Sportage V6 models)

1   Power Steering Pressure (PSP) switch
2   High-pressure line banjo bolt
3   Suction hose clamp
4   Power steering pump support bracket bolts

remove the support bracket.
9   Remove the serpentine drivebelt (see Chapter 1).
10 Working through the holes in the pump pulley, remove the two
power steering pump mounting bolts and remove the pump.

ALL MODELS

11 Installation is the reverse of removal, noting the following points:
  a) Tighten the pump mounting fasteners to the torque listed in this
     Chapter's Specifications.
  b) Use a new sealing washer(s) on the high pressure line fitting.
  c) Install and adjust the drivebelt as outlined in Chapter 1.
  d) Fill the power steering fluid reservoir with the recommended fluid
     (see Chapter 1). Bleed the power steering hydraulic system as
     described in Section 20.

20 Power steering system - bleeding

1   The power steering system must be bled whenever a line is disconnected. Bubbles can be seen in power steering fluid that has air in it
and the fluid will often have a tan or milky appearance. Low fluid level
can cause air to mix with the fluid, resulting in a noisy pump as well as
foaming of the fluid.
2   Open the hood and check the fluid level in the reservoir, adding the specified fluid necessary to bring it up to the proper level (see
Chapter 1).
3   Start the engine and slowly turn the steering wheel several times
from left-to-right and back again. Do not turn the wheel completely from
lock-to-lock. Check the fluid level, topping it up as necessary until it
remains steady and no more bubbles are visible.

21 Wheels and tires - general information

▶ **Refer to illustration 21.1**

1   All vehicles covered by this manual are equipped with metric-sized fiberglass or steel belted radial tires (see illustration). Use of other size or type of tires may affect the ride and handling of the vehicle. Don't mix different types of tires, such as radials and bias belted, on the same vehicle as handling may be seriously affected. It's recommended that tires be replaced in pairs on the same axle, but if only one tire is being replaced, be sure it's the same size, structure and tread design as the other.

2   Because tire pressure has a substantial effect on handling and wear, the pressure on all tires should be checked at least once a month or before any extended trips (see Chapter 1).

3   Wheels must be replaced if they are bent, dented, leak air, have elongated bolt holes, are heavily rusted, out of vertical symmetry or if the lug nuts won't stay tight. Wheel repairs that use welding or peening are not recommended.

4   Tire and wheel balance is important in the overall handling, braking and performance of the vehicle. Unbalanced wheels can adversely affect handling and ride characteristics as well as tire life. Whenever a tire is installed on a wheel, the tire and wheel should be balanced by a shop with the proper equipment.

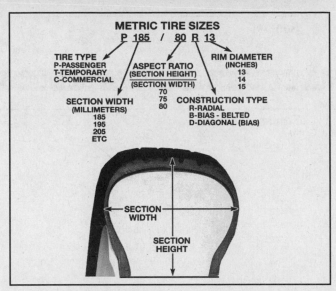

21.1 Metric tire size code

22 Wheel alignment - general information

▶ **Refer to illustration 22.1**

A wheel alignment refers to the adjustments made to the wheels so they are in proper angular relationship to the suspension and the ground. Wheels that are out of proper alignment not only affect vehicle control, but also increase tire wear. The front end angles normally measured are camber, caster and toe-in (see illustration). Toe-in and front camber are adjustable; if the caster is not correct, check for bent components. Rear toe-in is also adjustable, but rear camber and caster are not (if these angles are not correct, check for bent components).

Getting the proper wheel alignment is a very exacting process, one in which complicated and expensive machines are necessary to perform the job properly. Because of this, you should have a technician with the proper equipment perform these tasks. We will, however, use this space to give you a basic idea of what is involved with a wheel alignment so you can better understand the process and deal intelligently with the shop that does the work.

Toe-in is the turning in of the wheels. The purpose of a toe specification is to ensure parallel rolling of the wheels. In a vehicle with zero toe-in, the distance between the front edges of the wheels will be the same as the distance between the rear edges of the wheels. The actual amount of toe-in is normally only a fraction of an inch. Incorrect toe-in will cause the tires to wear improperly by making them scrub against the road surface.

Camber is the tilting of the wheels from vertical when viewed from one end of the vehicle. When the wheels tilt out at the top, the camber is said to be positive (+). When the wheels tilt in at the top the camber is negative (-). The amount of tilt is measured in degrees from vertical and this measurement is called the camber angle. This angle affects the amount of tire tread which contacts the road and compensates for changes in the suspension geometry when the vehicle is cornering or traveling over an undulating surface.

Caster is the tilting of the front steering axis from the vertical. A tilt toward the rear is positive caster and a tilt toward the front is negative caster.

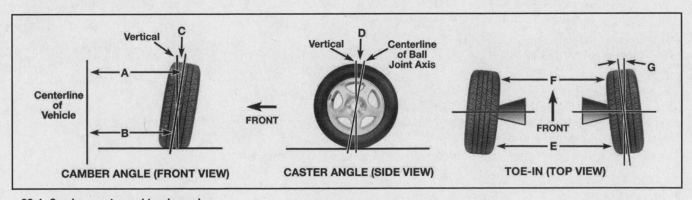

22.1 Camber, caster and toe-in angles

A minus B = C (degrees camber)
D = degrees caster

E minus F = toe-in (measured in inches)
G = toe-in (expressed in degrees)

Specifications

General

Power steering fluid type   See Chapter 1

Torque specifications	Ft-lbs (unless otherwise indicated)	Nm
Front suspension		
Strut		
Damper shaft nut*	50	68
Strut upper mounting nuts		
1997 and earlier models	22	29
1998 and later models	38	52
Strut-to-steering knuckle bolts/nuts		
1994 through 2004 except 2.0L DOHC	86	117
2004 and later (2.0L DOHC and 2.7L V6)	111	150
Stabilizer bar		
Stabilizer bar link nuts		
1997 and earlier models*	0.22 to 0.44 in (7 to 11 mm) of exposed thread	
1998 and later models (except Sportage)	45	61
Sportage	74 to 89	100 to 120
Stabilizer bar bracket bolts		
1994 through 2004 except 2.0L DOHC	40	54
2004 and later 2.0L DOHC		
(except Sportage)	22 to 33	30 to 45
Sportage	33 to 41	45 to 55
Control arm mounting bolts		
1994 through 2004, except 2.0L DOHC		
Pivot bolt	86	117
Rear mounting bolts		
Large	86	117
Small	50	68
Rear bushing nut	69 to 86	94 to 117
2004 and later 2.0L DOHC	96 to 111	130 to 150
Balljoint-to-control arm bolts/nuts	86	117
Balljoint-to-steering knuckle fasteners		
2004 and earlier, except 2.0L DOHC	40	54
2004 and later 2.0L DOHC (except Sportage)	43 to 52	58 to 71
Sportage		
Front pivot bolt	74 to 89	100 to 120
Rear pivot bolt	103 to 118	140 to 160
Driveaxle/hub nut*	See Chapter 8	
Subframe mounting nuts		
2002 through 2004 models (except 2.0L DOHC)	69 to 86	94 to 117
Sportage	37 to 48	50 to 65

*The manufacturer states that these fastener(s) must be replaced whenever removed.

Torque specifications	Ft-lbs (unless otherwise indicated)	Nm

➡**Note: One foot-pound (ft-lb) of torque is equivalent to 12 inch-pounds (in-lbs) of torque. Torque values below approximately 15 foot-pounds are expressed in inch-pounds, because most foot-pound torque wrenches are not accurate at these smaller values.**

Rear suspension

Strut		
Damper shaft nut		
2004 and earlier models except 2.0L DOHC	59	80
2004 and later 2.0L DOHC models		
(except Sportage)	30 to 41	40 to 56
Sportage	38 to 50	52 to 70
Upper mounting nuts		
2001 and earlier models	27	37
2002 through 2004 models except		
2.0L DOHC	22	30
2004 and later 2.0L DOHC and		
2.7L V6 models	22 to 30	30 to 40
Strut-to-steering knuckle nuts/bolts		
2004 and earlier models except		
2.0L DOHC	86	117
2004 and later 2.0L DOHC models		
(except Sportage)	81 to 96	110 to 130
Sportage	103 to 118	140 to 160
Stabilizer bar		
Stabilizer bar bracket bolts		
2004 and earlier models except		
2.0L DOHC	40	54
2004 and later 2.0L DOHC models		
(except Sportage)	13 to 19	18 to 26
Sportage	33 to 40	45 to 55
Stabilizer bar link nuts		
1997 and earlier models*	0.43 to 0.59 inch (11 to 15 mm) of exposed threads	
1998 through 2004 models except		
2.0L DOHC	45	61
2004 and later 2.0L DOHC models		
(except Sportage)	26 to 33	35 to 45
Sportage	74 to 89	100 to 120
Suspension arms		
Front and rear lateral arms		
2004 and earlier models except		
2.0L DOHC	86	117
2004 and later 2.0L DOHC and 2.7L V6 models		
Tie-rod adjusting nuts	37 to 43	50 to 58
Suspension arm-to-rear crossmember		
bolts/nuts	118 to 133	160 to 180
Trailing arms		
2004 and earlier models except		
2.0L DOHC	40	54
2004 and later 2.0L DOHC and		
2.7L V6 models	74 to 88	100 to 119

The manufacturer states that these fastener(s) must be replaced whenever removed.

Torque specifications (continued)	Ft-lbs (unless otherwise indicated)	Nm

→Note: One foot-pound (ft-lb) of torque is equivalent to 12 inch-pounds (in-lbs) of torque. Torque values below approximately 15 foot-pounds are expressed in inch-pounds, because most foot-pound torque wrenches are not accurate at these smaller values.

	Ft-lbs	Nm
Rear hub nuts		
2004 and earlier models except		
2.0L DOHC	205	278
2004 and later 2.0L DOHC models	148 to 188	200 to 255

Steering system

	Ft-lbs	Nm
Power steering pump mounting fasteners		
1994 through 2004 except 2.0L DOHC	38	52
2004 and later 2.0L DOHC	26 to 36	35 to 49
Steering gear mounting fasteners		
1994 through 2004 except 2.0L DOHC	34	46
2004 and later 2.0L DOHC	44 to 58	60 to 79
Tie-rod end-to-steering knuckle nut		
1994 through 2004 except 2.0L DOHC	29	39
2004 and later 2.0L DOHC (except Sportage)	12 to 25	16 to 34
Sportage	33 to 43	45 to 60
Steering column shaft-to-intermediate shaft U-joint pinch bolt		
1994 through 2004 except 2.0L DOHC	20	27
2004 and later 2.0L DOHC and 2.7L V6 models	132 to 168 in-lbs	15 to 19
Steering gear input shaft-to-intermediate U-joint pinch bolt		
1994 through 2004 except 2.0L DOHC	20	27
2004 and later 2.0L DOHC and 2.7L V6 models	132 to 168 in-lbs	15 to 19
Steering column mounting bracket fasteners		
1994 through 1997	120 in-lbs	13.5
1998 through 2004 except 2.0L DOHC	17	23
2004 and later 2.0L DOHC	120 to 156 in-lbs	13.5 to 17.5
Steering wheel mounting nut		
1994 through 2004 except 2.0L DOHC	36	49
2004 and later 2.0L DOHC (except Sportage)	26 to 33	35 to 45
Sportage	29 to 36	40 to 50

*The manufacturer states that these fastener(s) must be replaced whenever removed.

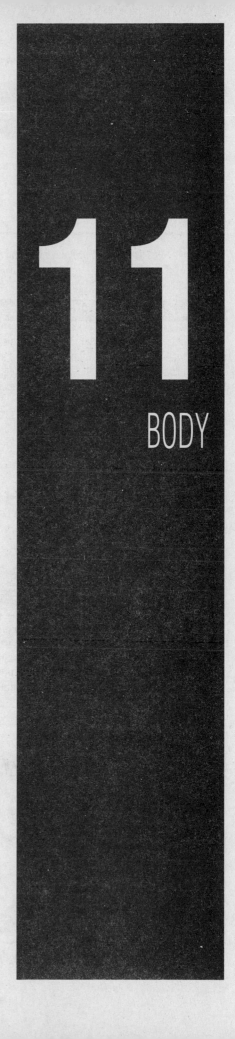

11

BODY

Section

1   General infromation
2   Repair minor paint scratches
3   Body repair - minor damage
4   Body repair - major damage
5   Upholstery, carpets and vinyl trim - maintenance
6   Fastener and trim removal
7   Hinges and locks - maintenance
8   Windshield and fixed glass - replacement
9   Hood - removal, installation and adjustment
10 Hood release latch and cable - removal and installation
11 Bumper covers - removal and installation
12 Front fender - removal and installation
13 Trunk lid and rear hatch, latch and lock cylinder - removal and installation
14 Trunk lid - removal and installation
15 Rear hatch - removal, installation and adjustment
16 Trunk release and fuel door lever - removal and installation
17 Door trim panels - removal and installation
18 Door - removal, installation and adjustment
19 Door latch, lock cylinder and handles - removal and installation
20 Door window glass - removal and installation
21 Door window glass regulator - removal and installation
22 Mirrors - removal and installation
23 Center console - removal and installation
24 Dashboard trim panels - removal and installation
25 Steering column covers - removal and installation
26 Instrument panel - removal and installation
27 Cowl cover - removal and installation
28 Seats - removal and installation
29 Rear shelf trim panel - removal and installation

1 General information

※※ WARNING:

The models covered by this manual are equipped with Supplemental Restraint Systems (SRS), more commonly known as airbags. Always disable the airbag system before working in the vicinity of any airbag system components to avoid the possibility of accidental deployment of the airbags, which could cause personal injury (see Chapter 12).

These models feature a unibody layout, using a floor pan with front and rear frame side rails which support the body components, and front and rear subframes which support suspension systems and other mechanical components.

Certain body components are particularly vulnerable to accident damage and can be unbolted and repaired or replaced. Among these parts are the hood, doors, tailgate, liftgate, bumpers and front fenders.

Only general body maintenance practices and body panel repair procedures within the scope of the do-it-yourselfer are included in this Chapter.

2 Repair minor paint scratches

No matter how hard you try to keep your vehicle looking like new, it will inevitably be scratched, chipped or dented at some point. If the metal is actually dented, seek the advice of a professional. But you can fix minor scratches and chips yourself. Buy a touch-up paint kit from a dealer service department or an auto parts store. To ensure that you get the right color, you'll need to have the specific make, model and year of your vehicle and, ideally, the paint code, which is located on a special metal plate under the hood or in the door jamb.

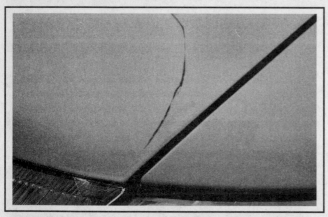

Make sure the damaged area is perfectly clean and rust free. If the touch-up kit has a wire brush, use it to clean the scratch or chip. Or use fine steel wool wrapped around the end of a pencil. Clean the scratched or chipped surface only, not the good paint surrounding it. Rinse the area with water and allow it to dry thoroughly

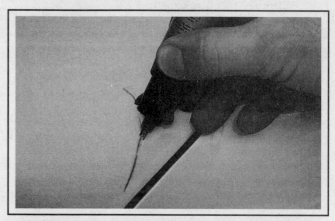

Thoroughly mix the paint, then apply a small amount with the touch-up kit brush or a very fine artist's brush. Brush in one direction as you fill the scratch area. Do not build up the paint higher than the surrounding paint

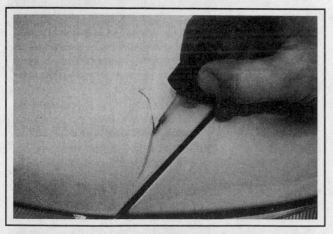

If the vehicle has a two-coat finish, apply the clear coat after the color coat has dried

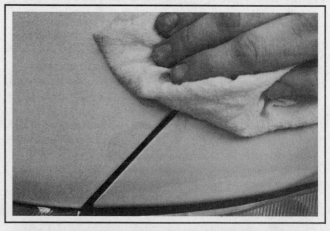

Wait a few days for the paint to dry thoroughly, then rub out the repainted area with a polishing compound to blend the new paint with the surrounding area. When you're happy with your work, wash and polish the area

3 Body repair - minor damage

PLASTIC BODY PANELS

The following repair procedures are for minor scratches and gouges. Repair of more serious damage should be left to a dealer service department or qualified auto body shop. Below is a list of the equipment and materials necessary to perform the following repair procedures on plastic body panels.

Wax, grease and silicone removing solvent
Cloth-backed body tape
Sanding discs
Drill motor with three-inch disc holder
Hand sanding block
Rubber squeegees
Sandpaper
Non-porous mixing palette
Wood paddle or putty knife
Curved-tooth body file
Flexible parts repair material

Flexible panels (bumper trim)

1 Remove the damaged panel, if necessary or desirable. In most cases, repairs can be carried out with the panel installed.

2 Clean the area(s) to be repaired with a wax, grease and silicone removing solvent applied with a water-dampened cloth.

3 If the damage is structural, that is, if it extends through the panel, clean the backside of the panel area to be repaired as well. Wipe dry.

4 Sand the rear surface about 1-1/2 inches beyond the break.

5 Cut two pieces of fiberglass cloth large enough to overlap the break by about 1-1/2 inches. Cut only to the required length.

6 Mix the adhesive from the repair kit according to the instructions included with the kit, and apply a layer of the mixture approximately 1/8-inch thick on the backside of the panel. Overlap the break by at least 1-1/2 inches.

7 Apply one piece of fiberglass cloth to the adhesive and cover the cloth with additional adhesive. Apply a second piece of fiberglass cloth to the adhesive and immediately cover the cloth with additional adhesive in sufficient quantity to fill the weave.

8 Allow the repair to cure for 20 to 30 minutes at 60-degrees to 80-degrees F.

9 If necessary, trim the excess repair material at the edge.

10 Remove all of the paint film over and around the area(s) to be repaired. The repair material should not overlap the painted surface.

11 With a drill motor and a sanding disc (or a rotary file), cut a "V" along the break line approximately 1/2-inch wide. Remove all dust and loose particles from the repair area.

12 Mix and apply the repair material. Apply a light coat first over the damaged area; then continue applying material until it reaches a level slightly higher than the surrounding finish.

13 Cure the mixture for 20 to 30 minutes at 60-degrees to 80-degrees F.

14 Roughly establish the contour of the area being repaired with a body file. If low areas or pits remain, mix and apply additional adhesive.

15 Block sand the damaged area with sandpaper to establish the actual contour of the surrounding surface.

16 If desired, the repaired area can be temporarily protected with several light coats of primer. Because of the special paints and techniques required for flexible body panels, it is recommended that the vehicle be taken to a paint shop for completion of the body repair.

STEEL BODY PANELS

▶ **See photo sequence**

Repair of dents

17 When repairing dents, the first job is to pull the dent out until the affected area is as close as possible to its original shape. There is no point in trying to restore the original shape completely as the metal in the damaged area will have stretched on impact and cannot be restored to its original contours. It is better to bring the level of the dent up to a point that is about 1/8-inch below the level of the surrounding metal. In cases where the dent is very shallow, it is not worth trying to pull it out at all.

18 If the backside of the dent is accessible, it can be hammered out gently from behind using a soft-face hammer. While doing this, hold a block of wood firmly against the opposite side of the metal to absorb the hammer blows and prevent the metal from being stretched.

19 If the dent is in a section of the body which has double layers, or some other factor makes it inaccessible from behind, a different technique is required. Drill several small holes through the metal inside the damaged area, particularly in the deeper sections. Screw long, self-tapping screws into the holes just enough for them to get a good grip in the metal. Now pulling on the protruding heads of the screws with locking pliers can pull out the dent.

20 The next stage of repair is the removal of paint from the damaged area and from an inch or so of the surrounding metal. This is easily done with a wire brush or sanding disk in a drill motor, although it can be done just as effectively by hand with sandpaper. To complete the preparation for filling, score the surface of the bare metal with a screwdriver or the tang of a file or drill small holes in the affected area. This will provide a good grip for the filler material. To complete the repair, see the Section on filling and painting.

Repair of rust holes or gashes

21 Remove all paint from the affected area and from an inch or so of the surrounding metal using a sanding disk or wire brush mounted in a drill motor. If these are not available, a few sheets of sandpaper will do the job just as effectively.

22 With the paint removed, you will be able to determine the severity of the corrosion and decide whether to replace the whole panel, if possible, or repair the affected area. New body panels are not as expensive as most people think and it is often quicker to install a new panel than to repair large areas of rust.

23 Remove all trim pieces from the affected area except those which will act as a guide to the original shape of the damaged body, such as headlight shells, etc. Using metal snips or a hacksaw blade, remove all loose metal and any other metal that is badly affected by rust. Hammer the edges of the hole in to create a slight depression for the filler material.

24 Wire-brush the affected area to remove the powdery rust from the surface of the metal. If the back of the rusted area is accessible, treat it with rust inhibiting paint.

25 Before filling is done, block the hole in some way. This can be done with sheet metal riveted or screwed into place, or by stuffing the hole with wire mesh.

26 Once the hole is blocked off, the affected area can be filled and painted. See the following subsection on filling and painting.

These photos illustrate a method of repairing simple dents. They are intended to supplement Body repair - minor damage in this Chapter and should not be used as the sole instructions for body repair on these vehicles.

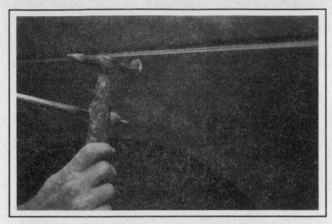

1 If you can't access the backside of the body panel to hammer out the dent, pull it out with a slide-hammer-type dent puller. Tap with a hammer near the edge of the dent to help 'pop' the metal back to its original shape, about 1/8-inch below the surface of the surrounding metal

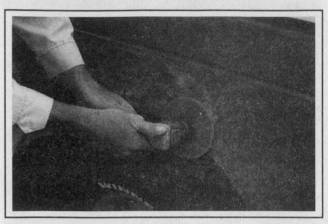

2 Using coarse-grit sandpaper, remove the paint down to the bare metal. Clean the repair area with wax/silicone remover.

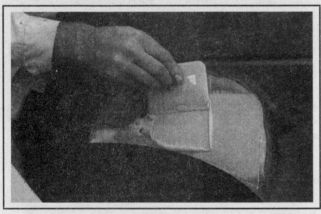

3 Following label instructions, mix up a batch of plastic filler and hardener, then quickly press it into the metal with a plastic applicator. Work the filler until it matches the original contour and is slightly above the surrounding metal

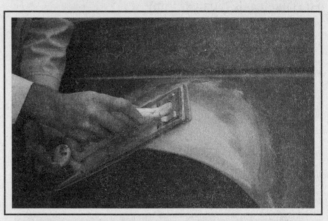

4 Let the filler harden until you can just dent it with your fingernail. File, then sand the filler down until it's smooth and even. Work down to finer grits of sandpaper - always using a board or block - ending up with 360 or 400 grit

5 When the area is smooth to the touch, clean the area and mask around it. Apply several layers of primer to the area. A professional-type spray gun is being used here, but aerosol spray primer works fine

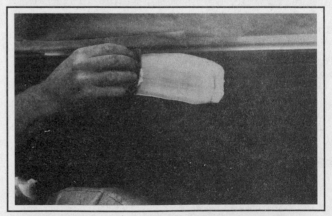

6 Fill imperfections or scratches with glazing compound. Sand with 360 or 400-grit and re-spray. Finish sand the primer with 600 grit, clean thoroughly, then apply the finish coat. Don't attempt to rub out or wax the repair area until the paint has dried completely (at least two weeks)

Filling and painting

27 Many types of body fillers are available, but generally speaking, body repair kits which contain filler paste and a tube of resin hardener are best for this type of repair work. A wide, flexible plastic or nylon applicator will be necessary for imparting a smooth and contoured finish to the surface of the filler material. Mix up a small amount of filler on a clean piece of wood or cardboard (use the hardener sparingly). Follow the manufacturer's instructions on the package, otherwise the filler will set incorrectly.

28 Using the applicator, apply the filler paste to the prepared area. Draw the applicator across the surface of the filler to achieve the desired contour and to level the filler surface. As soon as a contour that approximates the original one is achieved, stop working the paste. If you continue, the paste will begin to stick to the applicator. Continue to add thin layers of paste at 20-minute intervals until the level of the filler is just above the surrounding metal.

29 Once the filler has hardened, the excess can be removed with a body file. From then on, progressively finer grades of sandpaper should be used, starting with a 180-grit paper and finishing with 600-grit wet-or-dry paper. Always wrap the sandpaper around a flat rubber or wooden block, otherwise the surface of the filler will not be completely flat. During the sanding of the filler surface, the wet-or-dry paper should be periodically rinsed in water. This will ensure that a very smooth finish is produced in the final stage.

30 At this point, the repair area should be surrounded by a ring of bare metal, which in turn should be encircled by the finely feathered edge of good paint. Rinse the repair area with clean water until all of the dust produced by the sanding operation is gone.

31 Spray the entire area with a light coat of primer. This will reveal any imperfections in the surface of the filler. Repair the imperfections with fresh filler paste or glaze filler and once more smooth the surface with sandpaper. Repeat this spray-and-repair procedure until you are satisfied that the surface of the filler and the feathered edge of the paint are perfect. Rinse the area with clean water and allow it to dry completely.

32 The repair area is now ready for painting. Spray painting must be carried out in a warm, dry, windless and dust free atmosphere. These conditions can be created if you have access to a large indoor work area, but if you are forced to work in the open, you will have to pick the day very carefully. If you are working indoors, dousing the floor in the work area with water will help settle the dust that would otherwise be in the air. If the repair area is confined to one body panel, mask off the surrounding panels. This will help minimize the effects of a slight mismatch in paint color. Trim pieces such as chrome strips, door handles, etc., will also need to be masked off or removed. Use masking tape and several thickness of newspaper for the masking operations.

33 Before spraying, shake the paint can thoroughly, then spray a test area until the spray painting technique is mastered. Cover the repair area with a thick coat of primer. The thickness should be built up using several thin layers of primer rather than one thick one. Using 600-grit wet-or-dry sandpaper, rub down the surface of the primer until it is very smooth. While doing this, the work area should be thoroughly rinsed with water and the wet-or-dry sandpaper periodically rinsed as well. Allow the primer to dry before spraying additional coats.

34 Spray on the top coat, again building up the thickness by using several thin layers of paint. Begin spraying in the center of the repair area and then, using a circular motion, work out until the whole repair area and about two inches of the surrounding original paint is covered. Remove all masking material 10 to 15 minutes after spraying on the final coat of paint. Allow the new paint at least two weeks to harden, then use a very fine rubbing compound to blend the edges of the new paint into the existing paint. Finally, apply a coat of wax

4 Body repair - major damage

1 Major damage must be repaired by an auto body shop specifically equipped to perform body and frame repairs. These shops have the specialized equipment required to do the job properly.

2 If the damage is extensive, the frame must be checked for proper alignment or the vehicle's handling characteristics may be adversely affected and other components may wear at an accelerated rate.

3 Due to the fact that all of the major body components (hood, fenders, etc.) are separate and replaceable units, any seriously damaged components should be replaced rather than repaired. Sometimes the components can be found in a wrecking yard that specializes in used vehicle components, often at considerable savings over the cost of new parts.

5 Upholstery, carpets and vinyl trim - maintenance

UPHOLSTERY AND CARPETS

1 Every three months remove the floormats and clean the interior of the vehicle (more frequently if necessary). Use a stiff whiskbroom to brush the carpeting and loosen dirt and dust, then vacuum the upholstery and carpets thoroughly, especially along seams and crevices.

2 Dirt and stains can be removed from carpeting with basic household or automotive carpet shampoos available in spray cans. Follow the directions and vacuum again, then use a stiff brush to bring back the "nap" of the carpet.

3 Most interiors have cloth or vinyl upholstery, either of which can be cleaned and maintained with a number of material-specific cleaners or shampoos available in auto supply stores. Follow the directions on the product for usage, and always spot-test any upholstery cleaner on an inconspicuous area (bottom edge of a backseat cushion) to ensure that it doesn't cause a color shift in the material.

4 After cleaning, vinyl upholstery should be treated with a protectant.

→**Note: Make sure the protectant container indicates the product can be used on seats - some products may make a seat too slippery.**

❊❊ **CAUTION:**

Do not use protectant on vinyl-covered steering wheels.

5   Leather upholstery requires special care. It should be cleaned regularly with saddlesoap or leather cleaner. Never use alcohol, gasoline, nail polish remover or thinner to clean leather upholstery.

6   After cleaning, regularly treat leather upholstery with a leather conditioner, rubbed in with a soft cotton cloth. Never use car wax on leather upholstery.

7   In areas where the interior of the vehicle is subject to bright sunlight, cover leather seating areas of the seats with a sheet if the vehicle is to be left out for any length of time.

VINYL TRIM

8   Don't clean vinyl trim with detergents, caustic soap or petroleum-based cleaners. Plain soap and water works just fine, with a soft brush to clean dirt that may be ingrained. Wash the vinyl as frequently as the rest of the vehicle.

9   After cleaning, application of a high-quality rubber and vinyl protectant will help prevent oxidation and cracks. The protectant can also be applied to weather-stripping, vacuum lines and rubber hoses, which often fail as a result of chemical degradation, and to the tires.

---

6   Fastener and trim removal

▶ **Refer to illustration 6.4**

1   There is a variety of plastic fasteners used to hold trim panels, splash shields and other parts in place in addition to typical screws, nuts and bolts. Once you are familiar with them, they can usually be removed without too much difficulty.

2   The proper tools and approach can prevent added time and expense to a project by minimizing the number of broken fasteners and/or parts.

3   The following illustration shows various types of fasteners that are typically used on most vehicles and how to remove and install them

(see illustration). Replacement fasteners are commonly found at most auto parts stores, if necessary.

4   Trim panels are typically made of plastic and their flexibility can help during removal. The key to their removal is to use a tool to pry the panel near its retainers to release it without damaging surrounding areas or breaking-off any retainers. The retainers will usually snap out of their designated slot or hole after force is applied to them. Stiff plastic tools designed for prying on trim panels are available at most auto parts stores (see illustration). Tools that are tapered and wrapped in protective tape, such as a screwdriver or small pry tool, are also very effective when used with care.

Fasteners

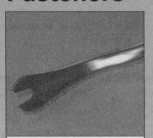

This tool is designed to remove special fasteners. A small pry tool used for removing nails will also work well in place of this tool

A Phillips head screwdriver can be used to release the center portion, but light pressure must be used because the plastic is easily damaged. Once the center is up, the fastener can easily be pried from its hole

Here is a view with the center portion fully released. Install the fastener as shown, then press the center in to set it

This fastener is used for exterior panels and shields. The center portion must be pried up to release the fastener. Install the fastener with the center up, then press the center in to set it

This type of fastener is used commonly for interior panels. Use a small blunt tool to press the small pin at the center in to release it . . .

. . . the pin will stay with the fastener in the released position

Reset the fastener for installation by moving the pin out. Install the fastener, then press the pin flush with the fastener to set it

This fastener is used for exterior and interior panels. It has no moving parts. Simply pry the fastener from its hole like the claw of a hammer removes a nail. Without a tool that can get under the top of the fastener, it can be very difficult to remove

7 Hinges and locks - maintenance

Once every 3000 miles, or every three months, the hinges and latch assemblies on the doors, hood and trunk should be given a few drops of light oil or lock lubricant. The door latch strikers should also be lubricated with a thin coat of grease to reduce wear and ensure free movement. Lubricate the door and trunk locks with spray-on graphite lubricant.

8 Windshield and fixed glass - replacement

Replacement of the windshield and fixed glass requires the use of special fast-setting adhesive/caulk materials and some specialized tools and techniques. These operations should be left to a dealer service department or a shop specializing in glass work.

9 Hood - removal, installation and adjustment

REMOVAL AND INSTALLATION

◗ **Refer to illustrations 9.2 and 9.4**

➡**Note: The hood is heavy and somewhat awkward to remove and install - at least two people should perform this procedure.**

1   Use blankets or pads to cover the fenders and cowl areas. This will protect the body and paint as the hood is lifted off.

2   Scribe or draw alignment marks around the bolt heads to ensure proper alignment during installation (see illustration).

3   Disconnect any cables or wire harnesses which will interfere with removal.

4   Have an assistant support one side of the hood while you support the other. Simultaneously remove the hinge-to-hood bolts (see illustration).

5   Lift off the hood.

6   Installation is the reverse of removal. If you position the hood so that the hinges fit within the scribe marks you made before loosening the bolts, in the same location they were in prior to removal, then the hood should still be aligned. Of course, if you're installing a new hood, or forgot to scribe the hinge positions, then you'll need to readjust the hood position.

ADJUSTMENT

◗ **Refer to illustration 9.10**

7   You can adjust the hood fore-and-aft and right-and-left by means of the elongated holes in the hinges.

8   Scribe a line around the entire hinge plate so you can judge the amount of movement.

9   Loosen the bolts and move the hood into correct alignment. Move it only a little at a time. Tighten the hinge bolts and carefully lower the hood to check the alignment.

10   Adjust the vertical height of the leading edge of the hood by screwing the edge cushions in or out so that the hood, when closed, is flush with the fenders (see illustration).

11   The hood latch assembly, as well as the hinges, should be periodically lubricated with white lithium-base grease to prevent sticking and wear.

9.2 Before removing the hood, draw a mark around the hinge plates

9.4 Support the hood with your shoulder while removing the hood bolts

9.10 The hood bumpers can be turned in or out to adjust the level flush with the fenders

10 Hood release latch and cable - removal and installation

SEPHIA AND SPECTRA MODELS

Latch

▶ **Refer to illustrations 10.1 and 10.2**

1 Remove the radiator grille opening cover (if equipped), then unscrew the latch retaining bolts and nut from the radiator support and remove the latch (see illustration).

2 Disconnect the hood release cable by disengaging the cable from the latch (see illustration).

3 Installation is reverse of the removal.

Cable

▶ **Refer to illustration 10.8**

4 Disconnect the hood release cable from the latch assembly (see illustration 10.2), then detach cable from any retaining clips securing it to the radiator support.

5 Attach a piece of wire or string to the latch end of the cable.

6 Loosen the left front wheel lug nuts. Raise the vehicle and support it securely on jackstands, then remove the wheel.

7 Remove the left inner fender splash shield (see illustration 11.2).

8 Working in the passenger's compartment, detach the hood release lever from the left side lower trim panel (see illustration).

9 Pull the grommet through the body and pull the cable into the passenger compartment. Ensure that the new cable has a grommet attached, then remove the old cable from the wire and attach the wire to the new cable.

10 Pull the wire back through the body, guiding the cable through the retaining clips under the fender.

11 Installation is the reverse of the removal.

➡ Note: Push on the grommet to seat it in the body completely.

SPORTAGE MODELS

Latch

▶ **Refer to illustrations 10.13, 10.14a and 10.14b**

12 Remove the radiator/grille cover fasteners (see Section 6 in Chapter 3) and remove the cover.

13 Remove the latch cover bolts (see illustration) and remove the cover.

14 Remove the hood latch bolts (see illustration), remove the latch and disengage the hood release cable from the latch (see illustration).

15 Installation is the reverse of removal.

Cable

▶ **Refer to illustration 10.17**

16 Disengage the release cable from the latch (see Steps 12 through 14).

17 Inside the vehicle, remove the hood release handle mounting screws (see illustration).

18 Remove the hood release handle and disengage the cable from the handle.

19 Inside the engine compartment, trace the route of the release cable and detach all cable clips, then pull the cable through the firewall.

20 Installation is the reverse of removal. Make sure that the grommet where the hood release cable goes through the firewall is seated securely.

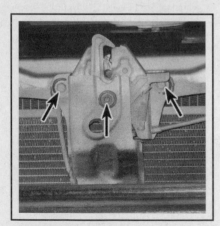

10.1 Hood release latch fasteners

10.2 Detach the cable housing from the latch, then remove the cable end from the slotted portion of the latch mechanism

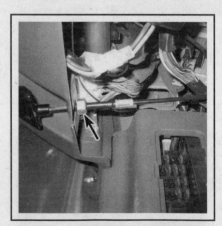

10.8 Loosen the hood release cable nut and detach the cable from the lower trim panel

10.13 Latch cover bolts (Sportage models)

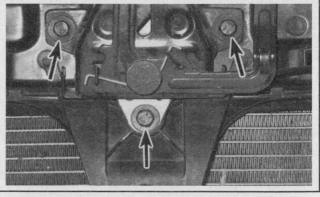

10.14a Remove the hood latch bolts, remove the latch . . .

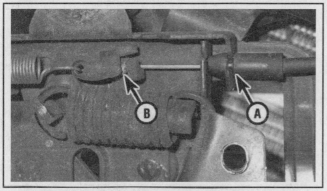

10.14b . . . then disengage the release cable grommet (A) and cable end plug (B) from their respective slots in the latch (Sportage models)

10.17 To disengage the hood release cable from the hood release handle, remove the handle mounting screws, disengage the cable grommet from its mounting slot, then slide out the cable end plug (Sportage models)

11 Bumper covers - removal and installation

SEPHIA AND SPECTRA MODELS

Front

▶ Refer to illustrations 11.2, 11.3, 11.4 and 11.6

1   Loosen the wheel lug nuts, raise the front of the vehicle and support it securely on jackstands. Remove the wheels.

2   Remove the fasteners securing the inner fender splash shield and detach the shield (see illustration). On later models, remove the upper radiator grille guard.

3   Working under the vehicle, detach the bolts or screws securing the lower edges of the bumper cover (see illustration).

11.2 Remove the fasteners securing the inner fender splash shield

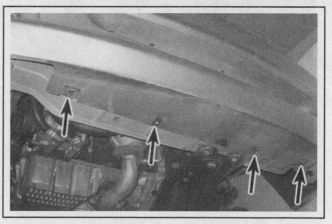

11.3 Bumper cover lower retaining fasteners

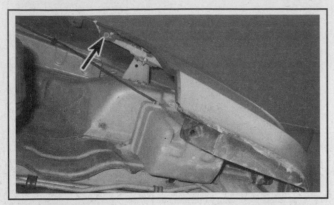

11.4 Working inside the fenderwell, remove the fastener securing the bumper cover to the fender

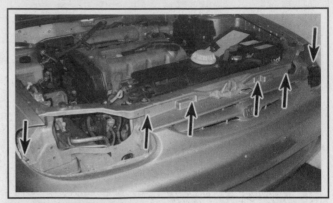

11.6 Bumper cover upper fasteners

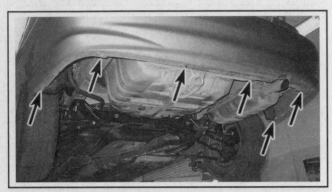

11.9 Remove the fasteners securing the lower portion of the rear bumper cover

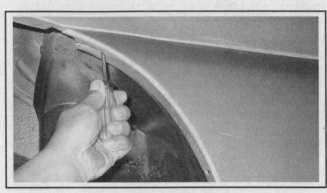

11.10 In each rear fenderwell, remove the fastener securing the front edges of the rear bumper cover

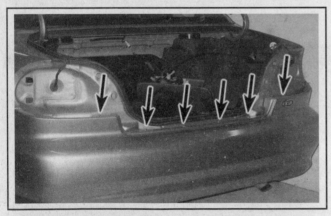

11.12 Remove the fasteners securing the upper portion of the bumper cover

4   Working in the front wheel opening, remove the retaining screws securing the bumper cover to the fenderwell (see illustration).

5   Remove the headlight housings (see Chapter 12).

6   Remove the fasteners securing the upper portion of the bumper cover (see illustration) and pull the bumper cover out and away from the vehicle.

7   Installation is the reverse of removal.

Rear

▶ **Refer to illustrations 11.9, 11.10 and 11.12**

8   Raise the vehicle and support it securely on jackstands. On later models, open the trunk and remove the inner trunk side and rear trim panels for access to the fasteners under them.

9   Working under the vehicle, detach the plastic clips and screws securing the lower edge of the bumper cover (see illustration).

10 Remove the screws securing the bumper cover in the rear wheel openings (see illustration).

11 Remove the taillight housings (see Chapter 12).

12 Open the trunk or rear hatch and remove the screws and clips securing the upper edge of the bumper cover (see illustration). Pull the bumper cover out and away from the vehicle.

13 Installation is the reverse of removal.

SPORTAGE MODELS

Front

▶ **Refer to illustrations 11.14, 11.17 and 11.18**

14 Open the hood, then remove the two upper mounting bolts from the bumper cover (see illustration).

15 Loosen the front wheel lug nuts. Raise the front of the vehicle and place it securely on jackstands. Remove the front wheels.

16 Remove the engine under cover/splash shield (see illustration 6.3 in Chapter 1).

17 Working inside the wheel housings, remove the screws that secure the upper rear corners of the bumper cover to the front fenders (see illustration).

18 Working underneath the front of the vehicle, remove the fasteners (see illustration) that secure the lower trailing edge of the bumper cover.

11.14 Upper front bumper cover mounting bolts (Sportage models)

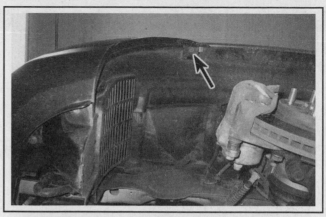

11.17 Front bumper cover retaining screw (left side shown, other side similar) (Sportage models)

11.18 Lower front bumper cover fasteners (not all fasteners shown) (Sportage models)

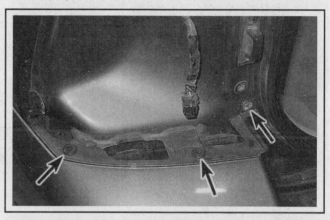

11.22 Upper rear bumper cover fasteners (Sportage models)

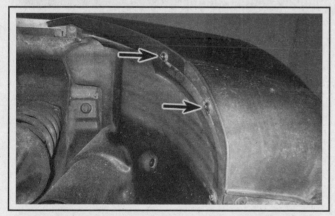

11.24a Lower bumper cover fasteners in rear wheel housing (Sportage models)

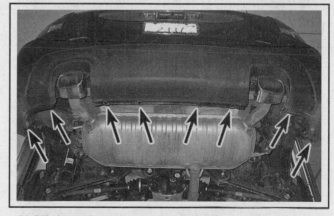

11.24b Lower bumper cover fasteners (Sportage)

19 Remove the bumper cover. Have an assistant help you.

20 Installation is the reverse of removal. Tighten the wheel lug nuts to the torque listed in the Chapter 1 Specifications.

Rear

▶ **Refer to illustrations 11.22, 11.24a and 11.24b**

21 Remove the rear taillight housings (see Chapter 12).

22 Remove the upper bumper cover fasteners (see illustration), where the taillight housings are located.

23 Loosen the rear wheel lug nuts. Raise the rear of the vehicle and place it securely on jackstands. Remove the rear wheels.

24 Remove the leading edge fasteners from the rear wheel housings and from the lower edge of the bumper cover (see illustrations).

25 Installation is the reverse of removal. Tighten the wheel lug nuts to the torque listed in the Chapter 1 Specifications.

12 Front fender - removal and installation

▶ **Refer to illustrations 12.3a, 12.3b, 12.3c and 12.3d**

1   Loosen the wheel lug nuts, raise the front of the vehicle and support it securely on jackstands. Remove the wheel.
2   Remove the front bumper cover (see Section 11).
3   Remove the fender mounting bolts (see illustrations).
4   Detach the fender. It's a good idea to have an assistant support the fender while it's being moved away from the vehicle to prevent damage to the surrounding body panels.
5   Installation is the reverse of removal.

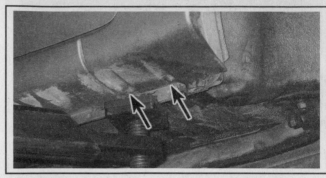

12.3a The lower rear corner of the fender is secured by two bolts

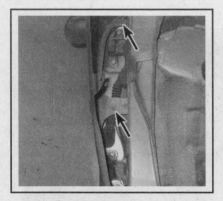

12.3b Open the door and remove the two fender-to-body bolts

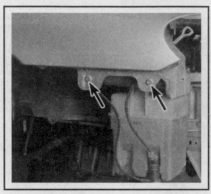

12.3c Remove the bolts at the front corner of the fender . . .

12.3d . . . and along the top portion of the fender

13 Trunk lid and rear hatch, latch and lock cylinder - removal and installation

TRUNK LID LATCH

▶ **Refer to illustrations 13.2 and 13.3**

1   Open the trunk and scribe a line around the trunk lid latch assembly for a reference point to aid the installation procedure.
2   Look upward through the trunk lid access hole and detach the rod from the lock cylinder (see illustration).
3   Remove the bolts retaining the trunk lid latch (see illustration).

4   Installation is the reverse of removal.

TRUNK LOCK CYLINDER

5   Open the trunk. Look upward through the trunk lid access hole and detach the rod from the lock cylinder (see illustration 13.2).
6   Remove the mounting bolt or clip and remove the lock cylinder from the trunk lid.

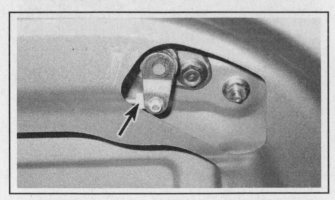

13.2 Detach the rod retaining clip then separate the rod from the lock cylinder

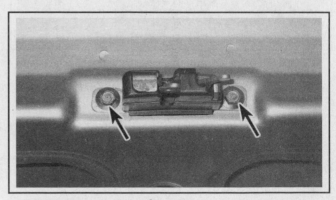

13.3 Trunk lid latch mounting bolts

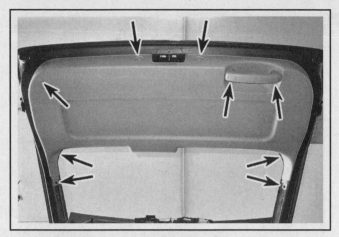

13.8 Rear hatch trim panel fastener locations

7 Installation is the reverse of removal.

REAR HATCH (SPORTAGE MODELS)

▶ **Refer to illustration 13.8**

8 Remove the rear hatch trim panel screws and plastic fasteners (see illustration), then carefully pry off the trim panel with a trim panel removal tool.

Rear hatch latch

▶ **Refer to illustration 13.11**

9 Disconnect the electrical connector from the latch.
10 Disconnect the outside handle rod and the actuator rod.
11 Remove the latch mounting bolts (see illustration) and remove the latch.
12 Installation is the reverse of removal.

Rear hatch glass latch

▶ **Refer to illustration 13.12**

13 Disconnect the hatch glass latch rod (see illustration).
14 Loosen the latch mounting bolts, disconnect the electrical connector, remove the mounting bolts and remove the latch.
15 Installation is the reverse of removal.

Rear hatch outside handle

16 Disconnect the outside handle rod and the latch rod (see illustration 13.12).
17 Remove the outside handle mounting nuts (see illustration 13.12) and remove the handle.
18 Installation is the reverse of removal.

Actuator

▶ **Refer to illustration 13.19**

19 Disconnect the electrical connector (see illustration).
20 Disconnect the outside handle rod and the glass latch rod.
21 Remove the mounting nuts and mounting bolt, reposition the actuator to access and disconnect the actuator rod and the key lock cylinder, then remove the actuator.
22 Installation is the reverse of removal.

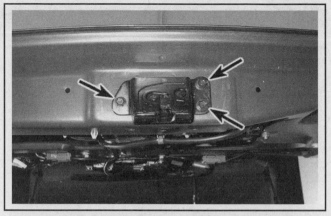

13.11 Rear hatch latch mounting bolts (Sportage models)

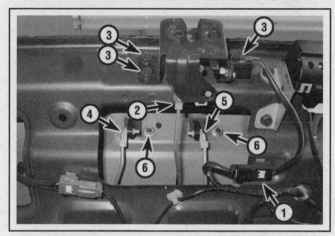

13.12 Rear hatch glass latch and outside handle details (Sportage models)

1	Electrical connector	4	Outside handle rod
2	Hatch glass latch rod	5	Latch rod
3	Latch mounting bolts (one bolt not visible)	6	Outside handle mounting nuts

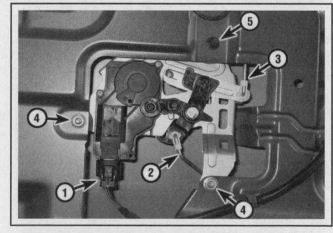

13.19 Actuator details (Sportage models)

1	Electrical connector	4	Mounting nuts
2	Outside handle rod	5	Mounting bolt
3	Glass latch rod		

14 Trunk lid - removal and installation

➡Note: The trunk lid is heavy and somewhat awkward to remove and install - at least two people should perform this procedure.

REMOVAL AND INSTALLATION

▶ Refer to illustration 14.3

1   Open the trunk lid and cover the edges of the trunk compartment with pads or cloths to protect the painted surfaces when the lid is removed.

2   Disconnect any cables or wire harness connectors attached to the trunk lid that would interfere with removal.

3   Make alignment marks around the hinge (see illustration).

4   While an assistant supports the trunk lid, remove the lid-to-hinge bolts on both sides and lift it off.

5   Installation is the reverse of removal.

➡Note: When reinstalling the trunk lid, align the lid-to-hinge bolts with the marks made during removal.

ADJUSTMENT

6   Fore-and-aft and side-to-side adjustment of the trunk lid is accomplished by moving the lid in relation to the hinge after loosening the bolts or nuts.

7   Scribe a line around the hinge plate as described earlier in this Section so you can determine the amount of movement.

8   Loosen the bolts and move the trunk lid into correct alignment. Move it only a little at a time. Tighten the hinge bolts or nuts and carefully lower the trunk lid to check the alignment.

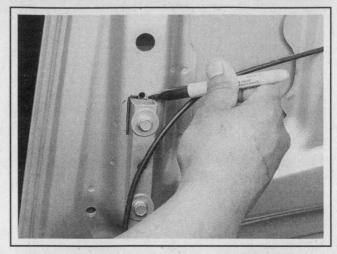

14.3   Draw around the hinge with a marking pen before loosening the bolts to ensure proper alignment of the trunk lid when it's reinstalled

9   If necessary after installation, the trunk latch assembly can be adjusted up and down as well as from side to side so the lid closes securely and is flush with the rear quarter panels. To do this, scribe a line around the latch to provide a reference point. Then loosen the bolts and reposition the latch as necessary. Following adjustment, retighten the mounting bolts.

10   The trunk lid latch assembly, as well as the hinges, should be periodically lubricated with white lithium-base grease to prevent sticking and wear.

15 Rear hatch - removal, installation and adjustment

➡Note: The rear hatch is heavy and somewhat awkward to remove and install - at least two people should perform this procedure.

REMOVAL AND INSTALLATION

Hatch

▶ Refer to illustrations 15.3 and 15.4

1   Have an assistant hold the rear hatch in the open position.

2   Disconnect all electrical connections, ground wires and harness retaining clips from the rear hatch.

➡Note: It is a good idea to label all connections to aid the reassembly process.

3   With an assistant holding the hatch, remove the rear hatch support struts (see illustration).

4   Mark around the rear hatch hinges with a pen or a scribe to facilitate realignment during reassembly (see illustration).

5   Remove the hinge-to-rear hatch bolts and lift off the hatch.

6   Installation is the reverse of removal.

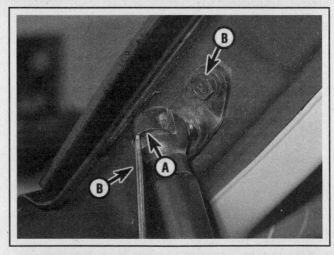

15.3   To detach the rear hatch support strut, pry off the socket clip (A) with a small screwdriver, then remove the mounting bolts (B) (one bolt not visible) (Sportage model shown, other hatchback models similar)

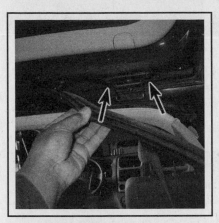

15.4 Rear hatch hinge bolt (Sportage models)

15.7 Rear hatch glass strut socket clip (Sportage models)

15.8 Rear hatch glass hinge bolt (Sportage models)

Hatch glass (Sportage models only)

▶ **Refer to illustrations 15.7 and 15.8**

7 Unclip the struts from their ball sockets (see illustration). Use a small screwdriver to pry off the clips (see illustration 15.3).

8 Remove the hinge bolts (see illustration) and remove the rear hatch glass.

9 Installation is the reverse of removal.

ADJUSTMENT

10 Having proper rear hatch-to-body alignment is a critical part of a well-functioning rear hatch assembly. First check the rear hatch hinge pins for excessive play. Fully open the rear hatch and move it side-to-side. If it has 1/16-inch or more play, the hinges should be replaced.

11 Rear hatch-to-body alignment adjustments are made by loosening the hinge-to-body bolts or hinge-to-hatch bolts and moving the door. Proper body alignment is achieved when the top of the hatch is parallel with the roof section, the sides of the hatch are flush with the rear quarter panels and the bottom of the hatch is aligned with the lower sill panel. If these goals can't be reached by adjusting the hinge-to-body or hinge-to-rear hatch bolts, body alignment shims may have to be purchased and inserted behind the hinges to achieve correct alignment.

12 To adjust the hatch-closed position, scribe a line or mark around the striker plate to provide a reference point, then check that the hatch latch is contacting the center of the latch striker. If not, adjust the side-to-side position first. Then adjust the up-and-down position of the striker so that the hatch panel is flush with the rear quarter panel and provides positive engagement with the latch mechanism.

16 Trunk release and fuel door lever - removal and installation

▶ **Refer to illustrations 16.1 and 16.2**

1 Detach the lever trim panel (see illustration).

2 Remove the lever retaining bolts (see illustration). Detach the cables from the lever.

3 Installation is the reverse of removal.

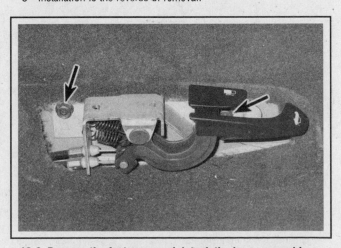

16.1 Remove the trim panel mounting screw, then remove the trim panel

16.2 Remove the fasteners and detach the lever assembly

17 Door trim panels - removal and installation

SEPHIA AND SPECTRA MODELS

▶ **Refer to illustrations 17.2, 17.3, 17.4, 17.5, 17.9a, 17.9b and 17.9c**

➡ **Note: This procedure applies to both the front and rear doors.**

1 Open the door and completely lower the window glass, then remove the mirror trim cover (see illustration 22.1).

2 Remove the fasteners at the front and rear edges of the door (see illustration). On later models, use a plastic trim tool or a screwdriver wrapped with tape to carefully pry off the armrest cover.

3 On manual window models, remove the window crank using a special tool (available at most auto parts stores) or by working a cloth back-and-forth behind the handle to dislodge the retaining clip (see illustration).

4 Remove the screw securing the inner door handle trim cover (see illustration).

5 In the pull handle pocket, remove the screw (see illustration).

6 Carefully pry around the door trim panel to disengage it from the retaining clips.

7 Grasp the trim panel, pull up and detach it from the door.

8 On models with power windows, disconnect the electrical connector and then remove the trim panel.

✳ CAUTION:

Do not allow the trim panel to hang from the electrical wires.

9 If necessary for access to the inner door, remove the handle bracket and inner door handle and carefully remove the plastic watershield (see illustrations).

10 Installation is the reverse of the removal procedure.

17.2 Remove the door panel mounting fasteners

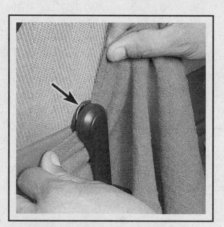

17.3 Work a cloth up behind the manual window regulator handle and move it back-and-forth until the retainer is pushed up so you can remove it

17.4 Remove the screw cap and screw securing the inner door handle trim cover

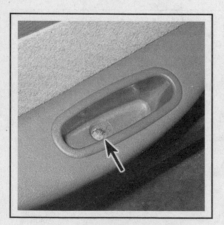

17.5 Remove the door panel screw inside the pull handle pocket

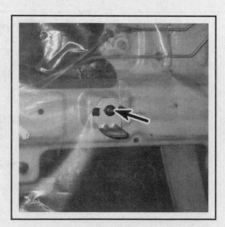

17.9a Remove the fastener securing the door handle bracket

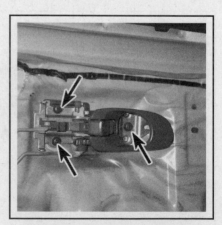

17.9b Remove the inner door handle mounting fasteners (typical)

17.9c Carefully peel the plastic watershield from the door

17.11 Use a trim removal tool to pry off the outside mirror trim cover (Sportage models)

17.12a Each of the door trim panel mounting screws is hidden behind a small trim cover (Sportage models)

SPORTAGE MODELS

♦ **Refer to illustrations 17.11, 17.12a, 17.12b, 17.13, 17.14 and 17.15**

11 Using a trim removal tool, carefully pry off the outside mirror trim cover (see illustration).

12 Remove the trim panel mounting screws (see illustrations).

13 Using a trim panel removal tool, carefully pry off the inside handle trim panel (see illustration).

14 Using a trim panel removal tool, carefully pry off the trim panel (see illustration). The trim panel is still secured to the door by five clips: one near the middle of the leading edge, on at the lower front corner, near the speaker, one near the middle of the lower edge and two on the trailing edge. Disconnect the electrical connectors for the power window switch, the power mirror and the door courtesy light and remove the trim panel.

15 If you wish to access the outside door handle/key lock cylinder, the door latch, the window regulator, remove the watershield from the door (see illustration).

16 When installing the trim panel, make sure that it snaps into place all the way around the perimeter. Installation is otherwise the reverse of removal.

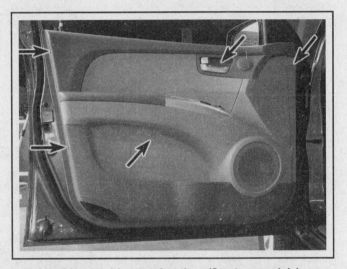

17.12b Trim panel fastener locations (Sportage models)

17.13 Before prying off the door trim panel, remove the inside door handle assembly

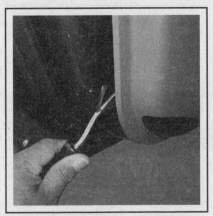

17.14 Use a trim removal tool to pry off the door trim panel (Sportage models)

17.15 Carefully peel back the watershield as necessary for access

18 Door - removal, installation and adjustment

➡ **Note: The door is heavy and somewhat awkward to remove and install - at least two people should perform this procedure.**

REMOVAL AND INSTALLATION

▶ **Refer to illustrations 18.6 and 18.8**

1   Lower the window completely in the door, then disconnect the cable from the negative battery terminal (see Chapter 5, Section 1).

2   Open the door all the way and support it on jacks or blocks covered with rags to prevent damaging the paint.

3   Remove the door trim panel and water deflector as described in Section 17.

4   Disconnect all electrical connections, ground wires and harness retaining clips from the door.

➡ **Note: It is a good idea to label all connections to aid the reassembly process.**

5   From the door side, detach the rubber conduit between the body and the door. Then pull the wiring harness through the conduit hole and remove it from the door.

6   Remove the door stop strut (see illustration).

7   Mark around the door hinges with a pen or a scribe to facilitate realignment during reassembly.

8   With an assistant holding the door, remove the hinge-to-door bolts (see illustration) and lift the door off.

9   Installation is the reverse of removal.

ADJUSTMENT

▶ **Refer to illustration 18.13**

10   Having proper door-to-body alignment is a critical part of a well functioning door assembly. First check the door hinge pins for excessive play. Fully open the door and lift up and down on the door without lifting the body. If a door has 1/16-inch or more excessive play, the hinges should be replaced.

11   Door-to-body alignment adjustments are made by loosening the hinge-to-body bolts or hinge-to-door bolts and moving the door. Proper body alignment is achieved when the top of the doors are parallel with the roof section, the front door is flush with the fender, the rear door is flush with the rear quarter panel and the bottom of the doors are aligned with the lower rocker panel. If these goals can't be reached by adjusting the hinge-to-body or hinge-to-door bolts, body alignment shims may have to be purchased and inserted behind the hinges to achieve correct alignment.

12   To adjust the door closed position, scribe a line or mark around the striker plate to provide a reference point, then check that the door latch is contacting the center of the latch striker. If not adjust the up and down position first.

13   Finally adjust the latch striker sideways position, so that the door panel is flush with the center pillar or rear quarter panel and provides positive engagement with the latch mechanism (see illustration).

18.6 Remove the bolt and detach the door stop from the door pillar

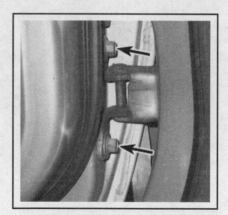

18.8 Remove the hinge-to-door bolts

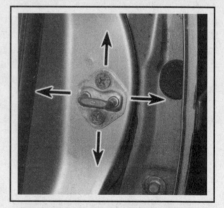

18.13 Adjust the door lock striker by loosening the mounting screws and gently tapping the striker in the desired direction

19 Door latch, lock cylinder and handles - removal and installation

❋❋ **WARNING:**

Wear gloves when working inside the door openings to protect against cuts from sharp metal edges.

SEPHIA AND SPECTRA MODELS

Latch

Removal

▶ **Refer to illustrations 19.2 and 19.3**

1   Remove the door trim panel (see Section 17).

2   Disconnect the lock cylinder, lock button and latch release operat-

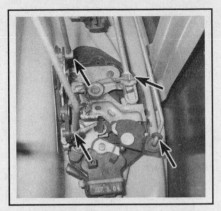

19.2 Disconnect the operating rods from the door latch

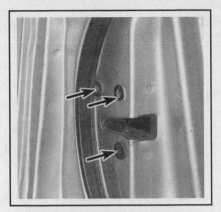

19.3 Remove the latch screws from the end of the door

19.7 Note how the operating rods are connected to the key lock cylinder and to the outside door handle, then disconnect them

19.10 To remove the lock cylinder, simply pull it out from the handle

19.13 Inside handle mounting screw (Sportage models)

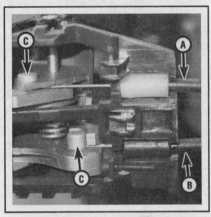

19.14 To disengage the inside handle lock cable (A) and connect cable (B) from the inside handle, pull out the cable grommets, then slide the cable end plugs (C) up and out (Sportage models)

ing rods from the door latch (see illustration).

3   Remove the three mounting screws from the end of the door and remove the door latch (see illustration).

Installation

4   Place the latch in position, install the screws and tighten them securely.

5   Connect the operating rods to the latch and secure with retaining clips.

Outside handle

▶ **Refer to illustration 19.7**

6   Remove the door trim panel (see Section 17).

7   Disconnect the operating rods, remove the mounting nuts and withdraw the handle from the door (see illustration).

8   Installation is the reverse of removal.

Lock cylinder

▶ **Refer to illustration 19.10**

9   Remove the outside door handle (see Steps 6 and 7).

10 Remove the lock cylinder from the handle (see illustration).

11 Installation is the reverse of removal.

SPORTAGE MODELS

Inside handle

▶ **Refer to illustrations 19.13 and 19.14**

12 Remove the door trim panel (see Section 17).

13 Remove the inside handle mounting screw (see illustration), then slide the handle rearward to disengage it from the door module.

14 Disconnect the lock cable and inside handle connect cable from the handle (see illustration), then remove the handle.

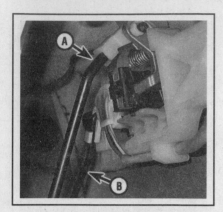

19.17 Outside handle rod (A) and lock rod (B) (Sportage models)

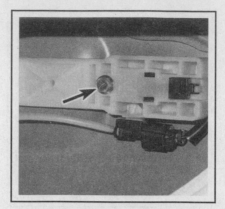

19.18a To detach the outside handle base from the door, remove this retaining bolt from inside the door . . .

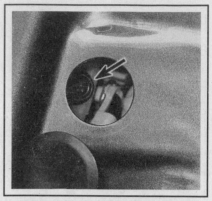

19.18b . . . then remove this trim cover in the end of the door and remove the other bolt (Sportage models)

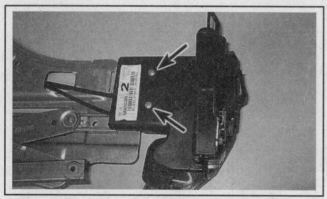

19.23 Latch mounting screws (Sportage models)

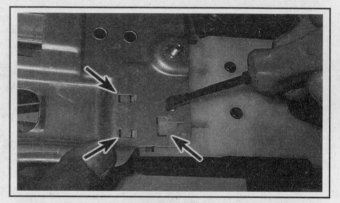

19.24 Use a small screwdriver to disengage these four lugs to detach the latch assembly from the door module

15 Installation is the reverse of removal.

Outside handle and key lock cylinder

▶ Refer to illustrations 19.17, 19.18a and 19.18b

16 Remove the door trim panel (see Section 17), the door window glass (see Section 20) and the rear window glass channel (see Section 20).

17 Disconnect the outside handle rod and the lock rod (see illustration).

18 Remove the outside handle base retaining bolts (see illustrations).

19 Remove the key lock cylinder and the outside handle lever from

the door, then remove the outside handle base from inside the door.

20 Installation is the reverse of removal.

Latch

▶ Refer to illustrations 19.23 and 19.24

21 Remove the door trim panel (see Section 17), the door window glass (see Section 20) and the door module (see Section 21).

22 Disconnect the lock cable and the inside handle cable.

23 Remove the two latch mounting screws (see illustration).

24 Disengage the lugs on the latch from the door module (see illustration) and remove the latch assembly.

25 Installation is the reverse of removal.

20 Door window glass - removal and installation

▶ Refer to illustrations 20.2 and 20.2b

✳✳ WARNING:

Wear gloves when working inside the door openings to protect against cuts from sharp metal edges.

1 Remove the door trim panel and the plastic watershield (see Section 17).

2 Raise the window glass just enough to access the window retaining bolts through the holes in the door frame (see illustrations).

3 Remove the bolts securing the glass guide channel.

4 Place a rag over the glass to help prevent scratching the glass and remove the two glass mounting bolts.

5 Remove the glass by tilting it slightly, pulling it up and out.

6 Installation is the reverse of removal.

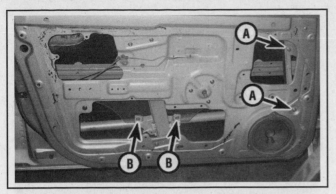

20.2a Door window glass details (Sephia and Spectra models)

A   *Glass guide channel nuts*   B   *Glass-to-regulator bolts*

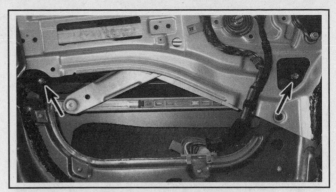

20.2b Door window glass-to-regulator bolt locations (Sportage models)

21 Door window glass regulator - removal and installation

※※ WARNING:

Wear gloves when working inside the door openings to protect against cuts from sharp metal edges.

1   Remove the door trim panel and, if applicable, the plastic watershield (see Section 17).

2   Remove the screws that retain the door window glass (see illustration 20.2a or 20.2b).

3   Lift the door glass and have an assistant hold the door glass upright.

POWER WINDOW MOTOR

◆ Refer to illustration 21.4

4   Disconnect the electrical connector from the window regulator motor (see illustration).

5   Remove the regulator/motor assembly mounting nuts. Remove the window regulator/motor assembly from the door.

6   Installation is the reverse of removal. Lubricate the rollers and wear points on the regulator with white grease before installation.

POWER WINDOW REGULATOR/DOOR MODULE ASSEMBLY

◆ Refer to illustrations 21.7, 21.11 and 21.12

7   Disconnect the electrical connectors from the power window motor (see illustration 21.4) and from the latch assembly (see illustration), then detach the clips that secure the wiring harness to the door module and set the harness aside.

8   Disconnect the lock rod and outside handle rod from the outside handle (see illustration 19.17).

9   Remove the power window motor (see illustration 21.4).

10 Remove the door speaker (see Chapter 12).

11 Remove the door latch fasteners (see illustration).

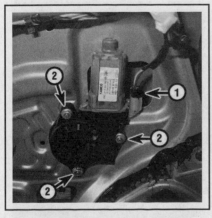

21.4 Power window motor details (Sportage shown, other models similar)

1   *Electrical connector*
2   *Mounting nuts*

21.7 Latch assembly electrical connector (Sportage model shown)

21.11 Door latch fasteners (Sportage model shown)

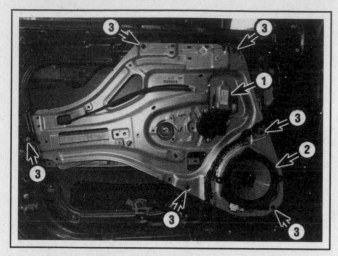

21.12 Power window regulator/door module assembly details (Sportage model shown):

1 Power window motor	3 Module assembly
2 Speaker	mounting bolts

12 Remove the door module bolts (see illustration) and remove the door module.
13 Installation is the reverse of removal.

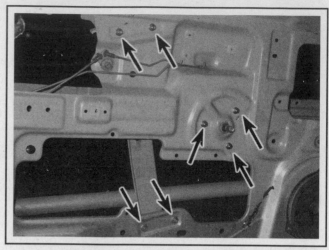

21.14 Door window glass regulator mounting nuts (manual regulator shown, power regulator similar)

MANUAL WINDOW REGULATOR

▶ **Refer to illustration 21.14**

14 Remove the mounting bolts and remove the regulator assembly through the service hole in the door frame (see illustration).
15 Installation is the reverse of removal. Lubricate the rollers and wear points on the regulator with white grease before installation.

22 Mirrors - removal and installation

OUTSIDE MIRRORS

▶ **Refer to illustrations 22.1, 22.3a and 22.3b**

1 Pry off the mirror trim cover (see illustration).
2 Disconnect the electrical connector from the mirror (if equipped).
3 Remove the three mirror retaining fasteners and detach the mirror from the vehicle (see illustrations).
4 Installation is the reverse of removal.

INSIDE MIRROR

▶ **Refer to illustration 22.5**

5 Push down toward the bottom of the windshield to release the mirror arm from the mounting bracket (see illustration).
6 Installation is the reverse of removal.
7 If the mount plate itself has come off the windshield, adhesive kits are available at auto parts stores to re-secure it. Follow the instructions included with the kit.

22.1 Pry the mirror trim panel from the door

22.3a Carefully peel off the foam insulation . . .

22.3b . . . then remove the mounting fasteners

22.5 Push the mirror arm down towards the bottom of the windshield to release it from the base

23 Center console - removal and installation

SEPHIA AND SPECTRA MODELS

▶ **Refer to illustrations 23.4a, 23.4b, 23.4c and 23.4d**

> ✳ **WARNING:**
>
> Most models covered by this manual are equipped with a Supplemental Restraint System (SRS), more commonly known as airbags. Always disable the airbag system before working in the vicinity of any airbag system component to avoid the possibility of accidental deployment of the airbag, which could cause personal injury (see Chapter 12).

1 Disconnect the cable from the negative terminal of the battery (see Chapter 5, Section 1).
2 Completely raise the parking brake lever.
3 On vehicles equipped with a manual transaxle, unscrew and remove the shift lever knob.

➡**Note: The shift knob on many later models is also secured with a screw on the front side.**

4 Remove the securing screws and detach the console (see illustrations).

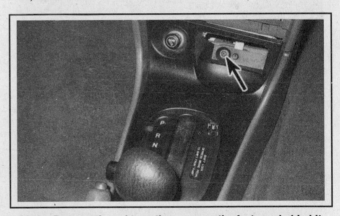

23.4a Remove the ashtray, then remove the fastener behind it

23.4b Carefully detach the clips and remove the trim ring from around the shifter, then detach any electrical connectors

23.4c Remove the console mounting fasteners at the front . . .

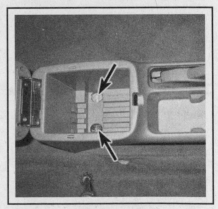

23.4d . . . and inside the console compartment

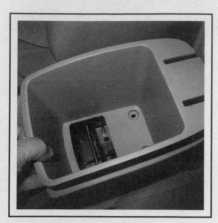

23.7 Remove the storage box (Sportage models)

23.8 Armrest hinge screws (Sportage models)

23.10 Pry up the blank trim panel or the seat heater switch panel (Sportage models)

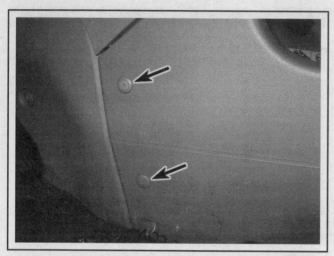

23.11 Push fastener locations, left side shown, two more on right side (Sportage models)

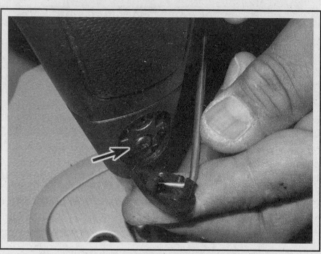

23.14 To remove the handle from the shift lever on automatic models, pry open this trim cover and remove the handle retaining screw, then pull the handle straight up (Sportage models)

5   Maneuver the floor console up and over the shift lever and parking brake handle and remove it from vehicle.

6   Installation is the reverse of removal.

SPORTAGE MODELS

▶ **Refer to illustrations 23.7, 23.8, 23.10, 23.11 and 23.14**

7   Remove the storage box fasteners and lift out the storage box (see illustration).

8   Remove the armrest hinge screws (see illustration) and remove the armrest assembly.

9   Carefully pry off the rear end cover.

10 On models without heated seats, pry out the blank trim panel (see illustration). On models with heated seats, pry out the seat heater switch panel, disconnect the electrical connectors and remove the seat heater switches.

11 Remove the four push fasteners (two on each side) from the front end of the console (see illustration).

12 Remove the screw from each side of the console.

13 Working inside the receptacle for the storage box, remove the two nuts from the back end of the console.

14 On models with an automatic transaxle, remove the shift lever handle (see illustration).

15 Lift up the console and verify that it's free of all fasteners, connectors and harnesses, then remove the console.

16 Installation is the reverse of removal.

24 Dashboard trim panels - removal and installation

❊❊ WARNING:

Most models covered by this manual are equipped with Supplemental Restraint Systems (SRS), more commonly known as airbags. Always disable the airbag system before working in the vicinity of any airbag system component to avoid the possibility of accidental deployment of the airbags, which could cause personal injury (see Chapter 12).

1 Disconnect the cable from the negative battery terminal (see Chapter 5, Section 1).

SEPHIA AND SPECTRA MODELS

Instrument cluster bezel

1997 and earlier models

▶ **Refer to illustration 24.2**

2 If equipped with a tilt steering column, lower the column. Remove the screws above the instrument cluster (see illustration).

3 Grasp the bezel securely and pull it away to detach the retaining clips from the instrument panel.

4 Installation is the reverse of removal.

1998 through 2003 models

▶ **Refer to illustration 24.5**

5 If equipped with a tilt steering column, lower the column. Remove the screws above the instrument cluster, then use a dull, flat-bladed tool around the edge of the panel to release it from the clips (see illustration).

6 Disconnect any electrical connectors from the bezel, then remove it from the instrument panel.

7 Installation is the reverse of removal.

Center trim panel (1994 through 1997 and 2004 and later models)

8 Use a trim stick to carefully pry around the complete edge of the center trim panel and detach it from the instrument panel

9 Installation is the reverse of removal.

Left side lower panel

▶ **Refer to illustration 24.10**

10 Remove the panel retaining screws (see illustration).

11 Detach the hood release lever and the 16-pin Data Link Connector, then detach the panel and lower it from the dashboard.

12 Installation is the reverse of removal.

24.2 Remove the screws retaining the instrument cluster bezel

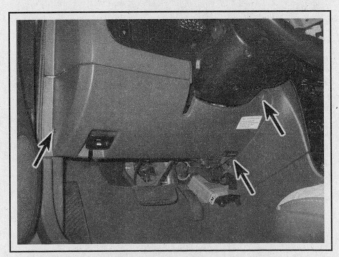

24.5 Remove the screws (A), then sharply pull the instrument cluster bezel back to detach the retaining clips (B) (typical 1998 through 2003 model)

24.10 Remove the screws retaining the lower panel

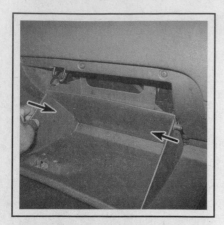

24.13 Squeeze the sides of the glove box bin until the bumpers on the bin have cleared the stops

24.14 Remove the glove box hinge screws

24.16 Carefully pry off the end trim cover with a trim removal tool (Sportage models)

Glove box

▶ **Refer to illustrations 24.13 and 24.14**

13 Open the glove box door. Squeeze the sides of the glove compartment bin together and pull the door down until the bumpers on the sides have cleared the stops (see illustration).

14 Remove the screws from the hinges and detach the glove box from the instrument panel (see illustration).

15 Installation is the reverse of removal.

SPORTAGE MODELS

Instrument panel end trim covers

▶ **Refer to illustration 24.16**

➡**Note: There is an end trim cover at each end of the instrument panel. This procedure applies to either one.**

16 Using a trim removal tool, carefully pry off the end trim cover (see illustration).

17 Installation is the reverse of removal. Make sure that the cover snaps into place.

Instrument cluster trim panel

▶ **Refer to illustration 24.19**

18 Tilt the steering column down to its lowest position.

19 Remove the two trim panel retaining screws (see illustration).

20 The cluster trim panel is still secured by several clips, one between the two screws you just removed and one at each lower corner. Using a trim removal tool, carefully pry off the panel at the two lower corners, then pry loose the hood of the trim panel.

21 Pull the trim panel toward you and disconnect the electrical connector for the trip sensor.

22 Installation is the reverse of removal. Make sure that the trim panel snaps into place.

Knee bolster trim panel and knee bolster

▶ **Refer to illustrations 24.24 and 24.25**

23 Disconnect the hood release cable from the hood release handle

(see illustration 10.17).

24 Remove the three retaining screws from the lower edge of the bolster trim panel (see illustration). The knee bolster trim panel is still secured by five clips: three across the upper edge of the panel and one about midway down each side of the panel. Using a trim removal tool, carefully pry off the trim panel.

25 If you need to access any component(s) located under the left end of the dash, remove the knee bolster bolts (see illustration) and remove the bolster.

26 Installation is the reverse of removal. Make sure that the trim panel snaps into place.

Center trim panel

▶ **Refer to illustration 24.27**

27 The center trim panel is retained by clips. Using a trim removal tool, carefully pry off the center trim panel (see illustration) and disconnect all electrical connectors

28 Installation is the reverse of removal. Make sure that all electrical connectors are connected and that the trim panel snaps into place.

Driver's and passenger's side center lower covers

▶ **Refer to illustration 24.30**

➡**Note: This procedure applies to either center lower cover.**

29 Remove the center console (see Section 23).

30 Remove the push fastener from the center lower cover (see illustration).

31 Remove the two retaining screws and remove the passenger's side center lower cover.

32 Installation is the reverse of removal.

Glove box

▶ **Refer to illustrations 24.33 and 24.34**

33 Remove the stops from the glove box (see illustration).

34 Disconnect the hinge pins (see illustrations), then remove the glove box.

35 Installation is the reverse of removal.

24.19 Instrument cluster trim panel retaining screws (Sportage models)

24.24 Knee bolster trim panel retaining screws (Sportage models)

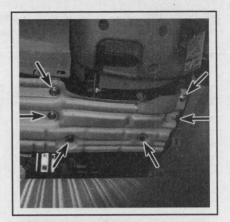

24.25 Knee bolster bolts (Sportage models)

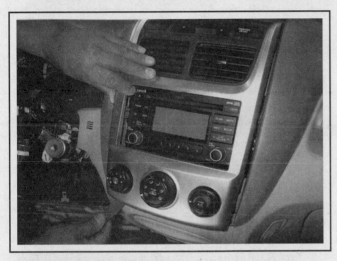

24.27 Carefully pry off the center trim panel (Sportage models)

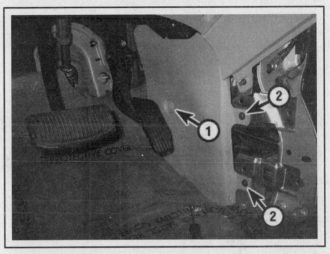

24.30 Center lower cover (driver's side) details (Sportage models)

1   Push fastener   *2   Retaining screws*

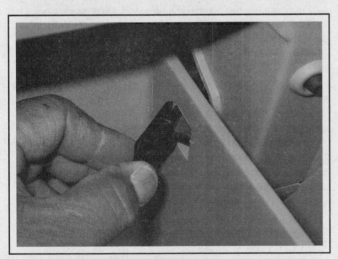

24.33 Pry up the rear of each glove box door stop and slide them to the rear, then pull them through the holes (Sportage models)

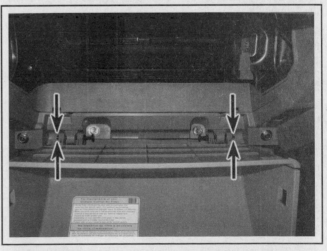

24.34 To disconnect the hinge pins from the glove box, squeeze the tabs on the end of each pin and pull them out (Sportage models)

25 Steering column covers - removal and installation

♦ Refer to illustration 25.3

✳✳ WARNING:

Most models covered by this manual are equipped with a Supplemental Restraint System (SRS), more commonly known as airbags. Always disable the airbag system before working in the vicinity of any airbag system component to avoid the possibility of accidental deployment of the airbag, which could cause personal injury (see Chapter 12).

1   Disconnect the cable from the negative battery terminal (see Chapter 5, Section 1).
2   On tilt steering columns, move the column to the lowest position.
3   Remove the retaining screws, then separate the halves and remove the covers (see illustration).
4   Installation is the reverse of the removal procedure.

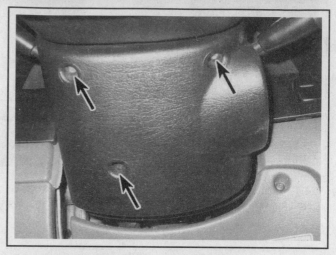

25.3 Steering column cover retaining screws

26 Instrument panel - removal and installation

✳✳ WARNING:

Most models covered by this manual are equipped with a Supplemental Restraint System (SRS), more commonly known as airbags. Always disable the airbag system before working in the vicinity of any airbag system component to avoid the possibility of accidental deployment of the airbag, which could cause personal injury (see Chapter 12).

➡Note 1: This is a difficult procedure for the home mechanic. There are many hidden fasteners, difficult angles to work in and many electrical connectors to tag and disconnect/connect. We recommend that this procedure be done only by an experienced do-it-yourselfer.

➡Note 2: During removal of the instrument panel, make careful notes of how each piece comes off, where it fits in relation to other pieces and what holds it in place. If you note how each part is installed before removing it, getting the instrument panel back together again will be much easier.

➡Note 3: It is not necessary, but it is suggested to remove both front seats to allow additional working space and lessen the chance of damage to the seats during this procedure.

SEPHIA AND SPECTRA MODELS

2003 and earlier models

♦ Refer to illustrations 26.9, 26.10a, 26.10b, 26.12a and 26.12b

1   Disconnect the cable from the negative battery terminal (see Chapter 5, Section 1).
2   Remove the steering wheel (see Chapter 10).
3   Remove the center console (see Section 23).

4   Remove all of the dashboard trim panels described in Section 24.
5   Remove the instrument cluster (see Chapter 12).
6   Remove the radio (see Chapter 12).
7   Remove the heater/air conditioner control assembly (see Chapter 3).
8   Remove the fasteners securing the steering column and lower it away from the instrument panel (see Chapter 10).
9   Remove the right and left side dashboard side covers (see illustration).
10 Remove both side kick panels (see illustrations).
11 Disconnect the electrical connectors under each end of the instrument panel, and at the center.

➡Note: A number of electrical connectors must be disconnected in order to remove the instrument panel. Most are designed so that they will only fit on the matching connector (male or female), but if there is any doubt, mark the connectors with masking tape and a marking pen before disconnecting them.

12 Remove the fasteners securing the instrument panel (see illustrations).
13 Pull the instrument panel towards the rear of the vehicle and detach any remaining electrical connectors interfering with removal.
14 Once all the electrical connectors are detached, lift the instrument panel then pull it away from the windshield and take it out through the passenger's door opening.

➡Note: This is a two-person job.

15 Installation is the reverse of removal.
16 Reconnect the battery. Refer to Chapter 5, Section 1.

2004 and later models

17 Disconnect the cable from the negative battery terminal (see Chapter 5).
18 Refer to Section 23 and remove the center console.

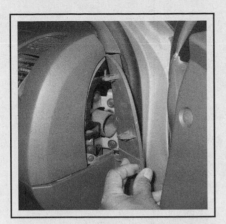

26.9 Carefully pry off the dashboard side covers

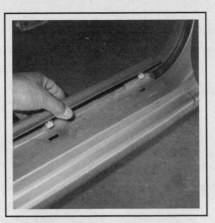

26.10a Carefully detach the clips securing the door sill and remove the sill . . .

26.10b . . . then remove the push fastener (arrow) and detach the clips to remove the side kick panel

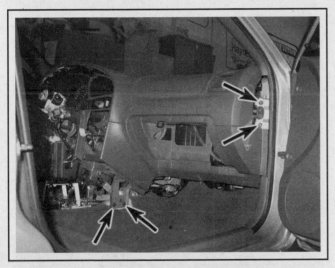

26.12a Remove the bolts from the support structure on the right . . .

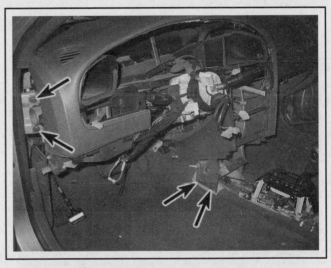

26.12b . . . and left sides of the instrument panel

19 Pull off the front door opening weatherstrips. Remove the cap and screw from each windshield pillar trim cover and pry them off.

20 Remove the front door threshold trim covers, then pry off the kick panels.

21 Carefully pry off the side covers from the ends of the instrument panel.

22 Remove the center instrument panel side covers.

23 Disconnect the hood release cable. Remove the lower instrument panel cover, disconnecting the switch wiring as you do so.

24 Refer to Chapter 10 and remove the steering wheel. Remove the steering column covers (see Section 25).

25 Unbolt the steering column from the cross bar and lower it to the floor.

26 Remove the guide and damper wire from the inside of the glove box. Remove the two hinge pins and remove the glove box.

27 Remove the 12 instrument panel screws. Disconnect all interfer-

ing wiring including the radio antenna cable. Remove the instrument panel assembly.

28 Remove the screws from the top of the instrument cluster bezel and remove it. Remove the instrument cluster, disconnecting the wiring as you do so.

29 Carefully pry out the center trim panel from the heater unit. Disconnect the wiring. Remove the four screws and lift out the heater control unit.

30 Remove the four radio mounting screws. Disconnect the radio wiring including the antenna cable, then remove the radio.

31 Remove the three bolts and seven screws from the lower instrument panel trim cover, disconnect the wiring and remove it.

32 Remove the 17 mounting bolts from the instrument fascia panel and remove it.

33 Installation is the reverse of removal.

26.35 Pry off the trim cap for each A-pillar trim panel retaining screw, remove the retaining screw, then pry off each trim panel (Sportage models)

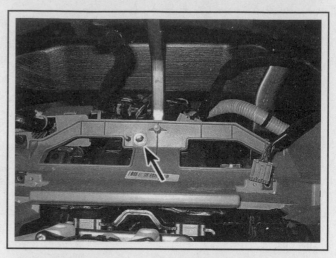

26.43 Instrument panel mounting nut location in the instrument cluster opening (Sportage models)

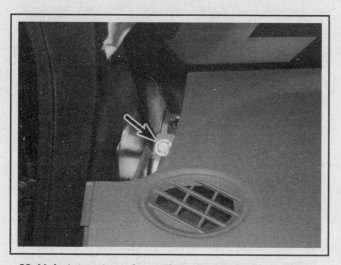

26.44 Instrument panel mounting nut, near the base of the left A-pillar (right A-pillar nut similar) (Sportage models)

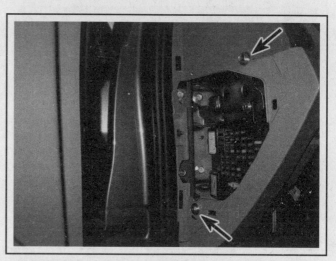

26.45a Instrument panel mounting bolts, left end (Sportage models)

SPORTAGE MODELS

▶ **Refer to illustrations 26.35, 26.43, 26.44, 26.45a, 26.45b and 26.46**

34 Disconnect the cable from the negative battery terminal (see Chapter 5).

35 Remove the left and right A-pillar trim panels (see illustration).

36 Remove both instrument panel end covers, the instrument cluster trim panel, the knee bolster trim panel, the center trim panel, the center lower cover (passenger's side) and the glove box (see Section 24).

37 Remove the steering column covers (see Section 25).

38 Remove the driver's side airbag and the steering wheel (see Chapter 10).

39 Remove the instrument cluster, the clock assembly and the radio (see Chapter 12).

40 Remove the heater/air conditioning control assembly (see Chapter 3).

41 Remove the front seats (see Section 28).

42 Disconnect the passenger's side airbag electrical connector.

43 Remove the nut located in the instrument cluster opening (see illustration).

44 Remove the bolt from the lower part of each A-pillar (see illustration).

45 Remove the bolts from the ends of the instrument panel (see illustrations).

46 Remove the bolts located in the glove box opening (see illustration).

47 Pull the instrument panel back and disconnect all electrical connectors for all harnesses that go between the firewall and the instrument panel.

48 With the help of an assistant, remove the instrument panel.

49 Installation is the reverse of removal.

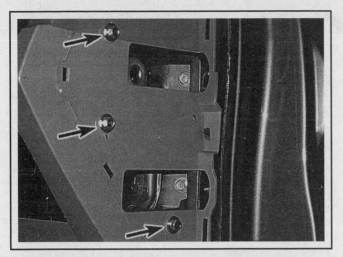

26.45b Instrument panel mounting bolts, right end (Sportage models)

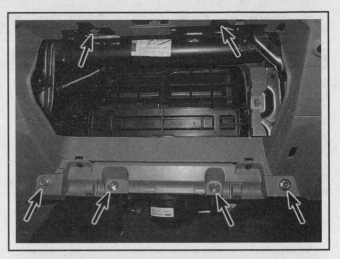

26.46 Instrument panel mounting bolts, glove box area (Sportage models)

27 Cowl cover - removal and installation

◆ Refer to illustrations 27.2a, 27.2b, 27.2c and 27.2d

1   Remove the windshield wiper arms (see Chapter 12, Section 11).

2   Remove the push pin fasteners and screws securing the cowl cover (see illustrations).

➡**Note: Use a small screwdriver to pop the screw covers up to access the screws (see illustration).**

3   Installation is the reverse of removal.

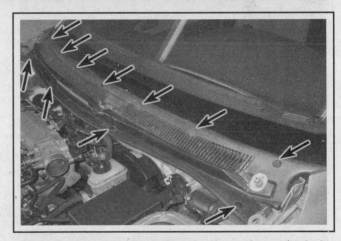

27.2a Remove the fasteners securing the cowl cover (typical Sephia model)

27.2b On Sportage models, peel back the rubber seal to expose the push fasteners. Remove all push fasteners . . .

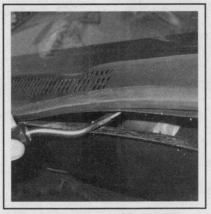

27.2c . . . then use a trim removal tool to pry off the cowl cover

27.2d On some models, you might have to remove trim covers to access the upper fasteners

28 Seats - removal and installation

> ### ✳✳ WARNING:
>
> Models covered by this manual are equipped with a Supplemental Restraint System (SRS), more commonly known as airbags. Always disable the airbag system before working in the vicinity of any airbag system component to avoid the possibility of accidental deployment of the airbag, which could cause personal injury (see Chapter 12).

> ### ✳✳ WARNING:
>
> The front seat belts on 2001 and later models are equipped with pre-tensioners, which are pyrotechnic (explosive) devices designed to retract the seat belts in the event of a collision. On models equipped with pre-tensioners, do not remove the front seat belt retractor assemblies, and do not disconnect the electrical connectors leading to the assemblies. Problems with the pre-tensioners will turn on the SRS (airbag) warning light on the dash. If any pre-tensioner problems are suspected, take the vehicle to a dealer service department. Also on these models, be sure to disable the airbag system (see Chapter 12).

FRONT SEAT

♦ **Refer to illustrations 28.1a and 28.1b**

1   Position the seat all the way forward, then all the way to the rear to access the seat retaining bolts (see illustrations). Detach any bolt trim covers and remove the retaining bolts.
2   Tilt the seat upward to access the underneath, then disconnect any electrical connectors and lift the seat from the vehicle.
3   Installation is the reverse of removal.

REAR SEAT

Sephia and Spectra models

♦ **Refer to illustrations 28.4 and 28.5**

4   Release the two latches at the front of the seat cushion and remove the cushion (see illustration).
5   Remove the seat back mounting bolts from both lower corners of the seat back (see illustration), then lift upward to remove the seat back.
6   Installation is the reverse of removal.

Sportage models

♦ **Refer to illustrations 28.7, 28.8a and 28.8b**

7   Flip up the trim covers, remove the left and/or right seat cushion frame hinge bolts (see illustration) and remove the left and/or right rear seat cushions.
8   Remove the left and/or right seat back mounting bracket bolts (see illustration) and remove the left and/or right seatbacks.
9   Installation is the reverse of removal.

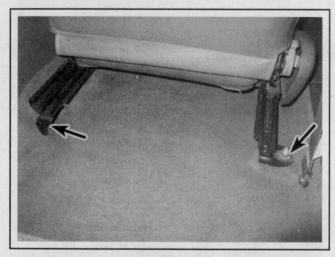

28.1a Remove the rear bolts from the front seat . . .

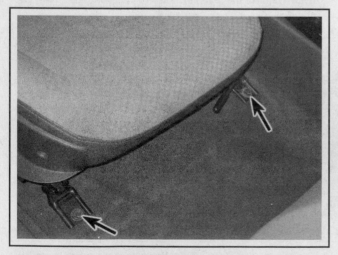

28.1b . . . then remove the front bolts (typical)

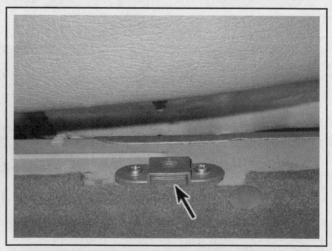

28.4 Remove the rear seat cushion by pushing the release buttons while lifting up on the seat cushion

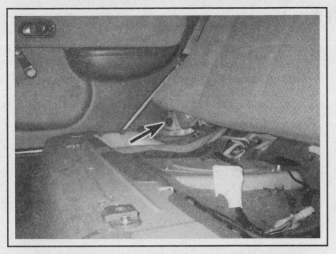

28.5 Remove the bolts from both sides of the seat back

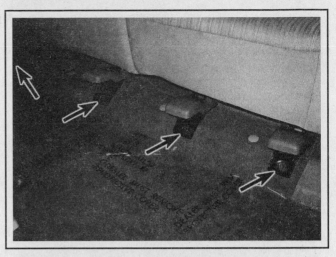

28.7 Rear seat cushion frame hinge bolts (fourth bolt not shown)

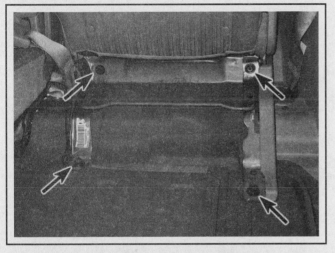

28.8a Left rear seatback mounting bracket bolts

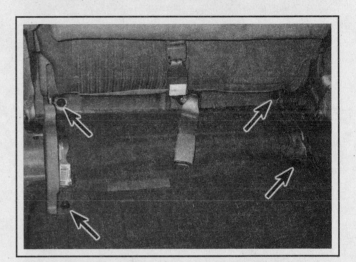

28.8b Right rear seatback mounting brackets bolts

29 Rear shelf trim panel - removal and installation

▶ **Refer to illustration 29.3**

1 Remove the rear seat cushion and seat back (see Section 28).
2 Remove the high-mounted brake light (see Chapter 12).
3 Detach the roof pillar trim pieces on both sides, then remove the retainers, child seat anchors (if equipped) and detach the shelf (see illustration).
4 Installation is the reverse of removal.

29.3 Remove the retainers along the front edge of the rear shelf trim panel

NOTES

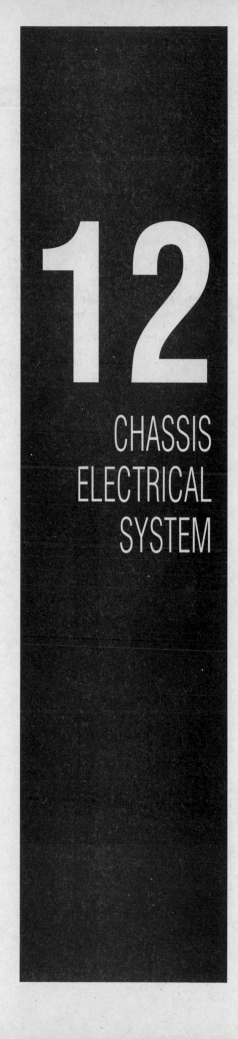

12

CHASSIS ELECTRICAL SYSTEM

Section

1 General information
2 Electrical troubleshooting - general information
3 Fuses - general information
4 Circuit breakers - general information
5 Relays - general information and testing
6 Turn signal and hazard flasher - check and replacement
7 Combination switch assembly - replacement
8 Key lock cylinder and ignition switch - replacement
9 Dashboard switches - replacement
10 Instrument cluster - removal and installation
11 Wiper motor - check and replacement
12 Radio and speakers - removal and installation
13 Antenna - removal and installation
14 Rear window defogger - check and repair
15 Headlight bulb - replacement
16 Headlight housing - removal and installation
17 Headlights - adjustment
18 Horn - replacement
19 Bulb replacement
20 Electric side view mirrors - general information
21 Cruise control system - general information
22 Power window system - general information
23 Power door lock system - general information
24 Daytime Running Lights (DRL) - general information
25 Airbag system - general information
26 Wiring diagrams - general information

1 General information

The electrical system is a 12-volt, negative ground type. Power for the lights and all electrical accessories is supplied by a lead/acid-type battery, which is charged by the alternator.

This Chapter covers repair and service procedures for the various electrical components not associated with the engine. Information on the battery, ignition system, alternator and starter motor can be found in Chapter 5.

It should be noted that when portions of the electrical system are serviced, the negative battery cable should be disconnected from the battery to prevent electrical shorts and/or fires.

2 Electrical troubleshooting - general information

♦ **Refer to illustrations 2.5a and 2.5b**

1 A typical electrical circuit consists of an electrical component, any switches, relays, motors, fuses, fusible links or circuit breakers related to that component and the wiring and connectors that link the component to both the battery and the chassis. Wiring diagrams are included at the end of this Chapter to help you pinpoint an electrical circuit problem.

2 Before tackling any troublesome electrical circuit, study the appropriate wiring diagrams to get a complete understanding of what makes up that individual circuit. Noting if other components related to the circuit are operating correctly, for instance, can often narrow trouble spots, down. If several components or circuits fail at one time, chances are the problem is in a fuse or ground connection, because several circuits are often routed through the same fuse and ground connections.

3 Electrical problems usually stem from simple causes, such as loose or corroded connections, a blown fuse, a melted fusible link or a failed relay. Visually inspect the condition of all fuses, wires and connections in a problem circuit before troubleshooting the circuit.

4 If test equipment and instruments are going to be utilized, use the diagrams to plan ahead of time where you will make the necessary connections in order to accurately pinpoint the trouble spot.

5 Basic electrical troubleshooting tools include a circuit tester, test light or voltmeter, a continuity tester, a set of test leads and a jumper wire (preferably with a circuit breaker), which can be used to bypass electrical components (see illustrations). Before attempting to locate a problem with test instruments, use the wiring diagram(s) to decide where to make the connections.

VOLTAGE CHECKS

♦ **Refer to illustration 2.6**

6 Voltage checks should be performed if a circuit is not functioning correctly. Connect one lead of a circuit tester to either the negative battery terminal or a known good ground. Connect the other lead to a connector in the circuit being tested, preferably nearest to the battery or fuse (see illustration). If the bulb of the tester lights, voltage is present, which means that the part of the circuit between the connector and the battery is problem free. Continue checking the rest of the circuit in the same fashion. When you reach a point at which no voltage is present, the problem lies between that point and the last test point with voltage. Most of the time the problem can be traced to a loose connection.

➡**Note: Keep in mind that some circuits receive voltage only when the ignition key is in the ACC or ON position.**

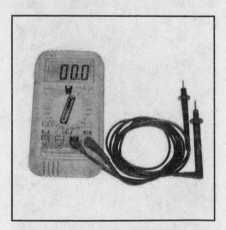

2.5a The most useful tool for electrical troubleshooting is a digital multimeter that can check volts, amps, and test continuity

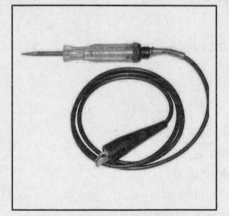

2.5b A simple test light is a very handy tool for testing voltage

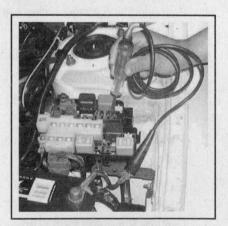

2.6 In use, a basic test light's lead is clipped to a known good ground, then the pointed probe can test connectors, wires or electrical sockets - if the bulb lights, the circuit being tested has battery voltage

FINDING A SHORT

7   One method of finding shorts in a live circuit is to remove the fuse and connect a test light in place of the fuse terminals (fabricate two jumper wires with small spade terminals, plug the jumper wires into the fuse box and connect the test light). There should be no voltage present in the circuit. Move the suspected wiring harness from side-to-side while watching the test light. If the bulb goes on, there is a short to ground somewhere in that area, probably where the insulation has rubbed through.

GROUND CHECK

8   Perform a ground test to check whether a component is correctly grounded. Disconnect the battery and connect one lead of a continuity tester or multimeter (set to the ohm scale), to a known good ground. Connect the other lead to the wire or ground connection being tested. If the resistance is low (less than 5 ohms), the ground is good. If the bulb on a self-powered test light does not go on, the ground is not good.

CONTINUITY CHECK

▶ **Refer to illustration 2.9**

9   Do a continuity check to verify that there are no opens in a circuit. With the circuit off (no power in the circuit), a self-powered continuity tester or multimeter can be used to check the circuit. Connect the test leads to both ends of the circuit (or to the power end and a good ground), and if the test light comes on the circuit is passing current correctly (see illustration). If the resistance is low (less than 5 ohms), there is continuity; if the reading is 10,000 ohms or higher, there is a break somewhere in the circuit. The same procedure can be used to test a switch, by connecting the continuity tester to the switch terminals. With the switch turned to ON, the test light should come on (or low resistance should be indicated on a meter).

FINDING AN OPEN CIRCUIT

10 When diagnosing for possible open circuits, it is often difficult to locate them by sight because the connectors hide oxidation or terminal misalignment. Merely wiggling a connector on a sensor or in the wiring harness may correct the open circuit condition. Remember this when an open circuit is indicated when troubleshooting a circuit. Intermittent problems may also be caused by oxidized or loose connections.

11 Electrical troubleshooting is simple if you keep in mind that all electrical circuits are basically electricity running from the battery, through the wires, switches, relays, fuses and fusible links to each electrical component (light bulb, motor, etc.) and to ground, from which it is passed back to the battery. Any electrical problem is an interruption in the flow of electricity to and from the battery.

CONNECTORS

12 Most electrical connections on these vehicles consist of multiple-terminal plastic connectors. The two halves of most connectors are

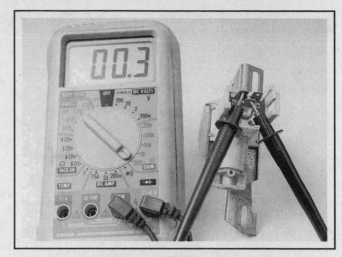

2.9 With a multimeter set to the ohm scale, resistance can be checked across two terminals - when checking for continuity, a low reading indicates continuity, a high reading or infinity indicates high resistance or lack of continuity

locked together by tabs molded into the plastic connector shells. So always look for the release tab(s) or locking tab(s) on a connector and release it/them before trying to disconnect the connector. If the connector is too dirty to find the release or locking tab(s), wipe it off. If a connector is in a dark area, use a flashlight. You might have to look closely (very closely!) at some connectors before you figure out how to separate the two halves, because the locking or release tabs are engaged in a way that is not immediately clear. And many connectors have not one but two sets of release or locking tabs.

13 Many of the important electrical connectors used on fuel, ignition and emission control systems are secured with Bosch-type wire retainers that surround three sides of the connector. Before you can disconnect one of these connectors you must separate the ends of the wire retainer from the connector, either by simply depressing the center part of the wire retainer or by prying the ends of the retainer out of their groove, depending on the type of connector.

14 Other connectors are usually locked together by release tabs that you simply depress to release, or by locking tabs that you spread apart or pry loose from some projection on the other half of the connector. Once you have figured out how to release a connector with locking or release tabs, carefully depress the release tabs or pry the locking tabs apart with a small screwdriver, then separate the connector halves. Pull only on the connector halves. Never pull on the wires or the wiring harness, because you might damage the wires and terminals inside the connector.

15 Each pair of connector terminals has a male half and a female half. This is particularly important to remember when you look at a connector terminal guide in a wiring diagram or wiring schematic, because you need to know whether you're looking at the wiring harness side or the component side of the connector. Connector halves are mirror images of each other, and a terminal that is shown on the right side end-view of one half will be on the left side end view of the other half. In other words, the terminal locations - and terminal numbering, if applicable - will be flipped.

3   Fuses - general information

FUSES

▶ **Refer to illustrations 3.1a, 3.1b, 3.1c and 3.2**

The electrical circuits of the vehicle are protected by a combination of fuses, circuit breakers and relays (for more information about circuit breakers, refer to Section 4; for more information about relays, refer to Section 5). Fuse and relay boxes are located in the engine compartment and in the left kick panel underneath the left end of the dashboard (see illustrations). On 2004 models with a 2.0L DOHC engine and on all 2005 and later models (except Sportage), the interior fuse and relay box is located under the left end of the dashboard; on these models you'll have to remove the knee bolster (see Chapter 11) to access the interior fuses. On Sportage models, the fuse and relay box is located at the left end of the instrument panel (see illustration). To access it, remove the left end cover (see Section 24 in Chapter 11). A wide array of mini and maxi-style fuses is used to protect various circuits. These fuses, which employ a blade terminal design, can be removed and installed without special tools. Each fuse protects a specific circuit or circuits, and the protected circuits are identified on the fuse panel cover. If the fuse panel cover is difficult to read, or missing, you can also refer to your owner's manual, which includes a complete guide to all fuses and relays in all three fuse/relay boxes.

If an electrical component fails, always check the fuse first. The best way to check a fuse is with a test light. Check for power at the exposed terminal tips of each fuse. If power is present on one side of the fuse but not the other, the fuse is blown. A blown fuse can also be confirmed by visually inspecting it (see illustration).

Be sure to replace blown fuses with the correct type. Fuses of different ratings are physically interchangeable, but only fuses of the correct rating should be used. Replacing a fuse with one of a higher or lower value than specified is not recommended. Each electrical circuit needs a specific amount of protection. The amperage value of each fuse is molded into the fuse body.

If the replacement fuse immediately fails, don't replace it again until the cause of the problem is isolated and corrected. In most cases, this will be a short circuit in the wiring caused by a broken or deteriorated wire.

3.1a The engine compartment fuse/relay box is located on the left side of the engine compartment. The functions and locations of the various fuses and relays are listed on the underside of the fuse/relay box cover

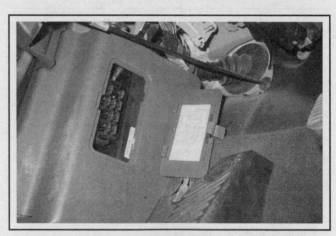

3.1b To access the fuse/relay box inside the passenger compartment, open the small access door in the kick panel on 2003 and earlier models

3.1c On Sportage models, the passenger compartment fuse and relay box is located at the left end of the dash (end cover removed)

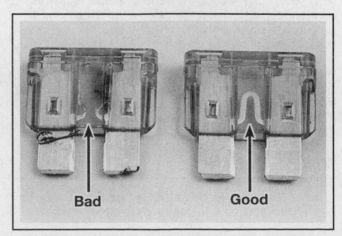

3.2 When a fuse blows, the element between the terminals melts - the fuse on the left is blown, the fuse on the right is good

4   Circuit breakers - general information

Circuit breakers protect certain circuits, such as the power windows or heated seats. The number of circuit breakers employed on your vehicle depends on its electrical accessories. Some circuit breakers are located in a fuse/relay box; others are located as stand-alone units under the dash and in other locations throughout the vehicle.

Because a circuit breaker resets automatically, a temporary or intermittent electrical overload in a circuit-breaker-protected system will cause the circuit to open momentarily, then close again. If a circuit-breaker-protected circuit does not close, or constantly opens and closes, check it immediately.

For a basic check, pull the circuit breaker up out of its socket on the fuse panel, but just far enough to probe with a voltmeter. The breaker should still contact the sockets.

With the voltmeter negative lead on a good chassis ground, touch each end prong of the circuit breaker with the positive meter probe. There should be battery voltage at each end. If there is battery voltage only at one end, the circuit breaker must be replaced.

Some circuit breakers must be reset manually.

5   Relays - general information and testing

GENERAL INFORMATION

1   Many electrical accessories in the vehicle utilize relays to transmit current to the component. If the relay is defective, the component won't operate properly.

2   Most relays are located in the engine compartment fuse and relay box (see Section 3).

3   Some relays are located in other parts of the vehicle, primarily in various wiring harnesses underneath the instrument panel.

4   If a faulty relay is suspected, it can be removed and tested using the procedure below or by a dealer service department or a repair shop. Defective relays must be replaced as a unit.

TESTING

▶ **Refer to illustrations 5.5a and 5.5b**

5   Most of the relays used in these vehicles are of a type often called "ISO" relays, which refers to the International Standards Organization. The terminals of ISO relays are numbered to indicate their usual circuit connections and functions. There are two basic layouts of terminals on the relays used in the vehicles covered by this manual (see illustrations).

6   Refer to the wiring diagram for the circuit to determine the proper connections for the relay you're testing. If you can't determine the correct connection from the wiring diagrams, however, you may be able to determine the test connections from the information that follows.

7   Two of the terminals are the relay control circuit and connect to the relay coil. The other relay terminals are the power circuit. When the relay is energized, the coil creates a magnetic field that closes the larger contacts of the power circuit to provide power to the circuit loads.

8   Terminals 85 and 86 are normally the control circuit. If the relay contains a diode, terminal 86 must be connected to battery positive (B+) voltage and terminal 85 to ground. If the relay contains a resistor, terminals 85 and 86 can be connected in either direction with respect to B+ and ground.

9   Terminal 30 is normally connected to the battery voltage (B+) source for the circuit loads. Terminal 87 is connected to the ground side of the circuit, either directly or through a load. If the relay has several alternate terminals for load or ground connections, they usually are numbered 87A, 87B, 87C, and so on.

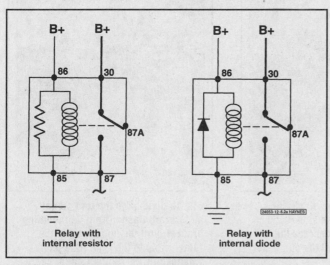

5.5a Typical ISO relay designs, terminal numbering and circuit connections

5.5b Most relays are marked on the outside to easily identify the control circuits and the power circuits (four-terminal type shown)

10 Use an ohmmeter to check continuity through the relay control coil.

   a) *Connect the meter according to the polarity shown in the illustration for one check; then reverse the ohmmeter leads and check continuity in the other direction.*

   b) *If the relay contains a resistor, resistance will be indicated on the meter, and should be the same value with the ohmmeter in either direction.*

   c) *If the relay contains a diode, resistance should be higher with the ohmmeter in the forward polarity direction than with the meter leads reversed.*

   d) *If the ohmmeter shows infinite resistance in both directions, replace the relay.*

11 Remove the relay from the vehicle and use the ohmmeter to check for continuity between the relay power circuit terminals. There should be no continuity between terminal 30 and 87 with the relay de-energized.

12 Connect a fused jumper wire to terminal 86 and the positive battery terminal. Connect another jumper wire between terminal 85 and ground. When the connections are made, the relay should click.

13 With the jumper wires connected, check for continuity between the power circuit terminals. Now there should be continuity between terminals 30 and 87.

14 If the relay fails any of the above tests, replace it.

6   Turn signal and hazard flasher relay - check and replacement

✳✳ WARNING:

Most models covered by this manual are equipped with a Supplemental Restraint System (SRS), commonly referred to as airbags. Always disable the airbag system before working in the vicinity of any airbag system component to avoid the possibility of accidental deployment of the airbag, which could cause personal injury (see Section 25).

1994 THROUGH 2004 MODELS (EXCEPT 2004 2.0L DOHC)

♦ **Refer to illustrations 6.5a, 6.5b and 6.6**

1 The turn signal and hazard flashers are controlled by the turn signal and hazard flasher relay, which is located above the passenger compartment fuse/relay box, above the left kick panel.

2 If the flasher unit is functioning correctly, you'll hear an audible click when it's operating. If one of the turn signal indicator lights on the instrument cluster flashes more rapidly than normal, a turn signal bulb for that side probably has a blown filament.

3 If neither turn signal indicator blinks, the problem might be a blown fuse, a faulty turn signal and hazard flasher relay, a broken switch or a loose or open connection. If the left or right turn signal fuse has blown, check the wiring for a short before installing a new fuse.

4 To access the turn signal/hazard flasher relay on some models, it may be helpful to remove the left kick panel (see illustrations 26.10a and 26.10b in Chapter 11).

5 Disconnect the electrical connector from the turn signal and hazard flasher relay (see illustrations).

6 Firmly pull the upper part of the relay to the right to disengage it from its mounting bracket (see illustration).

7 If the turn signal and hazard flasher relay is bad, take it with you when buying a replacement unit. Make sure that the replacement unit is identical to the original.

8 Installation is the reverse of removal.

6.5a The turn signal and hazard flasher unit is located on the under-dash fuse/relay box (1999 model shown)

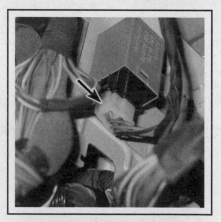

6.5b To disconnect the electrical connector from the turn signal and hazard flasher relay, depress this release tab and pull off the connector

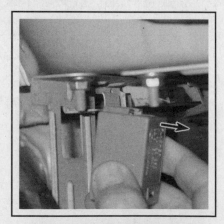

6.6 To disengage the turn signal and hazard flasher from its mounting bracket, pull the upper part of the relay firmly to the right (this photo was taken with the instrument panel removed - you won't be able to see this bracket from below)

2004 2.0L DOHC AND ALL 2005 AND LATER MODELS (EXCEPT SPORTAGE)

➡**Note: These models are not equipped with a conventional turn signal and hazard flasher relay. On these models, the turn signal and hazard flasher functions are controlled by the ETACS module, which is an integral component of the interior fuse and relay box located under the left end of the dashboard.**

9 Remove the left side lower panel (see Section 24 in Chapter 11).

10 Disconnect the electrical connectors from the fuse and relay box.

11 Remove the fuse and relay box mounting bolts (three on the left edge, two in the middle and two on the right edge).

12 Pull off the fuse and relay box and disconnect any electrical connectors from the back side of the box, then remove the panel.

13 If you're replacing the fuse and relay box, swap all fuses and relays to the new box.

14 Installation is the reverse of removal.

SPORTAGE MODELS

➡**Note: On Sportage models the turn signal and hazard flasher relay is an integral component of the passenger compartment fuse and relay box. If it's not working, replace the fuse and relay box.**

15 Remove the left instrument panel end cover (see *Dashboard trim covers - removal and installation* in Chapter 11).

16 Unbolt the passenger compartment fuse and relay panel (see illustration 3.1c).

17 Pull the fuse and relay box out of the dash and disconnect the electrical connectors from the backside of the box.

18 Transfer all the fuses and relays to the new fuse and relay box.

19 Installation is the reverse of removal.

7 Combination switch assembly - replacement

SEPHIA AND SPECTRA MODELS

◆ **Refer to illustrations 7.3 and 7.4**

❋❋ WARNING:

Most models covered by this manual are equipped with a Supplemental Restraint System (SRS), more commonly known as airbags. Always disable the airbag system before working in the vicinity of any airbag system component to avoid the possibility of accidental deployment of the airbag, which could cause personal injury (see Section 25).

1 Remove the steering wheel and the airbag clockspring (see Chapter 10).

2 Remove the steering column covers (see *Steering column covers* - *removal and installation* in Chapter 11).

3 Disconnect the electrical connector from the combination switch (see illustration).

4 Remove the combination switch retaining screws (see illustration) and remove the combination switch.

5 Installation is the reverse of removal.

SPORTAGE MODELS

◆ **Refer to illustration 7.7**

6 Remove the upper and lower steering column covers (see Chapter 11).

7 Disconnect the electrical connector from the turn signal switch or wiper/washer switch (see illustration).

8 Remove the two switch mounting screws and remove the switch.

9 Installation is the reverse of removal.

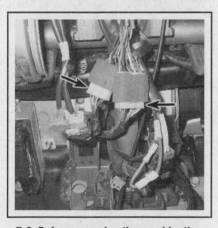

7.3 Before removing the combination switch assembly, disconnect these two big electrical connectors (later models have only one connector)

7.4 To detach the combination switch from the steering column assembly, remove these screws (typical)

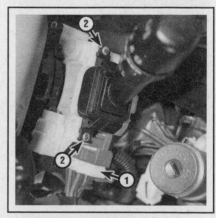

7.7 Windshield wiper/washer switch details (turn signal switch similar) (Sportage models)

1 *Electrical connector*
2 *Switch mounting screws*

8   Key lock cylinder and igition switch assembly - replacement

▶ Refer to illustrations 8.2 and 8.3

✳✳ WARNING:

Most models covered by this manual are equipped with a Supplemental Restraint System (SRS), more commonly known as airbags. Always disable the airbag system before working in the vicinity of any airbag system component to avoid the possibility of accidental deployment of the airbag, which could cause personal injury (see Section 25).

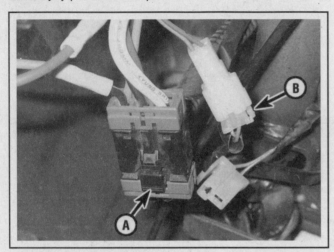

8.2 Depress this release tab (A) and pull the two halves of the ignition switch electrical connector apart, then disconnect the electrical connector (B) for the key lock cylinder buzzer

SEPHIA AND SPECTRA MODELS

1   Remove the steering column covers (see Chapter 11).
2   Disconnect the electrical connector from the ignition switch (see illustration).
3   Center-punch the shear-head bolts that secure the key lock cylinder housing to the steering column, then drill a hole in the center of each bolt with a 3/16-inch (5 mm) drill bit (see illustration) and unscrew them with a screw extractor.
4   Remove the ignition switch and key lock cylinder assembly from the steering column.
5   Before tightening the new shear-head bolts, insert the ignition key and verify that the steering wheel lock mechanism functions correctly and that the ignition key turns freely in the key lock cylinder. Then tighten the shear-head bolts until the heads break off.

SPORTAGE MODELS

▶ Refer to illustrations 8.7 and 8.8

6   Remove the knee bolster trim panel and the steering column covers (see Sections 24 and 25, in Chapter 11).
7   Turn the ignition key to the ACC position. Using an awl or a small screwdriver, depress the lock pin (see illustration) and pull out the key lock cylinder.
8   Disconnect the electrical connector from the ignition switch (see illustration).
9   Remove the ignition switch mounting screw and remove the switch.
10 Installation is the reverse of removal.

8.3 To detach the key lock cylinder from the steering column, drill out the bolts with a 3/16-inch (5 mm) drill bit, then unscrew the bolts with a screw extractor

8.7 Turn the ignition key to the ACC position, insert an awl or small screwdriver into this hole, depress the lock pin and pull out the cylinder

8.8 Ignition switch details (Sportage models)

1   Electrical connector
2   Switch mounting screw

9   Dashboard switches - replacement

✳ WARNING:

Most models covered by this manual are equipped with a Supplemental Restraint System (SRS), more commonly known as airbags. Always disable the airbag system before working in the vicinity of any airbag system component to avoid the possibility of accidental deployment of the airbag, which could cause personal injury (see Section 25).

SEPHIA AND SPECTRA MODELS

Interior light rheostat (pre-2004 models), trunk lid opener switch (2004 models) or power mirror switch

▸ **Refer to illustration 9.2**

➡Note: The photo accompanying this procedure depicts removal of an interior light rheostat (pre-2004 models), but the procedure for removing the trunk lid opener switch (2004 models) or power mirror switch is identical.

1   Remove the instrument cluster bezel (see *Dashboard trim panels - removal and installation* in Chapter 11).

2   To remove the interior light rheostat (or power mirror switch) from the instrument cluster bezel, depress the release tabs (see illustration) on the top and bottom of the rheostat (or power mirror switch), then push the rheostat (or power mirror switch) out of the cluster bezel from the back.

3   Installation is the reverse of removal.

Cruise control main switch, rear window wiper and washer switch (Spectra models only), rear window defroster switch or hazard flasher switch

▸ **Refer to illustration 9.5**

4   Remove the instrument cluster bezel (see *Dashboard trim panels - removal and installation* in Chapter 11).

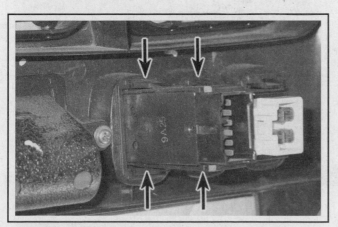

9.5 To remove the cruise control switch, rear window windshield wiper and washer switch, rear window defroster switch or hazard flasher switch from the instrument cluster bezel, depress the release tabs on the top and bottom of the switch, then push the switch out through the front of the cluster bezel

5   To remove the cruise control switch, rear window wiper and washer switch, cruise control main switch, rear window defroster switch or hazard flasher switch, depress the release tabs (see illustration) on the top and bottom of the switch, then push the switch out of the cluster bezel from the back.

6   Installation is the reverse of removal.

SPORTAGE MODELS

Rheostat/ESC/4WD lock switch assembly

▸ **Refer to illustration 9.8**

7   Remove the left instrument panel end trim cover (see Section 24 in Chapter 11).

8   Push out the switch assembly (see illustration) and disconnect the electrical connectors.

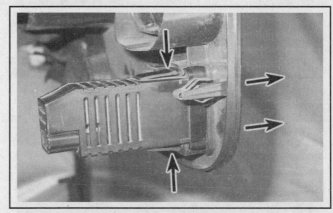

9.2 To remove the interior light rheostat (shown), trunk lid opener switch (2004 models only) or power mirror switch from the instrument cluster bezel, depress the release tabs on the top and bottom of the rheostat (or switch), then push the rheostat (or switch) out through the front of the cluster bezel

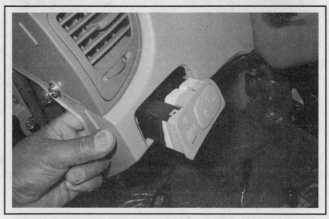

9.8 Remove the rheostat/ESC/4WD lock switch assembly by pushing it out of the instrument panel from the back (Sportage models)

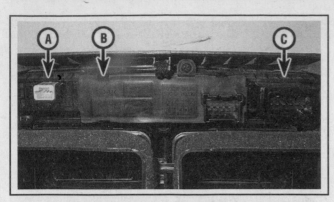

9.11 To remove the passenger airbag indicator light (A), the clock (B) or the hazard flasher switch (B) from the center trim panel, simply squeeze the lock tabs and push out the switch (Sportage models)

9 Installation is the reverse of removal.

Hazard flasher switch/clock/passenger seat airbag indicator light

▸ **Refer to illustration 9.11**

10 Remove the center trim panel (see Section 24 in Chapter 11).

11 Depress the lock tabs that secure the hazard flasher switch, clock or passenger seat air indicator light to the center trim panel (see illustration).

12 Installation is the reverse of removal. Make sure that the switch assembly snaps into place.

10 Instrument cluster - removal and installation

▸ **Refer to illustrations 10.2 and 10.3**

❊❊ WARNING:

Most models covered by this manual are equipped with a Supplemental Restraint System (SRS), more commonly known as airbags. Always disable the airbag system before working in the vicinity of any airbag system component to avoid the possibility of accidental deployment of the airbag, which could cause personal injury (see Section 25).

1 Remove the instrument cluster bezel (see *Dashboard trim panels - removal and installation* in Chapter 11).

2 Remove the instrument cluster mounting screws (see illustration).

3 Pull out the cluster and disconnect the electrical connectors from the backside (see illustration).

4 Installation is the reverse of removal.

10.2 To detach the instrument cluster from the dash, remove these four mounting screws (typical)

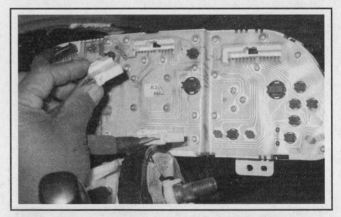

10.3 Pull the instrument cluster out from the dash far enough to access the backside of the cluster, then disconnect the electrical connectors and remove the cluster

11 Wiper motor - check and replacement

WIPER MOTOR CIRCUIT CHECK

➡**Note: If the following checks fail to locate the problem, have the system diagnosed by a dealer service department or other properly equipped repair facility.**

1 If the wipers work slowly, make sure the battery is fully charged and in good condition (see Chapter 5). If the battery is in good shape,

remove the wiper motor (see Steps 6 through 10 or 15 through 18) and operate the wiper arms by hand. Check for binding linkage and pivots. Lubricate or repair the linkage or pivots as necessary. Reinstall the wiper motor. If the wipers still operate slowly, check for loose or corroded connections, especially the ground connection. If all connections look OK, replace the motor.

2 If the wipers fail to operate when activated, check the fuse (see

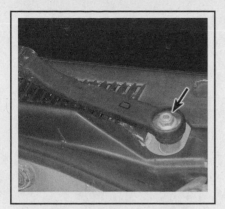

11.6a Remove the trim cover from each windshield wiper arm retaining nut, remove the retaining nut . . .

11.6b . . . then mark the position of the wiper arm in relation to its splined shaft

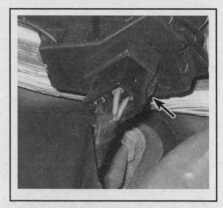

11.8 To disconnect the electrical connector from the windshield wiper motor, depress this release tab and pull out the connector

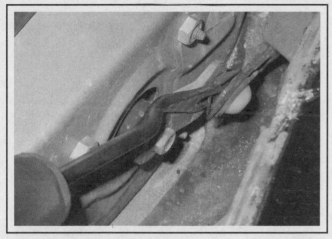

11.9 Carefully separate the windshield wiper linkage from the wiper motor arm with a trim panel removal tool (shown) or with some other suitable tool

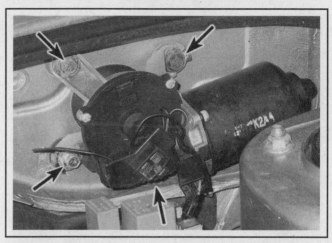

11.10 To detach the windshield wiper motor, remove the mounting bolts

Section 3). If the fuse is OK, connect a jumper wire between the wiper motor's ground terminal and ground, then retest. If the motor works now, repair the ground connection. If the motor still doesn't work, turn the wiper switch to the HI position and check for voltage at the motor.

➡**Note: Remove the cowl cover (see Chapter 11) and disconnect the electrical connector from the windshield wiper motor (see Step 8).**

3   If there's voltage at the connector, remove the motor and check it off the vehicle with fused jumper wires from the battery. If the motor now works, check for binding linkage (see Step 1). If the motor still doesn't work, replace it. If there's no voltage to the motor, check for voltage at the wiper control relays. If there's voltage at the wiper control relays and no voltage at the wiper motor, have the switch tested. If the switch is OK, the wiper control relay is probably bad. See Section 5 for relay testing.

4   If the interval (delay) function is inoperative, check the continuity of all the wiring between the switch and the wiper control module.

5   If the wipers fail to park (if they stop at the position that they're in when the switch is turned off instead of returning to their normal off position), turn the wiper switch to OFF and the ignition switch to ON, then check for voltage at the park feed wire of the wiper motor connector. If no voltage is present, check for an open circuit between the wiper motor and the fuse panel.

WIPER MOTOR REPLACEMENT

Sephia and Spectra models

Windshield wiper motor

◆ **Refer to illustrations 11.6a, 11.6b, 11.8, 11.9, 11.10, 11.11a and 11.11b**

6   Remove the retaining nut trim covers from the windshield wiper arm and remove the nuts (see illustration). Be sure to mark the position of each wiper arm in relation to the motor shaft (see illustration), then remove the wiper arms.

7   Remove the cowl cover (see Chapter 11).

8   Disconnect the electrical connector from the windshield wiper motor (see illustration).

9   Carefully pry the windshield wiper linkage loose from the wiper motor arm with a trim panel tool (see illustration) or with some other suitable tool.

10 Remove the windshield wiper motor mounting bolts (see illustration) and remove the wiper motor.

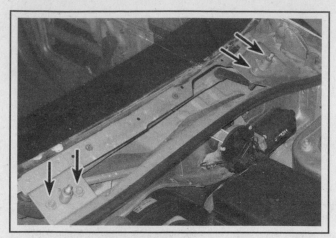

11.11a To detach the wiper linkage assembly from the cowl, remove these four nuts . . .

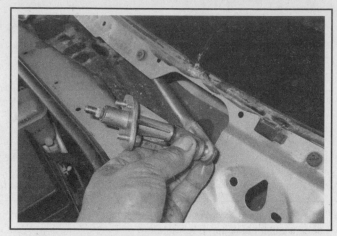

11.11b . . . and pull the linkage assembly out through the driver's side access hole

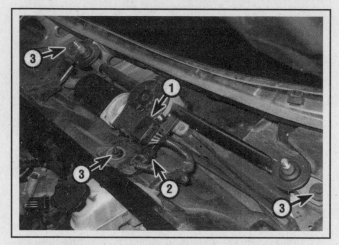

11.23 Windshield wiper motor/linkage assembly details (Sportage models)

11.25 Pry the linkage arm from the wiper motor crank arm (Sportage models)

1 *Windshield wiper motor electrical connector*
2 *Windshield de-icer electrical connector*
3 *Mounting bolts*

11 Remove the windshield wiper linkage from the cowl (see illustration) and remove the linkage through the driver's side access hole (see illustration).

12 Before installing the windshield wiper linkage, be sure to grease the pivot points.

13 Installation is otherwise the reverse of removal. Be sure to align the marks you made between the linkage arm and the motor mounting bracket and between the windshield wiper arm and the motor shaft.

14 Turn on the windshield wipers and verify that the wiper motor operates correctly in all modes (see your owner's manual if necessary).

Rear window wiper motor (2001 and later Spectra five-door models)

15 Remove the rear wiper arm trim cover and remove the wiper arm retaining nut (see illustration 11.6a), mark the relationship of the wiper arm to the wiper motor shaft (see illustration 11.6b), then remove the wiper arm.

16 Open the hatch, then, using a trim panel tool, carefully pry off the rear hatch trim panel.

17 Remove the three wiper motor mounting bolts.

18 Remove the rear window wiper motor.

19 Disconnect the electrical connector from the wiper motor.

20 Installation is the reverse of removal.

Sportage models

Windshield wiper motor

▶ **Refer to illustrations 11.23, 11.25 and 11.26**

21 Remove the windshield wiper arm mounting nut trim caps from both wiper arms. Remove the nuts that secure the wiper arms, mark the position of both wiper arms, then remove the arms.

22 Remove the weather stripping, then remove the clips that secure the cowl cover and remove the cowl cover (see Section 27 in Chapter 11).

23 Disconnect the windshield wiper motor electrical connector and the windshield de-icer electrical connector (see illustration).

24 Remove the windshield wiper motor/linkage assembly mounting bolts, lift out the assembly and place the windshield wiper motor/linkage assembly on a clean workbench.

25 Separate the linkage arm from the wiper motor crank arm (see illustration).

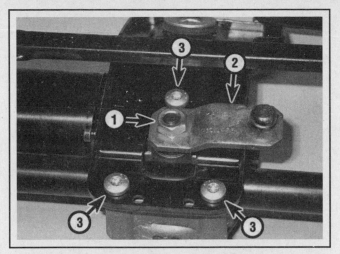

11.26 Windshield wiper arm details (Sportage models)

1   Crank arm nut   3   Wiper motor mounting bolts
2   Crank arm

26 Remove the crank arm nut (see illustration) and remove the crank arm from the motor.

27 Remove the motor mounting bolts and separate the motor from the linkage assembly.

28 Installation is the reverse of removal. When installing the wiper arms, make sure that they're aligned with the marks made in Step 21.

Rear wiper motor

▶ **Refer to illustrations 11.31 and 11.32**

29 Before removing the wiper arm, mark its position on the glass with masking tape, remove the rear wiper arm mounting nut trim cap and nut, then remove the wiper arm.

30 Remove the rear hatch handle retaining nut and remove the handle.

31 Open the tailgate window, then remove the rear wiper motor trim cover (see illustration).

32 Disconnect the electrical connector from the rear wiper motor (see illustration).

33 Remove the three wiper motor mounting nuts and remove the rear wiper motor.

34 Installation is the reverse of removal. Make sure that the wiper arms are correctly oriented.

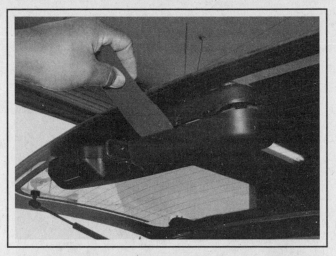

11.31 Remove the rear wiper motor trim cover (Sportage models)

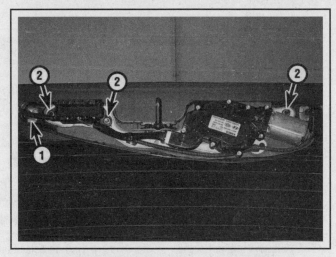

11.32 Rear wiper motor details (Sportage models)

1   Electrical connector   2   Mounting nuts

---

12 Radio and speakers - removal and installation

⁕ WARNING:

Most models covered by this manual are equipped with a Supplemental Restraint System (SRS), more commonly known as airbags. Always disable the airbag system before working in the vicinity of any airbag system component to avoid the possibility of accidental deployment of the airbag, which could cause personal injury (see Section 25).

RADIO

▶ **Refer to illustrations 12.2 and 12.3**

1   On 1994 through 1997 models and all Sportage models, remove the center panel bezel (see Chapter 11). On 1998 and later models, remove the instrument cluster bezel (see Chapter 11).

2 Remove the radio mounting screws (see illustration).
3 Pull the radio out of the dash and disconnect the electrical connector and the antenna cable from the backside of the radio (see illustration).
4 Installation is the reverse of removal.

12.2 To detach the radio from the dash, remove these four screws (typical)

SPEAKERS

Front door speakers

▶ **Refer to illustrations 12.6 and 12.7**

5 Remove the front door trim panel (see Chapter 11).
6 Remove the speaker mounting screws (see illustration) and pull the speaker out of its mounting receptacle.
7 Disconnect the electrical connector (see illustration) and remove the speaker from the vehicle.
8 Installation is the reverse of removal.

Rear speakers

9 Remove the rear shelf trim panel (see Chapter 11).
10 Open the trunk and disconnect the electrical connector from the speaker.
11 Remove the speaker mounting screws and remove the speaker.
12 Installation is the reverse of removal.

12.3 Pull the radio out of the dash and disconnect the electrical connector and the antenna cable

12.6 To detach the front door speaker from the door, remove these three mounting screws

12.7 To release the speaker electrical connector, depress the release tab and pull off the connector

13 Antenna - removal and installation

➡ **Note: Later models have antennas that are part of the rear window glass. Refer to Section 14 for information on checking and repairing these units.**

ANTENNA ASSEMBLY

▶ **Refer to illustrations 13.1, 13.2 and 13.3**

1 Unscrew the antenna mast from its mounting base (see illustra-

tion). If you're simply replacing the antenna mast, stop here and simply screw on a new antenna mast. If you're replacing the entire antenna assembly, keep going.
2 Unscrew the bezel nut from the mounting base (see illustration).
3 Open the rear deck lid, peel back the trunk carpet trim from the left rear corner of the trunk, disconnect the antenna cable electrical connector and remove the ground wire bolt (see illustration).
4 Remove the antenna support bracket nut and remove the antenna assembly.
5 Installation is the reverse of removal.

13.1 To detach the antenna mast from the antenna mounting base, simply unscrew it

13.2 To detach the antenna mounting base from the fender, unscrew the bezel nut

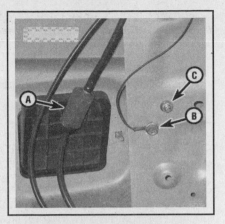

13.3 Peel back the carpet trim from the left rear corner of the trunk, disconnect the antenna electrical connector (A) and remove the ground wire bolt (B), then remove the bracket nut (C) and remove the antenna assembly

13.10 Before removing the antenna cable from the dash, carefully note how it's routed. When installing the new cable, try to route it exactly the same way

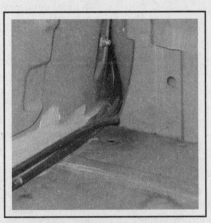

13.11a The antenna cable is routed through this hole in the left front corner of the trunk . . .

13.11b . . . and comes out on the other side to the left of the seat cushion

ANTENNA CABLE

▶ **Refer to illustrations 13.10, 13.11a and 13.11b**

❋❋ WARNING:

Most models covered by this manual are equipped with a Supplemental Restraint System (SRS), more commonly known as airbags. Always disable the airbag system before working in the vicinity of any airbag system component to avoid the possibility of accidental deployment of the airbag, which could cause personal injury (see Section 25).

6   Remove the radio and disconnect the antenna cable from the backside of the radio (see Section 12).

7   Remove the heater/air conditioner control assembly (see Chap-

ter 3).

8   Disconnect the antenna cable from the antenna mast electrical lead (see Step 3).

9   Inside the passenger compartment, remove the driver's seat and the rear seat cushion (see Chapter 11), then peel back the carpeting from the left side of the vehicle.

10   Trace the routing of the cable through the dash (see illustration), then carefully pull the cable out of the dash.

11   Open the trunk and, if you haven't already done so, pull back the carpeting from the left side of the trunk to expose the route of the antenna cable (see illustration), which is routed through a small hole in the left front corner of the trunk. Open the left rear door and note where the antenna cable comes out through the small hole at the left end of the rear seat cushion (see illustration). Pull the antenna cable out through this hole. (The two other cables routed through this hole are for the trunk latch and for the fuel filler neck door.)

12   Installation is the reverse of removal.

14 Rear window defogger - check and repair

1 The rear window defogger consists of a number of horizontal elements baked onto the glass surface.

2 Small breaks in the element can be repaired without removing the rear window.

CHECK

▶ **Refer to illustrations 14.4, 14.5 and 14.7**

3 Turn the ignition switch and defogger system switches to the ON position. Using a voltmeter, place the positive probe against the defogger grid positive terminal and the negative probe against the ground terminal. If battery voltage is not indicated, check the fuse, defogger switch and related wiring. If voltage is indicated, but all or part of the defogger doesn't heat, proceed with the following tests.

4 When measuring voltage during the next two tests, wrap a piece of aluminum foil around the tip of the voltmeter positive probe and press the foil against the heating element with your finger (see illustration). Place the negative probe on the defogger grid ground terminal.

5 Check the voltage at the center of each heating element (see illustration). If the voltage is 5 or 6-volts, the element is okay (there is no break). If the voltage is zero, the element is broken between the center of the element and the positive end. If the voltage is 10 to 12-volts the element is broken between the center of the element and ground. Check each heating element.

6 Connect the negative lead to a good body ground. The reading should stay the same. If it doesn't, the ground connection is bad.

7 To find the break, place the voltmeter negative probe against the defogger ground terminal. Place the voltmeter positive probe with the foil strip against the heating element at the positive terminal end and slide it toward the negative terminal end. The point at which the voltmeter deflects from several volts to zero is the point at which the heating element is broken (see illustration).

REPAIR

▶ **Refer to illustration 14.13**

8 ⁻ Repair the break in the element using a repair kit for this purpose (available at most auto parts stores). Make sure that the repair kit includes plastic conductive epoxy.

9 Prior to repairing a break, turn off the system and allow it to cool off for a few minutes.

10 Lightly buff the element area with fine steel wool, then clean it thoroughly with rubbing alcohol.

11 Use masking tape to mask off the area being repaired.

12 Thoroughly mix the epoxy, following the instructions provided with the repair kit.

13 Apply the epoxy material to the slit in the masking tape, overlapping the undamaged area about 3/4-inch on either end (see illustration).

14 Allow the repair to cure for 24 hours before removing the tape and using the system.

14.4 When measuring the voltage at the rear window defogger grid, wrap a piece of aluminum foil around the positive probe of the voltmeter and press the foil against the wire with your finger

14.5 To determine if a heating element has broken, check the voltage at the center of each element; if the voltage is 5 or 6-volts, the element is unbroken, but if the voltage is 10 or 12-volts, the element is broken between the center and the ground side. If there is no voltage, the element is broken between center and the positive side

14.7 To find the break, place the voltmeter negative lead against the defogger ground terminal, place the voltmeter positive lead with the foil strip against the heating element at the positive terminal end and slide it toward the negative terminal end. The point at which the voltmeter reading changes abruptly is the point at which the element is broken

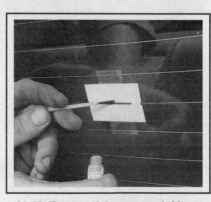

14.13 To use a defogger repair kit, apply masking tape to the inside of the window at the damaged area, then brush on the special conductive coating

15   Headlight bulb - replacement

✶✶ CAUTION:

Halogen gas filled bulbs are under pressure and can shatter if the surface is scratched or the bulb is dropped. Wear eye protection and handle the bulbs carefully, grasping only the base whenever possible. Do not touch the surface of the bulb with your fingers because the oil from your skin could cause it to overheat and fail prematurely. If you do touch the bulb surface, clean it with rubbing alcohol.

1994 AND 1995 MODELS

▶ **Refer to illustrations 15.1, 15.2 and 15.3**

1   Disconnect the electrical connector from the headlight bulb by squeezing the tabs and pulling the connector away from the headlight bulb (see illustration).

2   Rotate the headlight bulb retaining ring counterclockwise and remove it (see illustration).
3   Remove the bulb from the headlight housing (see illustrations).
4   Grasping the new bulb's base (NOT the bulb itself!), insert the bulb into the headlight assembly. Make sure that the tabs on the bulb's base are aligned with the slots in the headlight housing. Install the retaining ring, then rotate it clockwise to lock it in place.
5   Reconnect the headlight electrical connector.

1995-1/2 AND LATER MODELS

▶ **Refer to illustrations 15.6, 15.7, 15.8 and 15.9**

6   Turn the headlight bulb cover counterclockwise and remove it (see illustration).
7   Disconnect the electrical connector from the headlight bulb (see illustration).
8   Unsnap the headlight bulb retaining wire (see illustration).

15.1 To disconnect the electrical connector from the headlight assembly, squeeze the tabs and pull the connector straight back (1994 and 1995 models)

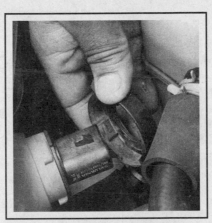

15.2 To remove the headlight bulb retaining ring, rotate the ring counterclockwise . . .

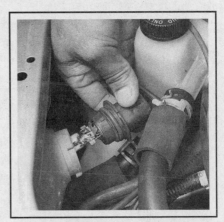

15.3 . . . then pull the headlight bulb out of the housing (1994 and 1995 models)

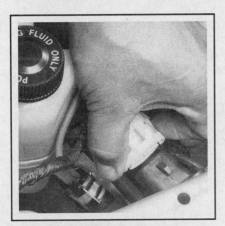

15.6 To remove the headlight bulb cover on 1995-1/2 and later models, rotate it counterclockwise (headlight housing removed for clarity)

15.7 Disconnect the electrical connector from the headlight bulb . . .

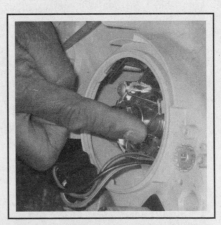

15.8 . . . unsnap the headlight bulb retaining wire . . .

15.9 . . . then pull the headlight bulb straight out (1995-1/2 and later models)

9 Remove the headlight bulb from the headlight housing (see illustration).

10 When installing the new bulb, make sure that the three tabs on the bulb's base are aligned with the three slots in the headlight housing.

11 Installation is otherwise the reverse of removal.

16 Headlight housing - removal and installation

1994 AND 1995 MODELS

1 Disconnect the electrical connectors from the headlight (see illustration 15.1) and from the front combination light (front turn signal/

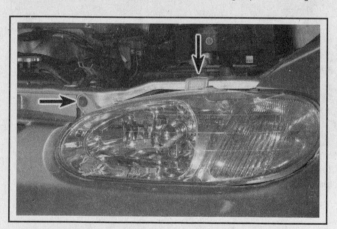

16.6 To detach the headlight/combination light assembly from 1995-1/2 and later models, remove these two bolts

parking light and side marker light).

2 Remove the grille mounting screws and remove the grille.

3 Remove the front combination light assembly mounting screws and remove the combination light.

4 Remove the headlight assembly mounting bolts and remove the headlight assembly.

5 Installation is the reverse of removal. Be sure to adjust the headlights when you're done (see Section 17).

1995-1/2 AND LATER MODELS (EXCEPT SPORTAGE)

▶ **Refer to illustrations 16.6 and 16.7**

6 Remove the headlight/combination light assembly mounting bolts (see illustration).

7 Pull out the headlight assembly, disconnect the headlight and combination light electrical connectors (see illustration) and remove the headlight assembly.

8 Installation is the reverse of removal.

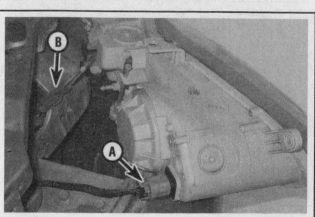

16.7 Pull out the headlight assembly and disconnect the headlight (A) and combination light (B) electrical connectors (1995-1/2 and later models)

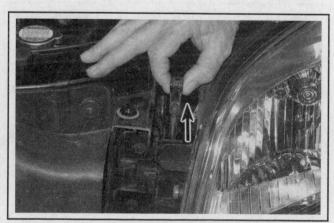

16.10 Pull up the headlight mounting bar to release the headlight housing (Sportage models)

SPORTAGE MODELS

▶ **Refer to illustrations 16.10 and 16.11**

9   Loosen the fasteners that secure the radiator/grille cover and raise up the end of the cover for the next step.

10 Pull up the headlight mounting bar (see illustration) and pull up the headlight housing.

11 Disconnect the electrical connector from the headlight housing (see illustration) and remove the headlight housing.

12 Installation is the reverse of removal.

16.11 Headlight housing electrical connector (Sportage models)

17   Headlights - adjustment

▶ **Refer to illustrations 17.1a, 17.1b and 17.3**

✳✳ WARNING:

The headlights must be aimed correctly. If adjusted incorrectly they could blind the driver of an oncoming vehicle and cause a serious accident or seriously reduce your ability to see the road. The headlights should be checked for correct aim every 12 months and any time a new headlight is installed or front end body work is performed. It should be emphasized that the following procedure is only an interim step that will provide temporary adjustment until a properly equipped shop can adjust the headlights.

1   On 1994 and 1995 models and on 2004 and later 2.0L DOHC Spectra models, the horizontal and vertical adjustment screws are located on top of the headlight housing. The outer screw on each headlight housing is for vertical adjustments; the inner screw is for horizontal adjustments. On 1995-1/2 through 2004 models, except 2.0L DOHC models, there is only one screw (see illustrations) on each headlight for vertical adjustments. On these models there is no horizontal adjustment screw.

2   There are several methods for adjusting the headlights. The simplest method requires masking tape, a blank wall and a level floor.

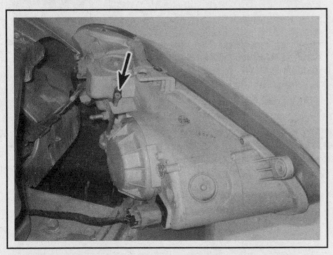

17.1a Vertical adjuster (1995-1/2 through 2004 models, except 2.0L DOHC)

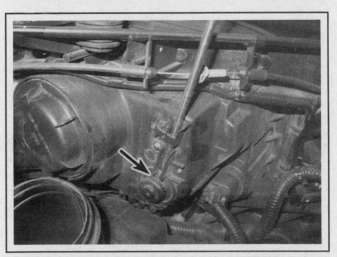

17.1b Headlight adjuster screw location (late model Sportage). This type of adjuster is turned by engaging the tip of a Phillips screwdriver with the crownwheel-type gear

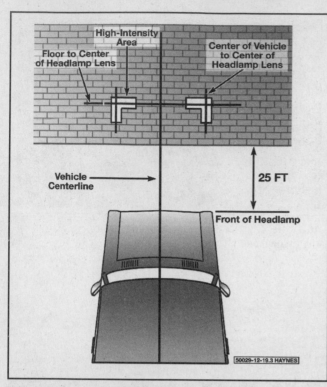

17.3 Headlight adjustment details

3 Position masking tape vertically on the wall in relation to the vehicle centerline and in relation to the centerlines of both headlights (see illustration).

4 Position a horizontal tape line in reference to the centerline of all the headlights.

→Note: It might be easier to position the tape on the wall with the vehicle parked only a few inches away.

5 Adjustment should be made with the vehicle parked 25 feet from the wall, sitting level, the gas tank half-full and no heavy load in the vehicle.

6 With the low beams turned on, position the high intensity zone so it is two inches below the horizontal line. On 1994 and 1995 models, adjust the horizontal position so the high intensity zone is two inches to the side of the vertical line, away from oncoming traffic.

7 With the high beams on, the high intensity zone should be vertically centered with the exact center just below the horizontal line.

→Note: It might not be possible to position the headlight aim exactly for both high and low beams. If a compromise must be made, keep in mind that the low beams are the most used and have the greatest effect on safety.

8 If you have any difficulty adjusting the headlights, have them adjusted by a dealer service department as soon as possible.

18 Horn - replacement

▶ Refer to illustration 18.3

→Note: On 1994 through 1997 models, the horn is located below the right front combination light. On 1998 and later models, the horn is located behind the grille (which is part of the bumper cover), on the radiator center support bracket.

1 On 1994 and 1995 models, remove the right combination light. On 1995-1/2 through 1997 models, remove the headlight/combination light assembly (see Section 16).

2 On 1998 and later models, remove the front bumper cover (see Chapter 11).

3 Disconnect the electrical connector(s) from the horn (see illustration).

4 Remove the horn mounting bracket bolt (see illustration 18.3) and remove the horn.

5 Installation is the reverse of removal.

18.3 Typical horn installation (1999 model shown, other models similar). To remove the horn, disconnect the electrical connectors (1) and remove the horn mounting bracket bolt (2)

19 Bulb replacement

SEPHIA AND SPECTRA MODELS

Exterior light bulbs

Front combination light (parking light/turn signal/side marker) bulbs

1994 and 1995 models

1 Disconnect the electrical connector from the front parking light/ turn signal/side marker bulb.

2 To remove the front parking light/turn signal/side marker light bulb from the combination light housing, turn it counterclockwise and pull it out.

3 Installation is the reverse of removal.

1995-1/2 and later models

▶ Refer to illustrations 19.5 and 19.6

4 Unbolt the headlight/combination light assembly (see Section 16)

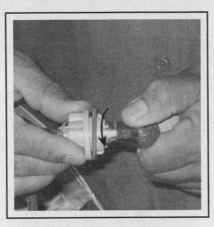

19.5 To remove the front parking light/turn signal/side marker light bulb holder, rotate it counterclockwise and pull It out

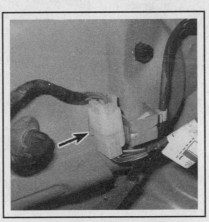

19.6 To remove the front parking light/turn signal/side marker light bulb from its bulb holder, push it in, rotate it counterclockwise and pull it out of the holder

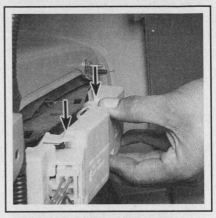

19.7a To release the bulb holder assembly from the rear combination light assembly on 1994 through 1997 models, depress these two release tabs . . .

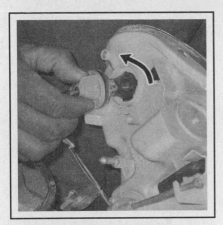

19.7b . . . and pull out the holder assembly. To remove a bulb from the holder, push it in, then rotate it counterclockwise and pull it out (1994 through 1997 models)

19.11 On 1998 through 2004 models (except 2.0L DOHC models), peel back the trunk carpeting, then disconnect the rear combination light electrical connector

19.12 To detach the rear combination light housing from 1998 through 2004 models (except 2.0L DOHC models), remove these two screws

and pull it out.

5   To remove the front parking light/turn signal/side marker light bulb holder, rotate it counterclockwise and pull it out (see illustration).

6   To remove the front parking light/turn signal/side marker light bulb from its bulb holder, rotate it counterclockwise and pull it out of the holder (see illustration).

Rear combination light (taillight) bulbs

1994 through 1997 models

▶ Refer to illustrations 19.7a and 19.7b

➡Note: The rear combination light (taillight) assembly houses the light bulbs for the brake lights, turn signal lights, back-up lights and side marker lights.

7   Working inside the trunk, remove the bulb holder assembly (see illustrations).

8   To remove a bulb from the combination light bulb holder assembly, push the bulb in, rotate it counterclockwise and pull it out.

9   To install a bulb in the combination light bulb holder assembly, push the bulb in and rotate it clockwise.

10 Installation is otherwise the reverse of removal.

1998 through 2004 models (except 2.0L DOHC models)

▶ Refer to illustrations 19.11, 19.12, 19.13 and 19.14

11 Working inside the trunk, peel back the carpeting, then disconnect the rear combination light electrical connector (see illustration).

12 Remove the rear combination light housing mounting screws (see illustration) and pull out the combination light.

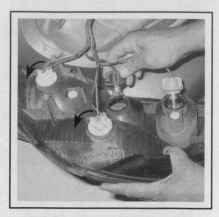

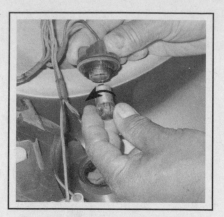

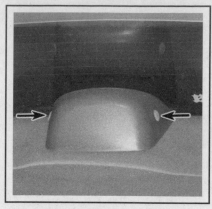

19.13 To remove a bulb holder from the rear combination light housing on 1998 and later models, rotate the holder counterclockwise and pull it out

19.14 To remove a bulb from a rear combination light bulb holder, push it in, turn it counterclockwise and pull it out of the holder

19.23 Remove these two push-fasteners from the high-mount brake light cover (see text) and remove the cover

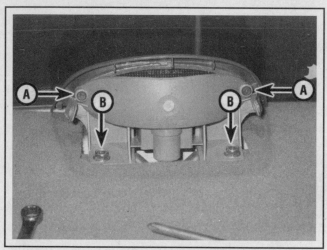

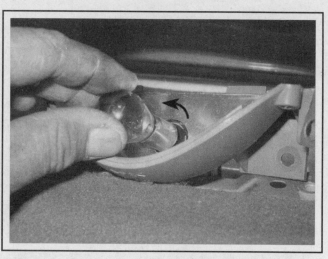

19.24 To detach the reflector from the high-mount brake light lens, remove the two screws (A). To detach the high-mount brake light assembly from the rear shelf trim panel, remove the two bolts (B)

19.25 To remove the bulb from the high-mount brake light reflector, push it in, rotate it counterclockwise and pull it out

13 To remove a bulb holder from the rear combination light assembly, rotate it counterclockwise and pull it out (see illustration).

14 To remove a bulb from the combination light bulb holder, push the bulb in, rotate it counterclockwise and pull it out (see illustration).

15 To install a bulb in the combination light bulb holder, push the bulb in and rotate it clockwise.

16 To install a bulb holder in the rear combination light assembly, align the three tabs on the circumference of the holder, insert the holder into its mounting receptacle and rotate it clockwise.

17 Installation is otherwise the reverse of removal.

2004 and later 2.0L DOHC models

18 Open the trunk, remove the screws on the tail lamp trim cover and remove it.

19 Disconnect the wiring from the lamp assembly.

20 Remove the four nuts, then remove the lamp assembly.

21 The bulbs for the stop and taillights, turn signals and back-up

lights can now be replaced.

22 Installation is the reverse of removal.

High-mount brake light

▶ **Refer to illustration 19.23, 19.24 and 19.25**

23 The high-mount brake light cover is secured to its mounting bracket by a pair of push-pull fasteners (see illustration). To remove each push-pull fastener, depress the center part of the fastener to release it from the locking legs of the fastener, then pull out the fastener.

24 Remove the high-mount brake light reflector mounting screws and bolts (see illustration), then tilt the reflector forward to access the bulb.

25 To remove the bulb from the high-mount brake light reflector, push it in, rotate it counterclockwise and pull it out (see illustration).

26 To install a new bulb in the high-mount brake light reflector, push it in and rotate it clockwise.

27 Installation is otherwise the reverse of removal.

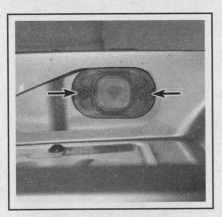

19.28 To remove a license plate light lens, remove these two screws

19.29 To remove the bulb from the license plate light reflector, simply pull it straight out

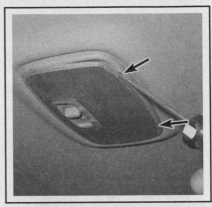

19.37 To remove the dome light lens, carefully pry it off at one of the two slots located along the perimeter of the lens

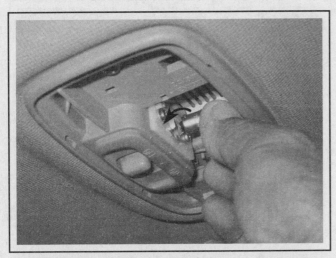

19.38 To remove the old bulb from the dome light assembly, push it in, rotate it counterclockwise and pull it out. To install it, push it in and turn it clockwise

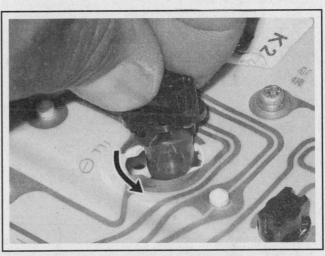

19.43 To remove a bulb from the instrument cluster, rotate it counterclockwise and pull it out. To install a new bulb, insert it into its hole and rotate it clockwise

License plate light

2004 and earlier models (except 2.0L DOHC)

▸ **Refer to illustrations 19.28 and 19.29**

28 Remove the license plate light lens (see illustration).
29 Pull the bulb straight out of the reflector (see illustration).
30 Push the new bulb straight into the reflector.
31 Installation is otherwise the reverse of removal.

2004 and later 2.0L DOHC models

32 Disconnect the cable from the negative battery terminal (see Chapter 5).
33 Open the trunk and disconnect the wiring from the light.
34 Remove the spoiler mounting screws and carefully lift off the spoiler.
35 Remove the stop light mounting nuts, then remove the light.
36 Installation is the reverse of removal.

INTERIOR LIGHTS

Dome light

▸ **Refer to illustrations 19.37 and 19.38**

37 Using a fingernail file or a small screwdriver, pry off the lens (see illustration). Be careful not to damage the plastic trim around the edge of the lens.
38 Remove the old bulb from the dome light assembly (see illustration).
39 To install the new bulb, push it into its receptacle and turn it clockwise.
40 Installation is the reverse of removal.

Instrument cluster illumination bulbs

▸ **Refer to illustration 19.43**

41 Remove the instrument cluster (see Section 10).
42 Lay the instrument cluster on a clean work bench.

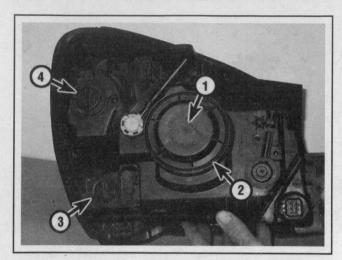

19.47 Bulb guide for headlight housing (2009 and 2010 Sportage model shown; refer to owner's manual for 2005 through 2008 models)

1   *Headlight bulb (high and low beam)*
2   *Parking light bulb (behind same cover as headlight bulb)*
3   *Front sidemarker bulb*
4   *Front turn signal bulb*

43 To remove a bulb from the instrument cluster, simply rotate it counterclockwise and pull it out (see illustration).

44 To install a new bulb in the instrument cluster, simply insert it into its hole and rotate it clockwise.

45 Install the instrument cluster (see Section 10).

SPORTAGE MODELS

Exterior light bulbs

Front parking light, front turn signal bulbs and front sidemarker bulbs

▶ **Refer to illustration 19.47**

➡**Note: The headlight housing shown in the accompanying illustration is from a 2009/2010 model. The parking light bulb is in a different location (upper outer corner) on 2005 through 2008 models than the unit shown here. The earlier housing does not include a front sidemarker light bulb. If you aren't sure about the location of any bulb in the earlier headlight housing unit, refer to your owner's manual.**

46 Remove the headlight housing assembly (see Section 16).

47 Rotate the bulb socket (see illustration) counterclockwise and pull it out.

48 To remove the bulb from the socket, push it into the socket, rotate it until the lugs on the bulb base are aligned with the slots in the socket and pull out the bulb.

49 Insert the new bulb into the socket, push it down and rotate it until it locks into place.

50 To install the bulb socket into the headlight housing, align the tabs on the socket with the slots in the headlight housing, insert the socket into the housing and rotate it clockwise until it locks into place.

51 Install the headlight housing.

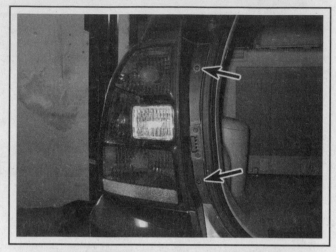

19.56 Taillight housing retaining screws (Sportage models)

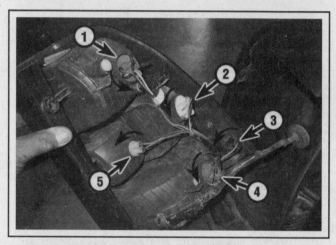

19.57 Taillight bulb guide (Sportage models)

1   *Brake and taillight bulb*   4   *Tail light bulb*
2   *Rear turn signal light bulb*   5   *Back-up light bulb*
3   *Rear sidemarker light bulb*

Fog light bulbs

52 Raise the front of the vehicle and place it securely on jackstands. Remove the engine splash shield.

53 Disconnect the electrical connector from the fog light bulb socket.

54 Remove the fog light bulb holder from the fog light.

55 Installation is the reverse of removal.

Taillight bulbs

▶ **Refer to illustrations 19.56, 19.57 and 19.58**

56 Open the hatch, remove the two taillight housing retaining screws (see illustration), then pull out the taillight housing.

57 To replace any taillight bulb (see illustration), turn the bulb holder counterclockwise and pull it out.

58 To remove the bulb from the socket, push it into the socket, rotate it until the lugs on the bulb base are aligned with the slots in the socket and pull out the bulb (see illustration).

59 Insert the new bulb into the socket, push it down and rotate it until it locks into place.

19.58 Push in and turn the bulb counterclockwise to align the lugs on the bulb with the slots in the socket, then pull out the bulb

19.61 License plate light lens screws (Sportage models)

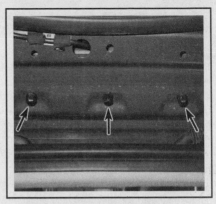

19.64 High-mount brake light retaining screws (Sportage models)

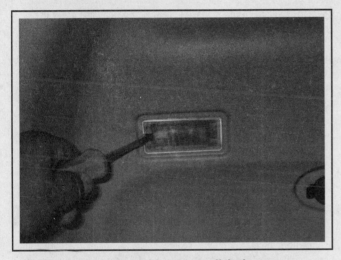

19.66 Use a small screwdriver to pry off the lens . . .

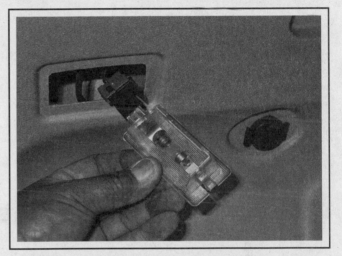

19.67 . . . then remove the bulb from the terminals

60 To install the bulb socket into the taillight housing, align the tabs on the socket with the slots in the headlight housing, insert the socket into the housing and rotate it clockwise until it locks into place. Installation is otherwise the reverse of removal.

License plate light bulbs

▸ **Refer to illustration 19.61**

61 Remove the lens retaining screws (see illustration) and remove the lens.
62 To remove the bulb, pull it straight out. To install a new bulb, push it straight in. .
63 Install the lens and tighten the screw securely.

High-mount brake light

▸ **Refer to illustration 19.64**

64 Open the hatch and remove the high-mount brake light retaining screws (see illustration). Pull out the high-mount brake light assembly, disconnect the electrical connector and remove the high-mount brake light.

65 Installation is the reverse of removal.

Interior bulbs

Front map light/glove box light/dome light/cargo area light

▸ **Refer to illustrations 19.66 and 19.67**

66 Using a small flat-blade screwdriver, carefully pry off the lens (see illustration).
67 Pull out the light assembly (see illustration), pull out the old bulb and install a new one.

✳ WARNING:

If it is necessary to pry out the bulb, pry only on the metal ends, not the glass.

68 Install the lens, making sure it snaps into place

20 Electric side view mirrors - general information

1   Most electric rear view mirrors use two motors to move the glass; one for up-and-down adjustments and one for left-right adjustments.

2   During mirror adjustment, the power mirror adjustment switch sends voltage to the left or right side mirror. With the ignition key turned to ON (engine not running), operate the mirror adjustment switch through all of its functions (left-right and up-down) for both the left and right side mirrors.

3   Listen carefully for the sound of the electric motors running in the mirrors.

4   If you can hear the motors but the mirror glass doesn't move, there's a problem with the drive mechanism inside the mirror.

5   If the mirrors do not operate and no sound comes from the mir-rors, check the fuse (see Section 3).

6   If the fuse is OK, remove the power mirror adjustment switch (see Section 9). Have the switch continuity checked by a dealership service department or other qualified automobile repair facility.

7   Test the ground connections.

8   If the mirror still doesn't work, remove the mirror and check the wires at the mirror for voltage.

9   If there is no voltage in any switch position, check the circuit between the mirror and the adjustment switch for opens and shorts.

10 If there's voltage, remove the mirror and test it off the vehicle with jumper wires. Replace the mirror if it fails this test.

21 Cruise control system - general information

1   The cruise control system maintains vehicle speed with an electrically operated motor located in the engine compartment, which is connected to the throttle body by a cable. The system consists of the Powertrain Control Module, the speed control actuator, the speed control cable, the speed control indicator light, the speed control actuator switches, the Brake Pedal Position (BPP) switch and the transmission range switch. The cruise control system requires diagnostic procedures that are beyond the scope of this manual, but there are some general procedures that will help you identify common problems.

2   Check the fuses (see Section 3).

3   Have an assistant operate the brake lights while you check their operation (voltage from the brake light switch deactivates the cruise control).

4   If the brake lights don't come on or stay on all the time, correct the problem and retest the cruise control system.

5   Visually inspect the control cable between the cruise control motor and the throttle linkage for free movement. Replace it if necessary.

6   Test drive the vehicle to determine if the cruise control is now working. If it isn't, take it to a dealer service department or an automotive electrical specialist for further diagnosis.

22 Power window system - general information

1   The power window system operates electric motors, mounted in the doors, which lower and raise the windows. The system consists of the control switches, the motors, regulators, glass mechanisms and associated wiring.

2   The power windows can be lowered and raised from the master control switch by the driver or by remote switches located at the individual windows. Each window has a separate motor, which is reversible. The position of the control switch determines the polarity and therefore the direction of operation.

3   The circuit is protected by a fuse and a circuit breaker. Each motor is also equipped with an internal circuit breaker, this prevents one stuck window from disabling the whole system.

4   The power window system will only operate when the ignition switch is turned to ON. There's also a main switch at the master power window control panel (in the driver's door) which, when activated, disables the switches at the rear windows and the switch at the passenger's window. So if there's a problem with the passenger window or with either of the rear windows, make sure that it's not simply a matter of flipping the main switch before proceeding.

5   The procedures listed below are general in nature, so if you can't find the problem using them, take the vehicle to a dealer service department or other qualified repair shop.

6   If the power windows won't operate, always check the fuses and relays first (see Sections 3 and 5, respectively). Also verify that there's voltage to the relay and that the relay is well grounded.

7   If only the rear windows are inoperative, or if the windows only operate from the master control switch, check the main switch for continuity in the unlocked position. Replace it if it doesn't have continuity (see *Door trim panel - removal and installation* in Chapter 11).

8   Check the wiring between the switches and the fuse and relay box for continuity. Repair the wiring, if necessary.

9   If only one window is inoperative from the main switch, try the other control switch at the window.

→Note: This doesn't apply to the driver's door window.

10 If the same window works from one switch, but not the other, check the switch for continuity.

11 If the switch tests OK, check for a short or open in the circuit between the affected switch and the window motor.

12 If one window is inoperative from both switches, remove the trim panel from the affected door (see *Door trim panel - removal and installation* in Chapter 11) and check for voltage at the switch and at the motor while the switch is operated.

13 If voltage is reaching the motor, disconnect the glass from the regulator (see Chapter 11). Move the window up-and-down by hand while checking for binding and damage. Also check for binding and damage to the regulator. If the regulator is not damaged and the window moves up and down smoothly, replace the motor. If there's binding or damage, lubricate, repair or replace parts, as necessary.

14 If voltage isn't reaching the motor, check the wiring in the circuit for continuity between the switches and motors. You'll need to consult the wiring diagram for the vehicle.

23 Power door lock system - general information

1   A power door lock system operates the door lock actuators mounted in each door. The system consists of the switches, actuators, a control unit and associated wiring. On some models, the power door lock system is part of the security alarm system. On these models, the power door lock system is more complex, and more difficult to diagnose. Therefore, home troubleshooting is limited to simple checks of the wiring connections and actuators for minor faults that can be easily repaired.

2   Power door lock systems are operated by bi-directional solenoids located in the doors. The lock switches have two operating positions: LOCK and UNLOCK. When activated, the switch sends a ground signal to the door lock control unit to lock or unlock the doors. Depending on which way the switch is activated, the control unit reverses polarity to the solenoids, allowing the two sides of the circuit to be used alternately as the feed (positive) and ground side.

3   The following general guidelines should help you quickly identify and repair typical problems. If you're unable to locate the trouble using these guidelines, consult a dealer service department.

4   Always check the fuses first (see Section 3 and your owners' manual).

5   Operate the door lock switches in both directions (LOCK and UNLOCK) with the engine off. Listen for the click of the solenoids operating.

6   Test the switches for continuity. Remove the switches and have them checked by a dealer service department.

7   Check the wiring between the switches, control unit and solenoids for continuity. Repair the wiring if there's no continuity.

8   Check for a bad ground at the switches and at the control unit.

9   If only one lock solenoid doesn't operate, remove the trim panel from the door with the bad solenoid (see *Door trim panel - removal and installation* in Chapter 11) and check for voltage at the solenoid while the lock switch is operated. One of the wires should have voltage in the Lock position; the other should have voltage in the Unlock position.

10 If the inoperative solenoid is receiving voltage, replace the solenoid.

11 If the inoperative solenoid isn't receiving voltage, check for an open or short in the wire between the lock solenoid and the control unit.

➡**Note: Wire harnesses typically break between the body and door, because repeatedly opening and closing the door fatigues and eventually breaks the wires.**

24 Daytime Running Lights (DRL) - general information

The Daytime Running Lights (DRL) system illuminates the headlights whenever the engine is running. The only exception is with the engine running and the parking brake engaged. Once the parking brake is released, the lights will remain on as long as the ignition switch is on, even if the parking brake is later applied. The DRL system supplies reduced power to the headlights during daylight operation to prolonging headlight life.

25 Airbag system - general information

GENERAL INFORMATION

1   Some 1995-1/2 and 1996 models, and all 1997 and later models are equipped with a Supplemental Restraint System (SRS), more commonly known as airbags. This system is designed to protect the driver, and the front seat passenger, from serious injury in the event of a head-on or frontal collision. 1995-1/2 and some 1996 and 1997 models use a pair of crash sensors mounted behind the front bumper, and a discriminating sensor located in the airbag diagnostic unit. Some 1996 and 1997 models, and all 1998 and later models use single crash sensor and a discriminating sensor built into the airbag diagnostic unit. The airbag assemblies are mounted on the steering wheel and inside the passenger's end of the dash 2001 and later models are also equipped with seat belt pre-tensioners. These are pyrotechnic devices that reduce the slack in the seat belts during an impact of sufficient force to trigger the airbags.

AIRBAG MODULE

Driver's side airbag

2   The airbag inflator module contains a housing incorporating the cushion (airbag) and inflator unit, mounted in the center of the steering wheel. The inflator assembly is mounted on the back of the housing over a hole through which gas is expelled, inflating the bag almost instantaneously when an electrical signal is sent from the system. A clockspring on the steering column under the steering wheel carries this signal to the module. This clockspring assembly can transmit an electrical signal regardless of steering wheel position. The igniter in the airbag converts the electrical signal to heat and ignites the powder, which inflates the bag.

3   For information on how to remove and install the driver's side airbag, refer to *Steering wheel - removal and installation* in Chapter 10.

Passenger's side airbag

4   The airbag is mounted at the top of the passenger's side of the instrument panel. It consists of an inflator containing an igniter, a reaction housing/airbag assembly and a trim cover.

5   The passenger's side airbag is considerably larger than the steering wheel-mounted unit and is mounted inside the dash, above the glove box. The airbag trim cover on top of the dash is textured and painted to match the instrument panel and has a molded seam, which splits when the bag inflates.

Side impact airbags

6   Extra protection is provided by side-impact airbags on later models. These are smaller devices that are on the outer sides of the seat backs. They deploy in severe side-impact collisions.

Side curtain airbags

7 In addition to the side-curtain airbags, extra side-impact protection is provided by side curtain airbags on later models. These are long airbags that come out of the headliner at each side of the car and come down between the side windows and the seats. They are designed to protect the heads of both the front and rear seat passengers

AIRBAG DIAGNOSTIC UNIT

8 This unit supplies the current to the airbag system (and seat belt pre-tensioners, on models so equipped) in the event of the collision, even if battery power is cut off. It checks this system every time the vehicle is started, causing the "SRS" light to go on, then off, if the system is operating correctly. If there is a fault in the system, the light will go on and stay on, or it will flash or the dash will make a beeping sound. If this happens, take the vehicle to your dealer or other qualified repair shop immediately for service.

DISARMING THE SYSTEM AND OTHER PRECAUTIONS

✳✳ WARNING:

Failure to follow these precautions could result in accidental deployment of the airbag and personal injury.

9 Whenever working in the vicinity of the steering wheel, instrument panel or any of the other SRS system components, the system must be disarmed. To disarm the system:

a) *Point the wheels straight ahead and turn the key to the Lock position.*

b) *Disconnect the cable from the negative battery terminal(s). Refer to Chapter 5, Section 1 for the disconnecting procedure.*

c) *Wait at least three minutes for the back-up power supply to be depleted.*

10 Whenever handling an airbag module, always keep the airbag opening side (the trim, or upholstered side) pointed away from your body. Never place the airbag module on a workbench or other surface with the airbag opening facing the surface. Always place the airbag module in a safe location with the airbag opening facing up.

11 Never measure the resistance of any SRS component or use any electrical test equipment on any of the wiring or components. An ohmmeter has a built-in battery supply that could accidentally deploy the airbag.

12 Never use electrical welding equipment on a vehicle equipped with an airbag without first disconnecting the airbag electrical connectors. The connector for the driver's side airbag is located near the bottom of the steering column; the connector for the passenger's side airbag is located inside the dash, near the glove box. The seat belt pre-tensioner electrical connectors are located behind the B-pillar trim panels.

13 Never dispose of a live airbag module or seat belt pre-tensioner. Return it to a dealer service department or other qualified repair shop for safe deployment and disposal.

AIRBAG MODULE REMOVAL AND INSTALLATION

Driver's side airbag module and clockspring

14 Refer to Chapter 10, *Steering wheel - removal and installation*, for the driver's side airbag module and clockspring removal and installation procedures.

Passenger's side airbag module

15 We don't recommend removing the passenger side airbag because there is no reason to do so unless it has been deployed and must be replaced, which should be handled by a dealer service department or other qualified repair shop.

26 Wiring diagrams - general information

Since it isn't possible to include all wiring diagrams for every year covered by this manual, the following diagrams are those that are typical and most commonly needed.

Prior to troubleshooting any circuits, check the fuses and relays to ensure that they're in good condition. Make sure that the battery is correctly charged and check the cable connections (see Chapters 1 and 5).

When checking a circuit, make sure that all connections are clean and tight, with no broken or loose terminals. If an electrical connector is difficult to disconnect, it's probably because the two halves of the connector are locked together on one or two sides of the connector. So stop and look for the locks, which are usually small plastic tabs that must either be depressed to unlock them, or must be released with a small screwdriver. If you have a problem finding the lock(s), clean off the connector with electronic parts cleaner, then look again. If you're trying to unplug a connector that's located in a dark area, use a flashlight to find the locks. When disconnecting an electrical connector, do NOT pull on the wires; pull on the two halves of the connector itself.

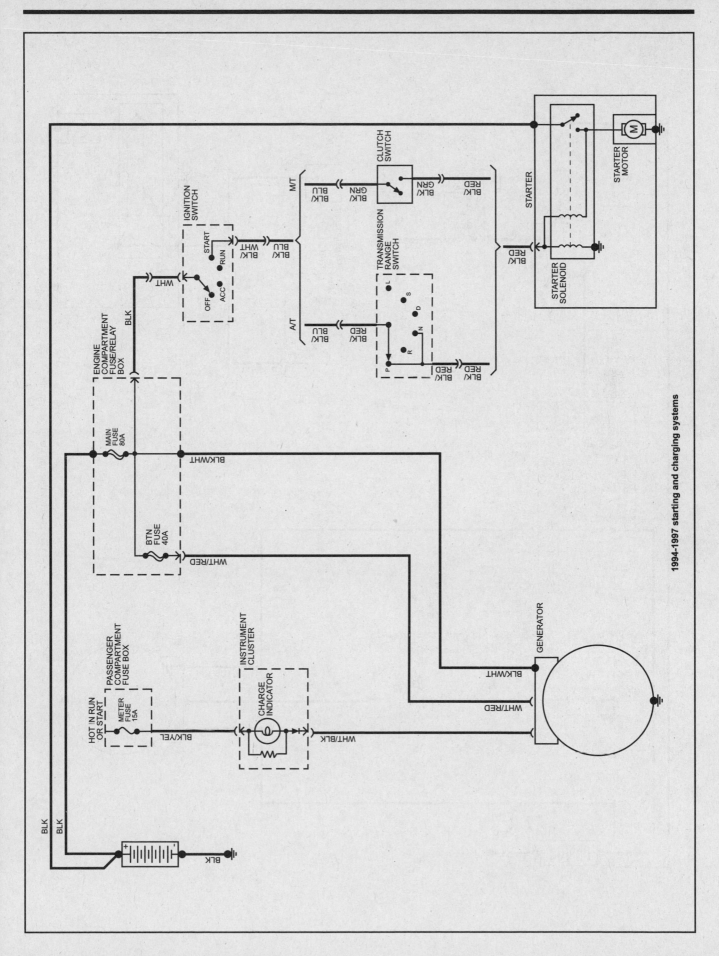

1994-1997 starting and charging systems

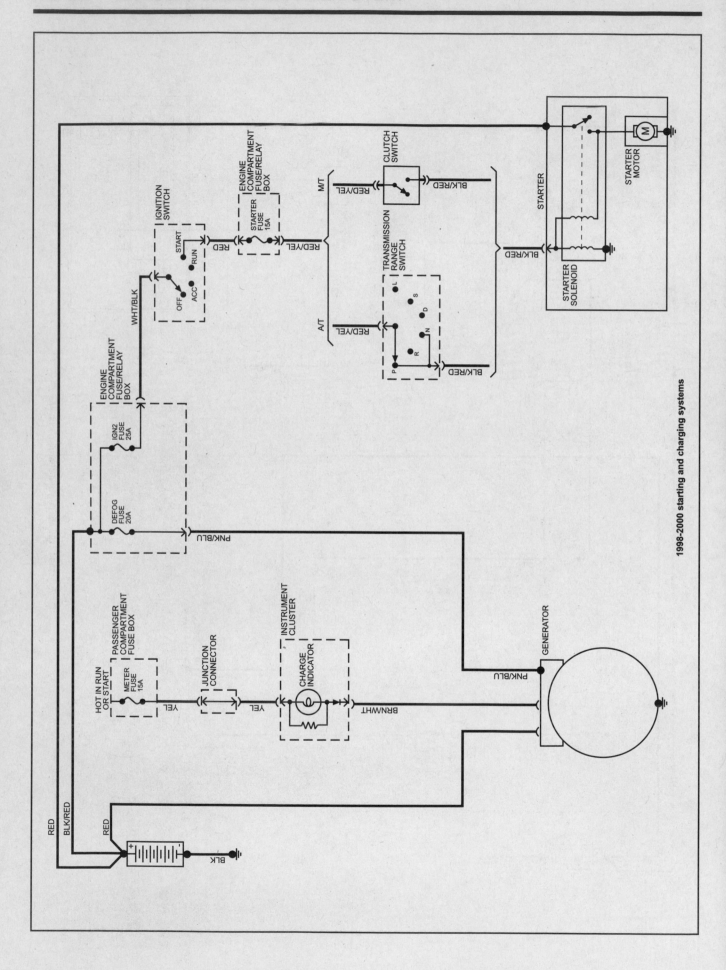

1998-2000 starting and charging systems

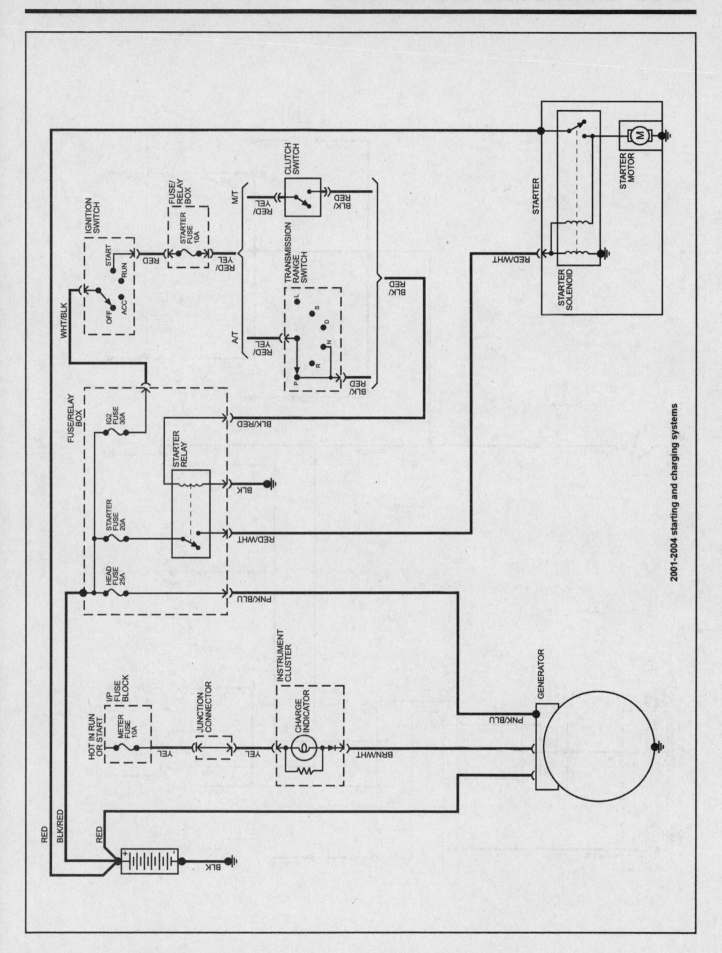

2001-2004 starting and charging systems

1994-1997 exterior lighting system (1 of 2) - typical

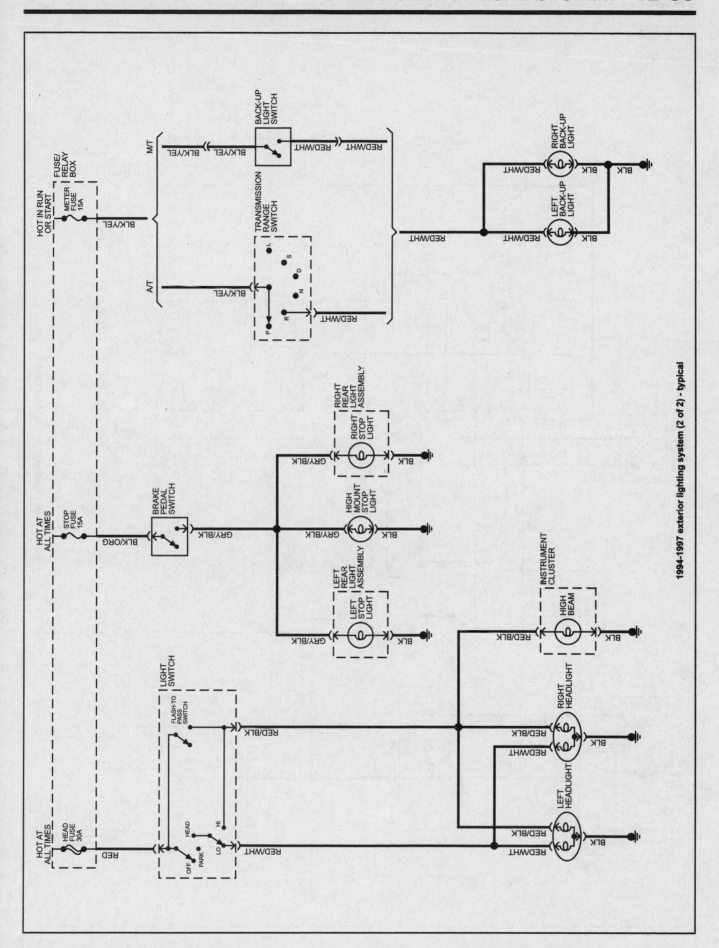

1994-1997 exterior lighting system (2 of 2) - typical

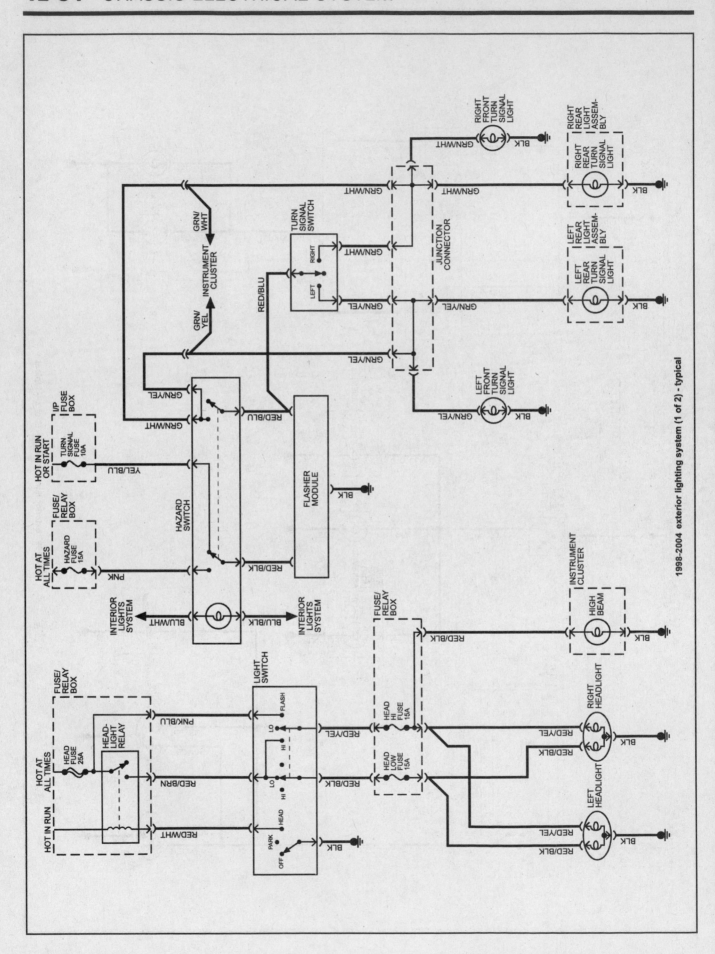

1998-2004 exterior lighting system (1 of 2) - typical

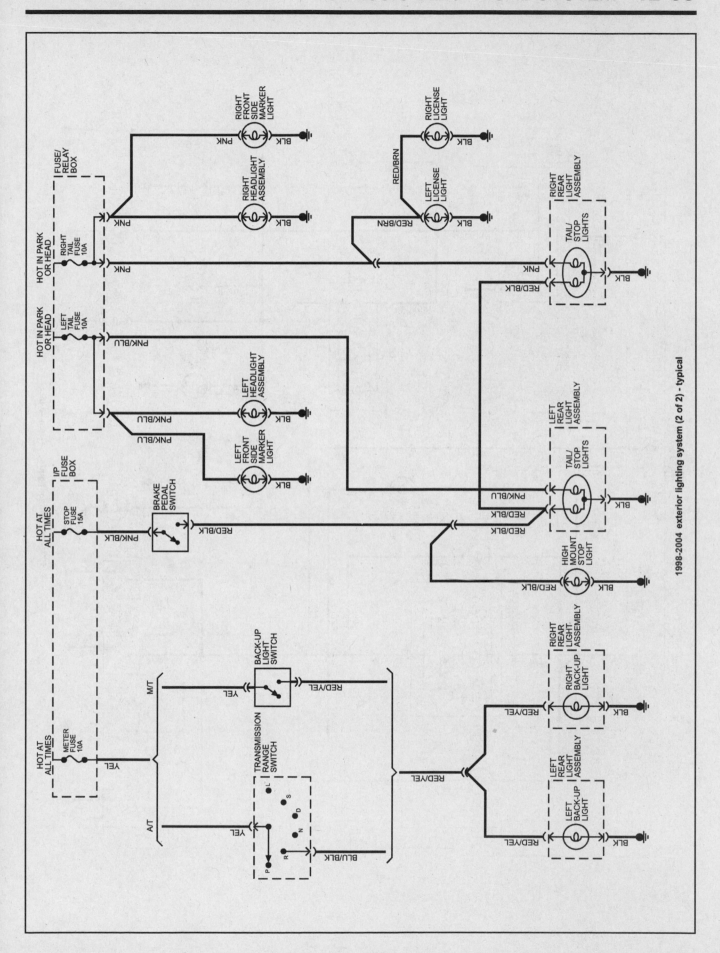

1998-2004 exterior lighting system (2 of 2) - typical

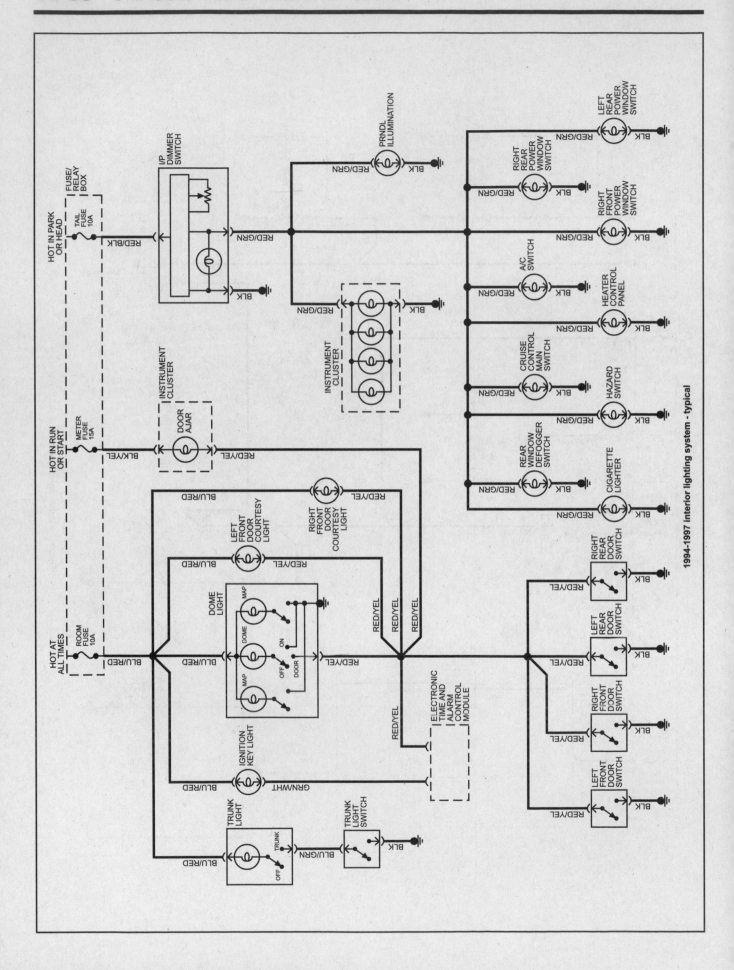

1994-1997 interior lighting system - typical

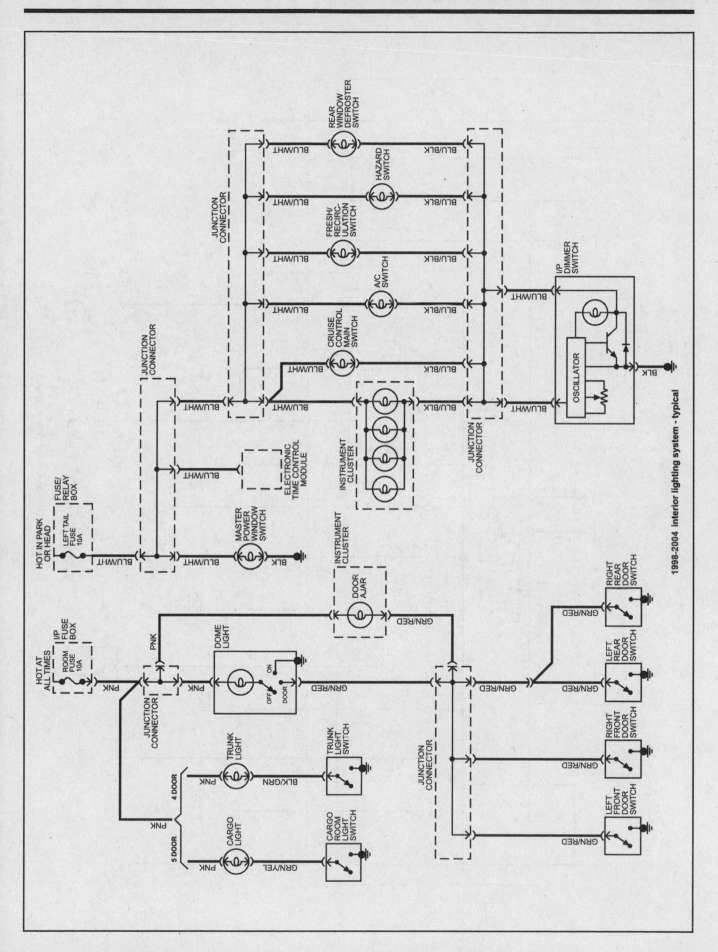

1998-2004 interior lighting system - typical

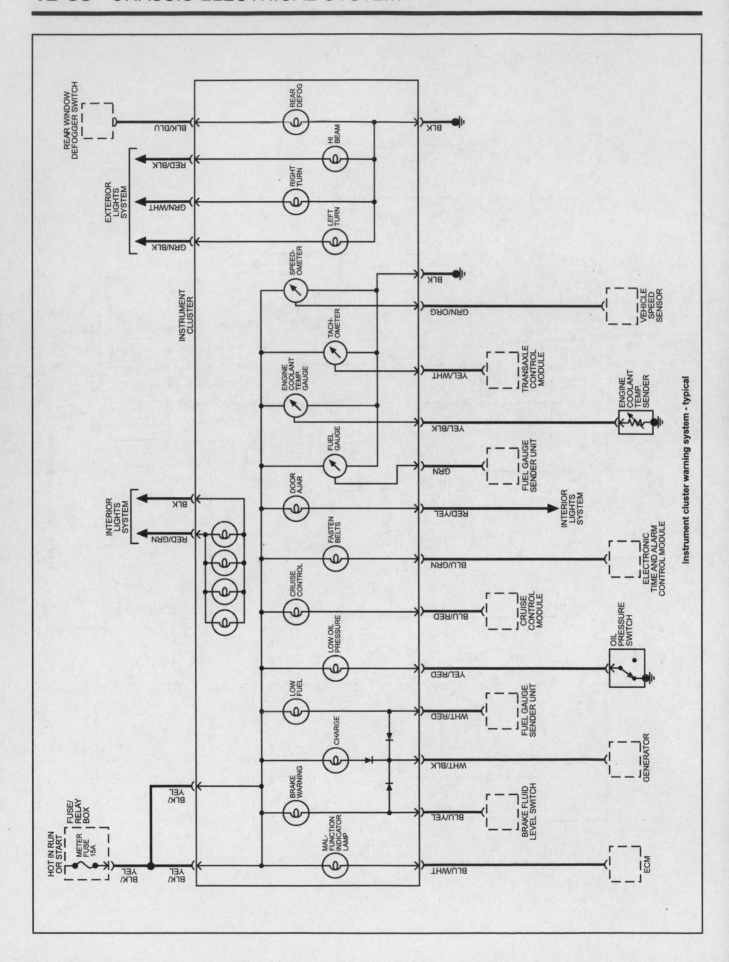

Instrument cluster warning system - typical

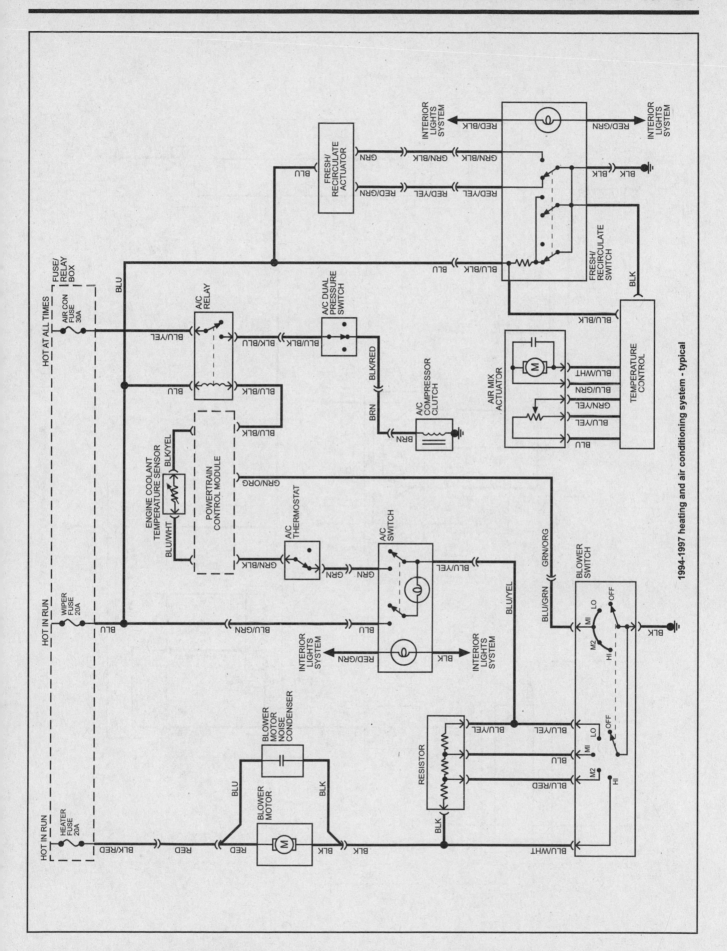

1994-1997 heating and air conditioning system - typical

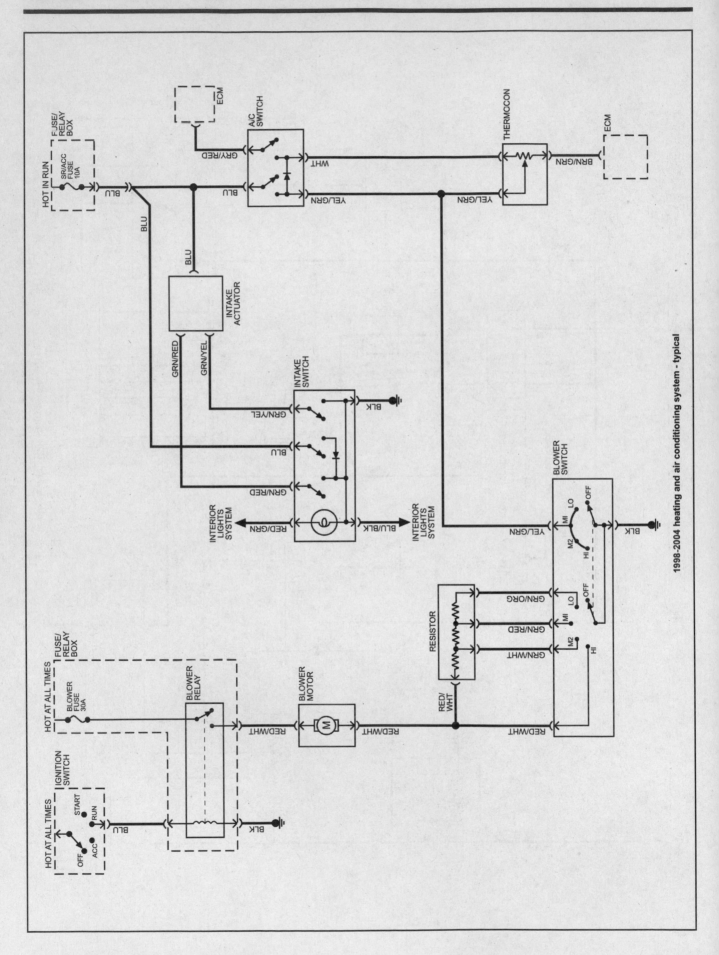

1998-2004 heating and air conditioning system - typical

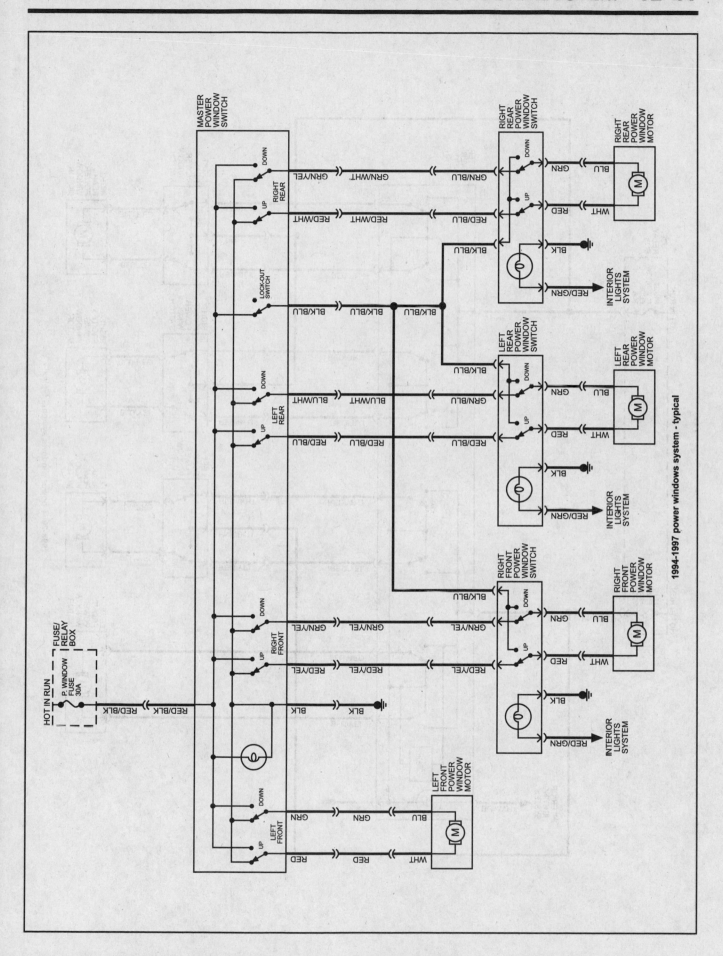

1994-1997 power windows system - typical

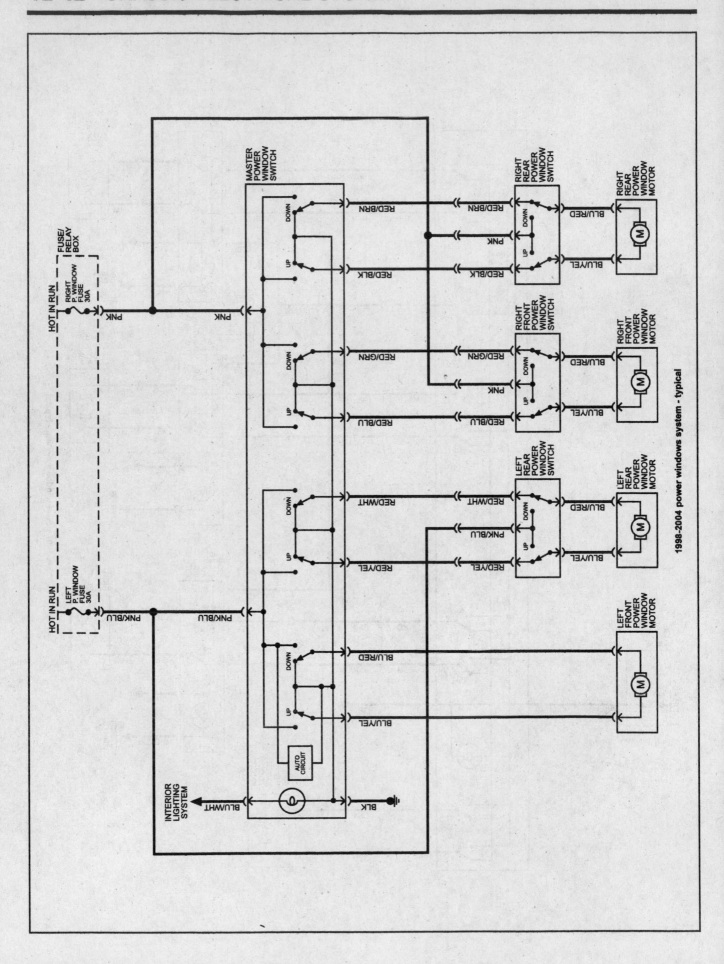

1998-2004 power windows system - typical

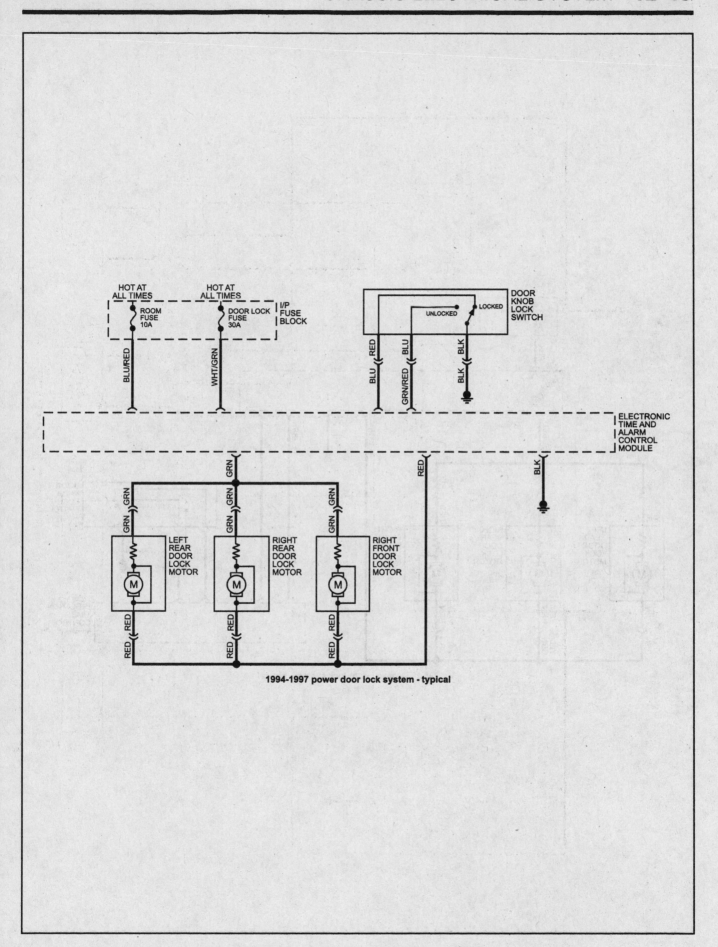

1994-1997 power door lock system - typical

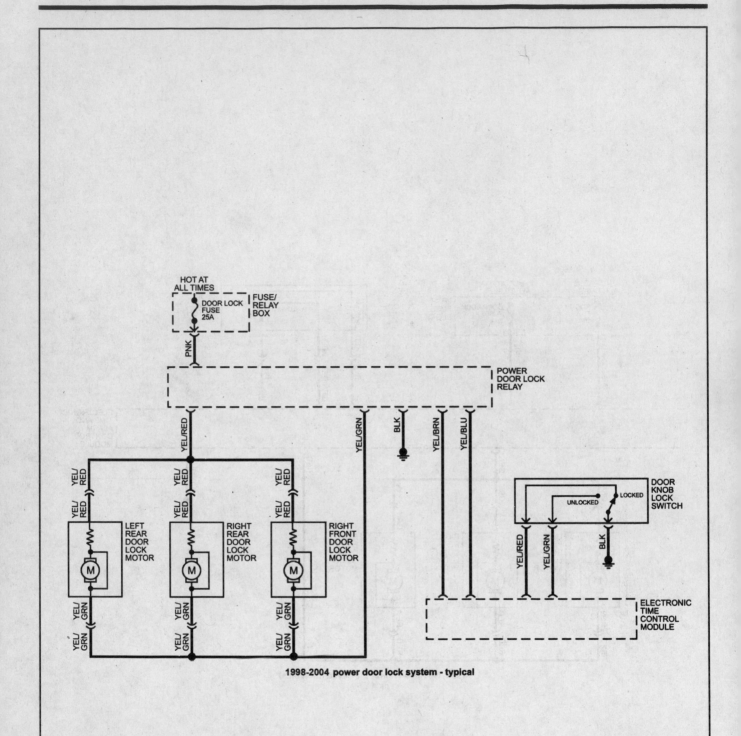

1998-2004 power door lock system - typical

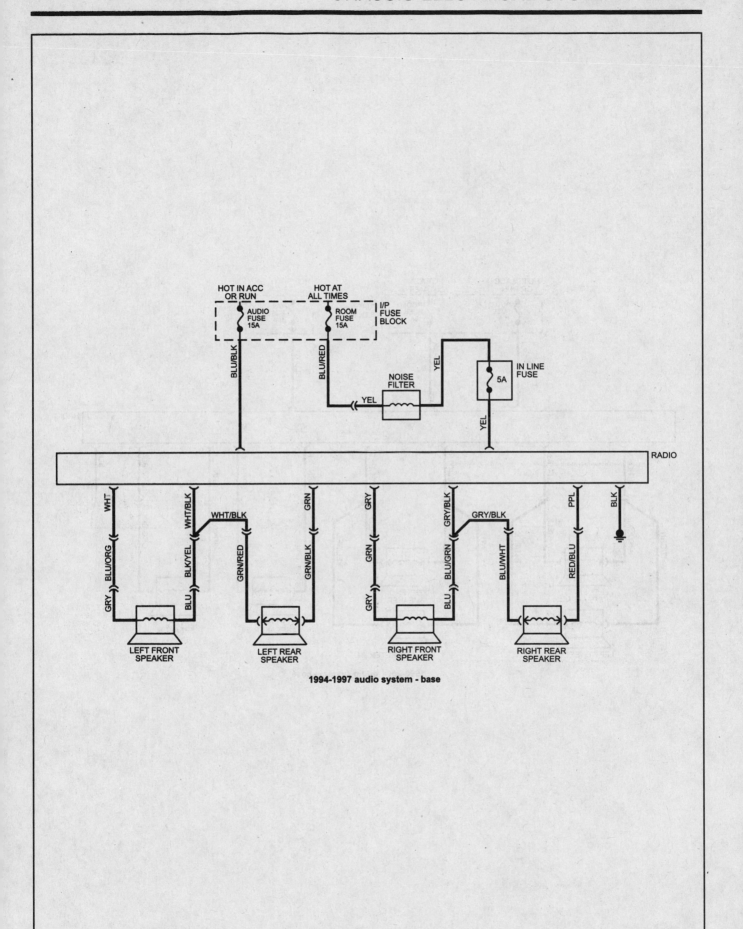

1994-1997 audio system - base

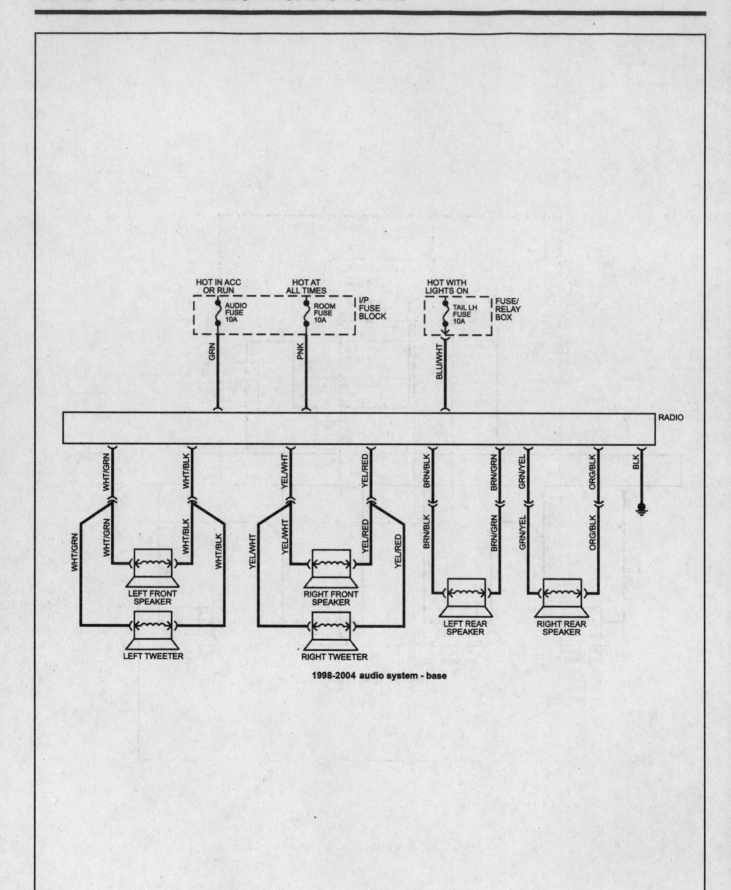

1998-2004 audio system - base

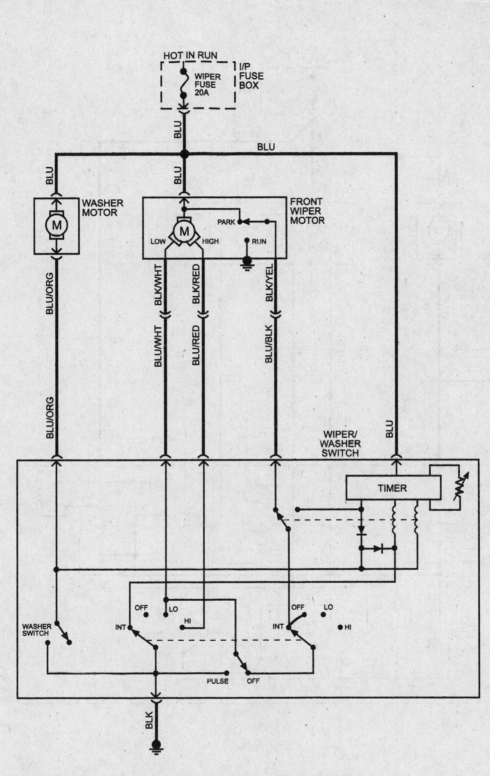

1994-1997 windshield wiper and washer system

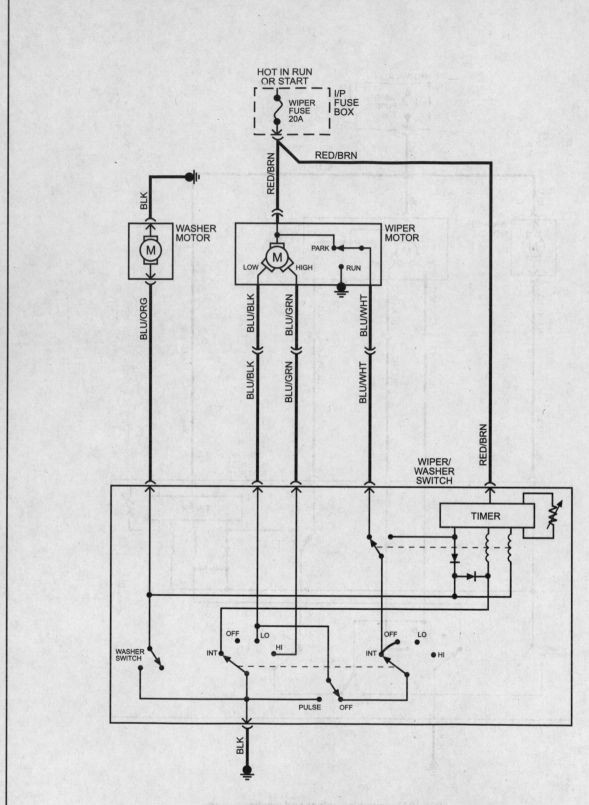

1998-2001 Sephia windshield wiper and washer system

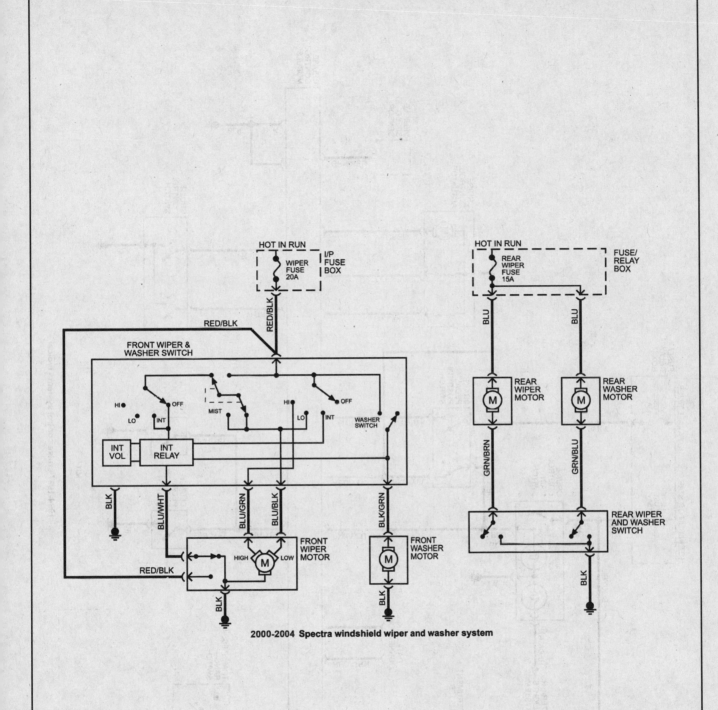

2000-2004 Spectra windshield wiper and washer system

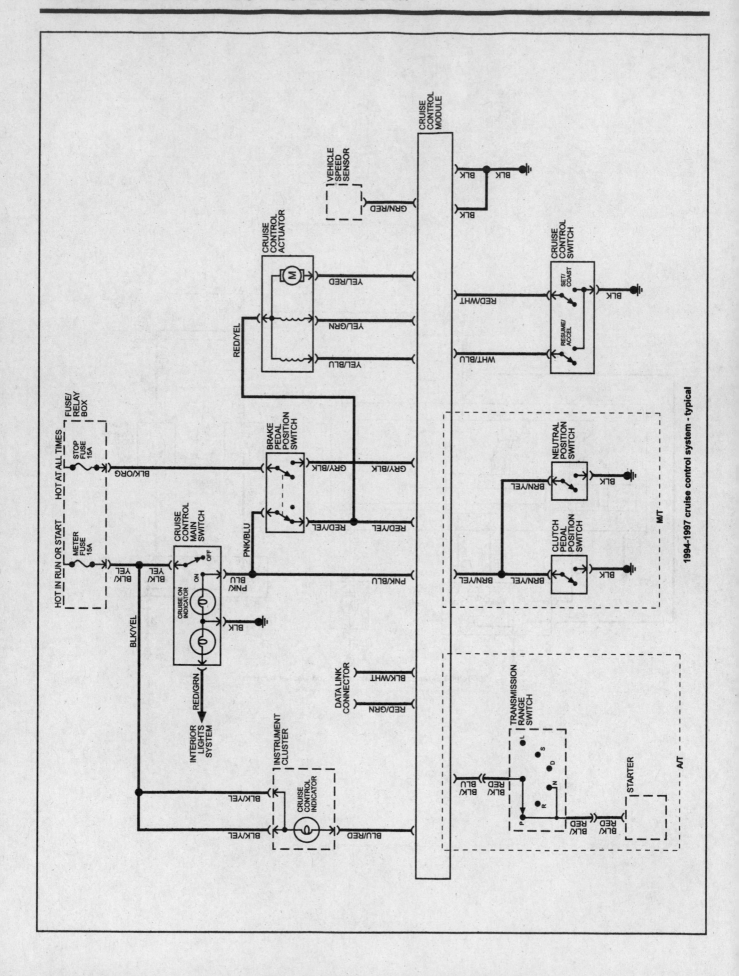

1994-1997 cruise control system - typical

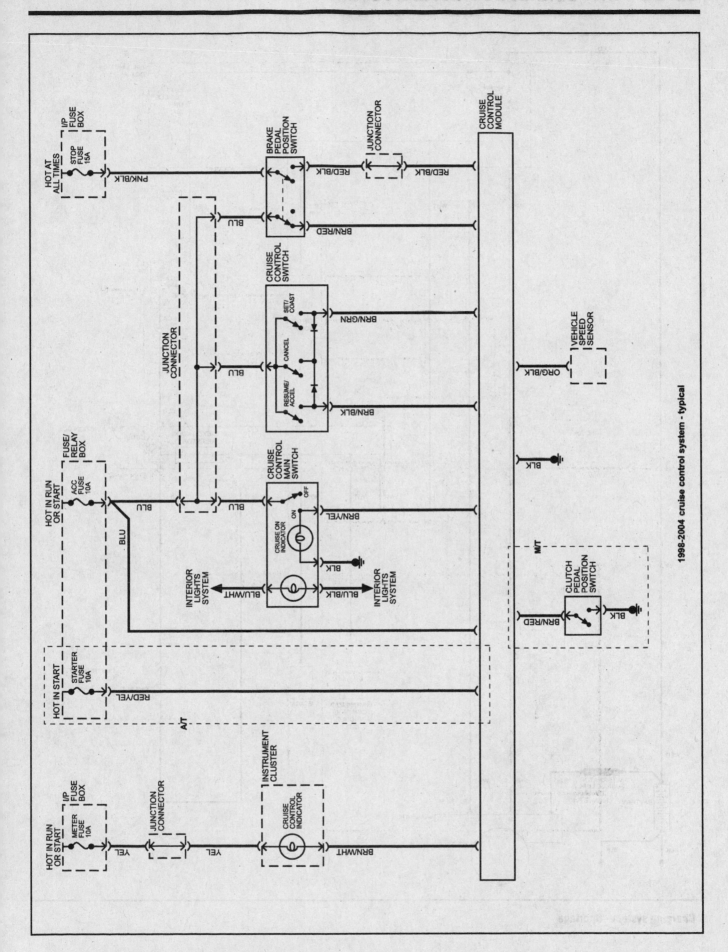

1998-2004 cruise control system - typical

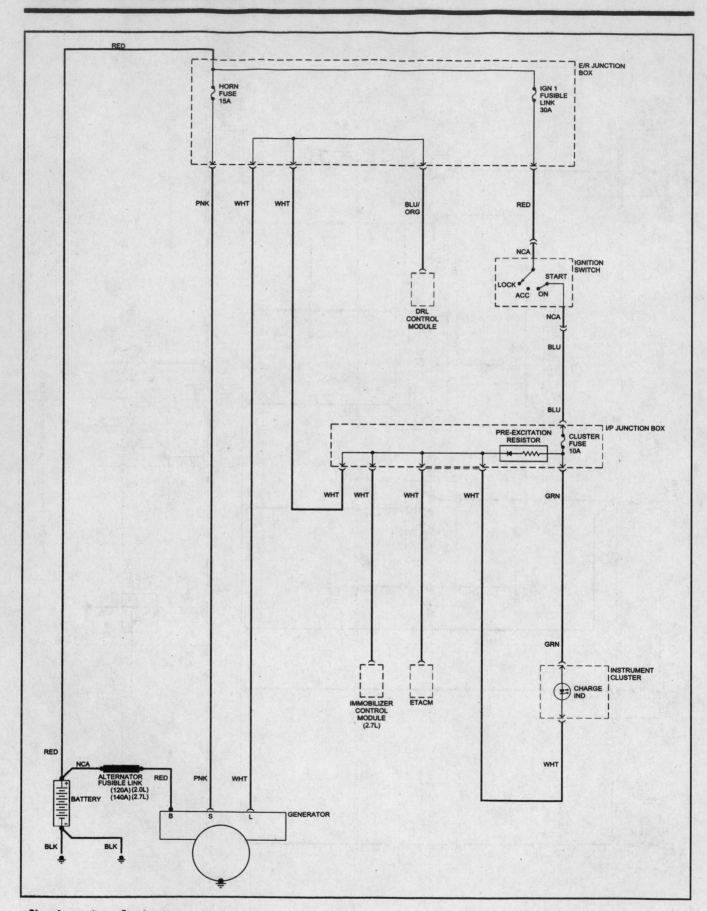

Charging system - Sportage

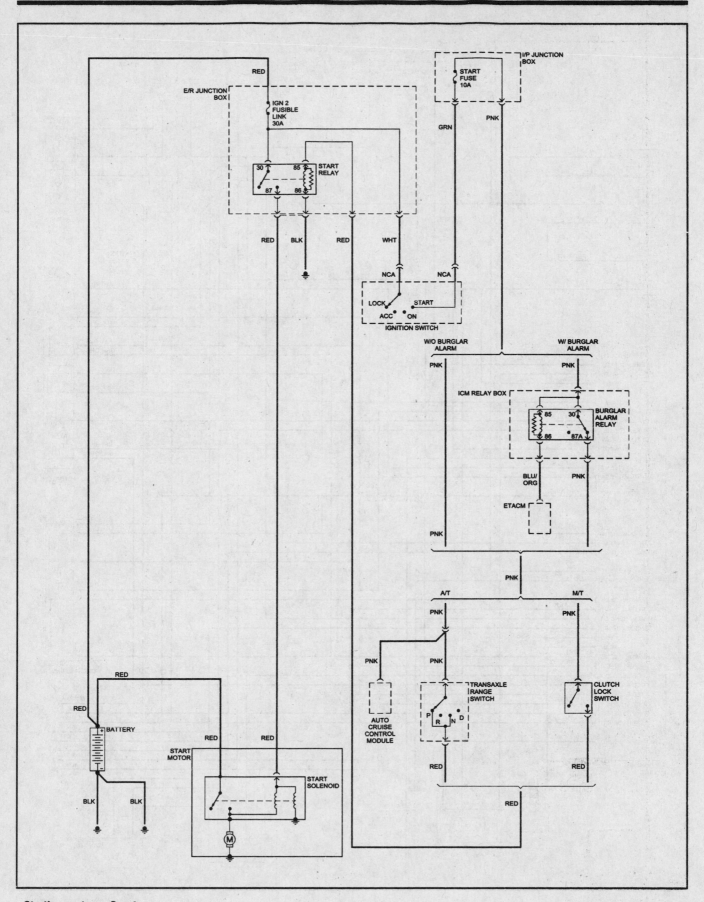

Starting system - Sportage

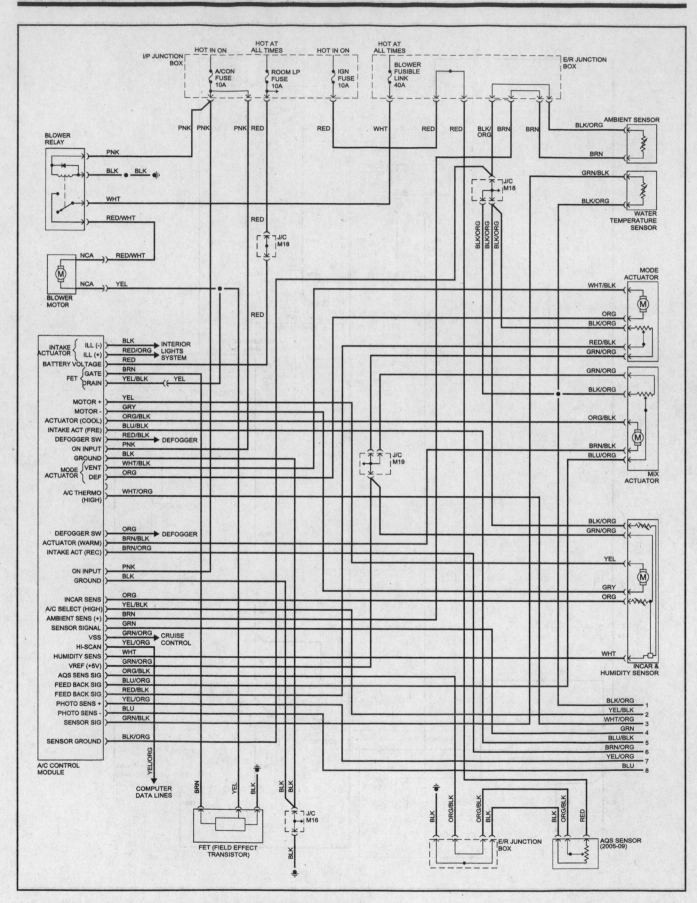

Air conditioning (automatic) and cooling fan system - Sportage (1 of 2)

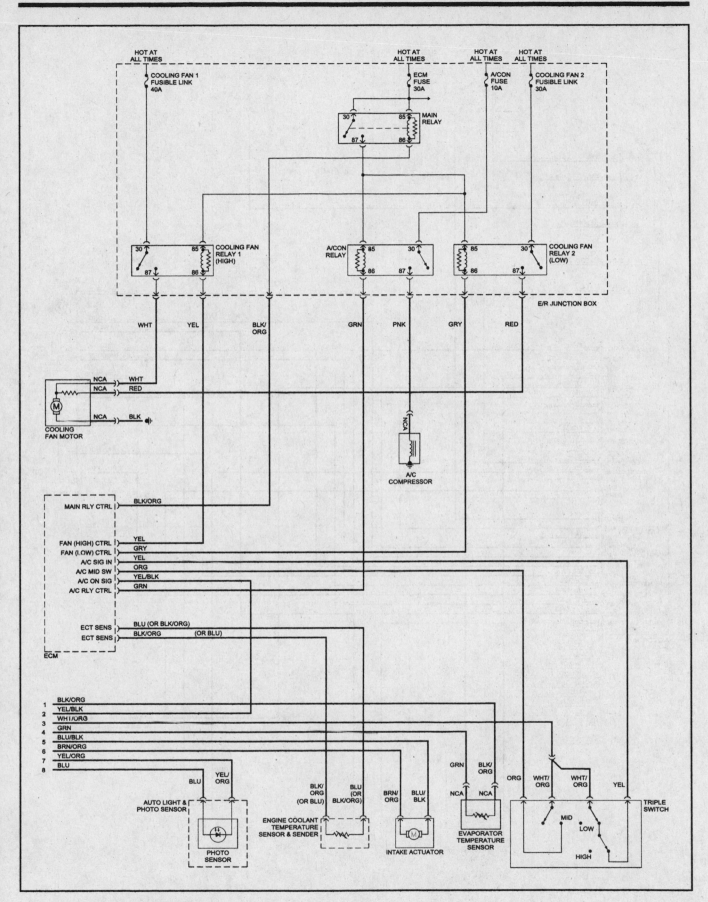

Air conditioning (automatic) and cooling fan system - Sportage (2 of 2)

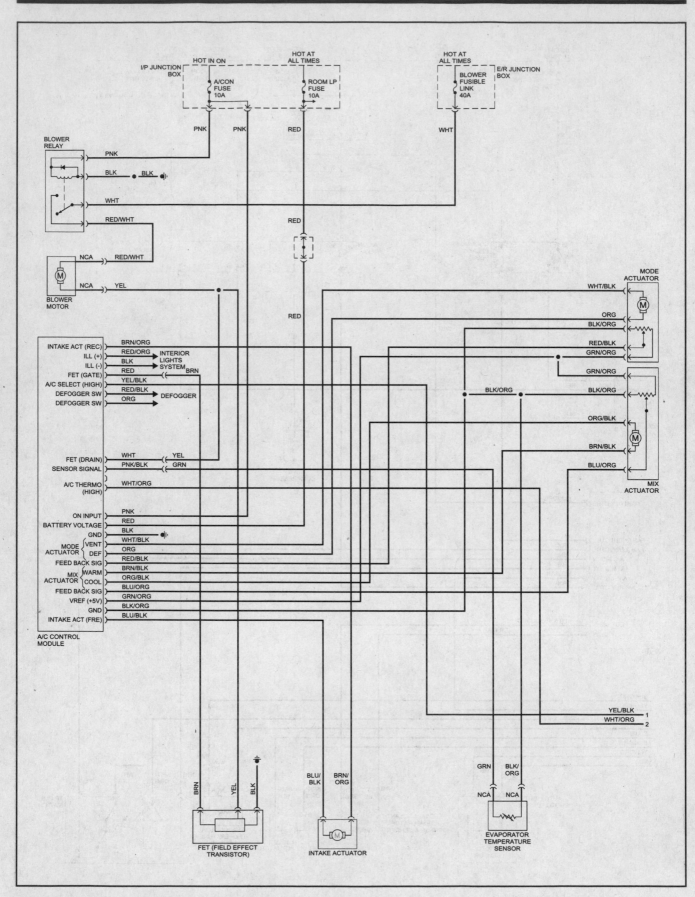

Air conditioning (manual) and engine cooling fan system - Sportage (1 of 2)

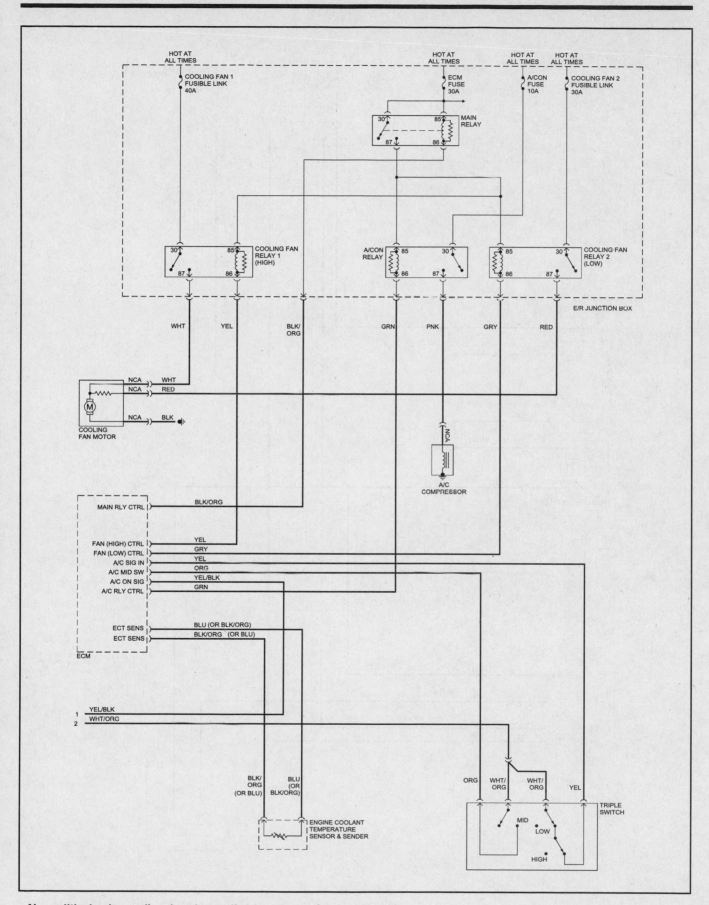

Air conditioning (manual) and engine cooling fan system - Sportage (2 of 2)

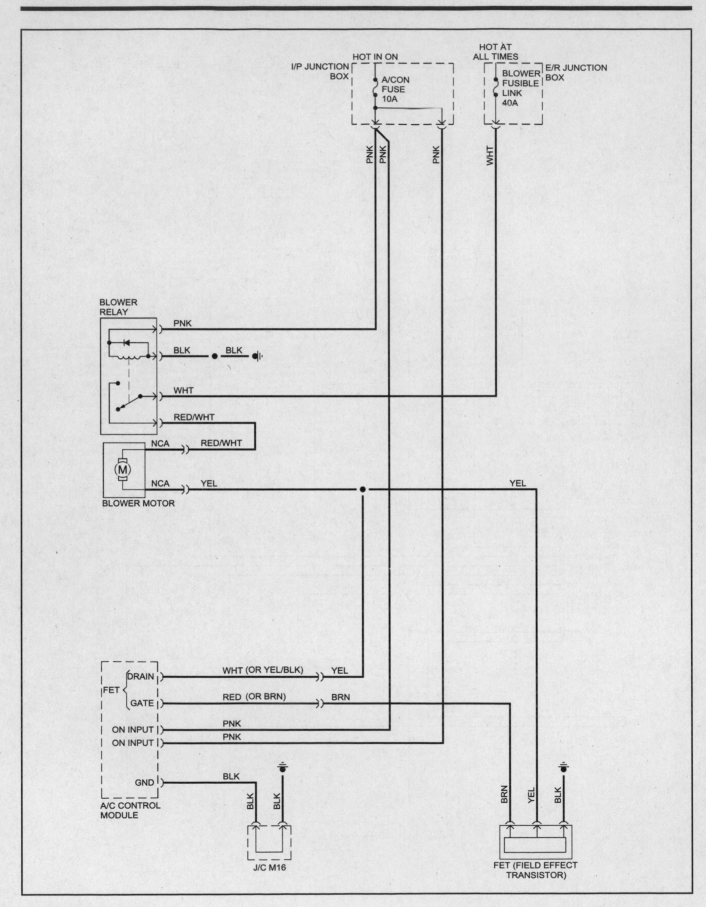

Heating system - Sportage

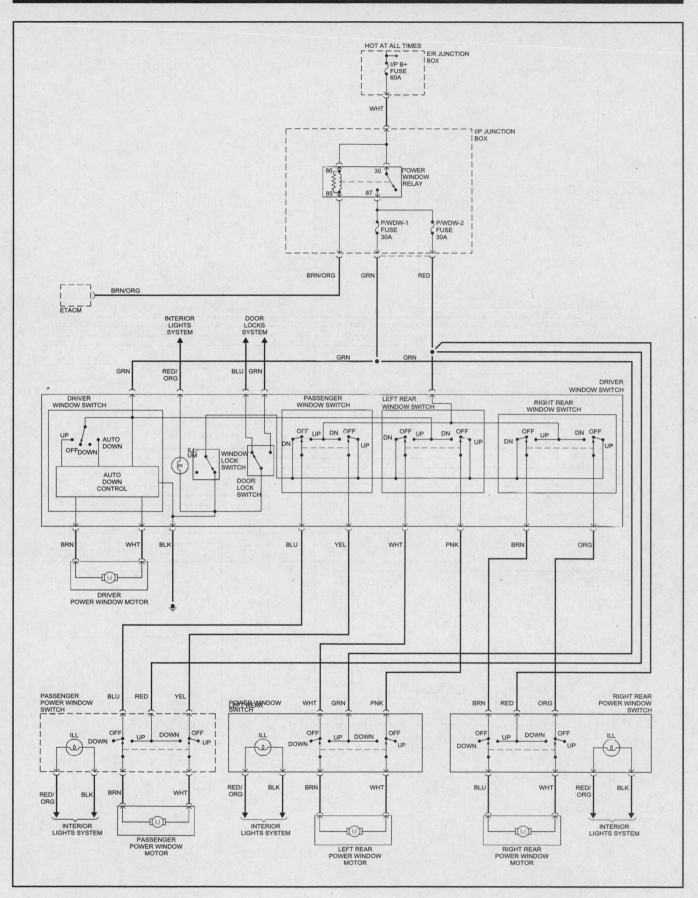

Power window system - Sportage

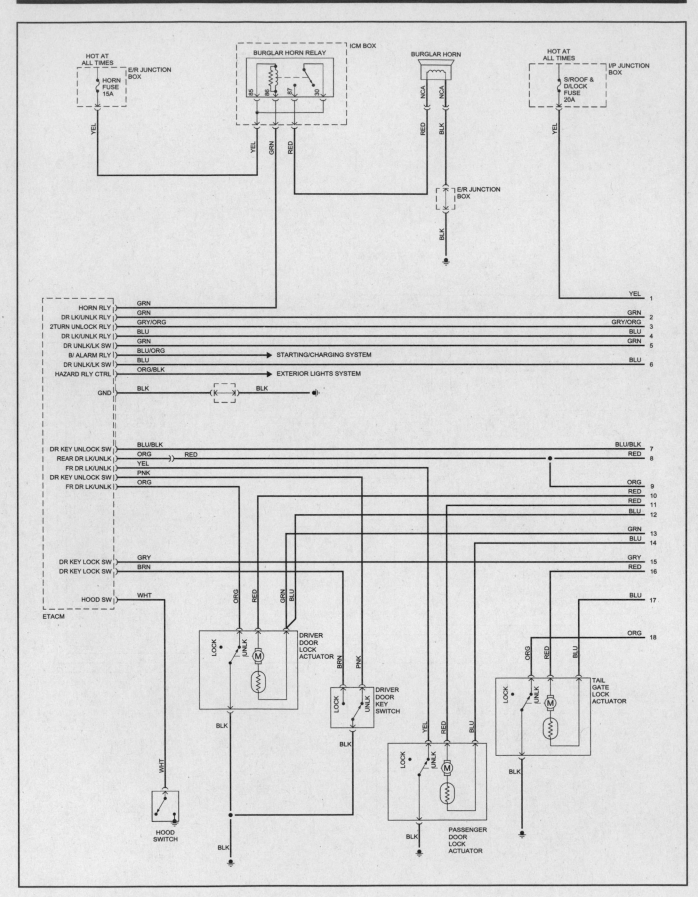

Power door lock system - Sportage (1 of 2)

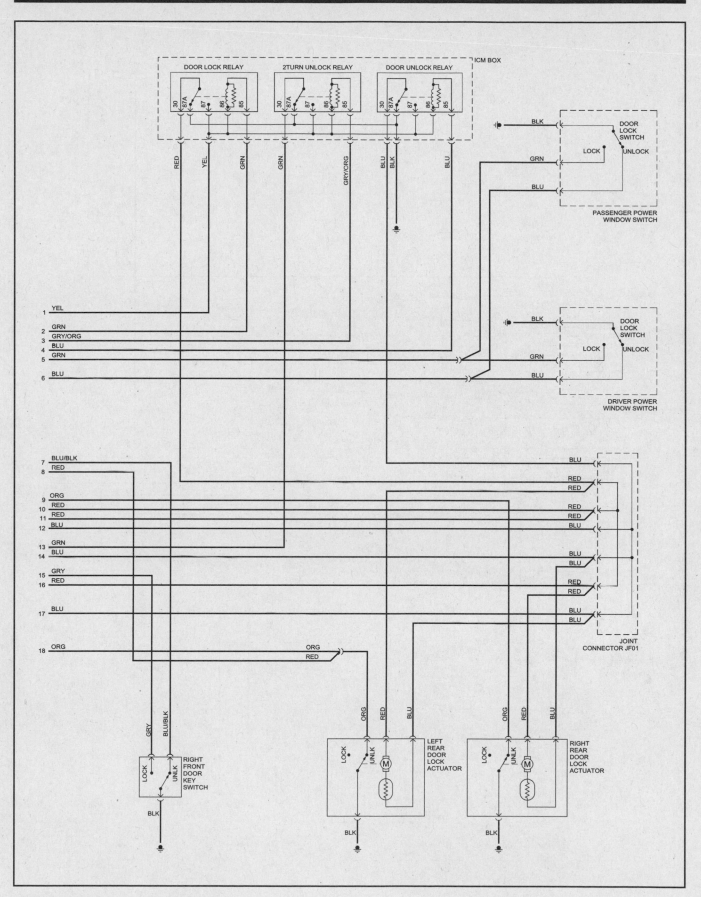

Power door lock system - Sportage (2 of 2)

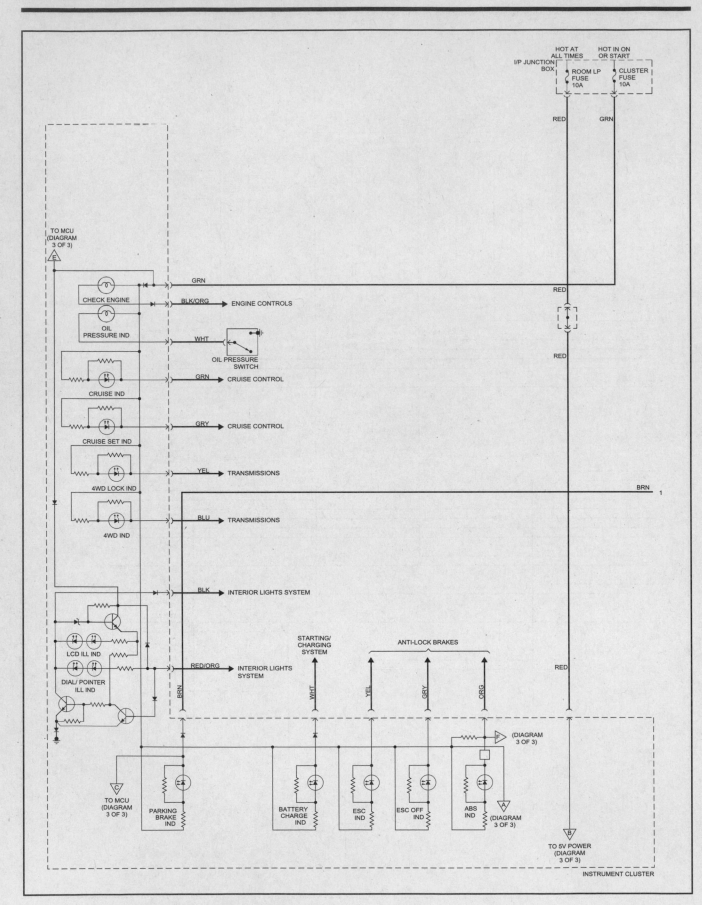

Instrument panel warning lights and gauges - Sportage (1 of 3)

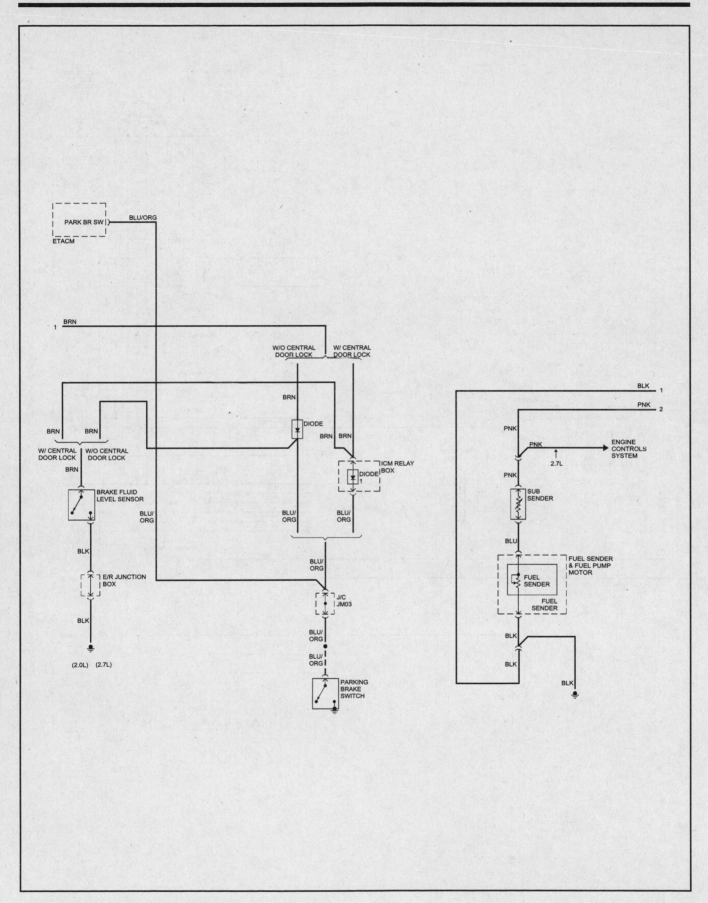

Instrument panel warning lights and gauges - Sportage (2 of 3)

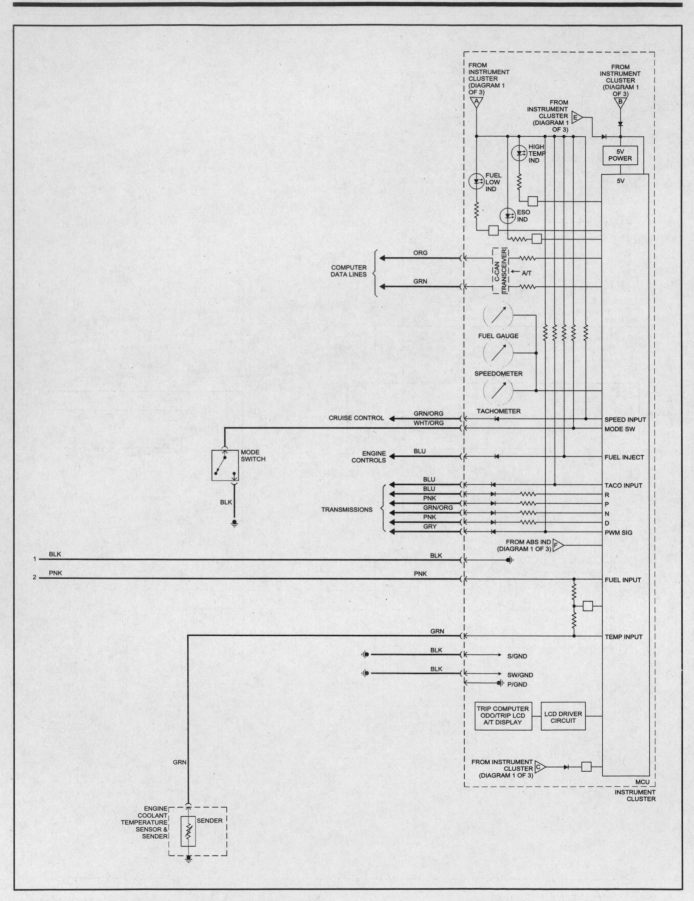

Instrument panel warning lights and gauges - Sportage (3 of 3)

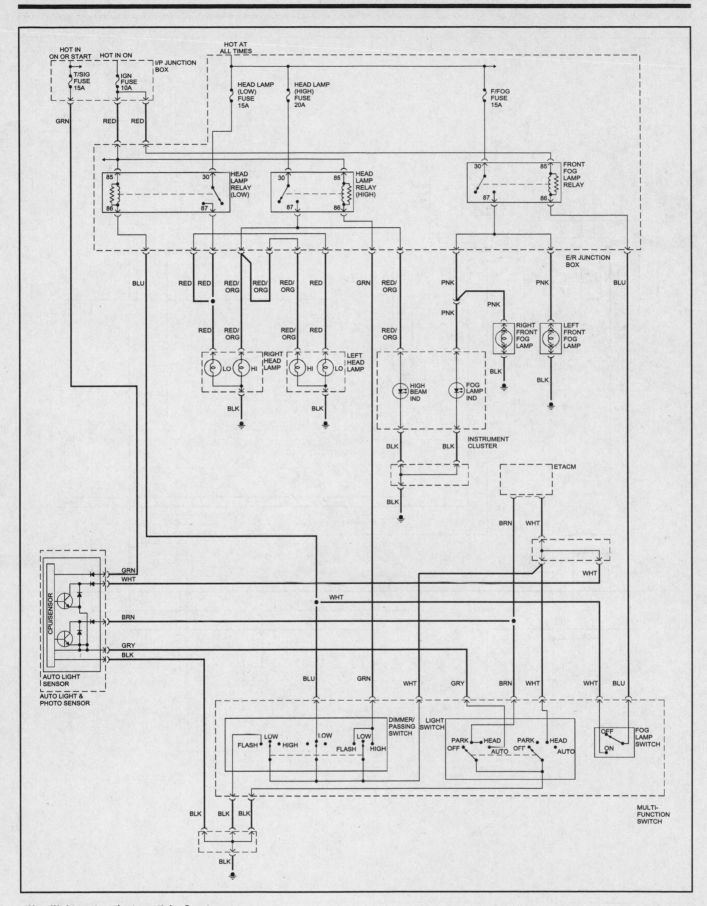

Headlight system (automatic) - Sportage

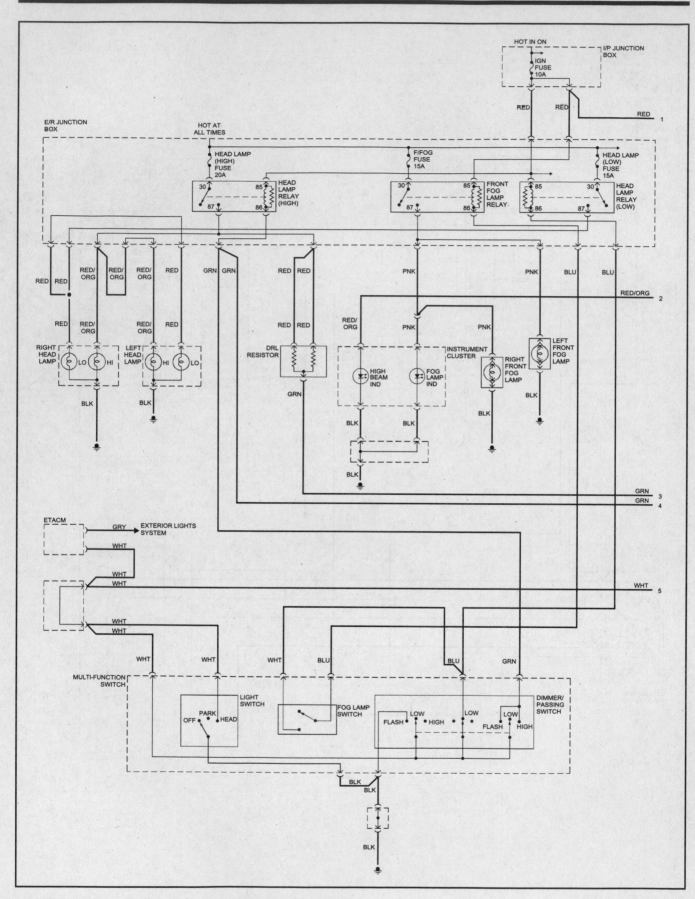

Headlight system (with Daytime Running Lights) - Sportage (1 of 2)

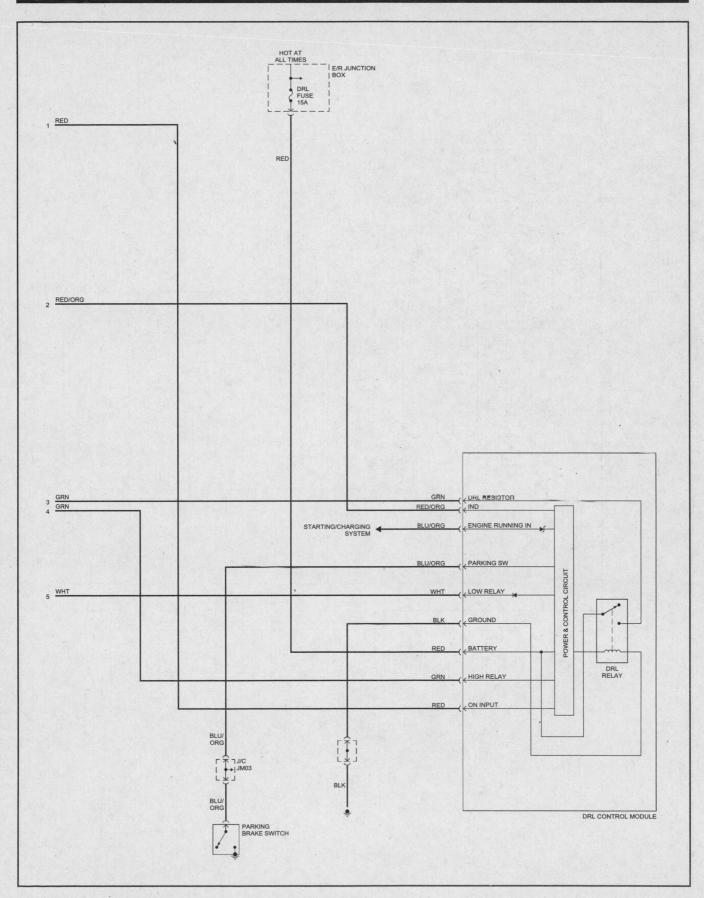

Headlight system (with Daytime Running Lights) - Sportage (2 of 2)

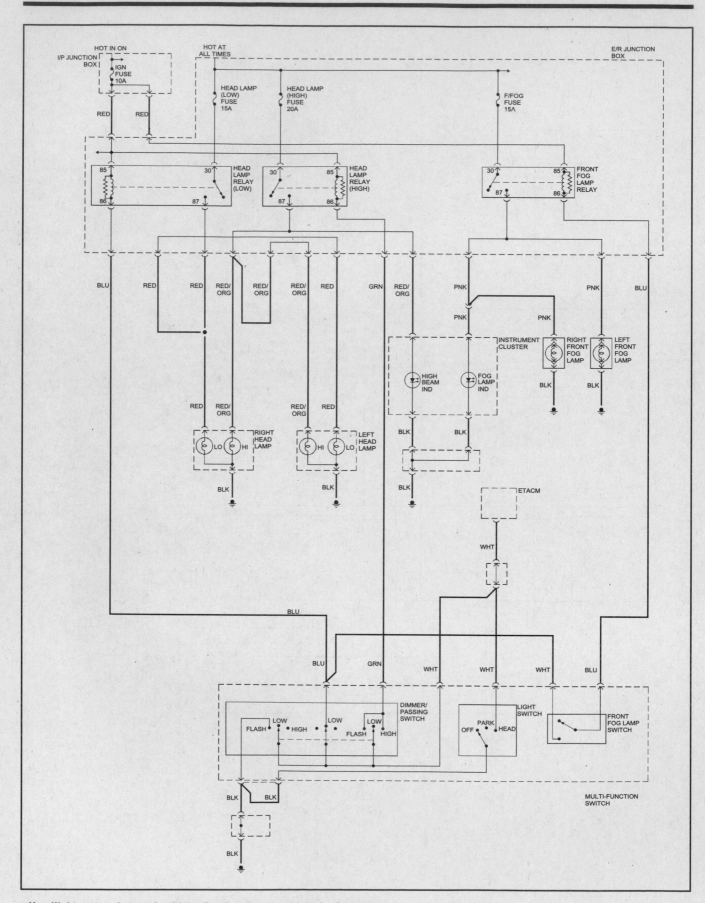

Headlight system (manual, without Daytime Running Lights) - Sportage

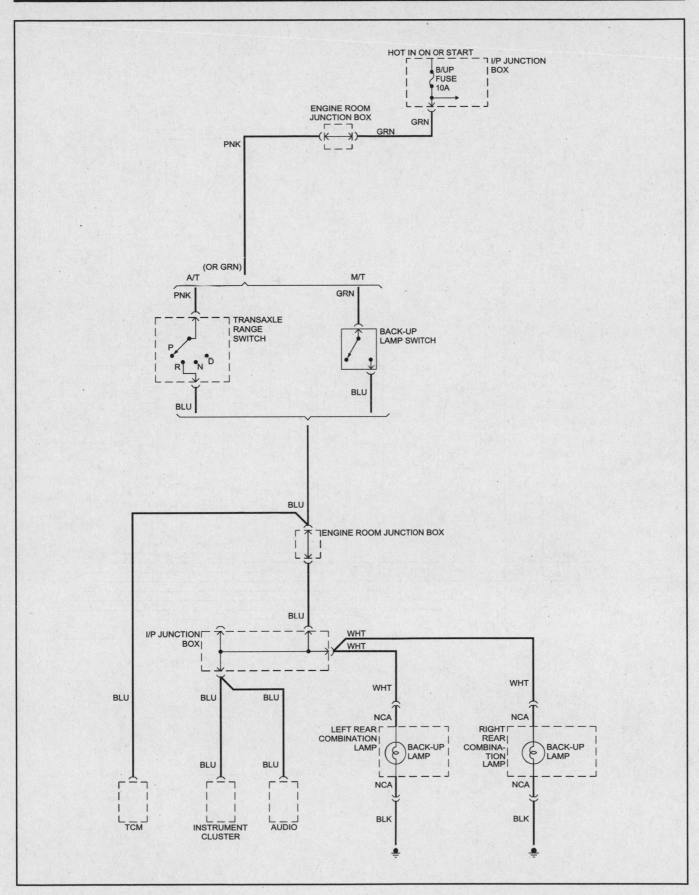

Back-up lights system - Sportage

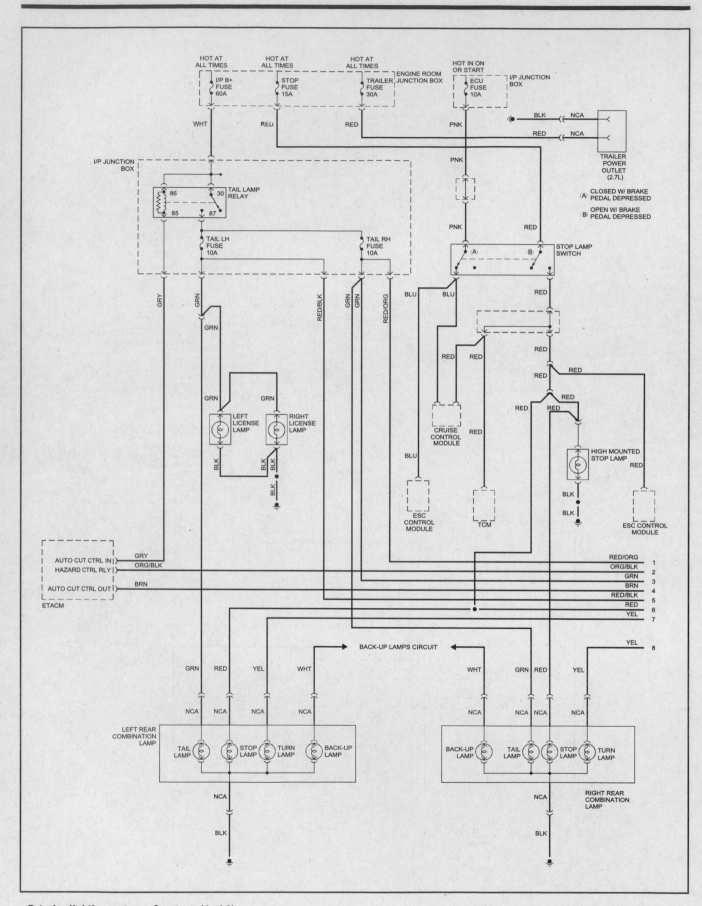

Exterior lighting system - Sportage (1 of 2)

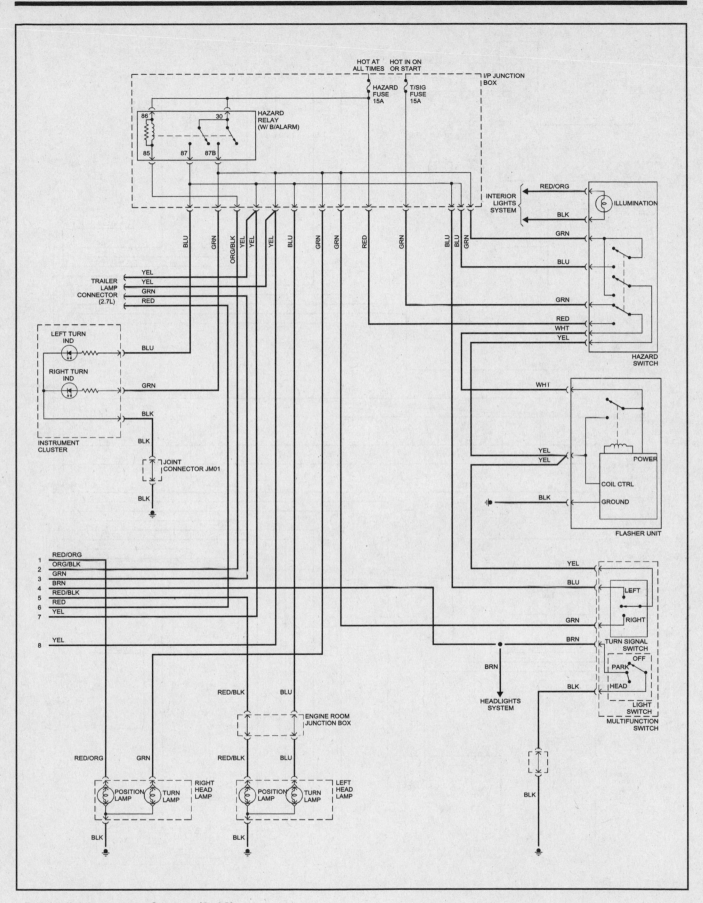

Exterior lighting system - Sportage (2 of 2)

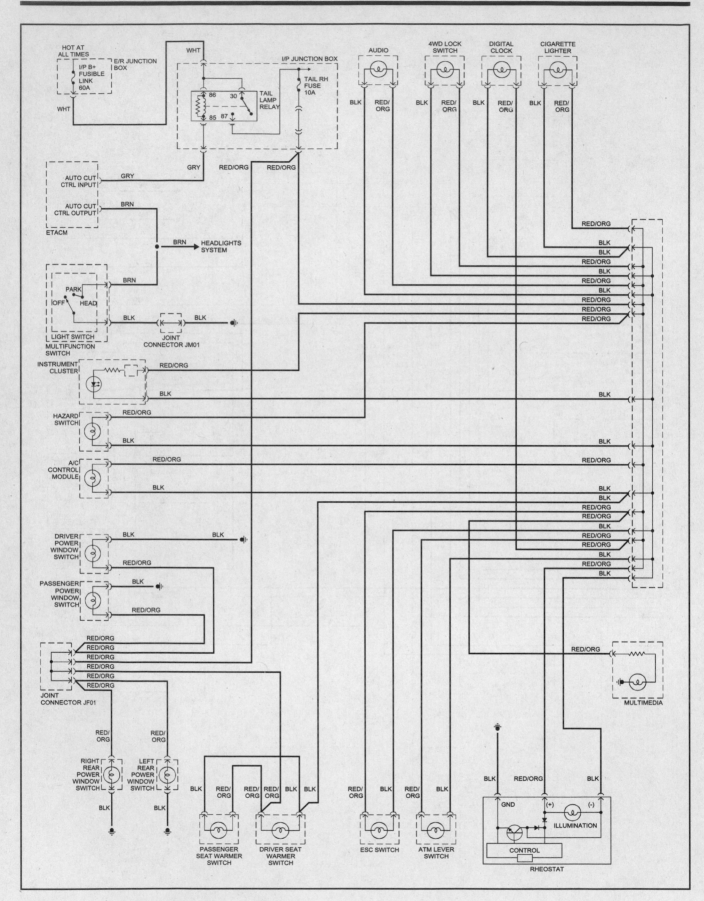

Instrument panel and switch illumination - Sportage

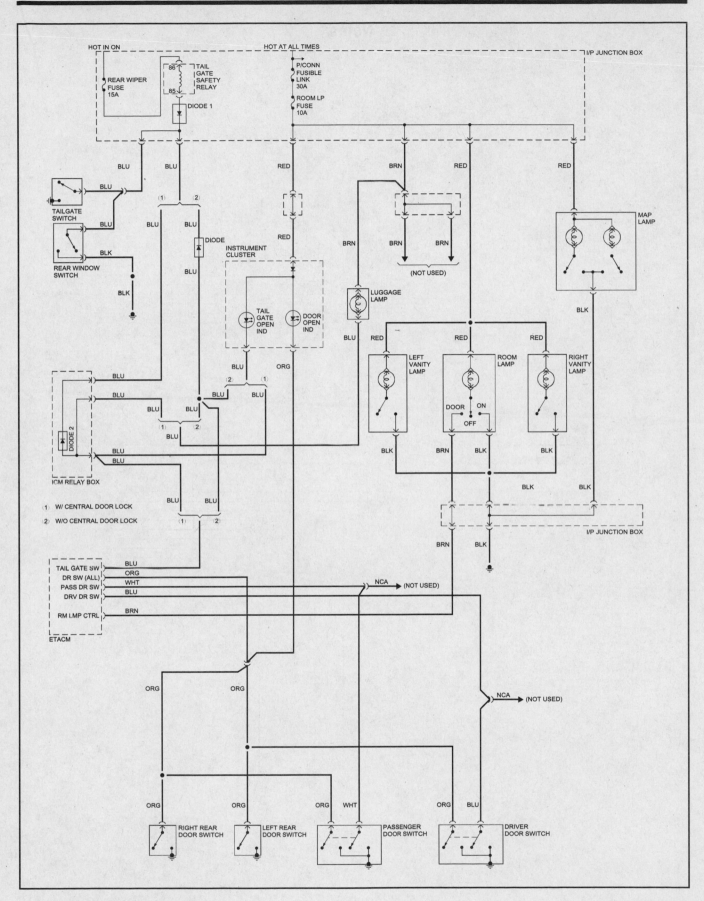

Interior lighting system – Sportage

Notes

GLOSSARY

AIR/FUEL RATIO: The ratio of air-to-gasoline by weight in the fuel mixture drawn into the engine.

AIR INJECTION: One method of reducing harmful exhaust emissions by injecting air into each of the exhaust ports of an engine. The fresh air entering the hot exhaust manifold causes any remaining fuel to be burned before it can exit the tailpipe.

ALTERNATOR: A device used for converting mechanical energy into electrical energy.

AMMETER: An instrument, calibrated in amperes, used to measure the flow of an electrical current in a circuit. Ammeters are always connected in series with the circuit being tested.

AMPERE: The rate of flow of electrical current present when one volt of electrical pressure is applied against one ohm of electrical resistance.

ANALOG COMPUTER: Any microprocessor that uses similar (analogous) electrical signals to make its calculations.

ARMATURE: A laminated, soft iron core wrapped by a wire that converts electrical energy to mechanical energy as in a motor or relay. When rotated in a magnetic field, it changes mechanical energy into electrical energy as in a generator.

ATMOSPHERIC PRESSURE: The pressure on the Earth's surface caused by the weight of the air in the atmosphere. At sea level, this pressure is 14.7 psi at 32°F (101 kPa at 0°C).

ATOMIZATION: The breaking down of a liquid into a fine mist that can be suspended in air.

AXIAL PLAY: Movement parallel to a shaft or bearing bore.

BACKFIRE: The sudden combustion of gases in the intake or exhaust system that results in a loud explosion.

BACKLASH: The clearance or play between two parts, such as meshed gears.

BACKPRESSURE: Restrictions in the exhaust system that slow the exit of exhaust gases from the combustion chamber.

BAKELITE: A heat resistant, plastic insulator material commonly used in printed circuit boards and transistorized components.

BALL BEARING: A bearing made up of hardened inner and outer races between which hardened steel balls roll.

BALLAST RESISTOR: A resistor in the primary ignition circuit that lowers voltage after the engine is started to reduce wear on ignition components.

BEARING: A friction reducing, supportive device usually located between a stationary part and a moving part.

BIMETAL TEMPERATURE SENSOR: Any sensor or switch made of two dissimilar types of metal that bend when heated or cooled due to the different expansion rates of the alloys. These types of sensors usually function as an on/off switch.

BLOWBY: Combustion gases, composed of water vapor and unburned fuel, that leak past the piston rings into the crankcase during normal engine operation. These gases are removed by the PCV system to prevent the buildup of harmful acids in the crankcase.

BRAKE PAD: A brake shoe and lining assembly used with disc brakes.

BRAKE SHOE: The backing for the brake lining. The term is, however, usually applied to the assembly of the brake backing and lining.

BUSHING: A liner, usually removable, for a bearing; an anti-friction liner used in place of a bearing.

CALIPER: A hydraulically activated device in a disc brake system, which is mounted straddling the brake rotor (disc). The caliper contains at least one piston and two brake pads. Hydraulic pressure on the piston(s) forces the pads against the rotor.

CAMSHAFT: A shaft in the engine on which are the lobes (cams) which operate the valves. The camshaft is driven by the crankshaft, via a belt, chain or gears, at one half the crankshaft speed.

CAPACITOR: A device which stores an electrical charge.

CARBON MONOXIDE (CO): A colorless, odorless gas given off as a normal byproduct of combustion. It is poisonous and extremely dangerous in confined areas, building up slowly to toxic levels without warning if adequate ventilation is not available.

CARBURETOR: A device, usually mounted on the intake manifold of an engine, which mixes the air and fuel in the proper proportion to allow even combustion.

CATALYTIC CONVERTER: A device installed in the exhaust system, like a muffler, that converts harmful byproducts of combustion into carbon dioxide and water vapor by means of a heat-producing chemical reaction.

CENTRIFUGAL ADVANCE: A mechanical method of advancing the spark timing by using flyweights in the distributor that react to centrifugal force generated by the distributor shaft rotation.

CHECK VALVE: Any one-way valve installed to permit the flow of air, fuel or vacuum in one direction only.

CHOKE: A device, usually a moveable valve, placed in the intake path of a carburetor to restrict the flow of air.

CIRCUIT: Any unbroken path through which an electrical current can flow. Also used to describe fuel flow in some instances.

CIRCUIT BREAKER: A switch which protects an electrical circuit from overload by opening the circuit when the current flow exceeds a predetermined level. Some circuit breakers must be reset manually, while most reset automatically.

COIL (IGNITION): A transformer in the ignition circuit which steps up the voltage provided to the spark plugs.

COMBINATION MANIFOLD: An assembly which includes both the intake and exhaust manifolds in one casting.

COMBINATION VALVE: A device used in some fuel systems that routes fuel vapors to a charcoal storage canister instead of venting them into the atmosphere. The valve relieves fuel tank pressure and allows fresh air into the tank as the fuel level drops to prevent a vapor lock situation.

COMPRESSION RATIO: The comparison of the total volume of the cylinder and combustion chamber with the piston at BDC and the piston at TDC.

CONDENSER: 1. An electrical device which acts to store an electrical charge, preventing voltage surges. 2. A radiator-like device in the air conditioning system in which refrigerant gas condenses into a liquid, giving off heat.

CONDUCTOR: Any material through which an electrical current can be transmitted easily.

CONTINUITY: Continuous or complete circuit. Can be checked with an ohmmeter.

COUNTERSHAFT: An intermediate shaft which is rotated by a mainshaft and transmits, in turn, that rotation to a working part.

CRANKCASE: The lower part of an engine in which the crankshaft and related parts operate.

CRANKSHAFT: The main driving shaft of an engine which receives reciprocating motion from the pistons and converts it to rotary motion.

CYLINDER: In an engine, the round hole in the engine block in which the piston(s) ride.

CYLINDER BLOCK: The main structural member of an engine in which is found the cylinders, crankshaft and other principal parts.

CYLINDER HEAD: The detachable portion of the engine, usually fastened to the top of the cylinder block and containing all or most of the combustion chambers. On overhead valve engines, it contains the valves and their operating parts. On overhead cam engines, it contains the camshaft as well.

DEAD CENTER: The extreme top or bottom of the piston stroke.

DETONATION: An unwanted explosion of the air/fuel mixture in the combustion chamber caused by excess heat and compression, advanced timing, or an overly lean mixture. Also referred to as "ping".

DIAPHRAGM: A thin, flexible wall separating two cavities, such as in a vacuum advance unit.

DIESELING: A condition in which hot spots in the combustion chamber cause the engine to run on after the key is turned off.

DIFFERENTIAL: A geared assembly which allows the transmission of motion between drive axles, giving one axle the ability to turn faster than the other.

DIODE: An electrical device that will allow current to flow in one direction only.

DISC BRAKE: A hydraulic braking assembly consisting of a brake disc, or rotor, mounted on an axle, and a caliper assembly containing, usually two brake pads which are activated by hydraulic pressure. The pads are forced against the sides of the disc, creating friction which slows the vehicle.

DISTRIBUTOR: A mechanically driven device on an engine which is responsible for electrically firing the spark plug at a predetermined point of the piston stroke.

DOWEL PIN: A pin, inserted in mating holes in two different parts allowing those parts to maintain a fixed relationship.

DRUM BRAKE: A braking system which consists of two brake shoes and one or two wheel cylinders, mounted on a fixed backing plate, and a brake drum, mounted on an axle, which revolves around the assembly.

DWELL: The rate, measured in degrees of shaft rotation, at which an electrical circuit cycles on and off.

ELECTRONIC CONTROL UNIT (ECU): Ignition module, module, amplifier or igniter. See Module for definition.

ELECTRONIC IGNITION: A system in which the timing and firing of the spark plugs is controlled by an electronic control unit, usually called a module. These systems have no points or condenser.

END-PLAY: The measured amount of axial movement in a shaft.

ENGINE: A device that converts heat into mechanical energy.

EXHAUST MANIFOLD: A set of cast passages or pipes which conduct exhaust gases from the engine.

FEELER GAUGE: A blade, usually metal, or precisely predetermined thickness, used to measure the clearance between two parts.

FIRING ORDER: The order in which combustion occurs in the cylinders of an engine. Also the order in which spark is distributed to the plugs by the distributor.

FLOODING: The presence of too much fuel in the intake manifold and combustion chamber which prevents the air/fuel mixture from firing, thereby causing a no-start situation.

FLYWHEEL: A disc shaped part bolted to the rear end of the crankshaft. Around the outer perimeter is affixed the ring gear. The starter drive engages the ring gear, turning the flywheel, which rotates the crankshaft, imparting the initial starting motion to the engine.

FOOT POUND (ft. lbs. or sometimes, ft.lb.): The amount of energy or work needed to raise an item weighing one pound, a distance of one foot.

FUSE: A protective device in a circuit which prevents circuit overload by breaking the circuit when a specific amperage is present. The device is constructed around a strip or wire of a lower amperage rating than the circuit it is designed to protect. When an amperage higher than that stamped on the fuse is present in the circuit, the strip or wire melts, opening the circuit.

GEAR RATIO: The ratio between the number of teeth on meshing gears.

GENERATOR: A device which converts mechanical energy into electrical energy.

HEAT RANGE: The measure of a spark plug's ability to dissipate heat from its firing end. The higher the heat range, the hotter the plug fires.

HUB: The center part of a wheel or gear.

HYDROCARBON (HC): Any chemical compound made up of hydrogen and carbon. A major pollutant formed by the engine as a byproduct of combustion.

HYDROMETER: An instrument used to measure the specific gravity of a solution.

INCH POUND (inch lbs.; sometimes in.lb. or in. lbs.): One twelfth of a foot pound.

INDUCTION: A means of transferring electrical energy in the form of a magnetic field. Principle used in the ignition coil to increase voltage.

INJECTOR: A device which receives metered fuel under relatively low pressure and is activated to inject the fuel into the engine under relatively high pressure at a predetermined time.

INPUT SHAFT: The shaft to which torque is applied, usually carrying the driving gear or gears.

INTAKE MANIFOLD: A casting of passages or pipes used to conduct air or a fuel/air mixture to the cylinders.

JOURNAL: The bearing surface within which a shaft operates.

KEY: A small block usually fitted in a notch between a shaft and a hub to prevent slippage of the two parts.

MANIFOLD: A casting of passages or set of pipes which connect the cylinders to an inlet or outlet source.

MANIFOLD VACUUM: Low pressure in an engine intake manifold formed just below the throttle plates. Manifold vacuum is highest at idle and drops under acceleration.

MASTER CYLINDER: The primary fluid pressurizing device in a hydraulic system. In automotive use, it is found in brake and hydraulic clutch systems and is pedal activated, either directly or, in a power brake system, through the power booster.

MODULE: Electronic control unit, amplifier or igniter of solid state or integrated design which controls the current flow in the ignition primary circuit based on input from the pick-up coil. When the module opens the primary circuit, high secondary voltage is induced in the coil.

NEEDLE BEARING: A bearing which consists of a number (usually a large number) of long, thin rollers.

OHM: (Ω) The unit used to measure the resistance of conductor-to-electrical flow. One ohm is the amount of resistance that limits current flow to one ampere in a circuit with one volt of pressure.

OHMMETER: An instrument used for measuring the resistance, in ohms, in an electrical circuit.

OUTPUT SHAFT: The shaft which transmits torque from a device, such as a transmission.

OVERDRIVE: A gear assembly which produces more shaft revolutions than that transmitted to it.

OVERHEAD CAMSHAFT (OHC): An engine configuration in which the camshaft is mounted on top of the cylinder head and operates the valve either directly or by means of rocker arms.

OVERHEAD VALVE (OHV): An engine configuration in which all of the valves are located in the cylinder head and the camshaft is located in the cylinder block. The camshaft operates the valves via lifters and pushrods.

OXIDES OF NITROGEN (NOx): Chemical compounds of nitrogen produced as a byproduct of combustion. They combine with hydrocarbons to produce smog.

OXYGEN SENSOR: Use with the feedback system to sense the presence of oxygen in the exhaust gas and signal the computer which can reference the voltage signal to an air/fuel ratio.

PINION: The smaller of two meshing gears.

PISTON RING: An open-ended ring with fits into a groove on the outer diameter of the piston. Its chief function is to form a seal between the piston and cylinder wall. Most automotive pistons have three rings: two for compression sealing; one for oil sealing.

PRELOAD: A predetermined load placed on a bearing during assembly or by adjustment.

PRIMARY CIRCUIT: the low voltage side of the ignition system which consists of the ignition switch, ballast resistor or resistance wire, bypass, coil, electronic control unit and pick-up coil as well as the connecting wires and harnesses.

PRESS FIT: The mating of two parts under pressure, due to the inner diameter of one being smaller than the outer diameter of the other, or vice versa; an interference fit.

RACE: The surface on the inner or outer ring of a bearing on which the balls, needles or rollers move.

REGULATOR: A device which maintains the amperage and/or voltage levels of a circuit at predetermined values.

RELAY: A switch which automatically opens and/or closes a circuit.

RESISTANCE: The opposition to the flow of current through a circuit or electrical device, and is measured in ohms. Resistance is equal to the voltage divided by the amperage.

RESISTOR: A device, usually made of wire, which offers a preset amount of resistance in an electrical circuit.

RING GEAR: The name given to a ring-shaped gear attached to a differential case, or affixed to a flywheel or as part of a planetary gear set.

ROLLER BEARING: A bearing made up of hardened inner and outer races between which hardened steel rollers move.

ROTOR: 1. The disc-shaped part of a disc brake assembly, upon which the brake pads bear; also called, brake disc. 2. The device mounted atop the distributor shaft, which passes current to the distributor cap tower contacts.

SECONDARY CIRCUIT: The high voltage side of the ignition system, usually above 20,000 volts. The secondary includes the ignition coil, coil wire, distributor cap and rotor, spark plug wires and spark plugs.

SENDING UNIT: A mechanical, electrical, hydraulic or electromagnetic device which transmits information to a gauge.

SENSOR: Any device designed to measure engine operating conditions or ambient pressures and temperatures. Usually electronic in nature and designed to send a voltage signal to an on-board computer, some sensors may operate as a simple on/off switch or they may provide a variable voltage signal (like a potentiometer) as conditions or measured parameters change.

SHIM: Spacers of precise, predetermined thickness used between parts to establish a proper working relationship.

SLAVE CYLINDER: In automotive use, a device in the hydraulic clutch system which is activated by hydraulic force, disengaging the clutch.

SOLENOID: A coil used to produce a magnetic field, the effect of which is to produce work.

SPARK PLUG: A device screwed into the combustion chamber of a spark ignition engine. The basic construction is a conductive core inside of a ceramic insulator, mounted in an outer conductive base. An electrical charge from the spark plug wire travels along the conductive core and jumps a preset air gap to a grounding point or points at the end of the conductive base. The resultant spark ignites the fuel/air mixture in the combustion chamber.

SPLINES: Ridges machined or cast onto the outer diameter of a shaft or inner diameter of a bore to enable parts to mate without rotation.

TACHOMETER: A device used to measure the rotary speed of an engine, shaft, gear, etc., usually in rotations per minute.

THERMOSTAT: A valve, located in the cooling system of an engine, which is closed when cold and opens gradually in response to engine heating, controlling the temperature of the coolant and rate of coolant flow.

TOP DEAD CENTER (TDC): The point at which the piston reaches the top of its travel on the compression stroke.

TORQUE: The twisting force applied to an object.

TORQUE CONVERTER: A turbine used to transmit power from a driving member to a driven member via hydraulic action, providing changes in drive ratio and torque. In automotive use, it links the driveplate at the rear of the engine to the automatic transmission.

TRANSDUCER: A device used to change a force into an electrical signal.

TRANSISTOR: A semi-conductor component which can be actuated by a small voltage to perform an electrical switching function.

TUNE-UP: A regular maintenance function, usually associated with the replacement and adjustment of parts and components in the electrical and fuel systems of a vehicle for the purpose of attaining optimum performance.

TURBOCHARGER: An exhaust driven pump which compresses intake air and forces it into the combustion chambers at higher than atmospheric pressures. The increased air pressure allows more fuel to be burned and results in increased horsepower being produced.

VACUUM ADVANCE: A device which advances the ignition timing in response to increased engine vacuum.

VACUUM GAUGE: An instrument used to measure the presence of vacuum in a chamber.

VALVE: A device which control the pressure, direction of flow or rate of flow of a liquid or gas.

VALVE CLEARANCE: The measured gap between the end of the valve stem and the rocker arm, cam lobe or follower that activates the valve.

VISCOSITY: The rating of a liquid's internal resistance to flow.

VOLTMETER: An instrument used for measuring electrical force in units called volts. Voltmeters are always connected parallel with the circuit being tested.

WHEEL CYLINDER: Found in the automotive drum brake assembly, it is a device, actuated by hydraulic pressure, which, through internal pistons, pushes the brake shoes outward against the drums.

Notes

A

ABOUT THIS MANUAL, 0-5

ACCELERATOR CABLE, REMOVAL, INSTALLATION AND ADJUSTMENT, 4-18

ACKNOWLEDGEMENTS, 0-4

AIR CONDITIONING

and heating system, check and maintenance, 3-16

compressor, removal and installation, 3-18

condenser, removal and installation, 3-20

pressure switch, replacement, 3-22

receiver-drier, removal and installation, 3-19

AIR FILTER

element, replacement, 1-26

housing, removal and installation, 4-14

AIRBAG SYSTEM, GENERAL INFORMATION, 12-27

ALTERNATOR, REMOVAL AND INSTALLATION, 5-12

ANTENNA, REMOVAL AND INSTALLATION, 12-14

ANTIFREEZE, GENERAL INFORMATION, 3-3

ANTI-LOCK BRAKE SYSTEM (ABS), GENERAL INFORMATION, 9-2

AUTOMATIC TRANSAXLE, 7B-1

diagnosis, general, 7B-2

driveaxle oil seals, replacement, 7A-2

fluid

    change, 1-35

    level check, 1-12

    type, 1-38

overhaul, general information, 7B-10

removal and installation, 7B-8

shift

    cable, removal, installation and adjustment, 7B-5

    interlock system, description and component replacement, 7B-7

    lever, removal and installation, 7B-6

throttle valve cable (1994 through 1997 models), check, adjustment and replacement, 7B-3

transaxle oil cooler, removal and installation, 7B-10

Transmission Range (TR) switch, replacement and adjustment, 6-23

AUTOMOTIVE CHEMICALS AND LUBRICANTS, 0-19

B

BACK-UP LIGHT SWITCH, MANUAL TRANSAXLE, CHECK AND REPLACEMENT, 7A-3
BALLJOINTS, REPLACEMENT, 10-9
BATTERY
cables, check and replacement, 5-4
check and replacement, 5-2
check, maintenance and charging, 1-18
precautions and disconnection, 5-2
BLOWER MOTOR RESISTOR AND BLOWER MOTOR, REPLACEMENT, 3-12
BODY REPAIR
major damage, 11-5
minor damage, 11-3
BODY, 11-1
BOOSTER BATTERY (JUMP) STARTING, 0-18
BRAKES, 9-1
Anti-lock Brake System (ABS), general information, 9-2
caliper, removal and installation, 9-8
disc, inspection, removal and installation, 9-9
fluid
change, 1-29
level check, 1-11
type, 1-38
general information, 9-2
hoses and lines, inspection and replacement, 9-19
hydraulic system, bleeding, 9-20
light switch, replacement, 9-23
master cylinder, removal and installation, 9-18
pads, replacement, 9-3
parking brake adjustment, 9-22
pedal, adjustment, 9-23
power brake booster, check, removal and installation, 9-21
shoes, drum brake/parking brake, replacement, 9-11
system check, 1-21
wheel cylinder, removal and installation, 9-17
BULB REPLACEMENT, 12-20
BUMPER COVERS, REMOVAL AND INSTALLATION, 11-9
BUYING PARTS, 0-8

C

CABLE REPLACEMENT
accelerator, 4-18
battery, 5-4
hood release, 11-8
throttle valve (1994 through 1997 models), check, adjustment and replacement, 7B-3
CALIPER, DISC BRAKE, REMOVAL AND INSTALLATION, 9-8
CAMSHAFT OIL SEAL(S), REPLACEMENT, 2A-14

CAMSHAFT POSITION (CMP) SENSOR, REPLACEMENT, 6-12
CAMSHAFT(S), LIFTERS AND ROCKER ARMS (FOUR-CYLINDER ENGINES), REMOVAL, INSPECTION, INSTALLATION AND ADJUSTMENT, 2A-16
CAMSHAFTS AND VALVETRAIN (V6 ENGINES), REMOVAL, INSPECTION, INSTALLATION AND ADJUSTMENT, 2B-9
CATALYTIC CONVERTER, GENERAL DESCRIPTION, CHECK AND REPLACEMENT, 6-27
CENTER CONSOLE, REMOVAL AND INSTALLATION, 11-23
CHARGING SYSTEM
alternator, removal and installation, 5-12
check, 5-11
general information and precautions, 5-11
CHASSIS ACCELERATION SENSOR, REPLACEMENT, 6-13
CHASSIS ELECTRICAL SYSTEM, 12-1
CHEMICALS AND LUBRICANTS, 0-19
CIRCUIT BREAKERS, GENERAL INFORMATION, 12-5
CLUTCH
components, removal, inspection and installation, 8-3
description and check, 8-2
fluid
level check, 1-11
type, 1-38
hydraulic system, bleeding, 8-3
master cylinder, removal and installation, 8-2
pedal
adjustment, 8-6
position switch, replacement, 6-13
release
bearing and lever, removal, inspection and installation, 8-5
cylinder, removal and installation, 8-3
start switch, check and replacement, 8-6
CLUTCH AND DRIVELINE, 8-1
COIL SPRING, REPLACEMENT, 10-5
COIL, IGNITION, CHECK AND REPLACEMENT, 5-6
COMBINATION SWITCH ASSEMBLY, REPLACEMENT, 12-7
COMPRESSOR, AIR CONDITIONING, REMOVAL AND INSTALLATION, 3-18
CONDENSER, AIR CONDITIONING, REMOVAL AND INSTALLATION, 3-20
CONTINUOUSLY VARIABLE VALVE TIMING (CVVT) SYSTEM, DESCRIPTION AND COMPONENT REPLACEMENT, 6-36
CONTROL ARM, REMOVAL, INSPECTION AND INSTALLATION, 10-8
CONTROL MODULE, IGNITION, REPLACEMENT, 5-6
CONVERSION FACTORS, 0-20
COOLANT
level check, 1-10
reservoir, removal and installation, 3-7
Temperature (ECT) sensor, replacement, 6-14
temperature sending unit, check and replacement, 3-11
type, 1-38

COOLING SYSTEM
check, 1-20
servicing (draining, flushing and refilling), 1-30
**COOLING, HEATING AND AIR CONDITIONING
    SYSTEMS, 3-1**
COWL COVER, REMOVAL AND INSTALLATION, 11-31
**CRANKSHAFT POSITION (CKP) SENSOR,
    REPLACEMENT, 6-14**
**CRANKSHAFT PULLEY AND FRONT OIL SEAL, REMOVAL
    AND INSTALLATION, 2A-15**
CRANKSHAFT, REMOVAL AND INSTALLATION, 2C-17
**CRUISE CONTROL SYSTEM, GENERAL
    INFORMATION, 12-26**
CYLINDER COMPRESSION CHECK, 2C-4
**CYLINDER HEAD(S), REMOVAL AND
    INSTALLATION, 2A-22, 2B-10**

D

DASHBOARD
switches, replacement, 12-9
trim panels, removal and installation, 11-25
**DASHPOT, CHECK, REPLACEMENT AND
    ADJUSTMENT, 6-29**
**DAYTIME RUNNING LIGHTS (DRL), GENERAL
    INFORMATION, 12-27**
DEFOGGER, REAR WINDOW, CHECK AND REPAIR, 12-16
DIAGNOSIS, 0-23
DIAGNOSTIC TROUBLE CODES (DTCS), ACCESSING, 6-5
DIFFERENTIAL (4WD MODELS)
lubricant
    change, 1-36
    level check, 1-14
    type, 1-38
removal and installation, 8-14
DISC BRAKE
caliper, removal and installation, 9-8
disc inspection, removal and installation, 9-9
pads, replacement, 9-3
DISTRIBUTOR
cap and rotor check and replacement, 1-33
removal and installation, 5-9
DOOR
latch, lock cylinder and handles, removal and installation, 11-18
removal, installation and adjustment, 11-18
trim panels, removal and installation, 11-16
window glass regulator, removal and installation, 11-21
window glass, removal and installation, 11-20
DRIVEAXLE
boot, replacement, 8-9
removal and installation, 8-7
DRIVEAXLE OIL SEALS, REPLACEMENT, 7A-2, 8-14

**DRIVEBELT CHECK, ADJUSTMENT AND
    REPLACEMENT, 1-27**
DRIVEPLATE, REMOVAL AND INSTALLATION, 2A-32, 2B-13
**DRIVESHAFT (4WD MODELS), CHECK, REMOVAL AND
    INSTALLATION, 8-13**
DRUM BRAKE SHOES, REPLACEMENT, 9-11

E

**ELECTRIC SIDE VIEW MIRRORS, GENERAL
    INFORMATION, 12-26**
**ELECTRICAL TROUBLESHOOTING, GENERAL
    INFORMATION, 12-2**
EMISSIONS AND ENGINE CONTROL SYSTEMS, 6-1
ENGINE, GENERAL OVERHAUL PROCEDURES, 2C-1
crankshaft, removal and installation, 2C-17
cylinder compression check, 2C-4
engine overhaul
    disassembly sequence, 2C-10
    reassembly sequence, 2C-19
engine rebuilding alternatives, 2C-7
engine removal, methods and precautions, 2C-7
engine, removal and installation, 2C-8
general information, engine overhaul, 2C-2
initial start-up and break-in after overhaul, 2C-19
oil pressure check, 2C-4
pistons and connecting rods, removal and installation, 2C-11
vacuum gauge diagnostic checks, 2C-5
ENGINE, IN-VEHICLE REPAIR PROCEDURES
Four-cylinder engines, 2A-1
    camshaft oil seal(s), replacement, 2A-14
    camshaft(s), lifters and rocker arms, removal, inspection,
        installation and adjustment, 2A-16
    crankshaft pulley and front oil seal, removal and
        installation, 2A-15
    cylinder head, removal and installation, 2A-22
    exhaust manifold, removal and installation, 2A-6
    flywheel/driveplate, removal and installation, 2A-32
    intake manifold, removal and installation, 2A-5
    mounts, check and replacement, 2A-33
    oil pan, removal and installation, 2A-25
    oil pump, removal, inspection and installation, 2A-28
    oil type and viscosity, 1-38
    rear main oil seal, replacement, 2A-32
    repair operations possible with the engine in the vehicle, 2A-2
    timing belt and sprockets, removal and installation, 2A-7
    Top Dead Center (TDC) for number 1 piston, locating, 2A-2
    valve cover, removal and installation, 2A-3
V6 engines, 2B-1
    camshafts and valvetrain, removal, inspection, installation and
        adjustment, 2B-9
    cylinder heads, removal, inspection and installation, 2B-10
    driveplate, removal and installation, 2B-13

exhaust manifold/catalytic converter assemblies, removal and installation, 2B-5
intake manifold, removal and installation, 2B-4
oil pan, removal and installation, 2B-11
oil pump, removal, inspection and installation, 2B-12
oil seals, replacement, 2B-9
powertrain mounts, check and replacement, 2B-14
repair operations possible with the engine in the vehicle, 2B-2
timing belt and sprockets, removal, inspection and installation, 2B-6
Top Dead Center (TDC) for number one piston, locating, 2B-2
valve covers, removal and installation, 2B-3

ENGINE COOLANT TEMPERATURE (ECT) SENSOR, REPLACEMENT, 6-14
ENGINE COOLANT, LEVEL CHECK, 1-11
ENGINE COOLING FANS AND SWITCH, CHECK AND REPLACEMENT, 3-5
ENGINE ELECTRICAL SYSTEMS, 5-1
ENGINE OIL
and oil filter change, 1-16
level check, 1-10
ENGINE OVERHAUL
disassembly sequence, 2C-10
reassembly sequence, 2C-19
ENGINE REBUILDING ALTERNATIVES, 2C-7
ENGINE REMOVAL, METHODS AND PRECAUTIONS, 2C-7
ENGINE, REMOVAL AND INSTALLATION, 2C-8
EVAPORATIVE EMISSIONS CONTROL (EVAP) SYSTEM, GENERAL DESCRIPTION AND COMPONENT REPLACEMENT, 6-32
EXHAUST GAS RECIRCULATION (EGR) SYSTEM, GENERAL DESCRIPTION AND COMPONENT REPLACEMENT, 6-35
EXHAUST MANIFOLD (FOUR-CYLINDER ENGINES), REMOVAL AND INSTALLATION, 2A-6
EXHAUST MANIFOLD/CATALYTIC CONVERTER ASSEMBLIES (V6 ENGINES), REMOVAL AND INSTALLATION, 2B-5
EXHAUST SYSTEM
check, 1-26
servicing, general information, 4-29

F

FASTENER AND TRIM REMOVAL, 11-6
FAULT FINDING, 0-23
FENDER, FRONT, REMOVAL AND INSTALLATION, 11-12
FILTER REPLACEMENT
engine air, 1-26
engine oil, 1-16
fuel, 1-37
FLUID LEVEL CHECKS
automatic transaxle, 1-12
brake fluid, 1-11

clutch fluid, 1-11
differential, 1-14
engine coolant, 1-10
engine oil, 1-10
manual transaxle, 1-13
power steering, 1-12
transfer case, 1-13
windshield washer, 1-12
FLUIDS AND LUBRICANTS
capacities, 1-39
recommended, 1-38
FLYWHEEL/DRIVEPLATE, REMOVAL AND INSTALLATION, 2A-32
FOUR-CYLINDER ENGINES, 2A-1
camshaft oil seal(s), replacement, 2A-14
camshaft(s), lifters and rocker arms, removal, inspection, installation and adjustment, 2A-16
crankshaft pulley and front oil seal, removal and installation, 2A-15
cylinder head, removal and installation, 2A-22
exhaust manifold, removal and installation, 2A-6
flywheel/driveplate, removal and installation, 2A-32
intake manifold, removal and installation, 2A-5
mounts, check and replacement, 2A-33
oil pan, removal and installation, 2A-25
oil pump, removal, inspection and installation, 2A-28
oil type and viscosity, 1-38
rear main oil seal, replacement, 2A-32
repair operations possible with the engine in the vehicle, 2A-2
timing belt and sprockets, removal and installation, 2A-7
Top Dead Center (TDC) for number 1 piston, locating, 2A-2
valve cover, removal and installation, 2A-3
FRACTION/DECIMAL/MILLIMETER EQUIVALENTS, 0-21
FUEL
filter replacement, 1-37
general information, 4-2
injection system
    check, 4-20
    general information, 4-19
lines and fittings, general information, 4-5
pressure regulator, replacement, 4-24
pressure relief procedure, 4-2
pulsation damper, removal and installation, 4-24
pump/fuel gauge sending unit
    component replacement, 4-9
    removal and installation, 4-6
pump/fuel pressure, check, 4-3
rail and injectors, removal and installation, 4-25
system check, 1-25
tank
    cleaning and repair, general information, 4-14
    pressure sensor, replacement, 6-15
    removal and installation, 4-12
FUEL AND EXHAUST SYSTEMS, 4-1
FUSES, GENERAL INFORMATION, 12-4

G

GENERAL ENGINE OVERHAUL PROCEDURES, 2C-1
crankshaft, removal and installation, 2C-17
cylinder compression check, 2C-4
engine overhaul
    disassembly sequence, 2C-10
    reassembly sequence, 2C-19
engine rebuilding alternatives, 2C-7
engine removal, methods and precautions, 2C-7
engine, removal and installation, 2C-8
general information, engine overhaul, 2C-2
initial start-up and break-in after overhaul, 2C-19
oil pressure check, 2C-4
pistons and connecting rods, removal and installation, 2C-11
vacuum gauge diagnostic checks, 2C-5
GLASS, DOOR WINDOW, REMOVAL AND INSTALLATION, 11-20

H

HATCH, REAR
latch and lock cylinder, removal and installation, 11-12
removal, installation and adjustment, 11-14
HAZARD FLASHER RELAY, CHECK AND REPLACEMENT, 12-6
HEADLIGHT
adjustment, 12-19
bulb, replacement, 12-17
housing, removal and installation, 12-18
HEATER AND AIR CONDITIONING CONTROL ASSEMBLY, REMOVAL AND INSTALLATION, 3-13
HEATER CORE, REPLACEMENT, 3-14
HINGES AND LOCKS, MAINTENANCE, 11-7
HOOD
release latch and cable, removal and installation, 11-8
removal, installation and adjustment, 11-7
HORN, REPLACEMENT, 12-20
HUB AND WHEEL BEARING ASSEMBLY, REPLACEMENT
front, 10-10
rear, 10-13

I

IDLE AIR CONTROL SYSTEM, COMPONENT REPLACEMENT, 6-30
IDLE SPEED CHECK AND ADJUSTMENT, 1-34
IGNITION SYSTEM
check, 5-5
coil, check and replacement, 5-6
control module, replacement, 5-6
distributor (1997 and earlier models), removal and installation, 5-9
general information, 5-5
switch/key lock cylinder assembly, replacement, 12-8
timing, check and adjustment, 5-10
INITIAL START-UP AND BREAK-IN AFTER OVERHAUL, 2C-19
INPUT SHAFT SPEED SENSOR, REPLACEMENT, 6-16
INSTRUMENT
cluster, removal and installation, 12-10
panel, removal and installation, 11-28
INTAKE AIR TEMPERATURE (IAT) SENSOR, REPLACEMENT, 6-17
INTAKE MANIFOLD, REMOVAL AND INSTALLATION, 2A-5, 2B-4
INTRODUCTION, 0-5

J

JACKING AND TOWING, 0-17
JUMP STARTING, 0-18

K

KEY LOCK CYLINDER AND IGNITION SWITCH ASSEMBLY, REPLACEMENT, 12-8
KNOCK SENSOR, REPLACEMENT, 6-17
KNUCKLE, REAR, REMOVAL AND INSTALLATION, 10-11

L

LUBRICANTS AND CHEMICALS, 0-19
LUBRICANTS AND FLUIDS
capacities, 1-39
recommended, 1-38

M

MAINTENANCE SCHEDULE, 1-2
MAINTENANCE TECHNIQUES, TOOLS AND WORKING FACILITIES, 0-9
MANUAL TRANSAXLE, 7A-1
back-up light switch, replacement, 7A-3
driveaxle oil seals, replacement, 7A-2
lubricant
    change, 1-36
    level check, 1-13
    type, 1-38
overhaul, general information, 7A-4

removal and installation, 7A-3
shift lever, removal and installation, 7A-2
MASS AIR FLOW (MAF) SENSOR, REPLACEMENT, 6-17
MASTER CYLINDER, REMOVAL AND INSTALLATION
brake, 9-18
clutch, 8-2
MIRRORS
electric side view, general information, 12-26
removal and installation, 11-22
MODULE, IGNITION, REPLACEMENT, 5-6
MULTI-FUNCTION SWITCH, REPLACEMENT, 12-5
MULTIPORT FUEL INJECTION (MFI) SYSTEM, GENERAL INFORMATION, 4-19

N

NEUTRAL POSITION SWITCH, REPLACEMENT, 6-18

O

OIL
engine, level check, 1-10
pan, removal and installation, 2A-25, 2B-11
pressure check, 2C-4
pump, removal, inspection and installation, 2A-28, 2B-12
seals (V6 engines), 2B-9
ON-BOARD DIAGNOSTIC (OBD) SYSTEM AND TROUBLE CODES, 6-2
OUTPUT SHAFT SPEED SENSOR, REPLACEMENT, 6-16
OXYGEN SENSORS, REPLACEMENT, 6-18

P

PACKAGE TRAY, REMOVAL AND INSTALLATION, 11-33
PADS, DISC BRAKE, REPLACEMENT, 9-3
PARKING BRAKE, ADJUSTMENT, 9-23
PARKING BRAKE SHOES, REPLACEMENT, 9-11
PARTS, REPLACEMENT, BUYING, 0-8
PISTONS AND CONNECTING RODS, REMOVAL AND INSTALLATION, 2C-11
POSITIVE CRANKCASE VENTILATION (PCV) SYSTEM
general description and component replacement, 6-35
valve check and replacement, 1-31
POWER BRAKE BOOSTER, REMOVAL AND INSTALLATION, 9-21
POWER DOOR LOCK SYSTEM, GENERAL INFORMATION, 12-27

POWER STEERING
fluid level check, 1-12
Pressure (PSP) switch, replacement, 6-20
pump, removal and installation, 10-19
system, bleeding, 10-20
POWER WINDOW SYSTEM, GENERAL INFORMATION, 12-26
POWERTRAIN CONTROL MODULE (PCM), REMOVAL AND INSTALLATION, 6-25
POWERTRAIN MOUNTS, CHECK AND REPLACEMENT, 2A-33, 2B-14
PRESSURE SENSOR, FUEL TANK, REPLACEMENT, 6-15
PRESSURE SWITCH, AIR CONDITIONING, REPLACEMENT, 3-22

R

RADIATOR, REMOVAL AND INSTALLATION, 3-8
RADIO AND SPEAKERS, REMOVAL AND INSTALLATION, 12-13
REAR DIFFERENTIAL (4WD MODELS)
lubricant
change, 1-36
level check, 1-14
type, 1-38
removal and installation, 8-14
REAR DRIVEAXLE OIL SEAL (4WD MODELS), REPLACEMENT, 8-14
REAR HATCH
latch and lock cylinder, removal and installation, 11-12
removal, installation and adjustment, 11-14
REAR KNUCKLE, REMOVAL AND INSTALLATION, 10-11
REAR MAIN OIL SEAL, REPLACEMENT, 2A-32
REAR SHELF TRIM PANEL, REMOVAL AND INSTALLATION, 11-33
REAR WINDOW DEFOGGER, CHECK AND REPAIR, 12-16
RECEIVER-DRIER, AIR CONDITIONING, REMOVAL AND INSTALLATION, 3-19
RECOMMENDED LUBRICANTS AND FLUIDS, 1-38
RELAYS, GENERAL INFORMATION AND TESTING, 12-5
RELEASE BEARING AND LEVER, CLUTCH, REMOVAL, INSPECTION AND INSTALLATION, 8-5
RELEASE CYLINDER, CLUTCH, REMOVAL AND INSTALLATION, 8-3
REPAIR OF MINOR PAINT SCRATCHES, 11-2
REPAIR OPERATIONS POSSIBLE WITH THE ENGINE IN THE VEHICLE, 2A-2, 2B-2
REPLACEMENT PARTS, BUYING, 0-8
ROTOR, BRAKE, INSPECTION, REMOVAL AND INSTALLATION, 9-9
ROUTINE MAINTENANCE SCHEDULE, 1-2

S

SAFETY FIRST!, 0-22
SCHEDULED MAINTENANCE, 1-1
SEAT BELT CHECK, 1-21
SEATS, REMOVAL AND INSTALLATION, 11-32
SHIFT
cable, automatic transaxle, removal, installation and
   adjustment, 7B-5
interlock system, description and component replacement, 7B-7
lever, removal and installation
   automatic transaxle, 7B-6
   manual transaxle, 7A-2
SHOES, DRUM BRAKE/PARKING BRAKE,
   REPLACEMENT, 9-11
SLAVE CYLINDER, CLUTCH, REMOVAL AND
   INSTALLATION, 8-3
SPARE TIRE, INSTALLING, 0-17
SPARK PLUG
check and replacement, 1-32
torque, 1-41
type and gap, 1-40
wire, distributor cap and rotor check and replacement, 1-33
SPEAKERS, REMOVAL AND INSTALLATION, 12-13
SPEED CONTROL SYSTEM, GENERAL
   INFORMATION, 12-26
STABILIZER BAR BUSHINGS AND LINKS, REMOVAL
   AND INSTALLATION
front, 10-7
rear, 10-14
STARTER MOTOR
and circuit, check, 5-13
removal and installation, 5-14
STARTING SYSTEM, GENERAL INFORMATION AND
   PRECAUTIONS, 5-13
STEERING
check, 1-23
column covers, removal and installation, 11-28
column, removal and installation, 10-16
gear boots, removal and installation, 10-17
gear, removal and installation, 10-18
knuckle and hub (front), removal and installation, 10-10
wheel, removal and installation, 10-14
STEERING, SUSPENSION AND DRIVEAXLE BOOT
   CHECK, 1-23
STOP LIGHT SWITCH, REPLACEMENT, 9-23
STRUT ASSEMBLY, REMOVAL, INSPECTION AND
   INSTALLATION
front, 10-4
rear, 10-10
STRUT/COIL SPRING, REPLACEMENT, 10-5
SUPPLEMENTAL RESTRAINT SYSTEM (SRS), GENERAL
   INFORMATION, 12-27
SUSPENSION AND STEERING SYSTEMS, 10-1
SUSPENSION ARMS (REAR), REMOVAL AND
   INSTALLATION, 10-12

T

THERMOSTAT, CHECK AND REPLACEMENT, 3-4
THROTTLE BODY, REMOVAL AND INSTALLATION, 4-21
THROTTLE POSITION (TP) SENSOR, REPLACEMENT, 6-21
THROTTLE VALVE CABLE (1994 THROUGH 1997 MODELS),
   CHECK, ADJUSTMENT AND REPLACEMENT, 7B-3
TIE-ROD ENDS, REMOVAL AND INSTALLATION, 10-17
TIMING BELT AND SPROCKETS, REMOVAL AND
   INSTALLATION, 2A-7, 2B-6
TIMING BELT CHECK, 1-31
TIMING, IGNITION, CHECK AND ADJUSTMENT, 5-10
TIRE AND TIRE PRESSURE CHECKS, 1-14
TIRE ROTATION, 1-20
TIRE, SPARE, INSTALLING, 0-17
TOOLS AND WORKING FACILITIES, 0-9
TOP DEAD CENTER (TDC) FOR NUMBER ONE PISTON,
   LOCATING, 2A-2, 2B-2
TORQUE SPECIFICATIONS
brake caliper mounting bolts, 9-25
cylinder head bolts, 2A-37, 2B-15
sparks plugs, 1-41
wheel lug nuts, 1-41
*Other torque specifications can be found in the Chapter that deals
   with the component being serviced*
TOWING, 0-17
TRANSFER CASE (4WD MODELS)
lubricant
   change, 1-36
   level check, 1-13
   type, 1-38
removal and installation, 8-15
TRANSAXLE, AUTOMATIC, 7B-1
diagnosis, general, 7B-2
driveaxle oil seals, replacement, 7A-2
fluid
   change, 1-35
   level check, 1-12
   lype, 1-38
mounts, check and replacement, 2A-33, 2B-14
overhaul, general information, 7B-10
removal and installation, 7B-8
shift
   cable, removal, installation and adjustment, 7B-5
   interlock system, description and component replacement, 7B-7
   lever, removal and installation, 7B-6
throttle valve cable (1994 through 1997 models), check, adjustment
   and replacement, 7B-3
transaxle oil cooler, removal and installation, 7B-10

TRANSAXLE, MANUAL, 7A-1
back-up light switch, replacement, 7A-3
driveaxle oil seals, replacement, 7A-2
lubricant
    change, 1-36
    level check, 1-13
    type, 1-38
overhaul, general information, 7A-4
removal and installation, 7A-3
shift lever, removal and installation, 7A-2
**TRANSMISSION RANGE (TR) SWITCH, REPLACEMENT
    AND ADJUSTMENT, 6-23**
TRIM PANELS, REMOVAL AND INSTALLATION
dashboard, 11-25
door, 11-16
rear shelf, 11-33
TROUBLE CODES, ACCESSING, 6-5
TROUBLESHOOTING, 0-23
TRUNK
latch and lock cylinder, removal and installation, 11-12
lid, removal and installation, 11-14
release and fuel door lever, removal and installation, 11-15
TUNE-UP AND ROUTINE MAINTENANCE, 1-1
TUNE-UP GENERAL INFORMATION, 1-9
**TURN SIGNAL AND HAZARD FLASHER RELAY, CHECK AND
    REPLACEMENT, 12-6**

U

UNDERHOOD HOSE CHECK AND REPLACEMENT, 1-24
UNIVERSAL JOINT (4WD MODELS)
general information and check, 8-12
replacement, 8-13
UPHOLSTERY AND CARPETS, MAINTENANCE, 11-5

V

V6 ENGINES, 2B-1
camshafts and valvetrain, removal, inspection, installation and
    adjustment, 2B-9
cylinder heads, removal, inspection and installation, 2B-10
driveplate, removal and installation, 2B-13
exhaust manifold/catalytic converter assemblies, removal and
    installation, 2B-5
intake manifold, removal and installation, 2B-4
oil pan, removal and installation, 2B-11
oil pump, removal, inspection and installation, 2B-12
oil seals, replacement, 2B-9
powertrain mounts, check and replacement, 2B-14
repair operations possible with the engine in the vehicle, 2B-2
timing belt and sprockets, removal, inspection and installation, 2B-6
Top Dead Center (TDC) for number one piston, locating, 2B-2
valve covers, removal and installation, 2B-3
VACUUM GAUGE DIAGNOSTIC CHECKS, 2C-5
**VALVE COVER(S), REMOVAL AND
    INSTALLATION, 2A-3, 2B-3**
**VARIABLE INDUCTION CONTROL SYSTEM (SPORTAGE
    V6 MODELS), DESCRIPTION AND COMPONENT
    REPLACEMENT, 6-37**
VEHICLE IDENTIFICATION NUMBERS, 0-6
VEHICLE SPEED SENSOR (VSS), REPLACEMENT, 6-24
VINYL TRIM, MAINTENANCE, 11-5
VOLUME AIR FLOW (VAF) SENSOR, REPLACEMENT, 6-24

W

WATER PUMP
check, 3-9
replacement, 3-10
WHEEL ALIGNMENT GENERAL INFORMATION, 10-21
WHEEL CYLINDER, REMOVAL AND INSTALLATION, 9-17
WHEELS AND TIRES, GENERAL INFORMATION, 10-21
**WINDOW GLASS REGULATOR, REMOVAL AND
    INSTALLATION, 11-21**
**WINDOW GLASS, DOOR, REMOVAL AND
    INSTALLATION, 11-20**
WINDSHIELD
and fixed glass, replacement, 11-7
washer fluid, level check, 1-12
wiper blade inspection and replacement, 1-17
wiper motor, check and replacement, 12-10
WIRING DIAGRAMS, GENERAL INFORMATION, 12-28
WORKING FACILITIES, 0-9